Nerzinskoi

Amur R

l'isne Tunguska

Erehorjarkot

L. Baykal

Ononn R

Houmari

CHINOIS

I des Etats

I. a Yeso

Loulco

Yelinguskoi

Kerlon R

Kulon L. Teitcicar

Nimguta Peuple
qui ont conquis la chine

Ningousta
Fourdan

Toko

Konghing

Jedo

de

Eke Aral
Ourat

Hami

Demare duru
Lamou Goncher

Naymam

Leabbing

Pinin

Méaco

TARTARIE

COBI

Muraille

Naymam

COREE

sing

JAPON

Ortous

Tayven

Pekin

Golfe de
Pecuolo

Kingkitao

Yimo

Contgchang

Ho

Changi

Petcheli

GRANI

Ho han

Sigan

Caifong

Hohan Ho

Sieu

Tunan

MITratico

Siau Leu

Sihans

Lingugam

Kiau Keu

Nankin

Leuo I.

o Dalu
huma

Thintu

Sung

Nantzhou

Vutchan

Hongtchou

Nangcheou

CHINE

Yaogund

Keilin

Telekiang

Yunan

Kaoutcheou

Canton

Tingtekou

Futcheu

Tropique du Cai

I. Formose

MER

Macao

Kai tanchan

Keshó

Cochinchine

Golfe
de
Cochinchine

Hayman I.

Araccan

S

Langham

Naun Tam

Pegu

Siam

Judia

Cochinchine

Taifo

I. de Luzon

Samar

Manille

PHILIPINES

Pref. de l'Inde
au dela
du Gange

Camboj
Ciampa

I. Mindanao

Tanasserim

G. de Siam

I. de Condor

ISLES

LES

Malacca

I. de Legor

Mt St Pedro
Borneo

I. Gilolo

MOLUQUES

I. Cocos

Detroit de Malacca

Ponciam

Malalno

BORNEO

Calebes

Achem

I. Nias

I. de Sumatra

Lava

180

Succadana

I.

I. Nassaw

Macassar

I. Ceram

Dt de la Sonde

Batavia

I. de Java

I. Maduro

Bali

I. de
Cumbava

INSIGHT GUIDES

Series Created by Hans Höfer

East asia

Edited by Scott Rutherford

Editorial Director: Brian Bell

APA PUBLICATIONS

Part of the Langenscheidt Publishing Group

L

CONTENTS

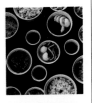

TRAVEL TIPS

INTRODUCTION

Arrival in Asia is a descent into abstractions. The Western mind, steeped in Aristotelian logic and preconceptions, can knit itself into a knot of pure bewilderment trying to recognize the undercurrents of East Asia. Foreign armies, armadas and adventurers have done so countless times. (One hopes that the days of invading armies, from outside and from within, are finished.)

Why does someone come to East Asia nowadays?

It is a long haul for the traveller coming from Europe or the Americas to Beijing, Hong Kong, Taipei, or Seoul, or if deep in the pockets, Tokyo. Travellers to East Asia generally come for two reasons: the pragmatist, for business or education; the romantic, to fulfil a dream or satisfy an incessant wanderlust.

The pragmatist comes because Asia is where the next century will be defined, and where much of the world's economic engine will be fuelled. The 21st century belongs to Asia, just as the 19th century was European, and the 20th century, American. Two of the world's largest three economies are Asian – China and Japan. China's share alone of the world's output is over 6 percent and growing; in fact, China is the world's second biggest economy after the United States. And China – with its one-billion-plus people – is just now rubbing the sleep from its eyes. It is the world's largest consumer market with nothing but future potential. With Japan, Korea, Hong Kong, and Taiwan nearby, China isn't lacking for inspiration.

Most paths in East Asia lead to China, whether in art, architecture, language, writing, philosophy. The Korean peninsula and Japanese archipelago have nurtured ancient Chinese culture into rich and unique civilizations of their own. (Although the Japanese are not keen to remember their Chinese or especially Korean heritage.)

The historical and political dynamics of East Asia are complex, changing, and usually subtle. These countries have at times been isolationist, not only against intrusions from outside the region, but amongst themselves. At the moment, Japan casts the biggest shadow across East Asia, if not all of Asia, representing an economic paradigm for other Asian peoples.

But beneath the envy and admiration for Japan's economic success is a lingering – and in some places, smouldering – bitterness about Japan's severe and brutal domination of Asia during World War II. The Koreans certainly have a strong memory of those times; many Japanese things are outlawed in Korea. On the other hand, most Japanese today seemed convinced that Japan was the principal victim of World War II. Other Asian countries will probably resist Japan's efforts to obtain a permanent seat on the Security Council at the United Nations, at least until the Japanese acknowledge that the economic high ground does not carry with it the moral high ground. So close in geography and yet so distant.

Preceding pages: the smoke and smell of temple incense; young couple, Guangzhou; traditional mask dancers, Korea; smiles of a fisherman; Mt Fuji over Tokyo; Hong Kong's Star Ferry. <u>Left</u>, old portrait of Confucius.

Hong Kong, that aberrant, fussy and vibrant city, spins on the pressured time of business and politics. Yanked from China in 19th-century colonial land grabs, Hong Kong has been a borrowed place on borrowed time, to borrow from novelist Han Su-yin. In many ways, it still is, despite its return to China in 1997, not exactly what the British had in mind when negotiations were started in the 1980s. The 1989 pro-democracy movement in China and subsequent government crackdown evaporated any confidence Hong Kong had in the possibility of an enlightened Beijing. Nearby Macau, the Portuguese outpost, reverts on better terms.

Perhaps Taiwan, that other detached limb of the Chinese dragon, may do likewise one day. Despite expulsion from the United Nations, of which it was a founding member, and the severing of diplomatic ties with most Western nations, Taiwan has propelled itself into a modern, productive industrial state, America's fifth largest trading partner despite the lack of diplomatic recognition. The Taiwanese are the best fed people in East Asia, and with more urban living space than the Japanese.

Neither Beijing nor Taipei dispute that Taiwan is an integral province of China. It's a question of perspective – and pride. Mainland China calls its capital city Beijing, which means northern capital. The Taiwanese call the same city Peiping, which means northern peace. The inference? Beijing is not the capital of China, at least at the moment.

However, Asian units of time are patience and fate, not ticks of the clock. China, after all, is nearly 50 centuries old. Its written language has been around since long before the collapse of the Pharaonic dynasties in Egypt. Another year – or 50 – is but a blink in time and history.

Right, temple image, Kwangju, Korea.

CHINA

Zhonghua Renmin Gongheguo is the official name of the People's Republic of China, but in everyday language it is simply Zhongguo – the Middle Kingdom. In the Temple of Heaven in Beijing, a marble altar signifies the center of the world, a place that only the Emperor was allowed to enter in order to communicate with heaven. According to the cosmological view of the world held in ancient Chinese cultures, the Middle Kingdom lay precisely below the center of the firmament. The peoples living on the dark peripheries of the earth's disk were regarded as barbarians. Perhaps they still are.

We of the West have for centuries regarded China as an empire at the edge of the world. The ancient Greeks wrote about the *Serers,* which means the "bearers of silk", and for more than a millennium there was only one link between Europe and China: the land route via the ancient Silk Road. Knowledge of China did not yield easily, nor quickly.

The variations of China's contours are as expansive as its vast territory, certainly too much for this book. Nevertheless, a book on East Asia must include something about China, the origin of everything East Asian. In *Insight Guide: East Asia* we'll introduce you to two of mainland China's most important cities, Beijing and Guangzhou, and one its most ancient cities and capitals, Xi'an. Beijing and Guangzhou (lazily known in the West as Canton) are thoroughly Chinese and thus thoroughly different, not only in latitude and appearance, but in cuisine, language, and attitude.

The foundations of modern China are probably the world's most complex and have the deepest roots anywhere. Yet even recent events give breadth and depth to its people and personality. The 19th century was a period of humiliation for China as the powers of industrialized Europe pushed China into a marginal existence, dividing up its territory and injuring its self-esteem. From this situation arose national and revolutionary forces working towards a strong China, a self-centred independence, often keeping itself at a long arm's length from the outside. The Chinese learn, always, never forgetting a lesson.

While you're walking the streets of Beijing and Guangzhou, don't forget an old Chinese proverb – "Seeing is easy, learning is hard". Or putting it another way, again through an old Chinese proverb, "None are as blind as those who don't want to see".

Preceding pages: the simplicity of dim sum. **Left,** autumn colours.

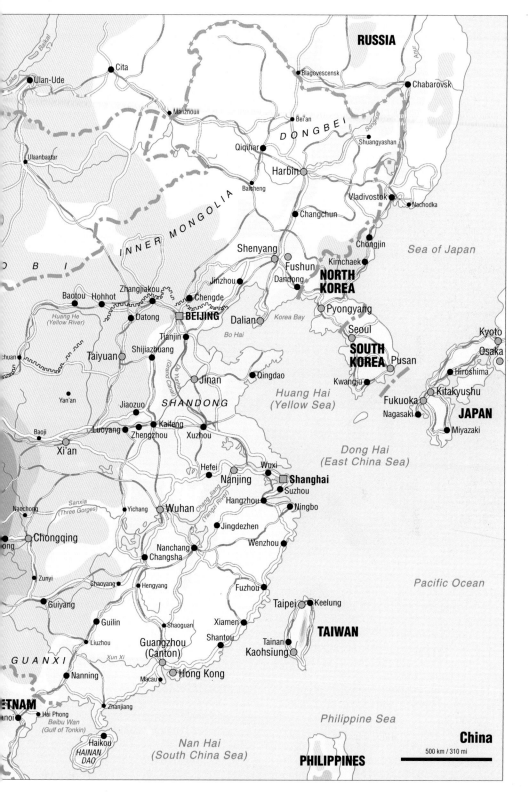

China

500 km / 310 mi

29

When the Chinese refer to their history, they might be speaking of already legendary times, for China's written history alone dates back over 4,000 years. Evidence of human life extends back considerably further – a fossilized skull unearthed in 1963 puts the earliest known human in China over half a million years ago.

Around the 4th or 3rd century BC, small tribes increasingly coalesced into bigger tribes, and eventually into small states. Stronger states, of course, consumed weaker

measurements, weights and coins, and the Chinese writing script. The Qin dynasty neglected agriculture in favour of countless construction projects, including the forerunner of today's Great Wall (which dates mostly from the later Ming dynasty). The resulting famines helped fuel a peasants' revolt that toppled the Qin dynasty.

The subsequent Han dynasty (202 BC–AD 220) lasted 400 years. Land ownership was expanded to include merchants and civil servants, who also gained executive powers

ones. New social classes and groups emerged, commerce between individual states increased, and the question of unification became a central source of conflict. By the beginning of the Warring States period (481–221 BC), the number of states competing for supremacy had been reduced to seven, the strongest called Qin.

The dynastic tradition: The Qin dynasty (221–206 BC) united the empire in 221 BC. The country was administratively divided into prefectures and administered by specially-chosen officials. Although in power but a short time, the dynasty's legacy included the standardization of transportation,

in a civil system based on merit, not patronage. Contact with other cultures increased as caravans began to travel on the Silk Road, bringing horses and gold to China in exchange for silk.

A new power appeared in the imperial court: the palace eunuchs, castrated males from the lower classes. Originally hired to look after the emperors' wives and concubines, they became important advisors, engaging in palace intrigues and power struggles until 1911, when rule by dynasty ended.

But like those before it – and those yet to come – the Han dynasty collapsed in AD 220, followed by nearly 400 years of war and social division. Eventually a new central government under the Sui dynasty (581–618) united the country. The Sui dynasty was overthrown in an army revolt and replaced by 300 years of the Tang dynasty (618–907), itself eventually – and not unexpectedly – toppled in a drawn out army rebellion.

Chinese civilization reached a peak under the Song dynasty (960–1279) with impressive developments in agriculture, a refined monetary system using paper money, and extensive trade extending to Africa and the

pire's capital. Distrusting the Chinese and not adapting to the Chinese ways, it is no wonder that the Mongols lasted less than a century as rulers of China.

Following the ejection of the Mongols in the late 1300s, the Ming dynasty (1368–1644) was a time of social, economic and governmental restoration. At first, the Ming dispatched an active maritime fleet, but the third Ming emperor decommissioned the fleet in the 15th century, considering it unnecessary for the Chinese to travel. The

Middle East. Confucianism became the political and ethical philosophy it is today, and civil servants replaced nobility and land owners as society's elite.

But trouble loomed in the north. The Mongols, united under Genghis Khan, had already conquered all of Central Asia, Russia and some Eastern European areas by the early 1200s. By 1279, China was added to the Mongol empire. Kublai Khan, the grandson of Genghis Khan, made Beijing his em-

resulting insularity was perhaps a reason why China did not acknowledge and confront the persistent European advance into Asia and China.

The Portuguese arrived in Guangzhou in 1517, firing a cannon salute, an unknown and provocative custom to the Chinese. The Spanish, Dutch and English soon followed.

Ignoring the Western advances into Asia, the Ming court focused on belligerent threats from northern nomads, and from Japanese pirates and expeditionary armies. The Great Wall was reinforced. This vigilance was expensive, and the peasantry became even more impoverished. Adding to the prob-

Left, an early view of the Imperial Palace. **Above**, Kublai Khan, and the Ming emperors Hongwu and Wanli.

lems, the eunuchs paralysed the imperial court with intrigue, and the Ming dynasty toppled early in the 17th century.

Initially invited from Manchuria to oust rebels out of Beijing following the Ming collapse, the Manchus went on to establish the Qing dynasty (1644–1911). By the middle of the 18th century, territory under the Qing dynasty covered more than 4.4 million square miles (11 million sq. km).

Early on, the Qing pulled China inward. After an initially promising start, Christian missionary activity was quenched by the imperial court at the end of the 18th century, as was most access to China by foreign merchant ships.

sia, Japan and Germany soon joined the colonial effort.

By 1900, China was threatened by the same fate as Africa: division by colonial powers. The so-called Boxer Rebellion, a reaction to the continual foreign humiliation and subjugation of China, sought to forcibly expel all foreigners – including the Manchu rulers – from China. Foreign troops defeated the Boxers in 1900, strengthening outside domination of China.

Weakened, the Qing dynasty was overthrown in a negotiated abdication in 1911 by a movement led by Dr Sun Yatsen, working from exile to free China from foreign control, and to replace the dynastic system with

For years, the Chinese had enjoyed a monopoly in the tea trade, taking in silver as payment. However, having now isolated itself, China refused to import much of anything. So in the early 1800s, the British started smuggling more opium into China, demanding payment in silver. Increasingly short of cash, the Qing finally ceased opium imports. The First Opium War (1839–42) was England's response; the British advanced to Nanjing and extracted concessions from China, including more open ports and exclusion of foreigners from Chinese jurisdiction. The Second Opium War (1856–60) brought British and French troops into Beijing. Rus-

democracy. But no other stable political order followed the Qing dynasty's demise. Warlords and feudal military rulers exploited the power vacuum.

A sovereign republic: A new left-wing intellectual movement emerged in China, culminating in a large student movement on 4 May 1919. The May Fourth Movement (as it was called) was a response to the Versailles Peace Treaty, which granted the former German territories in China to Japan, not back to China. Immediate effects of the movement were minimal, but it is regarded as a decisive turning point in modern Chinese history. Demands for complete national sovereignty increased significantly thereafter, and although the British sailed their gunboats up the Yangzi River one last time in 1927, new political forces – and strengthened Chinese nationalism – had emerged.

In 1921, the Communist Party in China was officially founded in Shanghai. The party's growth was fast, as was that of the Guomindang, or the National People's Party – the Nationalists – led by Dr Sun Yatsen.

The Nationalists and Communists mutually endured a brief coalition, but by 1928, Chiang Kaishek, now head of the Nationalist forces, succeeded in controlling all of China, having earlier broken off relations with the Communists, who retreated into the south-

with military campaigns against the Communists, who sought escape on the famous Long March northward. Walking 6,000 miles (9,600 km), only 10 percent of the over 100,000 people who began the march survived to its conclusion.

Chiang's campaign against the Communists was diverted by Japanese advances in the north. Provoking a confrontation near Beijing in 1937, the Japanese entered into war with China. Within days, Beijing fell to Japan, followed by Shanghai, Nanjing, and lastly Guangzhou.

With Japan's surrender in 1945, the Communists and Nationalists reverted to their mutual dislike, and a four-year civil war

ern mountains. There, under Mao Zedong, they developed a strategy that replaced the Soviet doctrine of urban proletariat revolution with that of a peasant revolution focused on land reform.

Although Chiang Kaishek had significantly strengthened Chinese sovereignty, corruption in the government and increased Japanese threats thwarted any land reform, a neglect strategically seized upon by the Communists. Chiang responded in the early 1930s

Left, the Qing Emperor receives a foreign envoy.
Above, Mao Zedong with his army at Yan'an during the civil war against the Nationalists.

between them ended only when the Nationalists and nearly 2 million refugees retreated to Taiwan.

Mao Zedong proclaimed the People's Republic of China in 1949. The nation's problems were immense, the peasants' quality of life dismal. Agrarian land reform redistributed land to the peasants in the early 1950s. Social reforms were extensive, though not always for the better, and industries were nationalized.

Initially, the economy improved. Encouraged, Mao introduced the "Great Leap Forward" in 1958, intending to put China on equal footing with economically advanced countries. Peasant cooperatives were to be the primary means for achieving this aim. But the "leap" was a disaster, with widespread and repeated crop failures, poorly conceived public works projects, and natural disasters leading to the death of perhaps 20 million people by the world's worst famine.

In 1966, student discontent turned into massive protests. Mao exploited these protests, initiating the "Great Proletarian Cultural Revolution" to unsettle his opponents. Party cadres provoked a mass movement of the Red Guards, tossing the country once again into chaos, at times close to civil war. Intellectuals, artists and politicians, including top party leadership, fell victim to the

terror of the Red Guards. Schools closed, artistic life stagnated, international relations evaporated. At the same time, Mao elevated himself in a personality cult unprecedented anywhere else in the world.

When the Cultural Revolution finally stalled in the early 1970s, premier Zhou Enlai quietly took over the reins of government, mediating between the moderate and radical factions. In 1973, he resuscitated political victims of the Cultural Revolution, including Deng Xiaoping, who became his deputy, and other pragmatists. Zhou Enlai also made great efforts to overcome China's international isolation: after China became a member of the United Nations in 1971, Richard Nixon visited the country in 1972.

The year 1976 was pivotal. Zhou Enlai died in January, leaving the moderate pragmatists in a precarious standing. Deng Xiaoping was removed from power by radicals known as the "Gang of Four", which included Mao Zedong's wife. However, when Mao died in September, the radicals were arrested and Deng restored to power.

The pragmatists initiated new policies that opened up the economy and dispersed some political power. Limited liberalization of political and artistic activity followed. Deng Xiaoping retired in 1987. China continued its return to the international order when Soviet leader Mikhail Gorbachev met with Deng Xiaoping in May of 1989 in Beijing, the first summit between China and the Soviet Union since 1959. Gorbachev's visit to China – highlighted by his own reform efforts at home – may have tipped over a long-smouldering powder keg. Earlier in April, before his visit, students began an extended pro-democracy demonstration in Tiananmen Square after the death of former party general secretary Hu Yaobang, who, two years earlier, had refused to counter or suppress student dissent. Protesters in Tiananmen Square swelled from 1,000 in April to more than a million by the third week of May. Martial law was imposed and military units were dispatched to Beijing. At first, protesters succeeded in peacefully keeping military convoys from entering Beijing's center, but on June 4, several thousand soldiers supported by tanks attacked the protesters in and around Tiananmen Square.

China's international reputation was severely damaged by the events at Tiananmen Square, including subsequent arrests and executions. China's leadership has been slow in reestablishing its international stature. Even in 1997, when Hong Kong was returned to Chinese control, Tiananmen remained a strong memory. The country's leaders seem uncertain, or even unconcerned, about how to relate to the world – it bullies its smaller neighbours over islands in the South China Sea, while demanding an equal footing, and respect, with the more economically powerful nations in Asia and in the world.

Left, concerned before the handover, Hong Kong. **Right**, Mao Zedong.

Ninety percent of China's population lives on just one-fifth of China's land, mostly in the east and south. In contrast, the vast empty areas in the north and west are sparsely populated, and often hardly habitable.

The Chinese consider themselves as Han, descended from the Han dynasty that was a pivotal point in Chinese history. Although over 90 percent of Chinese are ethnically Han, the distinction between Han and other racial groups is not black and white. The notion of being Chinese – Han Chinese – is to some degree a cultural concept, an acceptance of Chinese values. The Han Chinese are, of course, derived from a distinctive racial background, but over the centuries, the Han absorbed racial minorities.

The Han Chinese have traditionally populated the eastern part of the country, leaving the empty spaces to the west and north, at least up until modern times, to the minority ethnic groups. (Within China, only in Tibet is a national minority group actually the majority, with 98 percent of the population.)

Population headaches: China's population was counted for the first time about 2,000 years ago, in 4 AD. By 742 AD, during the Tang dynasty, China's population was just over 50 million people.

At around the same time as the invasion of Genghis Khan and the Mongols, around AD 1250, the 100 million mark was probably exceeded for the first time. By the middle of the 18th century, the number had doubled; a century later, in 1850, a population of 400 million people had been reached.

Shortly after World War II, there were half a billion people in China. Between the mid 1960s and the early 1980s, China's population increased by over 300 million, more than the total population of either the United States or the former Soviet Union. Today's population is over 1.2 billion people, nearly 20 percent of humanity. In recent years, China's population has increased annually by about 15 million people.

The governing and administrative challenges of such an immense population are mind-boggling. Gathering statistics for over a billion people, much less analyzing it, defies the imagination. Nevertheless, the statistics reveal much about China's options. The numbers are chilling, considering that less than ten percent of the world's agrarian areas are in China. For every 1,000 people, there are 21 births but just six deaths.

The government, in 1978, began a one-child-per-family program. Opportunities and incentives for those who have but one child are considerable. In cities, the program has been mostly successful. In the countryside, where large families are needed for farming, the program has had limited success.

Skewing any population statistics, however, is the preference for male heirs. In China, family lines are passed on through the male child. Partly because of this, and because – especially in rural areas – male offspring are more likely to support aging parents, sons are preferred to daughters. Female infants in the countryside have fallen victim to infanticide. From 1953 through 1964, the sex ratios at birth were a little under 105 males for every 100 female infants. Ultrasound scanners, which allow the determination of the sex of fetuses, were first introduced to China in 1979. As their use became widespread, especially amongst the middle and upper classes, the ratio climbed: 108 in 1982, 114 in 1990, and roughly 119 in 1992. Doctors are officially banned from disclosing the results of ultrasound scans, but they can usually be persuaded to tell. Also, private businessmen now offer the service, which can turn in handsome profits.

China's population is hard to sustain; most Chinese experts have said China can comfortably support a population of only 800 million. This is a major reason for the great emphasis China has placed on birth control.

Commission, a government agency, suggests several reasons. First, attitudes have not changed in rural areas; to a farmer, sons still provide the only security for old age. Second, sex education is still a taboo topic, especially in conservative rural areas where the grandmother educates her grandchildren according to her own beliefs.

In the cities, on the other hand, families actually prefer to have one child, as living space is restricted. Considering that living space in Shanghai or Beijing is, on average,

Although its original targets have proven excessively optimistic, the one-child policy has greatly reduced the rate of population increase. According to a 1993 estimate – comparing the average Chinese woman bearing five to six children in the 1950s, but only two in 1993 – the one-child policy had prevented 200 million births by 1993.

Yet problems still remain. Thirty percent of births are not planned, despite widespread use of condoms. The State Family Planning

Left, department store in Shenzen promotes consumerism. **Above**, summer dining at traditional home, Xiamen.

3.5 square meters, population-control measures are accepted.

Given the diverging sex ratio, many males will find themselves without female partners. The government has predicted that, if trends continued, there would be a 50- to 70-million-strong army of bachelors by 2000.

Little emperors: With so many hopes riding on them, particularly if they are male, children with no siblings are usually spoiled by doting parents and, especially, grandparents. These kids have been dubbed, literally, "little emperors". A Western equivalent might be "exceedingly spoiled brat". Even the Chinese consider them to be rude and spoiled.

The demographic shift to single-child families may have profound effects on Chinese society. Parents, growing up during the Cultural Revolution, excessively dote on their children amidst a limbo in values.

Traditional family values: Despite despotic little emperors dominating family life, the family – and traditional Confucian values – remains Chinese society's most important unit. In rural areas, common surnames identify an extended clan.

Land, that icon of family wealth, was passed on, equally, to a family's sons by the father. Over generations, the amount of land being passed on to each individual grew less and less, until family plots became exceed-

Although increasingly a rare occurrence in the cities, three generations may be living together in a rural family, with responsibility for elders falling to the sons. (Daughters, on the other hand, become members of her husband's family after marriage.) Families in the cities, however, are increasingly small and self-contained, like families in most of the world's modern cities.

"Women hold up half the sky", proclaimed Mao, but even under his rule, women rarely achieved high positions. The years since have seen further official affirmations of sexual equality, but surveys comparing the real status of women in the world rank China in the bottom third.

ingly small; average family wealth decreased.

At the turn of the century, and for the decades until the Communists took control in 1949, conditions for rural families were dismal, with scarce food, minimal health care and a continuing civil war. Rural conditions stabilized after 1949, with the quality of life gradually improving. In 1949, average life expectancy at birth was 35 years; by 1982, it was more than 65 years. Literacy jumped from 20 percent to nearly 80 percent. (This is not to disregard some central-government blunders, such as a colossal famine that killed 20 to 40 million people in the early 1960s because of poor planning.)

Age-old beliefs are largely to blame. According to Confucius, a woman without talent is virtuous. Besides regarding women as problematic and less innovative, employers are also concerned that if a woman becomes pregnant, she will be legally entitled to nine months' maternity leave.

Social life: Early morning, in a park in a Chinese city, men and women seem locked in solemn, slow-motion combat with invisible adversaries, swaying and turning and pushing into the air as they work through *taijiquan* routines. Some thrust swords into the air, while others inhale deep breaths and tighten muscles as they practice qong-fu.

Such group activities start young for the Chinese. Before their lessons begin, schoolchildren may "exercise" together. Taped music and a voice blare out from speakers. *Yi er san. One two three.* The children massage their eyes, in a routine to counteract eyestrain resulting from too much studying.

As their rich and varied cuisine reflects, the Chinese love to eat, and China's rise in living standards is apparent at meal times.

While meals in the home may be relatively simple, with a small selection of dishes from which to choose, restaurant meals can be veritable banquets. This is especially the case if the meal is accounted to entertainment expenses, or is being paid for by a

read under street lights. With little or no privacy at home, young couples may head for parks in search of romance. (While there are still arranged marriages in China, single people are increasingly free to marry as they please, particularly in urban areas.)

China's national and regional television stations are improving, but even though they feature foreign as well as domestic programs, their efforts rarely grip viewers.

Working life: "To get rich is glorious", announced Deng Xiaoping in 1978. The people responded with gusto.

Despite increases in urban wages, China's current income levels are still very low compared to the West. The figures are, however,

businessman who wants to impress – the Chinese do not usually split the tab. But whatever the offering, there should always be more food than the diners can eat. Otherwise, the host loses face. Sometimes banquets end with tables still piled with food. By one estimate, the Chinese waste enough food each year to feed 100 million people.

Until recently, dinner was the chief evening event. It may remain so for many people, who, after eating, leave claustrophobic homes for the street outside, to meet neighbors or

Left, hard-rock musicians, Shanghai. **Above**, a preference for traditional Chinese opera.

deceptive. This is partly because rents for most workers are still heavily subsidized, with apartments costing perhaps the equivalent of just a few dollars, literally, per month. The cost of living, too, is invariably lower in comparison with the West. (Urban life is rapidly becoming expensive, however, especially in Beijing, Shanghai, and Guangzhou.)

Two-thirds of China's people live in rural areas. Yet they are not all farmers. Increasingly, light industries are peppering the countryside, owned and operated by villages and towns in what the *Washington Post* called an industrial revolution more profound than that in the coastal urban areas. Typically called township-and-village enterprises, these small industries blend private-style management with government ownership.

For a decade and a half, annual growth rates of these enterprises has exceeded 20 percent, twice as high as China's economic growth. Employing over 100 million people, more than to be found in notoriously inefficient state-owned industries, town-and-village enterprises are easing the problem of rural people migrating to the cities in search of work.

Moreover, as agriculture becomes mechanized and automated, there are more people available to work in these small and vigorous regional industries.

seeking employment in the cities remains a city planner's headache.

The problem is especially acute in the south. In Guangzhou, a quarter of the population consists of migrant workers, the "floating population". It is estimated by the official press that China's floating population may exceed 100 million, nearly equivalent to the population of Japan and greater than that of France.

What drives the floating population are urban incomes that are twice that to be found in the countryside; moreover, one-third of the rural population is underemployed, if not actually unemployed.

The "iron rice bowl", as the system of

Many of these enterprises began as workshops in the commune system established in the 1960s. After Deng Xiaoping took power in 1978 and liberalized both agriculture and industry, rural incomes rapidly increased, as did buying power. These communal leftovers, at least those that survived, shifted to meet demand. Some are sweatshops, to be sure, and there is a conflict of interest for local governments, who are both owners and regulators of the enterprises.

While these township-and-village enterprises have offered new opportunities for the rural population and thus lessened the burden on cities somewhat, migrant workers

permanent jobs and guaranteed wages was once called, has proven over the years to be ineffectual, whether in industry or the civil service (which is the world's largest at nearly 40 million bureaucrats).

Not surprisingly, most state-run firms have proved to be uneconomical and unresponsive to China's increasing demand for commodities and services.

China has moved to stem the losses, cutting hundreds of thousands of jobs in state-run companies during the early 1990s. But the job cuts have met with resistance; sacked workers have assaulted managers. By contrast, the flourishing private sector is characterized by vitality and vigor; lunch breaks are short. Time is, after all, money.

Nationalities: There are over 50 officially-recognized minority groups in China, including those in Tibet and Xinjiang. Most minority groups live along China's strategic, sometimes troubled and usually sparsely-populated international borders.

Thus, when one of the minority groups needles Beijing, such as happens with Tibetans, the central government takes such deviations quite seriously. The minorities have often maintained close relationships with those of their group living on the other side of those borders. As a result, the central government cannot retain absolute control over some of these frontier peoples.

The defining elements of a minority are language, homeland, and social values. Perhaps eight percent of China's population is part of a minority group, with the largest being the 12-million-strong Zhuang, in southwestern China.

Given China's population of 1.2 billion, over 70 million people are non-Han Chinese. The constitution guarantees them certain national rights and privileges. One of the most important is the right to use their own language. To grant these minorities the right to live according to their own beliefs and traditions is, in the eyes of the Chinese, a sign of goodwill, and the renunciation of the expansionism of the old regime.

However, spoken and written fluency in standard Mandarin is the only way of becoming educated and improving social status. Schools for members of national minorities are not found everywhere, and universities teaching a minority language hardly exist.

This reflects an ancient concept, based on historical experience, that there is no other developed culture apart from the Chinese.

In reality, actually, the slow expansion of the Chinese nation from the original area on the Yellow River and its tributaries up to the South China Sea is linked to an equally slow assimilation of non-Chinese peoples into the Han Chinese society, considered culturally and technically more advanced than the surrounding cultures.

The small minorities that continue to live in less easily-accessible areas (known as "areas one flees to") have resisted the attraction of Chinese culture and civilization, and so have paid the price of slow progress within their own cultures.

At the same time, over the past century, Han Chinese have moved to the outlying regions in great numbers, usually becoming the majority group.

In the autonomous region of Xinjiang, Uighurs remain the largest existing ethnic group, but make up only 45 percent of the population. Only when grouped together with the Kazakhs, Kirghiz and others do Uighurs constitute an Islamic, Turkic-speaking majority. Forty years ago, 80 percent of the population fulfilled these criteria.

But now, the large cities have a majority of Han Chinese (except for Kashi); Urümqi, a city with over one million people and the capital of Xinjiang, is made up of around 80 percent Han Chinese.

In Inner Mongolia, the Han have predominated for decades, and now represent 80 percent of the population.

On the other hand, more Mongols live in this region than in the neighboring and namesake country to the north, Mongolia. It is mainly the nomadic population who are Mongolians; almost all settled farmers, entrepreneurs and people living in towns and cities are Han Chinese.

<u>Left</u>, people from the rural provinces, Guangzhou. <u>Right</u>, Kazakh woman, Xinjiang.

Ancestor worship: The ancestor worship of the Chinese is based upon the assumption that a person has two souls. One of them is created at the time of conception, and when the person has died, the soul stays in the grave with the corpse and lives on the sacrificial offerings. As the corpse decomposes, the strength of the soul dwindles, until it eventually leads a shadow existence by the Yellow Springs in the underworld. However, it will return to earth as an ill-willed spirit and create damage if no more sacrifices are

create an abode for the soul during the sacrificial ritual. It was usually the grandson of the honored ancestor who took on the role of substitute. About 2,000 years ago, genealogical tables were introduced as homes for the soul during sacrificial acts. Up until that time, the king and noblemen had used human sacrifices for ancestral worship. Even today, the Chinese worship their ancestors and offer the deities sacrifices of food. This is widely practised, for example, during the Qingming Festival.

offered. The second soul only emerges at birth. During its heavenly voyage, it is threatened by evil forces, and is also dependent upon the sacrifices and prayers of the living descendants. If the sacrifices cease, then this soul, too, turns into an evil spirit. But if the descendants continue to make sacrificial offerings and look into the maintenance of graves, the soul of the deceased ancestor may offer them help and protection.

Originally, ancestor worship had been exclusive to the king. Only later did peasants too begin to honor their ancestors. At first, people believed that the soul of the ancestor would search for a human substitute and

The original religion of the people actually focused on the worship of natural forces. Later, the people began to worship the Jade Emperor, a figure from Daoism who became the highest god in the popular religion after the fourteenth century. Guanyin, the goddess of mercy, originated in Mahayana (Great Wheel) Buddhism. Among the many gods in popular Chinese religion, there were also earth deities. The deities of streams and rivers were considered to be particularly dangerous and unpredictable. Apart from Confucianism, Daoism and Buddhism, there was also a working-class religion known as Daoist Buddhism.

Daoism: Central concepts of Daoism are the *dao*, which basically means way or path, but it also has a second meaning of method and principle; the other concept is *wuwai*, which is sometimes simply defined as passivity, or "swimming with the stream". The concept of *de* (virtue) is closely linked to this, not in the sense of moral honesty, but as a virtue that manifests itself in daily life when dao is put into practice. The course of events in the world is determined by the forces *yang* and *yin*. The masculine, bright-

ness, activity and heaven are considered to be yang forces; the feminine, weak, dark and passive elements are seen as yin forces.

Laozi, born in a village in the province of Henan in 604 BC, was the founder of Daoism. He lived at a time of crises and upheavals. The Daoists were opposed to feudal society, yet they did not fight actively for a new social structure, preferring instead to live in a pre-feudalistic tribal society.

Experts today are still arguing about Laozi's historical existence. Since the second

Left, ancestor worship, 19th century. **Above**, statue of Laozi, near Dazu.

century AD, many legends have been told about the figure of Laozi. One of them, for instance, says that he was conceived by a beam of light, and that his mother was pregnant with him for 72 years and then gave birth to him through her left armpit. His hair was white when he was born; he prolonged his life with magic.

The ordinary people were not particularly attracted by the abstract concepts and metaphysical reflections of Daoism. Even at the beginning of the Han period (206 BC–AD 220), there were signs of both a popular and religious Daoism. As Buddhism also became more and more popular, it borrowed ideas from Daoism, and vice versa, to the point where one might speak of a fusion between the two.

The Daoists and Buddhists both believed that the great paradise was in the far west of China, hence the name, Western Paradise. It was believed to be governed by the queen mother of the West (Xiwangmu) and her husband, the royal count of the East (Dongwanggong). Without making any changes to it, the Daoists also took over the idea of hell from Buddhism.

Confucius: While Laozi was active in the south of China, Confucius lived in the north of the country. For him, too, dao and de are central concepts.

For more than 2,000 years, the ideas of Confucius (551–479 BC) have influenced Chinese culture, which in turn sculpted the worldview of neighboring lands such as Korea, Japan and Southeast Asia. It is debatable whether Confucianism is a religion in the strictest sense.

But Confucius was worshipped as a deity, although he was only officially made equal to the heavenly god by an imperial edict in 1906. (Up until 1927, many Chinese offered him sacrifices.)

Confucius came from an impoverished family of the nobility who lived in the state of Lu (near the village of Qufu, in the west of Shandong Province). For years, Confucius – or Kong Fuzi (Master Kong) – tried to gain office with one of the feudal lords, but he was dismissed again and again. So he traveled around with his disciples and instructed them in his ideas. All in all, he is said to have had 3,000 disciples, 72 of them highly-gifted ones who are still worshipped today. Confucius taught mainly traditional literature, rites and music, and is thus regarded as the founder of scholarly life in China. The Chinese word *ru*, which as a rule is translated as Confucian, actually means "someone of a gentle nature" – a trait that was attributed to a cultured person. Confucius did not publish his philosophical thoughts in a book. They have, therefore, to be reconstructed from fragments of the comments he made on various occasions. The thoughts of Confucius were collected in the *Lunyu* (Conversations) by his loyal disciples.

Confucius believed that he would create an ideal social order if he reinstated the culture and rites of the early Zhou period (1100–700 BC). Humanity (*ren*) was a central concept at the time, its basis being the love of children and brotherly love. Accordingly, the rulers would only be successful in their efforts if they can govern the whole of society according to these principles. Confucius defined the social positions and hierarchies very clearly and precisely. Only if and when every member of society takes full responsibility for his or her position will society as a whole function smoothly.

Family and social ties – and hierarchy – were considered to be of fundamental impor-

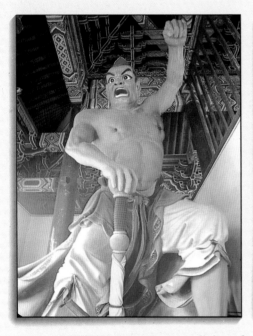

Confucianism is, in a sense, a religion of law and order. Just as the universe is dictated by the world order, and the sun, moon and stars move according to the laws of nature, so a person, too, should live within the framework of world order. This idea, in turn, is based upon the assumption that man can be educated. Ethical principles were turned into central issues.

Confucius was a very conservative reformer, yet he significantly reinterpreted the idea of the *junzi*, a nobleman, to that of a noble man, whose life is morally sound and who is, therefore, legitimately entitled to reign and lead people.

tance: between father and son (the son has to obey the father without reservations); man and woman (women have few individual rights); older brother and younger brother; friend and friend; and ruler and subordinate.

Buddhism: The Chinese initially encountered Buddhism at the beginning of the first century, when merchants and monks came to China over the Silk Road.

The type of Buddhism that is prevalent in China today is the *Mahayana* (Great Wheel), which – as opposed to *Hinayana* (Small Wheel) – promises all creatures redemption through the so-called *bodhisattva* (redemption deities). There were two aspects that were particularly attractive to the Chinese: the teachings of *karma* provided a better explanation for individual misfortune, and there was a hopeful promise for existence after death. Nevertheless, there was considerable opposition to Buddhism, which contrasted sharply with Confucian ethics and ancestor worship.

Buddhism was most influential in Chinese history during the Tang dynasty (618–907). Several emperors officially supported the religion; the Tang empress Wu Zetian, in particular, surrounded herself with Buddhist advisors. During the years 842 to 845, however, Chinese Buddhists also experienced the most severe persecutions in their entire

history: a total of 40,000 temples and monasteries were destroyed, and Buddhism was blamed for the economic decline and moral decay of the dynasty.

Since the seventh century, the ascetic Bodhisattva has been a popular female figure in China. She is called Guanyin, a motherly goddess of mercy who represents a central deity for the ordinary people. Guanyin means "the one who listens to complaints".

In Chinese Buddhism, the centre of religious attention is the Sakyamuni Buddha,

Left, demonic tutelary god, incense offering. **Above**, Buddha Sakyamuni.

the founder of Buddhism who was forced into the background in the sixth century by the Maitreya Buddha (who was called Milefo in China, or redeemer of the world). In Chinese monasteries, Sakyamuni greets the faithful as a laughing Buddha in the entrance hall. Since the fourteenth century, the Amitabha school had dominated the life and culture of the Chinese people.

The most influential Buddhist school was the so-called School of Meditation (Chan in China, Zen in Japan), which developed under the Tang dynasty.

It preached redemption through buddhahood, which anyone is able to reach. It despised knowledge gained from books or dogmas, as well as rites. Liberating shocks or guided meditation are used in order to lead disciples towards the experience of enlightenment. Other techniques used to achieve final insights were long hikes and physical work. The most important method was a dialogue with the master, who asked subtle and paradoxical questions, to which he expected equally paradoxical answers.

In 1949, the year the People's Republic of China was founded, there were approximately 500,000 Buddhist monks and nuns, and 50,000 temples and monasteries. A number of well-known Buddhist temples were classified as historical monuments.

By the beginning of the Cultural Revolution in 1966, it seemed as if the Red Guards were intent on completely eradicating Buddhism. The autonomous Tibet was hard-hit by these excesses. Only a few important monasteries and cultural objects could be protected, and completely or only partly preserved. Today, there are Buddhists among the Han Chinese, the Mongols, Tibetans, Manchus, Tu, Qiang and Dai (Hinayana Buddhists) peoples.

In the seventh century AD, another type of Buddhism, called Tantric Buddhism or Lamaism, was introduced into Tibet from India. With the influence of the monk Padmasambhava, it replaced the indigenous Bon religion, while at the same time taking over some of the elements of this naturalist religion. The monasteries in Tibet developed into centers of intellectual and worldly power, yet there were recurring arguments. Only the reformer Tsongkhapa (1357–1419) succeeded in rectifying conditions that had become chaotic.

Calligraphy, painting, poetry and music are regarded in China as the noble arts, whereas the applied arts are considered merely as honorable crafts. All the same, in the West, these skilled crafts have always held a special fascination and are usually considered to be true arts. When thinking of China, one thinks of silk, jade and porcelain.

Silk: The cultivation of the silkworm is said to go back to the third century BC. Legend has it that planting of mulberry trees and keeping silkworms was started by the wife of the mythical Yellow Emperor Huangdi. For centuries, silk held the place of currency: civil servants and officers as well as foreign envoys were frequently paid or presented with bales of silk.

The precious material was transported to the Middle East and the Roman empire via the Silk Road. The Chinese maintained a monopoly on silk until about 200 BC, when the secret of its manufacture became known in Korea and Japan. In the West – in this case the Byzantine empire – such knowledge was acquired only in the sixth century AD. The Chinese had prohibited the export of silkworm eggs and the dissemination of knowledge of their cultivation, but a monk is said to have succeeded in smuggling some silkworm eggs to the West.

Today's centers of silk production are areas in the south of China around Hangzhou, Suzhou and Wuxi; in this region, silk can be bought at a lower price. Hangzhou has the largest silk industry in the People's Republic, while in Suzhou, silk embroidery has been brought to the highest artistic level.

Porcelain: The Chinese invented porcelain sometime in the seventh century – a thousand years before the Europeans did. The history of Chinese ceramic artifacts, however, goes back to neolithic times. Along the Huang He (Yellow River) and Chang Jiang (Yangzi), 7,000- to 8,000-year-old ceramic vessels, red and even black clayware with comb and rope patterns, have been found. The Yangshao and Longshan cultures of the fifth to second millennium BC developed new types of vessels and a diversity of pat-

terns in red, black or brown. Quasi-human masks, stylized fish, and hard, thin-walled stoneware, with kaolin and lime feldspar glazes, were created. Later, light-grey stoneware with green glazes, known as *yue* ware – named after the kilns of the town of Yuezhou – were typical designs of the Han period. Even during the Tang dynasty, China was known in Europe and the Middle East as the home of porcelain.

The most widespread form of ancient Chinese porcelain was celadon – a product of a blending of iron oxide with the glaze that resulted, during firing, in the characteristic green tone of the porcelain. *Sancai* ceramics – ceramics with three-color glazes from the Tang dynasty – became world-famous. The colors were mostly strong green, yellow and brown. Sancai ceramics were also found among the tomb figurines of the Tang period in the shape of horses, camels, guardians in animal or human form, ladies of the court, and officials.

The Song-period celadons – ranging in color from pale or moss green, pale blue or pale grey to brown tones – were also technically excellent. As early as the Yuan period, a technique from Persia was used for underglaze painting in cobalt blue (commonly known as Ming porcelain). Some common themes seen throughout the subsequent Ming period were figures, landscapes and theatrical scenes. At the beginning of the Qing dynasty, blue-and-white porcelain attained its highest level of quality. Since the fourteenth century, Jingdezhen has been the center of porcelain manufacture, although today, relatively inexpensive porcelain can be bought throughout China.

However, antique pieces are still hard to come by because the sale of articles predating the Opium Wars is prohibited by the Chinese government.

Jade: With its soft sheen and rich nuances of color, jade is China's most precious stone. Jade is not a precise mineralogical entity but rather comprises two minerals: jadeite and nephrite. The former is more valuable because of its translucence and hardness, as well as its rarity. The Chinese have known jade since antiquity, but it became widely

Left, porcelain, Song dynasty, Xi'an.

popular only in the eighteenth century. Colors vary from white to green, but there are also red, yellow and lavender jades. In China, a clear emerald-green stone is valued most highly. According to ancient legend, Yu, as the jewel is known, came from the holy mountains and was thought to be crystallized moonlight. In fact, jade came from Khotan, along the southern Silk Road.

Nephrite is quite similar to jadeite, but not quite as hard and is more common. During the eighteenth century, nephrite was quarried in enormous quantities in the Kunlun mountains. It comes in various shades of green (not the luminous green of jadeite), white, yellow and black.

The oldest jades so far discovered come from the neolithic Hemadu culture (about 5000 BC). The finds were presumably ritual objects. Circular disks called *bi,* given to the dead to take with them, were frequently found. Centuries later, the corpses of high-ranking officials were clothed in suits made of more than 2,000 thin slivers of jade sewn together with gold wire. Since the eleventh century, the Jade Emperor has been revered as the superior godhead in Daoist popular religion. Today, the ring disk – a symbol of heaven – is still worn by some as a talisman; jade bracelets are often believed to protect against rheumatism.

In the jade-carving workshops in present-day China, there are thought to be as many as 30 kinds of jade in use. Famous among the jade workshops are those in Qingtian (Zhejiang province), Shoushan (Fujian province), and Luoyang (Hunan province). Masters of jade work include Zhou Shouhai, from the Jade-carving establishment in Shanghai, and Wang Shusen in Beijing, the latter specializing in Buddhist figurines. In government shops, jade can be trusted to be genuine. On the open market and in private shops, however, caution is advised. Genuine jade always feels cool and cannot be scratched with a knife. Quality depends on the feel of the stone, its color, transparency, pattern and other factors. If in doubt, a reputable expert should be consulted.

Lacquerware: The glossy sheen of lacquerware is not only attractive to the eye but is also appealing to the touch. The bark of the lacquer tree (*rhus verniciflua*), which grows in central and southern China, exudes a milky sap when cut, which solidifies in moist air, dries and turns brown. This dry layer of lacquer is impervious to moisture, acid, and scratches, and is therefore ideal protection for materials such as wood or bamboo. The oldest finds of lacquered objects date back to the fifth millennium BC.

Bowls, tins, boxes, vases, and furniture made of various materials (wood, bamboo, wicker, leather, metal, clay, textiles, paper) are coated with a skin of lacquer. A base coat is applied to the core material, followed by extremely thin layers of the finest lacquer that, after drying in dust-free moist air, are smoothed and polished. In the dry lacquer method, the lacquer itself dictates the form: fabric or paper is saturated with lacquer and pressed into a wood or clay mold. After drying, the mold is removed and the piece coated with further layers of lacquer. Vessels, boxes and plates were already being made in this way in the Han period.

During the Tang dynasty, large Buddhist sculptures were produced by the lacquerware process. If soot or vinegar-soaked iron filings are added to the lacquer, it will dry into a black color; cinnabar turns it red. The color combination of red and black, first thought to have been applied in the second century BC, is still considered a classic. In the Song and Yuan periods, simply-shaped monochromatic lacquerware was valued.

During the Ming period, the manufacture of lacquered objects was further refined. The cities of Beijing, Fuzhou, Guangzhou, Chengdu, Yangzhou and Suzhou were renowned for exquisite lacquerware, which was enriched and decorated with carving, fillings, gold paint and inlay.

The carved lacquer technique, which began at the time of the Tang dynasty, reached its highest peak during the Ming and Qing periods. The core, often of wood or tin, is coated with mostly red layers of lacquer. When the outermost coat has dried, decorative carving is applied, with the knife penetrating generally to the lowest layer so that the design stands out from the background in

century AD, was lost and then rediscovered in the thirteenth century. In the cloisonné technique, metal rods are soldered to the body of the metal object. These form the outlines of the ornamentation. The spaces between the rods are filled with enamel paste and fired in the kiln. Finally, metal surfaces not covered with enamel are gilded. During the Yuan dynasty, Yunnan was the center of cloisonné production. However, the golden age of this technique was the Ming period, when the techniques of melting enamel on porcelain were developed.

Ivory: As a craft material, ivory is as old as jade, and early pieces can be traced to as far back as 5000 BC. During the Bronze Age,

relief. Today, lacquerware is mainly produced in Beijing, Fuzhou and Yangzhou. The most well-known lacquerware is the Beijing work, which goes back to the imperial courts of the Ming and Qing dynasties. Emperor Qianlong (1734–1795) had a special liking for carved lacquerware; he was even buried in a coffin magnificently carved using this technique.

Cloisonné: The cloisonné technique – used to create metal objects with enamel decor – reached China from Persia in the eighth

wild elephants were not a rarity in northern China; some were tamed during the Shang dynasty. The old artist carvers regarded elephant tusks as a most desirable material from which to make jewelery, implements and containers. The once-large herds of elephants in the south of China thus shrank to a small remnant, and eventually ivory had to be imported. Ming dynasty carvings exemplified the excellent craft skills and superior taste; then, during Qing times, ivory carving was even further refined. Today's centers for ivory carving are Beijing, Guangzhou and Shanghai. All the ivory is imported from Thailand and several African countries.

What would England be without its countless church spires? Just as inconceivable would be China without its countless pagodas. In keeping with their original religious significance, they are mostly found in places of worship and monastic institutions, or at least near them, and are used for the safekeeping of relics. These tall and slender towers are also found on hilltops rising high over the landscape. Pagodas assume an aesthetic vividness as a result of their location and unique form, and this becomes one of the

the enrichment of Chinese architectural forms derived from Buddhism. The word *pagoda* is not Chinese, but was probably adapted from the Sanskrit word *bhagavan*, which has a similar meaning to the English word lord, commonly used to address divinity. In Chinese, a pagoda is called *ta*, which earlier was *tappna*, a Chinese rendering of the Indian word *stupa*. (Thus, Bai Ta is Bai Pagoda.)

China's capital city, Beijing, is known above all for its Imperial Palace complex, but the visitor's eye is irresistibly drawn to

enduring impressions of every traveler to China. Nevertheless, the variety of architectural styles, materials and forms are at first confusing for the uninitiated.

The first Buddhist missionaries spread the teaching of Buddha across northern India to China. Many Chinese monks later traveled the same route back to India to study ancient writings and to visit the places directly influenced by Buddha. In this way, reports of burial rites, religious art and the impressive monastic and temple architecture filtered into remote China.

By way of etymology, too, it can be concluded that the pagoda is representative of

another structure, in Beihai Park: Bai Ta, the White Dagoba, rising majestically to the west of the Imperial Palace and above the entire imperial city. The white, massive bell-shaped structure is set on a square base in the style of a Tibetan chörten; it was built in 1651 for the reception of the fifth Dalai Lama at the court of the emperor of China.

Who would have guessed that there was a connection, a common origin, between this building and Liuhe Ta (Pagoda of the Six Harmonies) on the Qiantang River, near Hangzhou? These two pagodas cover the entire span of Chinese pagoda design.

There are, of course, pagodas of boundless

diversity throughout Asia wherever the Buddhist religion is present. In the beginning, these buildings were nothing other than burial places. Indian rulers at the time of the Gautama Siddharta, the authentic Buddha, were buried in tombs that consisted of a semi-spherical solid core structure rising from a cylindrical plinth.

The style of Buddhist tombs resembling the Indian stupa can be found in Tibet. The Tibetan chörten were used for the burial of Lama high priests, including the Dalai and

with a surrounding gallery at each level – giving access to one small chapel after another – surmounted by a cylindrical core with a conical shape and a large "umbrella" sitting at its top. Above those are symbols from Buddhist teaching, such as the sun, recumbent half-moon and flames. The White Dagoba in Beijing belongs firmly to this Tibetan chörten tradition.

Chinese style: The diversity in the artistic development and stylistic form of pagodas throughout Asia evolved within China to the

Panchen Lamas; however, in the imaginative world of Tantrist Buddhism, which is dominant in Tibet, the building of a chörten is more meaningful than simply as a mere tomb. It is a symbolic ceremonial act, a result of which is the presence of Buddha manifesting itself in the finished building. The largest building of this kind is the chörten of Jiangzi, a monumental structure that also fulfills the function of a temple. A square four-story base structure rises from a polygonal plinth

characteristic elongation of the structure, while dispensing with the plinth. The Chinese pagoda is, to some extent, an overscaled representation of the umbrella-like superstructure built along the central shaft, which in the case of Tantric Buddhist buildings carried as many as thirteen "umbrellas", symbolizing the number of ways of attaining salvation. With Chinese pagodas, the shaft becomes a tower and the "umbrellas" become accessible storys.

The first pagoda structures found in China go back to the third and fifth century AD and were presumably constructed in timber; none of these survive. Later, in the north of China,

Left, beams and roof tiles of Beijing's Tiantan, or Temple of Heaven. **Above**, Temple of Heaven dome; White Dagoba, Beijing.

solid construction using bricks and tiles was adopted, whereas in the south – in the absence of alternative building materials – timber construction continued. The oldest surviving pagoda is found in the district of Dengfeng, near the old imperial city of Luoyang and close to the famous Shaolin monastery. This 40-meter-high (130-ft), twelve-sided Songyue Pagoda was built in AD 523; for over 1,400 years, it has withstood the ravages of weather, natural disasters and revolutions – from the Mongol invasion to the Cultural Revolution.

At the nearby Shaolin monastery, there is another rare sight: Talin, the Forest of Pagodas, a cemetery with more than 200 stone funerary pagodas – the last resting place of monks and abbots. These pagodas are only a few meters high and have, at chest height, a square core to which are attached memorial tablets or small recesses for offerings. Their function and symbolism correspond to the original Indian stupas, but not their architectural style.

Other ancient structures include what are possibly the best-known pagodas in China – the two Wild Goose pagodas in Xi'an. Dayan Ta, the Great Wild Goose Pagoda, was built at the instigation of and to the design of the monk Xuanzang who, in the seventh century AD, undertook an adventurous years-long journey to northern India. It is known to today's Chinese as a legend from the fictional trilogy, *Journey to the West*. The Great Wild Goose Pagoda is used to store his writings and was the religious focal point of a large monastery.

The curious name of this pagoda goes back to a legend supposedly brought back from northern India by Xuanzang. According to his account, it was here that Buddha – whose religious sect forbades the partaking of meat – successfully resisted the temptation of a wild goose. As a warning and reminder of this, a pagoda was erected on the very same spot where he had been tempted.

The smaller 13-story, 43-meter-high (141-ft) Xiaoyan Ta, or Little Wild Goose Pagoda, originally had another name but was simply re-christened, in the course of time, because of its striking similarity to its larger companion, the Great Wild Goose Pagoda. It is of approximately similar age but appears – because of its greater number of storys, its slender form, and its gently-curved topmost

point – much more graceful than the monumental and somewhat clumsy Great Wild Goose Pagoda. As solid-brick stepped pagodas, both are typical examples of the Tang-period style.

Tradition of architecture: Just as they adapted Buddhism by rapidly mixing the original teachings of Buddha with traditional superstitions and ancestor worship, so did the Chinese invest the genuine style of the Buddhist pagoda with their own forms and building traditions.

China has been known for its massive tower structures since the Han dynasty. This form of construction was used for city walls, as well as court and palace gates. Chinese

craftsmen developed timber-frame construction to its ultimate form, which can still be admired in the old palaces and temples. Posts and beams satisfy structural requirements and are often built without the aid of glue or nails. Corbels and brackets, artfully combined into incredibly complex structures, support the roofs. Walls resolve into openings or, at least, skillfully pierced surfaces that blend with the natural setting outside. Intricately designed curved roof shapes with finely carved figures encapsulate this style of building that, without a doubt, strongly reflects Daoist philosophy in its aim at complete harmony between people and nature.

The German poet Goethe, who was not unaffected by Chinese philosophy and culture, describes in a poem the unfamiliar turn of creative style. He tells of a Chinese on a visit to Rome; all the buildings, both ancient and new, seem heavy and clumsy to him. He wishes that the poor Romans could understand how fine columns of wood can carry an entire roof, and that carved and gilded beams are a joy to the eye of a sensitive and educated beholder.

Palace architecture: Early antecedents of Chinese palace architecture were found by archaeologists at Erlitou, near Luoyang. Excavations at the Shang dynasty site revealed a terrace that must have been the floor

of Chinese palace architecture are, of course, best observed at Gugong, the Imperial Palace, or some of the other palaces and temples in Beijing – most of which date from the Ming dynasty.

The Imperial Palace best exemplifies the contours of palace architecture. Large buildings like the three great Halls of Harmony, in the front part of the palace, rise from a terrace, which acts as a base but also serves a practical purpose – to protect the halls from any ingress of water. Old texts, however, point clearly to a symbolic and cosmological meaning: "The Heavens cover and the Earth carries." The terrace, in these terms, represents the Earth, and the roof, Heaven.

of some large hall. Architecture later made great strides in the Qin and Han dynasties. The basic plan configuration of later palaces was already fully developed. Timber-frame construction had been considerably refined. The infill panels between the posts and columns that carried the roof became subtle decorative screens. As during the Han dynasty, clay models of these were placed in graves as a parting gift.

Today, the main features and peculiarities

Left, the Great Wild Goose Pagoda at Xi'an, dating back to the Tang dynasty. **Above**, detail of a brick-built stepped pagoda.

The size of a terrace is determined by the ranking of the building in the total context; buildings along the central axis generally count for more than subsidiary ones. This architectural principle can be studied readily at the Imperial Palace. Taihedian, the Hall of Supreme Harmony, has the largest and most splendid terrace in the whole of the palace grounds; in three raised levels, the entire terrace is framed by a finely-decorated marble balustrade.

From the earliest days, the Chinese favored timber as a building material; it was not only easily transported, but it was also very practical. Heavy posts were capable of carrying the roof, while the wood could be carved for decoration and embellishment. For the columns of the Imperial Palace, the hard and precious *nanmu* wood (brought from the southwestern provinces) was used.

In summer, the infill panels between the load-bearing columns of simple houses were easily removed; in winter, the open timber grilles were covered with rice paper to keep the cold at bay. Corbel construction, between the tops of columns and the roof of palacial halls, reached the peak of fine craftsmanship. A visually-confusing impression of longitudinal and cross beams, which involved timber components originally intended just to carry the gutters, becomes

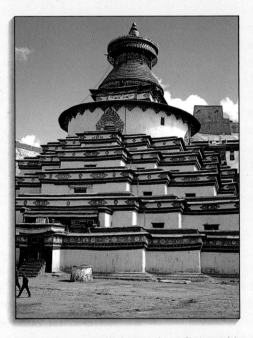

decorative embellishment in palace architecture – but without diminishing their function as load-dispersing elements of the structure. Corbel systems also give a clue as to the social status of the house owner – ordinary people were not permitted to have them.

The roofs of Chinese palaces lend these generally large and massive buildings an air of weightlessness; the slightly upturned eaves and gutters seem to let the entire roof float above the building. Another way of achieving this illusion of floating is the double roof: the roof is constructed in two stages, and the low wall separating the two suggests a small additional story.

The roofs of palaces are covered with glazed tiles. With the Imperial Palace, the emperor's color was yellow, while Tiantan, the Temple of Heaven, is appropriately covered in blue tiles. The tiles at the end are round or half-round decorated finials, and in the Imperial Palace, carry the dragon symbol.

Architecture and superstition: Very conspicuous on palace roofs is the ridge decoration: two dragon-like animals facing each other, while their gaping mouths seem to carry the ridge with their fish-like tails pointing heavenwards. Chinese mythology ascribes to the dragon the ability of being able to make rain. He thus protects the vulnerable timber building against fire.

The mythological beasts at the ends of the ridge of palace roofs have a similar significance: to protect the building from evil spirits. At the same time, the importance of the building can be derived from their number. Ten animals and one immortal decorate the ridge ends of the two-tier roof of Taihedian, in the Imperial Palace. The animals include a lion, dragon, phoenix, flying horse, and a unicorn, amongst others.

Lower down on most of these roofs, one will find a man riding a hen – another common figure intended to protect the building and occupants against disaster. Legend has it that this represents a tyrannical prince from the state of Qi (third century BC). After his defeat and death, the inhabitants of Qi are said to have fixed replicas of him riding on a hen to their roofs in order to keep away disaster and stigmatize the tyrant. Superstition has it that the evil tyrant on the hen cannot leave the roof because the hen cannot carry him in flight.

Such superstitious imaginings are often reflected in Chinese architecture. The so-called ghost wall, for example, was usually put up behind the entrance of all apartments and palaces to bar the entry of evil spirits, as they were believed to be able to move in a straight path only and not around corners. In the large palaces, Jiulongbi, the splendid Nine Dragon Wall, fulfilled this function. Even at the entrance to the government and party offices in Beijing (Zhongnanhai), there is a ghost wall directly behind the gate, complete with quotations from Mao Zedong.

Left, Tibetan Kumbun Chörten, Jiangzi. **Right**, Longhua Pagoda, Shanghai.

BEIJING:
NORTHERN CAPITAL

The country around Beijing was already settled in prehistoric times, proven by the discovery in the small town of Zhoukoudian, southwest of Beijing, of the skull of *Sinanthropus pekinensis* (Peking Man). More recently, since about a thousand years ago, the city has served as primary and subsidiary residence for a series of dynasties. Under the rule of the Mongol emperor Kublai Khan in the thirteenth century, it was known as Khanbaliq (City of the Khan), an especially splendid and magnificent winter residence of the emperors.

The city did not receive its layout, which still survives today, until the rule of the Ming dynasty. In traditional Chinese thought, the world was not imagined as the flat, round disk of the Ptolomaean vision in the West, but was conceived of as a square. A city, too – and especially a capital city – was supposed to be square, a reflection of the cosmic order and adhering to its geometrical definition, with a north-south and east-west orientation of roads and buildings. In no other city in China has this basic idea been fulfilled as completely as in ancient Beijing.

Geomantic design: The third Ming emperor Yongle is considered the capital's actual planner and architect. In 1421, he moved his government from Nanjing to the city of Beiping (Northern Peace) and renamed it as Beijing (Northern Capital). In a bad attempt at transliteration by Europeans, the city became known as Peking in the West – a name that persists in some instances, such as with the cuisine specialty, Peking Duck. (Nobody calls it Beijing Duck.)

The plans of Yongle followed the principles of geomancy, the traditional doctrine of "winds and water," which strives to attain a harmonious relationship between human life and nature. Screened from the north by a semicircle of hills, Beijing lies on a plain that opens to the south, an auspicious direction, as it was toward the south that the generos-

ity and warmth of *yang* was thought to reside. Likewise, all important buildings in the old city face south, thus protected from harmful influences from the north – whether winter Siberian winds or enemies from the steppes. Thus, it was not by chance that south-facing Qianmen the Outer Gate to the city – was the largest, most beautiful, and most sacred of its kind. The hill of Jing Shan, to the north of Gugong, the Imperial Palace, was probably created according to geomantic considerations as well.

A theoretical line from north to south divides the city east and west, with the axis centered on the Imperial Palace; important buildings and city features were laid out as mirror images on either side. Ritan (Altar of the Sun), for example, has its equivalent in Yuetan (Altar of the Moon). Planned in an equally complementary way were Xidan and Dongdan, the eastern and western business quarters, which today still serve as shopping streets.

Some of the most notable buildings of both old and new Beijing are to be found

on the north–south axis itself. From the north: Zhonglou and Gulou (Bell and Drum Towers), Jing Shan (Coal Hill), and the Imperial Palace. From the south northwards: Qianmen (Outer Gate), Tiananmen, and the Imperial Palace, lined up one after the other like pearls on a string. In the middle of this north–south chain of historically-significant buildings lies the heart of ancient Beijing, the Dragon Throne, from which the emperor, ritual mediator between heaven and earth, governed. This was considered the center of the physical world, thought of as a gigantic grid. The city, and the world, and everything within, are clearly given a defined place in a hierarchy, depending on how far they are from the center. This imperial throne is embedded in a majestic palace, which is also square and surrounded by high purple walls on all sides – the so-called Forbidden City. Around it lies the imperial city, which in earlier times also formed a square surrounded by walls.

Part of the old imperial city was defined by a chain of lakes. Today, the northern part forms the center of Beihai Gongyuan (Beihai Park). On the shores of the central and southern waters lies **Zhongnanhai**, since 1949 the Communist Party's forbidden city. Only highly-placed officials and important state guests are permitted inside.

Crowded around the old imperial city was a sea of mainly single-story houses. Curved like the crests of waves, the roofs of this inner city were not allowed to rise above the height of the Imperial Palace. Here, the tasteful homes of the wealthy and of influential officials were to be found. Even nowadays, this part of Beijing is still considered to be the actual inner city, or old city. However, only a few monumental gates of the mighty defensive walls that once surrounded Beijing have survived – Qianmen in the south and in the north, Deshengmen.

Adjoining the inner city to the south was an outer city. In Qing times, the former was residence for the Mongols, the latter for the Chinese. In the Chinese area, the doors of the houses were lower, **Palace gate.**

the *hutong* (as the alleys of Beijing were known) were narrower, and the rice bowls were less well-filled. Instead of tea, people drank hot water. Instead of satin boots, they wore sandals. However, bored Manchu officials and wealthy merchants sometimes fled their respectable surroundings for the Chinese district's tea and bath houses, brothels, specialty restaurants and bazaars – all competing for the favors and money of literati, monks, mandarins, and, from time to time, the occasional prince in clever disguise.

Even today, things are livelier to the south of Qianmen than in other parts of the city. The gourmet restaurants remain crowded. **Dazhalan**, a small street running at right angles to the boulevard of Qianmen Dajie, has old established shops and businesses of excellent reputation, and is still an attraction for people from the Beijing suburbs as well as the provinces. Not far away is **Liulichang**, a shopping street restored to its original style for tourists, which has almost everything that China can offer by way of art and kitsch. The number-one shopping district today is still **Wanfujing**, a street that runs in a northerly direction from the Beijing Hotel and is now lined with fashionable boutiques and fast-food restaurants, lending it the appearance of a street in Hong Kong or Singapore.

Outside these historic city districts, however, huge concrete tower blocks have sprouted. In the northwest lies the scientific and intellectual quarter, including China's most famous universities, Beijing and Qinghua.

The Chaoyang district, to the east, is the largest industrial area of the city. Bicycles still crowd the streets, but the cyclists are segregated from the motorized vehicle traffic, and today there is a flood of cars and buses that jams city streets and the multiple-lane ring highways that encircle Beijing. The local public transport system is insufficiently developed and hopelessly overcrowded, although the subway system is more tolerable for visitors, and faster.

The rhythm of the seasons is similar

Bird fanciers.

to that in central Europe. The summers are hot and long, winters cold and dry. When sandstorms whirl through the city in spring, Beijing hardly dares to breathe. The fine dust forces its way through cracks and crevices in homes, which are badly insulated. Moreover, vehicular exhaust, massive construction projects and industrial output have turned Beijing into a polluted city – the air is thick and dusty and leaves people red-eyed and scratchy-throated.

Yet an early morning walk through a park – any park – reveals undreamed-of impressions: the sound of a moon fiddle accompanied by an aria from a Beijing opera; the chirping of birds, their cages hung in the trees; the sight of graceful sword dancers and noiseless *taiji* practitioners; and more recently, gymnastics accompanied by disco music for the elderly. (Indeed, Beijing seems at times a city of dancing: ballroom, folk, disco.)

People in this crowded city grab every meter of available space and make use of it. Grassy spots by freeway entrance ramps are used for evening exercises.

The broad plazas outside the Forbidden City are turned into dance halls that would make Lawrence Welk proud. The steps and empty concrete expanses in front of office buildings are shared by grandparents and grandchildren.

Imperial Palace: In the ancient past, in the early morning when the fourth guard watch of the night was proclaimed by powerful strokes from Gulou, the Drum Tower, the mandarins in the imperial city would push aside their silken bed curtains, dress and tidy up, then step into their porter-carried litters, which bore them to the imperial morning audience in **Gugong**, the Imperial Palace. A eunuch would show them their place, arranged according to rank, and there, kneeling in silence, they would receive instructions from the emperor on the Dragon Throne.

Behind the walls, more than 10 meters (30 ft) high, and within the 50-meter-broad (160-ft) moat, life in the palace was dictated by a multitude of rules and taboos. (Entrance was denied to ordinary mortals, of course.) Today,

Emergency water container for fires.

the gateway serves as a gigantic entrance for visitors; it leads to one of the most fascinating displays of Chinese cultural history, and to what is probably the best-preserved site of classical Chinese architecture.

In 1421, after 17 years of construction, the Ming emperor Yongle moved into the palace, and up until the founding of the republic in 1911, the palace was residence and center of the world during the reign of 24 emperors – from the Ming dynasty up until the last emperor, Puyi. It has 9,000 rooms in which an estimated 8,000 to 10,000 people lived (including 3,000 eunuchs, as well as maids and concubines), all within an area of 70 hectares (180 acres).

The entire site can be divided into two large areas: **Waichao**, the Outer Court, in the south, and in the rear, **Neiting**, the Inner Residence.

Approaching from **Wumen** (Meridian Gate) are the three great halls and courtyards of the outer area. **Taihedian** (Hall of Supreme Harmony) is the first and most impressive of these, and at the same time it is the largest building in the palace. In its center is the skillfully-carved, gold-colored **Dragon Throne**, from which the emperor ruled over the Middle Kingdom. This was also where the most solemn ceremonies – the New Year's festivities or enthronement of a new emperor – were held. The courtyard held up to 90,000 spectators.

On the other side of the imposing architecture of the Outer Court, to the north and separated from it by **Qianqingmen** (Gate of Heavenly Purity), lies a labyrinth of gates, doors, pavilions, gardens and palaces. This was the residence of the imperial family, mostly female, as the emperor and castrated eunuchs were the only males permitted to enter here.

The center of this private section is formed by three rear halls, **Sanhougong**. However, the emperors did not live there after the Qing period, but carried on state business primarily in front of **Qianqinggong** (Palace of Heavenly Purity). Actual political intrigues and maneuvering took place in the inter-

Wumen Gate.

linked rooms to the left and right of this palace. Here, the more influential eunuchs and concubines were rivals for power and influence within the court; this was the scene of plots and intrigues, and of deaths – natural and unnatural.

The well in the northeast, just behind **Ningshougong** (Palace of Peace and Longevity), was the place of one such episode. A concubine of Emperor Guanxu had dared, in 1900, to oppose the ambitious Empress Dowager Cixi. As punishment, the concubine was rolled up in a carpet and thrown down into the narrow shaft of the well by eunuchs.

Government guides can be hired – for a princely sum – outside the Forbidden City, and there is also a helpful and informative audio tape that can be rented. Note that Westerners may be asked by Chinese tourists to pose repeatedly in family and group photos; although most people in Beijing have long since grown accustomed to seeing foreigners, most Chinese tourists are from outside Beijing, and foreigners are still something of a curiosity.

Nestling closely against the southern walls of the palace, near Tiananmen, **Zhongshan Gongyuan** (Sun Yatsen Park) continues to display the impressive imperial architecture and landscaping. In the park, there used to be a temple honoring the gods of the earth and of fertility. The triumphal arch near the southern entrance was originally set up in a different place in honor of the German ambassador, Baron von Ketteler, who was murdered at the beginning of the Boxer Rebellion.

The former shrine of the imperial ancestors, now known as the People's Cultural Park and functioning as something of a college for continuing education, dates from the Ming dynasty. Here, the ancestral tablets of the imperial forebears, which the emperor was required to honor, were kept.

On 1 October 1949, Mao Zedong, Chairman of the Communist Party, proclaimed the founding of the People's Republic of China from **Tiananmen** (Gate of Heavenly Peace). Today, his portrait gazes south from this spot onto **Tiananmen Square**, which was quadrupled in size during the 1950s so that up to a million people could gather in the square. Rallies of the Red Guards took place here during the Cultural Revolution, as did the 1989 democracy demonstrations, ending only when the government – after pulling the plug on the world's media – used the army and tanks to oust the demonstrators, resulting in many deaths.

In the center of the square is an obelisk, unveiled in 1958 as a monument to the heroes of the nation and a perfect example of the Socialist Realism style. In 1959, **Renmindahiutang** (Great Hall of the People), on the west side of the square, was officially opened. This is an impressive building in the Soviet Neo-Classical monumental style, and where the People's Congress meets. The massive facades of the **Museum of Chinese History** and the **Museum of the Revolution** border the square to the east.

After the death of Mao, a mausoleum for him was built. Even today, when the teachings of the little red book of quotations have long gone out of fashion, **Old Summer Palace.**

except for tourists, people from all over China visit **Mao's mausoleum**, filing respectfully past Mao's embalmed body, lying in a rose-hued, glass enclosure.

Just steps away from the mausoleum, visitors get a graphic picture of how socialism is being consigned to the dust bin of history by a feverish consumerism, as visitors are ushered through a small bazaar where everything from Mao busts to laundry detergent are for sale.

To the northwest of the Imperial Palace, in the grounds of today's **Beihai Gongyuan** (Northern Lake Park), was the winter residence of the Mongol emperor Kublai Khan. Now, only legends remain of his former palace on **Qinghuadao** (Jade Island), the site of **Bai Ta** (White Dagoba), 35 meters (115 ft) tall and a Buddhist shrine dating from 1651, built in the Tibetan style. At the foot of the shrine, on the shores of the wide lake that dominates the park, imperial cuisine in appropriate style is available in Fangshan, a gourmet restaurant. Tuancheng (Round Town), in the southern part of the grounds, was

Summer Palace.

once the administrative center of the Mongol Yuan dynasty. From here is a good view of Zhongnanhai (Southern and Central Lake), site of the Politburo and State Council grounds.

Summer palaces: The great aesthete and Qing emperor Qianlong, who ruled from 1736 to 1795, had a huge masterpiece of landscaping and architecture created in the northwest of Beijing: **Yuanmingyuan** (Garden of Perfect Purity), or more commonly in English, the Old Summer Palace. Structures here were in the Western style, built according to plans by an Italian Jesuit and based upon European models such as the palace of Versailles. Only ruins remain today; during the Second Opium War (1856–1860), British and French troops ravished the palace and reduced it to rubble.

The dynasty built a replacement nearby, in the grounds laid out by Qianlong as a place of retirement for his mother. The new summer residence took on special interest for the famous (or infamous) Empress Dowager Cixi, who

fulfilled a wonderful, if rather expensive, dream in 1888. Using absconded money that had been intended for the building of a naval fleet, she constructed **Yiheyuan** (Garden of Cultivated Harmony), or the Summer Palace. Originally a concubine of the third rank, Cixi had placed herself on the Dragon Throne after the death of the emperor and ruled in an unscrupulous and self-centered way for 50 years, in the name of her young child.

As in every classical Chinese garden, water and mountains (usually represented by rocks) determine the landscape of Yiheyuan: the lake **Kunming** covers three quarters of the total area of more than 30 square kilometers (10 sq mi); on its shore is **Wanshou Shan** (Hill of Longevity). Over bridges and up stairs, through gates and halls is the massive **Foxiangge** (Pagoda of the Incense of Buddha), which crowns the top of Wanshou Shan.

In the eastern corner is a special jewel of the classical Chinese art of garden design, **Xiequyuan** (Garden of Joy and Harmony), a complete and picturesque copy of a lotus pool garden from Wuxi.

In order to make it more difficult for strangers to spy into the grounds, **Renshoudian** (Hall of Benevolence and Longevity) was built right next to the eastern gate, **Dongmen**, now the main gate. Behind it lay the private apartments of Cixi; today, these rooms are also a theatrical museum. Here, Cixi used to enjoy operatic performances by her 384-strong ensemble of eunuchs.

Of light wooden construction and decorated with countless painted scenes from Chinese mythology, **Changlang** (Long Corridor) runs parallel to the northern shore of the lake, linking the palace's scattered buildings into one harmonious whole. It ends in the vicinity of **Qiuyangfang** (Marble Boat), a ridiculous mockery in which Cixi, looking out over the lake, had tea.

Tiantan: Twice a year, a splendid and magnificent procession of some 1,000 eunuchs, courtiers and ministers would leave Gugong, the Imperial Palace, for **Tiantan** (Temple of Heaven) to the **Tiantan.**

south. Only twice a year, then, would the western gate be opened for the emperor, and each time he would spend a night of fasting and celibacy in **Zhaigong** (Palace of Abstinence) prior to the ritual ceremonies of sacrifice the next morning. At the winter solstice he expressed thanks for the previous harvest, and on the 15th day of the first month he begged the gods of sun and moon, clouds and rain, thunder and lightning to bless the coming harvest.

Set in the middle of a park of 270 hectares (670 acres), Tiantan, an outstanding example of religious architecture, dates from the Ming period. Destroyed several times, including by lightning, it was last rebuilt in 1890, and has been open to the public since 1949. The temple grounds are square, although the northern edge follows a semicircle, a symbolic expression of the fact that the emperor, in offering his sacrifices, had to leave the square-shaped earth for the round-roofed heaven.

An exquisite example of Chinese wooden buildings, constructed without the use of a single nail, is the round, 40-meter-high (130-ft) **Qiniandian** (Hall of Prayer for Good Harvests). With its three levels and covered with deep blue tiles that symbolize the color of heaven, the roof is supported by 28 pillars. The four largest ones, in the center, represent the four seasons; the double ring of twelve pillars represents the 12 months, as well as the traditional divisions of the Chinese day, each comprising two hours.

In the south of the park lies a white, circular marble terrace, **Hianqiutan** (Altar of Heaven), and the so-called **Echo Wall**, famous for its acoustics.

Temples and shrines: As an imperial city, the Beijing of Ming and Qing times was not just a favored place for magnificent palaces and broad parks. Here, also, the great religions of China had impressive sacred buildings. Unfortunately, many of the Buddhist, Daoist, and Tibetan shrines and temples, along with mosques and churches, were damaged or destroyed during the Cultural Revolution, or were earlier turned into factories, barracks or schools after 1949.

Yonghegong.

However, the most important religious sites have been restored and reopened.

Fayuan Si (Temple of the Source of Buddhist Doctrine), a Buddhist shrine dating from the seventh century, is probably the oldest surviving temple in the city, located in the southwestern Xuanwu district. Today, it is a training center for Buddhist novices.

Just around the corner, on Niu Dajie, is the oldest mosque in Beijing, **Niujie Mosque**. The style of the building, which is almost a thousand years old, is an interesting combination of traditional Chinese architecture and elements of Arabic and Middle Eastern influence.

The most magnificent and most elaborately-restored sacred building in Beijing is **Yonghegong**, a Lamaist temple in the northeast of the old city. Originally the private residence of a prince, it was turned into a monastery when its owner was promoted to emperor in 1723; according to ancient Chinese custom, the former residence of a Son of Heaven had to be dedicated to religious purposes once he left. From the mid 1700s,

this was a center of Tibetan art and religion, which at the same time offered the central imperial power welcome opportunities for influencing – and controlling – ethnic minorities in Tibet and Mongolia. In the three-storied central section of **Wanfuge** (Pavilion of Ten Thousand Happiness) is a statue, 23 meters (75-ft) tall, of the Maitreya Buddha, which is supposed to have been carved from a single piece of sandalwood. Only a few steps away is the **Kongmiao** (Temple of Confucius), inviting a quiet look. Dating from the Yuan dynasty, it now houses part of the metropolitan museum.

On the other side of the Imperial Palace, due west along Fuxingmennei Dajie, **Baiyunguan** (Temple of the White Cloud) was once the greatest Daoist center of northern China. Today, a small group of monks lives here – only old and young. Due to the political climate between 1960 and 1976, a middle-aged generation of monks doesn't exist.

For a look at Beijing as a working city, not just a collection of temples and imperial buildings, walk through its narrow neighborhood streets. A bustling area, west from the top of Qianmen, is Dazhalan, a narrow and crowded *hutong* filled with vendors selling pirated CDs, T-shirts and electronics. An area of antiques is nearby on Liulichang. Visitors can also take a pedicab tour of a hutong here, which is a bit sanitized but nonetheless allows visitors to peer into a traditional, and fast-disappearing, way of life in Beijing.

The temples that lie at a distance from the dusty asphalt of the inner city and the suburbs have their own special charm. **Biyun Si** (Temple of the Azure Clouds), with its impressive Pavilion of 500 Luohan and its 35-meter-high (115-ft) stupa, lies at the feet of the **Western Mountains** and next to **Xiang Shan** (Fragrant Hill).

Not far away is the extensive complex of **Wofo Si** (Temple of the Reclining Buddha). Its main attraction is a reclining bronze figure depicting Buddha shortly before his entry into nirvana. A miniature train takes visitors from the bottom of the hill to the temple.

Left, Western Mountains, near Xiang Shan. Right, Bai Ta, the White Dagoba.

OUTSIDE BEIJING

Great Wall: It's been said that the only construction by human hands visible to the naked eye from space is **Wanli Changcheng**, the Great Wall. (It's difficult to find documentation of exactly who saw it from space, and when.)

It winds its way like an endless slender dragon from the Yellow Sea through five provinces and two autonomous regions and up into the Gobi Desert. The very earliest stages of the building of the wall date from the fifth century BC, but the present course was basically determined around 220 BC by Qin Shi Huangdi, the first Chinese emperor and the founder of the empire. He had smaller, previously-constructed sections linked and extended northwards to ward off the horse-riding nomads. Soldiers and peasants from all parts of the country were conscripted, spending several years of their lives building this "wall of ten thousand *li*" – Wanli Changcheng.

(One li is about 500 meters.) Blocks of rock weighing several hundred kilograms had to be heaved up the steep slopes, and many people paid with their lives for this project.

From ten in the morning until three in the afternoon, the pass of **Badaling**, the section of the wall that is most accessible from Beijing, turns into a tourist carnival. The avalanche of visitors streams past countless stalls selling souvenirs promoting this great symbol of Chinese civilization. Then it moves in two different directions, attempting to conquer the steep climb. From the high points are views of the breathtaking scenery, where the mighty wall climbs up and down in the midst of a fascinating mountain landscape.

The scenery at **Mutianyu** is almost as imposing. This part of the wall, some 120 kilometers (75 mi) to the north of Beijing, was restored a few years ago and is less busy than Badaling. Parts of the wall here remain as they were – it has not been rebuilt – so visitors have a better sense of its antiquity. The walk is **Great Wall.**

difficult but not treacherous. Cable cars take visitors from the bottom of the hills nearly to the wall itself.

Ming tombs: A visit to Badaling is normally combined with a trip to the **Shisan Ling**, the Ming tombs. Protected by a range of hills to the north, east and west, the tombs of 13 of the 16 Ming emperors lie in this geomantically-favorable spot. Entry from the south on the valley floor passes through numerous gates of honor along Shendao (Soul Path), flanked by the stone guardians of the tombs. The guard of honor of twelve human figures represents civil and military dignitaries and officials; there are also lions, horses, camels, elephants and mythical creatures – 24 stone figures form the animal guard of honor.

Two of the 13 tombs are open to the public. **Chang Ling** is the final resting place of Emperor Yongle. The mound of the tomb has not been excavated, and one can only admire the magnificent hall of sacrifice. In Yongle's day, in the fifteenth century, human sacrifice was by no means unusual; 16 imperial concubines accompanied him on his journey to the underworld. In Wanli's reign (1573–1620), this terrible custom was no longer practiced. The entrance to **Ding Ling**, the 27-meter-deep (89-ft) , dank vault of Wanli, was long sought for in vain, located only in 1957. His primary wife and one concubine are buried with the emperor.

Day trips: Tianjin, Chengde and Beidaihe attract many visitors from Beijing out for the day – usually on a day-trip by train. **Tianjin** has a population of seven million and is one of China's major cities. Some 140 kilometers (90 mi) to the southeast of Beijing, it is noted for its port and its carpets. Because of its architecture, Tianjin has more of a city atmosphere than Beijing.

Chengde, formerly Jehol, was the summer residence of the Qing emperors and, at the same time, a politically-important meeting place for the leaders of ethnic minorities. The "palace for escaping from the heat" – a translation of Chengde – is surrounded by a magnificent park.

XI'AN: CRADLE OF CIVILIZATION

The cradle of Chinese civilization anchors itself at the bend of **Huang He** (Yellow River), in the central provinces of Shaanxi and Henan. Here, in the fertile valleys of the loess-covered landscape, the ancestors of the Han Chinese settled in the third century BC. The fertile soil encouraged establishment of settlements, with the river irrigating the land. Too, the erratic personality of the river – flooding and changing course with regularity – forced people to work in close cooperation. Eventually, the first and strongest states of ancient China developed in this region.

Xi'an, capital of Shaanxi Province, lies in the protected valley of the river Wei, a few dozen miles west of the Wei's confluence with Huang He. From this valley, the emperor Qin Shi Huangdi unified China for the first time.

During the Tang dynasty (618–907), Xi'an was the largest city in the world. Chang'an (Heavenly Peace), as it was called back then, was linked to many central Asian regions and Europe via the Silk Road. Thousands of foreign traders lived in the city.

For more than 1,000 years, Xi'an served as the capital for nearly a dozen imperial dynasties. Following the demise of the Tang dynasty, however, Xi'an's importance began to evaporate. Its historical importance blossomed once again in 1936, when two generals of the Kuomintang kidnapped their leader, Chiang Kaishek, and forced him to cease his civil war with the Communists and cooperate with them against the Japanese – an incident considered to be pivotal in modern Chinese history.

Today, Xi'an is a modern industrial town known for its aviation and textile industries, and for its several universities and research institutes. About five million people call Xi'an home, and it is an important center for travel into China's interior. This old imperial capital is easily reached from all the important cities in China. A direct flight from Beijing takes about two hours, while the train journey of around 1,165 kilometers (725 mi) takes almost 24 hours.

Xi'an's climate has moderate seasonal variation. The winters are not too cold, while in summer, the temperature can rise to 30°C (85°F). At the beginning of spring and autumn, the days are pleasantly cool; the rainy season lasts from July to October.

Wheat and cotton is grown in the region around Xi'an. In some villages, one might find the traditional loess cave dwellings, which are increasingly being replaced with modern brick buildings.

Old imperial center: While the center of Xi'an retains its historical layout from the Tang dynasty, it is largely overwhelmed by modern buildings, heavy traffic and a persistent haze choked by exhaust of cars and buses that leaves residents with reddened eyes and sore throats. The air hangs heavy.

In its earlier days, the metropolis was surrounded by a large wall. The city itself stretched over nine kilometers (6 mi) from east to west, and nearly eight

Left, each figure had individual facial features. **Right**, demon deity, Longmen Shiku.

kilometers (5 mi) north to south. All roads in the town itself were built in a classic Chinese grid pattern, running straight north-south and east-west, meeting at right angles.

While the grid layout persists today, the layout of the ancient city is not quite identical with the modern one. Back then, Dayan Ta (Great Wild Goose Pagoda) was in the center of town. Although the walls built during the Tang dynasty are no longer there, 14 kilometers (8 mi) of the wall from the Ming dynasty still surround the center. The city has been rebuilding the 12-meter-thick (40-ft) walls, and the moat outside the wall has also been reconstructed and integrated within a park.

Modern Xi'an has wide, tree-lined avenues that give shade in the hot summers, and, too, help distinguish Xi'an from most other provincial capitals, which are bleak and monochromatic.

In the city center, where the city's two main roads intersect, is **Zhonglou** (Bell Tower). This renovated 23-meter-high (75-ft) tower, which dates from 1384, is encircled by downtown's shopping and commercial center. From Zhonglou east runs **Dong Dajie**, with many shops and restaurants. From Dong Dajie to the north is **Jiefang Lu**, leading to the railway station.

One of the biggest free markets in Xi'an is not far from Zhonglou, towards the south of the town. Its many snack bars are run by Hui Muslims selling delicious food, such mutton-filled sesame rolls.

A few minutes' walk from Zhonglou to the northwest is **Gulou**, the Drum Tower. Resembling the Bell Tower and dating from the eighteenth century, it was rebuilt after the 1949 Communist revolution. The Drum Tower highlights the Muslim quarter to the west. (Some 60,000 Hui Muslims live in Xi'an.) Lined with souvenir and other shops, alleys winding through the Hui neighborhoods lead to **Da Qingzhen Si** (Great Mosque). The mosque, which dates back to the Ming period and has been renovated several times, bears more resemblance to a Chinese temple with

Hu fu, a tiger figure from the Qin dynasty.

74

its inner courtyards. The main prayer hall is accessible only to Muslims.

Farther along the road, in the direction of Xi Dajie, is **Ximen** (Western Gate), one of the remaining 13 gates encircling the ancient city. In the hall above the gate are interesting historic exhibitions and displays.

Near the south gate of the city wall, **Nanmen**, and in a former Confucian temple is **Shaanxi Sheng Bowuguan**, the provincial museum, with more than 4,000 exhibits in three buildings, much of it relating to the Silk Road.

The first building has a chronologically-arranged exhibition about Chinese history from earliest times to the end of the Tang dynasty, with well-preserved artifacts (including unusual bronze objects). The museum's centrepiece is the collection of stele, with around 1,100 stone tablets on which ancient Chinese texts, including those of the Confucian classics, are engraved. The third section of the museum houses animal sculptures in stone, Tang dynasty stone friezes, bronzes and jewels, as well as Buddhist sculptures and ceramic tiles from the Han dynasty.

The museum, one of the best and most important in the nation, regularly holds special exhibitions.

Outside the city walls and about one kilometre from Nanmen, the 43-meter-high (141-ft) **Xiaoyan Ta** (Little Wild Goose Pagoda) was built in the eighth century. It was severely damaged during an earthquake eight centuries later, but was repaired in the late 1970s.

More significant than this pagoda, however, is the 73-meter-high (240-ft), seven-story **Dayan Ta** (Great Wild Goose Pagoda), anchoring the southwest end of Yanta Lu. It was built at the beginning of the Tang dynasty, in the seventh century. A noted monk, Xuanzang, went on a pilgrimage to India in 629, returning much later with many Buddhist scriptures, which were stored in the pagoda and translated into Chinese. Although only a few buildings remain of the original temple complex of 13 courtyards and over 300 rooms, a few monks have returned.

Below, Dayan Ta, Xi'an; right, countryside embroideries.

Near that pagoda, in the south of the city, is a true gem: **Shaanxi History Museum**. Opened in 1992, the modern museum is housed in a handsome building with clear and attractive displays, arranged in chronological order and labelled in English. There are displays of terracotta horses and soldiers, Ming and Qing pottery, and bronze cooking vessels that sit on tripods from the Shang and Zhou dynasties.

Terracotta warriors: The museums in the city proper give but a glimpse of Xi'an's greatest and most important attraction: **Bingmayong**, the underground Army of Terracotta Warriors.

This vast treasure lies 35 kilometers (20 mi) south of Xi'an, at the foot of Li Shan. In 1974, peasants digging a well uncovered these life-size figures of horses and warriors figures. (Visitors are sometimes invited to meet one of those farmers, if said visitors are willing to buy a book that he will autograph.)

The terracotta army is but part of a grand tomb, **Qin Shihuang Ling**, built by the first Chinese emperor, Qin Shi Huangdi. The main tomb of the emperor is about one kilometre to the west of the terracotta warriors. According to historic surveys, a splendid necropolis apparently depicting the whole of China in miniature is centred under the 47-meter-high (154-ft) mound. The necropolis itself is said to be immense in size; in order to open up the entire necropolis, 12 villages and half a dozen factories in the area would have to be relocated.

According to old records, the ceiling is said to be studded with jewels depicting the sky, and mercury was pumped in mechanically to create images of flowing rivers. (Trial digs have revealed high contents of mercury in the soil.) The official entrance to the tomb has yet to be found.

Several hundred thousand workers spent 36 years building the tomb, which the emperor, at the age of 13, ordered to be built shortly after he ascended the throne. It is also said that all of the workers and supervisors involved in its design and construction were buried alive within the tomb. Rumor has it that **At an unearthly attention for centuries.**

76

the emperor was so superstitious and fearful that he only had the necropolis built to deceive people and is, in fact, buried somewhere else.

Some of the approximately 7,000 terracotta figures from the excavations have been restored by archaeologists and are exhibited in a hall built above the excavation site. Scientists continue to dig for more figures, and visitors can watch the work in progress while walking the site's perimeter.

The figures are arranged in typical battle formation in 11 corridors, comprised of officers, soldiers holding spears and swords (many of them authentic weapons), and others steering horse-drawn chariots. Each figure is about 1.8 meters (5 ft 9 in) tall, and each head has been individually modelled with unique facial expressions.

In the main hall of the exhibit building is a model of the entire necropolis (main tomb and other tombs); videos are shown of the excavation work. There are now three buildings in which to view the terracotta figures and weapons; other areas might one day be excavated. Another building, set up as a small museum, contains a sensational exhibit: the miniature model of a bronze chariot, with horses and coachman, from the Qin dynasty. The carriage was discovered in 1980 and is similar to carriages used by Qin Shi Huangdi on his inspection tours, alive and above ground.

Outside Xi'an: On the way back to the city is **Huaqingchi** (Hot Springs of Huaqing), in use for over 3,000 years. There are baths and pavilions in the park area, which would be pleasant enough if not for the throngs of tourists. This is where, during the Tang dynasty, the most famous concubine in China, Yang Guifei, bathed. A reproduction of the bath she is said to have used can be seen. Farther up in the mountain is the place where Chiang Kaishek was recaptured by two of his own generals during an escape attempt, after he had been taken prisoner in 1936.

A visit to the neolithic settlement of **Banpo** is interesting, 10 kilometers (6 mi) to the east of Xi'an. Some relics,

including ceramics from the Yangshao culture, are exhibited. The excavated village shows the outlines of houses and cooking areas, and is part of the museum. There is still debate about whether the people living here 6,000 years ago were a matriarchal community.

Further afield, about 60 kilometers (40 mi) from Xi'an, is **Xianyang**, the capital during the reign of Qin Shi Huangdi. Few traces are left of the legendary palaces said to exist here then. There is a museum in a former Confucian temple that contains more than 3,000 artifacts from the time of the Warring Kingdoms, and also the Han and Qin dynasties. The collection of miniature terracotta horses and soldiers, from the Han dynasty and each about 50 centimetres (20 in) in height, is particularly impressive.

Seventy kilometers (40 mi) to the northwest of Xi'an is **Zhao Ling**, the tomb of Taizong, an emperor of the Tang dynasty. The tomb also contains, in addition to that of Taizong, 167 burial sites for the other members of the imperial family. The site, near the town of **Lingquan**, covers over 20,000 hectares (50,000 acres).

About 85 kilometers (50 mi) to the northwest of Xi'an is **Qian Ling**, the joint burial place of the Tang emperor Gaozong and his wife, the empress Wu Zetian. The tomb itself has not been opened – the approach to the tomb is guarded by a "ghost avenue" of large stone sculptures of animals and dignitaries. There is a group of 61 stone sculptures, with their heads missing, apparently representing foreign dignitaries. The peasants of the region and time are said to have knocked the stone heads off when there was a famine, which they believed was caused by the presence of these foreigners.

Six of the 17 smaller tombs nearby have been excavated. A few minutes from the main tomb are the tombs of Princess Yongtai and Prince Zhanghuai. The tombs contain exquisite frescoes from the Tang dynasty.

Yan'an: Mao Zedong's Long March from Jiangxi ended in the town of Wuqi **Excavations at Banpo.**

in 1936. The leaders then established their base of operations in Yan'an, staying for a decade. This small market town of just under 50,000 people is 270 kilometers (170 mi) to the north of Xi'an, where the Yan river cuts a path through the dry mountains.

Yan'an can be reached from Xi'an by overland bus (24 hours) or by plane (one hour). It can also be reached by plane from Beijing, Shenyang and Taiyuan. If taking the overland bus from Xi'an to Yan'an, stop at **Huang Ling** to visit the tomb of Huangdi, the Yellow Emperor. The tomb has long been a place of pilgrimage for Chinese.

Bao Ta, the pagoda that dominates Yan'an, originates from the Song dynasty and was restored in 1950.

Until the 1970s, when Yan'an was the national center of pilgrimage of the Cultural Revolution, it was as well known as Gugong, the Imperial Palace in Beijing. The headquarters of the military commission of the Chinese Communist Party, along with the houses of the communist leaders Mao Zedong and Zhu De, are still preserved in the Fenghuang mountains north of Yan'an. The Museum of the Revolution contains over 2,000 documents and objects from the Yan'an period, which is still praised by many older functionaries of the Chinese Communist Party as the "golden revolutionary era".

There are also some interesting Buddhist and Daoist temples in the area surrounding Yan'an.

Around Yan'an it is still possible to see the caves that are typical of this central loess landscape, and which were used during World War II by the leaders of the Communist Party and Red Army.

Hua Shan: In an easterly direction from Xi'an, 120 kilometers (75 mi) by train, is Hua Shan, one of the sacred mountains of China. Its name means "flowering mountain," and its cultural significance, extending far back into history, is Daoist. There are numerous temples on the mountain up to its top.

The ascent via the lower north summit to the 2,100-meter-high (6,900-ft) south peak starts at **Yuquan Yuan** (Garden of the Jade Spring), seven kilometers

Good-luck charm.

(4 mi) east of Huayin. The ascent takes at least half a day. Behind Yun Men (Cloud Gate), where there is a fine view, the path climbs steeply upwards; it's helpful not to suffer from vertigo. Many visitors and Daoist pilgrims ascend to enjoy the sunrise.

Luoyang: The train from Xi'an to Luoyang, east of Xi'an, takes about seven hours. The train passes through the town of **Sanmenxia** (Three Gate Gorge), where one of the largest hydroelectric power plants in China was built not so long ago.

While Xi'an was the capital of the Western Han dynasty (206 BC–AD 9), the imperial residence of the emperors of the subsequent Eastern Han dynasty (AD 25–220) was in 3,000-year-old Luoyang, sometimes called the Eastern Imperial City.

In fact, Luoyang, like Xi'an, served as the capital for several dynasties – ten, to be exact, flourishing during the Tang and Song dynasties, then gradually losing its importance to the increasingly prosperous coastal towns.

GUANGZHOU

The mythical origins of booming Guangzhou are not the most auspicious. As legend has it, five celestial beings, riding on the backs of five flying goats, landed here and founded Guangzhou. Goats don't do much for engendering civic pride in an economic powerhouse and gateway to the West. Yet the name Yangcheng, or Goat City, was once affixed to this city. Even today, the evening newspaper is called *Yangcheng Wanbao* (Goat City Evening News).

But goats are spunky and independent, and in Guangzhou, one grasps a palpable sense of China's energy, and of its breakneck pace in transforming itself into an international player. Guangzhou is a boisterous urban mass with all the blemishes one equates with modern cities: air thick with pollution, streets crowded with cars and trucks, blocks of cramped housing overflowing with people, and an invigorating chaos.

At the mouth of **Zhu Jiang** (Pearl River), Guangzhou lies 45 kilometers (28 mi) upriver from Humen (Tiger Gate), also called Bocca Tigris on old maps. Around five million people live in the greater metropolitan area, with over two million within the city's boundaries. Like many of China's cities, Guangzhou's population is probably much higher than official figures.

Climatically, Guangzhou is a temperate, subtropical city. The Tropic of Cancer runs a few miles to the north, and for a few days in July, the sun lies directly above the city. The rainy season parallels the hot summer months, when daily afternoon showers are typical.

Flying goats notwithstanding, Guangzhou probably was founded in 214 BC as an encampment by the armies of the Qin emperor, Qin Shi Huangdi (221–210 BC). At first the town was called Panyu; the name Guangzhou first appeared during the period of the Three Kingdoms (222–280). During the Tang period (618–906), the city was already an international port, but remained second to Quanzhou – Marco Polo's Zaytun –

for centuries. In 1514, the Portuguese flotilla commanded by Tome Pires reached Guangzhou. The province's name in the Cantonese dialect is Guangdong, from which the Portuguese derived the name of Cantào. From Cantáo came Canton, which came to be used in all European languages.

From 1757 to 1842, Guangzhou held a trade monopoly in China, as it was the only Chinese port opened to the foreigners. Traders were obliged to cooperate contractually with Chinese merchant guilds; this arrangement planted the seeds for the subsequent *comprador bourgeoisie*.

After the overthrow of the Ming dynasty by the Manchu in 1644, nationalist ideas survived longer in Guangzhou than in other parts of China. Yet, at the same time, close contact with overseas Chinese (*huaqiao*) ensured the continuation of an openness to the world and a desire for reform in the city. (Openness, in turn, would eventually spawn revolutionary zeal.) Trade with the East India Company increased, particularly the

Left, Guangzhou at dusk. Right, downtown tower.

importation of opium. The profits financed colonial expansion, however, and did not benefit the local Chinese population, and China's silver reserves were depleted to pay for the imports. This culture of dependency helped nurture revolutionary ideas and motivate secret societies, which preserved the ideals of the Ming period and fostered a determination to restore this last Chinese dynasty to power.

In 1839, the Chinese commissioner Lin Zexu ordered the confiscation and destruction of 20,000 chests of opium, leading to military intervention by Great Britain in the First Opium War (1840–1842). The resulting Treaty of Nanjing led to the opening to foreign trade in Guangzhou, Shanghai, Xiamen, Fuzhou and Ningbo, and the gift of Hong Kong to England. In 1858, in a reactionary fit by the Chinese, foreign traders were required to limit their base of operations to the island of Shamian, at the mouth of Zhe Jiang. After the Second Opium War (1856–1860), they settled in other parts of Guangzhou and continued trading.

Following the overthrow of the Qing dynasty in October, Guangzhou became the center of the movement led by Sun Yatsen (Sun Zhongshan) and the headquarters of the Kuomintang (KMT), the first modern party in China. In a period of cooperation between the KMT and the Communists, Mao Zedong worked and taught at Guangzhou's Institute of Peasant Movements, and Zhou Enlai and Lin Biao at the Military Academy.

The modernization of Guangzhou began in the early 1920s; most of the main streets defining the city today were built then. A feverish sense of urgency in construction – it took only 18 months to build 40 kilometers (25 mi) of road – is evident even today. Throughout the city, high-rises, hotels, bridges and new highways now seemingly materialize overnight. During that modernization in the 1920s, the remainder of the old city wall was pulled down, and a collection of junks on the river was removed.

Urban personality: The personality of Guangzhou differs significantly from that of the north. The language of

Colonial architecture, Shamian.

Guangzhou, Cantonese, is incomprehensible to northern Chinese, who typically speak Mandarin. Cantonese has nine tones, instead of the four tones in the Mandarin dialect. While it is urban, Guangzhou has been marked more by trade than industry, in contrast to Shanghai, although light industry is now important in Guangzhou.

The area around Guangzhou was overcrowded even 200 years ago, and many peasants from the region emigrated to Southeast Asia, America and Europe. As a result, Cantonese is the most common dialect among overseas Chinese. Likewise, the same is true for Cantonese cuisine, which is the most varied of all Chinese cuisines but is often mocked by other Chinese.

Thus the language, cuisine and boisterous, crowded look of Guangzhou is often familiar to foreigners – it is the look and feel of Chinatowns in North America, Europe and Australia.

Old Guangzhou: In the southwest of the city, the island of **Shamian** is a preserved relic of the colonial past. The small island was divided in 1859 into several foreign concessions, primarily French and British. After 10pm, Chinese were kept off the island by two iron gates and narrow bridges. The former Catholic and Anglican churches have been reopened for worship, and most of the former trade and consular buildings are now used as government offices.

Opposite the canal that separates Shamian from the town itself, and where houseboats are occasionally moored, begins the so-called **Bund**, which continues along the waterfront to **Haizhu**, the oldest steel bridge across the Zhu Jiang and built in 1933. About 100 meters to the east of the bridge, which connects the eastern end of Shamian with the mainland, is a memorial. Here, in 1925, Chinese demonstrators died in a hail of bullets fired by foreign troops guarding the foreign quarters.

About two kilometers further east, to the northeast of Haizhu, the 50-meter-high (160-ft) double towers of the **Catholic cathedral** are visible. Built in the early 1860s, the cathedral was left to

The bridge of Haizhu.

decay after 1949, and left to decay even more during the Cultural Revolution. In the 1980s, it was restored and now holds services under the auspices of the Patriotic Catholic Church, banned from having contact with the Vatican.

To the north of the bridge, half way down Shamian towards the mainland on Qingping Lu, is **Qingping Shichang** (Market), occupying the side alleys around the main roads of Renmin Nan Lu and Nuren Jie. This district has flourished since the reforms of 1978 and is always quite crowded with shoppers and those seeking a snack. One of the first places to develop under China's gradual adoption of market economics, the area was for years a capitalist oddity.

To the east is **Wenhua Gongyuan** (Culture Park), with roller-skating rinks, an open-air theater, theater halls, art exhibitions and performances by the School of Acrobats. Nearby is the well-stocked Department Store of the South (often called Nanfang Department Store), on the corner of Renmin Nan Lu, lined with shops and also known as Taiping Lu, in honor of the Taiping Rebellion of 1850–1864.

Xiajiu Lu leads to Guangdong, a restaurant. Behind it, in a narrow side alley named Shangxia Jie, is **Hualin Si**. This temple is said to have been founded by an Indian monk in 526, although the existing buildings date from the Qing period. There are 500 statues of Luohan – pupils of the Buddha – in the main hall. A statue of Marco Polo with brimmed hat, however, was lost during the Cultural Revolution.

Near the crossroads of Renmin Zhong Lu and the sixth section of Zhongshan Lu (Sun Yatsen Street), in Guangtalu south of Zhongshan Lu, is **Huaisheng Si**, a mosque dating back to 627 and founded by a trader who was said to be an uncle of Mohammed. At that time, Arab traders visited China, so the legend may well contain some truth, although it does not give sufficient evidence for an exact date of the foundation of the mosque. The 25-meter-high (82-ft) minaret, **Guang Ta** (Naked Pagoda), dominates the area, although new

Downtown skyline.

high-rises are competing for the skyline. The mosque is a cultural center for Guangzhou's 5,000 Muslims.

To the north of Zhongshan Lu, a fairly narrow street leads to **Liurong Si** (Temple of the Six Banyan Trees); its **Hua Ta** (Flower Pagoda) is a symbol of the city. Liurong Si, said to date back to the fifth century, was named in 1099 in a calligraphic tribute from the poet Su Dongpo (1031–1101).

The main hall contains statues of the Buddha, eight Luohan figures, the god of medicine, and the goddess of mercy, Guanyin. The statues date from the Qing period. Visitors can climb up the nine-story pagoda behind the main hall; unfortunately, the view is marred by numerous skyscrapers. Today, the temple is the local headquarters of the Chinese Buddhist Association.

A few hundred yards northeast is **Guanxiao Si**, a temple preserved during the Cultural Revolution on orders from Zhou Enlai. Local legend has it that the temple is older than the town; it dates from the time between 397 and 401. Some of the present buildings were, however, built after a big fire in 1269, and most probably only after 1832.

Dongtie Ta and **Xitie Ta** (Western and Eastern Iron pagodas) date from early in the city's history. There is a seven-meter-high (23-ft) stone pagoda behind the main hall, with sculptures of the Buddha placed in eight niches. It is thought to date from 967, but was only put in its present location at the beginning of Mongolian rule. The halls reflect several styles from different eras.

To the northwest, in a formal garden near Jiefang Bei Lu, **Sun Zhongshan Jiniantang** (Sun Yatsen Hall) is easy to spot with its eye-catching blue roof tiles. The hall, built shortly after the death of Sun Yatsen in 1925, now houses a large theater and lecture hall that can seat 5,000 people. **Yuexiu Gongyuan**, due north, is a beautiful example of a landscaped park. It is dominated by **Zhenhailou** (Tower Overlooking the Sea), a memorial to the seven great sea journeys undertaken by the eunuch Zheng He; between 1405 and 1433, he traveled

Sun Yatsen Memorial.

to east Africa, the Persian Gulf and Java. Today, the tower houses a museum on the history of Guangzhou.

Restored after the Cultural Revolution, **Chenjia Si** (Chen Family Temple) dates from 1894 and lies on the western part of Zhongshan Lu. It has six courtyards and a classic layout, and is decorated with friezes manufactured in Shiwan. Gardens surround a small lake with rowboats. There are also tennis courts, a swimming pool, badminton courts and a gym. The family name Chen is one of the most common in Guangdong Province. Families of that name from throughout the province donated money to build this temple.

Nearby, not far from the train station, is a shaded park devoted to the cultivation of orchids. The north of the town is dominated by **Baiyun Shan** (White Cloud Mountain), six kilometers (4 mi) away and accessible by cable-car.

Eastern districts: In the east of the city, on Zhongshan Lu, is the former Kongzimiao (Confucius Temple). It lost its religious function during the "bourgeois revolution" in 1912. In 1924, the **Peasant Movement Institute** (Nongmin Yundong Jiangxisuo) was opened here, in effect the first school of the Chinese Communist Party. The elite of the Communist Party taught here: Mao Zedong (his work and bedroom can be viewed), Zhou Enlai, Qu Qiubai, Deng Zhong, Guo Moruo and others. This is also where Mao developed his theory of peasant revolution.

After the collapse of the workers' uprising in 1927, the Communists were forced to retreat for a time from the cities. A park and memorial, **Lieshi Lingyuan** (Memorial Garden for the Martyrs), was created in 1957 in memory of the uprising and its nearly 6,000 victims. The temple is mostly of Ming-period construction.

Directly east of it is **Guangdong Geming Bowuguan** (Provincial Museum of the Revolution), a reminder of the role of the Kuomintang and its predecessors since the First Opium War.

South of Zhongshan Gan Lu are the old buildings of Guangdong University, where China's first modern author, Lu Xun, lectured in 1927. An exhibition is dedicated to him. Until 1927, the All Chinese Trade Union Federation was located nearby. Liu Shaoqi, the revolutionary and later president of the People's Republic – and a victim of the Cultural Revolution – worked there.

In the northeast, near the zoo on Xialie Lu, is a memorial park built in 1918 for the 72 victims of the uprising in 1911.

Outside Guangzhou: The town of **Foshan** (Buddha Mountain), with more than one million people, is home to **Zumiao** (Ancestor Temple), a famous Daoist temple whose history goes back to the Song dynasty. It was renovated in 1372, and contains a 2,540-kilogram (2-ton) bronze statue of the Northern God, Zhenwu, from around 1450. There is also a small museum on the grounds, which has relics dating back to the Han period. The buildings – most of which were built during the Qing dynasty – have been decorated with ceramics produced in the factory of **Shiwan**, located in a suburb. (Shiwan ceramics were also used in the Chen temple, in Guangzhou.)

Left, Flower Pagoda. Right, hotel bellboy.

HONG KONG AND MACAU

"Borrowed time, borrowed place" is the perfect description, coined by novelist Han Su-yin, of Hong Kong. Historically, the colony's citizens have tried to ignore the perpetual uncertainty of their future – their borrowed time – and have preferred to make their pile quickly in the fervent hope that destiny will unfold without severe or permanent disruptions. Hong Kong is reassuming the very real Chinese self that always lay just below the modern urbane facade; it believes its destiny is in the hands of fate, influenced perhaps by hefty doses of good *joss* (luck).

When George Orwell bestowed such considerable and ominous significance on the year 1984 so many years ago, the tiny colonial outpost of Hong Kong had no idea that 1984 would be its own year of destiny. The year was when Hong Kong's future was decided – in the form of an agreement between Great Britain and the People's Republic of China, initialled on 26 September in Beijing and signed on 19 December in the same city.

At midnight, on a rainy 30 June 1997 – the moment the 99-year lease on the New Territories, 90 percent of the colony, expired – the British Crown Colony, including the two areas of Hong Kong Island and the Kowloon Peninsula "ceded in perpetuity" in 1841 and 1856, were returned to China, the festivities broadcast live around the world. The Portuguese outpost in Macau followed two years later, but with a better deal than Hong Kong: residents of Macau retained dual citizenship in China and Portugal.

Some suggest that Portugal's lack of arrogance and righteousness persuaded China to give Macau's people the benefit of the doubt. Hong Kong residents, except for a select few, were not be allowed the same. In the end, the mainland Chinese, patient to the end, held most of the cards in negotiations.

During the often-acrimonious negotiations over almost two years, Britain, which clearly came out second best, managed to extract a 50-year guarantee from China (beginning in 1997) that, on paper, ensures Hong Kong's basic freedoms and autonomy – sort of. Hong Kong is now a Special Administrative Region of China, an arrangement conveniently accommodated by the official Beijing stance of "one country, two systems." In refugee-minded Hong Kong, where almost half the nearly 6 million population had fled from turbulent upheavals in China decades before, not to mention the rude shock of Tiananmen Square, trusting the Middle Kingdom for the 50 years after 1997 is more than a moot point of academic interest.

Preceding pages: Hong Kong Island's Central District, young ballerinas share a secret. **Left,** the Star Ferry against Central's skyline.

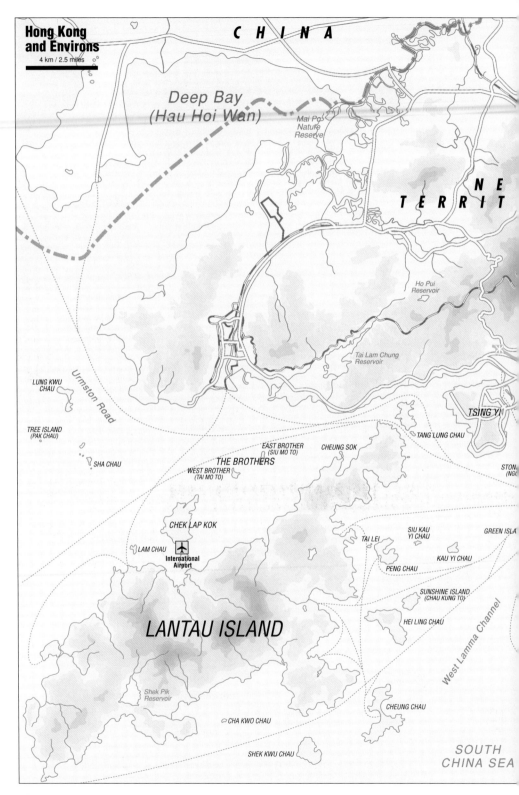

Hong Kong and Environs

4 km / 2.5 miles

C H I N A

Deep Bay (Hau Hoi Wan)

Mai Po Nature Reserve

N E

T E R R I T

Ho Pui Reservoir

Tai Lam Chung Reservoir

Urmston Road

LUNG KWU CHAU

TSING YI

TREE ISLAND (PAK CHAU)

SHA CHAU

TANG LUNG CHAU

EAST BROTHER (SIU MO TO)

CHEUNG SOK

THE BROTHERS

WEST BROTHER (TAI MO TO)

STON (NG

CHEK LAP KOK

TAI LEI

SIU KAU YI CHAU

GREEN ISLA

LAM CHAU

International Airport

KAU YI CHAU

PENG CHAU

SUNSHINE ISLAND (CHAU KUNG TO)

LANTAU ISLAND

HEI LING CHAU

West Lamma Channel

Shek Pik Reservoir

CHA KWO CHAU

CHEUNG CHAU

SHEK KWU CHAU

SOUTH CHINA SEA

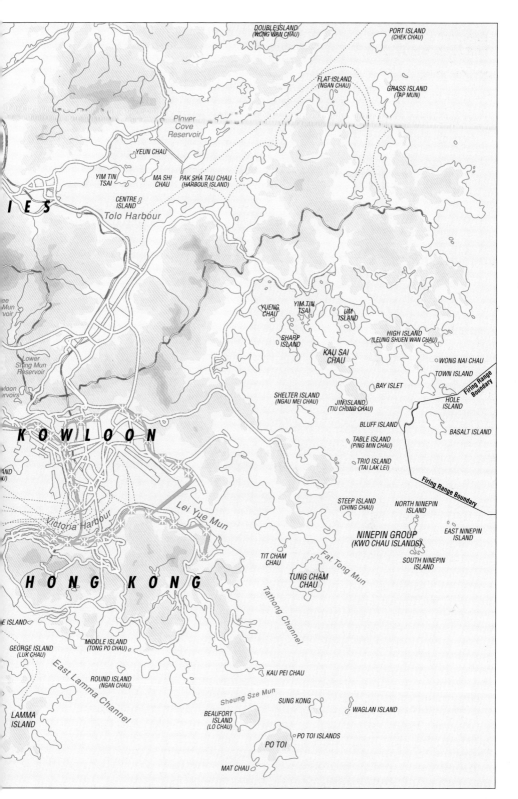

DOUBLE ISLAND
(WONG WAN CHAU)

PORT ISLAND
(CHEK CHAU)

FLAT ISLAND
(NGAN CHAU)

GRASS ISLAND
(TAP MUN)

Plover
Cove
Reservoir

YEUN CHAU

YIM TIN
TSAI

MA SHI
CHAU

PAK SHA TAU CHAU
(HARBOUR ISLAND)

I E S

CENTRE
ISLAND

Tolo Harbour

ee
Mun
voir

Lower
Shing Mun
Reservoir

oon
rvoirs

YUENG
CHAU

YIM TIN
TSAI

SHARP
ISLAND

UM
ISLAND

HIGH ISLAND
(LEUNG SHUEN WAN CHAU)

KAU SAI
CHAU

WONG NAI CHAU

TOWN ISLAND

Firing Range
Boundary

BAY ISLET

HOLE
ISLAND

SHELTER ISLAND
(NGAU MEI CHAU)

JIN ISLAND
(TIU CHUNG CHAU)

BLUFF ISLAND

BASALT ISLAND

TABLE ISLAND
(PING MIN CHAU)

K O W L O O N

TRIO ISLAND
(TAI LAK LEI)

Firing Range Boundary

AND
U)

STEEP ISLAND
(CHING CHAU)

NORTH NINEPIN
ISLAND

EAST NINEPIN
ISLAND

Lei Yue Mun

Victoria Harbour

NINEPIN GROUP
(KWO CHAU ISLANDS)

SOUTH NINEPIN
ISLAND

TIT CHAM
CHAU

Fat Tong Mun

H O N G   K O N G

TUNG CHAM
CHAU

E ISLAND

Tathong Channel

GEORGE ISLAND
(LUK CHAU)

MIDDLE ISLAND
(TONG PO CHAU)

ROUND ISLAND
(NGAN CHAU)

KAU PEI CHAU

East Lamma Channel

Sheung Sze Mun

SUNG KONG

WAGLAN ISLAND

LAMMA
ISLAND

BEAUFORT
ISLAND
(LO CHAU)

PO TOI ISLANDS

PO TOI

MAT CHAU

When Britain hauled down the Union Jack at midnight on 30 June 1997, Hong Kong's colonial status had lasted 150 years, five months and 10 days.

There cannot be many places where one can pinpoint the future as accurately as the past. One has visions of some bowler-hatted mandarin in deepest, darkest Whitehall, toting up the cost the morning after an all-night bash. If truth be known, Hong Kong was always a rather pesky, yet virtually self-governing, colonial possession to the British, and a problem only solved by the inscrutable oriental patience of the Chinese.

If Hong Kong was fiction instead of fact, its birth would have been an accident of history. In fact, it certainly was not. But its founding was controversial and unpopular with the mandarins back in London from the start. So distasteful did they find the affair that the man who did the deed was called back, censured and eventually sent to the 19th-century version of diplomatic purgatory, the consulate in Texas, bereft of the honours usually bestowed by grateful monarchs on those who add to the realm. Neither is he honoured in Hong Kong, though other lesser souls more in favour lived on as Hong Kong street names.

It all began on 20 January 1841, when Britain's sole remaining plenipotentiary in China, Trade Superintendent Captain Charles Elliot, annexed Hong Kong Island on his own volition and by force of arms – to obtain trade concessions, to recover compensation for thousands of chests of British opium confiscated earlier at Guangzhou, and to redeem a bent British pride.

The opium traders – for whom Elliot blockaded Guangzhou (colonially called Canton) and occupied three forts in order to secure "one of the islands… conveniently situated for commercial intercourse" – attacked Elliot after the fact because in their opinion his Convention of Chuen Pi was too conciliatory. They still had to pay customs charges to the Chinese, even though trading from desolate Hong Kong was far less convenient than trading from Guangzhou.

London was livid. Lord Palmerston, Queen's Victoria's Foreign Secretary, dismissed Hong Kong by calling it a "barren island with hardly a house upon it." It would never become a trading centre, he knowingly and wisely harrumphed.

The dubious honour of being the first Governor of this backwater Victorian white elephant fell to Sir Henry Pottinger (1843–44). In spite of the fact that London had been a bit lax in declaring sovereignty over its newest acquisition, Pottinger felt so strongly about Hong Kong's potential future that he encouraged permanent building and awarded

land grants. These practices he ordered stopped when he went north to take part in renewed hostilities against the stubborn Chinese. A long round of fighting ended at Nanjing – on 29 August 1842 with the signing of a Treaty of Nanking – when the Chinese capitulated just as Pottinger's forces were preparing to attack that city. At the time, Pottinger was being politically chastised for spending too much public money on "useless" Hong Kong development projects.

With the Treaty of Nanking, those arguments ended and London gladly accepted the Island of Hong Kong in perpetuity, so that Britain could have "a Port whereat they may careen and refit their Ships, when required, and keep Stores for that purpose…"

Previous to this time, Macau and Guangzhou's Whampoa were the major China trading ports, but with the eventual silting of Macau's harbour – located adjacent to the Pearl River Estuary – and the weakening of Portuguese power in Asia (and the growing strength of England), British traders wanted a place of their own to build godowns and process and sell profitable "foreign mud," as opium was nicknamed by the barren island. Though there was confusion over land sales, astute British traders instantly recognized that if Hong Kong did indeed become a prosperous colony, the key to success here would be land, and, of course, the local Chinese were way ahead. They readily sold land whether they had title to it or not. Good *joss* (luck) apparently was with the traders, because in June of 1843, Hong Kong was declared a Crown Colony.

The second of Britain's three bites occurred as a result of the Arrow War (more com-

Victoria Harbour, around 1860.

Chinese. By fortuitous accident, Hong Kong Island became England's China port, and became, almost from the beginning, both a swashbuckling embarrassment and lucrative money machine for England. Indeed, Hong Kong was founded for trade and continues to exist only for that commercial reason. The Treaty of Nanking was only the first of three "bites" the British lion took out of the Chinese dragon's rear.

During the six months Pottinger had been away from the colony fighting his battles, much progress had been made in settling this

monly known as the Second Opium War), when a Hong Kong-registered *lorcha* (a junk-rigged schooner with a foreign hull) named the *Arrow* was boarded off Guangzhou in 1856 by Chinese sailors. The *Arrow*'s crew was detained, and this impropriety irritated the British. Hong Kong's consul-general, Harry Parkes, retaliated in force, hoping to use this *casus belli* to force the Chinese to allow foreigners back in Guangzhou. (Entrance into Guangzhou was guaranteed by the 1842 Treaty of Nanking, but had never been asserted.)

The British fleet sailed up the Pearl River, breached Guangzhou's city walls and forced their way to the Chinese viceroy. Immediately British demands inspired by the *Arrow* incident were quickly met, but the key question of access to Guangzhou was not. The viceroy said he could not guarantee the safety of foreigners if they were allowed in the city.

Shortly thereafter, guerilla warfare broke out and foreign held factories in Guangzhou were attacked. Until that time, Hong Kong had been only a minor commercial dependence of Guangzhou. The *hongs* (the original trading houses, some of which still do business in Hong Kong today) transferred their headquarters to the security of the new British colony at Hong Kong. Local acts of terrorism continued to occur in Hong Kong,

Beijing was sacked by the allies. Lord Elgin, the British plenipotentiary who negotiated for the British this time, secured the cession of an additional 3.75 square miles (10 sq. km) of new territory consisting of Kowloon Point (on which the British had built a harbour defence fort in 1842) and Stonecutters Island (in the harbour).

With that second British "bite", Hong Kong now consisted of nearly 36 square miles (94 sq. km) of "sovereign" territory. The colony's harbour could now be defended on both sides and the colony's British residents had a convenient haven, Kowloon, across the water where they could engage in nefarious – mostly sexual – intercourse.

Guangzhou and along the vital Pearl River. British forces, this time joined by French allies, fought back and captured Guangzhou yet again. By the summer of 1858, allied forces had moved to the far north, where they eventually forced another Chinese capitulation and negotiated stronger concessions known as the Treaties of Tientsin. Foreigners now gained the rights to station diplomats in Beijing and travel at will throughout China. In 1860, under a subsequent Convention of Peking, Kowloon Point (Tsimshatsui) was leased in perpetuity from the Chinese. In that same year, another battle took place in the north and the emperor's Summer Palace in

England's third and last "nibble" of the Middle Kingdom occurred in 1898 – and it is this final morsel that long kept Hong Kong nourished and economically alive. By the mid 1880s, the British were concerned about the territory's security. What pushed Britain to force China's hand was a coaling-station grant to France on the southern China coast. After expressing Her Majesty's displeasure regarding this grant, Britain duly informed Beijing that for defence purposes (nothing was said about "balance of power" with France), the colony would require additional territory. Eventually a demarcation line was drawn from Deep Bay to Mirs Bay and

Britain forced China to lease the New Territories for 99 years from 1 July 1898.

In that third bite, the Crown Colony gained about 350 square miles (930 sq. km) spread over the mainland and 234 outlying islands. It also inherited an uncertain future.

For most of its history, and certainly the entire 20th-century part, Hong Kong's historical path has never deviated from the self-imposed limits of this lease. The year 1997 was well over the horizon in 1898, and it still seemed far, far away through the war-filled years up to the middle of this century. The date was blotted out of the collective psyche – a non-thing to be never spoken of – in the economically fat years of the 1960s and

1970s. Then, instead of exploding into the open, it slowly bubbled to the surface in mid-1982 with the lead up to Prime Minister Margaret Thatcher's visit to Beijing.

The British and the Chinese signed on the dotted line in 1984 after two years of, at times, quite acrimonious discussions. During this period, the Chinese bombarded the world, and particularly Hong Kong, with propaganda whilst the British kept a stiff upper lip with a self-imposed rule of silence.

Left, Princess Diana visiting during the old colonial days. Above, pro-democracy rally before the 1997 handover to China.

It is no secret that the British wanted to continue on after the magic date.

That was not to be. The British entered the negotiations with their mind set only on the rented area of the New Territories, the other parts having been signed over to England in perpetuity by treaty. As a negotiating point that the English may have overemphasized and misinterpreted, the Chinese claimed sovereignty over the entire colony, stating, as they had many times in history, the treaties were "unequal", meaning they were forced with gunboat diplomacy.

The British fought a rearguard action from the outset, and as 1997 approached, the fine points were still being negotiated. Chris Patten, the colony's last royal governor that one either loved or hated, instituted a directly-elected parliament, which the Chinese quickly dismissed, before and after the handover. Antiques and cash fled the country for havens elsewhere.

At the beginning of 1997, the reversion to Chinese sovereignty was an accepted fact, even to those tens of thousands who assembled in the night with lighted candles to commemorate the violence at Tiananmen Square, the last time they'd have the freedom to do so. A few weeks later, the night of 30 June became a media – not to mention political and social – extravaganza broadcast around the world. Even after the handover, questions remained, mostly of a cartographic nature. Would Victoria Harbour, named after a British queen, remain thus named? And what about Nathan Road, and Kennedy Town, and Hollywood Road?

Until 2047, the Chinese are designating all of Hong Kong as a Special Administrative Region, where the lifestyle, economy and laws can and often will be different from the rest of China. In many ways, visitors hardly noticed the difference afterwards, except for their arrival at the new Chek Lap Kok airport that opened on Lantau in 1998, replacing Kowloon's tired, and dangerous, Kai Tak. If not at the new airport, they arrived on the new express train direct from Beijing, which began service in 1997.

Two systems, one country was the catch phrase. Chinese leaders believe the return of Hong Kong – and the Portuguese colony of Macau in 1999 – is the first step in luring, if not overtly pressuring, Taiwan back into the fold. One country, three systems?

THE HONG KONG CHINESE

At first glance, Hong Kong is everything described in hackneyed epithets, but underneath its Western facade is a very Chinese mind that stubbornly refused to change during a century and a half of British rule. Chinese attitudes – Chineseness, if there is such a word – remain true to their Oriental traditions, despite colonial rule.

A Chinese in Hong Kong may have once kowtowed to a British lord in public (previously, literally – later, metaphorically), but often there was a humorous contempt for all *gweilo* (foreign devils) regardless of race, colour, and nationality. The term gweilo originated many years ago with the birth of Chinese xenophobia. Originally, it was derogatory, but in the past decades has been used by both Chinese and foreigners alike, a slang expression more commonly used than the polite *saiyahn* (Western person).

In spite of some feigned royalism, finding a Chinese who was *truly loyal* (in the British sense) to the Queen was perhaps as difficult as looking for a noodle in a haystack. It was just that British rule always appeared the benevolent lesser of other possibilities.

Perhaps the key to understanding the people of Hong Kong is to understand the mechanism which allows the society to successfully function in a noisy, claustrophobic circumstance. At bottom, they have always considered themselves a people living on borrowed land and borrowed time, where a *sense of place* is secured only by jostling and pushing. *I push and shove, therefore I exist.*

A close-knit traditional family structure also alleviates the discomforts of living in one of the world's most densely-populated areas. Generations live together in low-cost government housing estates, thousands jammed vertically into high-rises. (More than 50 percent of the population is housed in this way.) However, the larger the family, the larger the labour force, and the greater the family income, and so they can afford luxuries seemingly incongruous with their housing conditions.

Left: the smile of young ambition and Hong Kong confidence. **Right**, the ancient smile of gold investments and confidence.

Generational differences: Tenement life, however, is not domestic bliss. Clashes among close living family members are inevitable, especially between in-laws.

Contemporary concepts of child-rearing and nutrition have evolved, and children often become a focus of social discord. Younger Chinese parents, for example, are feeding their children more meat and milk. Consequently, new generations are becoming progressively bigger in build, and their modern parents are more liberal. Grandpar-

ents, however, still believe in traditional taboos concerning child-rearing and diet, preferring, for example, soybean gruel to formula. Therefore, they feel slighted when opinions are not heeded; after all, they have raised six or seven children of their own.

Cramped living (and working) conditions make life difficult for would-be young lovers. Moments alone are rare, and prying eyes – of brothers and sisters, parents and relatives, and colleagues and peers – are not a conducive environment for composing love letters or flirting, much less being sexually close. Dating and marriage are now by free choice. This, however, does not mean that parents do not have a say in marital decisions. Parental approval is usually sought, and the bride or groom is subjected to the scrutiny of relatives.

For economic reasons, the age of marriage in Hong Kong has been delayed. Women generally marry at the age of 24, and men at 26. Banquets for the entertaining of relatives can cost tens of thousands of dollars.

Concubinage (a form of polygamy) has been outlawed in Hong Kong since 1970, but it has metamorphosed into a more familiar creature. Concubines are now called mistresses, but are still publicly displayed as concubines were – as status symbols. One Hong Kong millionaire buys cars for his five

riches stashed away in banks. Rags to Rolls Royce stories abound in this free enterprise entrepôt, but in this fairy tale many of the beggars-turned-princes remain outwardly humble. A successful entrepreneur may be dressed in a greasy apron, chopping away at roast goose in a restaurant, and another may be hawking noodles and fishballs at a street corner. The owner of the colony's famous Yung Kee Restaurant (his roast goose is one of the world's 10 best dishes) started out with such a food stall; he now presides over a multi-storeyed, mega-dollar enterprise – a high-rise golden goose, if you will.

Another industry rich with Horatio Alger Wong stories is the garment business, one of

mistresses according to their rank: the first mistress has a Rolls-Royce, the second a Mercedes, and so on. The older generation of men who took concubines before the new law took effect are allowed to keep them, and their children are recognized and have legal rights to an estate.

Wealth: There are millionaires of every variety here. Some inherited the family business, some placed a right bet at the right time, and some lifted themselves by their sandalstraps through sheer effort. Some drive variously coloured Rolls-Royces to match their daily attire. Others wear the same old rags for years, and nobody suspects that they have

Hong Kong's major export industries. Many multimillion dollar garment businesses are known to have originated in family workshops employing five workers or less. By hard work, business acumen accumulated after several bankruptcies, and with a bit of good *joss* (luck), they hit the big time.

Industrious and efficient are some of the catchwords used to describe the colony's residents. Though the official work week is 44 hours, a 70-hour week is not unusual for many. Indeed, other Asian capitalists eye Hong Kong with envy. Laments one Taiwanese toy maker: "Our girls are only half as productive as workers in Hong Kong. Here people take work seriously and don't jabber at work like they do in Taiwan."

Flexibility: Hong Kong is also known for its resilience. One cliché often repeated is that despite the hardships Hong Kong faces, it is always resilient enough to bounce back. Little mention is made of the men, women and children who are responsible for such fiscal flexibility. When there is a manufacturing deadline to meet, people work nonstop for three or four days (and nights); when business is slack, they switch to other professions or survive through family support.

The root of this flexibility is a traditional Chinese pride. An additional incentive is provided by the lack of a welfare system in

ous drivers of Rolls Royces. This profligacy has made much impact – especially on Hong Kong youths, who seem to have adopted a temporal philosophy of get it while you can.

Several factors account for this *nouveau riche* air. One, of course, is the colony's obvious wealth. As its export business grows and industry burgeons, consumer goods loom tantalizingly within reach of a large portion of the population. All the trappings of an acquisitive society emerge.

A second factor, a more subtle one, is a feeling of transience that permeates all strata of Hong Kong society. Many who lost everything when they fled Communist rule in China decades ago have re-established them-

Hong Kong. If laid off, people cannot afford to wait around for government support; they have to move on to other jobs, even if at a lower status and pay.

Yet, traditional values are changing. Industriousness and thriftiness often give way to opulence and acquisitiveness. Indeed, humble Hong Kong has broken world records in the consumption of luxury goods. Its residents are proud of being the world's highest per capita consumers of French cognac, and they love being the world's most conspicu-

Left, gold and red are auspicious. **Above**, cool in Kowloon, dragon boat racer.

selves in the former colony, but the threat that their economic mobility may not last forever hangs over their bank accounts.

Not unlike its business community, Hong Kong's educational system is also highly competitive. Parents believe that their child's career is dictated by kindergarten credentials. For if a child fails to enter a top-rated kindergarten, she or he cannot get into a top elementary school. This eliminates any chance of going to a top-rated high school, which is a prerequisite to university.

A number of students commit suicide each year because they failed an important examination; many more contemplate this desperate move. Thus, parents make sure that their training starts early. They hire tutors to prepare their children for kindergarten entrance examinations, an ordeal which sometimes requires hours of testing to determine a child's Chinese, English and arithmetic skills. Surprisingly, the average standard of English in Hong Kong is not very high. The alphabet is pounded into little heads at the age of five or less, and children sing *London Bridge* and recite *Run Rover Run*, but they parrot both by rote, with little comprehension of what they are mouthing. When a Shakespearean play covered by the secondary school syllabus each year would be announced during colonial years, it was often literally memorised.

Land is scarce in Hong Kong, and real estate speculators regularly increase the price of every centimetre of soil; some grave sites cost tens of thousands of dollars. Therefore, the old woman prayed to Buddha in the morning and took communion from a Roman Catholic priest in the afternoon. By thus covering her beliefs she has assured herself a place in both heavens – and on the earth.

Superstition is perhaps the most common name for Hong Kong's religious bent, although it suggests a lack of validity. Unfortunately, the English language fails at accurately conveying the strongly-held beliefs in the occult and abstractions like fate. Almost every Chinese – Christian, Buddhist or athe-

Parochial schools are the most sought after educational institutions. Some parents convert to Christianity so that their children can enter these institutions.

To many Chinese in Hong Kong, religion is a pragmatic matter. Some get baptized into Christianity for personal gains – benefits from Christian charity organizations, social status, availability of grave sites in Christian cemeteries, and other practical considerations. One old woman born and raised a Buddhist was converted to Catholicism on her deathbed because a grave site in the Roman Catholic cemetery is much more spacious and cheaper than ordinary plots.

ist – believes in occult forces, believing that humans can control them by arranging furniture a certain way, by building a home in a divined location, by constructing walls to repel spirits, or by consulting for auspicious dates of major events. As gambling is a way of life for both rich and poor, it makes a difference whether a person gets off the bed on the right side, or whether the spouse says the right words. The Cantonese word for "book," for example, is poison to a gambler's ears, because that word (*shi*) sounds identical to the Cantonese word for "lose."

Above, harbour looks.

FENG SHUI

Though physically Hong Kong looks like a modern 20th-century city in the best Western tradition, such temporal surface similarities end there. In addition to written regulations and laws about construction of buildings, highways, bridges, tombs, homes and whatever else goes into a modern concrete city, Hong Kong people also honour unwritten spiritual laws called *feng shui* (pronounced *fung soy*). After government departments have completed their building plans, architects and contractors consult a *feng shui* man, a geomancer. His job is to determine the most auspicious location for not only the building, but also its doors, windows and desks.

Some people, corporations and organizations have, at times, tried to ignore the dictates of *feng shui*, which nearly always leads to trouble sooner or later.

Qi, yin and yang: *Feng shui* (which literally means "wind-water") is practised with a compass-like device that has eight ancient trigrams representing nature and its elements – heaven, water (the ocean), fire, thunder, wind, water (rain), hills and earth. These elements in turn represent eight animals (horse, goat, pheasant, dragon, fowl, swine, dog and the ox).

This Chinese science is based on the principle of *qi*, the spirit or breath that animates *yin* and *yang*, female-passive and male-active elements. The *feng shui* geomancer's job is to put all these spiritual and practical factors together to make a positive prediction.

Whether non-Chinese people here actually believe in *feng shui* doesn't matter. What is important is that Hong Kong can't be run without Chinese; therefore, government and private industry heed their ancient beliefs.

In Central District, at the site where Hutchison House, Bank of America Tower and a multi-storey carpark stand, a mass execution was conducted by Japanese during their occupation of the former British colony. When Hutchison House reached its full height, a Buddhist ceremony was conducted by the then deputy chairman of that giant conglomerate to appease the spirits of those who had died there.

Across the road, in a government carpark and in government offices on a building's top floors, pencil-pushers in the Transport Department reported seeing ghosts. These incidents of flying spirits became so acute that the dapper Brit who then ran the Transport Department, Brian Wilson, eventually led an exorcising procession of 70 chanting Buddhist monks and nuns through the carpark in 1974.

Hong Kong's Chinese traditional customs affect everyone, even progressive American businessmen. Before the Hong Kong Sheraton Hotel opened in 1974, its general manager, Robert Hamel, consulted a *feng shui* expert about the hotel's opening date; his local staff was reportedly very pleased.

Another American hotel chain up the street did not do likewise, and it was only after being plagued by bad *joss* incidents that its management called in a *feng shui* expert to set things, and *joss*, right.

The Regent of Hong Kong sheathed its lobby and mezzanine in 12-meter (40-ft) lengths of glass on a geomancer's advice. According to a *feng shui* source, the hotel rises at a site where

"a dragon enters the harbour for his bath." By designing a see-through lobby, there was no chance of disrupting the dragon's ritual – a mistake which would have created inexplicable bad *joss*.

Octagonal mirrors or deflectors called *pat kwa* are frequently hung outside windows of large office buildings and apartment houses. It is believed that these deflectors protect their occupants by repelling evil through the reflection of the mirrors.

A large part of *feng shui* is what nonbelievers might call common sense, or sound interior design that reflects good psychology. But talk to an expat who has lived in Asia for a while, and one is talking to someone who might have been a former sceptic but is now a believer. ∎

Right, the mirror in the *pat kwa* is meant to repeal evil spirits.

It has been said that when confronted with something they have never seen before or do not understand, the first impulse of a Chinese is to try eating it. Standing as Chinese food does on four millennia of uninterrupted civilization, not much has been lost.

Ancient Chinese cooking bears little resemblance to what you'll savour in Hong Kong today, but certain basic principles remain. Steaming, roasting, smoking and fermentation of meats were practised at least as early as 1000 BC, as was the now-forgotten

practice of "scorched" pig roasting without evisceration. Heavy, ornate, bronze cooking cauldrons and tripods from the Chou dynasty (1122–256 BC) have been unearthed intact. These items were used together as a double-boiler. Recipes of that time were also elaborate: a suckling pig, for example, was stuffed with dates, wrapped with hemp and mint and baked in a shell of clay. After the clay was removed, the pig was deep-fried until crisp, then steamed for three days, thereby producing a layer of fragrant oil.

Foods of northern and western China, for example, developed apart from the mainstream of China's southern coastal rice bowl.

This northern school, centred on the ancient and present capital of Beijing, was heavily influenced by Mongols who swept into Han China during the late 13th century.

The Mongols, who founded the Yuan dynasty in AD 1279, were a nomadic tribe. They lived in tents and dressed in furs and their tastes – based on what was available, that is, milk, butter and lamb – were quite different from the native Chinese, preferring a rough and simple cuisine: whole animals were roasted in stone pits or steamed with rock salt. They made fruit preserves and used pine nuts, rosewater, almond oil and sugar for seasonings; lamb dumplings were made with bean paste and dried tangerine peel; and lamb cakes included innards, ginger, and eggs.

Southern Chinese (mainly the Cantonese, but including sub-groups such as the local Hunan, Chiu Chow and Hakka) like to complain that Beijing-based food lacks smoothness and subtlety. Beijing folks, meanwhile, argue that southerners grind, chop and dilute the flavour out of their food.

The Chinese concept of a meal is very much a communal affair and one that provides a strong sensory impact. Dishes are chosen with taste and texture – a stomach-pleasing succession of sweet-sour, sharp-bland, hot-cool, and crunchy and smooth.

To most Westerners, Chinese food is basically strange. In fact, many dishes considered rare delicacies by Chinese make the Westerner ill. For example, monkey's brain (eaten directly from the skull of a freshly killed monkey), bear's paw, snake, dog, pigeon, frogs, sparrows, live baby mice (good for ulcers) and lizards. Unfortunately for the

lowed by other main courses. Soup – usually clear light broth – may be eaten after the heavier entrees to aid digestion. However, a thick full-bodied soup may be served as a main dish, and a sweet soup often serves as a dessert at meal's end. There are no inflexible rules when it comes to ordering your meal. The main thing is to enjoy the food.

Canton cuisine: The Cantonese live to eat and, at its most refined level, Cantonese gastronomy achieves a finicky discrimination that borders on cultism. Visitors to Hong

average Hong Kong Chinese who savours such gourmet fare, many of these delicacies are either banned by law or virtually impossible to obtain.

One mistake Westerners make is the unseemly swamping of their rice with soya sauce, a crude act that robs it of its character and function. A meal should include enough spicy and savoury dishes to make the neutral blandness of steamed rice an essential balancing agent. A typical Chinese meal invariably starts with a cold dish, which is fol-

Kong who think they are familiar with Cantonese food soon learn to their surprise that this discipline has little to do with sweet-and-sour pork – said to have been invented by ever resourceful inhabitants of Canton solely for sweet-toothed foreigners – or *chop suey* – said to have been invented in San Francisco. Also, despite Hong Kong's bent for things superstitious, fortune cookies do not exist here, another *gweilo* invention.

In the Cantonese method of preparation, food is cooked quickly and lightly – stir fried – in shallow water or an oil base, usually in a *wok*. The flavour of the foods is thus preserved, not lost, in preparation. Neither is

Left, clay-baked and Peking Duck. **Above**, inside one of the many floating Chinese restaurants.

the original taste of hot, spicy sauces . Many dishes, particularly vegetables or fish, are steamed. This discourages overcooking and preserves a food's delicate and "natural" flavours. Sauces are used to enhance flavours, not destroy them. The sauce usually contains contrasting ingredients like vinegar and sugar or ginger and onion.

A Cantonese restaurant is *the place* to eat fish, steamed whole with fresh ginger and spring onions and sprinkled with a little soy and sesame oil. Frogs are found in the rice paddies, and these "field chickens" are often served at banquets in South China. In Hong Kong markets they are sold live in plastic bags, and restaurants prepare them in many

delicious ways. The best frog course is deep-fried frog's legs cooked in a crunchy batter mixed with crushed almonds and served with sweet and sour sauce.

Beijing cuisine: Peking Duck is the most popular northern Chinese dish served in Hong Kong (and it is probably the most popular northern dish anywhere in the world). This duck dish is prepared by roasting it over an open charcoal fire and slowly basting it with syrup until the skin is crispy brown. When you partake of Peking Duck in a restaurant, part of the enjoyment of the meal is the "show" put on by the chef at tables as he swiftly carves the duck – *always* with a large

razor-sharp chopper (butcher's cleaver) and *never* with carving or paring knives.

Mongolian hotpot, called "steamboat" in the Singapore-Malaysia region, is of central Chinese Moslem origins. It is probably the second best known of the northern dishes, a winter food served between November and March in northern-style restaurants. The key preparation utensil for hotpot eating is a chafing dish with a small charcoal burning stove built-in underneath. A trough around this dish contains soup stock to which is added vegetables, cabbage and herbs. When the soup stock begins to boil, the entire stove is set into a hole cut in the table's centre .

Wafer-thin slices of various meats or fishes are cooked in small wire baskets dipped in this hotpot's bubbling broth. Rice is not usually served (unless you request it). Wheat is commonly grown in the north so northerners traditionally eat steamed bread (*pao*) or tasty onion cakes instead of rice.

Szechuan: Because Szechuan is one of China's westernmost provinces – and thus much exposed to the spicier delights of food in the Asian subcontinent – the cuisine of Szechuan is renowned for its spicy tastes and pungence. The ultimate Szechuan dish is smoked duck, a crisp-skinned specialty with the aromatic flavour of camphor-tea. It is prepared with a seasoning of ginger, cinnamon, orange peel, coriander and *hwa chiao*, pungent Szechuan peppercorns.

Szechuan food is a richly-spiced cuisine with a distinctive chilli sting. Characteristic dishes are succulent prawns seasoned with garlic and ginger, chilli bean paste and wine, garlic-laced eggplant that's mashed and then braised, and *ma-boo* bean curd braised in a powerful chilli sauce. Noodles or steamed bread are eaten in preference to rice.

Minced beef with vermicelli is known in Chinese as "Ants Climbing a Tree," and steamed Szechuan pork is an expensive winter specialty that combines abalone, pork, chicken, sea cucumber, ham, mushrooms and bamboo shoots. One of the best Szechuan soups is sour pepper soup, prepared with bean curd, chicken's blood and shredded bamboo shoots seasoned with chillies, peppercorns and vinegar.

<u>Left</u>, **the price of shark's fin at the local market varies with its quality.** <u>Right</u>, **the art of noodle making is a long process.**

HONG KONG ISLAND

However barren it was a century ago, nobody standing in the middle of Hong Kong Island could ever imagine it as anything but a great metropolis and an entrepot to the world's third largest port. Fifty-storey buildings are more common than 10-storey buildings.

Yet for all its urban pull, Hong Kong serves the same purpose it did nearly 150 years ago. The port, with its 7,000 visiting ships each year, was the colony's *raison d'etre*; along the old harborfront were all its important business and banking houses.

CENTRAL DISTRICT

The center of any great world capital is dominated by its government offices.

Hong Kong's **Central District** is no exception. Except that the *real* government of Hong Kong is its banks. So when one exits from the **Star Ferry** underpass, looking ahead at the great concrete vista to the south, one sees the spires of two of Hong Kong's three main banks – the modernistic US$1 billion Hongkong Bank (reputedly the most expensive building in the world), and to its right, the Standard Chartered Bank. Beyond, past the old Bank of China Building to the left of the Hongkong Bank, is the gleaming 368-meter-high (1,209-ft) Bank of China Tower (the sixth tallest in the world). The Bank of China's sharp angles point directly at the other financial institutions, a bad (or good, depending which side you're on) *fung shui* omen.

There are few truly historic buildings to give real character to Central. The colonial-style **Supreme Court Building** once housed the Legislative Council. The Victorian-Gothic **St John's Cathedral**, inaugurated in 1849 and Hong Kong's oldest Anglican church, is tucked away on Battery Path Road. The red brick **French Mission Building**, now housing government offices, is one of two other modest examples of 19th-century architecture, but is hardly worth the climb up the hill in the heat. The other is **Flagstaff House**, home to the **Museum of Tea Ware** (enter from Cotton Tree Drive) and reputedly Hong Kong's oldest surviving building.

But these buildings are aberrations. More to the Central style is **The Landmark** (they don't even call it a building), a structure opened in 1980 on Des Voeux Road on the site of the old Gloucester Hotel (which was demolished for the New Gloucester Building, which in turn was destroyed to make way for The Landmark). Five floors surround a vast 6,000-square-meter (20,000 sq ft) atrium with 100 shops.

The place to begin the Central tour is at the **Star Ferry Terminal**. Blinking to the right of the Hong Kong piers is the unmistakable polka-dotted **Jardine House**, whose distinctive round windows inspired the Chinese to nickname it the "House of a Thousand Orifices."

Just behind wonder is the **General Post Office (GPO)** and the government bookshop. Across the street to the west from the GPO and Jardine House are the shiny towers of Exchange Square, one of the most modern office complexes in the world and home of the Hong Kong Stock Exchange.

Even further west is the **Outlying District's Ferry Pier**, where locals hop a ferry to escape to one of the more peaceful outer islands, and the **Macau Ferry Terminal** and helipad, both in the **Shun Tak Centre**.

To the left is **City Hall**. This complex houses a concert hall and theater, a number of offices and, most important, billboards which advertise cultural programmes for the month.

Upon emerging from an underpass which fronts the Star Ferry Terminal, one finds oneself on Connaught Road Central. To the right, the swank **Mandarin Oriental Hotel** is connected by walkway over the Chater Road to Prince's Building and its shopping mall.

While in "lower" Central, one should also explore some of the side streets. Two interesting little streets – **Li Yuen Street East** and **Li Yuen Street West** – have stalls and shops that sell clothing, look-alike high fashion accessories and

Preceding pages: Hong Kong stock exchange. **Left,** Hong Kong Island, Central to Causeway Bay.

fabrics galore. Bargaining is expected here. Behind Queen's Road, the old waterfront road, climb up **Ice House** or **Wyndham** streets till they meet. That old, triangular-shaped ice storage building (circa 1911) is now the house of **Foreign Correspondents** and the **Fringe** clubs.

Lan Kwai Fong, a street which is also referred to as an "area" in Hong Kong's jargon, is the center of Hong Kong's trendy nightlife. Here chic restaurants mix with equally chic bars, pubs and discos.

WESTERN DISTRICT

If one was foolish enough to try to identify the real Hong Kong, one would think inevitably of **Western District**, which begins at Possession Street and sprawls west to Kennedy Town. More practically, Western's atmosphere emerges around **Central Market**, near the fringes of the busy Central district. Western was the very first district to be settled by the British. Today, there is virtually nothing British about this area; it is now a traditional Chinese urban society, known as a last refuge of the Hong Kong Chinese artisan.

As one probes deeper into Western, it's easy to forget colonial Hong Kong. The district past **Bonham Strand** (a marvellous street for printing shops) looks more like a set for an old *Fu Manchu* movie. City planners have classified this area as a slum, but architecturally this district – with its old 4-storey buildings topped by ornate balconies and carved balustrades – is more colorful and convenient than Hong Kong's more modern housing estates.

Minibuses and trams clank along the main streets, but walk as much as possible, all the way to Western's end, at **Kennedy Town**, where you'll find one of the colony's oldest Chinese settlements. Still very crowded, it has a Portuguese-style *praia*, a road which curves along original footpaths bordering **Belcher Bay**.

While returning to Central, don't miss a cruise down one of the most fascinat-

Work day scenes from Central.

ing of all local shopping areas: **Ladder Street**. Nobody knows when its broad stone steps were constructed, but old records say that this 65-meter (118-ft) "street" was built so sedan chair bearers could more easily carry their human cargo from Hollywood Road to residential Caine Road. Where Ladder Street meets Hollywood Road is the area's so-called Thieves Market. The lanes here are filled with bric-a-brac, real and fake antiques, and more stalls than one can ever browse through.

At the corner of Hollywood Road and Ladder Street is **Man Mo Temple**, built around 1840. Tourists regularly throng through Man Mo – but this doesn't inhibit the temple's regular worshippers, who animatedly create thick and redolent clouds with their burning joss.

THE PEAK

Victoria Peak – *The* Peak to those who have made it to society's top – wasn't always regarded with such awe. During the first six years of the former colony's history, hardly anybody traveled to those inhospitable heights.

It wasn't until 1888, when the **Peak Tramway** (actually a funicular railway) was opened, that The Peak became *the* Peak. Everybody who was (and is) anybody longs to live on The Peak. Its best flats and houses are rented out by the government – as Peak perks, if you will – to the colony's senior civil servants; or earmarked by the *hong* (Hong Kong's massive trading conglomerates) for their top executives.

The best way to see The Peak in all its bucolic glory is by walking around **Lugard Road**, which begins just opposite the Peak Tram's upper terminus at 395 meters (1,305 ft) above sea level.

The following two stops, **Macdonnell Road** and **Kennedy Road**, each lead to the entrance of the **Botanical Gardens** and **Zoological Gardens**, which house good collections of flora and fauna. An aviary here has about 700 birds of 300 species. The best time to visit is dawn, when locals are engrossed in *tai chi chuan* exercises. This rather curious

The harbour from the Peak.

exercise, which looks like a slow-motion ballet, is a shadow-boxing exercise that dates back to the time of Confucius, utilizing movements and breathing inspired by Buddhist meditation forms.

Descending by the steep Peak Tram, one realizes that the Tram is not just a tourist attraction. This is as much a local commuter vehicle as New York's IRT or London's Tube.

WANCHAI

In the celluloid version of *The World of Suzie Wong*, the *very* snobbish Sylvia Sims, at one of her Peak dinner parties, embarrassed the late William Holden to no end by speaking about the unfortunate denizens of **Wanchai**.

Wanchai nightlife was not meant for the Peak's *taipan*. In the late 1940s, it was a hangout for sailors. During the 1960s, Wanchai helped give rest, recreation and succor to thousands of American, Australian and New Zealand soldiers and sailors on R&R (rest and recreation) from Vietnam.

Wanchai's former red-light district now plays second fiddle to more liberated nightlife venues: gaudy big hostess clubs, discos, and raucous English-style pubs. Brightly-lit fruit markets, souvenir shops, second-hand bookshops, and tailors are open until midnight.

Nobody thinks about Wanchai for culture, but it does harbor the **Hong Kong Arts Centre** on Harbor Road: 15 floors of auditoria, rehearsal rooms, theater workshops, and the offices of numerous cultural organizations. Across the street is the **Academy for Performing Arts**.

Fenwick Pier, where visiting warships disgorge their sailors, is just up Harbor Road, behind the Academy for Performing Arts. This section of Harbor Road (called Wanchai North) has the HK$3 billion **Hong Kong Convention and Exhibition Centre**, a vast center which includes the Grand Hyatt and New World Harbour View Hotels.

Lucky mirrors: Two blocks to the south of Hennessy Road is a far more Chinese section of town, Queen's Road East.

Academy for Performing Arts.

Here are famous Chinese furniture-makers working right out on the street. Here also are two well-known Chinese temples. On Stone Nullah Lane, to the right off Queen's Road East, is **Pak Tai Temple**, home to a 3-meter-tall (10-ft) copper image dating to 1604. Closer to Central is Tik Loong Lane, which leads pilgrims to **Chai Kung Woot Fat Temple**, the Temple of the Living Buddha. Here, visitors who have overcome illnesses leave offerings in the form of mirrors with lucky inscriptions. Thus, the temple interior is dazzling.

HAPPY VALLEY

Western District was the first Hong Kong suburb occupied by Europeans, but they soon deserted it and moved to a spot which seemed healthier. Optimistically, they named this second living area **Happy Valley**.

In 1841, shortly after Happy Valley was settled, the colony's residents created the greensward and edifice which has made Happy Valley world famous.

This is the Hong Kong Jockey Club's **Happy Valley Racecourse**. During the October–May racing season, it attracts thousands of race-goers (about 35,000 a running). If you'd like to experience this, visitors' badges and information can be obtained from the Hong Kong Tourist Association.

CAUSEWAY BAY

Cruising down from Tai Hang Road to King's Road, opposite Victoria Park, one enters a fascinating and modern sector of the island: **Causeway Bay**.

Causeway Bay really was a bay until the 1950s, when the bay disappeared into a great land reclamation project.

The present-day "bay" is occupied by the **Hong Kong Yacht Club** on Kellett Island (which also was once a "real" island), and the **Typhoon Shelter**. To get there, cross Victoria Park Road in front of the Excelsior Hotel. At sunset hour, visitors are immediately be besieged by a gaggle of women. Don't get the wrong idea. All they are offering is

Happy Valley races.

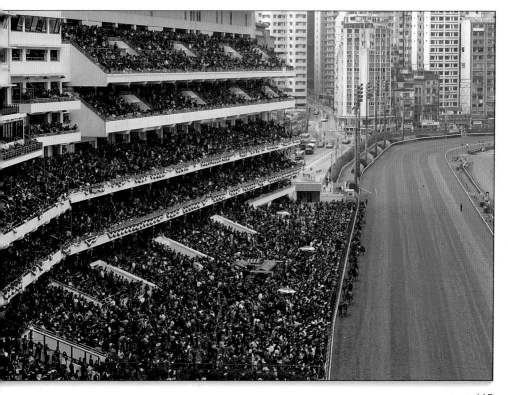

a chaste ride in one of their floating-restaurant *sampan*, decks filled beam to boom with tables and chairs. Bargain for the *sampan* before getting on.

Kitchen *sampans* pull up next, vying for orders and showing off their fresh prawns, crabs and fish. Seafood, noodles, congee, omelettes – just about anything edible – can be prepared before you in the precarious floating kitchens. This part of Hong Kong's waterfront also features the Noon-Day Gun. Nobody knows for sure why the gun is fired at noon everyday, now a Hong Kong tradition.

Causeway Bay's contemporary history began in 1973, when the Cross-Harbour Tunnel was opened. This underwater freeway is one of the largest tunnels in Asia. Its four lanes cross two kilometers of harbor water between Hong Kong and Kowloon.

With this tunnel came the inevitable: Causeway Bay was transformed into a thriving city. Street blocks behind the Excelsior Hotel have shopping outlets which sell goods at prices cheaper than stores located in Central or Kowloon.

One block to the east of Paterson Street, at right angles to the Plaza Hotel and Victoria Park, is **Food Street**, lined with diverse dining places with more than 200 chefs and menus listing some 2,000 dishes.

Across from Victoria Park is **Tin Hau Temple Road**, whose temple dates back to 1747. On Tunglowan Road, near the Park Theatre, is Queen's College, the oldest Anglo-Chinese school and founded in 1862. And on the northern side of this street is the Causeway Bay Magistracy. Daily courtroom sessions, conducted in English, are open to the public.

So much for modern Causeway Bay. "Old" Causeway Bay has existed since the beginning of Hong Kong. Here is **Jardine's Bazaar**, a marketplace which also dates back to those "foreign mud" and buccaneering days. Today, Jardine's Bazaar and nearby Jardine's Crescent are equally fascinating.

Indeed, each street in this area has special shopping wonders. **Pennington** **Causeway Bay.**

Street is known for its shops making paper effigies for funerals, Chinese medicine shops and old-style pawn shops (where the chief pawn-broker sits high up in a judgement seat like the Lord of Justice himself). On nearby **Irving Street**, one will find soya sauce and wine shops.

SOUTHSIDE

Southside Hong Kong is a region of rocky coasts and smooth white beaches; of little fishing villages and unhurried markets. Few office buildings or factories are anywhere in sight, but on summer weekends, every office, factory and farm worker in the colony seems to descend on the southside's shores.

Of Hong Kong's 36 gazetted beaches, the southside of the island has 14. A few, like **Rocky Bay** on the road to Shek O, have virtually no facilities, save an unparalleled view and an uncrowded beach. Others, like Repulse Bay, feature busloads of tourists, a McDonald's hamburger shop, and about as much peace and quiet as a complete carnival.

Shek O Beach is somewhere at middle ground. The road from Chaiwan skirts Mount Collinson on the left, and Tai Tam Harbour to the right. At a fork in the road, you can go left about 7 kilometers (4 mi) to **Big Wave Bay,** a beautiful beach, but with absolutely no public transportation to the beach. The Shek O beach and village, about the same distance from the fork, can be reached by public bus, and Big Wave Bay's beach is a 30-minute walk from Shek O.

Trekking at Tai Tam: After the first turn-off to Shek O, the road from Chaiwan continues in a curve to one of the most well-trodden hiking spots on the island: **Tai Tam Reservoir**. This was the first reservoir erected in Hong Kong, its earliest section completed in 1899. The two-hour walk in lovely areas surrounded by mountains, begins on Tai Tam Road, skirts around the different reservoirs, and ends at Wongneichong Gap Road near the **Hong Kong Cricket Club**.

Sea-side apartments along the harbour.

STANLEY and REPULSE BAY

Take public transportation or a car past Tai Tam Reservoir along the coast to Turtle Cove, then to **Stanley Village** Road and the village itself. Stanley was a thriving Chinese capital long before the British set foot here. In fact, a **Tin Hau Temple** here documents that the town was founded in 1770 by a pirate, Chang Po Chai, who captured the island. Today, **Stanley Market** attracts thousands of visitors on weekends, though it's open every day. Here, a few steps from New Street, is a large area with shops selling fashionable clothes (usually over-runs or seconds), rattan, fresh food, ceramic jugs, budget art, hardware, brass objects, Chinese products, vases – practically everything.

From Stanley, one can travel to the "capital" of the south side, **Repulse Bay**, directly on Repulse Bay Road. Repulse Bay Beach, now widened several times its original size and improved, has everything except peace and quiet. It once had one of the finest resort hotels in the East, The Repulse Bay Hotel, now replaced by a pastel colored commercial/residential complex, punctuated with a big designer hole in it and called The Repulse Bay.

Southside attractions: From Repulse Bay, the coast road curves westward over some of the colony's most beautiful scenery – to Deepwater Bay, Ocean Park and Aberdeen. (If going by bus, you must sit on the top deck to soak in this ride's magnificent vistas.)

ABERDEEN

Aberdeen has a character unlike any other town in the colony. Its charm, though, is questionable because this naturally ideal typhoon anchorage is home to about 20,000 of Hong Kong's 70,000 "boat people" and their 3,000-odd junks and *sampans*.

The term "boat people" has two meanings. One refers to Vietnamese refugees who came pouring into Hong Kong during the late 1970s, causing a momentary population panic.

Stanley.

(The panic was soon allayed when manufacturers realized that the Vietnamese were an ideal source of cheap labor. However, it wasn't until the latter part of the 1990s that the last of these boat people, many of whom had been incarcerated for years, were repatriated, often forcibly, to Vietnam.)

The more traditional boat people, on the other hand, are those who have been living on local waters for scores of generations, if not centuries.

The latter group of boat people consists of two main tribes: the Tanka (literally, the "egg people," because they used to pay taxes in eggs rather than cash) and the Hoklo.

Other Chinese have never accepted them (pre-Communist China wouldn't even permit them to settle on land), but Hong Kong is encouraging them to leave their boats. Schools for their children are opening up, housing estates are being constructed for them, and as land is gradually reclaimed from the harbor, the fishing people are being lured to work in factories.

At any rate, tourists are still seduced by the predictable and over-promoted 30-minute cruise through Aberdeen Harbour. They still enjoy the chaotic atmosphere, the incredible collection of sea life and the dynamism of this city upon the water. They also enjoy the opulent Chinese floating restaurants (take a *sampan* there), which are not in Aberdeen Harbour proper anymore, but in the yacht basin of Shumwan, across from the Aberdeen Boat Club and the Aberdeen Marina. It must be said, however, that Aberdeen has lost some of its innocence because of the swarms of tourists.

The four side streets between Aberdeen's Main Road and Chendu Road all have their own character. Northernmost Lok Yeung Road has a little shop selling pet food – not only for fish and birds, but also for caterpillars.

At Wu Pak Street there are a few good general markets. Finally, at Wu Nam Street, one can take a ferry four times a day to **Sok Kwu Wan**, a tiny settlement on **Lamma Island**, to sample that isle's good seafood.

Aberdeen's typhoon harbour.

KOWLOON:
NINE DRAGONS

Kowloon, though geographically a part of the Chinese mainland, was politically British soil until 1997, having been ceded to Britain in 1860 under the Treaty of Peking, which was negotiated as a Chinese concession at the time of the so-called Opium Wars. This was the second of three treaties that created the Crown Colony of Hong Kong.

The name Kowloon is made up of two Chinese words, *gau*, meaning nine, and *lung*, meaning dragon. Tradition says that a boy emperor who once lived here noticed there were eight hills, so he called them the Eight Dragons. A servant pointed out that an emperor is considered to be a dragon also; therefore, the eight hills plus the boy emperor were the nine dragons – *gaulung*. As was often the case, English pronunciation changed the name into something quite different: Kowloon.

Kowloon is a mere 10 square kilometres (3 sq mi), but it is this small area that most people remember after a visit to Hong Kong. Kowloon is *the* shoppers' paradise most visitors aim for in Asia, and also the site of most of the city's big hotels that cater to tourists and businesspeople.

At the tip of the peninsula, Tsimshatsui, is the Star Ferry terminal, and the Ocean Terminal/Ocean Centre/Harbour City complex. Then comes *the* "Golden Mile" with its myriad shops and hotels, and Kowloon's answer to the Suzie Wong style of nightlife. Next to Tsimshatsui is the Yaumatei district, where some people still live aboard junks, boats and barges.

Just beyond is Kai Tak, until 1997 the international airport and actually part of the New Territories, but looked upon as being in Kowloon. Nearby is the famous (in Hong Kong) Kowloon City Market, an incredible concentration of outdoor and indoor stalls centred on Lion Rock Road. A short walk away was where the Walled City once stood. **Old Kowloon.**

Farther east, in the middle of a huge housing estate, is the **Lei Cheng Uk Tomb**, discovered in 1955 during excavations for a housing estate. It dates back to between AD 100 and AD 200 and comprises three rooms, where one can still see shards of crockery and other relics from those ancient days.

TSIMSHATSUI

When exploring Tsimshatsui, start at the **Star Ferry terminal**. It's no longer the only starting point, because one can also drive through the **Cross-Harbour Tunnel** from Hong Kong Island, or whiz under the harbour on the Mass Transit Railway. But for a century, the only way to get off Hong Kong Island was the faithful Star Ferry, and the reason for going there was to catch the train to Europe. Where the old clock tower stands was this end of the Orient Express, the Far East terminus of the rail journey to and from London. Nearby is the **Peninsula Hotel**, where people stayed before boarding the train.

At the Star Ferry concourse are small shops, news vendors who hawk overseas newspapers, and a wharf for the harbour's tour boats.

Next to the Star Ferry wharves is **Star House**, containing the first of the shopping arcades. There is the large **Chinese Arts and Crafts** store, where everything from garments to porcelain may be purchased.

Adjoining the Star House/Hong Kong Hotel complex is the Ocean Terminal/Ocean Centre/Harbour City complex, on Canton Road, one of the largest air-conditioned and interconnected shopping centre in the whole of Asia. Adjacent to that complex is China Hong Kong City which houses the China Ferry Terminal.

A short walk from the Star Ferry takes you past the old **YMCA** (with modern additions, including a swimming pool) and the venerable Peninsula Hotel, built in 1928. Across the street is the egg-shaped **Space Museum**, **Planetarium** and **Space Theatre**. Next to it is the **Hong Kong Museum of Art** and the

Electronic items are usually a good buy.

Hong Kong Cultural Centre. Here, at the bottom of Nathan Road, one's overall impression of Tsimshatsui is tall buildings and advertising signs and shop shingles stacked one atop another as far as the eye can see. For a grand commercial impression, stand at this same spot after dark and enjoy the dazzling brilliance of neon-upon-neon.

Nathan Road was named after Sir Matthew Nathan, a major in the Royal Engineers who built the road and later became Hong Kong's governor, in 1904. During Nathan's time, this road was a meandering track lined with banyan trees (some of which can still be seen). Citizens used it to drive out to the countryside in horse-drawn buggies for Sunday picnics. Nathan's futuristic notion that Nathan Road would one day be part of a big commercial centre seemed so laughable then that his road was called Nathan's Folly.

Gold, diamonds, jade, pewter, ivory, watches, cameras, rugs, carpets, carvings, candelabras – speciality and sundry shops here stretch on and on.

Looking for food? Restaurants also exist all along Nathan Road and its side streets. Formal dining rooms and coffee shops are easily spotted in the major hotels, and there are innumerable others outside. At least five types of Chinese cuisine – Chiu Chow, Pekinese, Shanghainese, Cantonese and Szechuan – are available in addition to Korean, German, Hungarian, French, Malay, Indonesian, Italian, New York kosher, and others. Kowloon's Tsimshatsui is also the heart of Hong Kong nightlife.

The shoreline swings to the east after Tsimshatsui East, forming Hung Hom Bay. That strange looking upside down pyramid is the **Hong Kong Coliseum**, a 12,000-seat indoor stadium which has featured everything from the Ice Follies to rock-and-roll concerts and basketball. Across from it is the red-bricked **Hong Kong Polytechnic**.

YAUMATEI

Heading north on Kowloon's Canton or Jordan roads, you will surge with the

No-frills shopping in a factory outlet.

peninsula's traffic into the **Yaumatei District**, an area known for its large typhoon shelter, where Hong Kong's famous boat people anchor their floating homes.

It has been said that some citizens of Yaumatei's boat city live a lifetime without setting foot on shore. Inhabitants can get a haircut, medical aid or attend a church service – all without going ashore. And their children can attend floating schools.

At the junction of Kansu and Reclamation streets is the city's famous **Jade Market**, which has hundreds of stalls selling jade ornaments. If you plan to visit the market, opt for a morning trip and avoid the afternoon crowd. The closest MRT station is Jordan Road, where dealers offer jade in every imaginable form – from large blocks of the raw material to tiny, ornately-carved chips. In the multi-storey carpark at Yaumatei you'll find practitioners of an age-old Chinese craft, professional letter-writing. Here, a calligrapher will transcribe a letter in pen (or brush) and

Herbal drinks store in Temple Street.

ink, or on a typewriter, whichever is preferred. They handle love letters and business correspondence with equal ease and discretion.

Yaumatei's **Temple Street**, originally famous for its temples, is now renowned for its night market that lights up after the sun goes down.

In the Temple Street area are four temples, grouped together in Public Square Street. The colony's main **Tin Hau Temple** was built on these shores more than 100 years ago. Land reclamation has forced it to move inland, but Yaumatei's boat people hike to it regularly to worship sea gods, particularly Tin Hau, the protector of fisherfolk.

MONGKOK, SANPOKONG and KWUN TONG

Hong Kong is well-known as the most densely populated place on earth, especially within Kowloon, where there is a district with the highest population density of Hong Kong – **Mongkok**. Here live an estimated 165,000 people per

square kilometre. Many stories are told of how Mongkok got its name. In the first place, the word or name does not exist in any Chinese dialect. The *kok* part of it means "corner" in Cantonese, and one popular hypothesis notes that the name was supposed to be Wongkok, or Wong's Corner. But a sign painter inadvertently stencilled the "W" upside down, thus making it Mongkok instead. The shops along this stretch of Nathan Road boast many bargains not found on the pricier end of the Golden Mile.

Sanpokong, one of Kowloon's first manufacturing areas, is located just opposite the former Kai Tak Airport in a crowded and dirty jumble of streets bordered on one side by Choi Hung Road and on the other side by Prince Edward Road. Businessmen who visit the colony's factories know the place well.

For tourists, the only reason to go there would be to browse through factory outlet stores on Tai Yau Street and on side streets such as Ng Fong, Luk Hop, Pat Tat and Sheung Hei.

Kwun Tong is considered part of Kowloon administratively but is actually part of the New Territories. It houses numerous industrial facilities and therefore is one of the colony's newer centres for manufacturing, industry and housing estates. It is important enough to be serviced by four-lane highways (rare in Hong Kong) and ferries from Central, plus it is the final stop on the Mass Transit Railway.

Again, there is not much of interest to tourists except a few factory outlet shops and a fascinating **Temple of the Monkey God**, located at Saumauping Road in the Saumauping housing estate.

The Monkey God in Chinese religion is known and loved by children. He is an Oriental Santa Claus, Charlie Chaplin and Mickey Mouse reincarnated into one. Chinese children are raised on stories of the Monkey God, a rascal who raised so much hell on Earth that he was sent to Hell.

Worshippers at this temple seek health, peace and happiness. There is a medium here who speaks for the Monkey God, and an interpreter relays his **Crowded day at Wong Tai Sin Temple.**

messages to the faithful, because the medium uses a language unknown to anyone except himself, the interpreter and, of course, the Monkey God. The Mass Transit Railway (MTR) makes access to Kwun Tong easy.

KOWLOON CITY

The **Kowloon City Market** is centred on Lion Rock Road. Here you'll find anything from bananas to barbecues, shoes to swine, *cheongsam* and entire sets of porcelain dinnerware – up for sale at prices much less than in the regular tourist-oriented districts.

The **Wong Tai Sin Temple** sits a few yards from the MTR station of the same name. The temple is situated on Lung Chung Road amidst modern towering skyscrapers. Like many Chinese temples, this one is not merely a place of worship, but also a centre for community affairs. From a distance your eye is attracted to Wong Tai Sin's bright yellow roofing tiles, which were brought from Kwantung Province across the

Temple devotees wish for good luck in the new year.

border. Much of the temple's stonework was likewise imported from the same Chinese quarries that have supplied temple builders in China during the past centuries.

As you approach Wong Tai Sin, you may hear the shaking of a *chim*, a wooden cup full of prayer sticks. The chim is shaken until a stick falls out. The number of the stick is then carefully noted, and later, the worshipper will have his stick-fortune interpreted by a seer at one of the rented stalls.

Kowloon's answer to the "short time" hotels of Wanchai and Causeway Bay is found in **Kowloon Tong**, where they are known as blue motels. They are an economic anomaly in today's Hong Kong, having somehow escaped the so-called rent spiral.

In a city where small apartments are advertised for sale at over HK$15 million, and where a flat can cost HK$100,000 a month to rent, it seems strange that a trysting couple can have one of these little rooms for only a few hundred dollars an hour or so.

THE NEW TERRITORIES

The New Territories include the area right down to Boundary Street in Kowloon, but most people here say you're not really in the New Territories until you've travelled beyond Lion Rock Tunnel and Laichikok, but they are popularly considered to be in Kowloon, or New Kowloon. Start a New Territories tour by heading out toward **Castle Peak** or towards Shatin and Taipo. Alternatively, travel on Clearwater Bay Road which leads to the Sai Kung Peninsula.

On the Castle Peak side of the Kowloon peninsula is **Laichikok Amusement Park**, which has been entertaining people for decades and is one of the world's few places where you can enjoy Chinese opera and ice skating in the same compound. Another attraction, the **Sung Dynasty Village**, is a recreation of part of a village that existed in China 1,000 years ago. Everything in the place has been made exactly as it was in olden times, from the wine shop to the "bank" (the same kind in which the first paper money in the world was used). The village's impressarios stage special performances for visitors that include a traditional wedding ceremony and *kung-fu* demonstrations.

Just around the corner from Laichikok is **Kwai Chung**, the complex of five container terminals, and the industrial community of **Tsuen Wan**, a good example of the so-called New Town developments. It is the end of one MTR line and when you look at the skyline of this city with a population of a million people, it is difficult to imagine its romantic, violent, and essentially rural past.

The Tsuen Wan area has been inhabited since long ago, but the recent Chinese presence seems to have begun about the 2nd century AD. In the 13th century, the Chinese empire stretched to this area simply because the Chinese emperor was being driven south by invading Mongols. In 1277, he and his entourage arrived in Tsuen Wan. Later, be-

Inside a walled village.

tween 1662 and 1669, when the Formosan pirate Koxinga was building his empire, the Manchu government ordered a mass evacuation of coastal areas to save the populace from that marauder. Koxinga's forces demolished the vacated settlement of Tsuen Wan and it was not repopulated until the late 17th century.

The container terminals you now see were built entirely on reclaimed land. Leases have been granted on **Tsing Yi Island** to industrial enterprises such as tank farms, power stations and other ventures that require only initial access by water. When land access was needed, the government contributed to the cost of the bridge you now see spanning **Rambler Channel**.

From Tsuen Wan, heading out toward Castle Peak, you suddenly, surprisingly, find yourself in the country. The **Tuen Mun Highway** is a modern motorway with few views of the countryside, except for glimpses of gardens sliced by modern cloverleaf interchanges and flyovers. You end up in the new town of Tuen Mun, which is connected by a Light Rail Transport system to the old market town of Yuen Long.

About 22 kilometers (14 mi) along Castle Peak Road is **Dragon Garden**, where occasionally, by special arrangement, group tours are accepted at a small fee per person. This is a traditional Chinese garden, built by a wealthy Hong Kong businessman, and comprises grottoes, ponds, a neo-imperial mausoleum and a 15-meter (50-ft) sculpture of a dragon lying half submerged in a pond.

Near Castle Peak itself, adjacent to the LRT station, is a huge temple called **Ching Chuen Koong**, unusual in several ways. For one thing, it is home for aged people who have no relatives or means of support. Secondly, it is a repository for many Chinese art treasures, including lanterns more than 200 years old and a jade seal more than 1,000 years old. There is a library of 4,000 books, which document the history of the Daoist religion.

At the front of the altar is a 1,000-year-old jade seal kept in a glass case. The altar is protected by two statues that

Hakka woman.

were carved from white stone about 300 years ago for a temple in Beijing.

Near Tuen Mun, on the slopes of Castle Peak, is the much smaller, but just as interesting, **Pei Tu Temple**. Though it is fairly high up the slope, there is a paved road that runs almost to its entrance. This temple is dedicated to a character of Chinese mythology who was a monk, but not a totally honest one, and who was forever getting into trouble. One night he stayed with a family and in the morning took off with a prized golden statue.

A must on any trip around the New Territories is **Lau Fau Shan**, a huge fishmarket near Yuen Long. Here you'll find a restaurant with an entryway and walls decorated with thousands of oyster shells, each about 5 to 6 inches long.

Yuen Long is another redevelopment project, beginning as a traditional market town set in the middle of the largest flood plain in the New Territories. Its population, before redevelopment, was 40,000, and has now exceeded 1 million. Formerly a centre for privately-run

marketing, the town is rapidly taking on a labour-intensive, light industrial role.

Also near Yuen Long are the walled villages of **Kam Tin**. The most popular for visitors is the **Kat Hing Wai village** (often mistakenly referred to as the Kam Tin Walled Village).

There are 400 people living at Kat Hing Wai, all with the same surname, Tang. Built in the 1600s, it is a fortified village with walls 6 meters (18 ft) thick, guardhouses on its four corners, arrow slits for fighting off attackers, and a moat. The "authenticity" may seem spoiled by some of the modern buildings inside, complete with television aerials, but there is still only one entrance, guarded by a heavy wrought iron gate. You can enter the village for a nominal admission fee, but in ancient times, that gate was used to keep out undesirables. Something else that's only allowed by permission, and payment, is the taking of pictures of the elderly folk sitting around the gateway. The commercialism continues inside.

Choice burial sites: You'll see clusters of what appear to be huge pickle jars, with wooden lids, sometimes six or eight parked on a hillside. These pots contain the bones of dead Chinese. These people died and were buried long ago, but several years later, their bones are exhumed and placed in jars here to await consignment to their final resting place. This process takes a long time, because the exact arrangement of a grave is tremendously important and may take a long time to ascertain.

The graves, shaped like concrete armchairs, are sometimes huge. You can see them on hillsides, and if you stand by one you can usually view the sea or a pleasant valley. The *feng shui* (wind and water) placement of a grave is important. The departed relative is going to be stuck on that hillside forever; descendants chose a site with a good view and favourable breezes – conditions which are increasingly difficult to find even for the "living" in Hong Kong. These graves cost a comparative fortune, and it may take a hardworking family many years to save up enough money to purchase a tomb site.

In the New Territories are hard-working Hakka women dressed in *samfoo* (black pajama-like suits), their faces framed by black curtains around the brims of their wide hats. They come from a mysterious and very traditional matriarchal society and think nothing of labouring at jobs that Westerners consider to be for-men-only. Proceed with caution if tempted to photograph these women. They dislike photographers, and will literally chase a shutterbug across a field. Be prepared to shoot and run.

From Yuen Long and Kam Tin you can take a scenic route via **Shek Kong**, which once was a large British military garrison and airfield. From Shek Kong, **Route Twisk** begins, one of the best scenic drives in Hong Kong. Within minutes you are high up in forested mountains, apparently far from all human habitation. Route Twisk twists and turns for miles and then suddenly plunges right into the techno-industrial age of modern **Tsuen Wan**.

Another scenic rural route is from Shek Kong to **Fanling**, where there are several fine golf courses. Also nearby is **Luen Wo Market**, the region's traditional marketplace.

Fung Ying Sin Koon, a name meaning paradise, is a difficult-to-find – and thus rarely visited – temple. There is an intricate system of pathways and steps leading to the altar, and its grounds include many waterfalls and shady benches suitable for meditating.

Tai Po is a place name meaning "buying place," and the town certainly lives up to its name, serving as it has for many years as a place for farmers and fishermen to meet and exchange goods. But, like much of the old market towns, it too has been redeveloped. The old town lies at the northeastern end of Tolo Harbour, where the highway crosses the **Lower Lam Tsuen River**. On the northeast side of the river is the famous **Tai Po Market**, which includes a huge fish market and dozens of vegetable stalls.

The **Hong Kong Railway Museum**, complete with vintage stock, is housed in the former Tu Po Market station. Not far away, but with its own railway station, is **Tai Po Kau**. From here, or from

132

the train, you can see the departure and return of the fishing fleet. Like all the "new towns," Taipo is undergoing the transition from an old market town to a modern city.

To the east, **Mirs Bay** is largely undeveloped and well off the beaten track, its population of islanders cling to traditional employment forms such as fishing and vegetable-growing.

Whether entering **Shatin** by road or rail, you'll be amazed to find a bustling metropolis in the middle of the agricultural New Territories. Massive housing projects occupy fields where just a few years ago the greatest activity was water buffaloes pulling plows in rice paddies. The New Town Plaza is a massive shopping and entertainment complex, while Riverside Plaza Hotel along the banks of the Shing Mun is another addition.

The **Shatin Valley** has several places of worship, of which two are worthy of note. The **Temple of 10,000 Buddhas**, which can be reached by climbing 431 steps up the hillside above the Shatin Railway Station. There is a main altar

Monastery.

room with 12,800 small Buddha statues on its walls. The temple is guarded by huge, fierce looking statues of various gods. An additional 69 steps up the hill is the **Temple of Man Fat**. **Yuet Kai** was a monk whose greatest concern was to achieve immortality. When he died, he was buried, but, according to Chinese custom, his body was later dug up to be reburied in its final resting place. However, the body was found to be perfectly preserved and radiating a ghostly yellow glow. It was decided to preserve his body in gold leaf.

From either of these temples one can look down on the Hong Kong Jockey Club's **Shatin racecourse**. Thousands of punters (the grandstands hold 75,000) persistently go there every October through May horseracing season to bet money on the ponies and then pray for good fortune.

A great relief from this mad rush into the use-of-space age is afforded by a separate trip to another part of the New Territories called the **Sai Kung Peninsula**, including Clearwater Bay.

HONG KONG'S OUTLYING ISLANDS

It is regrettable that so few visitors make time to go to the outlying islands, for it is here that the real magic of Hong Kong is uncovered, an inheritance which brings Hong Kong in line with its apparently more traditional neighbours. Most of these places are only an easy ferry ride away from the chaotic Hong Kong that most visitors know.

LANTAU

Of all the outlying islands, the greatest in size, and perhaps in atmosphere, is **Lantau**, which has a land area twice that of Hong Kong Island. In some ways it is still not too late to experience on Lantau rural village lifestyles which have endured unchanged (except perhaps for television sets) unaffected by the fall of emperors, colonization and the decay of kingdoms and of the colonial empire.

However, in 1998 Hong Kong's new international airport, at **Chek Lap Kok** on the north side of the island, opened, along with a bridge to connect the island with the mainland. It won't be long before Lantau's atmosphere will change.

In Cantonese, *lantau* means "broken head," perhaps because its rugged dignity is dominated by the ragged and two part **Lantau Peak** that rises 935 meters (3,086 ft) high at the heart of lizard-shaped Lantau.

The island is cob-webbed with wandering pathways and dusty trails which spiral up, down and around its scenic mountains. A particularly good opening trail circles the blue **Shek Pik Reservoir**, on the west slopes of Lantau Peak. This 20,900-million-litre (5,500 million gal) reservoir gathers most of the freshwater carried from Lantau's heights by rushing streams and rivulets.

For those who land at **Silver Mine Bay**, Lantau's main ferry port, regular buses travel from there along Lantau's southern resort coast to the brightly painted red-and-gold **Po Lin Monas-**

Po Lin Monastery, Lantau.

tery. Here, in a large visitors' dining house, one can enjoy a good vegetarian lunch served by Po Lin's resident monks.

West of Po Lin, in the direction of **Tung Chung** on Lantau's north coast, is an excellent walking path that traverses mountain ridges, small canyons and over rushing streams en route to Lantau's **Yin Hing Monastery**, a haven rich with traditional Buddhist paintings and statues. This monastery sits on a slope and commands a fine view of the surrounding mountains, farming country and the blue South China Sea.

For those who would like to break up their Po Lin area tour with a local-style high-tea hour, there is a proper tea plantation and teahouse called the **Lantau Tea Gardens** just a short walk away from the Po Lin Monastery compound. The teahouse has rooms for rent, barbecue facilities and a free camping area.

On Lantau's northeast coast, meanwhile, is a meditative spot with a decidedly different aura. This is the **Trappist Haven of Our Lady of Liese** at **Tai Shui Hang**, which is looked after by a closed Christian order sworn to verbal silence.

Because the Trappist monks are protective of their privacy, they do not welcome casual visitors to their inner sanctums. Until recently, they did allow visitors to stroll through their grounds to admire the plump dairy cows they raise, but this thriving business has since been moved to the New Territories, supplying fresh milk to Hong Kong hotels. Expansive Lantau is also understandably famed for its many long, smooth and often empty beaches. The finest sandy sweeps are on the southeast coastline that arcs from **Cheung Sha** south of Silver Mine Bay to **Tong Fuk**. The most popular and crowded beach (probably because it is the easiest one to reach) is **Silver Mine Bay Beach**.

LAMMA

The third largest of the outlying islands, and somehow less well-known both to visitors and local people, is Lamma Island. It is nicknamed Stone-Age Is-

Fishing boat in the outlying islands.

land because of its archaeological association with some of the earliest settlements in Hong Kong.

Though it is just over eight square kilometres (5 sq mi), Lamma is rich in green hills and beautiful bays, and – because it's mountainous – there is a very small area of cultivation. Eroded mountain tops dominate the island's grassy lower slopes.

Lamma is an island totally devoted to fishing and has a small population, less than 6,000 people (which includes a surprising number of Europeans who want to get away from it all and commute to urban Hong Kong daily for work). Although Lamma has a regular ferry service, it has remained relatively undiscovered – much to the joy of those who moved out to it.

The nearest Lamma village to Aberdeen – from where a round trip by privately-chartered sampan will cost less than HK$200 – is **Sok Kwu Wan**, which lies on the eastern shore of the long fjord-like inlet known as **Picnic Bay** and is the haunt of Hong Kong's "Weekend Admirals" or "Saturday Sailors," the appropriate nautical names given to the colony's pleasure-junk captains.

Its quay is lined with excellent fresh seafood restaurants. It is possible to walk the entire length of the island to Sok Wan's sister town of **Yung Shue Wan**, at the north end of Lamma. This village sports many restaurants as well as bars. This trek follows a gentle hilly track up and down dividing valleys and treats hikers to a spectacular view across the sea to the **Lemas Islands**.

Both towns here offer the best of many Chinese worlds to the curious onlooker. Not isolated, yet underdeveloped, Yung Shue Wan has an excellent street market and the air is pungent with the smell of dried fish. Vegetable farms stretch up behind the village. At Sok Kwu Wan, visit the lovely **Tin Hau Temple**. The road which connects these two towns leads a walker first through neat patches of paddy and an occasional cluster of brightly-painted houses, then along **Hung Shing Ye Beach**, a long clean beach.

Hiking on Lantau.

CHEUNG CHAU

If it weren't for the distinctly Chinese junks and *sampan* which crowd Cheung Chau's curving little harbour, one's first sight of Cheung Chau would deceive the eye into believing that this is an Old World Mediterranean port – a neat little place with pastel homes set into pine-studded hills.

This dumbbell-shaped isle – with hills at either end and a village nestled in a connecting rod of land – is narrow enough that you can walk from **Cheung Chau Harbour** on its west side to **Tung Wan Harbour** on the east in just a few minutes or so.

Cheung Chau is a fishing island, with a few farms in its more distant reaches, and its main town is a tangle of alley-ways. There is little vehicular traffic, a Hong Kong phenomenon which gives the island an automatic serenity. Cheung Chau's sense of community is strong, but it does not exclude the visiting stranger. People here are more friendly than the hurried city dwellers in Hong Kong's Central District. Many Europeans and North Americans moved here to escape the claustrophobia of Hong Kong.

The island was once the haunt of pirates. One of the greatest pirates of all, Cheung Po Chai, used to hide out on this island when he was in danger. His tiny cave retreat can still be explored.

Once a year the whole island community comes together for a big Bun Festival, a celebration held to exorcise wandering and malicious ghosts, some from centuries ago during the pirate years, who have been unable to find peace and rest in this world.

The festival, known as *Ching Chiu* in Cantonese, originated many years ago after the discovery here of a nest of skeletons, probably the remains of people killed by pirates. Not soon after this discovery, the island was plagued by a series of misfortunes, and so the islanders called in a Daoist priest, who took a look and recommended that they should placate the restless spirits of the murdered people by making offerings to them once a year. So now they do.

Buildings on some outer islands are strictly low-rise.

MACAU

The first stop for visitors to Macau is usually **Penha Hill**, atop of which stands the magnificent **Bishop's Palace**, unoccupied for many years now but partly open to the public. From one vantage point there, one can see across the Old City to Macau's Inner Harbour, and less than a mile farther, China. From another point, you can see the Outer Harbour approaches and the island of Taipa, connected to the peninsula by a bridge.

At one stage in early Eurasian history, Macau was *the* Asian seat of Roman Catholicism. Bishops here controlled all of the church's missions from Goa to the Moluccas and Nagasaki. The Bishop's Palace complex also houses **Penha Church**. Though the present building dates only from 1935, the first chapel here was dedicated in 1622.

Perhaps the most striking Macau church is the facade of **St Paul's**, with its impressive grand staircase. Historians call it the finest monument to Christianity in the Far East.

Unfortunately, the site must have had bad *feng shui*. The first church at this site was destroyed by fire in 1601; the current facade was added before 1630. In 1835, another fire destroyed St Paul's adjacent college, a library reputed to be the best east of Africa, and, again, the church. In 1904, efforts were made to rebuild the church, but little was done.

If touring by taxi, the driver usually races on to one of the colony's Chinese temples, but ask him instead to head for **Monte Fort (St Paul's Fortress)**, which overlooks the facade and was built in the early 1620s. When Dutch ships attacked and invaded Macau in 1622, the then half-completed fortress was defended by 150 clerics and slaves.

Tours always include the Chinese temples of **A-Ma**, for which Macau is named; the Kun Iam Temple, famous for its table on which the first Sino-Lantau American treaty was signed in 1844; and the **Lin Fong Temple**. The temple of the goddess A-Ma squats be-

Macau and St Paul's from Monte Fortress.

neath **Barra Hill**, at the entrance to Macau's Inner Harbour. It is the oldest temple in this former Portuguese territory, said to date back 600 years to the Ming dynasty. The original temple was said to have been erected by Fujinese fishermen and dedicated to Tin Hau, the patron goddess of fishermen.

Kun Iam Temple is dedicated to Buddhism's goddess of mercy and dates back to 1627 on the site of an earlier 14th-century temple.

The third temple, the **Lin Fong (Lotus) Temple**, built in 1592, is quite near Macau's 19th-century Portas do Cerco (Border Gate). In the old days, it served as a guest house for mandarins travelling between Macau and Canton. Its most recent restoration took place in 1980, but it is still an excellent example of classical Buddhist architecture.

Most tours make a quick visit to the **Dr. Sun Yatsen Memorial House**. Though opened after he died, the memorial is near where he practised medicine at a nearby hospital. (He was one of the first Western-trained Chinese doctors in this area.) His birthplace is across the border in China.

Another classic is the **Leai Senado** (Loyal Senate) building on Macau's main square. This building was dedicated in 1784, its facade was completed in 1876, and it was restored in 1939. Half the offices on ground floor have been converted into a beautiful gallery for special exhibitions.

The church of **St Dominic** is one of the oldest and most famous, dating from the 17th century. (Spanish Dominicans had a chapel and convent on this site as early as 1588.) To gain entry, ring a bell to the right of the facade. When you get inside, you will note that many of the Christian motifs are of an Oriental style.

There are a couple of other places nearby that are not on the usual tourist route. One is the **Barra Fortress**, which has been turned into the deluxe **Pousada de Sao Tiago**, a hostelry that was developed within the fort's walls.

The **Guia Fortress and Lighthouse** (and also a chapel) is the first thing you see when you approach Macau by sea. This 17th-century, Western-style lighthouse – the oldest on the China coast – stands atop **Guia Hill** guarding coastal approaches. It is open to the public and even houses a small art gallery. There are also some interesting tunnels underneath the surrounding area.

Las Vegas of the East: Sleepy Macau is also vicariously known as the Las Vegas of the East, or, if you are a European, the Monaco of the East. Indeed, gambling is the main reason over 6 million visitors each year – 80 percent of them Hong Kong Chinese – make the 65-kilometer (40-mi) sea cruise across the Pearl River Estuary to Macau.

Macau's casinos, each one packed every day, feature Western and Chinese games of chance. If you tire of conventional craps, roulette, baccarat or blackjack, try a hand at Chinese *fantan*, *sikpo* (*dai siu*) and *pai-kao*. Also popular are Keno and slot machines.

Taipa Trotters: Despite – or perhaps because of – numerous rumours of trackside fixing and other foul play, greyhound racing seems to attract the Pearl River's hardest core gambling crowd,

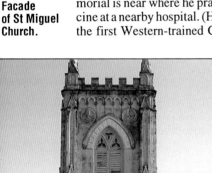

Facade of St Miguel Church.

notably in Macau's dog-racing venue, the Canidrome on Avenida General Castelo Branco.

Asia's Monaco wouldn't be complete without an annual auto race. So, like its glittering Mediterranean sister, Macau each year (on the last weekend in November) cordons off a twisting, through-the-streets grand-prix racecourse that starts and finishes on Avenida da Amizade, near the ferry piers. Racing drivers from around the world race Formula III cars for 32 laps around this 6 kilometer (3.8-mi) Guia Circuit.

Another Macau consists of the two islands of **Taipa** and **Coloane**. Previously, access to these islands was by small ferry boats which, in the case of Coloane, could only be approached at high tide. Taipa is now connected to the mainland by two beautiful arching bridges. Access is as simple as getting into a taxi or climbing aboard a minibus.

Taipa and Coloane's cobble-stoned villages have grown. Taipa has a number of high-rises, relieving some of the pressure on congested Macau. An interna-

tional airport has constructed on an artificial island off the east coast, but both islands are still rural and charming, with Iberian-style buildings around a central plaza, surrounded by typical Chinese farming communities.

Taipa was also at one period in the early 1700s the busy centre for Western trade with China, when an Imperial edict banned English and French ships at Canton and insisted they moor at Taipa instead. The major industries on Taipa in the old days were junk-building and the manufacture of firecrackers.

Taipa's Latin Orient ambience, however, still lives. Indeed, the small *praia* just below Largoda Carma rivals its larger and more famous predecessor on the Macau peninsula for beauty, elegance and romance. To preserve this 19th-century ambience, a **Casa Museu** (house museum) has been created (completed with period furniture) out of one of the five old houses.

Coloane, too, seems to have been forgotten for many years, but is now prominent because of its beaches. Coloane is almost twice as big as Taipa at 6.5 square kilometers (2.6 sq mi) in area. It is so close to mainland China that one can see quite clearly and easily a Chinese fishing village that sits only a quarter mile beyond a strip of water.

One of Coloane's beaches, **Kao Ho**, is the site for Macau's deep-water port. Situated on the northern end of the island, Kao Ho was once a traditional haven for South China Sea pirates. Most of the islanders patronized piracy, which apparently was their main source of livelihood. But one day the pirates overstepped their watery bounds. After a mass kidnapping of Chinese children from Canton, and a subsequent refusal of outrageous ransom demands by Coloane's buccaneers, Portuguese authorities went after the pirates and defeated them in a two-day battle in 1910. A memorial to this incident is set into a tiny square in front of the Portuguese **Chapel of St Francis Xavier**. This tiny chapel houses a relic, a 15-centimeter-long (6-in) piece of bone from the left arm of St Francis, plus the revered bones of Vietnamese and Japanese martyrs.

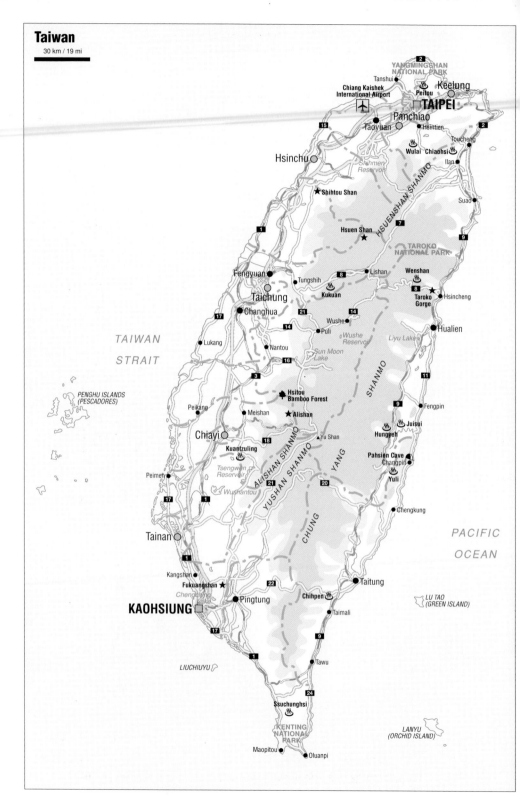

Taiwan

30 km / 19 mi

YANGMINGSHAN NATIONAL PARK
2

Tanshui
Peitou
Keelung
Chiang Kaishek
International Airport
TAIPEI
Panchiao
Hsintien
Taoyuan
2
Toucheng
15
Wulai Chiaohsi
Ilan
Hsinchu
Shihmen
Reservoir
HSUENSHAN SHANMO
Suad
9
Shihtou Shan
TAROKO
NATIONAL PARK
Hsuen Shan
7
Fengyuan
Lishan
Wenshan
Tungshih
8
Kukuan
Taroko
Gorge
Hsincheng
Taichung
Changhua
8
21
Wushe
14
Hualien
17
14
Puli
Wushe
Reservoir
Lukang
Nantou
Liyu Lake
Sun Moon
Lake
3
16
SHANMO
11
Hsitou
Bamboo Forest
9
Peikang
Meishan
Alishan
Fengpin
Chiayi
ALISHAN SHANMO
YUSHAN SHANMO
Yu Shan
Juisui
Hungyeh
Pahsien Cave
Kuantzuling
18
Changpin
Peimen
21
Tsengwen
Reservoir
Wushantou
20
Yuli
17
1
YANG
CHUNG
Chengkung
Tainan
1
TAIWAN STRAIT
PENGHU ISLANDS (PESCADORES)
PACIFIC OCEAN
Kangshan
Fukuangshan
Chengching
Lake
22
Taitung
KAOHSIUNG
Pingtung
Chihpen
17
LU TAO
(GREEN ISLAND)
Taimali
1
9
Tawu
LIUCHIUYU
24
Ssuchunghsi
KENTING NATIONAL PARK
LANYU
(ORCHID ISLAND)
Maopitou
Oluanpi

146

TAIWAN

Bao Dao – Treasure Island, what the early Chinese settlers first called this emerald island. Tales of the untold riches of this island, just off the east coast of mainland China, ignited an endless exodus centuries ago, often streaming from the southern region of Fujian province... Pirates and political exiles, traders and adventurers, farmers and fishermen.

Besides the island's intrinsic beauty, the Chinese also found that food grew abundantly and rapidly here, a significant concern for a people accustomed to the frequent famines and chronic food shortages of the mainland. Too, the island was fat with mineral resources.

Taiwan is frequently tagged as one of Asia's economic tigers, or dragons, if you will. So it is, and not that far behind Japan in providing an engine of growth for Asia. Yet despite the industrialization of the island, the essential features of the world's oldest, continuous and most culturally-accomplished civilization are all preserved in Taiwan. Being Chinese is a unifying force, it often seems, regardless of where one actually lives. Given the historical and cultural context of the binding nature of being Chinese, why the current animosity between Taiwan and the mainland government? Beijing considers Taiwan to be a renegade province, but Taipei considers itself the temporary refuge of a government in exile. Slowly, a half century of separation – together with the force of personality and political ideology – has led to a cultural gap of differing political, economic and social systems.

The social trait that the Chinese call *ren chingwei*, the flavour of human feeling, permeates all social relationships in Taiwan and China. Whether ren chingwei helps to resolve the governmental and ideological differences between Taipei and Beijing is a question of profound interest, especially after the return of Hong Kong to China's control.

Preceding pages: pagoda above the mist of Sun Moon Lake; young martial arts students.

Taiwan straddles the Tropic of Cancer about 190 kilometers (120 mi) off the shores of mainland China's Fujian province. Sparkling like an emerald in the cobalt waters of the East China Sea, the island occupies a strategic pivot between Japan, Korea, Hong Kong, the Philippines, and mainland China.

Shaped like a tea leaf, Taiwan stretches 400 kilometers (250 mi) from north to south and about 130 kilometers (80 mi) across its widest point. That makes this island of 19 million people about the size of Holland. Included within Taiwan's domain are several offshore islands: the Pescadores, Orchid Island, Green Island, and the militarily strategic Kinmen (Quemoy) and Matsu.

Two-thirds of Taiwan is corrugated by rugged mountains pushed up from ocean depths by prehistoric volcanic action. Traces of coral from the island's ancient sea-bed can still be found in igneous rock formations as high as 600 meters (2,000 ft) above sea level. Taiwan's Central Range runs like a bony spine along the island's north-south axis and includes at 3,997 meters (13,114 ft) the tallest peak in all of northeast Asia. The violent volcanic eruptions which formed these mountains left the island seamed from top to toe with the sulphurous brimstones of over 100 major hot springs, whose bubbling thermal waters constitute one of Taiwan's greatest recreational attractions – soothing hot mineral baths.

Long before the Chinese ever set foot on Taiwan, the island was inhabited by a colourful – and quarrelsome – array of primitive aborigine tribes who came to Taiwan from Mongolia, the Malay peninsula, and the South Pacific. Ancient artifacts from Taiwan's rugged eastern coastline indicate that aboriginal people were well established on the island at least 10,000 years ago, and probably much longer. Today, there are still over 250,000 ethnic aborigines scattered across Taiwan, including remnants of 19 different tribes. Nine of these tribes still have sufficient numbers and interest in their own origins to maintain their traditional tribal lifestyles in specially designated homelands tucked in the steep mountains and deep valleys of the Central Range. The largest tribe is the Ami,

who live in the mountains near the east coast town of Hualien and boast over 60,000 members. Their annual Ami Harvest Festival, held in Hualien in August, remains one of the island's most colourful and popular events.

Perhaps the most interesting and authentic tribe is the Yami, a seafaring tribe on offshore Orchid Island whose elegantly carved fishing boats give strong credence to claims of Polynesian roots. With their traditional costumes and feathered headgear, elaborately carved totem poles and other handicrafts,

and their inherent love of music and dance, Taiwan's native tribes form some of the brightest, boldest threads in the colourful cultural tapestry of Taiwan.

Among the most salient themes shared by all of these tribes is their veneration of the venomous Hundred Pacer snake as their spiritual ancestor. This deadly serpent gets its name from the fact that its victims rarely make it more than a hundred paces before dropping dead. The other motif which appears with the snake on almost all aborigine carvings, paintings, and weaving is the dismembered human head, a thematic remnant of their heyday as headhunters.

In AD 239, the Chinese kingdom of Wu launched a 10,000-man expedition to lay claim to the island, but the mission disappeared without a trace. Then, in 1430, the famous seafaring eunuch and Ming official Cheng Ho, whose armada sailed as far as India and Persia, "discovered" the island once again, claimed it on behalf of the Ming emperor, and gave it its present name, Taiwan, which means terraced bay.

The first Chinese to actually settle permanently on Taiwan were a refugee minority Islands and then to Taiwan itself, where by AD 1000 the Hakkas had begun to establish permanent settlements along the island's southern shores. To this day, the Hakkas remain a major dynamic force in Taiwan's booming economy, and they still command deep respect for their entrepreneurial and financial acumen.

Taiwan's wealth and beauty did not long remain a Hakka secret. During the 15th and 16th centuries, the island and its lucrative coastal trade became both target and haven

group called Hakka, a word which literally means "guests" or "strangers." For some unknown, or perhaps unexplained, reason, the Hakkas had been severely persecuted in China since ancient times and were driven from their ancestral homeland in northern China's Hunan province about 1,500 years ago. The Hakkas wandered far and wide, eventually settling down along the mainland's southeastern shores, where they engaged in fishing and trade. These activities soon brought them to the offshore Pescadores

Left, Taiwan native. **Above**, the Dutch command Fort Zeelandia on Taiwan about 1635.

for marauding pirates from China and Japan. After failing to wrest Macau from Portuguese rivals, the Dutch established a colony in 1624 on Taiwan's southern coast, where they built three forts.

In 1644, the militant Manchus commenced their relentless campaign to conquer the tottering Ming dynasty and claim the Dragon Throne as their own. The Ming emperor sought aid from a Taiwan-based pirate named Cheng Chi-lung and his son Cheng Cheng-kung, who nearly succeeded in driving the Manchu invaders out of China, but for superior Manchu numbers and resources. In 1661, the younger Cheng, known in Western chronicles as Koxinga, led his army of 100,000 men and armada of 3,000 war junks across the Taiwan Straits to safe refuge on Taiwan. Koxinga captured the island from the Dutch and established a civil administration based on Chinese laws and principles. When Koxinga died in 1662 at the age of 38, his mantle passed on to his son and then his grandson, who kept the island free of Manchu control until 1684.

Britain's Opium Wars with China in the 19th century brought Taiwan into the limelight once more. Dr. William Jardine, co-founder of Hong Kong's trading firm Jardine, Matheson, & Co., was profoundly alarmed by Beijing's attempt to forcibly forbid trade

wan was ceded to Japan, marking the start of 50 years of harsh colonial rule, in which the Japanese tried to eliminate local culture.

At the end of World War II, the island was formerly restored to Nationalist Chinese rule. Meanwhile, fighting continued on the mainland as Nationalist and Communist Chinese armies fought for control of China. Finally, Nationalist leader Chiang Kai-shek led his two best divisions, plus a rambling entourage of scholars and artists, merchants and magistrates, across the Taiwan Straits. In 1949, the Republic of China (ROC) formally transferred its government headquarters to the provisional capital of Taipei. The country set out on its new adventure.

in his firm's most profitable product – opium. In a letter to British Foreign Secretary Lord Palmerston, he wrote, "We must proceed to take possession of three or four islands, say Formosa, Quemoy, and Amoy, in order to secure new markets and new footholds in China." The Treaty of Tientsin, which ended the first Opium War in 1860, thus opened four ports in Taiwan to foreign trade: Keelung and Suao in the north, Tainan and Kaohsiung in the south.

By 1867, about three dozen foreign traders lived permanently on the island, mostly British, American, and German. Then, as a result of the Sino-Japanese war of 1894–95, Tai-

According to a report prepared by the Stanford Research Institute in 1986, Taiwan accomplished in the subsequent 30 years what it takes most developing countries over 100 years to achieve. It credits Taiwan's phenomenal growth directly to the enlightened *laissez-faire* and economic *savoir-faire* of the island's leaders. Nevertheless, Chiang Kai-shek maintained strict political discipline and social order.

The year 1965 proved a critical test of strength for Taiwan and its leadership. Financial aid from the United States, which had provided a springboard for economic development, was terminated. Nevertheless, the country's progress and growth continued to accelerate.

Chiang died in 1975. He was succeeded by the vice president, but in the following year, Chiang Kai-shek's son, Chiang Ching-kuo, was elected president.

Earlier, in 1971, the Republic of China – Taiwan – a founding member of the United Nations, lost its membership in the organization and was replaced by the People's Republic of China. In 1978, the United States announced the recognition of the People's Republic of China, and ceased official diplomatic relations with Taiwan.

Chiang Ching-kuo died in 1988. His successor as interim-president was Lee Teng-

hui. The National Assembly officially elected Lee as president in 1990; he was the island's first Taiwanese-born present. Despite political setbacks, Taiwan continued to thrive and survive. Its gross national product grew steadily by maintaining foreign trade through cultural contacts and trade associations, a remarkable achievement in the wake of diplomatic ostracism. Lee reinstate parts of the constitution placed in abeyance decades be-

Left, Chiang Kai-shek broadcasts news of his government's move to Taiwan in 1949. <u>Above</u>, Chiang Kai-shek Memorial Hall, venue for large-scale social and political activities.

fore, amended certain articles and added other new ones. Perhaps the most important was the free election of the second National Assembly, which assumed office in 1992. One of the new articles added to the constitution stated that the president and vice-president of the republic "will be directly elected by the entire voting population in the Taiwan area."

First official government contacts between Taipei and Beijing were in 1993, in Singapore, resulting in several signed agreements. But the second set of talks, scheduled for 1995, were cancelled by Beijing.

In 1996, Taiwan elected its first popularly-elected president, retaining Lee Teng-hui and thus giving Beijing a blow in the eye. Judging by its sabre rattling, China had feared that the 1996 popular election would increase Taiwan's claim of international legitimacy. Just before the elections, Beijing started military manoeuvres apparently intended to shake the confidence of Taiwan's voters. Most belligerent – and which initiated the American naval response of sending an aircraft carrier into the Taiwan Strait – was the launching of missiles into the ocean near the important seaports of Keelung and Kaohsiung, threatening trade routes.

Moreover, said Beijing, if Taiwan officially declared itself an independent nation (several Taiwanese politicians had threatened to make such a claim official), the mainland would not hesitate to use force against the island, despite the opinion of most military experts in the West that China is incapable of launching such an assault. In the end, Beijing lost considerable political capital with other nations, both in the region and globally. (China's insistence on claiming every island in the South China Sea down to Malaysia further irritated its regional neighbours: the Philippines, Malaysia, Brunei, Japan, Vietnam and Indonesia.)

Even more, China's actions reignited right-wing calls in Japan for a stronger, and more assertive, Japanese military.

Nonetheless, both Taipei and Beijing have okayed direct shipping between Taiwan and the mainland. Residents of Taiwan are allowed to visit relatives on the mainland. Taiwanese businesses have invested over US$20 billion on the mainland, mostly in the south, from where many Taiwanese originally came.

A Chinese painting appears as it does because it was painted by a Chinese artist. The aesthetics of painting are part of the Chinese cosmogony. Indeed, the Chinese assign painting and the complimentary art of calligraphy an important place in the natural order.

In historical terms, the earliest Chinese characters for writing were pictographic or ideographic. Indeed, they remain so today, although many characters are derived from these originals on a phonetic basis. The original forms of the characters are difficult to discern, as they have evolved into new shapes over the centuries. But the striking fact about Chinese writing is that, as the script developed, the older forms were not cast off. Many were preserved and used as they are today. This structural evolution of Chinese symbols was essentially completed by the fifth century.

Almost without exception, the artist of early China was a calligrapher, and from a privileged class. Otherwise, he would never have had the endless hours of time needed to acquire skill with the *maubi,* the brush used to write characters. In fact, competence with the brush was a necessary reflection of an education in ancient China.

Four treasures: The maubi combined a long, straight handle of wood or bamboo with a round tip that came to a point. It was soft, but firm and springy, and was probably made of rabbit, wolf or deer hair. Softer goat hairs were more often used by the painter than the calligrapher. The artist generally wrote on paper, which may have been invented as early as the second century AD. Lacking paper, he might have chosen silk for his canvas. Paper, however, provided an extremely sensitive surface that readily revealed the speed of the brush, the manner of its handling, and its charge of ink.

The artist's ink came in the form of a dry stick made from lampblack mixed with glue. After adding a little water, the stick was rubbed into an inkstone. Although grinding the ink was a slow process, it was a part of the

painting ritual – quieting and focusing the spirit before the art could commence.

These four treasures – maubi, paper, ink and inkstone, the tools of the calligrapher and painter – were the subject of much discussion and critique. The best brush would be made by famous craftsmen, with hairs from the pelt of an animal captured in the first weeks of March. The best inkstone would grind fine ink quickly and was "cold" enough to keep the fluid wet for long periods. It might come from a famous mountain miles

away. The choicest inks were made from the smallest particles of smoke, gathered at the greatest distance from the burning pine wood of *tung* oil, then beaten thousands of times to improve their quality.

The tools of the painter and calligrapher were essentially the same, as was their approach to painting and writing. The difference lay in the painter's use of color.

Calligraphy: Brush handling, by contrast, was all-important, and there was never a period of Chinese painting or a particular style in which good brushwork was not regarded as critical. Brush control reaches its finest in the subtle art of calligraphy, and the

Left, finishing touches on a character. **Right**, temple etching of an unusual form of ancient calligraphy.

Chinese have always regarded calligraphy as the highest of the arts. With its abstract aesthetic, it is certainly the purest.

Few examples of ancient calligraphy still exist. Most ancient inscriptions were rubbings taken from cast-metal vessels. The earliest examples of Chinese writing in Taipei's National Palace Museum are Shang-period oracle inscriptions, incised on tortoise shells or the scapulae of oxen. The earliest examples of work by famous calligraphers, on display, include the *Ping-fu tieh* (On Recovering from Illness), by Lu Chi, who lived from 261 to 303.

Painter's dao: The most obvious facet of Chinese painting is its expressions of a life nese sought to take their place within and participate in the natural order. Ritual was important as it involved actual participation, rather than just symbolic participation.

As Sze Mai-mai noted: "Painting and every other phase of Chinese life continued to be governed by the value of the ritual approach. It is worth noting, therefore, that the original purpose of ritual was to order the life of the community in harmony with the forces of nature (dao), on which subsistence and well-being depended. It was not only pious but expedient to perform regularly and properly the rituals of study, propitiation and celebration. These were acts of reverence. They were also literal attempts to bring

rooted in the *dao* – in nature. The concept of dao existed even before the formal teachings of the school of Daoism, and is a basic term of Chinese cosmology, expressive of the idea that all things have a common origin.

The Confucianists and Daoists differed more in their preoccupations than on their concept of dao. The Daoists were concerned with humanity's direct, mystical relationship with nature, the Confucianists with an individual's role in society. Both reflect, however, humanity's oneness with nature's larger harmony, the oneness of dao.

The Chinese universe was an ordered, harmonic whole. Perceiving this order, the Chi- heaven down to earth, for they were patterned on the rhythmic transformations in the skies and in nature, in the hope that a like order and harmony might prevail in society."

The painter's preoccupation with the dao occurred at both the ritual level of the Confucianist school and the mystical level of the Daoists. The Chinese painter was often a pillar of society, well-educated, with a responsible government position and considerable duties to his family. He was a man of the world. Yet, as an artist, he needed peace and quiet. Chinese literature and poetry abound with references to this conflict between the weight of responsible citizenship and the withdrawal to relative seclusion that marks the life of an artist. As a system, Daoism was better suited to the individual effort of painting, as it focused on the relationship between the individual and nature – on the creative act itself, between the painter and his subject, and the magical link between the two – art. Laozi's disciple, Zhuangzu, elaborated: "Dao has reality and evidence but no action or physical form. It may be transmitted but cannot be received. It may be obtained but cannot be seen."

Such concepts apply equally to the painter, as Chang Yenyuan wrote: "He who deliberates and moves the brush intent upon making a picture, misses to a still greater extent the

or provides definition where lines would be too strong – in mist or in the far distance.

The strokes, by contrast, are so important that they have even been given labels. There are hemp-fiber strokes, big ax-cut strokes, lotus leaf-vein strokes, raveled-rope strokes and others. It is critical that every line, stroke or dot in a painting be alive and have a validity that plays a part, yet can be separated from the painting as a whole. Each swish of the brush can thus be judged on its own merits, and a painting is perfect in whole and in parts. This is quite unlike the West, where an individual mark contributes to a marvelous whole, but can scarcely be subjected to a meaningful appraisal in itself.

art of painting, while he who cogitates and moves the brush without such intentions, reaches the art of painting. His hands will not get stiff; his heart will not grow cold. Without knowing how, he accomplishes it."

Techniques: The paintings of the Chinese, far more than those of other traditions, are essentially based on line-work. Their color is primarily symbolic and decorative. Tone is more important, but it plays a supporting role. It either fills the forms defined by lines

Above, *Autumn Colors on the Chiao and Hua Mountains*, a mural painting by Chao Mengfu, Yuan dynasty, 1295.

What is less obvious, but far more important in the sweep of history, is the debt of painting to calligraphy. The isolation of the strokes in any painting, with their self-contained beauty and the many special qualities of the calligraphic line, stand as evidence.

Living lines have always been central to the Chinese painter's art. His years of training as a calligrapher made it difficult for him to make marks that did not exhibit their own beauty. To capture the harmony of the parts brought the painter closer to achieving the harmony of the dao. Calligraphy remains obscure to those who can't see that a dot may be full of life, a line may burst with energy.

Westerners usually cringe when first encountering the somewhat shrill tones of traditional Chinese opera. Indeed, the tones are quite different and unexpected. To the ears of aficionados, however, the high-pitched notes lend emotional strength to the song lyrics, and the prolonged wails accentuate the singers' moods.

The music provides the beat and the backing for a visual spectacle of electric shades of painted faces, glittering rainbow of costumes, exquisite pantomime and impossible acrobatics. The unique blend of sound and spectacle that results is called *jingxi*, capital opera, or better known as Beijing opera.

Beijing opera was formally established in 1790, and in the city for which it is named. That was the year the most famous actors from all corners of the Chinese empire gathered in Beijing to present a special variety show for the emperor. The performance proved so successful that the artists remained in the capital city, combining their ancient individual disciplines of theater, music and acrobatics into the form of Beijing opera that continues today.

The first venue for these spectaculars were the tea houses of the capital city. With greater popularity and increased complexity of performances, the tea houses evolved into theaters. Yet the carnival atmosphere of the small tea houses persisted, and continues to do so even today.

Foreigners visiting an opera in Taiwan may be stunned to find that audiences eat, drink and gossip their way through the operas in tried-and-true fashion, only to fall silent during famous scenes and solo arias. It may seem rude to Western viewers, but when the Chinese attend an opera, they go intent on enjoying themselves.

Since audiences in Taiwan and in other Chinese communities know all the plots of the operas by heart – and all the performers by reputation – they know exactly when to pay undivided attention to the stage action and when to indulge in other pleasures.

It is in terms of technique, however, that Chinese opera emerges unique among the world's theatrical forms. The vehicles of expression blend singing, dancing, mime and acrobatics, and utilize sophisticated symbolism in costumes, makeup and stage props.

Each of the vehicles of Chinese opera is an art form in itself. The use of face paint, for instance, is divided into 16 major categories representing more than 500 distinctive styles. Despite the complexity and enormous array of facial ornamentation, proper application of the paint imparts a character with a distinct identity. "The moment we see the face, we know exactly who he is and the nature of his character," says a devoted opera fan.

History credits the invention of the makeup techniques to Prince Lanling, who ruled over the northern Wei kingdom during the sixth century. As his own features were so effeminate, the prince designed a fierce face-mask to improve his appearance and his chances on the battlefield. The ruse worked wonders. Lanling easily defeated enemy forces that far outnumbered his own. His savage mask was later adapted for dramatic use during the ensuing Tang dynasty. To facilitate the actors' movements and their ability to sing, the design was painted directly onto their faces.

Each color applied possesses its own basic properties: red is loyal, upright and straightforward; white denotes craft, cunning and resourcefulness, even a clown or a criminal; blue is vigorous, wild, brave and enterprising; yellow dominates an intelligent but somewhat reserved character; brown suggests strong character with stubborn temperament; green is reserved for ghosts, demons and everything evil; and gold is the exclusive color of gods and benevolent spirits.

The extensive use of pantomime in Chinese opera virtually eliminates the need for elaborate stage sets. The few backdrops and

sleeve can be remarkable when flicked by expert wrists. To express surprise or shock, a performer simply throws up his arms. The sleeves fly backwards in an alarming manner. An actor wishing to convey embarrassment or shyness daintily holds one sleeve across the face, as if hiding behind it. Determination and bravery can be emphasized by flicking the sleeves quickly up around the wrists, then clasping the hands behind the back. The message is universally understood. The range of symbolic gestures made possi-

props that are incorporated in a performance are put to ingenious uses.

Water-sleeves and props: One inventive prop that is actually part of a performer's costume is the water-sleeve, often used to mime emotion and imply environmental conditions. These long, white armlets of pure silk are attached to the standard sleeves of the costume and trail down to the floor when loose.

Although it is merely an extra length of cloth, the expressive power of the water-

Left, putting on the delicate colors of the painted mask. **Above**, the obligatory family dispute scene of every Chinese opera.

bly by the water-sleeve is endless. These complement other expressive gestures in mime. Performers dust themselves off to indicate that they have just returned from a long journey. They form the sleeves into a muff around the clasped hands as protection against the cold weather of a winter scene. To cope with hot summer weather, the sleeves are flapped like a fan.

Simple devices like the water-sleeve, with its wide range of expression, make stage props generally unnecessary. The few that are used have obvious connotations.

Spears and swords come into play during battle and action scenes. The long, quivering peacock plumes attached to the headgear of some actors identify them as warriors. Ornate riding crops with silk tassels tell any tuned-in Chinese audience that the actors are riding horses. Black pennants carried swiftly across the stage symbolize a thunderstorm, but four long pennants held aloft on poles represent a regiment of troops. A character riding a chariot holds up two yellow banners horizontally about waist high, each painted with a wheel. An actor who appears bearing a banner with the character for *bao*, which means report, is a courier delivering an important message from afar.

Chinese opera also employs single props for a variety of uses. As simple an item as a

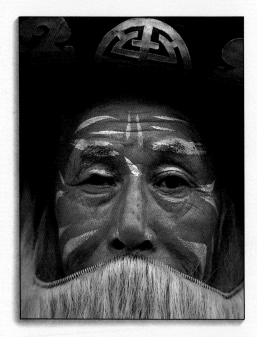

chair is exactly what it appears to be when sat upon. But when placed upon a table, a chair is transformed into a mountain. Or it can be used as a throne. If an actor jumps off a chair, he has committed suicide by flinging himself into a well. After that, long strips of paper may be hung from just above his ears to indicate he has become a ghost.

While neon-colored costumes and dazzling makeup can enthrall audiences for hours, the long intervals of song and dialogue can invariably induce bouts of boredom. But just as attention begins to drift, the performances are punctuated by rousing feats of athletics and prestidigitation. In fact, it is

often difficult to distinguish the magic tricks from the acrobatics.

Chinese operas don't unfold on a stage. They leap, bound and bounce into action. Performers appear to have an uncanny knack for doing one midair somersault more than is humanly possible before they return to earth. Hands become feet and inverted stomachs become grotesque faces, as two or more acrobats link arms and legs to become one fantastic creature.

The most thrilling portions of Chinese opera are indisputably the battle scenes. They employ every form of martial art and acrobatic maneuver conceivable – and then some. Sabers, axes and fists fly through the air in a manner that would end in buckets of bloodletting amidst novices. The stars of Chinese opera can fling a sword high in the air – and somehow, quite miraculously, catch it in the razor-thin slit of its scabbard.

Traditionally, female roles in Chinese opera were performed by impersonators, but modern performances usually employ women as women. Yet the old impersonators perfected such stylized feminine gestures that aspiring actresses find themselves in the odd position of having to learn to imitate a man imitating a woman.

Taiwan opera: In addition to Beijing opera, an offshoot simply called Taiwan opera has become popular on the island. Taiwan opera is usually performed outdoors on elevated stages in public markets. The shows incorporate sparkling, colorful costumes and elaborate backdrops. The innovations in Taiwan opera range from the use of Taiwanese dialect, instead of the difficult Hubei dialect of Beijing opera, to disco-colored robes and Western makeup techniques. These changes have expanded the popularity of Chinese opera to the average person on the street.

Traditional Chinese puppet shows are also staged frequently throughout Taiwan, and are based on the themes, roles, music and costumes of Beijing opera. Before television had arrived in Taiwan, puppet shows were one of the primary forms of entertainment. As in opera, costumes and makeup indicate the type of character.

Left, conspicuous painted masks depicting personality are a distinguishing feature. **Right**, up close, the painted mask is nearly a work of art requiring skill to apply.

Chinese folk religion is a blend of practices and beliefs that have developed out of animism, ancestor worship, Confucianism, Daoism, Buddhism and various folk beliefs. In Taiwan, these forms of worship are generally similar to those still practiced by Chinese elsewhere in Asia. But despite the common thread that runs through traditional beliefs and rituals, and the fact that the island is comparatively small with good communications, local practices in Taiwan differ considerably from region to region, even within a few kilometers from one another.

Although Taiwan has separate Buddhist, Daoist and Confucian temples, the common person blends the practices of all three with a measure of superstition and ancestor worship. To further confuse matters, peasant devotees refer to this religious blending by the umbrella term Buddhism, even as they regularly visit local folk-religion temples to worship heroes and deities unknown to Buddhism. Indeed, there is little concern for strict dogmatism in folk religion.

Religious solemnity is not a quality of temples, which are often retreats from the heat and where women and the elderly meet and chat with acquaintances, relax, or play cards. Some village temples even double as schools, stores and recreation centers.

Because the supernatural and human worlds coexist in the popular folk religion of Taiwan, temples represent the place where the two worlds can meet and communicate, as folk-religion temples are the residences of the deities. The living devotees provide the resident deities with incense, oil and food offerings; in exchange, they receive advice and protection against demonic influences responsible for such earthly sorrows as plagues, disasters and illnesses.

Any number of requests might be put to a deity. Devotees may ask for something as minor as assistance for a child in passing a school examination, or as dire as a cure for a terminally-ill family member. An unemployed man might ask for a job, a pregnant woman may request an easy delivery. These problems can be put to "specialists" such as the goddess of fertility, or to "general practitioners", who can hear any requests. Although devotees do not always leave the altar satisfied, most do feel renewed hope and comfort. Even Chinese who are skeptical about the gods' powers perfunctorily carry out rituals, just to stay on the safe side.

Temples: Taiwan's temples were originally built in the 18th and 19th centuries by craftsmen. They range in size from small shrines containing one or two images or tablets to

large establishments with several main halls flanked by minor ones, each holding separate altars and murals. As a rule, a temple is named after the chief deity on the main altar. Even if the temple has a literary label or is home to a score of other gods, the locals still refer to it by the name of its principal deity.

Insight into Chinese folk religion can be gleaned from the architecture and decor of the temple buildings themselves. One important element is the temple roof, of ornate design and skilled craftsmanship. Indeed, temple roofs are alive with images of deities, immortals, legendary heroes and mythological animals, all of which serve to attract good

Left, the altar of Matsu's main shrine at Deer Ear Gate. **Right**, a devotee prays.

fortune – and repel evil from the temple and surrounding community.

The center right of a temple usually is crowned with one of four symbols: a pagoda, which represents a staircase to heaven; a flaming pearl, which symbolizes the beneficial *yang* spirit; the sun, usually flanked by two dragons, a magic gourd, which is said to capture and trap evil spirits; or else the three Star Gods of Longevity, Wealth and Posterity. These roof symbols usually reflect the role of the temple's main deity. Often one of these symbols tops the main gate, while another crowns the main hall.

Below this central and symbolic image are the fantastic and often gaudy assortment of

on a main altar. Confucian temples, severe by comparison, do not contain any images. (The image of Confucius can be found on an altar of a folk-religion temple, however.)

The interior decoration of folk-religion temples varies considerably. Many of them contain fascinating murals depicting scenes from Chinese mythology and history. Pillars and balustrades may be intricately-carved works of art. Most temples have guardians painted on the outside faces of the main doors; these pairs can vary from ferocious generals to more benign-looking military and civil mandarins, or even young scholars.

Altars: The main altar of a typical folk-religion temple bears the image of its major

figures associated with Chinese temples. The eaves slope down, then rise again in sudden curves, with colorful dragons, phoenixes, fish and flowers flying from the tips. The phoenix, a mythical bird said to appear only in times of extreme peace and prosperity, and the dragon, symbol of strength, wisdom and good luck, are the two most auspicious symbols in Chinese mythology.

These exterior features are, at first glimpse, very much the same in Buddhist and folk-religion temples. Inside, however, the differences are obvious. Buddhist temples and monasteries, in general, contain few images, with one to three significant gilded Buddhas

deity, attended by images of aides, officials or servants. Fronting the principal deity is a smaller image of the same god; this miniature is taken from the temple occasionally to bless devotees as they stand in their home doorways, or is carried during festivals to other neighboring temples.

In addition to the main altar, most temples also have two secondary altars flanking the main one; in some larger temples, there are further altars along the side walls. Beneath the main altar, at ground level, are two forms of small altar. One contains a tablet dedicated to the tutelary or protective spirit of the temple itself; the other contains stone or wooden "white tigers" – the bringers or destroyers of luck. A common offering for these tigers is a slab of fatty pork.

There are always five items on the table before a temple's main altar. A large incense pot is flanked by two decorative vases and two candlesticks. The incense pot itself is a primary religious object; in some temples, it is regarded as the most sacred. It is filled with ash accumulated by years of worship, and is the repository for the spirit of the venerated Jade Emperor. When a new temple is constructed, ash is taken from an existing temple and placed in the incense pot of the new temple. In some temples, the main incense pot is situated just to the outside of the main entrance; it is here that devotees begin their round of prayers and offerings. They place one or three sticks of incense in each pot throughout the temple, depending upon the seniority of the concerned deity.

Offerings: In addition to incense, offerings include food, drink, oil and objects made of paper. The type of food provided depends upon the season, the appetite of the particular deity, and the pocketbook of the devotee. Food is normally left at the temple only long enough for the deity to partake of its aroma, a period often defined as the length of time it takes for an incense stick to burn down. Afterwards, the food is taken home to the dinner table of the devotee and family. Leftovers not retrieved are later "disposed of" by the temple keepers. In some temples, only fruit and vegetables are offered to the gods. In season, boxes of mooncakes – baked pastries stuffed with sweet bean paste – are placed on temple altars. Bowls of cold, cooked rice are often left before minor deities, including underworld gods. Tea or wine, in rows of three or five small cups, is occasionally offered. Nothing is ever presented in groups of four, the number of death.

Another form of offering is paper money, tied in bundles and placed under the image or on the altar table. This so-called hell money represents either large sums of cash drawn on the Bank of the Underworld, or else lumps of fake gold or silver taels, the currency used in Chinese imperial times.

Left, one of the ubiquitous old temples in the Penghu (Pescadores) Islands. **Right**, pig and pineapple meal for the spirits that roam during the Feast of the Hungry Ghosts.

In addition to the gods, ancestors are also commonly at the receiving end of offerings and tokens of respect in temples. Traditionally, ancestral tablets were kept in family homes, and respects were paid at a living-room altar. These tablets bear the ancestors' names and photographs, and it is important that they be given regular offerings lest they become hungry ghosts. Increasingly, however, families have paid temples to house the ancestral tablets on a special altar and assume the responsibility for offerings and prayers, especially if there is a possibility of neglect at home.

According to traditional thinking, upon death a soul is hastened through the various

courts and punishments of purgatory in order to be reborn again. Also, there is the belief that the underworld is remarkably similar to the human world.

Thus, when someone dies, relatives do their best to see that the spirit of the deceased enters the underworld in comfort. Food offerings give symbolic sustenance, and hell money and paper artifacts represent houses, cars, clothes and often servants. These substitutes are transported to the underworld by smoke from the burning paper and representations. Failure to care for the spirit of a deceased family member sets another hungry ghost loose in the world.

Consider the case of the curious goatherd, who one day noticed that several of his billy goats were behaving in an unusually randy manner, mounting the nearest females repeatedly in remarkably brief spans of time. Concerned by their amorous behavior, perhaps even a bit envious of their prowess, the goatherd, in time-honored scientific tradition, kept careful watch on his horny herd for a few weeks. He soon detected a pattern. Whenever a billy goat ate from a particular patch of weeds, the goat's promiscuous proclivities peaked.

Before long, Chinese herbalists had determined what goats had long known: that a plant of the *aceranthus sagittatum* family was one of the most potent male aphrodisiacs in their catalogue of confections. So they called the herb *yin-yang-huo* – horny goat weed is the best translation possible.

Many of China's most efficacious herbal remedies were gradually discovered in precisely that manner. If a dog nibbled on certain weeds that induced vomiting, the curious Chinese experimented with the emetic properties of those weeds. Centuries of such observations and experimentation have provided Chinese medicine with the world's most comprehensive pharmacology of herbal remedies.

Historians have traced the beginnings of herbal medicine to Shen Nung, the legendary emperor known as the Divine Farmer for his teaching of agricultural techniques, around 3500 BC. "Shen Nung tasted the myriad herbs, and so the art of medicine was born," proclaimed a Han-dynasty historian. References to various diseases and their herbal remedies first appeared on Shang dynasty oracle bones, circa 1500 BC, that were unearthed this century in China. Their discovery proved that medicine was a formal branch of study in China as long as 3,500 years ago.

Later, books on medicine were among the few tomes spared from destruction during the infamous burning of books by Qin Shi Huangdi, in 220 BC.

The first volume that summarized and categorized the cumulative knowledge of disease and herbal cures in China appeared during the Han dynasty, in the second century BC. *The Yellow Emperor's Classic of Internal Medicine* contained the world's first scientific classification of medicinal plants, and is still used by Chinese physicians and scholars today.

The quintessential herbal doctor Sun Ssu-mo appeared on the scene 800 years later, during the Tang dynasty. He established a pattern of practice still followed by Chinese physicians today. Previously only the high and mighty had access to professional medical care, but Sun applied the Confucian virtue of *ren*, or benevolence, to his trade. He established the great tradition of *renshu renhsin* (benevolent art, benevolent heart) that has guided Chinese physicians ever since.

Sun Ssu-mo was also medical history's first dietary therapist. In his famous study *Precious Recipes*, he wrote, "A truly good physician first finds out the cause of the illness, and having found that, he first tries to cure it by food. Only when food fails does he prescribe medication."

In fact, Sun diagnosed the vitamin-deficiency disease beriberi 1,000 years before European doctors identified it in 1642. Sun prescribed a strict dietary remedy that sounds remarkably modern: calf and lamb's liver (rich in vitamins A and B), wheat germ, almonds, wild pepper and other vitamin-packed edibles.

Another milestone in the history of Chinese herbal medicine was the publication of *Ben Tsao Gang Mu* in the 16th century. Known to the West as *Treasures of Chinese Medicine*, this authoritative pharmacology was compiled over a period of nearly three decades, through research and study by the physician Li Shin-chen. He scientifically classified and analyzed 1,892 entries, including drugs that were derived from plants, animals and minerals.

The book became popular in Western medical circles during the 1700s and 1800s, and was used by Charles Darwin for classifying the various species in nature.

The theory and practice of traditional Chinese medicine takes an approach to disease and therapy that is diametrically different from Western ways. The Chinese prefer preventive techniques; the West concentrates on cures, The Chinese regard medicine as an integral part of a comprehensive system of health and longevity called *yangsheng*, which means "to nurture life". The system includes proper diet, regular exercise, regulated sex and deep breathing, as well as medicinal therapies and treatments. Unlike Western medicine, which has become increasingly fragmented into specialized branches, Chinese medicine remains syncretic. The various combinations of therapies from different

problem. Payments were stopped. Only when he cured the patient at his own expense did his normal fee resume. The system stressed the importance of preventive care. It also served as a powerful deterrent to malpractice, as doctors profited by keeping their patients healthy and happy rather than sick and dependent.

Modern families in Taiwan and in other Chinese communities can no longer afford to keep a physician on the payroll, but the precept of prevention prevails. The Chinese

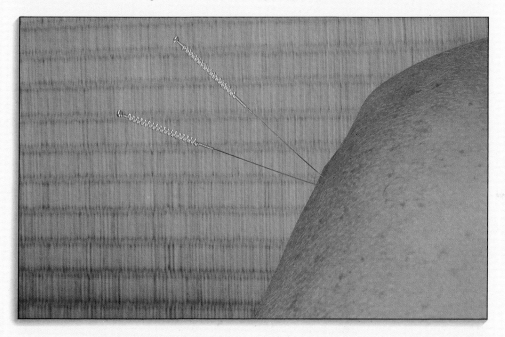

fields in yangsheng must be mastered by every Chinese physician.

In fact, prior to the twentieth century, most Chinese families retained family doctors much as modern corporations retain lawyers. The doctor was paid a set monthly fee and made regular rounds to dispense herbal remedies and medical advice specifically tailored to the individual needs of each family member.

When a member of the family fell seriously ill, the doctor was held fully responsible for failing to foresee and prevent the

Above, acupuncture needles.

trace and treat root causes of weakness and disease rather than their superficial symptoms. The physician draws a medical picture that encompasses everything from the weather and season to a patient's dietary and sexual habits. True causes are often far from the symptoms.

For instance, Chinese medicine traditionally traces eye problems to various liver disorders. Such symptomatic connections are rarely established in the West, where the eyes and the liver are treated by two specialists separated by medical training.

The theoretical foundations of Chinese medical arts, like those of the martial arts, are rooted in the cosmic theories of *yin* and *yang*, the Five Elements (earth, water, metal, wood, fire), and the concept of *qi*, or vital energy. Essentially, Chinese doctors manipulate a patient's internal balance of vital energies by using herbs, acupuncture and other methods to "clear energy stagnation, suppress energy excess, tonify energy deficiency, warm up cold energy, cool down hot energy". By reestablishing the optimum internal balance of vital energies and restoring harmony among the body's vital organs, a physician can keep his patient healthy.

Herbal therapy encompasses more than 2,000 organic medicines listed in the Chinese pharmacology, but only about 100 are commonly used to treat people. The rest are reserved for only the rarest conditions. Many common ingredients of the herbal pharmacy are standard ingredients of Western kitchens: cinnamon, ginger, licorice, rhubarb, nutmeg, orange peel and other spices and condiments. Herbal prescriptions routinely contain at least a half-dozen ingredients, some added simply to counteract the side-effects of more potent additives.

Acupuncture is probably the most widely used of Chinese therapies in the West. Acupuncturists stick fine steel needles into "vital points" along the body's "vital-energy" network. More than 800 such points have been identified, but only about 50 major spots are used in common practice.

The insertion of a needle in each point produces a specific therapeutic effect on a specific organ, gland, nerve or other body part. The points are connected to the internal organs and glands by energy channels called meridians. While many of the secrets of acupuncture still mystify physicians in the West today, they acknowledge that it can be effective in treating certain ailments.

Acupuncture has also proven to be effective as a local and general anesthetic. In recent years, patients have undergone painless appendectomies, major operations and even open-heart surgery while remaining alert and wide awake under acupuncture anesthesia. In most ways, acupressure utilizes the same points and principles as acupuncture, but is applied with deep finger pressure rather than needles.

Massage, called *tui-na* (push and rub), is applied to joints, tendons, ligaments and nerve centers, as well as to vital-points and meridians. With regular application, tui-na can be effective in relieving and gradually eliminating arthritis, rheumatism, sciatica, slipped discs, nerve paralysis and energy stagnation and dissipation.

Skin-scraping involves the use of a blunt spoon or coin, dipped in wine or salt water, and rubbed repeatedly across vital-points on a patient's skin, usually on the neck or back, until a red welt appears. In cases of heat stroke, colds, fever, colic and painful joints, the practice draws out what Chinese physicians call "heat energy", releasing it through the skin and hopefully eliminating the cause of the problem.

Blood-letting requires a sharp, thick needle with a triangular point that is used to prick open the skin at a vital-point related to the diseased organ. The release of blood induces "evil qi" and heat energy to travel along the meridians and eventually escape through the open point.

Suction cups made from bamboo or glass are briefly flamed with a burning wad of alcohol-soaked cotton to create a vacuum, then pressed over a vital-point, usually along the spine. They stick tightly to the flesh by suction. Skin and flesh balloon into the cup, drawing out evil energies by pressure. The method has been found very effective in the treatment of arthritis, rheumatism, bruises, abscesses, and any ailments related to excessive exposure to wind or dampness.

Moxibustion is the term for a treatment in which a burning stick of *moxa,* made from wormwood and resembling a thick cigar, is held directly over the skin at particular vital-points. The herbal energy radiates from the glowing tip into the vital-point and transmits therapeutic benefits along the meridian network, eventually to the diseased organ.

As bizarre as bloodletting, moxibustion and other Chinese medical treatments may sound, much less be in reality, all of these techniques are utilized with apparent success in Taiwan. For many common ailments, the Chinese approach puts faith in natural, organic curatives. However, Chinese medicine does not dispute the superiority of Western medicine in the treatment of acute traumatic ailments, injuries and emergency cases.

Right, a practitioner of traditional medicine applies suction cups made of bamboo to pressure points along the spine.

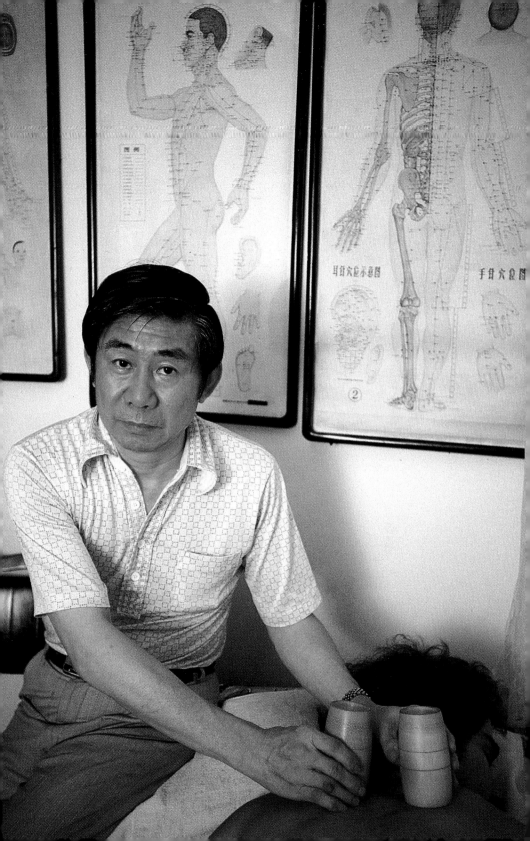

TAIPEI

The changes that forever altered the face of Taipei during the 1970s were truly dramatic. All the blessings and evils of modernization gripped the city in a frenzy of growth, which, for better or worse, continues today.

Yet this veneer of 20th-century sophistication does not mask one implacable fact: Taipei remains one of the most staunchly traditional cities of Asia. For all its modern appointments, Taipei has not succumbed to the creeping Westernization that has woven itself into social fabric of Asian cities like Hong Kong and Singapore.

Exhaust from the vehicles, combined with smoke from the industrial complexes that ring the city, has added another modern malaise to Taipei.

Yet for all its newly acquired ills, the underlying currents of traditional Chinese culture continue to make Taipei an attractive destination for travelers.

Administrative beginnings: Historically, Taipei's outskirts have attracted more interest than its center. When Koxinga drove the Dutch from Taiwan in 1661, he appointed a general named Huang An to command army and naval forces stationed at Tanshui, at the mouth of the Tanshui River and northwest of modern Taipei. New farming methods were introduced along the river banks, and soldiers were sent to reclaim land.

An emperor of the Qing dynasty was the first to designate the area as an administrative center, in 1875. The Japanese furthered the area's administrative reputation when they took control of Taiwan in 1895. In 1920, 23 years after plans had been drawn, Taipei was formally recognized as a city.

Into the city: Modern visitors to Taipei, like the settlers of old, experience the city's outskirts first. **Chiang Kaishek International Airport** (CKS) is located in Taoyuan, about 40 kilometers (25 mi) southwest of the capital. The airport's modern glass-and-concrete terminal is one of Asia's largest. Buses and taxis whisk new arrivals along the fast, clean

North-South Highway, linking airport and points north to Taipei.

Taipei is divided into northern and southern districts by Chunghsiao Road, site of the Taipei Railway Station. Chungshan North and Chungshan South roads slice the city into eastern and western portions. Depending upon which side of this north–south axis a street lies, it is assigned either East or West. Very long main roads are divided into sections. Section 1 is near the city center, while Section 5 is quite a distance out. Addresses therefore provide at least a rough indication of where one must look on the map.

One of the city's easiest landmarks for orientation is the **Grand Hotel**. Located atop a ridge at the northern end of the city, this 530-room hotel looks somewhat like an ancient palace, built in the classical imperial style of old China. The massive multi-story new wing is crowned by the largest classical Chinese roof on earth.

The Grand Hotel is as good a spot as any to begin touring Taipei. East of the

Grand Hotel about half a kilometer is the **Revolutionary Martyrs' Shrine**, on Peian Road. Open daily, the entire complex is built in the palace style of the Ming dynasty. Each structure attempts to reproduce a similar hall or pavilion in Beijing. Dedicated to the fallen heroes of China's wars, the arched portals of the main gate open onto a vast courtyard, past guest pavilions, drums and bell towers. Two gigantic brass-studded doors open onto the main shrine, where the names of the heroes are inscribed beside murals depicting their feats. The late Chiang Kaishek considered this a favorite retreat, frequently spending entire afternoons strolling through the grounds and halls. A changing of the guard occurs every hour.

Only a short taxi ride in the opposite direction, to the southwest of the Grand Hotel, is **Kong Miao**, the Confucius Temple, on Talung Street. A tranquil retreat compared to the city's other places of worship, absent are the throngs of worshippers supplicating their gods with prayer and offerings, the cacophony of gongs and drums, and the gaudy idols. Absent, too, are images of Confucius. The tranquility is fitting – Confucius preached the virtues of peace and quiet. The architecture of the temple is subtle yet exquisite, and highlighted by magnificent roofs.

By contrast, the **Paoan Temple**, on Hami Street and next to the Confucian Temple, is a gaudy monument to traditional Chinese folk religion. This 250-year-old Daoist temple sports carved dragons writhing in solid rock on the main support columns, and an interior crowded with the images of many deities. Buddhist elements are also apparent in the architecture, in testimony to the syncretic nature of Chinese religion.

Just south of the Grand Hotel is the **Taipei Fine Arts Museum**, with 24 galleries of modern art, and the **Lin An Tai Homestead**, an original 30-room family home of a wealthy merchant from the Qing-dynasty era and built in the 1820s. Designed for the very young lovers of Chinese history and culture – but adults will like it, too – is **Children's Grand Hotel.**

Paradise, which includes a World of Yesterday and a World of Tomorrow.

Located in the eastern part of the city is an important memorial to Chiang Kaishek's mentor and the founder of the Republic of China, Dr. Sun Yatsen – the only common denominator between the rival Communist and Nationalist regimes, which both revere him as the founder of modern China. On Section 4 of Jenai Road and a long taxi ride away, the main building of the **Sun Yatsen Memorial** boasts a sweeping, gracefully-curved Chinese roof of glazed yellow tile. A six-meter-high (20-ft) bronze statue of Sun Yatsen graces the main lobby.

Downtown walkabout: The best place to begin a downtown walking tour is from the **Taipei Railway Station**. This is not just a station, but an impressive and spacious palace, with four floors below street level. Close to the railway station are the bus terminals.

Over the years, the downtown area has been remodeled at the same time as the construction of the new underground rail arteries. Many old buildings were removed, giving space to modern skyscrapers. One pride of Taipei is the 245-meter-tall (800-ft) **Shin Kong Tower**, just opposite the train station and overshadowing the Taipei Hilton. High-speed elevators shoot visitors upwards at 540 meters per minute (1,770 ft/min), topping out in 35 seconds at the observatory on the 49th floor (out of 51). A Taipei landmark since 1994, the tower's unobstructed view on clear days is a popular excursion. The inner wall of the observatory is adorned with old black-and-white lithographs depicting Taipei of yesteryear.

Tempting is shopping in one of the large shopping malls. But first consider the Chinese way of daily shopping. East towards the Tanshui River is the narrow and unique **Tihua Street**, perhaps Taipei's most important historical street and paralleling Yenping Road. In the mid 1800s, the first merchant established his business in this area; most of the houses are from the first decade of this century. Back then, goods arrived

Busy back street.

mainly by boat on the Tanshui River.

West from the railway station and opposite the **main post office** (which offers a good philatelic section) stands the ugly **North Gate**, one of the four remaining city gates. Located at the intersection of Chunghsiao and Chunghua roads, just before Chunghsiao crosses the river, the gate was erected in 1984, looking somewhat out of place amidst the tangle of expressway flyovers that are modern Taipei.

Behind the museum is **Taipei New Park**, "newly" opened in 1907 and featuring ponds, pagodas and pavilions. The best time to walk the grounds of New Park is at dawn, when thousands of the city's residents stretch, dance, exercise and move through various forms of *taiji, shaolin* and other disciplines. Visitors are welcome to join in with the groups for an invigorating start to a day in Taipei. (Evenings, however, are best spent somewhere else by visitors.)

To the east of the New Park are most of the important government ministries and offices. From the park's southwestern end, it is only a short distance to the governmental center of Taiwan.

Most prominent is the **Presidential Building**, fronting an enormous plaza that is the site of the annual and colorful celebrations during the Double Tens: October 10, or National Day. The five-story complex, finished in 1919, has a central tower 60 meters (200 ft) high.

At the south end of Chungshan Road is the impressive **East Gate**, the biggest of the original five gates of the nineteenth-century city wall. In 1966, it was renovated and underwent considerable ornate embellishment on its once-very-simple facade.

A massive monument to the late president, the **Chiang Kaishek Cultural Center** is located at Chungshan South Road, close to the East Gate. Dedicated in 1980, the fifth anniversary of Chiang's death, the enormous 76-meter-high (250-ft) Memorial Hall dominates the landscaped grounds. Inside is an imposing 25-ton bronze statue of the late president. From morning until late evening, the adjacent park is full of life – seniors chatting under a shady tree or feeding the beautiful fat carps in the placid fish ponds, mothers with children strolling the walkways, newlyweds taking the inevitable wedding photos.

The **National Museum of History**, on Nanhai Road, contains 10,000 Chinese art objects dating from 2000 BC to modern times, including a fine sampling of Chinese currency. This interesting museum is less crowded than its counterpart, the National Palace Museum. After touring its exhibits, visitors can stroll the grounds of the **botanical gardens** next door, containing hundreds of species of trees, shrubs, palms and bamboo. Adjacent to the Museum of History are the **National Science Hall** and **National Arts Hall**.

West of the Chiang Kaishek memorial and near the river is the oldest and most famous of Taipei's myriad temples, **Lungshan**, or Dragon Mountain, a reference to the large collection of toothsome creatures on its busy roof. The temple is on Kuangchou Street, close to the Tanshui River in the heart of old Taipei and southwest of the Taipei Rail-

Chiang Kai-shek Memorial.

way Station. It was built early in the eighteenth century to honor Taiwan's patron deities, Kuanyin and Matsu.

Markets: A good way to absorb the city's traditions is to take in the public markets. Most are open from dawn until midnight, selling an amazing variety of fresh vegetables, fragrant fruits, meats, fish, poultry, spices and condiments. At night, the fresh-produce vendors retire from the scene, to be replaced by scores of food stalls on wheels. These instant cafes serve every conceivable kind of Chinese snack food, at reasonable prices. The most exotic night market of all is the two-block-long lane in the Wanhua district called **Snake Alley** by tourists, which flock to the street by the bus load. Only a few minutes' walk from the Lungshan temple, this alley's main thoroughfare is known to everyone else as Huahsi Street.

The Western sobriquet stems from the nature of business conducted by some of the street's vendors, their shops stacked with cages of hissing snakes. The vendors flip open the cage tops and deftly whip out snakes to sell. Customers watch as the chosen snake is strung live on a wire, stretched taut and literally unzipped open before their eyes with a small knife.

Blood and bile from the squirming snake are squeezed into a glass containing potent spirits and herbs. For customers who are keen on seeking an additional "kick", the vendor will even add a few drops of poison venom to the mixture. The carcasses of the gutted snakes are left to hang in the night, while the concoction is drunk by men who believe the potion strengthens the eyes and the lower spine, eliminates fatigue and, inevitably, promotes male sexual vitality. Later, the meat is taken back to the kitchen for snake soup, a tasty and nourishing dish.

North of the city: Nestled in the foothills, several kilometers to the northeast of the Grand Hotel and past the Martyrs' Shrine, is the most popular and important attraction in Taipei, if not in all of Taiwan. An imposing complex of beige-brick buildings, topped with green and

Fortune teller, Snake Alley.

imperial-yellow slate roofs, houses the **National Palace Museum**. The building is impressive, and the treasures within are unimaginable. Next to the museum is a small, but perfectly styled and very attractive, *chin-shan-yuan* Chinese garden, worth a stroll.

Displayed in the Palace Museum – the exhibitions change from time to time – are some 6,000 works of art representing the zenith of 5,000 years of Chinese creativity. And these are just a fraction of the more than 700,000 paintings, porcelains, bronzes, rubbings, tapestries, books and other art objects stored in nearly 4,000 crates located in vaults that are tunneled into the mountain behind the museum.

The National Palace Museum opened in 1965. But the history of its treasures, which reads like a John le Carré thriller, can be traced back more than 1,000 years, to the beginning of the Song dynasty (AD 960–1279). The founder of that dynasty established the Hanlin Academy, intended to encourage literature and the arts.

The emperor's brother and successor later opened a gallery, where some of the items in the current collection were first housed. The gallery was then established as a government department for the preservation of rare books, old paintings and calligraphy. This imperial gallery was the prototype for Taipei's contemporary collection.

The Song collection was transported from Beijing to Nanjing during the Ming dynasty, then back again, foreshadowing the collection's many moves in the twentieth century. The collection expanded considerably during the Qing dynasty (1644–1911). The Qing emperors were avid art collectors. The majority of items in the present collection are the result of their effort to seek out China's most important treasures.

But the real intrigues began in November, 1924. The provisional Nationalist government in Beijing gave the last surviving Manchu emperor, Puyi, and his entourage of 2,000 eunuchs and ladies two hours to evacuate the Imperial Palace. Then the government had 30 **National Palace Museum.**

young Chinese scholars and art experts identify and inventory the overwhelming collection of art treasures that had been hoarded within the palace for more than 500 years.

It took the scholars two years just to sort out and organize the collection. In the meantime, the government formally established the National Beijing Palace Museum and began displaying some of the treasures.

By the time the task of identifying all the priceless objects was completed in 1931, the Japanese had attacked northwst China, in Manchuria, and threatened - Beijing. The art collection had, and still has, enormous symbolic value to whomever possesses it, bestowing a measure of political and social legitimacy upon its owners. To prevent the Japanese from seizing the collection, the government carefully packed everything in 20,000 cases and shipped it, in five trains, south to Nanjing.

Thus began a 16-year-long odyssey. The priceless treasures were shuttled back and forth across the war-torn face

Carved wooden cups.

of China by rail, truck, ox cart, raft and foot, always a few steps ahead of pursuing Japanese and, later, Communist troops. Incredibly, not a single item was lost or damaged. A representative selection of the best items was shipped to London for a major art exhibition in 1936 – prompting an uproar among China's intellectuals, who feared the foreigners would never return the works. But all made it back to China. The following year, the Japanese occupied Beijing and threatened Nanjing.

Once again, the precious collection was loaded aboard trucks and transported in three shipments over hills, rivers and streams to China's rugged western mountains.

After the Japanese surrender in 1945, the Nationalist government brought the pieces back to Nanjing. But when Communist control of the mainland appeared imminent in 1948, 4,800 cases of the most valuable pieces were culled from the original 20,000 cases and sent for safekeeping to Taiwan. They were stored in a sugar warehouse in Taichung, where they remained until the Chungshan (Sun Yatsen) Museum Building, in Waishuanghsi, opened in 1965.

Among the items cached are 4,400 ancient bronzes, 24,000 pieces of porcelain, 13,000 paintings, 14,000 works of calligraphy, 4,600 pieces of jade, 153,000 rare books from the imperial library, and 390,000 documents, diaries and old palace records. Massive steel doors lead to the catacombs in the mountain, where the steel trunks are stacked one atop the other. One semicircular tunnel is 190 meters (610 ft) long, the other 150 meters (490 ft). The temperature must be maintained at a constant 18°C (64°F), and humming dehumidifiers line the corridors.

Almost directly opposite the National Palace Museum, just a few minutes' walk away, is the **Chinese Culture and Movie Center**, which provides insight into medieval Chinese architecture, costume and folk art. Feature films are also sometimes made here; the architectural compositions and other motifs conform perfectly to the Chinese idea of typically Chinese.

THE NORTH

Taipei's sights and traffic monopolize most of a traveler's time in the northern part of Taiwan. But an excursion beyond the city will offer another side of life on the island. Taiwan's northernmost tip, especially, is a microcosm of Taiwan, with its mountains, waterfalls, volcanic past, beaches, paddy fields, villages and temples.

The fastest route of escape from Taipei lies up nearby **Yangming Shan**. About 40 minutes' drive via winding roads north of the city, Yangming is known as the local Beverly Hills. Large numbers of wealthy industrial tycoons, movie stars and entrepreneurs, as well as expatriate businesspeople, live here in luxurious villas clinging to the cliffs in the cool climes above Taipei.

The mountain-top is crowned by **Yangmingshan National Park**. This well-maintained park features walkways that wind through colorful gardens of trees, bushes, fragrant flowers and grottos. From the middle of February until the end of March, an annual spring-flower festival is held in the park, with the entire mountain awash with cherry blossoms and carpeted with bright, flowering azaleas.

A less lofty but an equally-entrancing retreat a few minutes from Taipei is the suburb of **Peitou** (pronounced *bay tow*). It nestles snugly in lush green hills north of the city, and can be reached via twisting back roads from Yangming Shan, or from Taipei via a much-less-scenic route that passes through the suburb of Tienmou. (Peitou will soon be a stop at the MRT's Red Line.)

Peitou literally means Northern Sojourn. It has a Japanese feel that has lingered ever since the Japanese turned the town into a resort for their officers and magistrates at the turn of the century. More recently, Peitou was notorious as a getaway for large groups of men from Japan. The attractions were Peitou's therapeutic hot springs, and women tending aching muscles.

Butterfly kite over Yangming Shan.

After walking through the center of town, with its city park and Chinese pavilion, strollers will come to a traffic island. The right-hand fork proceeds past the New Angel Hotel, near to which Chiyen Road offers access to a challenging diversion, a climb up tranquil **Phoenix Mountain**.

Those who venture up Chiyen Road to the mountain eventually come to a large double staircase guarded by two enormous lucky dogs. The stairs lead to the **Chen Memorial Garden**, whose chief attraction is its tranquility. The paved pathway behind the garden is the start of the exhausting mountain ascent. From the summit, there are sweeping views of Taipei, Peitou and the surrounding countryside.

The western horizon of northern Taiwan is dominated by a 475-meter-high (1,560-ft) mountain, the **Goddess of Mercy Mountain**, as its profile resembles that of Kuanyin (Guanyin) from a distance. Visitors who make the steep climb to its peak will be rewarded by breathtaking views of the northern coast.

Northern routes: The drive along Taiwan's northern coastline rewards visitors with its scenic natural sights, and with charming farm towns and fishing villages. The entire route can be covered comfortably in a single day of driving from Taipei.

On the way to Tanshui, alongside the Tanshui River, is **Kuantu** with its eye-catching, red-colored 550-meter-long (1,700-ft) bridge. Directly on the river and close to a cliff is an extremely large temple complex, **Kuantu Matsu**, one of the most important of its kind in Taiwan. It is worth a stroll around, with a viewpoint high above the river accessed via a tunnel through the cliff.

The terminus of the North Coast Highway is a town with a rich historical heritage, **Tanshui**. The town was the main point of contact in northern Taiwan between the Chinese and foreign traders during its heyday as the island's major port, in the nineteenth century. The North Coast Highway rounds the northernmost nib of Taiwan. From here on, the China Sea extends to the hori-

Jam session, Yangming Shan National Park.

zon. After passing Fukwai Cape, at Taiwan's northernmost point, a natural wonder appears: **Shihmen** (Stone Gate), an impressive natural erosion form, with an eight-meter-high (25 ft) opening. Even more evidence of the forces of nature are apparent at **Yehliu**, literally Wild Willows. The white, yellow and brownish sandstone promontories here, directly in front of the pounding ocean, have been etched into all manner of artistic shapes by weather and erosion. The terrain is other-worldly, attracting crowds of curious onlookers from the big city of Taipei.

Taiwan's northernmost city and second-largest port is **Keelung**, junction for the North Coast and Northeast Coast highways, and the northern terminus of the North-South Highway. Its natural harbor has 40 deep-water piers and three mooring buoys that can handle large vessels. Only Kaohsiung, in the south, has more extensive port facilities.

Keelung's main point of interest is an enormous white **statue and temple of Kuanyin**. The 22.5-meter (74-foot)

statue is propped up on a 4-meter-high (14-ft) pedestal that enables the deity to watch over the entire city.

Fulung, the next stop on the Northeast Coast Highway, belies the notion that Taiwan's best beaches lie only in the southern reaches of the island. The white sand beach here hugs the northern shore of a cape that juts into the ocean. Enthusiastic strollers will find that the shoreline stretches for kilometers.

A principal attraction of this lovely region is the **Chiaohsi hot springs**. Small restaurants scattered about the town specialize in fresh seafood. Two temples cater to the faithful in Chiaohsi.

Less than 10 minutes' drive into the hills behind the Chiaohsi is **Wufengchi** (Five Peaks Flag Scenic Region). Vendors around the parking lot sell the area's sought-after products of dried mushrooms, preserved plums and other fruits, fresh ginger and medicinal herbs.

Among the latter is a furry little doll with four "legs" formed by roots, and two "eyes" made with buttons. The vendors call it Golden Dog Fur. It's actually

Northern coast.

a fern-plant that roots in stone and grows from remote cliff sides. When rubbed into cuts, scrapes, lacerations, sores and other festering skin wounds, it stops the bleeding immediately and promotes rapid healing with a minimum of unsightly scarring.

Near the Taipei suburb of **Hsintien**, south of the city, is the **Chihnan Temple**, one of the most important landmarks in the north. This Temple of the Immortals has been under constant construction and expansion for nearly 100 years. Perched on a lush green hillside, it exemplifies the concept of a temple as a magic mountain peak. There are supposedly 1,000 steps along the winding approach to the temple. The temple is home for about 50 Buddhist monks.

Near Chihnan Temple, keep an eye on the rolling green hills – many are coated with tea bushes, producing fine Chiense teas. And if they are in flower, stop and take a closer look at the camelia-like blossoms.

South of Taipei: Southwest of Taipei are several other places well worth a stop. Only 20 kilometers away from Taipei is the busy old town of **Sanhsia**, with streets snaking around old brick buildings and the famous Tsushih Temple, originally built in 1770. The temple was in ruins after World War II, but it is now reconstructed, with new and perfectly-carved stone decorations, making it one of the finest examples of Chinese temple art.

A short hop away is the small town of **Yingko**, a potter's heaven. Some of the factories allow tours, giving a chance to watch how "muddy" clay will be transformed into a beautifully-painted Chinese vase, worth a dominant position in the Ming or Qing court. Many shops line the narrow, usually crowded streets, selling everything from simple earthenware to the finest porcelain, from ordinary teapots to delicate figures. Some is predictable, some is exquisite.

Several other attractions within hailing distance of Taipei – and all to the south – beckon travelers. Fifty kilometers (30 mi) away to the southwest, down Highway 3 and near the town of Tahsi, is **Tzu Hu** (Lake Mercy), tempo-rary resting place of the late Chiang Kaishek. His body rests above ground in a heavy granite sarcophagus in his former country villa, awaiting the day when political conditions permit returning his body to his birthplace in mainland China, in Zhejiang province.

One of the main attractions to the south of Taipei, beyond Tahsi and near Lungtan, is **Window on China**. On a site covering 10 hectares (25 acres), the most important buildings and temples in Taiwan, as well as many notable buildings in mainland China, have been erected in miniature.

Totalling 130 in all, the buildings are on a scale of 1:25, and are populated by some 50,000 miniature – and artificial – people, some of whom perform parades or dances to music. A recently-added section features famous buildings from all parts of the world. Vegetation is provided by countless bonsai trees grown to proportionally-correct sizes. It goes without saying, of course, that one should not visit here on local holidays or weekends, unless thick crowds are enjoyed.

Yehliu sculpture.

CENTRAL TAIWAN

Central Taiwan boasts the most varied terrain on the island. From the summit of snow-capped Yu Shan, the Jade Mountain, the landscape drops 3,952 meters to the harbor at Taichung. The alluvial plain that divides the highlands from the Taiwan Strait is filled by vast green rice fields, and plantations of bananas, pineapples, papayas, sugar cane, tea and other crops.

Taichung: The urban center of central Taiwan is Taichung, whose name means, not coincidentally, Central Taiwan. The pace and pressure of modern metropolitan Taipei are replaced here by a quieter, slower life. Taichung is what Taipei once looked like.

Taiwan's third-largest city and on the island's western side, Taichung has a population of around 100,000 people. Located on the plain about 20 kilometers (13 mi) from the coast and 100 kilometers (60 mi) south of Taipei, Taichung enjoys the island's best year-round climate, without the seasonal extremes of heat and cold that mark the north and south.

Although Taichung is neither as scenic nor as diverse as Taipei, it has numerous points of interest. The **Martyrs' Shrine**, on Shuangshih Road northeast of Chungshan Park, was erected in 1970. Its design provides a superb example of the harmony and balance inherent in classical Chinese architecture. Many locals claim it is even more outstanding than the martyrs' shrines in Hualien or Taipei. Protected by two bronze guardian lions, the Martyrs' Shrine commemorates 72 Chinese beheaded in 1911 by the tottering Manchu court, on the eve of the republic's revolution.

Across the island: North and east of Taichung, the **Central Cross-Island Highway** stretches for 200 kilometers (120 mi), from Tungshih through Taroko Gorge to the eastern coast. The Chinese claim no visit to Taiwan is complete without a trip across this road, for it displays – with striking beauty – the full gamut of the island's rainbow hues: lush tropical valleys and snow-capped peaks, alpine forests and rocky ravines, steamy hot springs and roaring rivers, mountain lakes and the shimmering sea.

The highway was completed in 1960 at the cost of 450 lives. Ten thousand laborers, most of them retired servicemen who had fought on the mainland in the 1940s, struggled four years to complete the road.

Lishan: Lishan – Pear Mountain – is on the crest of the Central Range, near the Central Cross-Island Highway's halfway point. Highway 7, to Ilan in the northeast, begins here.

Lushan Hot Spring snuggles in the valley below Wushe. Lushan village straddles a turbulent stream traversed by a suspension footbridge. Hot-spring inns lie along the banks of both sides of the river. Lushan is famous for its tea, medicinal herbs, petrified-wood canes, wild-blossom honey and dried mushrooms. Potent medicinal deer-horn shavings, tanned deer skins and other products that are either very expensive or unavailable in Taipei are common here.

Buddha on Changhwa, southwest of Taichung.

Sun Moon Lake: Taiwan's most enduringly popular honeymoon resort is Sun Moon Lake, 750 meters (2,500 ft) above sea level and in the western foothills of the Central Range. Entirely enfolded in mountains and dense tropical foliage, the lake takes the shape of a round sun when viewed from some of the surrounding hills, or of a crescent moon when seen from other heights.

The lake was formed in the early 20th century, when the occupying Japanese built a dam for hydroelectric production. Prior to that, there had been a major tribal settlement in this area; traces remain on the lake's south shore.

Its beauty notwithstanding, Sun Moon Lake's popularity often leaves it crawling with bus-loads of package tourists from Taipei and abroad. The best way to enjoy the scenic beauty of Sun Moon Lake is to rise at daybreak and walk, drive or take a cab along the road that winds around the lake. At dawn, the crowds are still snoozing, and early birds have the lake to themselves.

A good starting point for an exploration of the lake is the Sun Moon Lake Hotel, perched on a high embankment overlooking the lake. Heading east and south, the road leads first to the majestic **Wenwu**, a temple of martial and literary arts. This Daoist shrine, dedicated to Confucius and the two great warrior deities Kuan Kung and Yueh Fei, is built into the hillside in three ascending levels. The temple complex is interesting for its complicated layout, with various pavilions and side halls connected by ornate passages and stairways.

High on a hill near the southern end of the lake, the **Hsuanchuang Temple** houses some of China's most precious Buddhist relics. This temple was built for safekeeping and preservation of the relics, known as *ssu li-tze*.

Atop a hill beyond the Hsuanchuang Temple stands the ornate, nine-tiered **Tzuen**, the **Pagoda of Filial Virtue**. It was erected by Chiang Kaishek in memory of his mother, and hence the name. An uphill walk through cool glades of bamboo, fern, maple and pine leads to the foot of the pagoda. From

Sun Moon Lake.

here, there are spectacular views of the entire lake and surrounding scenery.

Mountain tops: East of Chiayi, the resort area of **Alishan** and the peak of Yu Shan (Jade Mountain) rise from the mists of the Central Range.

Alishan's popularity is due primarily to the famous sunrise view from the summit of nearby **Chu Shan** (Celebration Mountain). Indeed, it is a spectacular event. As visitors stand shivering in their jackets 2,490 meters (8,170 ft) above sea level, gazing into the graying mist, the sun suddenly peers over the horizon. Golden shafts of light pierce the dawn, skipping across the thick carpet of clouds that cover the valleys to the east. This sea of clouds springs to life like a silver screen the moment the sun glances across it, undulating in vivid hues of gold and silver, red and orange.

On holidays and weekends, the summit is overcrowded with excited and noisy visitors – several thousand of them. Such days are not the days to witness an idyllic sunrise. On any given day, nonetheless, hundreds of people make the predawn ascent, usually by tour bus. By 7am, most of them will be back at the hotel for breakfast.

More often than not, however, fog and mist are so thick atop the peak that sunrise watchers find themselves floating within the clouds rather than in clear skies above them. And even if the weather on Alishan is terrible – if there are rain and clouds – most visitors will depart quite delighted. Drifting mountain mists are regarded as possessing extraordinary curative powers, due to their high concentration of *qi.*

Qi (pronounced *chee*) is the life-force or vital energy, the most fundamental of all Chinese physical and spiritual concepts. Qi is considered the basic force that animates all forms of life. The most potent qi, it is believed, rises in the atmosphere and clings as mist to the mountains, like cream rising to the top of milk. From time immemorial, Chinese have cultivated the custom of *denggao* – ascending high places. They believe the qi found in the mist strengthens their longevity and virtue. One of the most ancient of all Chinese characters –

hsien, for immortal – combines the symbols for man and mountain. And while the practical and urban Chinese are unlikely to become mountain-top ascetics, they are convinced of the restorative powers of high-altitude mists,

Rain and mist, however, may not hold the same delight for foreign visitors as for the Chinese. Not to worry; there are other reasons to visit the Alishan area. The region is blanketed with thick forests of red cypress, cedar and pine, some of them thousands of years old. When these ancient plants finally fall to rest, the Chinese let sleeping logs lie. The great gnarled stumps and petrified logs form some of Alishan's most exotic sights. Some of these suggest romantic images and have been named accordingly: Heavenly Couple and Forever United in Love are two examples. The walking paths and grottoes behind Alishan House incorporate several of these formations, and there are many more on the trails.

Alishan is the billeting post of mountaineering expeditions to **Yu Shan**, the Jade Mountain.

At 3,952 meters (12,966 ft) in altitude, Yu Shan is the highest mountain in Asia east of the Himalaya, south of the Russia's Kamchatka Peninsula and north of Borneo's Mount Kinabalu. Yu Shan is far more visited than the others, however. Indeed, as Taiwan's favorite alpine resort, Yu Shan can lure visitors by the thousands. Even higher than Japan's majestic Mount Fuji, this peak was called New High Mountain during the 50 years of Japanese occupation. Its original name was restored by the Chinese in 1945.

Prior permission to climb this peak, now within a national park, is required from the Alpine Association, in Taipei. Treks to Yu Shan, of course, require proper alpine clothing, hiking shoes, backpacks and sufficient stamina.

From Alishan village, there is a road leading 20 kilometers (12 mi) to **Tungpu**, a remote hot spring nestled in the mountains at 2,600 meters (8,500 ft) above sea level. There is a rustic hostel there for overnight stays; another hostel is high on the mountain slopes, at about 3,300 meters (10,800 ft) elevation. Four full days should be allotted for this breathtakingly-beautiful trip.

Using his head: After journeying into the mountains, other trips might seem anticlimactic. But temple-lovers, especially those proceeding south from Chiayi, or heading to or from Alishan by road, may want to stop at **Wufeng Temple** to pay respects.

Wufeng, perhaps the only historical personage revered by both Chinese and the ethnic minorities, was an eighteenth-century Chinese official.

Born in 1699 to a merchant family in mainland Fujian province, he emigrated to Taiwan as a youth and studied, in great detail, the customs and dialects of indigenous people. Appointed official interpreter and liaison between Chinese settlers on the plains and recalcitrant tribes in the mountains, he worked tirelessly to end feuding between the two clashing camps.

The tribes followed the disturbing practice of invading the plains every year, after reaping the bounty of their mountains, to harvest Chinese heads as sacrifices to their gods. Wufeng, wise at the age of 71, devised a courageous scheme to end the practice.

On a certain day and at a certain place, he told his tribal friends that they would see "a man wearing a red hood and cape, and riding a white horse. Take his head. It will appease your gods." The tribal warriors followed his instructions, lopping off the head of the mysterious rider. Only after removing the red cowl did the warriors discover that the man they had killed was none other than their old friend, Wufeng.

This act of self-sacrifice so moved and terrified the local chief that he called a conclave of all 48 of the tribal headmen in the Alishan region. They agreed to ban the practice of head-hunting forever because of the sacrifice.

About 15 kilometers (9 mi) south of Wufeng Temple, a short distance off Highway 3 to Pingtung, is the rustic hotspring spa of **Kuantzuling**. Resting in a low mountain pass between Chiayi and Wushantou Lake, it is renowned for its therapeutic mineral waters.

Dawn, Alishan.

THE SOUTH

Known in Taiwan as Cheng Cheng-kung – Lord of Imperial Surname – Koxinga was a Ming loyalist at odds with the new Manchu Qing court. He fled to Taiwan, landing near Tainan in 1661 with 30,000 troops in 8,000 war junks. He besieged the Dutch fort at Anping, eventually driving the Dutch from the island. The Ming stronghold that he established lasted three generations, until his grandson finally capitulated to the Manchu court.

Koxinga brought more than troops to Taiwan. He carried a camphorwood icon of Matsu, which still sits in the shrine to this goddess at Luerhmen (Deer Ear Gate), where Koxinga first landed. Moreover, his entourage included about 1,000 writers, artists, musicians, craftsmen and master chefs, whose function it was to launch a Chinese cultural renaissance in Taiwan. (A similar group followed Chiang Kaishek in 1949.)

Today, **Tainan** remains highly conscious of its rich cultural legacy. Under a forward-thinking administration, Taiwan's fourth-largest city of around one million people is focusing into a tourist mecca. Light industry, agriculture, fishing and tourism are all encouraged in the area, but large industrial plants and their accompanying pollution are kept at arm's length. The goal is to maintain a clean and cultured city, a showcase for visitors. The authorities are especially determined to protect the scenic beauty and delicate ecological balance of Tainan's tropical coastline.

Temples are the hallmark of Tainan. In fact, there are 220 major temples and countless minor shrines scattered throughout the town and surrounding countryside.

It is perhaps appropriate to begin at **Koxinga's Shrine**. Set in a garden compound of tropical trees and breezy pavilions, the shrine was built in 1875 by imperial edict from the Manchu Qing court in Beijing. Left in ruins following the Japanese occupation, the shrine was restored after World War II, and again in 1962.

Three blocks from Koxinga's Shrine is Tainan's **Confucian Temple**, the oldest temple for the sage in Taiwan. It was built in 1665 by Cheng Ching, Koxinga's son, as a center for the Chinese cultural renaissance in Taiwan. Restored 16 times since then, it still stands out as Taiwan's foremost shrine to Confucius, reflecting a classical architectural style otherwise seldom seen on the island.

Tainan's residents believe that their behavior is reported to the emperors of heaven and hell by Cheng Huang, the city deity. His small, old, and very original temple – **Cheng Huang Miao** – is located on Chingnien Road, between Chienkuo and Poai roads.

The open beam-work on the temple ceiling is noteworthy. Unlike other ceilings, this one is varnished rather than painted, its surface etched with fine filigree. Relics and ritual objects hang everywhere, among them two giant abaci. The hardwood beads of each abacus are the size of melons. One hangs to the right of the main shrine, the other

Koxinga statue at temple.

from the beams over the front door. These are used by the city deity to tally the merits and demerits of each citizen for his annual report to the emperors of heaven and hell.

An indispensable stop on any Tainan temple tour is the **Temple of the Jade Emperor**, one of the oldest and most authentic Daoist temples in Taiwan. Located near the corner of Mintsu, a highly-detailed facade of stone, carved in deep relief, graces the entrance to the central hall of this gaudy complex. Inside, the Jade Emperor is represented by an austere stone slab engraved with his name. The Temple of the Jade Emperor is one of the most ritually-active temples on the island.

Koxinga landed at **Luerhmen** (Deer Ear Gate), a shallow bay north of Tainan, off of Highway 17. The spot is consecrated by the elaborate **Matsu Temple**, built upon the site of an older structure. Matsu's shrine, within the main hall, is protected by enough writhing dragons to frighten away an army of devils. Her two fierce guardians, one red and one green, stand fully armed in classical martial-arts postures. Sitting before the large central icon of Matsu are a row of smaller, black camphorwood icons bedecked with finery. The one in the center is said to be over 1,000 years old, brought to Taiwan from the Chinese mainland by Koxinga.

In **Anping**, a 20-minute taxi ride from downtown Tainan, are more reminders of Tainan's military past. **Fort Zeelandia** was first built by the Dutch in 1623, then heavily reinforced between 1627 and 1634. Bricks were held in place with a mixture of sugar syrup, glutinous rice and crushed oyster shells. This ingenious mixture must have worked, for much of the original foundation is still intact.

Two kilometers to the south of the canal, which is crossed via a bridge, stands **Yitsai Chincheng**, an old Chinese fort once used for Tainan's coastal defenses. As with Fort Zeelandia, silt and sand accumulations have left this edifice far from the shoreline it once guarded.

Bell ringers, Deer Ear Gate.

Kaohsiung: Taiwan's economic showcase and a city of superlatives, **Kaohsiung** is Taiwan's largest international seaport, its major industrial center, and the only city on the island besides Taipei with an international airport. The port is the world's third-largest container port after Hong Kong and Singapore, and it also has a large drydock for ship repairs and maintenance.

With over one million inhabitants, the city is Taiwan's second largest, and the only one besides Taipei to enjoy the status of a special municipality – equal to a province, and administered by the central government. A city of humble origins, Kaohsiung has experienced meteoric economic growth, but the concentration of heavy industry has caused considerable pollution. Kaohsiung is trying to attract and develop high-technology industries in its central districts, moving smokestack factories out to suburban industrial zones. The city is often shrouded with smog.

The city center is dominated by modern tower blocks, including the **Grand 50 Tower**, whose 50 stories make it one of the tallest buildings in Taiwan. Another overview of the city is atop **Shou Shan** (Longevity Mountain Park), which overlooks Kaohsiung harbor near the fishing wharves. On most days, the views of the city itself are disappointing.

Temple-addicts may want to include three complexes on their rounds in Kaohsiung. The **Three Phoenix Palace**, on Hopei Road, is the largest temple in the city, devoted to the demon suppressor, Li Na-cha. Stone lions stand sentry at the foot of the steps, which lead up to an elaborately-carved stone facade. The **Holy Hall of Martial and Literary Arts**, a three-story Daoist temple dedicated to the deity Kuan Kung and his literary counterpart, Confucius, is on Fu-Yeh Street. Not far away, on Yeh-Huang Street, is the **Shrine of the Three Mountain Kings**. This 300-year-old Buddhist temple is dedicated to three brothers, private tutors to a man who saved the life of the Chinese emperor.

Ship scraps: Kaohsiung is the world's largest scrapper of old ships. Armies of

Kaohsiung steelworks and harbor.

laborers bearing acetylene torches, saws and wrenches break down about 200 steel-hulled, ocean-going ships each year. They harvest an enormous quantity of scrap steel, nautical devices, copper wire and other parts. The scrap wharf is located at **Little Harbor**, 10 kilometers (6 mi) south from downtown.

As Taipei's leading industrial and export city, Kaohsiung is naturally a good place for shopping. Best buys are modern manufactured goods, clothing and other contemporary items, rather than arts and crafts. A good street for window-shopping and absorbing local color is narrow **Hsinle Street**, which runs parallel to Wufu Road, between Love River and the harbor area.

As Taiwan's number-one fishing port, Kaohsiung naturally offers excellent fresh seafood. A fine culinary evening can be enjoyed on Chichin Island, which can either be reached by ferry from the Kushan terminal, or by car, arriving at the south end via the harbor tunnel. The island is 11 kilometers (7 mi) long, but only 200 meters wide. At the northern end, dozens of seafood restaurants stand cheek-by-jowl. Whether kept on ice or alive in tanks waiting for customers to make their choice, the sheer variety of seafood is unbelievable.

After Taipei, Kaohsiung has Taiwan's most active night life. The busy but pleasant **Liuho night market**, some blocks south from the railway station, offers plenty of food stalls and many bargains. Midnight ramblers on the prowl find amusement on **Fleet Street**, a one-block section of Chienhsin 3rd Road, between Wufu 4th and Kungyuan. Fleet Street caters to Kaohsiung's transient merchant seamen.

Into the hills: No visitor should miss **Fokuang Shan**, at least an hour's drive northeast of Kaohsiung in lush rolling hills. Better known as Light of Buddha Mountain, this is the center of Buddhist scholarship in Taiwan. The complex consists of several shrine halls surrounded by cool colonnades, pavilions and pagodas, bridges and footpaths, libraries and meditation halls, ponds and grottoes, and exquisite Buddhist statu-

Shrine hall, Fokuang Shan.

ary. Near the entrance, the tallest Buddha image on the island – 32 meters (105 ft) high – is surrounded by 480 life-sized images of disciples.

Outlying islands: Kaohsiung is also the gateway to offshore islands under the jurisdiction of the Taiwan government.

It is easy to discover **Penghu**, the Pescadores Islands, the Isles of the Fishermen, situated between Taiwan and the mainland. The 16th-century Portuguese sailors who first put Taiwan on European maps – as Formosa – also gave these islands their name. Nearly every army that has attacked Taiwan has used the Penghu as their springboard. During the Mongul Yuan dynasty, Chinese pirates used these islands as a base from which to sack ships plying coastal waters. Ming authorities finally suppressed the piracy and established a trading post here, and early Hakka settlers stopped here en route to Taiwan. Then, in rapid succession, the Dutch, Koxinga, the Manchu Qing, and the Japanese took control of the archipelago, en route to the island of Taiwan.

Today, Penghu forms Taiwan's only island-county. Half of the archipelago's population of 150,000 live in **Makung**, the county seat on the main island of Penghu. Fishing is the primary source of income; the only crops that grow on these flat, windswept islands are peanuts, sweet potatoes, and sorghum, used for making potent Kaoliang liquor. Makung has a number of attractions, including the old town wall and its gates, and a number of old temples.

East and south of Kaohsiung: Shortly after Fengshan, an extremely large bridge crosses the Kaoping River. In the dry season, only a little bit of running water is visible, but in typhoon season, the whole river bed is filled with raging waters. From the pleasant town of **Pingtung**, worth exploring with its farmer markets and temples, Highway 22 runs directly to **Santimen**, 50 kilometers east of Kaohsiung.

The coastal crescent that occupies Taiwan's southern reaches is known as the **Hengchun Peninsula.** Two arms reach into the sea: Oluanpi (Goose Bell

Penghu Island harbor.

Beak), longer and to the east, and Maotoupi (Cat's Nose Cape), stubbier and more westerly. The broad bay between the two points harbors some of the island's best swimming beaches.

The roadside resort valley of **Kenting** lies between Kenting Park in the hills and Kenting Beach on the shore. There is a choice of several hotels in the area. Close by is also one of the three nuclear power stations owned and operated by the Taiwan Power Company.

In the low hills above the two-pronged peninsula sprawls **Kenting National Park**, a lovely haven for exotic flora and strange formations of coral rock. Offshore, the merging of waters of the Pacific Ocean, Taiwan Strait, South China Sea and Bashi Channel create a pastel tapestry of green and blue swirls.

Kenting National Park was first established by the Japanese in 1906, who combed the earth to find exotic species of plants to transplant here all that could thrive in this climate. The Chinese have continued to expand the collection: currently there are more than 1,200 species growing in the 50-square-kilometer (20-sq-mi) park. Paved paths and marked scenic routes interlace the park, and most trees and shrubs are identified in Latin as well as in Chinese.

Scenic points include the 100-meter-long (330-ft) tunnel through contorted rock called the Fairy Cave, and the deep gorge, opened like a sandwich by an ancient earthquake, known as One Line Sky. In the Valley of Hanging Banyan Roots, visitors enter a preternatural world where thick banyan roots stretch 20 meters (60 ft) through cliffs of solid stone to reach the earth, their green canopies whistling in the wind high above. From First Gorge, confirmed trekkers can enter the dense groves of the **Tropical Tree Preservation Area**. It takes a little over an hour to make the walk.

On the ocean side of town, **Kenting Beach** features an unspoiled white-sand beach that stretches about 200 meters (650 ft). The clear azure water is warm and gentle, perfect for swimming from April to October.

Kenting Beach weekend.

THE EAST COAST

On the Pacific side of the great Central Range, which bisects Taiwan from north to south, lies the island's rugged eastern coast, unsurpassed for its contours of land, sea and sky. Insulated by a wall of mountains from the industrial and commercial developments of the western plains, eastern Taiwan remains an enclave of old-fashioned island culture, a refuge where the flavor of human feelings retains its natural taste.

South to Hualien: "Breathtaking" is not a cliché when applied to the roller-coaster, 110-kilometer-long (70-mi) route between **Suao** and Hualien to the south. It is literally a cliff-hanger, with the crashing breakers of the Pacific Ocean eroding the rocks 300 to 450 meters (1,000 to 1,500 ft) below the highway. Chiseled into sheer stone cliffs that rise in continual ridges, the road was first built in 1920, along the route of the original footpath that was hewn out

of rock in 1875. At first, there was only one lane to cope with the convoys of automobiles, taxis, buses and trucks. Now, traffic can move freely in both directions, even if the road occasionally gets rather narrow. The journey takes between two and three hours, but the traveler is rewarded with magnificent views and a rush of adrenaline.

Hualien: Those who visit Hualien will find it a pleasant, cheerful town. With 90 percent of the Hualien area dominated by mountains, the city itself – the largest settlement on Taiwan's east coast – fills the narrow strip of flat land separating the mountains from the sea. Hualien's greatest claim to fame is marble. Uncountable tons of pure marble are contained in the craggy cliffs and crevices of nearby Taroko Gorge.

Hualien is home to Taiwan's largest ethnic minority, the Ami, numbering about 150,000. During the annual Ami harvest celebration, in late August and early September, the town is particularly festive. At other times, authentic performances of traditional tribal dances are staged for visitors in a large marble factory along the road to Taroko Gorge, and in the **Ami Culture Village**, about a 15-minute drive from downtown.

But these centers offer more kitsch than class. Those seeking authentic glimpses of Ami life should visit the little coastal town of **Fengpin**, a short drive south of Hualien. The harvest festival's opening ceremonies are especially exciting at Fengpin.

Taroko Gorge: Nine out of 10 people who visit Hualien usually tour Taroko Gorge, one of the most spectacular natural wonders of the world. By car, cab or bus, the route from Hualien heads north for 15 kilometers (9 mi), through vast and green plantations of papaya, banana and sugar cane. When the road reaches **Hsincheng**, it cuts westward, straight into the cavernous, marble-rich gorge of Taroko.

Taroko means beautiful in the Ami dialect, and visitors at once realize that the people who named the site were not exaggerating. A gorge of marble cliffs, through which flows the torrential Liwu River, Taroko winds sinuously for 20 **Suao Harbor.**

kilometers (12 mi) from the coast to its upper end at Tienhsiang.

The first scenic points along the route are the **Light of Zen Monastery** and the **Shrine of Eternal Spring**. The latter is a memorial to the 450 retired servicemen who lost their lives constructing this road, known as the Rainbow of Treasure Island. The shrine is perched on a cliff overlooking the boulder-strewn river, with a view of a waterfall pouring through a graceful moon bridge.

At **Swallow's Grotto**, the cliffs tower so tall on either side of the road that direct sunlight hits the floor of the gorge only around noon. The Fuji Cliff reels visitors' heads as they look up its sheer stone face, echoing the roar of the river below. The **Tunnel of Nine Turns** is a remarkable feat of engineering – it cuts a crooked road of tunnels and half-tunnels through solid marble cliffs.

The final stop on the Taroko Gorge tour is **Tienhsiang**. Here, amidst natural beauty, is the Tienhsiang Lodge, where overnight lodging and meals are available. A suspension bridge near the lodge leads across the river to an exquisite pagoda perched on a peak. A few minutes' drive beyond Tienhsiang, a series of steps at the mouth of a tunnel lead down to the dramatic setting of the **Wenshan Hot Springs**.

South from Hualien: Scenery along the East Coast Highway heading south from Hualien grows more gentle and pastoral. On one side, the deep-blue waters of the Pacific either crash frothily against rocky capes or nuzzle the beaches of quiet coves. Inland, the Central Range forms a massive windscreen, sheltering brilliant green plantations and terraced paddies that cover arable land.

Along the coastal route, a large, seated Buddha image, facing the sea some 15 kilometers (9 mi) south of Hualien, draws the attention of those not "templed out." Another 25 kilometers (16 mi) further is **Chichi**, the first good swimming beach south of Hualien. The small bay here has clear water for swimming, and sometimes the waves break perfectly for body-surfing. The beach is of black sand.

Taroko Gorge.

Taitung: Reached from the north by both Highway 9 and Highway 11, the sleepy seaside city of Taitung is pleasant and airy. At about the same latitude as Kaohsiung on the opposite coast, Taitung is the economic hub for the lower portion of the east coast.

Taitung is not much of a traveler's destination in itself. But it makes a convenient springboard for excursions to nearby places such as the Chihpen hot springs, Lu Tao (Green Island) and Lanyu (Orchid Island), and the East Coast Highway.

South from Taitung: Tucked against the mountain-side at the mouth of a rugged canyon, along the rocky Chihpen River, is **Chihpen**, one of Taiwan's oldest, quaintest and most remote hot-spring resorts. Dubbed the Source of Wisdom by the Japanese, it was developed as a resort by the Japanese around the beginning of this century.

The Chihpen Valley, which cuts into the steep mountains behind the spa, is reminiscent of the gorgeous wild gorges hidden deep within the remote mountain ranges of western Sichuan province, on the mainland. Here are thick forests and clear streams, steep cliffs and cascading waterfalls, bamboo groves and fruit orchards, robust mountain dwellers and exotic flora and fauna.

The biggest treat in the Chihpen Valley is the **Chinghueh Temple** (Clear Awakening Monastery), located up a steep hill about a kilometer from the lower hot-spring area, next door to the Royal Chihpen Spa Hotel. A brace of big elephants in white plaster stand at the foot of the steps to the elegant shrine hall. While Daoist temples display the dragon and tiger, the elephant is strictly a Buddhist motif.

Perhaps no stretch of major road in Taiwan is as untrammeled as Highway 24, which cuts inland and westward from Chihpen to cross the mountains towards Kaohsiung. Travelers will see a lot from the window of a coach, but it is far more convenient and pleasurable to cover this portion by private car or taxi. There is the train as well, but this spends a lot of its time in tunnels.

Island outposts: For the traveler with a taste for offbeat destinations, two islands easily reached from Taitung offer worlds far from the mainstream of Chinese civilization.

Within sight of Taitung, about 30 kilometers (20 mi) due east, is **Lu Tao**, or Green Island. The 16-square-kilometer (6-sq-mi) island has only recently been developed for tourism; it wasn't so long ago that a holiday on Lu Tao meant sitting out a long prison sentence.

The waters and reefs around Lu Tao are excellent for swimming, scuba diving, fishing and shell collecting.

Lanyu, or Orchid Island, is the most unlikely jewel in the waters surrounding Taiwan. An island of 45 square kilometers (17 sq. mi), it is 60 kilometers (40 mi) east of Taiwan's southern tip and 80 kilometers (50 mi) southeast of Taitung. Lanyu is home to 4,250 Yami, Taiwan's smallest minority tribe. With colorful costumes and a strongly-matriarchal society, the Yami are often regarded as the northernmost extent of Polynesian ancestry, long isolated from technology's intrusions.

Left, Shrine of Eternal Spring.
Right, Suao-Hwalien Highway.

Sariwŏn
Chaeryŏng
Sinch'ŏn
Haeju
Ongjin
Kaesŏng
Tongduch'ŏn
Üijŏngbu
SEOUL Kuri
Puch'ŏn Kwach'ŏn
Kwangmyŏng
Ansan Anyang
Suwŏn
Ŏsan
Songt'an
P'yŏngt'aek
Ch'ŏnan
Yesan
Choch'iwŏn
Kongju Ch'ŏngju
Taech'ŏn
Puyŏ
Nonsan
Kanggyŏng
Kunsan Iri
Kimje
Chŏngup
Namwon
Songjŏng Naju **KWANGJU**
Sunch'ŏn
Mokp'o Pölgyo
Kangjon Changhūng
Haenam
Yŏsu

SONGNAM
Wŏnju
Chech'ŏn
Yongwol
Ch'ungju
Mt. Soghi (Sŏngni)
▲1058m
TAEJON
Kimch'ŏn Kumi
Mt. Umang
▲1126m **CHŎNJU**
Mt. Togyu Mt. Sudo
1508m ▲1317m
Mt. Kaya
1430m **TAEGU**
Yongch'ŏn
Miryang
Mt. Kaji
1240m
Chinju Ch'angwŏn
Kosŏng Kimhae
Masan **MASAN** Chinhae
Samch'ŏnp'o Pusan
Ch'ungmu

Sea of Japan
(Tonghae)
Mt. Hyangno
1293m▲
Sa-myŏng Mt. Sŏrak Sokch'o
▲1198m 1708m▲
Ch'unch'ŏn Mt. Tuno
1422m Kangnŭng
Hongch'on
Mt. Kanwang
▲1461m Tonghae
Samch'ŏk
Mt. Taebaek
▲1561m
Mt. Sobaek Uljin
1439m
Yongju Mt. Ilwol
▲1219m
P'yŏnghae
Sangju Andong
Ŭisŏng Yŏngdŏk
Mt. Pohyon
▲1124m
P'ohang
Yŏngch'ŏn
Kyŏngju
ULSAN

**REPUBLIC
OF KOREA
(SOUTH KOREA)**

*Yellow Sea
(Huang Hai)*

NORTH KOREA
SOUTH KOREA

SOUTH KOREA
JAPAN

*Western Channel
(Pusan Strait)*

Korea

*Eastern Channel
(Tsushima Strait)*

Strait

PIGŬM I.
TAEHŬKSAN
ISLAND

KŎCH'AGUN Is.

Cheju Strait

Cheju
Mt. Halla
▲1950m

Republic of Korea
80 km / 50 miles

KOREA

Part of the beauty of Korea is provided by its history. Squeezed as it is between its bigger neighbours – Japan, China and Russia – Korea has survived invasions, wars and colonial rule, while remaining fiercely distinct. No small accomplishment.

Until 1945, Japanese colonial overlords aggressively worked for half a century to eliminate Korean culture, including the Korean language and Korean family names, replacing them with Japanese. Tens of thousands of Koreans were shipped to Japan as slave labour; many of their descendants remain in Japan, more Japanese than Korean but without the rights of citizenship. Korea's success as an economic powerhouse following World War II, and the Korean War, is as astounding as Japan's own postwar progress.

Yet as with Japan, Korea shares a common cultural heritage with the ancient Chinese kingdom. Indeed, all three nations are closer than they like to admit.

In modern times, the peninsula was first known as the Hermit Kingdom because of its 19th-century policy of retreating from foreign influence. It was not until the 1988 Summer Olympics, in Seoul, that the Koreans burst into the international scene as a world player. In two short weeks, millions of viewers around the world saw Korea as it is – a modern and vibrant nation, with a long and rich cultural heritage, coming of age as an economic and political power.

Today, part of Korea's attraction is its pulsating modernity. In Seoul, the country's capital for 600 years, skyscrapers reach towards the heavens and traffic jams stall the human race below. Neons light the city at night and workers pile into vehicles early in the morning. Yet in the neighborhoods of Seoul and throughout the countryside, women still hang peppers to announce the birth of a baby boy, children bow to their grandparents, fortune-tellers warn of future trouble and offer portents of luck, Buddhist monks wander the streets for alms, and families take to the mountains to worship the natural beauty of their land.

The country is dotted with Buddhist temples and contains some great Buddhist treasures. It also has a rich Confucian legacy from its Yi dynasty period, when it was said that the Koreans were more Confucian than the Chinese. Perhaps they still are, suggest the Chinese themselves. Raised on the strictures of Confucianism and the tolerance of Buddhism, and fashioned by a land of bitter winters and roasting summers, not to mention outside intrusions over the centuries, the Koreans have emerged a proud and strong people.

Preceding pages: paddies of rice at harvest time, winter storm in Seoul.

So far as it is now known, the Korean peninsula was first settled by wandering tribes from central and northern Asia some 30,000 years ago. These hardy nomadic people had their own language, a variant Ural-Altaic speech related to Turkish, Hungarian and Finnish. This uniquely Korean tongue, despite a later overlay of Chinese ideographic writing and vocabulary plus some elements shared with Japanese syntax, has remained an important factor contributing to national unity. This was especially so after the belated invention of an efficient phonetic alphabet, called *han'gul*, in the 15th century.

As population increased during the Bronze and Iron ages, and the people settled into sedentary occupations such as farming and fishing, their social organization developed from tribal to clan level. Patriarchal chiefs of allied clans met in council over important issues such as war, a practice that led eventually to selection of a king who was merely first among equals. The outspokenness and self-reliance of Koreans had taken firm root by the 1st century BC.

It was during this period, too, that the major influx of informative influence from China began. In addition to agricultural and manufacturing skills, there came the writing system that brought with it classical Chinese literature. The most important borrowings from the mainland, however, consisted of religio-philosophic creeds and the social system these implied or dictated.

The Golden Horde: The Silla kingdom, which first unified the peninsula under one government in AD 668, is generally regarded as a predominantly Buddhist monarchy, but it was actually guided by firm Confucian tenets of ritual and conduct, as was the succeeding Koryo dynasty, assuming power in 936.

During Koryo times, the Buddhist clergy did indeed attain powerful influence in government. It was during this period too that the Mongol armies of the Great Khan swept over the country in 1213. The suffering and destruction were unprecedented, and when the Korean king sued for peace, he was forced to take a Mongol princess as bride, and to declare himself a vassal of the Khan, and willing to assist the Mongols in their abortive attempts to invade Japan. Under the Mongols, the Koreans gained knowledge of astrology, medicine, artistic skills and cotton cultivation. As the Golden Horde weakened and receded, it was easy to blame Buddhist ascendancy in the government for Korea's national disaster.

When anti-Mongol general Yi Song-gye rebelled and proclaimed himself founder of a new dynasty in 1392, one of his immediate concerns was to eradicate Buddhist power at court. Confucianism of a peculiarly ortho-

dox and dogmatic type was installed in power, leading to the calcification of an already rigid social system.

The new dynasty started off well, nonetheless, and during the reign of the fourth monarch, King Sejong the Great (1419–1450), a cultural renaissance and some attempt at administrative reforms ushered in what many Koreans like to think of as a Utopian age.

Japanese invasion: In 1592 and 1598, legions of the Japanese warlord Hideyoshi launched two successive invasions of the peninsula, bent on an invasion of China from Japan via Korea. This attempt was futile and devastating to Korea, for the invading armies clashed with Chinese forces on Korean soil. Less than 40 years later, Korea was ravaged by the Manchu forces bent on overthrowing China's Ming dynasty, to which Korea maintained a tenacious loyalty.

Stunned by this double disaster into a state of near traumatic shock, Korea withdrew from all outside contacts, assuming the role of Hermit Kingdom for over two centuries. Divisive feuds festered among political factions, while idealistic reformers found themselves stymied by isolation and lack of practical knowledge. A vital new trend towards modernization and reform at the end of the 19th century achieved too little too late to prevent Korea from becoming a pawn in the contention between a declining China and an awakening Japan, with Russia and Western powers on the sidelines.

During the Russo-Japanese War of 1904, Japan consolidated 20 years of creeping encroachment upon Korea's sovereignty, and in 1910 the peninsula was formally annexed as part of the island empire. The Japanese occupation attempted not mere annexation, but complete assimilation. The usurpers behaved with unparalleled greed, arrogance and brutality, not only in exploiting Korea's resources to a ruinous extent, but in trying to extirpate the very foundations of the country's national identity: the language, customs and culture of thousands of years. The long-dormant nationalism of Korea's intelligentsia, awakening from centuries of apathy and self-destructive bickering, arose to fight the Japanese, in ways ranging from assassination and guerrilla warfare to nonviolent demonstrations and passive sabotage.

When Tokyo finally surrendered to the Western allies in 1945 following defeat in World War II, Korea regained its independence, only to be partitioned five years later, followed by a civil war that proved far more cataclysmic than any earlier invasion.

The Cold War between the US and Soviets led to the establishment of the 38th parallel as the official demarcation line between the Communist north and the south of the peninsula. The stage was set for civil war, and North Korean troops crossed the 38th parallel in strength in 1950. The Americans moved

NATIVES OF KOREA.

Left, Confucius is *Kongja* to Koreans. <u>Above</u>, residents in a Korean village.

in to help the south and the Korean War, including eventual and massive intervention by the Chinese, dragged on until a truce was signed in 1953.

The war dealt a fatal blow to any hopes of a speedy, peaceful reunification of Korea. The creation of the demilitarized zone made the border between the Korean states one of the most effective artificial barriers in the world, and the fighting had inevitably hardened the hostility on both sides.

In the south, the period following the war was one of stagnation and slow recovery. President Yi's government collapsed in 1960, following widespread student demonstrations and violent intervention by the authori-

army and ran as the candidate of the Democratic Republican Party. In 1967, Park won a re-election and two years later, he secured a constitutional amendment to open the way for a third term, to which he was elected in 1971, narrowly defeating Kim Dae-jung.

Park declared martial law on 17 October 1972, and called for a program of reforms. The constitution was redrawn. Under the terms of the new constitution, Park was appointed to a new six-year term as president, with no limit on future terms.

Park's rule came to an end in 1979 when he was killed by his own intelligence chief, who claimed he had assassinated Park in order to restore democracy. He was convicted, along

Capture of Heijo Korla by the Japanese Army

ties. The subsequent government proved incapable of retaining power and fell to a military coup in 1961.

The coup leaders imposed an absolute military dictatorship and Major General Park Chung-hee emerged as its chairman. Park was a 43-year-old career officer of rural origin. By 1960, he had risen to become deputy commander of the Second Army, but had always remained apart from the main political factions within the army.

Under Park's leadership, the military government continued to rule until 1963, when it could no longer resist pressures for a return to civilian government. Park retired from the

with six accomplices, and executed.

The long-term legacy of Park's 18 years in office comprised two trends: Park's idea of Korean-style democracy placed a strong emphasis on administrative efficiency, and he presided over a series of development programs that made Korea one of the most remarkable economic successes of the 1960s and 1970s. The immediate period of transition after his sudden death, however, was a period of uncertainty and contention.

Under the 1972 constitution, the prime minister Ch'oe Kyu-ha, became acting president. On 6 December he was named to serve out Park's term. Between Ch'oe's election and his inauguration on 21 December, an abrupt change occurred within the military establishment when the agency responsible for investigating Park's murder arrested the Army Chief of Staff, General Chong Sunghwa, who was accused of complicity in the assassination of Park.

The arrests of military opponents marked the first step in a phased assumption of power by Chun. Suppression of civilian opponents in 1980 led to a popular revolt in the city of Kwangju after special forces sent to control student demonstrations overreacted and brutalized protesters. At least 200 students and civilians were killed.

In January, Chun became the first head-of-

state to be received by newly-elected American President Ronald Reagan. The haste with which Washington appeared to endorse Chun's takeover led Korean dissidents and students to conclude that America, which had 40,000 troops in Korea, had backed the new military coup from the outset. This perception was the basis for the anti-Americanism which characterized anti-government protests during Chun's rule and which remains in the 1990s.

Left, lithograph of 19th-century attack by Japanese troops. Above, monument to a 20th-century war.

By the time Chun's rule neared its close, the opposition was weakened by factional strife and the campus protest movement was alienating students and the public with its leftist slogans and violent protest tactics. However, when Chun anointed fellow coupmaker Roh Tae-woo as his successor, religious dissidents called for protests and hundreds of thousands of ordinary Koreans joined student activists in taking to the streets to demand direct popular elections. Roh accepted all the protesters' demands. In December, Roh won the election.

Roh took power in 1988 in what was the first peaceful transfer of power in Korean history. The pent-up frustrations of a rapidly developing society, held down by years of dictatorial rule, appeared to explode at once. For three years in succession widespread labour disputes rocked the nation. Wages rose so fast that Korea found itself no longer able to sell many of its products overseas competitively. Yet the country still managed to achieve growth rates which are the envy of the developing nations.

In 1988, Korea staged the summer Olympics. For two weeks, Korea shed its wartime rubble-and-ashes image and was seen by the world as a fast-paced, modern nation that it is. In the wake of the Games, Seoul developed full diplomatic ties with East European nations and the former Soviet Union.

While Korea advanced economically and diplomatically, politics appeared to drag. Where North Korea was concerned, old habits which characterized earlier authoritarian rulers prevailed. Starry-eyed dissidents who travelled illegally to North Korea to encourage unification – after Roh had declared the North to be a "brother" and no longer the "enemy" – received heavy jail terms.

In the 1990s, scandals and corruption reigned; shoddy construction caused the collapse of department stores, bridges and subway tunnels. Most surprisingly, the iron-hand rule of the military alumni came to a humiliating end: in 1997, both Roh and Chun were convicted of treason for, amongst other things, their role in the Kwongju massacres and sentenced to prison.

Famine in North Korea led to a test of wills and pride, as the Communist nation was in desperate need of food, but unwilling to accept it directly from the south. It went through China first.

To understand today's Koreans and their intriguing, paradoxical country – to survive potentially terminal cultural shock, and to learn to get along smoothly in this fascinating nation – it's necessary to give some consideration to the questions of who they are, how they become that way, and why they act the way they do.

The qualities that have enabled Koreans to survive, and which have become their most strongly ingrained attributes, are primarily three: patience, flexibility, and stubbornness. To these may be added a robust, satiric, and sometimes uncouth sense of humor.

outside influences, it seems, and were there to be developed and orchestrated by proximity and events. Buddhism encouraged the cultivation of patience. Likewise, the Confucian system became in practice a pragmatic philosophy, presupposing adaptability in pursuit of advantage. And Daoism suggests a stubbornness embodied in its metaphor of water as the strongest of elements, since it gradually wears away even the hardest stones.

Koreans still find it difficult to speak of the Japanese annexation with any degree of equa-

ness. To these may be added a robust, satiric, and sometimes uncouth sense of humor.

Korean patience does not mean passivity, nor does flexibility imply lack of strong individuality. The third trait, stubbornness – sometimes dignified by calling it perseverance – explains and modifies the other two.

It would be easy but misleading to make a neat generalization here and say that these three basic Korean qualities are derived from the three major outside influences, and to speak of Chinese patience, Japanese adaptability, and American stick-to-it-iveness. But it goes deeper than that: these counterpointed national themes appeared earlier than the

nimity and they shudder at the suggestion that they resemble their island neighbors. The Japanese did influence Korea in many ways – they stepped into a vacuum in social structure, political organization, education and administration – but the price was so severe that even today, Japanese songs and movies are still banned in Korea.

During the occupation, when Christian missionaries from America, Britain, Canada and Australia offered an alternative, many Koreans quickly took up the calling. The Japanese recognized the Christians as leading subversives, but did not directly seek to dismantle the churches until World War II because of their links to foreign powers. Although there was far wider acceptance of Japanese rule than modern Koreans wish to remember, the dream of independence never died for the majority.

Korean anger against foreign powers and frustration over her own weakness underlie the painful memory of both the colonial period and the subsequent division of the peninsula into northern and southern halves.

In some ways, this sorrow sometimes rocks the stability of the southern portion of the cern with manner than with matter. As the essayist Lee O-young: "In Korea, they say there is no logic… instead there is emotion, intuitional insight and a soulful spirit."

Korean etiquette consists of an elaborate system of formalized gestures designed to produce pleasant feelings and smooth relations. This is done by ensuring maintenance of proper *kibun* (mood or aura) through adroit employment of *nunch'i* (intuiting another's feelings through observation), and behaving with suitable *mot* (style or taste).

peninsula – students inevitably blame the current government for maintaining the status quo – but it also serves to strengthen the society. Koreans hold onto one another like parents do their children to fend off foreign influence and maintain their traditions. National pride and resilience results, a force far stronger than armies.

Manner over matter: Despite the economic urgency of importing modern science and technology, Koreans still show more con-

Left, the older and wiser. **Above**, a Korean courtesan of the 1880s. **Right**, bride surrounded by doting relatives.

Somewhere along the line, amidst the maze of honorifics and the anxiety to determine whether one must talk up, down, or straight-from-the-shoulder to a given individual, any idea of truth, fairness, or brass-tacks agreement becomes distinctly secondary.

Despite the differences, most Occidental visitors receive a favorable impression of Koreans as a warm, friendly, sympathetic and cheerful people, the proverbial salt of the earth – an impression that usually remains, even after the strange experiences some will encounter in a clash of cultural values. The whole abrasiveness of such a clash is not felt, because the foreigner is considered in the same category as classless people, or *sangnom*: "unpersons" and outcasts who are not expected to know how to behave in a proper Korean manner, and upon whom it would be pointless to waste anger.

From the vantage point of the foreign sangnom, a Korean can be seen in his best light – without all the hangups he has to deal with among his compatriots – as a courteous, considerate, and tenaciously loyal friend. The Korean is gregarious, fun-loving, hearty, even bibulous; yet the Korean remains a devoted family man, a hard worker, and a solid citizen. He is very likely highly cultured – taxi drivers know Beethoven symphonies, schoolboys gather tasteful

been longer and heavier than that of the Irish. This human family may be indissolubly united, but each link in the chain represents a unique, idiosyncratic national entity, with its own customs created or adapted to special circumstances, and in these differences reside the main points of interest for the traveler.

In Korea, the hallmark of nationality has for a long time probably been symbolized by family ritual. The ancient Chinese called their Korean neighbors the ceremonious people of the east, admitting that the Koreans had outdone the Sage's own people in adherence to Confucian formalities.

Passage of life: Marriage used to occur only after the ministrations of a matchmaker who

wildflower bouquets – with great respect for learning and refinement. He is fiercely nationalistic, not shallowly patriotic, and exhibits a touching reverence for the natural beauties of his mountain-riven, storm-tormented land.

But visitors may sometimes glimpse the other side of the coin: an intoxicated Korean becomes angry or tearful, not euphoric. Korean songs are sad and their poems piercingly nostalgic. It is why they try so hard to be happy, to seize the fleeting moment before it is past.

Koreans have been called the Irish of the Orient, yet the burden of their history has

blended astrology with canny pop psychology and sociology. Nowadays, the dating game is played among the young, with rather stricter rules perhaps than in the West. Traditionally, marriage occurred quite young. A girl's family sent her bedding and trousseau chest to the boy's home, and the boy's family reciprocated with gifts. On the nuptial day, the bride was carried in a palanquin to the groom's house and the couple – often meeting for the first time – shared a cup of rice wine to pledge their troth. This ritual is now seen only in staged form at folk village shows, for the custom of the *yesik-chang* (wedding hall) pervades town and country.

These marriage factories, often huge buildings with dozens of weddings going on simultaneously in various-sized chambers, provide everything from flowers to Western-style music. Crowds of friend and relatives gather in pew-like seats, with no compulsion to retain order or quiet; children frequently scamper and shout up the aisles. The only trace of the old days remaining is the family-only room at the back, where time-honored bows are performed and wine shared. The public part of the ceremony is the bridal procession, a short homily by a family and the indispensable group photography. Guests bring gifts, usually cash in white envelopes.

bles piled high with fruit, rice cakes, cookies, candies and other goodies set out among brass candelabra.

After the ceremony comes a feast with drinking, music, and dancing for all, including the guest of honor, to the endurance of the last one to give in. Traditional funeral customs called for the coffined body to be placed in the house, where ritual wailing goes on by servants, shirt-tail relations, or paid mourners, while the family provides a convivial party resembling an Irish wake. On the third day, a procession accompanies the coffin on a bier borne by laborers, fueled by frequent stops for rice wine, to the grave site preceded by the wooden tablet (or pennant) lettered in

After marriage the birth cycle was expected to resume and keep the family busy with rituals. No further scheduled event was indicated until the 60th birthday, or *hwan'gap*, one of the most important events in any Korean's life. The 60th birthday is celebrated with all possible pomp and ceremony. The elder sits virtually enthroned on cushions, receiving the kowtows of children and grandchildren. Behind him are low ta-

Left, respectful progeny gather around at a hwangap, or 60th birthday, c. 1930. **Above**, a child on his first birthday, honored with fruit, rice cakes and cash.

Chinese with the name of the deceased, which will later be enshrined in the house.

Though such old-fashioned funerals may still be encouraged in the countryside (but should not be photographed by strangers), they are obviously impractical in big cities, where the choice is cremation for the poor.

Though the funeral completes the life cycle, it does not end the cyclical pattern of Korean family ritual, for twice a year – on the *ch'usok* autumn harvest holiday and in spring on *hansik* (or cold food) day, now coincidental with Arbor Day – family members gather at the grave and set up tables covered with fruits and rice cakes that are eaten later.

Most East Asian countries adhere to a spiritual mainstream, but Korea denies a simple religious label. Strong traditions of shamanism, Confucianism, Daoism, Buddhism, and Christianity infuse society. Though many Koreans subscribe exclusively to one religion, they also allow other spiritual beliefs to play an occasional role in their lives.

Shamanism: If one could peer into the souls of Korean people, one would find fascinating elements of shamanism, the folk worship of a pantheon of household, village and animate and inanimate forces in nature.

Koreans, like other Asians, maintain ancient traditions such as the *kut*, or exorcising ceremonies. These practices have not been fully institutionalized into a religion, but shamanism has been kept very much alive in Korea – as in the deification of Sanshin, a non-Buddhist mountain god, who has found his way into special shrines located within the courtyards of Buddhist temple complexes.

Daoism: Daoism has been practiced in Korea for more than 1,300 years, but active examples of its presence are rare these days. Though Daoist texts were often studied in the past, and though some of Korea's Buddhist temples temporarily served as Daoist temples, few remnants of early Daoist art survive today. Daoism achieved its greatest height in Korea during the Unified Silla dynasty (AD 668–918). Practitioners aren't so dedicated today, but Daoism is experiencing something of a renaissance as a number of modern schools draw upon its teachings.

Buddhism: When it comes to the arts and innovative thought, Buddhism stands out as one of the most important of this country's cultural fountainheads. This religion stresses finding a practical and moderate way towards self-actualization while on earth. The Mahayana school of Buddhism, with its acceptance of local deities as a means of drawing the masses to temples for an eventual study of more orthodox doctrines and practices, proved to the liking of the Koreans.

Buddhism is Korea's largest single religion. One may find Buddhist influences in modern-day Korea subtle but pervasive. In the thought patterns of Koreans, for example, the principle of *karma* allows many to take a passive view of the world. The individual who is caught by the negative effects of some past action may justify his or her problem as being out of his or her control.

Confucianism: Confucianism has become a way of life in Korea. Confucius – or *Kongja*, as the Koreans refer to him – was never a breaker of traditions but a conservative reactionary who rallied for a return to China's Golden Era, the early days of the Chou dynasty (1112 BC–256 BC). His greatest innovative moment came when he proclaimed that the ultimate measure of political success was not sheer might but a ruler's virtue and his people's contentment. Confucius was the region's first and greatest moralist.

Today, Confucianism thrives more in Korea than in any other nation, and though Confucianism has been greatly discredited since the turn of the century by both foreign and domestic intellectual movements, its basic values and premises still dominate the lives of all Koreans. Ancestor worship continues to be practised much as it has been for more than 1,000 years. In Korea, even an "old fool" is first and foremost an elder. To rebel against the word of an elder is to invite social censure – a conservative and powerful force which is very effective in Korea's small and closed society.

Christianity: First-time visitors to Korea often gaze with wonder at the many purely Christian church steeples and crosses that punctuate populated skylines. As with all the faiths, there is a discrepancy between claimed membership and government estimates. Over nine million, or by government reckoning, almost half of all Koreans who follow a particular religion, are avowed Christians.

Today, Christianity plays a disproportionate role in power circles, both government and opposition, considering its small percentage of the Korean population.

Other religions: About 500,000 Koreans belong to a wide variety of "minor" religions. The most well-known internationally is the Unification Church, a movement started by Moon Sun-myung, a North Korean refugee, in 1954.

__Right__, honoring Confucius at a special ceremony.

For insights into a nation's character, look at its art, particularly its architecture. For example, in the three principal East Asian countries – China, Korea and Japan – the eaves of buildings have curved upwards for centuries. A subtle difference, however, exists in the manner of these upturns.

China's traditional architecture is vertical in feeling, its roofs reflecting a nation out to conquer or control nature. Korean roofs form soft curves which float ever so gently heavenwards, flowing with nature's rhythms. And Korean ceramics appear less perfected, warmer and more approachable, so that the viewer touches the potter's hand in spirit.

Pottery and ceramics: The Korean potter created beautiful elongated curves which soar with controlled energy. These unknown craftsmen decorated their porcelains with a pale, gray-green celadon glaze which sometimes became "kingfisher," a bluish-green considered a "secret color." More than 60 shades can be distinguished by the attuned eye, but the most highly admired are "sky blue after rain," and "sea water washed by rain and wind."

White porcelains were developed for upper-class use. Upon large jars, artisans painted sparsely, creating simple designs with iron-impregnated copper or malachite containing copper oxide or cobalt, "Mohammedan blue." Unlike Ming dynasty blue-and-white ware potters, the Korean craftsman never went to the same excess of treating his pot's surface as though it were an easel for painting. Rather, he limited his decorations to hints of nature – such as a single, blossoming spray, a pair of fish, a dragon, or curving leaves with grapes. The underglaze painting with iron is casual rather than pretentious and so suggests an earthy Korean spirit.

Sculpture: When Buddhism swept out of India and over central and eastern Asia, the artists of each of a dozen countries responded by creating cave sculptures, free-standing images of Buddhas, and temples. They represented the human body thinly disguised as

a deity with certain sacred marks, such as long ear lobes, a depression between the eyes and a pronounced "protuberance of wisdom" on top of the head.

Korea's earliest bronze statuettes of Buddha appear relatively flat and linear, also inspired by the calligraphic line; soon its natural genius in metallurgy and its skilled stone chiselers initiated their own directions.

Korea excels in granite sculptural work. The Korean peninsula is dotted with Buddhist figures carved in rocks in the moun-

tains. Perhaps due to the fact that the country's terrain is 70 percent mountainous, Koreans have developed a special love for stone and a skill in using it both as building material and for sculptural pieces.

Koryo paintings: Almost as remarkable as uncovering the rich treasures of golden crowns from Korea's 5th and 6th century and rediscovering its 12th- and 13th-century pale green celadon wares has been the unveiling (in the late 1970s) of 93 Koryo-period paintings – Buddhist icons of unsurpassed beauty. It was thought that such art had vanished. Sad to say, though, all these beautiful Korean art works are now owned by Japanese. Tucked

Left, *Kwanseum-posal with Willow Branch*, **Koryo painting of mineral colors on silk, 14th-century.**
Right, **Koryo origins dot the countryside.**

away in various temples and shrines, these rarely seen paintings on silk were largely labeled as Chinese paintings, but the paintings reflect Northern Sung works in style, when Buddhism's influence was deep. Korean artists carried the lines of gold and the brilliant areas of clothing (scarlet, malachite green and sapphire blue) into further refinement and grace, as well as in complexity.

An entirely different approach to art is revealed in Yi dynasty folk paintings. Charmingly naive and unpretentious, they reflect the actual life, customs and beliefs of the Korean people. Today, they are still relegated to special museums, such as Emille Museum at Songni-san, because the national

and *yin,* male and female, along with five directions (north, south, east, west and center), five colors (black, red, white, blue and yellow), and five material elements (water, fire, metal, wood and earth).

During the peak of Buddhist influence, cosmological symbolism played a minor role in Korean art. The lotus, the official religious flower, and other such Buddhist symbols dominated art. However, with the suppression of Buddhism in 1392, Daoism, Buddhism and shamanism had become homogenized so that they were hardly separable in popular thought. For example, it is difficult to determine the exact origin of the 12 zodiacal images used in art.

museums are perpetuated by a Confucian-type bureaucracy.

Korean folk art – with its blue dragons, white tigers and magical fungi – is based on symbolism which developed and evolved over a long period of time and was understood by all the people. Even today, a basic understanding of this complex system is essential to appreciate this lively art.

Symbols: In the mists of China's remote antiquity, symbolic directions arose as part of a cosmology derived either from Daoism or an even more ancient shamanistic system of concepts. Among the most important were the correlatives of heaven and earth, *yang*

The major symbols used and their meanings are as follows:

Four Sacred Animals of Good Luck: Turtle, dragon, unicorn, and phoenix.

Ten Symbols of Longevity: deer, crane, turtle, rocks, clouds, sun, water, bamboo, pine and the fungus of immortality (*pullocho*).

Fertility Symbols: pomegranate, jumping carp, 100 babies and finally Buddha's hand citron.

Special Guardians: tiger (front gate or front door), dragon (gate or roof), *haet'ae* (fire or kitchen), rooster (front door) and dog (storage door).

Individual Associations: peach (longevity),

pomegranate (wealth), orchid (scholar, cultural refinement), lotus (Buddhist truth, purity), bat (happiness), butterfly (love, romance), bamboo (durability), peony (noble gentleman, wealth) and plum (wisdom of age, hardiness or independence, beauty, loftiness). The list could go on and on.

Music and movement: Music and dance are by far the most highly developed of the performing arts in Korea, including, of course, the modern Western introductions, which have a great appeal to Koreans of the younger generation. There are no traditional dramatic forms except those that appear as forms of dance. For the traditional Korean, the enjoyment of these art forms is in the participation

never left out of any discussion of Korean dance. One is a state of mind called *hung*. It is joie de vivre; it is how you feel when the spirit moves you and the "feeling" in "once more with feeling."

The other is an elusive spiritual quality called *mot*. It is charm, grace, that certain something – even a bit of sexuality – all rolled into one. Without *mot*, even the most perfectly executed dance is but a pretty piece of choreography.

Korean dance in itself never tells a story; it strives only to communicate its mood. Whatever stories emerge are told verbally or through acting that is supplemental to the dance, as in the masked dance dramas.

and not in merely watching the polished choreographic versions so commonly seen on stage.

Hung and Mot: Korean dancers move with a total lack of emphasis on what Westerners call technique. There is a complete absence of movements like those of ballet requiring years of vigorous physical training. For the Koreans, those years are spent teaching the body to express outwardly the inner mood of the dance wished to be performed.

This brings us to two concepts that are

Left, Yi-dynasty painting of a *kisaeng* house. **Above**, flutist plays in royal costume.

Subtle microtones, startling vibratos: Most of the music uses a five-note scale rather than the more familiar seven notes. Except for the octave, the intervals between pitches are not the same as we are used to hearing, and thus Westerners sometimes avoid the music.

No system of harmony is used, but this lack is more than made up for by melodic ornamentation including unusual attacks and decays, subtle microtones and highly complex rhythms.

Korean instruments are traditionally divided up into classes according to the material of which they are made: skin, silk, bamboo, metal, earth, stone, gourd and wood.

Spicy. Fiery. Earthy. Cool. Korean food is diverse and provocative. Its bold and subtle tastes, textures, and aromas are sure to elicit comments, sighs, and even tears at every meal.

Most foreigners associate pungent garlic and hot chili pepper with Korean cuisine. It is true that garlic-eating has been heartily appreciated by Koreans since the race's first breath, but little is it known – even in Korea – that the chili pepper did not even exist in this country until the 16th century when it was introduced by Portuguese traders.

women gather in groups throughout the country to cut, wash, and salt veritable hills of cabbage and white radish. The prepared kimch'i is stored in large, thick earthenware crocks and then buried in the backyard to keep it from fermenting during the winter months. Throughout the dark and cold winter, these red-peppered, garlicked and pickled vegetables are a good source of much-needed vitamin C.

During other eating seasons, a variety of vegetables such as chives, pumpkin and egg-

However these two ingredients may have reached Korean plates and palates, they are now used in many dishes – most liberally and notoriously in *kimch'i*. For the newcomer, learning to eat this dish is the first step to becoming a connoisseur of Korean food.

Kimch'i culture: Kimch'i is *the* dish that has made Korean food famous. Next to rice (*pap*), it is the most important component in any Korean meal. It is not known when or how kimch'i originated, but like curry in India it's in Korea to stay. So institutionalized is kimch'i that one of Korea's most important annual social events is *kimjang,* or autumn kimch'i making. At kimjang time,

plant are used to make more exotic types of kimch'i. The summer heat makes it necessary to prepare a fresh batch almost daily, often in a cool, light brine. Raw seafood, such as fish, crab and oysters are "kimch'i-ed" too, and indeed, in Korea, a woman's culinary prowess is often determined first and foremost by how good her kimch'i tastes.

Exotic herbs: Not all Korean food ingredients are quite so bold tasting as the garlic and chili pepper. In actuality, the earliest Korean dishes consisted of understated ingredients. To Koreans, almost every plant and animal in their diet has a herbal or medicinal quality and certain dishes are purposely eaten to warm or cool the head and body. Wild aster, royal fern bracken, marsh plant, day lily, aralia shoots and broad bell flowers are just a few of the many wild and exotic plants included in the typical Korean's diet. Others, such as mugwort, shepherd's purse, and sow-thistle, are also seasonally picked and eaten.

More common table vegetables – such as black sesame leaves, spinach, lettuce and mung and soy beans – are typically grown in the backyard, but others are found only in the wild. All are collectively called *namul* when

spinach, sliced radish or dried seaweed (*miyok-guk*). The latter is said to be benefi-cial to lactating mothers.

A seafood dish of some kind is usually included with various "side dishes" which are called *panch'an*. This may be a dried, salted and charbroiled fish or a hearty and spicy hot seafood soup called *mae-un-t'ang*. A delicious mae-un-t'ang usually includes firm, white fish, vegetables, soybean curd (*tubu*), red pepper powder, and an optional poached egg.

they are individually parboiled, then lightly seasoned with sesame oil, garlic, soy sauce, and ground and toasted sesame seeds.

Another vital part of the Korean meal is soup (*guk*), which is said to be one of Korea's earliest culinary techniques. Soup will al-ways be found at a proper table setting. Especially popular is *twoenjang-guk*, a fer-mented soybean paste soup with shortnecked clams stirred into its broth. Also popular are a light broth boiled from dried anchovies, and vegetable soups rendered from dried

Bulgogi and kalbi: Probably the most popu-lar Korean entré ordered or automatically served to Westerners is *bulgogi* (barbecued beef). Most beefeaters – whether Texans or Koreans – are unanimous in their apprecia-tion of this dish which is strips of red beef marinated and grilled over a charcoal bra-zier. Another popular meat dish is tender and marbled *kalbi* short ribs which are marinated and barbecued in the same way as bulgogi.

To Koreans, however, rice – not meat – is considered to be the main dish of the meal. In fact, one of the most common street greet-ings, "*Pam mogoss-o-yo?*" literally means "Have you eaten rice?"

Left, dinner for two. **Above,** cabbage and turnip vendors during annual autumn *kimjang.*

When Koreans sit down to a traditional meal, they relax on a clean lacquered paper floor. The meal comes to them on a low table. Usually the food is served in a collection of small metal bowls which are neatly arranged. The utensils used are a pair of chopsticks and a flat soup spoon.

Westerners may be surprised to find that Koreans often will eat a bowl of rice and maybe have an extra helping even though tastier side dishes remain unfinished. Don't let this preference for rice bother you; if you run out of a particular item, the lady of the house will bring more. When you've had enough to eat, place your chopsticks and soup spoon to the right of your bowl; do not

shelter during the Korean War three decades ago, today it is operated as a wine-house by several aging ladies. The quality of the potent rice *makkolli* is excellent, so kul-jip never lack customers.

There are only a few other bomb-shelter wine houses in Seoul but there are many places to drink – probably more per capita than in most other countries. Within a few minutes' walk of kul-jip are a beer hall with draft and bottled beer, a market wine shop serving several alcoholic beverages, and a roadside drinking cart, where passers-by can duck in for a quick snort on their way home.

Drinking is an important part of Korean culture. There are few proscriptions against

leave them stuck in the rice or resting on any of the bowls. A dish of sliced and chilled fruit is usually served as a dessert. Depending on the season, muskmelon, strawberries, apples, pears and watermelon are among the fresh and sweet selections. At major celebrations, steamed rice cakes *(tok)* are presented as tasty ritual food.

Toasting the spirits: Deep within a cave beneath a hill in northern Seoul, four men sit around a low round table, drinking small bowls of a milky white liquor they pour from a battered aluminium teapot.

Welcome to *kul-jip* ("cave-house") one of Seoul's most unusual drinking spots. A bomb

alcohol here and many social reasons for imbibing, so most Korean men – and a growing number of women – drink. Drinking with Koreans provides opportunities for a foreigner to penetrate Korean culture. This is partly because of the salience of drinking in the culture and partly because, like anywhere else, alcohol removes inhibitions and speeds social and cultural interaction.

On floating cups and kisaeng: History doesn't reveal when Koreans first discovered fermentation, but drinking was an important part of the culture even in Korea's early dynasties. During the Silla dynasty, the king and his court relaxed at *P'o-Sok-jong* drinking bower outside Kyongju. Here a spring bubbled up into an abalone-shaped stone channel. The drinkers set their cups afloat in the channel and competed to compose poems before the cups drifted all the way round.

Later Korean dynasties continued drinking. Probably the most popular surroundings were what is today known as the *kisaeng* party. Kisaeng were female entertainers who played musical instruments, sang, danced, composed poetry and practiced calligraphy to amuse the male aristocracy at palace parties. They also poured drinks, served the men food, and flirted. According to tradition, high-class kisaeng took lovers but weren't promiscuous. At one point in the Yi dynasty, there were more than 20,000 kisaeng.

Today, few kisaeng can play classical instruments, compose poetry or write with a brush. Instead, most kisaeng parties include a band with drums and electric guitar, and the kisaeng and their guests a-go-go dance around the table after eating. The main patrons are Korean businessmen, who are more than willing to pay large sums to entertain customers, and Japanese tourists.

Never drink alone: Confucians also might be surprised to find that although bowing while drinking has been largely forgotten, other elements of traditional etiquette still remain. The cardinal rule is that one doesn't drink alone. Furthermore, a drinker doesn't pour his own glass, but waits until his companion fills it for him. In this tradition, to serve oneself would be an act of arrogance and greed.

Generally, in a gesture of respect and friendship, a drinker will give his cup to another, conveying it politely with both hands. His companion receives the cup with both hands and holds it thus while it is filled to the brim. He may then drink. After emptying the cup, he again uses both hands to return it to the owner. Then, grasping the wine vessel with both hands, he refills the cup for the owner, returning the favor.

In a group, several drinkers in succession may offer their cups to a single person, leaving an array of brimming cups before him. A person who has given up his cup can't drink until the recipient returns it or someone else gives him his. So whoever has received

a cup has an obligation to empty it and pass it on without inordinate delay.

The working man's brew: A popular Korean brew is makkolli, a milky liquor that most rural households ferment at home from rice. Reputed to be highly nutritious, farmers found that a few cups during the long working day helped stave off hunger.

Makkolli was inexpensive in the cities as well, making it the working man's drink. For many people, until the early 1970s, going drinking usually meant going to a *makkolli-jip*, an establishment that served makkolli.

Makkolli-jip vary in style and quality, but are generally comfortable unpretentious places where nobody can put on airs.

The two most important factors about any makkolli-jip are the quality of the makkolli, and the kinds of side dishes, *anju*, that it serves since all drinking in Korea involves eating. The things that go best with makkolli range from fresh oysters, peppery octopus, dried fish, squid or cuttlefish, to soybean curd, soups, bean pancakes, scallion pancakes and omelettes.

The other beverage with long-standing popularity is *soju*, a cheap distilled liquor of around 25 percent alcoholic content, with a quality somewhere between gin and kerosene. Price and the high alcoholic content make it Korea's cheapest drink.

Left, a Korean businessman's lunch. **Right**, local beer and spirits.

According to Korean legend and history, a she-bear and a tigress who wished to be incarnated as human beings were once granted a herbal prescription by Hwan-ung, the heavenly king. Each was given a bunch of mugwort and 20 bulbs of garlic and told to retire from the sunlight for 100 days. Only the she-bear carefully followed the king's advice, and emerged from her cave as a woman. She was then granted a son by Hwan-ung and gave birth to Tan'gun Waggom, the great ancestor of Choson (Korea).

rean pharmacology. Some knowledge of Chinese herbal medicine had been previously transmitted to Japan when, as early as AD 414, a Silla doctor named Kim Pa-chin was sent to cure Japan's King Inkyo and was given a large reward for his medical favors.

Around the middle of the Three Kingdoms Period (57 BC–AD 936), Korea started to publish its own pharmacology with original prescriptions, which combined Korean and Chinese medical knowledge. The use of indigenous herbs came into prominence dur-

This tale illustrates the close bond Koreans have with nature and also their belief in the power of herbs. Mugwort and garlic have long been vital ingredients in the Korean diet, and other basic herbs have for centuries been recognized as preventative and curatives for human illnesses.

Chinese herbal medicine and acupuncture were officially introduced in the 6th century to the Koguryo court by a Han named Chih Tsung. Chih's knowledge dramatically expanded the possibilities in the field of Korean medicine. This knowledge was carried to the neighboring kingdoms of Paekche and Silla, and was assimilated with ancient Ko-

ing the Koryo (936–1392) and Yi (1392–1910) dynasties. More than 150 medical manuals were published during the Yi dynasty, and one of the most valuable of these, the *Uibang Uch'wi*, was stolen by a Japanese warlord Kato Kiyomasa, during one of the Hideyoshi invasions of the 1590s. This pharmaceutical manual is still retained in Japan as a national treasure.

Hanyak or Yak-guk: In 1880, Western medicine was introduced by doctors from China and Japan. However, despite the pervasiveness of 20th-century medicine, *hanyak*, traditional Korean medicine, remains extremely popular. Western-style pharmacies (*yak-guk*), replete with men dressed in starched white gowns, waiting behind drug counters, can be found on just about any modern, commercial street in Korea.

Hanyak shops are also visible almost everywhere – many of them distinguished by their fascinating window displays of snakes, enormous white ginseng roots being pickled in belljars full of Korean wine, and a random collection of deer antlers, dried reptiles and insects. Raw herbs are also sold at most marketplaces. In addition, Korean-style thera-

t'ang) and snake wine (*paem sul*) are commonly prescribed potions – albino snake for longevity, yellow python for a cure-all, and viper for neuralgia and tuberculosis. Dog meat soup (*posin t'ang*; *posin ha-da* means to build up one's strength) is also a very popular body rejuvenator, especially when it's prepared from the meat of white and black dogs. Many small shops and cafes specialize in these soups, but Westerners may find a more palatable tonic in an *insam ch'at chip*, a ginseng teahouse.

peutic pressure-point massage, *chi ap*, and acupuncture, *ch'im*, and a variety of other traditional healing techniques are still practiced throughout the country.

Some of the common ingredients used in prescriptions are iris root for feeblemindedness, snakeberry leaves to help regulate the menstrual cycle, and chrysanthemum roots to cure headaches. Not all of the antidotes are vegetarian, though. Snake meat soup (*paem*

Korean herb vendors display their medicinal wares in numerous colorful ways. <u>Left</u>, the window of a herb shop in Seoul. <u>Above</u>, an array of herb vats at Taegu.

Aromatic Teahouses: The cozy herb teahouse is usually identified by white, anthropomorphic ginseng roots painted on its door and by the pungent aroma of hot cinnamon and ginger tea. Inside the shop, belljars of dried herbs line the shelf. Although ginseng tea is the most popular, other homemade brews are served as well. There are, to name a few delicious concoctions, aromatic ginger tea (*saeng kang ch'a*) made with boiled and strained ginger root and raw sugar; *t'ang*, fresh white ginseng root blended with water and sugar; and porridges such as *chat chuk*, made of pine nuts, water, rice flour and salt or sugar to taste; and *kkae chuk*, toasted black sesame seeds, water, rice flour and salt or sugar. (Beware, however, of large heapings of sugar.)

Herbs are steeped in earthenware pots (metal is said to deplete herbal potency) over a low-burning *yont'an* (coal briquette) for at least an hour or two until an essence is thus extracted. Besides tasty teas and porridges, fresh fruit juices and fruits, such as sliced persimmons, strawberries and tangerines soaked in *soju* (25- to 50-percent proof drinking alcohol), are also served.

Panax Ginseng: Among the herbs in Korea, *panax ginseng*, referred to as *insam* in Korean, is by far the most popular. As far back as the 3rd millennium BC in China, herbal

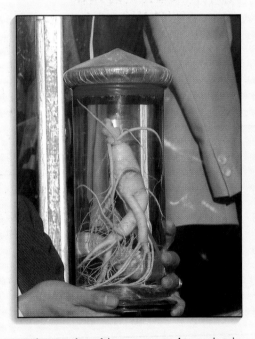

potions and poultices were used to maintain and restore the internal *um-yang* (i.e. the positive-negative, acid-base, male-female) forces to proper balance by stimulating or repressing either aspect. Ginseng, which originally grew wild along ravines and in the forests of Korea and Manchuria, was found to be bursting with *yang* energy. It became a vital ingredient used in a vast range of medications prescribed in the first Chinese pharmacology.

The exchange of medical knowledge with China encouraged trade in herbs. Ginseng flowed into China until the Koryo dynasty, when supplies began to diminish, and was exported during the Yi dynasty as a tribute to Chinese royalty. To boost the supply, ginseng cultivation was encouraged.

Ideal climatic conditions, especially between northern 36 degrees to 38 degrees latitudes, where an optimum mountain-forest simulated environment is maintained, have allowed the production of a cultivated root that is considered to be the standard.

Extreme care is administered in nurturing the root. In the preparation of *yakt'o* (soil for herbs), only a moderately rich mulch of deciduous chestnut or oak leaves is used. Hand-thatched mats are erected to shade red (*hong*). Approximately 60 percent of the best ginseng is selected for the red variety, which is further processed to preserve the potency of its chemical components.

Although panax ginseng is also cultivated in neighboring China, Russia and North Korea, only the Republic of Korea exports the product on a grand scale. Valued more precious than gold in ancient times, Korean ginseng today is still considered a costly commodity and is sold in the hanyak shops at varying rates, depending on the grade of the product. While white ginseng is readily accessible, only about one percent of the better-quality red ginseng is marketed domestically by the government Office of Monopoly (which also exclusively controls the production of all ginseng-related commodities).

If consumed regularly in small doses, scientists who have studied the substance claim the root will help stimulate the central nervous system. Larger doses, however, depress the nervous system by buffering out physical and chemical stress, and by promoting cell production, which counteracts anemia and hypertension. Ginseng thus reportedly increases physical and mental efficiency, and enhances gastrointestinal motility and tone. It is also a common Western notion that ginseng increases one's libido. The Koreans, however, rely on much more potent aphrodisiacs, such as powdered deer antlers.

Ginseng comes conveniently packaged in 20th-century products. For internal rejuvenation are pills, capsules, extracts, jellies, instant teas, soft drinks, jams, candies, chewing gums, and ironically, even cigarettes.

Left, perhaps nothing is more symbolic of Korea than preserved ginseng roots. Right, healthy eating at a 60th-birthday feast.

SEOUL

"If you have a horse, send it to Cheju Island; if you have a son, send him to Seoul." So an old Korean saying advises. Send a horse to Cheju Island where the grass is green and lush. Send a son to Seoul to go to school. Indeed, the city swarms with thousands of students attending its 18 universities and 15 colleges. Send a child to Seoul to get a job: all the head offices of any enterprise – commercial, financial, governmental – are in Seoul, home to one quarter of the country's population.

By government designation Seoul is officially a *t'ukpyol-si* or special city. Other provincial capitals are referred to as *chikhal-si*, or self-governing city, which entitles them to administer their affairs separate from the provincial government. Seoul is *the* central city and has been the capital for more than 5,000 years (the word *seoul* means capital), the eye, as it were, of the Korean vortex.

Centers of the vortex: Topographically, the city's center is wooded **Nam-san** (South Mountain), a 900-foot (270m) elevation that gazes across midtown at conically shaped **Pugak-san** (North Peak Mountain). Between these peaks sprawled the old walled city. The 10-mile (16-km) encircling wall made of earth and dressed stone is gone, but a few crumbling stretches on Pugak-san and Nam-san, and other restored patches that were rebuilt for tourist visibility, have survived. The original wall was pierced by nine gates. Five still stand, and the two largest – **Namdae-mun** (Great South Gate) and **Tongdae-mun** (Great East Gate) – are regal presences in the midst of the modern city's swirl. They are reminders of the capital as it was once laid out.

Some think the center of the city is **City Hall Plaza**, the fountain square bounded on the north by **City Hall**, on the south by the **Plaza Hotel**, on the east by the entrance to Ulchi-ro (one of the main east-west streets), and on the west by **Toksu Palace** (a remnant of the old dynasty that founded the city). Running under the plaza are two subway lines. Traffic running in and out of the square from three major arteries swings round the fountain; pedestrians descend underground to cross the square through its underpasses; and, if traffic allows, you can stand in the middle of the north-south street, **T'aep'yong no**, and look south to Namdae-mun and north to **Kwanghwa-mun** (Gate of Transformation by Light), the reconstructed gate in front of the 20th-century capitol building. This is City Hall Plaza – a link between the old and new.

Other centrists claim that the Kwanghwa-mun intersection is Seoul's center. This is the next crossing north of City Hall Plaza and it's dominated by a looming **statue of Yi Sun-sin**, Korea's great 16th-century naval hero.

From that intersection, T'aep'yong-no runs south, Sejong-no to the north, Sinmun-no west and Chong-no east – yes, the streets change name as they cross. Even more perplexing is that the Kwanghwa-mun intersection is not directly in front of the Kwanghwa-mun

Preceding pages: cherry blossoms in spring. **Left,** proud traditions. **Right,** downtown Seoul.

gate for which it is named – that's another long block north of here. People who believe that this intersection is *the* center of the city probably think so because it is the entrance to Chong-no, or Bell Street, the city's original main commercial street. When he established Seoul as the capital in 1394, Yi dynasty founder Yi Song-gye, whose royal name was T'aejo, hung a bell there. The bell was rung at dawn and dusk to signal the official opening and closing of the city gates. The bell hanging inside the Poshin-gak belfry at Chong-no intersection today was rebuilt in 1984 and is rung only on special holidays.

The governmental heart of the old walled city was **Kyongbok Palace** (Palace of Shining Happiness), which was T'aejo's residence and seat of power, and was used by him and his successors until 1592, when it was burned during the war with Japan. If you inquire more minutely, you will discover that Kyongbok's throne hall, the **Kunjong-jon** (Hall of Government by Restraint), rebuilt in 1867, was the very center of Taejo's governmental heart. Here the king sat to receive ministers ranged in orderly ranks before him, made judgements, and issued proclamations. The hall faces south down Sejong-no and once commanded an unobstructed view through Kwanghwa-mun to Namdaemun. In 1991, the government launched a 10-year project to restore the palace, rebuilding some buildings such as the **Kangnyongjon** (residence of the king) and **Kyotaejon** (residence of the queen), destroyed by the Japanese, and removing some pagodas which the Japanese built. Flanking the palace gate are two stone *haet'ae*; mythical animals from Korean lore, which have witnessed Seoul's changes and additions ever since they were carved and placed here in the 15th century to guard the old palace from fire.

Seoul chic: Many people think Seoul's real center today is modern **Myong-dong**, an area of narrow alleys that starts a 10-minute walk southeast from City Hall Plaza directly across from **Midopa Department Store**. Myong-dong's

National Folklore Museum, Kyongbok Palace.

main thoroughfare, a one-way street, is lined on both sides with swanky shops that sell chic clothes and accessories, and it ends at the top of a low hill before **Myong-dong Cathedral**.

Myong-dong alleyways come alive in the evening when they are crowded with after-work strollers window-shopping – "eye-shopping" in Korean – past the fancy displays of shoes and handbags, tailor-made suits and custom-made shirts, dresses in the latest fashions, handcrafted jewelry, and cosmetics.

Getting around: Administratively, Seoul is divided into 22 wards – *ku* – with each ku again segmented into various precincts – *dong*. A dong is an area of considerable size, but the term is often used simply to identify where you live or where you're going. People hoping to share a taxi ride, for example, stand at the side of the street shouting, "*Hannam-dong!*", "*Tonam-dong!*", "*Yaksu-dong!*" and other dongs at passing taxis.

Knowing the address of a particular house does not guarantee that you will find it – at least, not quickly. Addresses are given as such-and-such ku, ku-and-such-and-such dong, and a house number. And house numbers seldom follow in numerical sequence; rather, they are assigned according to when the house was built. Thus , all Koreans get a lot of practice in drawing maps

Only downtown, in fact, will you hear the names of certain streets used regularly. It's handy, however, to have some idea of which streets these are. The east-west streets include: **T'oegye-ro**, which runs east from Seoul railway station and follows the northern foot of Nam-san until it joins Ulchi-ro beyond Seoul stadium; **Ulchi-ro** ,which runs east from City Hall Plaza (west from City Hall Plaza runs another main artery, Seosomun-ro); **Chong-no**, which runs east from Kwanghwa-mun intersection to Tongdae-mun and beyond; **Sinmun-no**, which runs west to **Sodae-mun** (this is the West Gate, but no gate stands there now); and a block south of Kwanghwa-mun intersection is **Ch'onggyech'on**, which runs east in

the shadow of the elevated Samil-lo expressway.

The north–south streets are: **Namdaemun-no**, which curves northeast from Namdae-mun until it intersects Chong-no (where its name becomes An'gukdong-no); and **T'aep'yong-no**, which runs from Namdae-mun north to the Kwanghwa-mun intersection, where its name becomes **Sejong-no**. (A word to those who may be confused: The Chinese character for "road" is romanized to *-no*, *-ro*, or *-lo* according to the ending of the preceding word to reflect how it is properly pronounced.)

With increasing traffic congestion, however, the subway is the handiest means of transport in Seoul, with numerous lines. These lines connect to the national railroad lines to nearby cities such as Inch'on, Uijongbu and Suwon. Visitors will be happy to hear that signs and maps at subway stations are clearly marked in English, which makes doing the city underground relatively simple. Line No. 1 is marked coded red on subway maps and, predictably for the first subway line, begins at Seoul railway station. The first stop from here is City Hall, which brings you right out onto the city plaza and within easy reach of Toksu Palace, the Plaza, President, Westin Chosun and Lotte hotels, the British Embassy and the American Cultural Center.

Shoppers going to **Tongdae-mun Market** or movie-goers heading for the Hollywood, Piccadilly and Danseongsa theaters should get off at stops further down the line.

Virtuous longevity: For "modern" and exploratory openers, begin your tour of Seoul at the central and historical Toksu Palace (Palace of Virtuous Longevity), whose gate faces City Hall Plaza. Toksu is not the oldest of the surviving palaces – it was built as a villa toward the end of the 15th century – but it is important for its role at the unhappy end of the Yi dynasty. King Kojong, who was forced to abdicate in favor of his son Sunjong in 1907, lived in retirement and died here in 1919 after having seen his country annexed by the Japanese in 1910 and

Namdaemun-no, Seoul.

his family's dynasty snuffed out after 500 years.

Among the most conspicuous structures on the palace grounds, regularly open to the public, is a **statue of Sejong**, the great 15th-century king who commissioned scholars to develop a distinctive Korean writing system, different from the traditional Chinese characters, and officially promulgated in 1446. There are also a royal audience hall and two startlingly European-style stone buildings, with Ionic and Corinthian columns designed by an Englishman in 1909, which once housed the National Museum of Modern Art, now relocated south of the city. The palace grounds offer a welcome relief from the modern bustle, especially in the fall when its aisle of *gingko* trees are aflame in gold.

In front of Kyongbok Palace is the **National Museum**, the largest museum in the country, displaying over 100,000 items from ancient times through the Choson Kingdom period. These include Paekche tiles, Silla pottery, gilt Buddhas, Koryo celadons and Yi calligraphy and paintings. The building, once the central government offices, boasts the largest and finest collection of Korean art in the world. Inside the palace grounds is the **National Folklore Museum** of Korea, which houses artifacts of everyday use and dioramas showing how they were used.

About a block east of Kyongbok lies **Ch'angdok Palace** (Palace of Illustrious Virtue), built in 1405 as a detached palace, burned down in 1592, rebuilt in 1611, and used since then as the official residence of various Yi kings, including the last one Sunjong, until the latter's death in 1926. The best preserved of Seoul's palaces, Ch'angdok has a throne room hall surrounded by long drafty corridors leading past reception rooms furnished with heavy upholstered European chairs and sofas.

Nakson-jae, a small complex of buildings within Ch'angdok's grounds, is still the residence of descendants of the royal family: ensconced there are an elderly aunt of Sunjong; the wife of the last crown prince, Sunjong's son (who

Rush hour in Seoul, and National Museum.

never ruled), her son, and his wife. In the formal back gardens of Nakson-jae, a series of stair-stepped, granite-faced tiers planted with azaleas, it is possible to feel totally isolated from the sounds of modern Seoul.

Behind Ch'angdok lies the extensive acreage of **Piwon**, the Secret Garden, so called because it was formerly a private park for the royal family. In wooded and hilly terrain, footpaths meander past ponds and pavilions and over small bridges. The most picturesque of these sites is **Pando-ji** (Peninsula Pond) shaped like the outline of the Korean peninsula. From its shore extending out over the water stands a small, exquisite fan-shaped pavilion from which Injo, the 16th king, could cast a line for a bit of quiet fishing.

Piwon and portions of Ch'angdok Palace may be visited by joining one of several daily guided tours at the Piwon entrance. Nakson-jae is open to the public twice a year for royal ceremonies.

Honoring the sage: Strangely, the teachings of Confucius, who lived in China about 2,500 years ago, became more deeply rooted in Korea than in their native land, especially during the Choson dynasty (1392–1910), when they formed the basis of Korean society. Even today, many aspects of Confucianism live on in Korean society, such as the emphasis placed on education, respect for one's elders and ancestral worship.

Twice a year, in the second and eighth lunar months, many people still gather at the **Songgyun'gwan** shrine located on the grounds of **Songgyun'gwan University** to the northeast of Piwon. The Sokchon honors the spirit of Kongja (Confucius), the man whose principles formed the basis of government and code of behavior in Yi-dynasty Korea.

Buddhism's hub: The Confucian Yi court tried hard to extinguish the spirit of the Buddha throughout the country, but it failed miserably. Buddhist temples abound. City temples, though, are hardly places of quiet retreat. **Chogye-sa**, founded in 1910 and the headquarters of the official sect of Buddhism in Korea, is right downtown off **An'guk-**

Candid lanterns Chogye-sa.

dong-no. As the center of Buddhism in the country, it hums with activity, and on the occasion of Buddha's birthday, on the 8th day of the 4th lunar month, it becomes the hub – and hubbub – of Buddhist festivities in Korea.

Foreigners, tho Waeguk Saram: When the first Western foreigners appeared in significant numbers in Korea, they were not allowed to live within the city walls. In the 1880s, however, King Kojong permitted foreign missionaries, traders and legations to buy land in **Chong-dong**, just inside the western wall and behind and to the north of Toksu Palace. Many of the structures they built still stand and are still in use: the **Chong Dong Methodist Church**, which Korea's first modern president Syngman Rhee attended, and the **Ewha Girls' High School**, founded by Methodist missionaries.

All that remains of the Russian legation are the ruins of a white tower near the present Kyonghyang Shinmun (newspaper) building, but the American ambassador's residence, the British Embassy and an adjoining **Anglican Cathedral** are still in use. The cathedral is a graceful Italianate building, its square belfry visible from City Hall Plaza over the intervening walls. The British Embassy, a red-brick structure dating from the late 1800s, was given a US$6 million face-lift and expansion during the early 1990s.

The American ambassador's residence, behind walls and a heavy gate emblazoned with a red-white-and-blue American seal, is a low one-story Korean-style house. Its most recent renovation added a replica of P'osok-jong, a channel in the shape of an outsized abalone shell carved from stone.

In ancient times, a Silla king and his courtiers sat around the contours of the real P'osok-jong (in Kyongju), which was filled with running water. Through the channel floated wine cups. When a bobbing cup hesitated in front of king or courtier, it was his turn either to compose an impromptu poem or down the hesitant wine as a fine for lack of instant inspiration. A frequent result was a tipsy

Chogye-sa devotees, Buddha's birthday.

king and an equally tipsy court. It is not known if successive American ambassadors have continued this tradition.

Cruising It'aewon: It'aewon is an urban area that runs down from the southern flank of Nam-san and eastward from the fenced edge of **Yongsan Garrison**, the site of the headquarters of the Eighth U.S. Army.

The main thoroughfare that bisects the army base into north–south posts similarly bisects It'aewon into an uphill Nam-san side and a downhill-toward-the-Han-River side. Foreigners, not all of them Western, now occupy multistory apartment buildings higher up the mountain – a location that gives them a sweeping view of the **Han River** and mountain ridges south of the city.

Today, It'aewon merchants attract shoppers from civilian ranks as well, and visitors hail from all over the world. By day, bargain-hunters swarm through the hundreds of clothing, eel-skin, brassware, shoe and antique stores, where they stock up on competitive Korean-made goods.

But now It'aewon is a mere shadow of its former self. New department stores cast long shadows over the street stalls; by night, a midnight closing time, strictly enforced since its introduction in 1990 to combat drunk-driving and rising crime, has forced many of the small establishments to close down.

Market focus: The life of an urban villager, especially that of a housewife, revolves around the local market. Though Korean households have refrigerators these days, the housewife (or housemaid) still shops everyday for the basic ingredients.

Tonam-dong market is typical. This market lies along both sides of a roadway, which shoppers on foot share with bicycles, handcarts and an occasional motorcycle delivering goods.

The shops are more like open stalls because few of them have fixed doors. Sellers of one commodity tend to cluster together, so you'll find a neat segregation of products: fruit sellers are ranged in a double row down on roadway, then all the fish dealers, all the

A shop in Joongang market.

grain stores, all the vegetable stalls, all the umbrellas, all the dresses and skirts and so on.

The Tonam-dong market also includes a large two-story building, which on the first floor features open shops selling ready-to-wear clothes, household goods, accessories, cosmetics, kitchenware, plastic goods, textiles in a rainbow of colors, and a whirl of patterns.

Take the previous description of Tonam-dong market, multiply it by 50, and you have **Namdae-mun Sijang** (Great South Gate Market, located east of the gate itself); then take Namdae-mun Sijang, multiply it by another 50 and you have **Tongdae-mun Sijang** (Great East Gate Market), a large area that stretches south of Chong-no 5-ka and 6-ka.

The local pub: In the evening, another aspect of market life unfolds: the *sul-jip* or drinking house. A sul-jip should not be thought of as a bar, cocktail lounge, or beer hall, though those too certainly abound in the city. Rather, a sul-jip is a mini-restaurant and social hall. Indeed,

a stranger could pass through the market unaware that behind a tiny sliding door is a narrow room with four small oil drum tables, a cluster of tiny stools, and space for 16 customers sitting (and up to three standing at a counter).

Here the men who live and work in the market gather for a few after-work snacks and bowls of *makkolli* rice wine. A certain amount of makkolli-sipping leads to loud singing (accompanied by banging metal chopsticks against the edge of a table).

Labyrinthine arcades: Although the markets undoubtedly contain anything you'd want to buy and would find if you searched long enough, the city offers other somewhat more convenient if less colorful shopping places: modern department stores – Midopa on Namdae-mun-no and right next door to the Lotte. Just up the road is Sinsegye opposite the old Bank of Korea building. On Samil-lo, by Ch'onggyech on 2-ka, is the swish store, Printemps.

There are long streets of shops underground, along Chong-no and Ulchi-ro,

Department store in central Seoul.

and smaller and more pricey arcades underneath the Westin Chosun, Lotte and Plaza hotels. Above ground there is the **Nagwon Arcade** at Chong-no 2-ka and a four-block arcade running north-south from Chong-no 3-ka to T'oegye-ro 3-ka.

Underground labyrinthine shopping arcades lie invisibly beneath some of the city streets: the **Sogong Arcade** runs from under the corner of the Plaza Hotel, turns left at the Westin Hotel and continues between the Lotte and Midopa department stores to the edge of Myong-dong; the **Hoehyon Arcade** starts in front of the **Central Post Office** and runs up to T'oegye-ro; and other mini-arcades exist where pedestrian underpasses allow room for a few stores. These arcades offer clothes, jewelry, calculators, typewriters, cameras, and souvenir items, including reproductions of antique porcelain.

The time-honored location for antique dealers is **Insa-dong**, along a narrow street called by foreigners **Mary's Alley** that leads south from An'guk-

dong Rotary to **Pagoda Park**. (Who Mary was nobody remembers now.) Some shops offering fine Koryó celadon, Silla pottery and Yi furniture are still flourishing there, but many have fled to other sections of the city, notably to Ch'onggyech'on 8-ka. Ch'onggyech'-on is well worth a visit, even by someone who isn't in the market for antiques. It's actually part of **P'yonghwa Sijang** (Peace Market), itself an extension of Tongdae-mun Sijang.

Martial amusements: Age-old Korean martial arts such as *t'aekwon-do, hapki-do*, and *yu-do* are taught in schools and centers nationally, and these days around the world. A favorite t'aewon-do viewing spot is the **Yuksamdong World T'aewon-do Headquarters**, across the Third Han River Bridge.

Later Seoul: Since the Olympic "clean-up" of street traders, deemed by the city fathers to be unsightly and unhygienic, Seoul's pavements have certainly been easier to negotiate, but the city has lost some of its spontaneous charm. Amid the rising forests of multi-story apartment complexes south of the river, you can find, lit at night by carbide flames, the ubiquitous handcarts loaded with tangerines and chewing gum, dried cuttlefish and peanuts.

And even here the *yont'an* man pulls his cartload of coal briquettes through the streets to deliver a family's household heating fuel supply.

In contrast to the older residential sections of Seoul on the north side of the river, the old neighborhoods of diverging alleyways, the southern section of the city, spreading out from the foot of bridges newly constructed across the Han, are carefully grid-ironed, their streets ruled into right angles.

Here dwellers buy everyday necessities in "proper" stores – modern supermarkets where onions come prepackaged in plastic bags. To some, the beige and gray complexes (**Chamsil, Hyondae, Yongdong, Yoido**) lack in color and charm; yet, even they offer a kind of beauty, a beauty revealed at night by a drive eastwards along the north bank of the Han River from the First Bridge.

Left, Seoul Tower. **Right**, going fishing: Han River shore.

BEYOND THE SEOUL AREA

Beyond Seoul's secure city walls there are numerous day outings away from the hustle of urban life. Stroll down to any bus, subway or train terminal, set off in virtually any direction from Seoul, and you'll be amazed at the classical intrigues which await only minutes outside this sprawling city.

Namhansan-song, the South Han Mountain Fortress, is a popular weekend hiking area about 30 kilometers (20 mi) southeast of Seoul proper. This grand highland redoubt – with 8 kilometers (5 mi) of stone walls – was originally built about 2,000 years ago during Korea's Paekche dynasty. Most of the fort's now-visible structures, however, date to the 17th and 18th centuries, when the fortress served Yi kings of that period as a retreat from invading Chinese armies. In 1637, Namhansan-song was the site, following a six-week-long siege, where King Injo, the 16th Yi monarch, surrendered himself, some 14,000 of his men, and in the end, Korea, to a huge Manchu invasion force.

This spectacular place is located just east of **Songnam**, and may be reached via National Route 3 (en route to Kwangju), or through Songnam off the Seoul-Pusan Expressway.

Pukhansan-song, the North Han Mountain Fortress and Namhansan-song, are the two major ancient fortresses in the Seoul area. This one, similar in design and setting to Namhansan-song, is located above the sprawling northeast suburbs of Seoul along the high ridges of **Pukhan Mountain**.

Pukhansan-song was first built during the early Paekche period and at various times fell into martial disuse. Following severe attacks during the 16th century by armies of Ch'ing China, the Yi King Sukjong refurbished its battlements. These same walls were partially destroyed during the Korean War, but have since been restored to honor their historic importance. A neat village has bloomed alongside a stream in the cra-

ter-like center of the fortress, and meadows and small forests on its less-populated fringes are favored picnic sites. On the road back to Seoul, if you take the northern access highway, look carefully to your left and right. You may see shamanistic spirit posts (a rarity these days) peeking out at you through the brush and pines.

Gambling: Thousands of miles away from country idylls, but nevertheless a lovely spot from which to view Seoul over a proper drink, is the well-known **Walker Hill Resort** complex. This nightlife area of Las Vegas-style revues, gambling (in the **Sheraton Walker Hill**), and resort amenities is located above Seoul's eastern suburbs and overlooks a picturesque bend in the Han River. From Walker Hill's glittering lounges and gardens, you can see Seoul's city lights twinkling in the urban west. Walker Hill was named after Gen. Walton H. Walker, former commander of the U.S. Eighth Army and killed in a traffic mishap during the Korean War.

Kwangnung: The impressive Confucian-style burial tombs of King Sejo (1456–1468), the 7th Yi king, and his wife, Queen Yun Chon-hi, are probably the most aesthetically and idyllically located tombs in the Seoul area. These monumental mounds are located about 30 kilometers (20 mi) northeast of central Seoul and just past Uijongbu (a town and military camp made famous in the American movie and television serial *M*A*S*H).* The tombs are hidden in a forest of old trees, which shade trickling streams and wide greens ideal for a picnic.

Honnung and Honinnung: These tombs of the 3rd and 24th Yi kings lie in the southeast skirts of Seoul, in Naekokdong and near a green belt area where melons, strawberries, eggplant, peppers, corn and rice are cultivated. In late spring, summer and autumn, shady fruit stands are set up in fields so people can sit and enjoy refreshing breezes, sunshine and fresh-from-the-earth fruit before hiking up to the nearby Honnung, the tombs of King T'aejong (1367–1422) and Queen Wonkyong (1364–1420), and Innung, the tombs of King Sunjo (1790–

1834) and Queen Sunwon (1789–1837). All the tombs are guarded by granite statues and by fantastic animal sentries. If you are in Korea on 8 May, you may want to attend a *chesa* (ancestor worship) ceremony conducted annually at Honnung by Yi dynasty descendants.

Ceramics: The soulful pottery kilns of two of Korea's finest potters are about 70 kilometers (40 mi) south of Seoul near **Ich'on** (also just north of National Highway 4). In **Sukwang-ni, Sindungmyon**, a couple of miles north of Ich'on proper, you can observe Koryo celadons being created by ceramics master Yu Kun-hung, or you can marvel at Ahn Dong-o's Yi-dynasty whiteware as they're pulled hot from his traditional kilns. These gentlemen's fine work can be purchased on the spot or in prominent ceramic art galleries in Seoul. At the other end of the potting spectrum, you will find, here and there in the great Ich'on area, row upon row of the ubiquitous shiny, brown, tall and oblong *kimch'i* pots. These utilitarian wares are hand-thrown and fired in old adobe huts.

A morning excursion 45 kilometers (28 mi) south of Seoul to the **Korean Folk Village** near Suwon will give you a full day to tour the 240 homes, shops and other attractions in this authentically rendered Yi-dynasty village. Visit ceramic and bamboo shops, drink rice wines in a wayside tavern, then join the staged wedding procession of a traditionally costumed (and transported via palanquin) bride and groom, who are trailed by a colorful, whirling farmers' dance band. Even in a day you may not be able to view all the fascinating exhibits in this sprawling museum.

If you have time, consider one of the following day-trips which involve longer distances and time, but which provide experiences equal to the worthy effort.

Suwon, the capital of **Kyonggi Province**, is an old fortress-city 50 kilometers (30 mi) south of Seoul in the vicinity of **Mt. Paltal**. Suwon's name, which means "water-source" or "water-field," derives from its location in an area which was traditionally known for its fine artesian wells of water.

Traditional tombsite guardians, Taenung.

These days, Suwon is renowned for its recently restored castle walls and support structures, and – in a tastier realm – for its luscious strawberries (called *ttalgi* in Korean). The city is also famous for its *kalbi*, or barbecued short ribs, but it's the strawberries – in late spring through summer – that come to most Korean minds when you mention the word Suwon.

King Chongjo wanted to move the Korean capital from Seoul to the Suwon site in the 18th century, but because of various personal and political problems, he was never able to accomplish that kingly feat.

Chongjo created a beautiful fortified city here – complete with proper parapets and embrasures, floodgates, observation platforms and domes, parade grounds, command bunkers, cannon stands and an archery range. Chongjo's original fortress, known as the "Flower Fortress," was heavily damaged by the weather and by bombing during the Korean War, but in 1975 the Korean government undertook a major restoration of his dream city. The project took nearly half a decade and cost several millions of dollars.

One particularly lovely spot near the North Gate, **Changan-mun**, is a strikingly landscaped reflecting pond, **Yong-yon**, which sits below an octagonal moon-watching pavilion called **Pang-hwasuryu-jong**.

This meditative spot was ordered to be created by the aesthetically inclined King Chongjo when he initiated his Suwon fortress-city master plan in 1794. These days it's a gem of a place much-favored by neighborhood *haraboji* (grandfathers), who sit inside its gabled cupola lighting long-stemmed pipes, drinking sweet rice wine, and bouncing patriarchal thoughts off nearby castle walls. The whole classical effect is officially labeled "The Northern Turret."

Sogni-san National Park, a mountain retreat in North Ch'ungch'ong province, is superb any time of the year, but is most favored by discriminating Korean weekenders in the autumn, when its trees are aflame with color. Oaks,

Suwon's southside city gate.

maples and gingkos try to outdo each other in their autumnal radiance. As one romantic Korean travel writer once wrote of Sogni-san: "The tender green for spring, abundance of forests for summer, yellow leaves for autumn, and snow for winter – all deserve appreciation."

Indeed, since ancient times Sogni has been a preferred resort area, and appropriately, the word *sogni* means "escape from the vulgar." To achieve this Sogni escape, travel from Seoul to the city of **Taechon** by train, then transfer by bus or car through **Okch'on** to the Sogni area. Alternatively, you can also motor directly by car or bus from Seoul via Ch'ongju city. It's about a three-hour motorcar journey one-way, longer if you are rubbernecking and driving.

Sogni-dong is a mountain village famous for the semi-wild tree-mushrooms cultivated in this area and sold in roadside stands. Seoulites who know try to arrive in Sogni village at lunchtime, when they can enjoy a fabled Sogni mushroom lunch. Such a lunch can feature as many as six completely different mushroom dishes served with a dizzying array of side dishes, kimch'i and rice. Be sure to buy a bag of these tender air-dried morsels for future munchings at home.

Biggest Buddha: Following this mushroom overdose, proceed uphill to Sognisan's biggest attraction, **Popju-sa**, a large temple complex dominated by a massive Miruk Buddha of the Future, fashioned of modern poured cement. This 27-meter-high (88-ft) image, completed in 1964, is often declared by the informed tour guides as the biggest Buddha in Korea.

This sprawling temple complex was first built at the base of Mt. Sogni in the 6th century, shortly after Buddhism had been carried into Korea from China. Records note that work began in 553 during the 14th year in the reign of the Silla king Chinhung.

The original founder and spiritual master was the high priest Uisang, who had returned home from studies in India. Uisang contributed several Buddhist books – many of them scriptural – to Popju-sa's first library.

Remnants of this favored temple's days of spiritual grandeur can be found on all parts of the compound.

Consider for practical openers the famed **Ch'olhwak**, a massive iron rice pot, which was cast in 720 during the reign of Silla king Songdong, when some 3,000 priests were living – and eating – here.

This grand mass facility is 1.2 meters (4 ft) high, 2.7 meters (9 ft) in diameter, and 10.8 meters (35 ft) in circumference. These days you'll find perhaps only a small proportion of that number of gray-robed, sutra-chanting monks here, so the pot's former utilitarian purpose is no longer present.

Other Popju-sa curiosities include a large *deva* lantern surrounded with relief *bodhisattva*, a second stone lantern supported by two carved lions, and, outside the temple, a large "ablution trough" carved in the shape of a lotus. To the left side of the main entrance you'll also find a huge boulder that has come to life with a serene Buddha sculpted into a wide and flat facade.

Sogni-san National Park.

242

INCH'ON

Inch'on – which until the 1880s was a fishing village called Chemulp'o – was for a long time the only Korean place foreigners were allowed to visit.

Today, It is a booming harbor and Korea's fourth largest city. The number of trading ships calling at Inch'on has increased with every passing year, and consequently the 39-kilometers (24-mi) stretch between Seoul proper and the port of Inch'on has become the most important sea, road and rail supply route in Korea.

In the current century, Inch'on has become most well-known as the place where Gen. Douglas MacArthur, commander of US Pacific forces, directed a brilliant amphibious landing which turned the bitter Korean War around for South Korea and its allies.

That landing began at dawn on 15 September 1950. Historian David Rees writes in his important book, *Korea: The Limited War,* that "the successive objectives of the operation called for the neutralization of Wolmi-do, the island controlling Inch'on harbor, a landing in the city, seizure of Kimpo Airfield, and the capture of Seoul." Despite fierce objections from his subordinates, MacArthur's strategy proved to have that winning element of surprise.

Freedom Hill looms over an earnest seaport abustle with international trade. Atop the hill, jaunty in sculpted khakis, is a 10-meter-high (32-ft) statue of Gen. MacArthur, gripping a pair of binoculars in his right hand.

The fastest and easiest way to get to Freedom Hill is to take the Seoul Subway train due west through industrial suburbs and rice fields that sprawl alternately between Seoul and the setting sun. Once you arrive at Inch'on-dong station, take a cab or hike up to Freedom Hill above this town of steep streets and endless ocean terminals.

The ocean view from up there is overtly industrial, but sea breezes are crisp, and besides the MacArthur statue, you'll find a whitewashed replica of the Statue of Liberty.

Fishermen on Inch'on.

SORAK-SAN NATIONAL PARK

Sorak-san, the Snow Peak Mountain, is now more formally known as the **Sorak-san National Park**. It is not just a lone mountain top, but actually a series of peaks in the midsection of the spectacular **Taebaek Sanmaek**, or Great White Range, Korea's most prominent geographical region.

Inje, the renowned gateway to inner Sorak, is a good place to begin. En route you'll encounter (at **Chang Su Dae**) numerous nature trails (abloom in the spring and ablaze in the fall), veil-like waterfalls, red-bellied frogs, creeks and, at **Osaek Yaksu**, mineral water springs famed for their therapeutic properties. Some travelers like to pause at Chang Su Dae and hike up to the Taesung waterfalls, then upward to **Paekdam-sa**, a charming Buddhist temple smack in the interior of Inner Sorak. Further east on the Han'gye Pass road, at the very top of this spectacular pass, is yet another trek – this one all the way to the top of Sorak's supreme peak, **Taechon-bong** – the third-highest mountain in Korea at 1,708 meters (5,604 ft). You can navigate onward and enter the Sorak-dong resort complex by its back door. The Osaek Yaksu medicinal springs at the far east end of the Han'gye Pass road are well worth a stop and the recuperative soak.

Before you head into the bush, stroll up the main flagstoned and fir-lined path which leads to **Sinhung-sa**, an ancient temple originally built near its present location in AD 652. The first Sinhung-sa, then called **Hyungsong-sa**, or the Temple of Zen Buddhism, was destroyed by a forest fire in 707, rebuilt in 710, burned again in 1645, rebuilt a third time at its present location in 1648.

Just before reaching the actual temple compound is a neatly kept and fenced-in cemetery full of unusual bell-shaped tombstones, erected to honor former illustrious Zen monks who spent much time meditating in this area.

A remote temple accessible only by foot.

In the temple itself, which sits on a pleasant little bluff with a superb view of the surrounding mountains, you'll pass through lattice doors carved and painted with a floral motif. You'll then come eye-to-eye with a standard **Amit's Buddha**, flanked by Kwanseum and Taiseiji *bodhisattva*.

Next, proceed up this spiritual path to the **Kejo Hermitage**, about three kilometers up along a singing stream bed. Kejo Hermitage, a subsidiary of the mother Sinhung Temple, is partially built into a granite cave at the base of **Ulsan-bawi**, a spectacular granite formation that dominates this part of the Sorak area. Like much of Sorak, and like the famous **Diamond Mountains** across the DMZ in North Korea, Ulsan-bawi's face is rich with anthropomorphic images. Indeed, about halfway up the Kejo Hermitage, an enterprising fellow with a high-powered telescope sells lingering peeks at one particularly erotic formation at Ulsan-bawi's midsection.

Fronting the Kejo Hermitage and Ulsan-bawi is another geologic curiosity that has become a major tourist attraction over the years. This is the famed **Rocking Rock**, a massive boulder which rocks back and forth in its secure place when given a solid nudge. Being photographed in front of this tipsy ball of granite is a touristic must.

If you enjoyed your ramble to the Rocking Rock, then you're ready for a more challenging trek – this time to the **Kumgang Cave** above the aforementioned Pison-dae (Flying Fairy Peak).

From this restful camp at the base of Pison-dae, devoted Buddhist pilgrims head up a smaller path to Kumgang Cave, which is located near the top of Pison-dae and requires a serious genuflection to exercise.

After negotiating 649 stairs to reach this charming cave-shrine, your heart will be pounding in your head, but the extraordinary view from up here – and from a halfway-point promontory – will be your earthly reward.

Inside the cave is a small Buddha surrounded by burning candles, incense and food offerings.

Rocking Rock.

THE EAST COAST

Snow country and a ski resort. Highland hot springs overlooking rice terraces and pine forests. The bluest waters and whitest sand beaches in Korea. Stalactite- and stalagmite-filled caverns.

At the southern end of Korea's East Coast are **P'ohang** and **Ulsan**, recently created industrial cities where steel, automobiles and ships are manufactured at astonishing production rates. To the north – along postcard-perfect pine bluffs, inland lagoons, and cabana-dotted beaches – are seaside retreats.

You can begin your tour of the East Coast at several points up and down the East Sea, but probably the most central place to use as pivot point for travel is Kangnung, the major city in east **Kangwon Province**, reached by train or bus. The most interesting way to make the 230-kilometer (140-mi) journey from Seoul is by private car. Once you get into more mountainous areas, notice the unusual pointy-topped silos of Korean design, bright ears of corn drying along rooftops, and hops plantations which are distinguished by the lacy network of string trellises built to support these twining vines, from which *maekju* (beer) is made.

Land of 10,000 Buddhas: One road-to-Kangnung detour you must make is just beyond little **Chinbu** village, about 40 kilometers (25 mi) west of Kangnung. This sidetrip carries you along paved and dirt roads to **Mt. Odae National Park**, a charming mountain area and the location of two of Korea's most well-known temple complexes, **Woljong-sa** and **Sangwon-sa**. The road leading to 1,563-meter-high (5,128-ft) **Odae-san** is literally dotted with tiny hermitages, Zen meditation niches, and other impressive remnants of Buddhism which date to the 7th century and Korea's impressive Silla dynasty.

Woljong-sa, which sits on the southern fringe of Odae-san about 8 kilometers (5 mi) off the expressway, is a sprawling temple complex distinguished by a su-

perb nine-story octagonal pagoda and an unusual kneeling Buddha sculpture. The tiered pagoda, which rises 15 meters (50 ft), is capped with a sculpted lotus blossom and a bronze finial of intricate design; the kneeling Buddha, meanwhile, has well-weathered features, and (because of an unusual cap he's wearing) looks very much like a European tin soldier.

Korean-style schussing: The Taekwallyong mountain region is where Korea's most modern and well-equipped ski resort is located. Throughout the **Taekwallyong** area are various ski spots with names such as Talpanje, Chirmae and Third Slope. Most are located in the vicinity of a small town called **Hwoenggye**, but the newest and favorite slopes have been developed in a place called **Yongpyong**, or **Dragon Valley**. The Dragon Valley Ski Resort sprawls over 50 acres and is equipped with chairlift systems, snow-making machines, a ski school, ski rental facilities, and even lighting facilities for ambitious night skiing.

Monks at Sangwon-sa, Odae-san.

Kangnung is a sleepy seaside town rich in traditional architecture and hospitable people, the key trading and terminal point in this part of Korea.

The Kangnung area abounds with precious distractions worth touring, but perhaps the most prominent are:

• A classical Confucian academy and shrine – **Hyangkyo** and **Taesungjon** – in the northwest suburbs of Kangnung on the grounds of the Myungnyun middle and high schools. This hilltop structure, which was built in 1313, destroyed by fire in 1403, then rebuilt in 1413, has low, brooding rooflines and tapering colonnades typical of Koryo dynasty structures in other parts of Korea.

• **Kyongp'o-dae Lake** and Kyongp'o-dae Beach. This resort just a few miles north of Kangnung has long been a popular Korean recreational spa. Waters off Kyongp'o-dae Beach are often busy with zig-zagging speedboats and sailing craft, and on shore are numerous tented seafood restaurants.

Black Bamboo Shrine: Another fine Confucian place, this one just a little

way north of Kangnung, is **Ojuk-hon** (Black Bamboo Shrine), birthplace of the prominent Confucian scholar-statesman-poet Yi I (1536–1584). Yi I, more popularly known by his pen name Yulgok (Valley of Chestnuts), was one of a group of Neo-Confucianists who became powerful in the 16th century.

A merciful apparition: On Wontongp'ojon's sea side, dominating all natural and man-made items in the area, is a 15-meter-high (49-ft) high white-granite statue of Buddhism's bodhisattva of Mercy, known in Korea as the goddess **Kwanseum-posal**, in China as Kwan Yin, and in India as Avalokitesvara (though Avalokitesvara is an earlier male counterpart). This particular goddess of mercy faces the southeast atop a 2-meter-tall (6-ft) pedestal of granite and open lotus blossom.

Continue north past **Uisang-dae** and its tiny pink lighthouse to **Sokch'o** town. Private and government enterprise have developed several sand beach areas north of Sokch'o, but the all-time favorite languishing spot is **Hwajinp'o Beach**, about halfway between Sokch'o and the DMZ (demilitarized zone). Korea's presidents have traditionally maintained summer villas here. Beyond Sokch'o are several quaint fishing villages, exotic inland lagoons quackingly alive with fish and waterfowl, and broad, dune-like beaches.

Not to miss: Mentioned below are some of the sights and sites along the southeast coast the visitor should not miss.

• The strangely beautiful **Songnyu Cave**: Just south and then inland from **Uljin** town, Songnyu-gul, which is actually a proper limestone cavern adrip with bizarre stalactites and stalagmites, is, as one tour leader describes it, "a spelunker's delight."

The easiest way to get there if you don't have a car of your own is to catch a local bus from Uljin and travel 8 kilometers (5 mi) south to the Songnyu-gul bus stop. From there the cavern is about a 2-kilometer (1.2-mi) walk west on a dirt path or road across attractive rice paddies and along a curving riverbank.

Kwanseum-posal (Bodhisattva of Mercy), Naksan Temple.

• **The Paegam Hot Springs**: Approximately 30 kilometers (20 mi) south of Uljin is **P'yonghae**, a quiet farming town where you can book a taxi or chance a bus to Korea's picturesque **Paegam** mountain and hot springs. We say chance a bus, because the irregular buses that crawl up to the Paegam springs on a rocky and dusty road through beautiful highland country are invariably overcrowded with people, animals and domestic goods.

• **Juwang Mountains**: Korea hands who like to travel and embark on a get-away-from-it-all journey head to the **Mt. Juwang National Park** due west of Yongdong and southeast of Andong via Chongsong. This 720-meter-high (2,362-ft) East Coast mountain in north Kyongsang Province can usually be reached only by country bus; but according to visitors who have made the effort to get there, the trip is well worth the bouncing hassle.

• **P'ohang**: At the southern end of your East Coast adventure looms P'ohang, a seaport and resort area that since 1968 has been the apple of Korea's industrial eye. This is because P'ohang is the location of the model P'ohang Iron and Steel Company (POSCO), Korea's successful producer of industrial steel and its by-products.

If you're interested, tours can be arranged by contacting the Korea National Tourism Corporation or the POSCO public relations office.

• **Ullung-do**: Few foreigners venture out to this island 270 kilometers (170 mi) northeast of P'ohang. Indeed, because of its location, Ullung-do is one of Korea's best-kept secrets. But, look out – the word is getting around as tourism to this island is now being promoted by the national government.

Some of the best sights and travel experiences in Korea are on this island, which is about halfway between Korea and Japan (and is the farthest east one can go and still be in Korea). Embark on the *Han II Ho* speedboat ferry in P'ohang, and six hours later you'll be strolling into **To-dong** town on Ullung-do's southeast coast.

Blue-green Ullung-do.

THE WEST COAST

Korea's jagged West Coast, cut by the whimsical Yellow Sea, is dotted with myriad peninsula islets floating offshore, and bordered by sandy beaches overlooking quiet pine glens. Along this coast, village fishermen and seasonal beach-goers regulate their activities according to tidal changes, because the tide differential is so extreme. In certain areas at low tide, the Yellow Sea exposes vast mud flats 5 meters (17 ft) to 7 meters (25 ft) offshore – a distance second in tide extremes only to the Bay of Fundy in Canada's Nova Scotia.

Travellers en-route to the coast may find **Onyang**, about 18 kilometres (11 mi) west of Ch'on-an on Highway 21, to be a refreshing stop along the way. A hot spring and **Hyonch'ungsa Shrine**, which is dedicated to Korea's great 16th-century naval hero, Admiral Yi Sun-sin, have long attracted visitors, but since the **Onyang Folk Museum** in **Kongok-ni** opened in 1978, tourist traffic to Onyang has increased. Touted as having the best all-around collection of Korean folk art in the world, the privately-owned Onyang Folk Museum boasts over 7,000 traditional Korean folk articles – only a portion of the vast collection Kim Won-dae has accumulated over the past two decades.

Nature lovers may flee to popular **Mallip'o Beach** on the western tip of a peninsula, which flares into the Yellow Sea like a snarling dragon. Just north of Mallip'o Beach lies **Ch'ollip'o**, another kind of haven for flora and for people fond of flora. On a 200-acre sanctuary, more than 7,000 varieties of plants, almost exclusively of temperate climates, thrive on a stable climate, the longer springs and autumns in this region.

Veteran westerners in Korea have long favoured the West Coast's Taech'on Beach, or **Taech'on-dae**, as a spring-through-fall resort haven. This fun spot is about 14 kilometres (9 mi) from the town of Taech'on, and is reached by bus or train from Seoul. Taech'on.

The Beach (Taech'on to the locals) is unofficially divided into two sectors – a northern stretch called KB, or the "Korean Beach," and a southern stretch called the "Foreigners' Beach." This was originally a Christian missionaries' resort. The Korean Beach – where discos and wine houses coexist with sleepy fishermen's huts – is a nonstop boogie scene during the peak summer season, but the Foreigners' Beach maintains an air of residential dignity.

Paekche capitals: Further inland from Taech'on, away from frolicking surf and missionary resorts, lie the ancient towns of **Kongju** and **Puyo**. Kongju was once the capital of the Paekche Kingdom until the capital was moved south to Puyo. Both Kongju and Puyo have retained the limelight in the 20th century because of the Paekche relics which have recently been excavated in the central and southeastern provinces.

Paekche historical remains abound in Puyo and are displayed in the **Puyo National Museum**. Prehistoric stoneware vessels, shamanistic instruments, gilt-bronze and stone Buddhist statues, gold and jade ornaments and other treasures attest to the development and excellence of Paekche craftsmen, who were influenced by central Asian and Chinese artists.

Paekche legacy extends itself beyond the museum. Along the serene Kum River at **Paengma-gang** (White Horse River), remnants of the grandeur and the fateful fall of the Paekche kingdom of some 1,300 years ago are preserved. You can have a picnic on the flat rock (Nan-sok, or Warm Rock) on the river bank at **Saja**, just as the Paekche kings once did. On the opposite side of the river is the picturesque **Nakhwa-am** (Rock of the Falling Flowers) bluff with a pavilion on its brow.

From these Paekche visions, head southeast along Highway 23 to Kwanch'ok Temple outside of Nonsan.

Unjin Miruk: As you scale up the stone steps on the P'anya hillside to **Kwanch'ok-sa** (Temple of the Candlelights), all the superlative descriptions you've ever heard regarding the **Unjin**

Papering a screen, Chonju.

Miruk – the 1,000-year-old, largest standing stone Buddha in Korea – stir visitors with anticipation.

Curiosity is piqued when, at the top of a flight of stairs, your first glance at the Unjin Miruk is through the clear, horizontal window of the temple (if the temple doors are open). All you can see of the Buddha of the Future is its face – its eyes peering back at visitors through the holy sanctum.

Chonju, which is 93 kilometres (58 mi) south of Seoul, is the provincial capital of Chollapuk-do. It is the ancestral home of the descendants of Yi Songgye, founder of the Yi dynasty, and is famous for its paper products (fans, umbrellas and proper papers), *pi pim pap*, and food in general.

Paper-making was introduced to Korea by the Chinese about 1,000 years ago. The Koreans, however, became so adept at this fine craft that both Chinese and Japanese calligraphers came to favour Korean papers over their own.

Technology has encroached on the handmade paper-making industry, but

in Chonju, villagers still actively perpetuate this tradition in their homes and in makeshift factories. The sound of new paper pulps swishing in water drifts out of windows, and in many backyards white sheets of fresh paper hang like drying laundry.

The entire process may be observed at Oh Dong-ho's factory at the end of Chonju's main street – just before a small bridge and to the left along a red brick wall.

Horse ears and frozen fairies: The winding road on to **Mai-san** (Horse Ears Mountain) is a joyful cruise in its paved condition. There are charming and classical sights at nearly every highway turn. Just five minutes outside of Chonju, for example, you will see on the left a series of hills covered with hundreds of traditional Korean grave mounds. This is an unusually crowded pre-Christian-style cemetery.

The famous Mai-san "Horse Ears" are not visible until you get quite close to Chinan town. There, over to the right yonder, they spring up from behind a large knoll above a meandering riverbed. Once you reach Mai-san, your expedition has just begun.

The hike through narrow **Chonghwang Pass** between the two horse ears is a stair-climbing, heart-thumping rise up 132 steps. Up there, near **Hwaom Cave**, you can rest a while and enjoy a panoramic view of Chinan and environs. Continue into a small valley on the south side of the ears, veer to the right (while negotiating another 181 steps in segments) and you will come to one of the most bizarre Buddhist temples in Korea. Built by the hermit monk Yi Kap-yong, this **T'ap-sa** (Pagoda Temple) religious site is a collection of stone pagodas, some of them 9 meters (30 ft) high. All were built without mortar and have stood in surrealistic splendor in this narrow valley since the early part of this century.

Kumsan-sa (Gold Mountain Temple), on the western slope of **Moak-san**, is reputedly the most beautiful temple in **Chollapuk-do**. It is about 34 kilometers (21 mi) southwest of Chonju. The complex was burned during the 1592 **Unjin Miruk statue.**

Hideyoshi invasion, then finally rebuilt in the early 17th century.

Today, its main hall, **Miruk-jon**, stands three stories high, making Kumsan-sa the tallest temple in Korea. This spaciousness is devoted to housing 10 designated cultural assets from Silla, Paekche, and Koryo periods. Miruk-jon, a worship hall for the god Avalokitesvara, is one of these 10 priceless treasures.

Inside Miruk-jon, a huge golden Maitreya (Buddha of the Future) stands 12 meters (39 ft) tall, holding a red lotus blossom in its left palm. It is flanked by two crowned bodhisattvas, Taemyosang and Pophwarim. Below the statues, behind the wooden grill, a stairway leads down to the Matreya's feet. Devotees and visitors alike can walk down the steps to kiss the candlelit Maitreya's feet and make an offering.

Kwangju, the ancient provincial capital of **Chollanam-do**, is a low-key city where at night, in many areas of the central city, vehicular traffic ceases and streets become pedestrian malls busy with strolling people engaged in people-watching or even shopping. More often than not, these strolling people also eat. In fact, Kwangju competes with Chonju for honours such as "best food in Korea" and "the most food served in Korea." The country's best rice wine is served here.

Mudung (Peerless Mountain) hovers like a guardian over Kwangju. A resort area has been created at its base among acacia trees and beside a whispering stream. Along Mudung's right flank are two factory buildings, which are used for tea production during spring and autumn tea-harvesting seasons.

The two-story **Kwangju Museum** was built to house Yuan dynasty booty that was discovered in a sunken 600-year-old Chinese ship, in the Yellow Sea in 1976. This archaeological find is exhibited on the ground floor gallery.

Upstairs on the second floor is a gallery of Cholla treasures, which includes 11th- to 14th-century bronze Buddha bells, Yi dynasty scroll paintings, and fine white porcelain.

Pagodas of Yi Kap-yong, Mai-san.

THE SOUTH

In 1592, the Japanese warlord Toyotomi Hideyoshi dispatched 150,000 troops to begin an ambitious assault on the Chinese empire. Korea had the bad fortune of being in the way and of being loyal to China. When the Korean government refused to grant Japan free access across its frontiers, the Japanese fought their way through. After six years of war, they finally retreated, failing to conquer China, but thoroughly devastating Korea. Thousands of Koreans were killed or taken to Japan as slaves, vast tracts of crucial farmland razed, the country's social order left in shambles, and much of Korea's great cultural legacy destroyed or stolen.

Taegu: The logical starting point for a swing through Korea's southern crescent area is **Taegu**, capital of North Kyong-sang Province. Taegu serves as a clearing house for a variety of produce harvested in this agriculturally rich province and it is an industrial center as well. It is a uniquely Korean compromise between urban and rural extremes: big enough to offer good hotels, restaurants and contemporary entertainment, yet small enough to retain a relaxed ambiance that is all but lost in Seoul or Pusan. Traditionally-styled clothing is still very much in evidence, especially (for no apparent reason) in the environs of **Talsong**, an earthwork fortress dating back to the prehistoric Sam-Han era. The fort is now a popular park, complete with a small zoo.

Yak-chong Kol-mok, "medicine alley," is the site of one of Taegu's more notable sensory delights. The street is a center for wholesale purveyors of traditional medicines.

Taegu also has its own brand of nightlife which, if lacking the polish of posher establishments in Seoul, is well-endowed with enthusiasm. Most afterhours partying in Taegu is centralized in several blocks near the "old station" at the center of town. A spirited confusion of side alley vendors, eclectic shop

Many of the original city gates still remain.

fronts, nightclub bands, band throngs intent on entertaining themselves.

For tamer daylight diversions, there is **Su-song Reservoir** on the southern outskirts of the city. In winter, the reservoir's ice is crowded with skaters.

Taegu has several other recreational areas: **Tong Chon Resort** and **Mang-wuli Park** are out past the train station, on the Naktong River where the Communist attack that began the Korean War was finally halted. **Ap-san Park** includes a cable car ride up to the summit of **Ap-san** for a panoramic view of the Taegu plain. Near the old train station is Taegu's small reconstructions of old government buildings. The original structures were built in 1601 as part of a complex of administrative buildings, which remained in use until 1965.

The **Sobuju-c'ha-jang** (West Depot) will get you to **Yong-yon-sa**, a tiny temple that is perched high in the mountains with an exquisite set of guardian deva paintings, miles of hiking trails, cordial inns, and an invigorating stream for bathing.

The bus to **Unumn-sa** from **Nambu-ju-ch'a-jang** (South Depot) is a challenging, but rewarding, test of stamina. Unmun-sa is a restful sanctuary for a community of Buddhist nuns. **Chikji-sa**, easily reached from Taegu via Kimch'on, is a gem of a temple. Chikji-sa's shrines are populated with a bewildering array of finely-carved statues.

Pusan: Wedged between a range of mountains and the sea, the big port city of **Pusan** is a raucous melange of masts, loading cranes and buildings; honking cabs, train whistles, and the throbbing air horns of passing ferries; suited businessmen, deck hands, navy cadets and fish mongers.

For those willing to dare the murky water of Pusan harbor, **Songdo Beach** is just a stone's throw southwest of **City Hall**. Even if you prudently abstain from swimming, it offers an interesting alternative to staying in town, as there are several inns and hotels with a uniquely Pusan flavor. Somewhat cleaner waters are available at three sandy beaches to the east of the city. The most popular is

Chikji-sa.

Haeun-dae, which has good hotels and a properly bustling resort town.

A few small Buddhist temples are scattered around town, and two large, important ones are within easy reach by bus or taxi; **Pomo-sa**, the closer of the two and the headquarters of the Dyana sect, is a mountain temple a few miles from Tongnae Hot Springs.

T'ongdo-sa is half an hour to the north along the highway to Taegu. With a total of 65 buildings, T'ongdo-sa is Korea's largest temple. Many of the buildings are dispersed throughout the surrounding mountainside, so the temple does not appear especially expansive on first encounter.

In addition to the many fine statues housed in the shrines, an excellent collection of artwork is on display in the temple museum. Woodblock prints are available for purchase.

Regular ferries run from a terminal behind Pusan's city hall throughout the Hallyo Waterway to Ch'ungmu and Yosu, to the port cities of **Masan** and **Chinhae**, and to the island of Koje-do. The waterway is sheltered from the open sea by hundreds of islands, which are the ancient peaks of an inundated mountain range.

Ch'ungmu is deservedly the most popular local destination out of Pusan. The dock of this still rustic resort town is small, but always busy with ferries returning from neighboring islands, small private fishing trawlers, tourist excursion boats, and all manner of hired craft which take water-sportsmen out for an afternoon of fishing or skindiving.

The many tidy restaurants in town serve a variety of seafood. Clams, oysters, soft-shelled crabs and unidentifiable mollusks are thrown into everything, to the delight of those who have an appetite for submarine curiosities and to the horror of those who don't.

On the way to Ch'ungmu, you will pass between the mainland, to the north, and the island of Koje, to the south. **Koje-do** is Korea's second-largest island (after Cheju) and one of the most beautiful areas of the country. The ferries to Ch'ungmu stop at several of the larger towns on the northwest coast of Koje-do. With careful scheduling it is possible to spend much of a day exploring the beaches, hillsides, and pastoral towns of the island, catch a ferry (or bus) and arrive at the more accommodating Ch'ungmu by evening.

KYONGJU

It's the massive burial mounds – brown and dusted by frost in the winter, and carpeted with a dark-green nap in the summer – which punctuate any visit to **Kyongju**, between Taegu and Pusan. The mounds – memorial tombs known as *nung* to Koreans – represent for now and all time the glory that was Silla.

Kyongju was well known to Asia's ancients as Kumsong, the home of powerful and opulent shaman kings. Today, it's an easy-going resort town where rice cultivation and tourism are more important than wars of conquest.

Its distinction as a one-time seat of power, however, cannot ever be forgotten. This 210-square-kilometer (80-sq-mi) valley is literally dotted with 1st- to

Kyongju's Tumuli Park.

8th-century and later burial tombs, tiered pagodas, fortress ruins, granite standing and relief sculptures, palace grounds and other remnants of the rich Three Kingdoms Period. Some of the major sites are:

Sillan tombs at Tumuli Park. In this unique "park" of 152,000 square meters (182,000 sq yds) on the southeast side of Kyongju are located some 20 tombs of varying sizes, and which were originally heaped into place as early as the middle of the first century.

The largest of the tombs, that of King Mich'u (r. 262-285), has been identified in ancient chronicles as the **Great Tomb**. However, a secondary tomb, the so-called **Ch'onma-ch'ong**, or Heavenly Horse or Flying Horse tomb, is probably the most well-known gravesite in **Tumuli Park** (sometimes called the Tomb Park). This tomb, about 30 meters (90 ft) in diameter and 13 meters (40 ft) high, was excavated in 1973, and in its collapsed wood and stone burial chambers were found numerous and important treasures.

Kyongju National Museum: Many of Kyongju's treasures are in the open air where they can be seen, touched, experienced. Visitors here can see some of the finest examples of more than 80,000 items unearthed during recent and old-time digs in this area: metal work, paintings, earthenware, calligraphic scrolls, folk art objects, weapons, porcelains, carved jades, and gold, granite and bronze sculptures.

Pulguk-sa: This sprawling temple complex about 16 kilometers (10 mi) due east of Kyongju on the western slopes of Mt. T'oham is one of the oldest surviving Buddhist monasteries in Korea, and it is also Korea's most famous temple. Its renown comes not from its age or size but probably because it stands, flawlessly restored, an example of Silla-era architecture.

Sokkuram, northeast of Pulguk-sa, is a grotto temple set amongst pines and maples, which enshrines a white granite Sakyamuni Buddha image considered by some art historians to be the most perfect Buddha image of its kind.

CHEJU-DO: SOUTHERN PARADISE

In a 1970s travel article about "undiscovered worldwide tourist destinations," *Newsweek* nicknamed **Cheju-do** the "Island of the Gods" and raved about its people, culture, seafood, climate, beaches, golf courses, horseback riding, challenging hiking trails, sports fishing grounds and volcanic peaks and craters. The Korean government prefers to call Cheju-do "Korea's Hawaii" and "The Hawaii of the Orient."

On this egg-shaped island, which lies about 150 kilometers (90 mi) south of Pusan in the channel between Korea and Japan, offshore waters are of the same aqua-turquoise color as those of Hawaii. These colors in turn lap against the same type of black lava shelves, jagged outcroppings and steep cliffs which rim the Hawaiian isles.

Cheju-do boasts to be home of the world's longest known lava tubes – the **Snake** and **Manjang caverns** located at **Kim Nyong**, between Cheju and Songsanp'o. The Manjang cavern, the longer of the two tubes, is 6,976 meters (7,629 yds) long, and with a diameter that ranges from 3 to 20 meters (10–66 ft). During the summer, tourists can join local guides on lamplight tours of these caverns filled with bats, spiders, centipedes and unusual lava formations.

Once winter sets in, icy offshore winds knife across Cheju-do and shatter all Polynesian allusions, but this splendid island – which since ancient times has been renowned for its winds, women and stones – is worth any traveler's detour. When weather gods are cooperating, Cheju-do is one of Asia's great vacation idylls.

The first Westerners to visit and tell the outside world about Cheju-do (and Korea proper) were Dutch sailors who shipwrecked at **Mosulp'o** on Cheju's south shore in 1653.

It wasn't until 1958 – an incredibly late exploratory date by contemporary tourism standards – that the first really

Rape (mustard) blossoms at Sogwip'o.

significant group of tourists descended on Cheju-do. The island is now criss-crossed with paved streets and high-ways, and dotted by hotels and *yogwan* (inns). Six major hotels on the island even have casinos.

Among the island attractions one shouldn't miss are:

• Cheju-do's superb beaches. Favorite crescents of sand are located at **Hyopje, Kwakji, Hamdok** and **Songsan** along Cheju's upper half, and at **Hwasun**, the aforementioned Chungmun and P'yoson in the south sector.

• The **Hallim weavers village** on the northwest shore, where Koreans trained by Colombian Roman Catholic priests and nuns are creating some of the finest Irish woolens outside of Ireland.

• The series of waterfalls on both the east and west sides of lovely **Sogwip'o**. The strong **Chongbang Falls** right in Sogwip'o town is often referred to as the only waterfall in Asia that plunges directly into the sea.

• The **Tol-harubang**, or grandfather stones. These carved lava rock statues, 52 in all, are seen on all parts of Cheju-do. However, nobody is quite sure what to make of these phallic fellows with funny smiles. Anthropologists say they probably represent legendary guardians who once flanked the entrances to Cheju's largest townships. Other schol-ars compare them to mysterious statu-ary found in some parts of the southern Korean peninsula, Tahiti, Okinawa, Fiji and even Easter Island. Suitable places to study these images up close are at the entrance to the **Samsonghyol Museum** in Cheju City or in front of Kwandok-jok-jong (a 15th-century pavilion).

Diving women: Cheju-do's diving women, called *haenyo*, have been a sym-bol of this island and its purported ma-triarchal culture.

When sea and weather conditions are favorable, scores of the haenyo, who range from teenagers to wrinkled grand-mothers, can be seen bobbing offshore between free dives for seaweed, shell-fish and sea urchins. Remember to ask for permission before photographing the haenyo up close.

The other side of Songsanp'o.

Japan

250 km / 155 miles

JAPAN

In Japan, one constantly hears of the "special" Japanese character, or the "special" Japanese snow – an excuse used several decades ago to keep out imported skis or the "special" Japanese appreciation of nature, hard to imagine at times amidst the racket of loudspeakers and tour buses, and the rank commercialization of what is considered a special scenic spot in Japan. The fact is, Japan is *more* different – even "more unique" if that were grammatically possible to say – than any place else on this planet, and no one with experience here, least of all the Japanese, would disagree.

Asian travellers are often very surprised to find Japan much more like the West than their own lands. Conversely, Western travellers – once they get past the shock of learning that not all Japanese run around in *kimono* or live in wood-and-paper huts, *or* work for Sony or Toyota – come to believe that what may appear to be Western on the outside is on the inside as "inscrutable" as they ever imagined Asia to be.

Usually, neither group is disappointed in what it discovers, or thinks it discovers, but never is either group correct in its analysis. Japan may be Westernized but it is not Western – not at home, not in the office, not on the golf course. Never. Likewise, although Japan is geographically in, and derives much of its social and cultural origins from Asia, many leagues of deep blue water and many centuries of social and commercial isolation have until only the mid 19th century separated these islands from the rest of the Orient, not to mention the rest of the world. Nonetheless, most of Japanese culture is derived from the Korean Peninsula and, of course, China itself.

There are few places that can so regularly endear and enrage the visitor at the same time. No matter how long one has lived in Japan, or how well one speaks the language, or handles the *hashi* or chopsticks, one is and always be an outsider. This, however, also gives the traveller a lot of elbow room in making mistakes and creating embarrassing situations. We're all outsiders, in the end.

And a final word: Don't expect serenity and Zen-like vistas. Japan is not especially attractive, save for the most remote regions. The cities are a chaos of architectural design and layout, and the countryside is a web of power lines and public works. Even the rock gardens of Kyoto are usually packed with students and tourists.

Having said that, few travellers leave Japan without leaving part of themselves there, too. Most usually return for yet another look.

<u>Preceding pages</u>: sunset over a smouldering Sakurajima, southern Kyushu; downtown Naha, Okinawa.

The earliest Japanese records describe the creation of the Japanese archipelago by the gods Izanagi and Izanami, who accomplished the task by dancing around a heavenly pillar and meeting in conjugal embrace. The source of the story is late, from the 8th century, by which time there had already been considerable cultural influx from Korea and China.

Archaeological remains of a neolithic period include pieces of pottery more than 10,000 years old. The entry of continental culture is evidenced in the appearance of wheel-thrown pottery and bronze implements during the Yayoi Period (ca.300 BC–AD 300).

It is difficult to say how much of a Bronze Age Japan had, for the iron culture of Han China seems to have arrived fast on the heels of bronze. In the first centuries AD, powerful kings and a hierarchical military society arose in central and western Japan. The aristocracy of this time were buried in immense tumuli with stores of helmets, swords, mirrors and jewels. The sword, mirror and "curved jewel" (*magatama*), which are the regalia of Japan's historical emperors, probably have their origin in this prehistoric culture. The largest of the tombs, called the tomb of Emperor Nintoku, is near the city of Sakai (Kansai), a keyhole-shaped island surrounded by three moats. In terms of area, it is the largest funerary construction in the world.

Nara Period, 710–794: Beginning in the 7th century with the active importation of Chinese culture and learning, the construction of Buddhist temples and the establishment of a state with a written code of government in the Yamato valley (present-day Nara Prefecture), Japan at last entered recorded history. No writing system seems to have existed before the 5th century, when Chinese ideographic characters (which had already been in existence for at least 2,000 years) were brought into use.

Buddhist icons had arrived in Japan from Korea during the 6th century, rousing debate in court and a brief civil war between advocates of the new religion and adherents to the native Shinto. The primacy of Buddhism was firmly established by Prince Shotoku Taishi, Imperial Regent from 593, who promulgated a Buddhist moral code and built numerous temples. Shotoku never condemned Shinto, but he devoted himself fully to Buddhism.

Nara witnessed a great cultural flowering. The Japanese court sent envoys across the Japan Sea to China at great risk, instructing them to bring back books and scholars of government, philosophy and religion. The sight of Chang'an, the Chinese capital, and the scale on which the Chinese did things must have overwhelmed the Japanese. The Sui emperor is reported to have gone on

outings on the Yellow River in a fleet of pleasure boats drawn by 80,000 men. This splendour could not be emulated, but Japan's first permanent capital was planned to match in every way possible the model of Chang'an. In 710, the capital Heijo-kyo was established at Nara. Palaces, government offices, storehouses and great temples were erected.

Heian Period, 794–1185: In 794, the capital was moved to present-day Kyoto and named Heian-kyoto, Capital of Peace and Tranquillity. The move seems to have been made this time to give the government a fresh start away from the great temples like Todai-ji, which had come to dominate Nara politics.

The new capital was also built on the Chinese model. A century later official contact with China was halted.

During the period that followed, heavily Chinese-influenced court culture incubated in the Heian capital, cut off from the outside world, even from the Japanese provinces. The Heian period represents on one hand the stagnation and inevitable decline of institutions begun in Nara, but on the other, a time of brilliance at court – within its tiny, cloistered society, a kind of classical age of Japanese aesthetics. The major poetry anthologies and literary diaries date from this period. Women were the revolutionary force in Heian literature, writing in a new Japanese vernacular liberated from the stodginess of academic Chinese.

The undisputed masterpiece of Heian literature, and of all Japanese prose, is the *Tale of Genji*, written around the year 1000 by Murasaki Shikibu, a lady-in-waiting to the empress. It is a narrative of over a thousand pages and termed by some the world's first novel. The pages of Genji gives a vivid sense of the rarified air of the author's environment. Daily life was taken up entirely by ceremony. An infinitesimal error of taste could cause a stir and social alienation.

In the eyes of residents of the capital, the countryside just a few hours journey away was a barren and forbidding place of exile, and so military clans were entrusted with the subjugation of the distant provinces. In the 10th century, these clans consolidated power, improving the nation's administration.

Kamakura period: Taira clan absconds with the emperor in a 12th-century insurrection.

Kamakura Period, 1185-1333: *Samurai* means "one who serves". In the regime established at Kamakura by Yoritomo, and in the ranks of the samurai caste throughout the country, loyal service to one's lord was the single ethic governing all individual conduct. The samurai served with his sword, and there developed a cult of the sword, as well as a cult of the god of war, Hachiman. The custom of ritual suicide, *seppuku* or *harakiri* (meaning "belly-slitting") also has its roots in this period.

The warrior nation under the Kamakura shogunate was mobilized twice to defend Japan, in 1274 and 1281, when forces of the

Mongol ruler Kublai Khan, who was then sovereign of the world's largest empire, attacked the shores of Kyushu. Both battles were decided by fateful typhoons which shipwrecked and scattered the invading fleet. The storms that had saved the day were called *kamikaze*, "divine winds", a word that was revived the next time Japan encountered the threat of a foreign invasion, by the Allies in World War II.

The years from 1336–92 are called the Northern and Southern Courts Period. Civil wars were waged, ostensibly in dispute over the throne, but more often than not actually for territorial gain and the slow consolidation of military power.

a custom first practised by zen monks in the Kamakura Period, became the center of a cult in which art objects, teas and tea wares were admired and compared.

The tea ceremony, called *chanoyu*, has since become the greatest single influence on the applied arts and Japanese tastes in general. While shogun Yoshimasa practised tea in his suburban-Kyoto retreat, the Onin War, another large-scale regrouping of feudal estates, raged in the streets of Kyoto. Ten years of fighting, from 1467–77, led to no satisfactory resolution, but caused destruction on a scale previously unseen and ushered in another century of disorder, usually referred to as the Warring States Period. The

Ashikaga/Muromachi Period, 1333–1587: The family of Ashikaga Takauji, who had turned on Kamakura to support Godaigo and then banished Godaigo himself, managed to hold on to a position of relative strength based in Kyoto during 56 years of anarchy. The Ashikaga Period was not characterized by good government, as the shoguns pursued a sweet life of aesthetic pastimes and left administration to ministers who pursued personal gain.

The arts flourished in Kyoto. Trade opened up again in China, bringing in pottery and monochrome paintings of a style which would have great influence in Japan. Tea drinking,

actors in this period of turmoil were not only local samurai forces but also armies of monks from the powerful temples around Kyoto. Three great generals finally distinguished themselves from the fray, and their campaigns unified Japan.

Momoyama Period, 1573–1603: Nobunaga, one of the three generals, was assassinated by one of his retainers at the height of his power, and control of one third of Japan was left to his general, Toyotomi Hideyoshi. Through generous bribes and prolonged sieges, Hideyoshi subjugated the remaining clans and brought a tenuous peace to Japan for the first time in 100 years.

Hideyoshi laid the groundwork for a more centralized feudal society. One of his edicts forbade farmers to bear arms and samurai to farm. The resulting "sword hunt" of 1587 served to separate the samurai class from the peasantry and make the sword an emblem of rank. It also reduced peasant uprisings.

Edo Period, 1603–1868: Hideyoshi spent his life in empire-building campaigns, and died in 1598 without leaving an able heir. In the battle over succession that followed, Tokugawa Ieyasu developed the strongest backing, winning a decisive victory at the battle of Sekigahara, in 1600.

The 258 years of Tokugawa rule were the most peaceful period in Japanese history.

After a final ban on Christianity, the Tokugawa severed all connections between Japan and the rest of the world, regulating the size of sea-going vessels, executing any Japanese who went abroad and returned, and limiting trade contact to a handful of Dutchmen and Chinese in the port of Nagasaki. This law, like all enacted by the shogunate, was a strategy to guarantee their static and absolute rule. But Japan in the Edo Period was far from unchanging.

Ironically, the ones to benefit most were the merchants, who sat on the bottom rung of the Confucian social ladder. Commercial empires were built, several of which survived today. The Mitsui conglomerate, for

With time the shogunate located in Ieyasu's castle-town of Edo (presently-day Tokyo) developed into an immense administrative institution regulating in every detail the strictly hierarchical, four-class society of samurai, farmers, artisans and merchants. This social order was derived from the moral philosophy of neo-confucianism, which served as the state creed.

Left, portrait of Minamoto no Yorimoto, Kamakura Period, and an ink painting of the Muromachi Period. **Above**, Commodore Perry's visit to Uragawa, Kanagawa, early Edo Period, opened Japan to the world.

example, began as Edo's first off-the-rack clothier in the late 17th century. The samurai, on the other hand, were soldiers without wars to fight.

A striking development during the Edo Period was the appearance of a popular culture of theatre, literature, music and art catering to the bourgeois tastes of the merchant townspeople. The locus of this artistic activity was in the licensed prostitution and entertainment districts, referred to as the *ukiyo*, or floating world. Its idols were *geisha* and *kabuki* actors, who were immortalized in *ukiyo-e*, pictures of the floating world. The ukiyo-e woodblock prints were originally produced as no more than theatre advertisements and souvenirs.

Samurai too were drawn into the decadent life of the "gay quarter" despite repeated edicts forbidding them to mix in the fun, closing theatres and condemning frivolity. The arts of the floating world show a radically new outlook, in which philosophical depth is replaced by this-worldly materialism and sensuousness.

Meiji Period, 1868–1912: In 1853, American Commodore Perry anchored in Uraga Bay and announced America's demand that Japan open its ports to trade. The shogunate, in financial straits and militarily unable to repel the foreigners, was forced into conces-

Victory at war with China in 1895 and with Russia in 1905 changed Japan's image of itself among world nations and surprised the West. The defeat of the Russian navy in particular announced that Japan was a power to be reckoned with. Japan had learned its lessons well watching the imperial expansion of Western nations. The Sino-Japanese War yielded the island of Taiwan, and Russia yielded the southern half of Sakhalin. In 1910, Japan annexed Korea.

Taisho Period, 1912–25: Emperor Meiji died in 1912, marking the end of Japan's first era as a modern nation. His son, Taisho, reigned for 14 years (1912–26), removed from politics and the public eye.

sions. The ever-weakening shogunate signed treaties with America and European nations.

In 1868, the imperial capital was moved to Edo, which was renamed Tokyo, and monarchy was restored under Emperor Meiji. In the first two years, the samurai class was abolished and *daimyo* estates were repossessed. Ports were opened and a policy of across-the-board Europeanization was embarked upon in Japanese institutions.

Meiji was a time of frenetic change and experimentation. Much of the population followed the government in trying on a Western suit of clothes, giving rise to the adjective *hai-kara* (from "high-collar").

Showa Period, 1926–89: With the death of the Taisho emperor in 1926, Hirohito succeeded to the throne, beginning the Showa Period. The nation continued to pursue a policy of military expansion. Political reality contrasted starkly with the carefree young society of Taisho.

Harsh reality overshadows the memory of the Showa Period (1930s). Military extremists led the nation deeper into a war for Asian domination. Japan withdrew from the League of Nations, isolating itself. In 1937, Japan lurched into an all-out invasion of China, in which tens of millions of Chinese died. Although direct involvement of Western nations apart from Russia would not come for another four years, World War II in Asia was in full swing. One day after the bombing of Pearl Harbor in 1941, the U.S. and Britain declared war on Japan.

Upon surrender in 1945, Japan was reduced to its borders as they had stood at the beginning of Meiji. The emperor renounced his divinity. A new constitution was written under direction of Gen. Douglas MacArthur.

Prevented from developing a military, Japan's government and industry were able to focus on economic and industrial development, and do so they did. With direct planning by the government, and a system that nurtured favoritism amongst corporations,

government and industry, not to mention the financial sector, denied that Japan had any worry about its progress.

Heisei Period, from 1989: The Showa emperor died in 1989, ending any direct connection between the imperial family and the brutal military actions of Japan in Asia. His son, Akihito, was but a child during World War II. But Japan's half-century of aggression in Asia continues to shadow the country, assisted by politicians who continue to claim most of the atrocities are fabrications, and by a government that continues to remove all negative references to Japan's actions in World War II from text books. This lack of self-reflection and reality has hin-

not to mention in banking and government, Japan's economy grew into one of the world's most dynamic. Not only did Japanese industry revolutionize manufacturing techniques, the products it manufactured set the global standards for both quality and aesthetics.

By the 1980s, Japan seemed unstoppable. Real estate values escalated, especially in Tokyo, and both individuals and corporations took out loans based upon inflated land values. The economy overheated, and despite warnings from foreign analysts, both

Left, World War II blessings. Above, earthquake damage in Kobe, 1995.

dered Japan's call for a permanent Security Council seat in the United Nations.

Japan's superheated economy – the so-called bubble economy – collapsed at the beginning of the 1990s, sending Japan into a recession and banking crisis that lingered into the late 1990s. Known for life-time employment, Japanese companies slashed their work forces, a shock to Japan's postwar sense of affluence and security. Adding to this loss of innocence were an earthquake in 1995 that killed nearly 6,000 people in Kobe, displaying the government's emergency ineptness, and gas poisonings in Tokyo's subway system, in the heart of the city.

Of whatever size or purpose, the group defines for the Japanese their individual purpose and function. And the group known as the Japanese – *nihonjin*, or if especially nationalistic, *nipponjin* – is the mother of all groups. (Not exactly an irreverent comment, given that Amaterasu Omikami, or Great Heaven-Shining Mother, is the foremother of the Japanese themselves.)

Television commentators and musing politicians repeatedly refer to *ware-ware Nipponjin*, or "we Japanese", and the implicit definition of what "we Japanese" are or aren't, do or don't do, believe or not believe. The compulsion to define identity even shows up in advertising.

"Don't understand us too quickly," the Japanese will warn visitors, by definition outside of any group of which the Japanese feel themselves a part. Indeed, they often seem to prefer that foreigners not understand too much about them at all. There is a certain pride amongst Japanese in their collective feeling that outsiders simply don't understand – so they'll proclaim – simply because they are not Japanese.

Origins: The Japanese sense of uniqueness extends down to a basic racial identity, of a race and culture distinct from others – if not superior. But the objective evidence strongly points to origins from the mainland.

Theories regarding the racial origins of the Japanese cite both the north and the south – Manchuria and Siberia, and the South China or Indochina regions – as likely possibilities. Students of the subject differ as to which origin to favor. The southern physical type is, of course, the Malay; the northern type is the Mongolian. Today, both north and south Asia are considered equally valid as likely origins of the Japanese. Still, the precise configuration of the migrations and the cultural traits associated with areas of origin are subject to argument. (Toss in, too, other theories about migrations from Polynesia.)

There was considerable human immigration later – in addition to cultural and artistic influences – from Korea, a point vehemently

denied by Japanese nationalists and racial purists, despite the overwhelming archaeological and anthropological evidence. Whereas archaeology in many countries is considered the most neutral of disciplines, without political overtones of any kind, in Japan it is rife with factions and hot-tempered rivalries. One group of "experts" in Japan has steadfastly refuted and rejected most modern dating methods, particularly when used to authenticate theories proposing a Japan–Korea connection.

In any case, it may also be possible that the Korean and Japanese languages were mutually understandable, if not identical, some 2,000 years ago, and that a close affinity between the people on the Korean peninsula and the Japanese archipelago may have approached a common culture.

Unique or arrogant?: Perhaps the most substantial insulator of Japanese from the outside is the language, spoken only in the islands. In fact, the grammar and syntax are considerably easier than most germanic or romance languages. The Japanese will retort, however, that it is one of the world's most difficult. The language isn't, but the

Left, on a flower-picking expedition, Tohoku.
Right, Kyoto temple smiles.

context of usage can be confusing for those not brought up within the Japanese culture. To fully understand the Japanese and their ways, knowing the language is essential. An "expert" on Japan who doesn't speak the language fluently is a fraud.

There is much in the Japanese language that buttresses a fundamental notion: There is an undercurrent in Japanese thinking – and in Japanese traditions – that all things Japanese, including the race, are "special", if not unique, among the world's things. And most Japanese certainly believe that outsiders will never be able to fully appreciate, much less understand, the distinctions and nuances of *being* Japanese, and of Japanese ways. Stay

call such behavior insincere is, to the Japanese, simply ignorant, and hurtful. It doesn't have to be approved of by foreigners – *gaijin,* or if especially polite, *gaikokujin.* However, if one is to be effective in Japan, the special – and unique? – Japanese way must be learned and applied with grace and skill.

Notable, both for the linguistic hedging and for the insight into Japanese thinking, is the difference in how Japan and the rest of Asia, if not the world, remember history. If the past is not flattering, it is best forgotten, think the Japanese. But Japan's neighbors – especially Korea, Philippines and China – think differently. Collectively, the Japanese seem unable to recall five decades of brute

in Japan long enough, listen to the conversation and media, and it seems that only Japan has earthquakes, typhoons, tasty rice, misery, hot weather, bad memories of war, trees that change color in autumn, snowfall and fast trains.

Living on egg shells: In a country where physical crowding and complex interpersonal relationships have, over the centuries, shaped the language and social manners, even the slightest chance of offending, or disappointing, or inconveniencing someone else is couched in a shower of soft words, bows, and grave smiles. (Or worse, giggles, a sure signal of acute embarrassment.) To

Japanese aggression capped by a Pacific war killing 20 million people. But with the Imperial army's own documents magically appearing from hiding, and as aging veterans publicly purge their nightmares, forgetting is increasingly difficult to do. What rankles its Asian neighbors most, however, is the regularity with which Japan's conservative politicians denounce factual history. In 1994, Japan's minister of justice publicly declared that the 1937 Rape of Nanking – when between 100,000 and 300,000 Chinese were slaughtered by an out-of-control Japanese army – was merely an unsubstantiated fabrication. A myth.

Obligations: If apologies are linguistic puzzles, other expressions of social necessity too are interesting, if not curious.

Strangely, the very word for "thank you" – *arigato* – literally means, "You put me in a difficult position." *Oki no doku,* which is an expression of sympathy, means "poisonous feeling." And who but the Japanese would think of expressing regret or apology with *sumimasen,* which, in strictly literal translation, means, "This (situation/inconvenience) will never end"?

Then there is that virtually untranslatable word, *giri.* To violate it is simply unthinkable. Giri is often translated as a sense of duty and honor, but such a definition ignores the

– are nowadays as far flung from the original homestead as education, job opportunities and jet planes can take them. And although nostalgia for the *furusato* (hometown) and simpler living has taken on a trendy air recently, the urban nuclear family is increasingly defining the contours of Japanese life.

In many marriages today, the husband still maintains a higher status and exercises greater authority in the family by virtue of being the sole provider. He shows little inclination in helping around the house or taking care of the children, except when it suits him.

Like her grandmother, the Japanese woman feels obligated to show appreciation to the family through acquiescence and service.

subtle communal and personal responsibilities behind giri. In Japan, there are unspoken responsibilities inherent in acceptance within a group, whether in a friendship or with coworkers in an office, or in the sharing of communal village life. When the responsibility beckons – and the member of any group will recognize it without articulating it – the individual must meet that responsibility, putting aside one's work or desires.

Family: Extended families – often cited as the core of Japan's traditional social stability

Left, forget about the girl, Kyushu. **Above**, Meiji-era schoolboys, and Tokyo University, or Todai.

Unlike her grandmother, she is more willing to regain control over her own life by getting a divorce. Although comparatively low, rising divorce rates reflect the growing desire of spouses, particularly wives, to exert personal aspirations and concerns over those of the family.

Some wives file for divorce when husbands retire from their jobs, demanding half of the husband's severance pay. Increasingly, some couples divorce before they even get started on a proper married life. It's called a Narita Divorce. Modern Japanese women have often spent more time traveling overseas than their new husbands; their first joint jaunt overseas, usually the honeymoon, is ripe with tension and ends in disaster because the woman is more self-reliant than the man. After returning home to Narita, Tokyo's international airport, they divorce.

Slowly, and from causes more economical than ideological, women have been restructuring their own opportunities; with increased travel and exposure to foreign media, they've seen the alternatives to a submissive role. The number of women subscribing to the standard pattern of a brief period of initial employment, followed by several decades of full-time devotion to a home and children, followed by a return to the job market as a part-time or temporary worker, is declining.

Increasingly, women are demanding to be allowed to work after marriage and after giving birth to children.

Some 95 percent of Tokyo's women have been through high school, and over a third hold college degrees. But until the late 1980s, the vast majority of these highly qualified graduates may not have wanted careers, considering the working lives of men.

Education: Japanese social institutions in general, and schools in particular, are arranged hierarchically in terms of their ability to bestow economic and social status. No institution ranks higher in this regard than Tokyo University.

Entrance to higher education is determined by dreaded examinations, which are administered by the individual universities; for each school applied to for admission, a complete set of entrance exams must be endured. The more prestigious a school is, the greater the number of applicants seeking admission and the more difficult the examination.

To help them reach this goal, parents will budget a considerable amount of their monthly income to send children to *juku,* private cram schools that are a multibillion-yen business. For the most disciplined of students, every night and weekend is spent at juku, having their brains crammed with exam-passing information.

Perhaps, more importantly, schools reform undisciplined brats into socially-predictable, and responsible, persons. The schools pound down the nail that sticks out. From the earliest days of school, the educational system focuses on developing such basic Japanese values as harmonious relations with others and establishing group identity, through membership in a limited number of social and vocational groups.

Education is respected in Japan, and so are educators. In fact, the honorific for teacher – *sensei,* as in Nakamura-sensei – is the same as for physicians. Unfortunately, the responsibility and professional pressure is considerable upon teachers, especially at the high school level, when students are preparing for their university examinations. Holidays are rare for the teachers.

Even the Japanese themselves admit their educational system's shortcomings. The excessive emphasis on entrance examinations is a cause of much national concern and debate. Because of the emphasis on conformity and passing exams, students lack initiative and creative abilities. As a result, Japanese corporations, for example, must go to America and Europe for original research-and-development work.

Reforms are being considered, but not terribly fast. The rigidity of certain facets of the formal education system and the alienation of increasing numbers of young people, along with increased awareness of violence in the schools and bullying of some pupils, are also increasing concerns.

Left, even rebels seek solace. Right, young businessman in Naha, Okinawa.

RELIGION

Polls asking Japanese in which religion they believe consistently yield results that total well over 100 percent – most say they are followers of both Shinto and Buddhism.

Ask a Japanese how many gods there are, and the answer may be one or one thousand. Ask about the nature of the *kamisama*, or deities, that are worshipped, and a confused silence may result. There is no Japanese equivalent of the Bible or Koran, unless one counts the *Kojiki* (Record of Ancient Matters), which describes the mythological origins of the Japanese; even the most ardent ultranationalist does not accept the eighth-century chronicle as divine writ, however.

Until recently, nearly every home was equipped with a *kamidana* god-shelf with Shinto symbols, or else a *butsudan* Buddhist household altar containing memorials for the family's ancestors, before which offerings of flowers, food, drink or incense are made daily. Many had both. Likewise, people passing by any of the thousands of Shinto shrines or Buddhist temples throughout the country still tend to drop in for a brief devotion before going on their busy way again.

It is hard to attribute all this to simple custom; the Japanese definitely seem to have a sense of religious piety and spiritual yearning, although it is far different from that in the West. The main difference seems to be that the line between the sacred and the profane is much less clearly drawn in Japan. In many ways, community life and religion are one and the same. Similarly, the distinction between good and bad, or sinful and righteous, is less clear in Japanese society. It is said that the West considers most things as black or white; in Japan, there is a lot of gray.

Shinto: A basic understanding of the Japanese religious sensibility must begin with Shinto – not a "national religion" in any current official sense (although it once was zealously nationalistic), but rather one that influences virtually every aspect of Japanese culture and society. It is hard to give any simple definition of Shinto (lit. way of the

gods), since it is not a systematized set of beliefs. There is no dogmatic set of rules, nor any holy script. The term *shinto* was not even invented until after the introduction of Buddhism, a date traditionally given as AD 552, and then only as a way of contrasting the native beliefs with that imported faith.

In general, it can be said that Shinto shares with many other animistic beliefs the truth that all natural objects and phenomena possess a spiritual side. It is this animism, mixed with ancestor worship – a shared trait with

Buddhism – that characterizes Shinto, then. A tree, for example, was revered by the ancient Japanese as a source of food in nuts and fruit, of energy in firewood, of shelter, and even of clothing. For that reason, when a great tree was felled to provide wood for the Buddhist temple complexes at Nara or Kyoto, it was not used for several years, in order to give the spirit within time to safely depart. Mountains, forests and even the oceans were also similarly revered.

As for ancestor worship, the Yamato "race" always believed that it had descended from heaven, and so worshipped Amaterasu Omikami – the sun goddess, she who ruled

Left, Shinto priest reciting prayers to various deities, Tohoku. **Right**, a Buddhist family tomb in northern Hokkaido.

the heavens – as the ancestress of the imperial family, if not all the people. The *Kojiki* is basically a justification for their conquest of the "Middle Land Where Reeds Grow Luxuriously" and their rule over other apparently related groups, such as the inhabitants of Izumo on the Japan Sea, who were said to be descendants of Amaterasu's brother, the rowdy storm god, Susanoo no Mikoto.

It should be recognized that the term *kami*, although usually translated as "god," is quite different from the Western concept of divinity. The classic definition, as originally understood in Japan, was made by the eighteenth-century scholar Motori Norinaga: "Anything whatsoever which was outside

analogy, you might say this world is plus, while the after-world is minus. There was no concept of sin, nor of divine retribution, nor of absolution for offenses committed. Just about the worst thing that could happen was the pollution of a ritual. Otherwise, as far as the afterlife was concerned, it was commonly thought that the dead would eventually be reborn into this world, just as spring returns after winter.

There are 13 mainstream Shinto sects and numerous sub-sects in Japan today, but since the American occupation following World War II, they have not been controlled by the government. In fact, it was only during the period from the Meiji Restoration of 1868

the ordinary, which possessed superior power, or which was awe-inspiring, was called kami."

In ancient Shinto there was also a belief in a kind of soul – *tamashii* – that lived on after death. An unrefined form of ancestor worship also existed, remnants of which can be seen in the observances of the spring and autumn equinoxes. It can also be seen in the *Obon,* which, although primarily Buddhist in other parts of Asia, has both Shinto and Buddhist overtones in Japan.

Primitive Shinto had concepts of heaven and hell, as well, although they were hazily conceived at best. To use electricity as an

through the end of World War II that the government took any direct part in Shinto.

It was during the Meiji Restoration that the government introduced *kokka* (national) Shinto as a political tool for controlling the people through the policy of *saisei it'chi* – the "unity of rites and politics." Although the emperor was said in the Meiji constitution to be "sacred and inviolable," the nature of his sacredness was never officially defined; the most common interpretation, however, was that, through prayer, he became one with his divine ancestor Amaterasu and the other gods, and could therefore intercede on behalf of his people.

Yasukuni-jinja, a Shinto shrine just north of the Imperial Palace in central Tokyo, is an example (a particularly notorious one) of the national shrines set up by the authorities. It is here that the spirits of every soldier who died in the name of the emperor since 1853 are enshrined (including war criminals executed by the Allies after World War II). Visits made here – official or not – by the prime minister and other members of government are often violently opposed by those who believe the constitution now supports the separation of church and state.

Buddhism: The traditionally-accepted date for Buddhism to have arrived in Japan is AD 552. While this may be true, it wasn't until

with through entry into the blissful state of *nirvana,* or Buddhahood.

Buddha's followers came to believe that one who really knows the truth, lives the life of truth, and thus becomes truth itself. By overcoming the conflicts of the ego, then, one can attain a universal, cosmic harmony. *Mahayana,* meaning Greater Vehicle, was the form of Buddhism that became established throughout most of East Asia. It holds that every being, sentient or non-sentient, shares a basic spiritual communion, and that all are destined for Buddhahood. Although all beings are separate in appearance, they are one and the same in reality. Every person's present situation is determined by past

centuries later that it ceased to be the exclusive province of aristocrats. This is somewhat ironic in view of the beliefs of the religion's founder, Sakyamuni – born a prince in eastern India (now part of Nepal) around 500 BC – who advocated a middle way between indulgence and asceticism.

The Buddha, as he came to be known (though this is a misnomer), blamed all the world's pain and discontent on desire, and claimed that through right living, desire could be negated and the "self" totally done away

Left, schoolgirl, Heian-jingu, Kyoto. **Above**, Shinto shrine, Rishiri Island.

deeds, Buddhists believe; this is the principle of *karma.*

Since the main Mahayana sutras only appeared around 100 BC, it is not known how closely they reflect the original thoughts of the Buddha. But by the time it reached Japan's shores through China, Buddhism had changed tremendously from Sakyamuni's simple message. It was to undergo even more radical change when it encountered the beliefs held in the Japanese archipelago.

As early as the sixth century, for example, *Ryobu* Shinto began to emerge as a syncretic compromise with Buddhism. In this hybrid belief system, kamisama were regarded as temporary manifestations of the Buddhist deities. In time, Buddhist thought became influenced by the indigenous beliefs, deviating so far from the original, that some scholars doubt whether the Japanese version really deserves to be called Buddhism. For example, although the goal of nirvana is to break the cycle of reincarnation, most Japanese Buddhists seem to believe that the souls of the dead are eventually reborn. As the famed folklorist Yanagida Kunio once pointed out, if asked where people go after they die, the typical Japanese will usually answer *Gokuraku*, which translates as Paradise. Contrast this with the more orthodox Buddhist belief in death as a permanent state;

tains have always held in Japanese religious lore. Certain peaks – Omine near Nara, and, of course, Fuji – are especially sacred; each year, thousands of pilgrims dressed in white ascend them. Such considerations also lay behind the choice of the mounts of Koya and Hiei, near Kyoto, as the respective sites for the headquarters of the Shingon and Tendai Buddhist sects.

The contemporary Japanese concept of an afterlife, then, appears to be quite similar to that held before Buddhism arrived. Excepting those Japanese Buddhists whose particular sect specifically countermands such a concept, most seem to believe that the life force passed on from one generation to the

in fact, a euphemism expressing someone's death is *Hotoke ni natta* ("He became a Buddha").

In practice, however, Japanese usually return to their *furosato*, or ancestral home, for the two equinoxes, as well as during the midsummer Obon, or Feast of the Dead observances. The purpose of attending Obon is to be present when the family's ranking male ceremoniously offers food to the spirits of departed ancestors – spirits that supposedly return to earth for the occasion.

From where do they return? Yanagida says most people will answer "the mountains." This may derive from the special place moun-

next continues eternally, although little energy is spent in explaining exactly how.

Amida Buddhism: There are today an estimated 56 main divisions, and 170 subdivisions, in Japanese Buddhism.

The single most popular sect is Jodo Shinshu, founded by Shinran (1173–1262), who preached an "easy road to salvation" by means of the *nembutsu* prayer to the Amida, a bodhisattva who made a vow eons ago to save all who placed faith in him or her, and to guide them to the Blissful Land of Purity.

About half of the Japanese Buddhists belong to either Jodo Shinshu, or to Jodo, another form of Amidaism established by

Honen (1133–1212). True believers of Jodo Shinshu think that it is not even necessary to be "good" in order to be reborn into the Western Paradise, and that the laity can become Buddhas as easily as priests, even without the faith Honen claimed essential.

Amidaism is perhaps the form of Buddhism closest to the core Japanese beliefs, In its slight concern for moral judgement and exaltation of natural inclinations beyond considerations of good and evil. This, no doubt, helps account for its popularity.

Back in the Kamakura Period, when religion was a much more vital social force than it is today, the Amidaists directly contended for converts with the followers of the obstinate reformer Nichiren (1222–82). Nichiren claimed that he was the man selected to spread the "True Word" that would lead men to the "Primeval Gateway". He gloried in street preaching, and neither exile nor the threat of execution could faze him.

His highly nationalistic thinking is well-known; he predicted the Mongul thrust at Japan and noted that Buddhism had constantly been spreading eastward toward the land where it would achieve its ultimate maturity: Japan.

Nichiren's followers have been called "Buddhist Calvinists," and are usually to be found among the *petite bourgeoisie* and lower classes. During the 14th century, they often engaged in pitched battles with Shinran's followers, usually farmers or townspeople.

Today, many of Nichiren's followers in Japan belong to the *Soka Gakkai,* a controversial organization whose political arm, the *Komei-to,* or Clean-Government Party, has considerable strength in the National Diet.

Zen emptiness: The impact of that particularly eclectic form of Buddhism called Zen on Japanese culture is considerable, reaching far beyond the temple and entering into cultural and social areas of all kinds, including gardening, ink painting, calligraphy, the tea ceremony, and even military strategies.

Two Buddhist priests in the twelfth and thirteenth centuries – Eisai, founder of the Rinzai Zen sect, and his disciple Dogen, who established the Soto Zen sect – are given the lion's share of credit for bringing the principle of "emptiness" into Japanese Buddhism.

Left, jizo images for protection of children, Kyoto. **Right**, Buddhist beneath sacred waterfall.

Soto sect followers rely almost solely on *zazen*, or sitting meditation; they reject scripture and seek to emulate Sakyamuni, who reached the state of enlightenment while meditating without conscious thought in such a position. In contrast, the Rinzai sect also utilizes *koan* riddles, such as the famous "What is the sound of one hand clapping?" Koan must be tackled with something beyond logic and non-logic, and the riddles' function is to stimulate (or perhaps divert) the mind into a similar state.

Zen was influenced by both Daoism and the Wang Yangming school of neo-Confucianism, which stressed the "prime conscience" and the importance of action. They

would describe the "Great Ultimate" as being akin to the hub of a well: empty but the point from which all action flows. For various reasons, Zen sects proved better able than the others to satisfy the spiritual needs of the samurai.

Whether through zazen or the use of koan posed by the Zen master, the goal is for the disciple to be provoked, excited or irritated to the point where one makes a non-intellectual leap into the void and experiences reality and the unity of all things directly. If successful, one will then view everything anew with a light from within, and there will no longer be any contradictions or duality.

The earliest preserved and distinctly Japanese works of art are those of the late Yayoi Period. These were small, tubular clay figurines called *haniwa*, some of which were set up like fences around imperial mausolea. Whatever their purpose may have been – substitutes for people buried alive in the tombs, or magical instruments to ward off evil spirits or bandits – their immediate interest lies in their utter simplicity and charm.

Although many of them are only cylinders, some of the haniwa (and there are

Aesthetic impulses: The haniwa figures are also important for another reason. We find in them – at the very beginning of the culture – many of the salient characteristics of almost all Japanese art.

Decorative, narrative, human. The decorative extends from modest fence posts to elaborately gilded and painted screens and walls in palaces and castles, to pin-ups in a swordsmith's shop. The narrational can range from rolls and rolls of scrolls illustrating one of the world's biggest (and greatest) novels

hundreds) are figures of men and women (dancers, warriors, singers), horses, monkeys and birds. Most are very simple, with only a few details of decoration – a sword or a necklace, perhaps. They have large hollow spaces for the mouth and eyes, which prevented them from cracking when being fired, and which adds not only to their charm, but to their mystery, too.

Who are they? What are they saying? Some emotion or song seems to have been eternally suspended here, and while the will to know them may be strong, the recognition of the eternally human, of the eternally here and now, is more compelling.

– *Genji Monogatari,* or *Tale of the Genji* – to a single illustration of a young boy playing a flute before a warrior. As for the human: in Japanese art it embraces everything, from demons to gods, from animals to, well, people.

Nara and Kamakura sculpture: Before the Nara Period, there are some superb examples of sculpture (such as the Kuze Kannon and the Kudara Kannon, both at Horyu-ji, in Nara). To recommend only one, mention must be made of the Miroku in Koryu-ji, in Kyoto. This is a delicately-carved wooden statue of the Buddha of the Future. The young person (gender is blurred in Buddhist art, but one assumes the figure is of a boy) has one leg crossed over the other, his chin rests on a couple of extended fingers, and one detects the slightest hint of the most gracious, lyrical smile imaginable. The Miroku is a hint of the greatness to come.

In the Nara Period (646–794), with Japan's full-scale welcome of things Chinese, the native response to the real is fused with its spiritual aspirations without ever abandoning the former. Work is done in wood, clay, bronze or by using the curious technique of hollow lacquer.

(Toshodai-ji) and of the Buddha's disciples (Kofuku-ji) are utterly remarkable for the realism of their portraiture.

It was also during this time that the 16-meter-high, bronze Daibutsu (the Great Buddha) was created. It is a sorry sight from what it must have originally looked like, housed as it is now in a much smaller hall and worn by age. It was originally gilded with bronze, and incised with designs that can now only be barely discerned on some of the lotus petals upon which the figure sits. This is the great

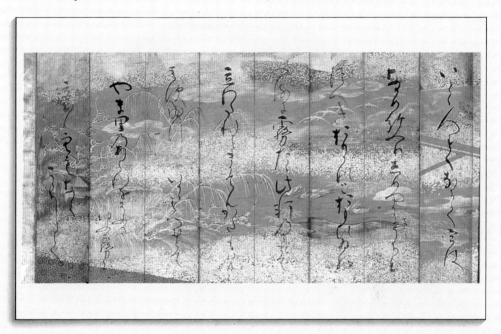

Sculptures – gods and humans alike – are spiritually powerful because they are so real (they probably had real models). And though it cannot now be seen, they were originally colored. The patinas of age may lend them a spiritual depth, but one should not forget their original splendor. While the Buddha and some of the deities are ruled by convention (the beatific smile, various hand gestures for the former, terrifying gazes for the latter), the portraits of the blind monk Ganjin

Left, earthenware pot, Jomon Period, and a bodhisattva from the Asuka Period. Above, *Excerpts from the Tale of Genji,* 17th century.

tourist attraction at Todai-ji, in Nara, which should not be missed.

The Nara Period ended with the move of capital to Kyoto. With that, the beginning of the Heian Period (794–1185), Japanese sculpture declined as other arts ascended, and did not revive until the Kamakura Period, several centuries later. While Nara Period sculpture was both human and ideal, that of the Kamakura Period was wholly human, passionate, personal and emotional.

For example, the Kamakura Period (1185–1336) produced more portraits of monks and of demons (warriors, really) than of aloof gods. The Kamakura Period also produced its Daibutsu, which, though somewhat smaller than that in Nara, is equally affecting. Now sitting uncovered in the Kamakura hills, its impressiveness has been enhanced by time and exposure to the ocean air.

Painting: In the Heian Period, life itself became an art, and works of art became its decorative attendant. Kyoto's Byodoin may have been meant as a model of the next world, but it only showed that life in this one was already exquisite.

Japanese painting had long existed, but it had not flowered into great sophistication, particularly in the form of long, unfolding (and hand-held) scrolls. These paintings, called *Yamato-e*, might depict the changing

their delicacy of line reveal the Japanese gift of design. With the Genji scroll are the conventions of the removed roof, the "dash for the eye and a hook for the nose," and the floating, golden clouds that rhythmically lead the eye from scene to scene. It is a splendid example of the great Japanese graphic sensibility that is still seen today in advertising and comic art.

In the Kamakura Period, war and religion came together. This was the great period of Zen art, when *suiboku* (water-ink, painting with black *sumi* ink) comes to the fore. One of the world's masterpieces of *suiboku-ga* can be seen in the National Museum in Tokyo: Sesshu's *Winter Landscape*, a bold

seasons, famous beauty spots, or illustrate well-known stories. The best Yamato-e were of the latter type, depicting popular legends, warrior tales, or works of great literature, such as the *Ise Monogatari* and the *Tale of the Genji*. The popular legends might include a satirical look at pompous officials turned into battling frogs and rabbits, or a man who can't stop farting, or a look into the punishments that await evil-doers in hell. Post-Heian warrior tales drew on the many heroic or sentimental tales collected in the *Heike Monogatari* and other stories (as Western artists drew theirs on Homer and Virgil).

The scrolls are easy to follow, and with

landscape of a traveler dwarfed by nature, a lonely town and mountain all around, and a vertical streak of ink that cuts the sky. Because of his line, his sense of composition, and the moods he can evoke, Sesshu seems at times to be a contemporary artist, though he died in 1506 at the age of 86.

The Momoyama Period (late 16th century) is Japan's age of Baroque splendor, when, as one scholar says, "The simper of the late Ashikaga court went down before the swagger of men like Nobunaga." It is the one of the high points of Japan's decorative genius. It is filled with gold and silver, with very bright, flat colors (no shading or outlining), with lush scenes painted on screens and walls of flower-viewing parties, of lovely women and sight-seeing spots.

This is not to imply that monochrome was abandoned during Momoyama. Far from it: there was a great deal of superb *sumi-e* (ink picture) screens and paintings done at this time. The overwhelming impression, however, is of gold.

Floating world: The Edo Period (1603–1868) is the great age of popular art, even though much great decorative art was being made for the aristocracy or the military classes, especially by Koetsu, Sotatsu and Korin. The latter's gorgeous *Irises* – all violet and gold – is an excellent example in the Nezu

vein in the early eighteenth century; at first, the prints were either monochromatic or hand-colored with an orange-red. In time, two colors were used, then four, and so on.

Although the names of hundreds of ukiyo-e artists are known, it should be remembered that the production of these prints was a cooperative effort between many highly-skilled people. There was the artist who created the design and suggested colors, the carvers of the many blocks, the actual printers, and finally the publishers.

Early ukiyo-e, especially those by the first great master, Moronobu, are usually portraits of prostitutes from the Yoshiwara district of old Edo, or else illustrations for

Museum of Art, in Tokyo. The merchant class, however, was developing its own pleasures in fiction, drama (*kabuki*) and art, and mass appeal soon became more important than ever.

The art most associated with Edo Tokyo is *ukiyo-e* (literally, "pictures of the floating world"). Once again, the sublunary, fleshy human existence was a key element. Although wood-block printing had been used to reproduce sutras, for example, the technique first began to be used in a more popular

Left, erotic woodblock print. **Above**, *View on a Fine Breezy Day*, by Hokusai, Edo Period.

books; with polychrome printing, in ukiyo-e a number of "genres" became established. There were, for example, portraits of prostitutes (*bijin ga*), kabuki actors in famous roles, the ever-present scenes of renowned places, and of plant and animal life.

Ukiyo-e, suffice it to say, is one of the world's great graphic art forms, but until very recently, the Japanese themselves never considered ukiyo-e to be "art". It was a publishing form, and not art until foreigners started collecting them. Only in the past few decades have Japanese collectors begun to realize the value of ukiyo-e, long appreciated by outsiders.

Japan is a country of regional cuisines, and, too, of seasonal cuisines. In fact, sampling local dishes is a fundamental purpose of traveling for many Japanese.

Two types of places that particularly deserve attention for their pure Japanese ambience are the *izaka-ya*, or pub, often with a string of red lanterns above its door, and the *taishu-sakaba*, a much larger tavern-like establishment that may also sport red lanterns. These red lanterns – *akachochin* – signify a traditional Japanese place for eating and meal, whether in the snow-blanketed mountains or on the sea shore. Some of the better restaurants serving kaiseki ryori have succeeded in creating exactly such an atmosphere regardless of outside environment, with brush works, flower arrangements, and views of waterfalls cascading over well-hewn rocks into placid pools. The effect at once elevates the senses and the pleasure of kaiseki ryori.

The ingredients must be as fresh as the dawn. That's a prime requisite of good food in general, of course, together with a good

drinking. Specialties include Japanese-style fried fish, shellfish, broiled dishes, *tofu* (bean curd) dishes, *yakitori* (skewered and broiled meat), fried rice-balls, and simple *sashimi*.

Kaiseki ryori: At least one meal in Tokyo should be *kaiseki ryori*, a centuries-old form of Japanese cuisine served at restaurants, or in ryokan, in several elegant courses. Ingredients depend upon the season and region. One might spend a lifetime sampling every regional variation.

Fastidiously prepared, kaiseki ryori is so aesthetically pleasing that it's virtually an art form. Ideally, the food's visual appeal would be heightened by a proper setting for the recipe and a good cook. Rejoice in the fact that Japan has plenty of all three.

Japanese cuisine focuses on flavor and its subtleties, and on the food's presentation. Rather than create distinctive flavors for their dishes, Japanese chefs seek above all to retain natural flavors. And rather than alter the appearance of their ingredients, they strive to enhance their visual appeal through artful arrangements and subtle tactile stimulation of hands and mouth. Many of Japan's most enjoyable and popular dishes are common and reasonably priced. Among them are such everyday dishes as *yakimono* (fried dishes), *nabemono* (pot dishes), *agemono* (deep fat fried dishes), *nimono* (boiled dishes) and a wide variety of noodle dishes. (The suffix -*mono* can be roughly translated here as "things", as in "fried things".)

Noodles: Noodles are eaten in Japan throughout the year and nearly throughout the day – and night.

Japanese noodles are of three main types: soba, *udon*, and *somen*. Soba noodles, made of buckwheat, are thin and brownish. Udon noodles, made of wheat, are usually off-white, and thick to very thick. Somen noo-

dip made of *mirin* (sweet *sake*), and *katsuobushi* (shaved flakes of dried bonito). Soba noodles in this form, when served chilled on a *zaru*, a type of bamboo tray, are called *zarusoba,* a delicious summer meal. Soba is not only tasty, but extremely nutritious, the more so in proportion to its *sobako* (wheat flour) content. Another hot weather favorite – just as soba is, but entirely different – is the thin, off-white wheat noodle called somen, noted for its delicate flavor and adaptability to a variety of garnishes.

dles, also made of wheat, are as thin as vermicelli. Udon is usually eaten in hot dishes, and soba and somen may be eaten hot or cold, depending upon season. Additionally, eaten only cold is a type called *hiyamugi* (iced noodles), made of the same ingredients as udon but much thinner.

Most common are soba, from buckwheat flour and particularly delicious if not over-burdened with non-buckwheat flour extender. It is usually served with *wasabi* (Japanese green horseradish), thinly sliced scallions, a

Left, imported fare, and traditional packaging of eggs. Above, fast counter fare, Japanese style.

One of Japan's great cold weather favorites is udon, a somewhat thick to very thick wheat noodle served in a hot soy-base broth with scallions, other vegetables, and an egg. Udon, a real body-warmer, is particularly appreciated for its excellent texture.

Unlike pasta that's turned around on a fork, Japanese noodles are drawn into the mouth with chopsticks and *slurped* down. Experts say the noodles taste better that way.

Sushi and sashimi: Taste and visual pleasure converge in sushi and sashimi, both of uncooked seafood. Japanese simply adore sushi and sashimi.

A good sushi shop, or *sushi-ya,* can be

both expensive and confounding if one doesn't know what to ask for. Try, instead, a *kaiten sushi-ya,* where small dishes of sushi pass by on a conveyor belt along the counter. It lacks a certain elegance, but in a kaiten sushi-ya, the uninitiated can study the sushi offerings at leisure, and sample it for less cost. Then, later, armed with new-found expertise, visit a proper sushi-ya.

Good sushi requires the ingredients should be of good quality, that the rice be properly vinegared and steamed, and that the topping should be absolutely fresh.

Nabemono: If hot-pot dishes are your pleasure, Japan is the place to be. Every part of Japan, without exception, has its own dis-

tinctive *nabe-ryori* (pot dishes). Nabemono are winter dishes, essentially, and include: *ishikari-nabe* (Hokkaido Prefecture), containing salmon, onions, Chinese cabbage, tofu, *konnyaku* (a jelly made of root starch), and *shungiku* (spring chrysanthemum).

Popular for a quick meal is Tokyo-style *oden-nabe*, a potpourri containing potatoes, tofu, konnyaku, boiled eggs, octopus, carrots, daikon, kelp, and a wide variety of other ingredients.

Make a note of oden, which are often presented as pick-and-chose in convenience stores. It is one of the better winter body-warmers and a hearty dish.

Tsukemono: Never is one served a Japanese meal without *tsukemono*, or distinctive Japanese-style pickles. Historically, pickles probably owe their origins to the practice of pickling foods in anticipation of famines.

Ingredients used in Japanese pickles vary somewhat with the seasons and are of considerable variety. Common ingredients are Chinese cabbage, bamboo, turnips, *kyuri* (Japanese cucumbers), hackberry, daikon, ginger root, *nasu* (Japanese eggplant), *myoga* (Zingiber Mioga), *udo* (a type of asparagus), *gobo* and many others. Besides taste and nutrition, tsukemono add color to a meal, and also offer a wide range of textures, from *crunch* to *squish,* that might be missing from the main dishes. Furthermore, pickles can serve to clear the palate for new tastes – such as in a round of sushi, in which a bite of pickled ginger root rids the mouth of the aftertaste of an oily, white-skinned fish such as *aji* (mackerel), and prepares it for the delicate sweetness of, say, an *ebi* (prawn).

Bento: Like most modern countries, Japan is increasingly a land of fast-food. The traditional Japanese box lunch, *bento*, or more respectfully, *obento,* has become a form of fast-food in itself, with both convenience stores and *bento-ya* offering wide selections to take out. A bento box is used, flat and shallow and with small dividers to separate rice, pickles, and whatever else.

A special type of bento that has become an art in itself, not to mention a pursuit for the connoisseur, is the ekiben (from *eki* for train station and bento), sold at train stations and featuring regional specialities. If traveling by train, it is worth seeking out ekiben, which are often packaged in distinct ways.

A popular summer dish is *unagi,* or broiled eel served on rice. It's said to help one withstand the hot and humid days of the Japanese summer – *doyo no iri.*

With the drinks: At a traditional Japanese pub, the ubiquitous izaka-ya, try the likes of *saba* (mackerel), *sanma* (mackerel pike), *nijimasu* (rainbow trout), *nishin* (herring), *iwashi* (sardines) and *katei* (turbot). Try them *shioyaki*-style (salt broiled), with a good cold Japanese beer or a very dry sake. Japanese ginger-fried pork and beef are other simple but satisfying fried dishes enormously popular in any season.

<u>Left</u>, seafood restaurant. <u>Right</u>, pickle shop.

TOKYO

Japan has always been a country of villages. Tokyo is the biggest village, and one can easily reduce Tokyo itself into a gathering of smaller villages, most of them anchored around major train stations. Indeed, these stations are the foundation for understanding Tokyo's layout and personality.

Most of Tokyo's smaller villages lie on a circular rail line called **Yamanote-sen**, or Yamanote Line. There are 29 stations on the Yamanote, and it takes about an hour to make the complete loop, actually an oval in shape. Look at the layout of the Yamanote-sen, and of the placement of the stations along the way, and orientation in Tokyo becomes so much easier.

The important stations on the line – and the ones with which to become most familiar – are Tokyo, Ueno, Shinjuku, and Shibuya.

In the center of the oval defined by the Yamanote-sen, a bit off-center to the east, are the grounds of what once was the Edo castle. The Imperial Palace has replaced the castle, but the old symmetry of the castle defenses – moats and gates – are evident still today.

TOKYO STATION

While not Japan's busiest station – Shinjuku is quite possessive of the honor – **Tokyo Station** is nonetheless sizable, with 19 platforms side by side, including the terminus for the shinkansen, or bullet train. Deep beneath the station are additional platforms for more subway and JR lines.

The **Marunouchi** side is fronted by the original Tokyo Station, built in 1914 of red brick in an Old World, European style. Air raids in 1945 damaged the station, taking off the top floors; renovations, finished in 1947, left it somewhat lower.

From the Marunouchi entrance of Tokyo Station, a wide boulevard slices through corporate buildings towards the grounds of the Imperial Palace.

Yaesu side: On the other side of Tokyo Station, the **Yaesu** entrance opens onto a boulevard of rather undistinguished office buildings, many of them banks and corporate headquarters. Extending from the Yaesu central exit is Yaesu Dori, which intersects the major arteries of Chuo Dori and Showa Dori, running south to Ginza and north to Ueno.

Chuo Dori crosses Nihombashi-gawa over **Nihom-bashi**, or Nihon Bridge. (The Nihom/Nihon variation is a phonetic one of pronunciation.) An infuriatingly ugly elevated **Shuto expressway** directly above was erected just before the 1964 Tokyo Olympics.

Both the concrete-lined river and expressway diminish the significance of the original 1603 arched wooden bridge: the center of Edo Tokyo, and the zero point for the five main roads leading out of Edo. The present stone bridge, erected in 1911, retains little – actually none – of its Edo-era ambience. **Nihombashi**, as the area was known and still is, was a stage of gossip and public humiliation, including those about to be executed.

Preceding pages: Shinto shrine, Hokkaido. Left, high-rises over west Shinjuku. Right, the old Tokyo Station.

On the eastern periphery of Nihombashi, towards the Sumida-gawa, the **Tokyo City Air Terminal** is a downtown check-in facility for flights departing Narita. Not only can airline and baggage check-in be done here, but clearance of immigration, too.

Ryogoku: The site of Tokyo's sumo arena, called the **Kokugikan**, is in the area called Ryogoku, on the other side of Sumida-gawa and northeast of Tokyo Station. A lot of very large people live in Ryogoku – it is the home of many of the *sumo beya,* or stables, as the training center/dormitories for the *rikishi,* or wrestlers, are called.

Near Ryogoku is the **Fukagawa Edo Tokyo Museum**, a spectacular hall that encompasses a massive reconstruction of a part of *shitamachi* Edo from the nineteenth century. It is like walking on to the set of a samurai drama: there is even a life-like dog relieving himself by the guard tower. Every 20 minutes, the lighting cycles through night and day. There are numerous historical displays and detailed models of entire towns.

IMPERIAL PALACE

The Imperial Palace, or **Kokyo**, is a functional palace, where the emperor and his family reside. Much of the palace grounds – including the palace itself – are closed to the public and secluded behind massive stone walls, old trees and Edo-period moats.

Most of the 110-hectare complex is forested or given to private gardens and small ponds. The Imperial Palace building itself is an expansive, low building of concrete, veiled with a green roof. It was completed in 1970 to replace the wooden residence destroyed in a 1945 Allied air raid.

Kokyo Gaien, the palace's outer garden to the southeast, is an expansive area of green and impeccably-sculpted pine trees planted in 1889. Approaching from Marunouchi, this is the area first encountered after crossing Hibiya Dori. A large gravel-covered area leads to a famous postcard scenic – literally – of **Niju-bashi**, a distinctive bridge across an inner moat and one of the most widely-

Niju-bashi, Imperial Palace.

recognized landmarks in Japan. Tourists come here by the bus-loads for a quick group portrait in front of the bridge and moat.

Visitors are also permitted in the **Kokyo Higashi Gyoen**, the East Imperial Garden of the palace. It is open most days and can be entered through Otemon, Hirakawa-mon and Kitahanebashimon, three of the eight gates into the palace grounds. Inside are remains of the defenses of Edo-jo, and the foundations of the castle's *donjon*, the primary lookout tower of the shogun's residence.

Unfortunately, today nothing substantial remains of the old Edo castle – except for some turrets and donjon foundations, in addition to the moats and gates – nor do we have any surviving visual images of the castle.

GINZA

Of all places in Japan, **Ginza** has perhaps the greatest name recognition in the world, after Tokyo and Kyoto. During the super-heated bubble economy of the late 1980s, land in Ginza was literally priceless, the most expensive real estate anywhere. Likewise, an evening's entertainment in the exclusive and unmarked clubs of its back alleys too seemed nearly priceless.

Chuo Dori, sometimes called Ginza Dori, is one of two main arteries through Ginza. A few blocks past the overpass separating Ginza from Nihombashi and Yaesu is a monument to the original site of Ginza. Further on, numerous fashionable boutiques, immense department stores and galleries line the wide boulevard. The Mitsukoshi store anchors **Ginza 4-chome**, where Chuo Dori intersects Harumi Dori, the second main artery. (Most Tokyo districts are subdivided into *chome*; Ginza has eight.) **Harumi Dori** extends from Hibiya Koen, down through Ginza and Tsukiji and across the Sumida-gawa.

Along Harumi Dori towards Tsukiji, just past Showa Dori, the **Kabuki-za** is clearly a venue of kabuki. The current building was built in 1925, in what is known as the Momoyama style, which

Chuo Dori, Ginza.

has roots in the castles of the late 1600s.

Deeper into Tsukiji towards the Sumida-gawa is the famous **Tsukiji fish market**, where merchants arrive long before dawn to select the best of the day's fresh catch. Other produce is also auctioned here; in fact, there is a storage refrigerator here large enough to chill ten-days' food supply for the entire city.

In the opposite direction on Harumi Dori from Tsukiji, back past Ginza 4-chome, Ginza's potential for shopping ecstasy abounds. A popular meeting place is the **Sony Building** – note the waiting and expectant faces outside; inside are the latest in electronics, and an Toyota display room.

An elevated expressway over Harumi Dori defines the boundary between Ginza and **Yurakucho**. Towering on the opposite side of the expressway are the tall, curving exteriors of the Seibu and Hankyu department stores, with a popular animated clock on the exterior and facing the intersection. Just beyond are elevated train tracks extending from **Yurakucho Station**, constructed in 1910; the *shinkansen* and Yamanote-san trains snake along the overhead tracks. On the Yurakucho side of the tracks – directly across from the Yurakucho Denki Building, with the American Express office at street level – is the **Tourist Information Center**, or **TIC**. If expecting to travel in Japan, hit this place for extensive information about Japan.

Along **Hibiya Dori** is the towering **Imperial Hotel** (or in Japanese, *teikoku hoteru*). Always a place of impeccable standards by which other hotels are measured, the first Imperial Hotel opened in 1890. Its modest structure was replaced by a wonderful Frank Lloyd Wright design. The day after it opened to the public in 1923, the destructive Great Kanto Earthquake hit Tokyo. The hotel was one of the few structures to escape destruction. The Wright building was replaced by the modern structure in 1970. It's indeed a shame the Wright building wasn't kept in Tokyo; if going to Nagoya, there it is, relocated and reassembled as before.

Rainy dusk, Ginza 4-chome crossing.

300

KANDA and AKIHBARA

If there is a book, however old and in whatever language, that seems unattainable, it can be found in the **Jimbocho** station area of **Kanda**. There are stores specializing in art books, second-hand books, comic books – in English, French, German, Russian... Anything and everything.

West along Yasukuni Dori leads to its namesake, **Yasukuni-jinja**, in the **Kudan** area. What is said to be Japan's largest *torii* – eight stories high, made of high-tension steel plates, and weighing 100 tons – boldly announces the shrine. Its entrance nipping the northern tip of the Imperial Palace grounds, at Kitanomaru Koen, this Shinto shrine is Japan's most controversial. Proponents say it honors those who died for Japan; opponents say it glorifies Japanese aggression, and that it honors convicted war criminals. Pincered between the two extremes are politicians, who must decide whether or not to attend annual ceremonies at the shrine.

Akihabara: The neighborhood of Akihabara epitomizes the old Edo tradition of merchants or craftsmen of a particular commodity congregating together. Indeed, Akihabara is singularly devoted to the sales of electrical and electronic things. Today, its prices may be the cheapest in Japan, but rarely do they beat prices of similar components for sale overseas.

Akihabara's fame for electrical things originated shortly after World War II. A black market for scarce electrical and radio components evolved near the station. Now, Akihabara accounts for around 10 percent of Japan's domestic electrical and electronic sales.

UENO

North of Tokyo Station and Akihabara, exactly eight minutes on the Yamanote train, is **Ueno Station**. It's a subjective and subtle impression, but the area around the station seems somehow more down to earth, if not grittier, than other parts of urban Tokyo. It was once

Akihabara shop, and Ueno Koen.

the commoner's part of town, in what was called Shitamachi. Nowadays, there's an aspect of urban life around Ueno not typically noticeable in Japan – the homeless men that camp out in Ueno Koen; foreigners overstaying on expired visas, hustling passers-by with altered, counterfeit telephone cards; the park itself lacking the showcase polish expected of an urban park in one of the world's richest cities.

West of the station, **Ueno Koen** (Ueno Park) is perhaps Tokyo's most distinctly "park" park: sprawling grounds with trees, flocks of scrounging pigeons, monuments and statues, homeless Japanese (and until a few years ago, illegal immigrants from the Middle East), a zoo, a big pond with waterfowl, national museums. It's not quite as tidy and pristine as one might expect in Japan; the park seems tired and in need of scrubbing and a few more trash cans, always a scarce item in Japan.

Behind the shrine and down a slope is a road that acts as a natural divider between the park and **Shinobazuno-ike**, once an inlet and now a pond (*ike*) dense with lily plants. A small peninsula juts into the pond, with a Buddhist temple to Benten – a goddess of good fortune and the only female amongst the Seven Deities of Good Luck – perched on the end. A promenade follows the pond's squarish two-kilometer circumference. The **Shitamachi Museum** (look for it in the cluster of buildings near the pond, at the park's south entrance) is a hands-on exhibit of Edo commoners' daily life in Shitamachi, as this part of Edo Tokyo was once known.

The **National Museum of Western Art** is anchored by a collection of nearly a thousand pieces, and the **Tokyo National Museum** offers a superbly-displayed collection of Asian art and archeology. Arching over the outside entrance to the museum grounds is an immense samurai estate gate.

ASAKUSA

From the mid 1800s until World War II, Asakusa was the center of all fine things

Asakusa Kannon gate.

in Tokyo, a cultural nucleus of theater and literature, and of cuisine and the sensual delights. Imagine today's Shibuya, Ginza, Roppongi and Shinjuku tossed together, countrified and without the benefit of neon, fast-food and loudspeakers.

Anchoring Asakusa was **Senso-ji**, or **Asakusa Kannon**, perhaps the oldest Buddhist temple in the region, and a draw for people from around Japan, who brought with them spending money to make Asakusa prosper.

The south entrance to the temple, on Asakusa Dori, is a large gate, **Kaminari-mon**, or Thunder Gate, dating from 1960. (It had burned down a century before.) Here begins **Nakamise Dori** (lit. inside the shops), where two rows of red buildings funnel temple-goers northwards through a shopping arcade before spilling out onto the temple grounds.

In the other direction, east of Senso-ji, is the **Sumida-gawa**, which empties into Tokyo Bay. The exit for the Ginza Line, Tokyo's first subway line that opened in 1927, surfaces near the **Azuma-bashi** (bridge). Just north of the bridge is **Sumida Koen**, a recent attempt to open up the river front.

SHIBUYA, HARAJUKU and ROPPONGI

Shibuya is one of the trendiest neighborhoods in Tokyo, although many resident foreigners might nominate Roppongi to the east, mostly because Roppongi caters to foreigners, and has done so with high style for decades. Shibuya, on the other hand, caters to Japanese youth with money to spend, and there's a lot of both here.

The most popular exit of **Shibuya Station**, opening to the northwest, is named after a hound dog. And outside of that entrance, one will find a statue, erected in 1964, of said dog, an Akita named Hachiko. For a rendezvous in Shibuya, Hachiko's statue is the preferred rendezvous spot.

Beyond the Hachiko entrance is an immense intersection. Looking straight ahead, note the tall cylindrical building: the **Shibuya 109** building, a good refer-

Shibuya.

ence for orientation. The crowded road to its right leads up a gentle hill to Tokyu department store, and adjacent to it, the **Bunkamura**, a performance hall built during the roaring 1980s. Something's always going on inside – art, music, cinema, theater – and the interior spaces are a refreshing retreat on a hot day.

At the top of the hill, bearing to the left, is the huge **NHK Broadcast Center**, a 23-story building with two dozen TV studios and an equal number of radio studios. NHK is the government-run, viewer-subsidized (or taxed, more accurately) television and radio broadcaster. In addition to two subscription satellite channels, there is the standard NHK broadcast channel and an educational channel, with dowdy professors and chalkboards and charts of chemical molecules. Over 1,500 shows are produced in the broadcast center weekly.

Open to the public inside the center is the **NHK Studio Park**, a well-designed introduction to television broadcasting, with a number of interactive exhibits. Intriguing is a 3-D high-definition tel-evision presentation. Overhead observation windows look down upon sets for the ever-popular samurai dramas, which in fact rarely seem to be in production during visitor hours.

Yoyogi Koen served as the Olympic Village during the 1964 games. Before that, however, the area was a barracks, called Washington Heights, for the American army. Everything was eventually torn down, but rather than erecting something new, the site was turned into the park. It now includes a wild bird park, playground, and on weekends, some of the spunkiest Japanese anywhere. Too, there is some of the worst music, as wannabe rock groups give free "concerts," all at the same time, hoping to establish a following of adolescent girls that will cascade into Japan-wide popularity.

Yoyogi Koen is an extension of one of Japan's most famous Shinto shrines, **Meiji-jingu**. The shrine deifies Emperor Meiji and Empress Shoken. (Their remains, however, are in Kyoto.) The emperor, of course, was restored to rule in the 1868 Meiji Restoration, when the **Harajuku traffic.**

Tokugawa shogunate collapsed. The emperor died in 1912, the empress, two years later. The original shrine, built in 1920, was destroyed during World War II; the current shrine buildings were reconstructed in 1958. The shrine itself is constructed of Japanese cypress from Kiso, said to be the best lumber in Japan.

The walk to the shrine passes through a tunnel of these trees, and beneath three large *torii* gates, said to include one of the largest wooden gates in Japan: 12 meters high with pillars over a meter in diameter. Cypress wood, over 1,700 years old, from Taiwan was used.

Harajuku: The entrance to Meiji-jingu is near **Harajuku Station**, architecturally interesting for a Japanese train station. Leading from the station are a number of hip, groovy and rad avenues. (Harajuku itself was once a post station on the road from Kamakura, in the less-hip eleventh century.)

For some reason, narrow **Takeshita Dori**, a small side street between the station and Meiji Dori, has become a teeny-bopper avenue of shops and

Harajuku hip.

eateries. Positively for the young, it is without breathing room on weekends.

More room is found instead on the wide and upscale **Omote Sando**, a boulevard running from the southern end of Harajuku Station, where one finds the entrance to Meiji-jingu. Omote Sando has a European feel about it, from the expansiveness of the boulevard (at least for Japan), to the zelkovea trees that line it, to the style of architecture in some of the buildings.

Roppongi: In the lower middle of the oval defined by the Yamanote-sen, and just to the southwest of the Imperial Palace, is an area favoured by Tokyo's expatriate community: **Minato-ku**, a Tokyo ward made up of Aoyama, Akasaka, Roppongi, Azabu and Hiroo. The area is peppered with embassies and high-priced expat (and company-subsidized) housing, and liberally spiced with nightclubs and restaurants.

Up on a hill served by the Hibiya-sen, **Roppongi** is the heart of the area's social life, and night life, and courting life. It crawls with both foreigners and Japanese on the prowl for the opposite sex. Its main avenues are bright and loud, the back alleys lined with drinking establishments laced by themes meant to nurture nostalgia, or homesickness, in strangers in a strange land. But don't confuse the activity here with the blatant sex trade of Shinjuku's Kabukicho. In Roppongi, it's only upscale food and drinks, buttressed by probing smiles.

Check the horizon to the south, towards Shiba: the red-and-white **Tokyo Tower** juts skyward, looking industrial and out of place. Finished in 1958, its primary purpose was to broadcast television signals. Subsequent lyrical allusions to the Eiffel Tower or dynamic elegance were fabrications of creative writing. It's an ugly projection into the skyline, but the views from the observation decks are quite excellent.

SHINJUKU

After building Edo castle and settling down, Tokugawa Ieyasu had the **Shinjuku** area surveyed at the urging of some entrepreneurs. He then established a guard post – near today's Shinjuku 2-chome – along the Koshu Kaido, a road that led west into the mountains. Shinjuku (lit. new lodging) quickly became one of the largest urban towns in Edo, filled with shopkeepers, wholesale distributors, inns and tea houses. Shinjuku was also known for the male sensual delights, with over 50 "inns" catered by "serving girls". Unlike those in Asakusa, the women of Shinjuku were without licenses, and thus were considered as less than equals.

In its early days, when the line through Shinjuku was but 21 kilometers long, only about 50 people used the station at Shinjuku daily. Surrounding the wooden station was a forest of trees. The year was 1885. Nowadays, it's said by the Japanese that **Shinjuku Station** is the world's busiest train station. Maybe, maybe not, given the Japanese propensity for superlatives. It is a furiously busy place – approaching three million people daily – and congested, and can test the traveler's patience.

As with most large urban stations in Japan, there are multitudinous shops and restaurants filling every unused space in the multi-level labyrinth, above and below ground. There are also four massive department stores within Shinjuku Station itself, two of which have their own private train lines leading from Shinjuku: Keio, with a line that opened in 1915, and Odakyu, its line beginning in 1927.

To the East: If the four department stores within the station are somehow lacking, tumble out the station's east entrance onto **Shinjuku Dori**, where there are more department stores, and thousands of regular stores, and tens of thousands of people. This entrance of Shinjuku Station is a popular meeting and rendezvous spot.

This side of the station is, of course, a superb rambling area, which one can do for hours with little purpose. Many of those who have a purpose enter **Kabukicho**, north of Yasukuni Dori. After World War II, residents of this area sought to establish a sophisticated entertainment area of cinemas and dance halls, and perhaps most importantly, a kabuki theater. Hence, Kabukicho. But somewhat optimistically, naming of the neighborhood preceded construction of the kabuki theater, which was in fact never built.

The cinemas were, however, and for many years Tokyo's best cinema-viewing was in Kabukicho; European films were very popular during the 1960s, especially with intellectuals, wannabe intellectuals, political radicals and radical wannabes. Eventually, they moved elsewhere, leaving Kabukicho to the *yakuza*. Kabukicho is most famous nowadays for its rowdy nightlife and (expensive) sexual entertainment, which tends towards voyeurism rather than participation or solicitation. Still, it is popular for just strolling, ironically.

West Shinjuku: For more stately pursuits, follow Yasukuni Dori under the tracks to the west side of Shinjuku. (One could also exit the station directly to avoid the east side altogether.)

Given the shakiness of Tokyo's land, not to mention the experience of several devastating earthquakes, tall buildings in Tokyo have been limited. But Shinjuku sits atop rather solid ground, giving architects the confidence to build what they claim are earthquake-proof buildings that utilize sophisticated techniques for stress dissipation and structure stabilization.

Continue to the twin-towered building of the **Tokyo Metropolitan Government Office**. Conceived and started at the beginning of the so-called bubble economy in the 1980s, the buildings were designed to make a statement, simply put: Tokyo was now one of the world's great urban centers. (Still, it can be noted, only 85 percent of Tokyo residences have access to sewage systems.) Around 13,000 city employees fill the buildings each day.

The main building has two twin upper towers. Finished in 1991, these two towers are 48 floors high, or 243 meters (797 ft). At the top of both towers, expansive observation windows offer without doubt the finest views in Tokyo, and they're free. Construction of the building has been criticised as bubble-economy excess.

Tokyo Metropolitan Government Building.

SOUTH OF TOKYO

YOKOHAMA

With a population of over three million, Yokohama is second in size only to Tokyo. Happily, however, many of those areas worthy of exploring are concentrated in a relatively small area and can be covered, for the most part by foot, within a single day.

Another thing that makes Yokohama (only a 30-minute train ride from Tokyo) alluring is the fact that its broad, relatively uncrowded streets (except on weekends) and laid-back atmosphere provide a perfect antidote for Tokyo's claustrophobia and fast pace.

Start a walking tour of central Yokohama at **Sakuragicho Station**, which is the terminus for the Toyoko Line, originating at Tokyo's Shibuya Station. Other ways to get here from Tokyo are aboard the JR Yokosuka or Tokaido lines from Tokyo, or the Keihin Kyuko Line from Shinagawa. In both cases, you have to transfer onto the Negishi Line at Yokohama Station. Incidentally, Sakuragicho was also the last stop on Japan's first railroad, which began service to Shimbashi in Tokyo in September 1872.

Central Yokohama is in a state of great flux at the moment, as work proceeds down near the harbor on the massive **Minato Mirai 21** project, which will totally revamp the port area by the turn of the century.

Within its 190 square kilometers (75 sq. mi), it includes the 73-story **Landmark Tower**, at 296 meters (970 ft) one of the tallest buildings in Japan. The International Zone will feature a huge convention complex, and the Amenity Zone will be devoted to landscaped parks. Nearby are the *Nippon Maru*, a tall ship, and the neighboring **Maritime Museum**. Also close by is the **Yokohama Art Museum**, with its excellent collection of modernist sculpture.

When Commodore Perry and his Black Ships arrived in 1853, Yokohama was just a poor fishing village next to a rank swamp. Under the terms of a treaty negotiated in 1858 by the first U.S. envoy to Japan, Townsend Harris, the Port of Kanagawa, smack on the Tokaido – or the East Sea Road between Edo Tokyo and Kyoto – was to be opened to foreign settlement. But the shogunate reconsidered and built an artificial island on the mud flats of Yokohama instead.

That attempt to segregate the "red-haired barbarians" proved fortuitous for all concerned, since Yokohama's superb natural harbor helped international trade to flourish. The wild early days of the predominantly-male community centered around such recreational facilities as Dirty Village, the incomparable Gankiro Teahouse, and the local race track. Periodic attacks by sword-wielding, xenophobic samurai added to the lively atmosphere.

Eventually, foreign garrisons were brought in and the merchants could concentrate in a more sedate environment. **Honcho Dori** became the center of commercial activities. The wide street

Left, Daibutsu, Kamakura. Right, Yokohama park.

is still bracketed with banks and office buildings. There is, for example, the stately **Yokohama Banker's Club** and, on the right four blocks down, the lovely red-brick **Yokohama Port Opening Memorial Hall**, which miraculously survived the Great Kanto Earthquake of 1923 and the fire bombings of World War II. Also in this area are numerous prefectural offices, and near the waterfront, the **Yokohama Custom House**.

The **Yokohama Archives of History**, on the site of the former British consulate, houses a museum with various exhibits about Yokohama's fascinating history, and a library with related audiovisual materials.

Across from it is the **Yokohama Port Opening Square**, where the Japan-US Treaty of Peace and Amity was signed in 1854, and the **Silk Center**, with a delightful museum on the history of that mysterious fabric; at one time, Yokohama owed its prosperity primarily to silk, in which the local Indian community was intimately involved.

A little bit farther down the same road is the **New Grand Hotel**, which, although slightly down at the heel, is still a civic institution and the best spot for a break over coffee and cake. Next to it is the somewhat garish 106-meter (348-ft) **Marine Tower**, and a doll museum.

Yamashita Park is well worth a visit. Among the attractions at the park are the Girl with the Red Shoes, a statue dedicated to international friendship among children. If serendipity brings you here on a clear summer night, you are likely to hear a rock band wailing away on a temporary stage several hundred feet offshore. The former passenger liner and hospital ship, *Hikawa Maru*, is permanently moored here, and can be visited. Conveniently, there is a beer garden on deck, and boat tours of the harbor leave from next to the ship. Occasionally, distinguished visitors such as the *Queen Elizabeth II* are also to be found in port.

No visit to Yokohama would be complete without a meal in Chukagai, or **Chinatown**. This dozen or so blocks is

Yokohama Port, and Marine Tower.

the largest Chinatown in Japan, and is nearly as old as the port. The area within its five gates accounts for 90 percent of the former foreign settlement.

Chinatown also takes pride in the historical role it had in providing staunch support to Sun Yatsen when he was here in exile, trying to rally support for revolution on the Chinese mainland.

On days when a baseball game is on at nearby **Yokohama Stadium**, the area is visited by more than 200,000 people, the majority intent on dining at one of the approximately 150 local restaurants. Most also sneak in at least a peak at the exotic shops selling imported Chinese sweets and sundries from elsewhere in Asia. There are also many herbal medicine and tea shops. Although in most Chinatowns, from San Francisco to London, restaurants prepare food for Chinese tastes, in Yokohama everything is adjusted to Japanese taste buds, with a tad of French influence. Top chefs recruited from Hong Kong and Taiwan have to be deprogramed to an extent.

Back in the old days, the waterfront Bund often stood in contrast with the **Bluff**, or Yamate Heights, where the leading foreign merchants lived in palatial homes. **Nanmon Dori** in Chinatown was the central street that ran through the international settlement and connected the two. It became a local tradition – known as **Zondag**, from the Dutch word for leisure – that on every Sunday, the flags of the many nations were flown and brass bands would strut down the road.

Virtually every guidebook ever written about Yokohama urges readers to visit the famed **foreign cemetery** *(gaijin bochi),* where around 4,200 foreigners from 40 countries who somehow found their way to Japan are buried. The adjacent **Yamate Museum**, with quaint displays on the life of early foreign residents, sits near where Japan's first brewery was located.

Many expatriates prefer Yokohama over Tokyo, as both its waterfront is accessible, unlike that of Tokyo, and it retains a cosmopolitan ambiance.

Dancing in Yamashita Park.

KAMAKURA

Kamakura lies cradled in a spectacular natural amphitheater, surrounded on three sides by wooded mountains and on the fourth by the blue Pacific. For roughly 150 years, from 1192, when Minamoto no Yoritomo made it the headquarters of the first shogunate, until 1333, when imperial forces breached its seven "impregnable" passes and annihilated the defenders, Kamakura was the de facto political and cultural capital of Japan.

During those years, the warrior administration based here built impressive temples and commissioned notable works of art, a great deal of it Zen-influenced. Despite the endemic violence of Japan's middle ages, most survived and can be viewed today, including 65 Buddhist temples and 19 Shinto shrines – interspersed with walks through quiet surrounding hills.

Kamakura is only an hour from Tokyo Station, and 30 minutes from Yokohama, on the JR Yokosuka Line.

For that reason much of it resembles an open-air madhouse on weekends. Visitors customarily begin their sightseeing from **Kamakura Station** or Kita-Kamakura, the station nearest the five great Zen temples. A different approach to the city is recommended, however.

Take the private Odakyu Line from Shinjuku and get off either at Fujisawa or Enoshima. This offers a chance to ride the delightful **Enoden** (Enoshima Dentetsu) electric trolley line and consequently slip gently into a Kamakura frame of mind. The Enoden, which began operations in 1902, starts from **Fujisawa** and ends at Kamakura Station, with 13 stops in between. For about half its 10-kilometer (6-mi) length, the cars run along the ocean, and when they are not crowded, the conductors even allow surfers to bring their boards aboard.

Hop off the Enoden at **Hase**, the station closest to **Daibutsu**, the Great Buddha. There's little chance of missing the colossus. At 11 meters (40 ft) in height – minus the pedestal – and weighing 93 tons, this representation of the compassionate Amida is unlikely to get lost in a crowd. Because the features of the statue were purposely cast out of proportion when it was built in 1252, stand four to five meters in front of the statue to get the full impact of the art work. For a fee, crawl around inside the statue.

Astonishingly, the Great Buddha has survived, almost intact, the onslaughts of earthquakes, typhoons and *tsunami* – like the one that in 1495 ripped away the wooden building that once enclosed it.

Central Kamakura: On the east side of the station is **Wakamiya Dori**, the broad boulevard that leads under three massive *torii* archways to the Tsurugaoka Hachiman-gu, to the north. Parallel to Wakamiya Dori is **Kamachi Dori**, Kamakura's modest answer to the Ginza. The area abounds with all kinds of trendy shops and eating places, and many of the Japanese-style restaurants here and elsewhere in the city have incorporated Zen principles of cooking. Quite crowded on weekends.

Folk-craft shops encourage serious browsing. But Kamakura is most fa-

Detail at a Kamakura Shrine.

mous for *Kamakura-bori* (lacquerware), which originated in the area in the thirteenth century for the production of utensils used in religious ceremonies. Learn more about this art at the **Kamakura-bori Kaikan,** on the right as you start up Wakamiya Dori towards Tsurugaoka Hachiman-gu.

The approach into **Tsurugaoka Hachiman-gu** crosses a steep, red half-moon bridge that separates the Gempei Ponds. The three islands on the right – the Genji side – signify the Chinese character for birth, that is, the victory of Yoritomo and his followers, while the four in the Heike pond stand for the death of the rival Taira.

Art and archery: Behind the Heike Pond is the **Kanagawa Prefectural Museum of Modern Art**, and a little past the Genji Pond is the **Kokuhokan** (National Treasure Hall). Each month, the Kokuhokan teasingly changes the limited displays of the 2,000 treasures from the temples of Kamakura, which are in its possession. Continuing up the avenue towards the main shrine, cross a 25-meter (82-ft) dirt track, along which every September 16 mounted archers gallop and unloosen their arrows at targets in the ancient samurai ritual of *yabusame.*

Nichiren: The area due east of Kamakura Station is largely the province of temples of the Nichiren sect. Although most foreigners have heard of Zen, few know much about Nichiren (1222–82) and his teachings, despite the fact that the iconoclast priest founded the only true Japanese Buddhist sect. Nichiren was an imposing personality who, in his lifetime, was nearly executed, exiled twice and set upon by mobs on more than one occasion, and who continues to generate feelings of both respect and disdain centuries after his death.

The temples of **Hongaku-ji, Myohon-ji, Chosho-ji, Myoho-ji**, and **Ankokuron-ji** are all Nichiren temples and are worth a visit. The Myohon-ji, for example, although only 10 minutes from the station, seems a world apart, as does much of this side of Kamakura.

Main hall, Tsurugaoka Hachiman-gu.

FUJI AND HAKONE

Sweeping up from the Pacific to form a nearly perfect symmetrical cone, 3,776 meters (12,388 ft) above sea level, the elegantly-shaped **Fuji-san** watches over Japan. But the mountain loses its temper on occasion. Fuji's last eruption in 1707 covered Edo Tokyo, some 100 kilometers (60 mi) away, with ash.

Although climbers are known to set out to challenge the mountain throughout the year, the "official" climbing season for Fuji begins on July 1 and ends on August 31. The mountain huts and services found along the trails to Fuji's peak are open only then, and casual hikers are advised to pick this period to make the journey to the top. Expect thick crowds to the top.

The five main trails – Kawaguchi, Subashiri, Fujinomiya, Fuji-Yoshida, and Gotemba – are each divided into ten stages known as *go*. The Kawaguchi trail is the most popular route up, and Subashiri seems to be the preferred way down, but Fujinomiya is more convenient if coming from the direction of Kansai, to the southwest. The ascent should take about 9 hours from the first *go* to the tip of the cone.

Fuji Five Lakes: The Five Lakes district skirts the northern base of Fuji and provides an ideal year-round resort, offering a range of outdoor recreational activities such as camping and water sports during the summer months, and skiing and skating in the winter. From east to west, the lakes are **Yamanaka, Kawaguchi, Sai, Shoji** and **Motosu**. (A *ko* added to the end of these names signifies "lake".)

Yamanaka-ko, which is the largest in the group, and the picturesque Kawaguchiko are the most frequented of the five, but some of the best spots are hidden near the smaller and more secluded Motosu-ko, Shoji-ko and Sai-ko. Some recommended visits include the **Narusawa Ice Cave** and **Fugaku Wind Cave**, both formed by the volcanic activities of one of Fuji's early eruptions; the delicate **Shiraito Falls**; and **Koyodai** (Maple Hill), which offers one of the best views of the surrounding area. The primeval forests of **Junkai** and **Aokigahara** are also worth noting.

Hakone: Local history has it that when Toyotomi Hideyoshi, one of Japan's great warriors and the first to unite the country, seized Odawara Castle in 1590, he ordered a rock mineral bath to be built in the neighboring mountains, where his men could ease their travel-weary bodies. This area is known as Hakone, the backdrop of Fuji.

The optimal tour starts at Odawara Station, where the **Hakone Tozan Densha** (mountain railway) begins its nine-kilometer (5-mi) zig-zag up to **Gora**. This amazing single-track train, built in 1919, climbs and clangs its 40-minute journey up the steep slope.

Hakone-Yumoto, the first stop on the line and the gateway to Hakone's 16 hot springs, nestles in a shallow ravine where the Hayakawa and Sukumo rivers flow together. An overnight stay at one of the inns here is highly recommended, as are the hot springs.

Twenty minutes up from Yumoto lies **Miyanoshita**, the oldest and the most thriving of the spa towns. The original *Taiko no Iwayu,* the rock bath attributed to Hideyoshi, can be found here, although it is no longer in use.

Miyanoshita is also the home of the famed **Fujiya Hotel** and **Naraya Ryokan**. Fujiya, dating from 1878, is the second-oldest existing hotel in Japan. Naraya, the Japanese-style of the two, has a fine reputation and is also used by the imperial family.

Outdoor art: The Tozan Tetsudo also makes a stop at **Chokoku-no-Mori**, an outdoor sculpture garden where the works of Picasso, Rodin, Leger and Takamura Kotaro and many others are on permanent display.

The **Suginamiki**, or Ancient Cedar Avenue, makes for a wonderful stroll. This was part of the **Tokaido Highway**, down which the grand processions of the shogun lords made their way to the capital. Near here stood the Hakone Sekisho, a barrier originally built in 1618 to defend Edo and keep an eye on the comings and goings on the highway. **Right, Hakone and Fuji-san.**

OSAKA AND KOBE

Many Japanese look askance at Osaka, as if it belonged to another, somewhat unrelated, part of the planet. Its humor is different and a bit more rollicking than Tokyo, and greetings are to the point: *Mokarimakka?* Making money? Even the language and intonation has a distinct, earthy flavor, raising eyebrows of disdain in sophisticated Tokyo.

Osaka's business connection is documented as far back as the fourth century, when Emperor Nintoku made Naniwa (Osaka) his capital. He astutely decided to rebate all taxes to local businesses for three years, after he was informed of an impending recession. His ploy worked rather well, and the Osaka business ethic was conceived, as was its unique language of the merchants, *akinai kotoba*.

The city's stellar port and river connection to the capital in Kyoto played a central role in its economic and cultural development. Merchants from around the country – and from China and Korea – flooded the city. Osaka grew in strength and economic power, culminating with the shogunate of legendary Toyotomi Hideyoshi (1536–98), who chose Osaka as his seat of government, built himself a fine castle, and then turned the city into Japan's foremost commercial and industrial center. For the next 270 years, Osaka was the kitchen of Japan, with raw materials pouring in and high-quality finished products flowing out. Kyoto and fledgling Edo (Tokyo) were consumers, Osaka the provider.

Downtown: Osaka has an extensive, user-friendly subway and train system that makes exploring the city a pleasure. Their are two sides of the Osakan coin: one side centers on Umeda, in Kita-ku around Osaka Station, and the other on Namba, in Chuo-ku around Namba Station. While only 10 minutes apart by subway, they are worlds apart in mind and manner. Osaka's newer face, Umeda is where most of the new skyscrapers, office blocks, hotels and shopping centers are sprouting. Namba is the unpretentious side of the city, where residents say is the real Osaka. Most Osakans will say that Umeda is where one works, but Namba is where the good times are. It's where the friendly, funny *Osaka-ben* (Osaka dialect) is spoken with pride, and where Osakans feel most at home.

Umeda: Since most trains (except the *shinkansen*) arrive at the Osaka Station complex in Umeda, it is from here that a tour of the city should start. Explore the vast subterranean shopping network that connects the three clustered train stations with Osaka's three main north–south subway lines; it's the largest in Japan and one of the largest in the world. Corridors connect department stores with hotels and hundreds of shops and boutiques, and uncountable eateries.

Up on the street from the station complex is Midosuji, Osaka's main north–south boulevard. South on the other side of the river is **Nakanoshima**, one of the most important pieces of real estate in the city. This narrow island is the center of city government, and the home to many major Osaka companies. A footpath runs most of the way around Nakanoshima, offering splendid views of the river and city. An hour or two here is well worth the time.

From Midosuji, follow the path east along the river, passing in front of Osaka city hall, library, and the quaint, red-brick central public hall. Across from the public hall is the superb **Museum of Oriental Ceramics**, housing the famous Ataka collection of Chinese and Korean porcelain.

Back on Midosuji, continue south under the *ginkgo* trees. Japan's thriving pharmaceutical industry started in Osaka with the import of Chinese herbal remedies. Most of Japan's drug companies still have their headquarters here along Doshomachi, just off Midosuji.

Continuing south on Midosuji is the district of Honmachi, where Midosuji and Honmachi boulevards cross. Just north of the crossing is **Semba**, the apparel wholesale area of Osaka. Most large wholesalers have outgrown their Semba homes, but some 800 small wholesalers still operate in the Semba Center Building, a two-story structure entirely under a 930-meter-long expanse of elevated highway. Many of Osaka's most venerated businesses got their start in Semba, and many Japanese say that there is no one quite as astute in business as a Semba-trained businessman, who can manipulate a soroban faster than a calculator.

Follow Midosuji south until the next major crossing, Nagahori. The first landmark to look for is the **Sony Tower**, at the mouth of Osaka's premier covered-shopping street, **Shinsaibashi**, which extends south toward Takashimaya department store and Namba Station. Here are ancient little shops sitting in apparent ignorance of the outrageously fancy boutique plazas towering on either side.

South on Shinsaibashi is one of the most fascinating stretches in Osaka, the **Dotonbori** amusement quarter. At the Dotonbori Canal, Shinsaibashi ends and Ebisusuji begins. At this point, the *son et lumire* **Kirin Plaza Building**, architecturally akin to something out of Blade Runner, stands on the left.

Venture about halfway across the bridge, squeeze in along the stone rail-ing, and then sit tight for one of the best nonstop parades in the country – Osakans from every walk of life out for a walk. There is more to Dotonbori than just the passing crowds, however. For hundreds of years, this was the theatrical heart of Japan, with six *kabuki* theaters, five *bunraku* playhouses, and a myriad of other halls at one point, where the great storytellers and comics of Osaka performed. Today, most of the old theaters have been replaced by cinemas, among which the elegant old **Shochiku-za** is an architectural link to the golden age of black-and-white films. The venerable **Naka-za**, with its kabuki and geisha dances, and the vaudevillian **Kado-za** are still active, but they are the last of the legitimate theaters left in Dotonbori. Several years ago, the Bunraku Puppet Theater moved from its old Asahi-za home to the **National Theater**, a few blocks to the east.

Just south of Naka-za, the alley named Hozenji Yokocho is lined with scores of traditional Osaka eating and drinking establishments. (Some can be quite ex-

Dotonbori Canal.

pensive, so confirm prices before ordering.) Continue down the alley to **Hozen-ji**, one of the most visited and venerated temples in Osaka. Local businessmen come to pray for good business, young couples ask for happy futures, and older people pray for good health. A very serviceable temple, indeed, with something for everyone.

Namba Station offers little that is remarkable, save the vast underground shopping arcade of Namba City and Ranbow Town. Three main subway lines connect at Namba Station, also t e terminus for both the Kintetsu and Nakai railways serving Nara, Wakaya a and points south. Namba is also o e of the best connecting points to the **K nsai International Airport**. Both JR Wes and Nankai Railroads serve the airpor from here.

Osaka Castle: The hard-to-miss Osaka-jo is reached by following the footpath to the eastern end of Nakanoshima, then up the spiral ramp onto Tenjin-bashi. Walk north across the bridge, then right at the police box. A short jaunt ends at the entrance of **Sakuranomiya Koen**. A few blocks north of this point sits funky **Tenmangu Jingu**, dedicated to the god of learning. As its name implies, Sakuranomiya (Cherry Garden) Koen has nearly 20 kilometers of trails lined with cherry trees. If lucky enough to be there on the second week in April, you'll get a good look at Japan's national flower, the cherry blossom, along with uncountable numbers of Osakans at their merriest while drinking and singing under the trees.

Follow the footpath along the river to the **Osaka mint** (about a kilometer) and the mint museum. Then take the foot bridge (Kawasaki Bashi) over the river to Osaka-jo, the castle, straight ahead. Up and then down through an underpass, and then up onto an overpass eventually leads to it. (One might also have taken a taxi and relaxed.)

Osaka-jo is one of the most visited sites in the city. It is an ode to everything that was great in the past and a symbol of the possibilities of Osaka in the future. The main *donjon*, towering above the vast expanse of gardens and stone

walls, is a replica of the original built by Toyotomi Hideyoshi, in 1585. With the conscripted help of all the feudal lords of the nation and the labor of tens of thousands, the massive castle was completed in three years. Much of the original grounds, moats and walls still stand.

KOBE

The *kanji* characters for Kobe translate as god's door. But Kobe, 30 kilometers (20 mi) east of Osaka, is more like a doorsill – a long and narrow ledge squeezed between the mountains and Osaka Bay. Kobe is best known for its port, pearl and fashion industries, and, of course, for its beef. It boasts no world-class attractions and is consequently bypassed by most tourists, despite its long history of trade and foreign contact, and a Hong Kong-like topography.

In 1995, Kobe was jolted by a massive earthquake that killed 6,000 people in the Kansai region. Entire neighborhoods, especially in the western sections of the city, were flattened when Japanese-style homes – wooden post-and-beam frames with heavy tiled roofs – collapsed and burned in the resulting gas fires. Buildings and elevated roads, mostly of contemporary concrete construction, collapsed. All transportation and port facilities were also damaged, especially Kobe's port facilities, built on reclaimed land.

Although the earthquake was destructive beyond belief, and the government's inept emergency response equally beyond belief, the dire predictions that Kobe would take several years to rebuild have not proven true.

By 1997, Kobe had, for the most part, returned to normal. Yes, damage from the earthquake can still be seen in empty blocks and boarded buildings, but the trains are running, and the port is busy, and shops and restaurants are open.

The cardinal point on the Kobe compass is **Sannomiya**, a popular shopping and entertainment district. North from **Hankyu Station**, look for Kitanozaka Dori, which leads uphill past the India Social Club to **Kitanocho**. Here, on the high ground, rich foreign traders once staked out impressive residences at the turn of the twentieth century, their growing influence freeing them from the foreign ghetto originally allocated near the wharfs. Presenting a fanciful potpourri of European and American architectural styles, several of these *ijinkan* – now sharing the hill with trendy boutiques and restaurants – are open to the public. Westerners tend to find the interiors unexceptional (and full of cheap souvenirs for domestic tourists), but standouts include the impeccably-restored **Kazamidori**, and the **Choueke House**, which offers an intimate glimpse into the life-style of one long-time resident family.

While in the neighborhood, try to locate the mosque and synagogue, and the Catholic, Baptist and Russian Orthodox churches, all within a few blocks of one another – a unique assemblage for an Asian city this size.

Extending west from Sannomiya, parallel shopping arcades extend to **Motomachi Station** and beyond. The one directly under the tracks – the remnants of a black-market that surfaced amid the post-war rubble – is a mecca for bargain-hunters seeking second-hand and imitation goods.

South of Motomachi Station and just west of the elegant Daimaru department store, look for the dragon gate announcing Kobe's two-block-long **Chinatown**. This small but vibrant enclave, like Kitanocho, surpasses in its aura of foreignness anything that can be seen in the historic ports of Yokohama and Nagasaki, thus cementing Kobe's reputation as the most non-Japanese corner of the country.

From Chinatown, it's a short walk south to **Meriken Koen** and the waterfront. The park was named for the American consulate that once stood nearby. The surrounding redeveloped wharf frontage is the site of the strikingly-designed **Maritime Museum**. It is an informative, user-friendly resource with audio explanations in English. A visit here should also include a ride to the top of adjacent **Port Tower** and the 45-minute harbor cruise. The Kobe Meriken

Kobe Port.

320

Park Oriental Hotel towers over the entire reclaimed area.

In a feat of near science fiction, and with a biblical dimension, Kobe has "recycled" its surplus mountains to build up from the sea floor two of the world's largest artificial islands. This massive undertaking was to assure Kobe as a prime trading port – it already has sea links with 150 countries – and its position as a world leader in efficient handling of containerized cargo.

For an intriguing look at the cultural side of foreign trade, drop in at the nearby **Kobe City Museum**, housed in a doric-columned former bank. This small, admirable museum focuses on Japan's early encounters with the West and features a rare collection of *namban* (southern barbarian) art, works inspired by contacts with the first Portuguese and Spanish traders arriving here in the sixteenth and seventeenth centuries.

For those who do not relish tramping about, a bus shuttle for tourists retraces a similar route and offers a day-pass. Taxis, alas, are not recommended, due

Into the Inland Sea.

to the short-distance trips – and possibly because many of the drivers are seasonal workers in the local sake distilleries. In fact, Kobe cabbies are undoubtedly the surliest in the nation, a rude awakening if expecting otherwise.

The Portliner monorail from Sannomiya provides a convenient elevated loop ride around **Port Island**. Here – and on neighboring **Rokko Island**, also reachable by a monorail from JR Sumiyoshi Station – visitors can get a first-hand look at the future of container vessels. Moreover, the center of the island has been zoned to accommodate a hotel, sports and convention facilities, plus an amusement park and spacious sea-view apartments for 20,000 residents. Port Island is also where the jet-boat shuttle from **Kobe City Air Terminal** (KCAT) departs for the 30-minute ride to the Kansai International Airport, in Osaka Bay.

Port Island, incidentally, offers a good vantage point from which to gaze back nostalgically at the "old" Kobe, especially at night.

KYOTO

Kyoto defines traditional Japan. As Japan's artistic and cultural depository, Kyoto ranks with Athens and Beijing as a living museum. The city sits on a flat plain enclosed by a horseshoe of mountains on three sides. Open to the south, between the rivers **Katsura-gawa** to the west and **Kamo-gawa** to the east, Kyoto is Japan's seventh largest city, with a population of 1.4 million. With several colleges and universities, it is the educational center of western Japan.

For nearly 1,100 years, from 794 until 1868, Kyoto was home of the emperor and thus capital of the nation. Japan's first permanent capital was established in Nara in 710, but by 784, the intrigues of power-hungry Buddhist priests forced the Emperor Kammu to move the capital to Nagaoka, between Nara and present-day Kyoto. It wasn't until 988 that the use of *kyoto* (capital) began to appear in official records; a century later, Kyoto was the city's proper name.

Kyoto (then Heiankyo) was built to a scale model of the Tang dynasty's (618–906) capital of Chang'an (now Xi'an), in China. The city extended in a regular grid pattern, still in evidence today, for 5.2 kilometers (3.2 mi) from north to south, and 4.4 kilometers (2.7 mi) east to west. Walls with 18 gates and a double moat surrounded the city. And because of the persistent trouble with priests in Nara, temples were forbidden inside Heiankyo – many of Kyoto's most venerated temples are in the hills surrounding the city. A decision by the Americans not to bomb Kyoto during World War II – its historical heritage was considered too important – assured that these ancient structures stand today.

Kyoto has some 1,500 Buddhist temples, 300 Shinto shrines, 100 museums, two imperial villas, one palace and castle, plus 5,000 arts and crafts shops. Don't even think of visiting them all. Most people encounter Kyoto first from **Kyoto Station**, most likely having taken the *shinkansen* from Tokyo, less than three hours away.

Just east of Kyoto Station and across the Kamo-gawa, **Sanjusangen-do** has served as the backdrop for countless pictures of Japanese archery. Its archery festival, on January 15th, is famous across Japan. The temple, last rebuilt in 1266, houses 33 alcoves, between 33 pillars under a 60-meter-long (200 ft) roof. Inside is a thousand-handed Kannon, bodhisattva of mercy and compassion, and her 1,000 disciples. Each face is different: Japanese look for a face resembling their own – or that of a relative – to whom to make an offering.

North on the other side of Shichijo Dori is the **Kyoto National Museum**, exhibiting artifacts of history, art and crafts. East up the slope (*zaka*), on the east side Higashioji Dori, leads to **Kiyomizu-dera**. The temple's main hall (*hondo*) sits perched out over the mountain side on massive wooden pilings. The veranda, or *butai* (dancing stage), juts out over the valley floor.

Back across Higashioji Dori sits **Rokuharamitsu-ji**, one of Kyoto's gems. At the rear of the main hall, built

Golden Pavilion.

in 1363, is a museum with two fine Kamakura-period (1185–1333) sculptures: Taira-no Kiyomori, of the Heike clan, and Kuya, founder of the temple. The eyes of Kiyomori, presaging the tragic destruction of his clan, sum up the anguish often seen in Kamakura-period art. Kuya, who popularized the chanting of the lotus sutra, is shown reciting magic syllables, each of which becomes Amida, the savior.

North are the brilliant-orange buildings of **Yasaka-jinja**, affectionately called Gion-san after the adjoining Gion pleasure quarter. One of the tallest granite *torii* in Japan, at nine meters (30 ft) in height, marks the portal to the shrine. The unusual main hall is built in the residential Gion-style.

Crossover Sanjo Dori and continue north through **Okazaki Koen**. This park holds museums, halls, a library and zoo. An arching 24-meter-high (80 ft) torii leads from Okazaki Koen to the vermilion-colored gate of **Heian-jingu**, more of an architectural study than a Shinto center. The shrine, dedicated to Kyoto's first and last emperors, is a replica of the original Imperial Palace, built in 794 and last destroyed by fire in 1227. The shrine was erected in 1895 to commemorate Kyoto's 1,100th anniversary. The shrine displays the architecture of the Heian period, when Chinese influence was at its zenith.

Passing through the shrine's massive gate, it's hard to imagine that the shrine is but a two-thirds scale version of the original Imperial Palace. The expansive, white-stone courtyard carries the eye to the Daigoku-den, or main hall, where government business was conducted. The Blue Dragon and White Tiger pagodas dominate the view to the east and west.

Follow **Tetsugaku no Michi**, or the Philosopher's Walk, north past the temple of Zenrin and the Nomura Museum. The walk, named for the strolling path of Japanese philosopher Kitaro Nishida (1870–1945), snakes about two kilometers along the bank of a narrow canal to Ginkaku-ji. The quiet path – save for the crowds of tourists at times

Purification at Heian-jingu.

– is noted for its spring cherry blossoms and fall foliage. Along the path are interesting homes, shops, tea rooms and small restaurants.

Philosopher's Walk ends at the Silver Pavilion, or **Ginkaku-ji**. The Ashikaga-era shogun who erected it in 1489 died before its completion, and it remains sans silver, but with an exquisite pavilion and Zen garden.

Imperial ways: Due west and back across Kamo-gawa, the **Kyoto Imperial Palace** remains the emperor's residence and thus under the control of the Imperial Household Agency, which dictates every nuance and moment of the imperial family's life.

Originally built as a second palace for the emperor, the Kyoto Imperial Palace was used as a primary residence from 1331 until 1868, when Tokyo became the new residence with the fall of the shogunate, and with the Meiji restoration of the imperial system.

From the palace, a few blocks west is **Nishijin**, the weaver's quarter. The Nishijin Textile Center has excellent displays of working looms and woven goods. Here, try on a kimono. South is **Nijo-jo**, a castle begun in 1569 by the warlord Oda Nobunaga, and finished by Tokugawa Ieyasu, ally to Oda Nobunaga, to demonstrate his military dominance over the city. In 1867, it served as the seat of government from where Emperor Meiji abolished the shogunate. Rectangular in dimensions, the castle's magnificent stone walls and gorgeous gold-leafed audience halls reflect the power of the Edo-period shoguns. The corridors of the castle's Ninomaru Palace feature "nightingale" (creaking) floors to warn of intruders.

Further south and back near Kyoto Station are two notable temples. As was the case with many of Kyoto's historical treasures, Japan's great unifier, Toyotomi Hideyoshi (1536–98), was responsible for establishing **Nishi Hongan-ji**. Its Chinese influences are many, and historians sometimes consider it the best example of Buddhist architecture still around. The *hondo*, or main hall, was rebuilt in 1760 after fire

Ginkaku-ji, the Silver Pavilion.

destroyed it. To the east, **Higashi Hongan-ji** was established in 1603 when the first Tokugawa shogun, wary of the Jodo-shinshu sect's power at Nishi Hongan-ji, attempted to thwart their influence by establishing an offshoot of the sect. Only the main hall and founder's hall are open to the public. The present buildings were erected in 1895, after fire destroyed the predecessors.

Zen paths: To the north and west of the city center, skirting the foothills, are three renowned Zen temples that should not be missed. Established as a small monastery in 1315, **Daitoku-ji**'s present buildings were built after 1468, when one of the several fires in its history burned down the temple. It is the holy of holies, where Zen married art. Some eight of Daitoku-ji's 22 subsidiary temples are open to the public. The three best-known are Daisen, Zuiho and Koto. In **Daisen-in** is Kyoto's second most famous, maybe the best, Zen garden. Unlike the abstractions of other gardens, the Daisen garden more closely resembles the ink-wash paintings of Zen

Rock-garden homework, Ryoan-ji.

art. Look for the mountains, rivers and islands in the water, which appears to flow under the veranda.

Walk west along Kitaoji Dori, past Funaokayama Koen, to the best-known temple in Kyoto, if not all Japan: **Kinkaku-ji**, or the Golden Pavilion. It's a replica built in 1955 of a fifteenth-century structure, and last recovered in gold-leaf in 1987. Each of the pavilion's three stories reflect a different architectural style. It is probably the youngest temple in Kyoto. The original was burned down in 1950 by a man who entered the Buddhist priesthood after being seduced by the pavilion's beauty. Thinking that his sense of aesthetics might approach perfect if he burned down the very object that had enchanted him in the first place, he did exactly that. The author and right-wing nationalist Mishima Yukio fictionalized the burning episode in his 1956 book, *Kinkakuji*.

Further west, visit **Ryoan-ji**, or Temple of the Peaceful Dragon, early in the day, before the peace is shattered by the bus-loads of tourists. Here is the

most famous Zen rock garden (*karesansui*, or dry landscape) in the world, and one of Kyoto's main tourist attractions. The sixteenth-century garden is an abstract of an ink-wash painting executed in rock and stone. No one knows the exact meaning of its fifteen rocks (one is always out of sight) and raked gravel, but speculations abound.

A little past Ryoan-ji, **Ninna-ji**'s formidable gate, with its fierce-looking nio guardians, is one of the best in Japan. Walking back east, tenth-century **Kitano Tenman-gu** is one of Kyoto's most earthy shrines. Its restrained wooden architecture enshrines Sugawara Michizane, a ninth-century scholar and statesman.

Westward: Out in the western hills, **Arashiyama** was once the playground of Heian aristocrats, and is today punctuated by quaint temples. Visitors cross over the Hozu-gawa on picturesque Togetsu Bridge to the restaurant and shop-lined promenade along the river.

One of the most famous strolling gardens in Japan lies inside Katsura Rikyo,

or the **Katsura Imperial Villa**, due west of Kyoto Station on the west side of Katsura-gawa. Its garden features a number of splendid tea houses overlooking a large central pond. Katsura, with its severe refinement, has exercised more influence on contemporary architecture than perhaps any other building in Japan.

Southward: Just a few blocks south of Kyoto Station, **To-ji** boasts one of the nation's enduring postcard images: the five-story Goju-no-to. This pagoda was rebuilt in 1644 and stands at 55 meters (180 ft) as Japan's tallest pagoda. The temple itself was established in 796, around the same time as Kyoto. Built next to the old city's main gate, which faced south, the temple became the main Buddhist temple in Japan. Its main hall, or *kondo*, reflects Buddhist traditions from India, China, and Japan.

To the east, up against the hills, **Tofuku-ji** rests as one of the best places for autumn foliage. It contains Japan's oldest, and perhaps most important, Zen-style gate, from the fifteenth century. Yet its 25 subsidiary temples are rarely visited, and the grounds are usually quiet.

A few block south of Tofuku-ji is one of Japan's icons. Almost everyone has seen pictures of tunnel-like paths of hundreds of bright-red torii. Actually, there are over 10,000 torii covering the paths of **Fushimi Inari Taisha** – the fox shrine founded in the ninth century in honor of the fox that farmers believe is the messenger of the harvest god. To experience Fushimi, walk the full four-kilometer (2.5 mi) course, which takes about two hours.

Old quarters: Along the Kamo-gawa in central Kyoto, **Gion** is Kyoto's famous pleasure-quarter, or *geisha* district. But in Kyoto, they're known as *maiko* and *geiko*, not geisha. Along Gion's narrow streets, one won't see geiko, but there's a good chance to catch sight of a maiko hurrying to entertain a guest, especially around Gion Shimbashi. The neighborhood of old wooden buildings near **Gion Shimbashi**, the bridge over Kamo-gawa, is a national preservation district. **Minami-za**, built in the early 1600s, is the oldest theater in Japan.

Left, Fushimi Inari. Right, Kyoto autumn.

THE SOUTH

HONSHU

Himeji: A 15-minute stroll from the shinkansen station, along a road lined with modern sculptures, brings visitors to the main attraction in the city, **Himeji Castle**. It is called the White Egret Castle, as it quite resembles a nesting crane, majestically resting on the banks of the Senba River. It is the largest, and most elegant, of the dozen existing Japanese medieval castles. Best of all, it is easily accessible to travelers.

The castle's construction was a Herculean task, requiring 393,000 kilograms (400 tons) of wood, 75,000 tiles weighing 3 million kilograms (3,000 tons), and a huge number of large stones. These stones weren't easy to come by, and tales of their procurement live on in the ramparts. Several ancient stone coffins, mined from nearby tombs, can be seen in one part of the precincts.

Hiroshima: The best way to see Hiroshima is through the window of a street car. As most other Japanese cities tore up their streetcar tracks, their cars were added to Hiroshima's collection – the city has acquired an eclectic collection of cars, many dating back to the 1940s and with a few from abroad.

One moment – 8.15am, 6 August 1945 – irrevocably changed world history. The atomic flash, signalling Hiroshima's instant destruction and the ultimate loss of over 200,000 lives, has been reflected in the subsequent lives of people everywhere, shaping their political, military and technological milieu. The immediate and lasting impact on Hiroshima gives concrete reality to nuclear war, just as the city's renewal demonstrates in steel and concrete the incredible path of reconstruction the entire nation undertook in a few short years following the war.

The **Heiwa Kinen Koen** (Peace Memorial Park) is adjacent to the **Genbaku Domu** (Atomic Dome), said to be ground zero of Hiroshima's atomic explosion.

Southern Honshu train.

At its maximum intensity, the temperature here approached that on the sun's surface, and almost everything within sight was vaporized instantly. The building with the skeletal dome once housed the Industrial Promotion Hall, and was one of the few remaining structures in the vicinity.

Shimonoseki: The western limit of Honshu, Shimonoseki is the gateway to Kyushu and to Korea as well, with *shinkansen* service to Hakata and daily ferries to Pusan, South Korea. There isn't much to linger over here, but the largest aquarium in Asia, the **Shimonoseki Suizokukan**, and **Akamon Shrine** may be of interest to those waiting for a boat.

SHIKOKU

The least developed and least visited of Japan's four main islands, Shikoku's attractions (and drawbacks) are attendant on its relative isolation. The island can provide a more "Japanese" experience than Honshu or Kyushu: its people are less familiar with foreigners and its

Fishing boat, Uwajima.

places have been less influenced by the homogenizing aspects of modern culture, although a bridge connecting it with Honshu a decade ago is changing that. It is also more diffused; places likely to be of interest to international travelers are relatively far apart and more difficult to get to than in more widely traveled pathways.

The most numerous and distinctive visitors to Shikoku today, arriving by plane as often as not, are *ohenrosan*, devout Buddhist pilgrims making the rounds of the 88 holy temples and shrines established by the priest Kobo Daishi 1,200 years ago.

Takamatsu: This city, the capital of Kagawa Prefecture, is the main railway terminal and port in eastern Shikoku.

About 20 minutes by train from the center of Takamatsu is **Yashima.** The architectural embodiments of Shikoku's past – an open-air *kabuki* theater, a vine suspension bridge, thatch-roofed farmhouses, and a variety of other traditional buildings – have been collected and preserved in **Shikoku Mura** (village).

Kotohira: One of the most famous and popular shrines in Japan is here – **Kotohiragu**, also called Kotohira-san. It is dedicated to Okuninushi no Mikoto, the Guardian of Seafarers.

The **Kanamaruza**, restored to its original 1835 condition, is the oldest existing *kabuki* theater in Japan. Its stage, resonating with the echoes of thousands of performances, is exciting to visit even when empty, but even more so in the third week of April when the nation's best kabuki actors bring it alive.

Kochi: The capital of Kochi prefecture, **Kochi** is best known for the role its leading families played in forging the alliance between the Satsuma and Choshu clans and the ensuing imperial restoration. Its most renowned citizen from this period is Sakamoto Ryoma, who was assassinated in 1867.

The steep cliffs of the **Ashizuri** and **Muroto** capes, continuously battered by fierce seas, offer some of the most beautiful scenery on Shikoku.

Matsuyama: Near this city is the **Matsuyama-jo**, one of the most spectacular castles in Japan, built in 1603 (rebuilt to the same specifications following a fire in 1854) atop a mountain. The industrial city's other principal attraction is the **Dogo Onsen Honkan**, as famous for its waters as its literary associations. Dogo Onsen retains the flavor of an old fashioned bath house.

KYUSHU

Fukuoka/Hakata: During the Nara and Heian periods, the Fukuoka area was the principal Japanese port for trade with China and Korea. In 1281, Kublai Khan sent a force of 150,000 soldiers, the largest amphibious assault in history prior to World War II. After 53 days of fighting, during which the Mongols overwhelmed fanatical Japanese resistance, a terrific typhoon, the famous *kamikaze* (divine wind), sank most of the invading fleet.

Fukuoka, with a population of over one million, competes with Kitakyushu for designation as the largest city on the island of Kyushu.

Harvesting pearl oysters, Shikoku.

In its role as the crossroads between Japan and China, Fukuoka was the place that Zen Buddhism first touched the archipelago. **Shofuku-ji**, founded in 1195 by Eisai on his return from years of study in China, is the oldest Zen temple in Japan. The **Sumiyoshi-jinja**, the oldest extant Shinto shrine on Kyushu, was built in 1623. Other points of interest in Fukuoka include the **Fukuoka-shi Bijutsukan**, an art museum housing a collection of Japanese art, and **Ohori Koen**, a park containing the remains of Fukuoka Castle, and reconstructions of its turret and gates. **Karatsu**, **Imari**, and **Arita**, west of Fukuoka, are pottery towns whose fame dates to the 16th century, and are of significant interest to those interested in Japanese ceramics.

Nagasaki: A city of over half a million, Nagasaki clings to steep hills wrapped around a very active deep-water harbor, competing with Kobe for designation as Japan's San Francisco. Like San Francisco, it has a lively **Chinatown** (Shinchimachi) and a spirit of receptiveness to new and even outside ideas.

A simple stone obelisk stands at the epicenter (usually called hypocenter here) of the atomic blast which devastated Nagasaki on the morning of 9 August 1945. The **International Culture Hall** (housing the **Atomic Bomb Museum**) contains photos, relics, and poignant details of the blast and its 150,000 victims.

Beppu: If you want to "go to hell" and enjoy the trip, head for Beppu on the northeastern coast of Kyushu. The resort town is famous for its *jigoku*, variously colored ponds of water and mud that steam and boil, as well as its spas. A popular destination for Japanese tourists, Beppu is gaudy and commercial.

Kagoshima: This prefecture, in the far south of Kyushu, consists of two peninsulas, Satsuma and Osumi. **Kagoshima**, the southernmost metropolis in Kyushu, is famous for **Sakurajima** and its active volcano, which has erupted over 5,000 times since 1955. Half a million people live within 10 kilometers (6 mi) of Sakurajima's crater, often carrying umbrellas for the falling ash.

Southern
Kyushu
farmland.

OKINAWA

The 100-odd *Nansei* (Southwestern) islands in the Ryukyu chain stretch like an immense bow for 1,000 kilometers (620 mi) from Kyushu to within sight of Taiwan. In pre-modern times, most of these far-flung islands shared a similar and distinct Ryukyuan culture.

The center of tourist activity in the main city of **Naha** is **Kokusai Dori** (International Road). But only a short distance away are typically Okinawan neighborhoods. Perhaps the quickest way to get a feel for the differences between Okinawa and the rest of Japan is to visit an Okinawan pub and relax to the frequently plaintive sounds of the *sanshin*, the three-stringed snakeskin-covered Okinawan banjo known elsewhere as the *jabisen*.

Okinawan crafts are also a delight. Don't miss the **Tsuboya** pottery-making district off Himeyuri Dori in Naha, where kilns can be visited.

A mighty palace: The first castle on **Shuri**, the magnificent mountain overlooking the countryside and the oceans beyond, was established in 1237. Under the second Sho dynasty, which was established in 1469 by King Sho En, it became a mighty palace complex. Shuri remained the political and cultural center of the Ryukyus until 1879, when the last Okinawan king was forced to abdicate by the Meiji government.

During the Battle of Okinawa in 1945, Shuri was the headquarters of the Japanese army. It was destroyed during the fighting and Ryukyu University now stands on the former site. Reminders of the bloodiest battle of the Pacific War are hard to pass by in the southern part of the island, where major Japanese units made their last stand.

Spots not to miss in the far south are the tunnel labyrinth at **Romogusuku**, near Naha Airport, which was the last headquarters of the Imperial navy and in which over 4,000 men committed suicide, and the **Himeyuri no To** (Lily of the Valley Tower), where a group of

Naha Port.

high school girls and teachers committed suicide by jumping into a well.

Northward: The central portions of Okinawa Island are largely occupied by military bases, most important of which is the large U.S. air base at Kadena.

The **Motobu Peninsula** was the site of the 1975 World Ocean Exposition. Several exhibitions concerning Okinawan culture or the ocean are open daily except Thursday. The ruins of **Nakijin Castle** are a 20-minute drive away.

The outer islands: Your best bet for experiencing the Ryukyuan way of life as it used to be is to visit the outer islands or *Sakishima*, which are reached by ferry or air from Naha.

Kerama, only 35 kilometers (20 mi) west of Naha, with numerous sea snakes among its gorgeous coral reefs, is a fine scuba-diving haunt. **Kumejima**, 3 hours by ferry from Naha's Tomari Port, has preserved several fine traditional homes in **Nakazato** and elsewhere.

Further afield is the Miyako group of eight islands. **Miyakojima**, the main one, is an hour by air or 10 hours by boat from Naha. Nearby **Irabu Island**, which can be reached by boat from **Hiraya**, offers scenery and fine diving.

The **Yaeyama group**, best reached by air (the ferry from Naha only docks about once a week), was relatively isolated from the rest of the Ryukyus. It will appeal to those interested in folklore or the outdoor life. The main island of **Ishigakijima** has one of the largest and most beautiful coral reefs in this part of the Pacific.

Spectacular jungle: A short ferry or hovercraft ride from Ishigaki harbor will take you to **Taketomi**, a flat island famed throughout Japan for the star-shaped sand at **Cape Kondoi**. A ferry or jetfoil will also whisk you to the large island called **Iriomote**, a touch of New Guinea in Japan.

Except for the two towns of **Ohara** on the southeast and **Funaura** on the north, the island is primarily tropical rain forest designated as a national park, with a unique wild feline, the Iriomote cat. Thankfully, development on the island has been limited, with only one resort.

Average day on Okinawa.

HOKKAIDO

"Boys, be ambitious!" These were the parting words of Dr. William S. Clark, first president of Hokkaido University, in 1876. This injunction still applies to the traveler venturing to Japan's northern island, where the temples and castles of the south give way to mountains, forests and farms. Hokkaido has only been part of the Japanese nation since it was settled in the 19th century, as an example of the progressive Meiji Restoration development.

The roots of Hokkaido's people are in farming, fishing, hunting and shark trading. The visitor will find the residents here more direct and friendlier than their southern counterparts, and due to the Meiji-era Westernization, quite sophisticated. Hokkaido is also home to Japan's last indigenous people, the Ainu, of Caucasian ancestry and with no genetic connection to today's Japanese. With a population of only 20,000, the Ainu are today a phantom culture with a forgotten language, looked upon by Japanese as a sightseeing curiosity and whose main occupation – besides fishing and farming – is dressing up and posing for photographs at tourist sites. A brutal statement, but unfortunately true.

Transportation around the island by bus or train is spotty. Most Japanese tourists visit via the tour-bus route.

Hakodate: To the south of Sapporo – and just across the Tsugaru Strait from Aomori and Honshu's northern tip – is Hakodate. Wait until dark and take the rope-way up the nearby mountain. From there, gape at one the region's most beautiful night views. Hakodate is Hokkaido's historic city, with Japanese settlers as early as the thirteenth century, Russian visitors around 1750, and a foreign enclave, at Motomachi, in 1854. Don't miss the fish market at dawn, when the squid fleet and the crab trappers return to port.

Shikotsu-Toya: Between Hakodate and Sapporo, near Sapporo's Chitose Airport, the Shikotsu-Toya area is Hokkaido's most accessible national park. Closest to Sapporo is **Shikotsu-ko**, a huge caldera lake.

Toya-ko, south of Shikotsu, is round and a popular lake. Tour boats visit its four islands, where the view of **Yotei-zan** at 1,890 meters (6,200 ft) due north is best. Toya-ko resort is boisterous in summer, with fireworks during the August festival season. There are many *ryokan*, whose hot-spring baths have lake views.

The best route from Toya-ko east to the tourist mecca of **Noboribetsu** is by bus through gorgeous Orofu re Pass. Noboribetsu's weirdest sight is at the Dai-Ichi Takimoto-kan Hotel, where 40 indoor hot-spring baths can hold 1,000 bathers simultaneously.

Sapporo: In southwest Hokkaido, Sapporo is the island's capital and its largest city with 2 million people. The city's downtown revolves around Japan's liveliest, most charming boulevard, **Odori Koen** (Odori Park), running east and west through downtown.

In the first week of February, this broad avenue of parks and fountains **Sapporo.**

contains Sapporo's world-famous Snow Festival. (Book accommodation months in advance.) This festival includes snow statues and ice sculptures made by corporate, professional and amateur teams. In summer, beer gardens spring up on the lawn, and people linger outdoors long into the night.

Sapporo is laid out in a grid, so uncommon amongst Japan's villages, towns and cities. Just northwest of Sapporo Station, itself a few blocks north of Odori Koen, is Hokkaido University, and the Sapporo Brewery is due east. Otherwise, go south from Sapporo Station – to the botanic garden (detour west), the **Tokeidai** (clock tower, detour east), and then Odori Koen. Farther south is **Tanuki-Koji**, a vibrant strip of restaurants and shops. Finally, south of Odori Koen is **Susukino**, Sapporo's night life and strip-joint district, where Ramen Yokocho is a circus of Sapporo-style "fast-food."

Other Sapporo sites include the Snow Dairy and Asahi Brewery, two restored historical sites – the Kotani Tondenkei Oku (Settlers House) and Hokkaido Settlers Village – the Sapporo Art Forest, and Sheep Hill Tower.

Akan National Park: To the east along the southern coast of Hokkaido is the port city of **Kushiro**, where ultramodern architecture contrasts with one of Japan's most congenial dockside scenes. Kushiro itself is noted mostly for the migrating cranes that put on mating displays in the fields outside the city.

Akan-ko is famous with the Japanese for *marimo*, odd and green algae balls – also known as "God's fairies" – that will either delight, or bore, you. Tour buses dominate this park, which makes a car or a bicycle a plus. Two volcanoes, **Oakan-dake** and **Meakan-dake**, tempt climbers, with Meakan the preferred jaunt, partly because an onsen awaits the weary climber.

Also on the Akan circuit, and less touristy, is **Kussharo-ko**, the largest inland lake in Hokkaido (80 sq km) and home to Kusshi, Japan's very own "Nessie." Three congenial onsen surround Kussharo: Kawayu, Wakoto, and

Dairy farm, central Hokkaido.

Sunayu, whose hot sands provide a welcome novelty. **Io-san**, or Mount Sulphur, steams and reeks impressively. **Bihoro Pass**, above Kussharo's west shore, is a breathtaking vista.

Wilder and colder than Akan and Shikotsu-Toya, **Taisetsuzan** is the biggest national park in Japan (230,900 hectares/570,500 acres), anchored directly in the center of Hokkaido and to the west of Akan.

This is a landscape of volcanic peaks and steep highlands, magnificent gorges, carpets of alpine wildflowers and inevitable sightings of the park's rich wildlife – deer, fox, bears and exotic birds. Hokkaido's highest peak, **Asahi-dake**, at 2,290 meters (7,500 ft), is here.

Shiretoko Hanto: A beautiful, barely-civilized finger of volcanic peninsula jutting into the **Sea of Okhotsk**, Shiretoko Hanto is nearly the end of the earth, and that sensation can be vividly felt in places like **Seseki**, a south-coast hot spring that steams on a rocky shore. There are no hotels in sight, no tourist shops, nor any place to eat. A car or bike

is necessary for exploring most of Shiretoko, and many places require backpacks and sleeping bags for overnight stays.

Starting from the fishing and onsen village of **Rausu**, a trip along the south coast is rugged and lonely, but adequately relieved by the pleasures of scenic seaside *rotemburo* (outdoor bath).

The north shore, starting from the mundane spa town of **Utoro**, offers more visitors' amenities. From Utoro, there are sightseeing boats and roads east. **Iwaobetsu** is a lovely and unspoiled onsen, from which one can hike to the top of **Rausu-dake**, the peninsula's highest mountain at 1,660 meters.

North coast: The best route away from the Shiretoko is west along the northern coast, through the village of Shari and towards **Abashiri**, with its interesting but quirky prison museum, pleasant walks along Tofutsu-ko, and the Natural Flower Gardens.

North alongside the Sea of Okhotsk, through the attractive Abashiri Quasi-National Park, is **Wakkanai**, which lies at the northernmost tip of Hokkaido. In spring, the break-up of the ice to the north of Wakkanai is a mainstay of national television news.

Rishiri and Rebun: The small volcanic islands of Rishiri and Rebun are just west of Wakkanai, but before boarding the ferry, visit **Sarobetsu alpine wildflower refuge**, a rainbow of color as far as the eye can see, especially in July. This is one of Hokkaido's real wonders, remote, natural, uncrowded.

Across the water, both Rishiri and Rebun offer delights for the biker, hiker, camper and fisherman. It's possible lodge at a *minshuku* (home-style inn) on either island and get up early in the morning with your host to go fishing in the Sea of Japan.

Hiking is excellent, with Rishiri the best with a climb up **Rishiri-san**, poking up from the ocean 1,720 meters (5,620 ft), like Neptune's elbow. On Rebun, which is comparatively flat, hike from Sukotan-misaki to Momiwa, or bike from Kabuka to Funadomori to make the most of the rewarding coastline scenery.

Left, autumn colors. **Right**, sunrise over Kussharo-ko.

INSIGHT GUIDES
TRAVEL TIPS

FLY SMOOTH AS SILK TO EXOTIC THAILAND ON A ROYAL ORCHID HOLIDAY.

Watching exquisite cotton and silk umbrellas being hand-painted in Chiang Mai. Lazing in the shade in sun-drenched Phuket. This

ROYAL
ORCHID
Holidays

Let your message travel with Insight Guides

With 200 titles covering the world, Insight Guides can convey your advertisement to sophisticated international travellers.

HÖFER MEDIA PTE LTD

Singapore: 38, Joo Koon Road, Singapore 628990
Tel: (65)-865-1629/30   Fax: (65)-862-0694

London: PO Box 7910, London SE11 8LL, United Kingdom
Tel: (44 171)-620-0008, Fax: (44 171)-620-1074
e-mail: insight@apaguide.demon.co.uk

INSIGHT GUIDES

CHina

Getting Acquainted

The Place

China is the third-largest country in the world after Russia and Canada. Topographically, the country is 35 percent mountains, 27 percent high plateau, 17 percent basin or desert, 8 percent hilly areas, and 13 percent plains. Only about 11 percent of the land area is agriculturally useful. The highest population densities are along the coast.

Local Time

Despite its immense size, there is but one time zone throughout China: GMT +8 hours, adjusted to daylight saving time in summer.

Climate

The largest part of China is in a moderate zone with separate seasons. There are distinctive climatic differences resulting from monsoons, the expanse of the land area, and the considerable differences in altitude. While it is generally warm and humid in southeastern and central China, the north and northeast are relatively dry. The best times for traveling: spring (May) and fall (September/October).

China covers 35 degrees of latitude, resulting in a great variation of regional climates. In many areas, the summer is hot and rainy, with a high level of humidity, while the winter is dry. In northern China, more than 80 percent of rainfall occurs in the summer months, but only 40 percent of the annual rainfall occurs in southern China during the same period.

There are frequent typhoons in southeast China during the rainy season, between July and September. North of the Chang Jiang (Yangzi), the winter can be extremely cold.

The northeast has hot, dry summers and long, cold winters. Summer in the desert regions of Xinjiang and Inner Mongolia is also hot and dry, while winter is cold and dry. In central China, the summers are hot and humid, with a lot of rainfall in the late summer months. In the low lying regions of the Yangzi, winter is somewhat milder than in the central Chinese loess mountain regions or in Sichuan, which is surrounded by mountains. In the regions around Beijing, Xi'an and Zhengzhou, there are occasional sand storms in winter and spring.

On the Tibet-Qinghai Plateau (average altitude: 4,000m/13,100ft), summer is short and moderately warm, while winters can get very cold; there is little rainfall throughout the year, and the differences in day and night temperatures are great. A mild climate with warm summers and cool winters generally prevails on the Yunnan-Guizhou High Plateau, with little rainfall, and very rare frosts.

Southern China has a sub-tropical climate. Rainfall is distributed around the year; the summers are long, humid and hot, and the winters are short with cooler temperatures.

The People

The People's Republic of China is the world's most populous nation. Around 1.2 billion people live in China. About 20 percent of the population live in urban areas. A little over 90 percent of the population are Han Chinese; the remaining percentage, or around 70 million people, includes 55 national minorities who differ fundamentally in their customs, traditions, languages and culture from the Han Chinese. The minorities have been exempted from China's strict population controls.

Culture & Customs

Chinese politeness has always been a formal one that follows strict rules. Chinese people can seem, however, quite impolite by Western norms in public situations. Nevertheless, travelers are advised to remain polite towards their Chinese counterparts, and to refrain from shouting or being insulting. Stay calm in all situations but indicate politely and firmly what your problem or inquiry is about.

Politeness is definitely a foreign word when it comes to public transport. Whether on the underground or the bus, the overcrowded conditions always encourage a struggle. No priority is given to pedestrians on the roads; be careful when crossing the road, as you have no right-of-way.

For Chinese, it is bad to lose face, especially in front of a foreigner. Don't put a Chinese in a position where they might lose face. Any criticism should be done discreetly and tactfully.

It is usually not the custom in China to greet people with a handshake, though it is commonly used with foreigners. Moreover, embracing or kissing when greeting or saying goodbye is highly unusual. Generally, Chinese do not show their emotions and feelings in public. Consequently, it is better not to behave in too carefree a manner in public. Too, it is advisable to be fairly cautious in political discussions.

It is very important for the Chinese to have good connections; someone who has no connections (guanxi) is only half Chinese. It is important for the Chinese to make contacts, and to keep them. This is equally important to foreigners on business. One should expect lots of invitations and gifts. Qingke, the wining and dining of guests, is an old Chinese tradition and is still used today to thank friends for a favor or to make new business contacts. If invited by a Chinese, you are obliged to return the invitation.

It is considered quite normal in China to eat noisily and belch during a meal. This doesn't mean that a foreign guest must do likewise. An increasing number of Chinese, particularly in the big cities, don't find it very pleasant either. In many simple restaurants, bones and other remnants are thrown on the table or the floor. It is also quite common for people to spit, despite official campaigns to try and restrain this and other such habits. It is important for foreign visitors to know that these things are customary and not at all bad manners.

Names: The family name comes first, the given name second. Mao Zedong's family name is Mao, for example, and the given name is Zedong. Only among family and very good friends is it usual to use given names. Therefore, address men or women whom you may meet by their family name, with an honorific following the family name: *xiansheng* for men, *furen* for women. The same goes for the form of address referring to the person's position, which is sometimes used in China. For instance, Manager Li in Chinese is Li *jingli*, and Professor Wang is Wang *jiaoshou*.

Government & Economy

The People's Republic of China is, according to its constitution, a socialist state. It was founded on 1 October 1949. The national flag is red with five stars: the large star at the center symbolizes the Chinese Communist Party, while the smaller stars represent the four main social classes that participated in the revolution. The state emblem is Tiananmen (Gate of Heavenly Peace), illuminated by five stars, on a red background. It is surrounded by a corn wreath with a cog-wheel below.

The capital of the country is Beijing. All provinces and autonomous regions are strictly subordinate to the central government. Administratively, China is divided into 23 provinces (including Taiwan, considered by China as a misbehaving province), five autonomous regions (Inner Mongolia, Xinjiang, Tibet, Ningxia and Guangxi), and four locally-governed cities (Beijing, Tianjin, Shanghai and Hong Kong). The provinces and autonomous regions are further subdivided into districts, counties and towns, which are further subdivided into districts.

The **autonomous regions** are mostly populated by members of ethnic minorities who have the right to determine their own affairs – within the framework of a central state policy. They can follow their own customs and traditions and use their own language.

The **National People's Congress** is the highest governing body. Only the people's congresses at the lowest local level are directly elected, though the method of election can be called neither free nor secret, as the party retains the right to propose candidates. The People's Liberation Army, overseas Chinese and the national minorities send their own representatives to the congress.

The **Communist Party** has the leading role within both state and society. It was founded in 1921. Since the Cultural Revolution, increasingly the party has been held in low esteem among the population, because of privileges for high functionaries, misuse of power and bureaucracy.

Mao Zedong led the party from 1935 until 1976; after his death, Hua Guofeng became party leader. By 1978, Deng Xiaoping had virtually consolidated his position. Two potential successors to Deng have come and gone – Hu Yaobang, who took over as general secretary in 1981, and was forced to resign, and his successor, Zhao Ziyang, who was sacked after the 1989 democracy movement. Even after officially retiring from politics in the early 1990s, Deng Xiaoping has held on as China's *de facto* leader. There is no mechanism for an orderly succession of power.

The **Four Modernizations**, which are official party policy, are the modernization of agriculture, industry, science and technology, and defence. China is aiming to transform itself from a backward agricultural country into an industrial nation by the year 2000. This target is to be reached with structural reforms in the economic and political sectors that are intended at loosening the centralized economic and government system. Socialist planning is to be combined with a market economy.

Planning the Trip

What To Bring

As anywhere, it is best to take your usual toilet articles and medicines. Hotel shops will have a good choice of Western goods. Elsewhere, items such as tampons or sanitary napkins are still difficult to find.

Photographic items – film and batteries – are available, but may be cheaper and fresher if bought before arriving. It is worth taking a small flashlight, especially for individual travelers who may stay the night in modest hostels. Chinese-made batteries tend not to last long. An electrical adapter may be useful too; many of the older hotels have sockets which require a three pin plug and the hotel service often only has a limited number of adapters available.

Electricity

Electricity is 220 volts, 50 cycles AC. Plug types span those used in Australia, Europe and North America/Japan. Unless staying in an international-class hotel, obtain adapters before arriving in China. If traveling away from the tourist centers, it is worth taking battery-operated equipment.

What to Wear

Simple and appropriate clothing is advisable for visitors. In the summer months, take light cotton clothes that are easily washed and not too delicate. Something modestly warm is useful, even in the hottest season, as the air conditioning in the hotels is often vigorously used. Footwear should be comfortable and strong.

Most Chinese wear ordinary clothes to evening performances at the Beijing opera, the theater or circus. It is best to follow this custom, especially at some of the venues. In rural areas, the floor is often of compressed mud, making high-heeled shoes foolish. In contrast, urban discos and clubs are the venue for more fancy dress.

Rain gear is useful, especially during the summer months – China's rainy season is from May to August. In the north, winters tend to be very dry and cold. Day temperatures of between –15° to –20°C are common.

Entry Regulations
Visas & Passports

All foreigners need an entry visa. If part of a group, the tour operator will often obtain it; group visas will usually be issued for groups with at least 10, and the guide accompanying your group will keep the visas. Individual travelers can apply at any Chinese embassy, and the procedure is usually straightforward, taking about a week. The duration depends upon current regulations, and upon your own country's regulations for visiting Chinese citizens. Typical is a 30-day single-entry visa. The passport must be valid for six months after the expiration of the entry visa.

Traditionally, it has been easier to obtain visas in Hong Kong, including long-term, multiple-entry visas, than anywhere else. Quicker, too. With the return of Hong Kong to China, the situation will no doubt soon change. Will entry through Hong Kong be the same as through other ports of entry into China, or will there be a limited-entry visa for, say, only Hong Kong and maybe Guangzhou? As of early 1997, China had not announced its future policies. If planning to visit Hong Kong after July 1997, don't assume the same ease of access as before.

If your visa runs out while in China, it can be extended by the local Public Security Bureau – the ubiquitous police (*Gongan Ju*).

There was a time when many areas were off limits to foreigners, or else special travel permits, exceedingly difficult to obtain, were required. Nowadays, most of the country is open to foreigners, except some delicate border areas.

Customs

On arrival, each traveler must complete a form declaring foreign currency and valuables such as cameras, antiques and jewelry. The declaration must be handed in on departure; if required, the listed objects must be shown to verify that they haven't been sold within China.

Tourists can freely import two bottles of alcoholic beverages and 600 cigarettes, as well as foreign currency and valuables for personal use without restrictions. The import of weapons, ammunition, drugs and pornographic literature (broadly interpreted) is prohibited. On departure, antiques such as porcelain, paintings, calligraphy, carvings and old books must carry the red lacquer seal of an official antique shop. Otherwise, they can be confiscated by the customs officials without compensation.

Health

The best prevention is to ensure maximum hygiene while traveling, especially in restaurants and roadside snack bars. Never eat raw, uncooked or partially-cooked food, including salads outside of top-end hotels. Animal or human excrement is still frequently used as fertilizer, so that bacteria on uncooked vegetables can easily be ingested. Also suggested if traveling outside of a tour group: acquire chopsticks and a tin bowl with lid for train journeys and meals in small roadside restaurants. Drink only boiled or bottled water, even though the tap water is drinkable in some places and hotels. The adjustment to a different climate and different food frequently leads to colds or digestive problems that, although rarely serious, can nevertheless impede one's enjoyment.

Tibet, the northwest, and the tropical province of Yunnan make particularly high demands on the body. Heart disease and high blood pressure can lead to serious problems in Tibet. Along the Silk Road, expect high temperatures and dry conditions.

If planning to visit areas outside of Beijing, Shanghai, Guangzhou and Hong Kong, consider carrying emergency evacuation insurance. If injured in the deserts of western China, for example, medical and transportation costs could leave you indebted into the next decade. Two of the largest emergency evacuation companies are SOS Assistance and Asia Emergency Assistance. They have offices in many major cities throughout the world, or contact them in Hong Kong:

International SOS Assistance, 507 Kai Tak Commercial Bldg, 317 Des Voeux Road, Central, Hong Kong. Tel: 2541 6483, Fax: 2544 1677.

Asia Emergency Assistance (AEA), Allied Resources Bldg 9F, 32-38 Ice House Street, Central, Hong Kong. Tel: 2810 8898, Fax: 2845 0395, In Beijing: 505 5352.

Illnesses

Travelers to East Asia may be exposed to potential illnesses or diseases from a number of sources. The most frequently reported illness, and this should come as no surprise, is traveler's diarrhea.

Other diseases are unique to East Asia or the tropics, transmitted by insects, contaminated food and water, or close contact with infected people. Diseases are not restricted to clearly-defined geographical areas. To reduce the risk of infection:

- reduce exposure to insects
- ensure quality of food and water
- be knowledgeable about potential diseases in the visited region

Insect-Transmitted

Malaria: Transmitted to humans by a mosquito, which bite at night from dusk to dawn. *Symptoms:* Fever and flu-like symptoms, chills, achiness, and tiredness. Up to one year after returning home, travelers should consult a physician for flu-like illness. *Risk:* Little or no risk in urban areas and popular tourist destinations; there is no risk in provinces bordering Mongolia, and in the western provinces of Heilungkiang, Kirin, Ningsia Hui Tibet, and Tsinghai, nor in Hong Kong. Risk exists in rural areas not visited by most travelers. In areas of risk, transmission is highest from May to December; in the south, transmission occurs year-round. Whether taking preventative drugs or not, travelers in risk areas should reduce exposure to malaria-carrying mosquitoes, which bite mainly during the evening, from dusk until dawn.

Taking drugs to prevent malaria is recommended only for travelers to rural areas and who will have outdoor exposure during evening hours. What medication to take is not as easy as it was a decade ago. There is increasing evidence that mosquitoes in many parts of the world, including in parts of northern Thailand and Burma, are developing resistance to traditional preventive drugs such as choloroquine and Mefloquine (Lariam).

Moreover, some individuals have extreme reactions to many of the more recent preventative drugs. Consult medical authorities or a physicians knowledgeable in travel medicine for recommendations.

Dengue fever: Primarily an urban – in or around human habitations – viral infection transmitted by mosquitos. The mosquitoes are most active around dawn and dusk. *Symptoms:* sudden onset of high fever, severe headaches, joint and muscle pain, and a rash, which shows up 3 to 4 days after the fever begins. *Risk:* Occurs in parts of southern China and Taiwan. The risk is minimal for most travelers. Those who have lived several years in high-risk areas are more susceptible than short-term visitors. There is no vaccine or specific treatment available.

Japanese encephalitis: A mosquito-borne viral disease in rural areas, often in rice-growing areas. *Symptoms:* none, or headache, fever, and other flu-like symptoms. Serious complications can lead to a swelling of the brain (encephalitis). *Risk:* Occurs in rural China and Korea, and occasionally in Hong Kong and Taiwan. The mosquito bites in the late afternoon and early evening. Low or minimal risk for most travelers. Transmission is usually seasonal during the rainy season. There is no specific drug for treatment, but there is a preventative vaccine, which should be considered for persons who plan long-term – 4 weeks or more – visits to rural areas.

Yellow fever: Not in China or Asia.

Contamination

Food and water-borne diseases are the primary cause of illness to travelers, and many travelers to China might expect some degree of discomfort, especially diarrhea, which is caused primarily by viruses or bacteria. Transmission is usually through contaminated food or water.

Hepatitis A: A viral infection of the liver transmitted by ingestion of fecal-contaminated food or drink, or through direct person-to-person contact. *Symptoms:* Fatigue, fever, no appetite, nausea, dark urine and/or jaundice, vomiting, aches. There is no specific treatment, although an effective vaccine is available, especially for those who plan to travel repeatedly or reside in risk areas. Immune globulin is recommended only for short-term protection.

Hepatitis B: All countries in Asia, including China, report high levels of infection. Hepatitis D is a viral infection of the liver transmitted through the exchange of blood or blood-derived fluids, or through sexual activity with an infected person. Unscreened blood and unsterilized needles, or contact with potentially-infected people with open skin lesions, are sources of infection. An effective vaccine is available, which should be started six months prior to travel.

Typhoid fever: A bacterial infection transmitted by contaminated food and/or water, or even directly between people. Travelers to East Asia are susceptible to typhoid fever, particularly in smaller towns or rural areas. *Symptoms:* Fever, headaches, tiredness, no appetite, and constipation (rather than diarrhea). Be cautious in selecting food and water. Bottled or boiled water and eating only well-cooked food lowers the risk of infection. Typhoid fever is treated with antibiotics. Vaccination is recommended for travelers off the tourist routes, especially if staying for six weeks or more. Available vaccines protect 70–90 percent of users.

Cholera: Although some cases have been occasionally reported in China, the risk is virtually nonexistent. An acute intestinal infection caused by bacteria, most often through contaminated water or food. *Symptoms:* Abrupt onset of watery diarrhea, dehydration, vomiting, and muscle cramps. Medical care must be sought quickly when cholera is suspected. The available vaccine is only 50 percent effective, and is not recommended for the majority of travelers.

Schistosomiasis (bilharzia): An infection from a flatworm larvae that penetrates the skin, including unbroken skin. *Risk:* Schistosomiasis is found in some areas of China, including rivers and lakes of southeastern and eastern China, especially along the Chang Jiang (Yangzi River) and tributaries. The risk comes from bathing, wading, or swimming in contaminated freshwater. There is no easy way to identify infested water. If exposed, immediate and vigorous drying with a towel, or the application of rubbing alcohol to the exposed areas, can reduce risk. Water treated with chlorine or iodine is virtually safe; saltwater poses no risk.

Money Matters

The Chinese currency is called *renminbi* (people's currency) and is often abbreviated RMB. The basic unit is the *yuan*. Ten *jiao* make one yuan, and ten *fen* make one *jiao*. Thus, 100 fen make one yuan. Notes are currently issued for 2, 5, 10, 50 and 100 yuan. Coins include 1 yuan, 5 jiao, and 1, 2 and 5 fen.

Before China abandoned, in 1994, its dual-currency system – RMBs and FECs, or Foreign Exchange Certificates, which foreigners were required to use – there was a reasonably active black market in currency exchange. Since the RMB is not completely convertible on the world markets, a black market still exists, although it is highly illegal and the black-market exchange rates are laughable and not worth the risk of being short-changed, receiving counterfeit bills or being arrested.

Most of the world's primary currencies are accepted in banks and hotels. Eurocheques, however, are not accepted anywhere, including branches of European banks.

Increasingly, many places frequented by foreigners take the usual **credit cards** such as American Express, Visa, Diners Club, and MasterCard. Don't expect much utility from them outside of the major cities, however. Also, most transportation costs – domestic air and train tickets – must be paid for in cash.

Cash advances may be obtained from major branches of the **Bank of China**, including the head office of the Bank of China, 410 Fuchingmennei Dajie, Tel: 6601 6688, or the Beijing branch at 19, Dong An Men St, Tel: 6519 9115/4.

Forget about **wire transfers** of money to China. It'll take about a month and a considerable amount of patience with paperwork.

Public Holidays

In contrast to the traditional festivals, such as the Spring Festival (Lunar New Year), which follow the lunar calendar and thus vary in timing from year to year, important official holidays follow the Gregorian calendar.

1 January: New Year's Day
February: Variable. Lunar New Year (Spring Festival)
8 March: International Women's Day
1 May: International Labor Day
4 May: Youth Day (May 4th Movement)
1 June: Children's Day
1 July: Founding of Communist Party
1 August: Founding of People's Liberation Army
1 October: National Day

Most shops are open on holidays. School holidays in China are between 1 August and 30 September. This also applies to universities.

Don't plan on travel – or border crossings – during holidays, unless reservations have been made and confirmed long before. Especially make no plans during the Spring Festival, which is three days long, when everyone is traveling to hometowns.

Getting There
By Air

BEIJING

The international airport connects Beijing to all parts of China and to the world's major cities. Beijing's airport is 27km (25 mi), a 25-minute drive, from the center.

Taxis are on the left as you leave the terminal. Air China has a coach service to its offices at Xidan, west of Tiananmen Square and Dongsi, in the northeast of the city. This is recommended only if you have light baggage. Most major hotels offer limousine or bus transfers. Passengers on international arrivals must fill out arrival cards, customs and health declarations. Travelers with tuberculosis and AIDS carriers are barred from entry.

If leaving on a domestic flight from Beijing, check in at least 30 minutes before the flight or you will lose your seat. (29 minutes before the flight is not good enough.) International flight check-in should be done at least one hour before the flight. Foreigners leaving China by air are required to pay a 90 yuan airport tax. Domestic flight tax is 15 yuan.

GUANGZHOU

The major airports are in Guangzhou and Shenzhen. Guangzhou's Baiyun Airport is 10km (6 mi) and a 30-minute drive from the city. The domestic and international terminals are housed in separate buildings. Shenzhen's Fuyong Airport is about 25km (15 mi) from Shekou, at the western end of Shenzhen, and 55km (34 mi) from the center of Shenzhen. Domestic flights operate between Guangzhou and Shenzhen and major cities in China.

Guangzhou is connected via international flights to Bangkok, Hanoi, Ho Chi Minh City, Hong Kong, Jakarta, Kuala Lumpur, Manila, Surabaya, Singapore, Sydney and Vientiane.

With the exception of Singapore Airlines, MAS and Garuda, which have offices selling tickets in Guangzhou, tickets for international flights on Chinese and foreign carriers must be purchased from the CAAC main office. Tickets for domestic flights are sold at the offices of the Chinese carriers and also at the CAAC main office. Bear in mind that buying a return ticket on a domestic route is difficult, except to cities like Beijing and Shanghai.

HONG KONG

Hong Kong is served by more than 30 airlines, plus a dozen other charter and cargo companies. Kai Tak Airport in Kowloon is about 20 minutes by car from most hotels in Kowloon and less than 40 minutes' drive via the Cross-Harbor Tunnel to Hong Kong Island. The new airport at Chek Lap Kok on Lantau island, scheduled for completion in late 1997, will replace Kai Tak.

The terminal building at Kai Tak doesn't win any architectural awards, but recent massive renovation efforts have eased many bottlenecks. Upon arrival, airplanes are parked alongside modern passenger bridges. Immigration, customs and baggage check points are all within a short walking distance, and free baggage carts are available.

By Rail

BEIJING

Beijing has five railway stations with lines running to most major cities throughout China. Beijing's new West Railway Station, the largest station in Asia, opened in 1996, providing badly need relief for the overloaded Beijing Railway Station.

If arriving via the **Trans-Manchurian** or **Trans-Mongolian** railways (often called the Trans-Siberian, which goes to Siberia, not China), all the same health and customs procedures apply as if arriving via an international flight.

There is a choice of two routes. The Chinese train – which is better equipped and maintained – takes 5 days via Ulan Bator through Mongolia, entering China via Erlian. The Russian train, which goes through Manchuria and takes a day longer, enters China at Manzhouli. Both trains leave once a week from Moscow.

Depending upon the type of train, there are two or three classes. Food is not included in the ticket price. Initially, the food on the train is fairly reasonable, but becomes increasingly monotonous as the journey continues.

If you want to interrupt the train journey in Russia for longer than 24 hours, you need a tourist visa and you have to show a hotel booking.

Note: Military installations must not be photographed, in Russia and in China. Film will be confiscated and a few hours of inconvenience enjoyed.

For train tickets from Beijing to other parts of China, go to the foreigners' booking office. One word of caution: train tickets must be bought at the point of departure; return tickets cannot yet be purchased.

GUANGZHOU

There are trains to most large cities in China. Four daily trains link Guangzhou and the Hunghom station on the Kowloon side of Hong Kong, with two extra trains added during special festivals, the Guangzhou Fair and other peak periods. Traveling time is 2 hours. There is also a direct train between Foshan and Hong Kong, with a traveling time of 3 hours.

In Guangzhou, most hotels and the CTS office can help get train tickets. In Hong Kong, tickets can be purchased through travel agents, hotels, CTS offices or at the lobby of the Hunghom railway station (Tel: 8333 0660). If tickets to Guangzhou are sold out, take the Kowloon-Guangzhou Railway (KCR) to the border terminus of Lo Wu (a short 40-minute journey, with three departures an hour from 6am–9pm). The Shenzhen station is right across the border. There are a dozen trains a day between Shenzhen and Guangzhou. Traveling time is 2 hours. Trains arrive in Guangzhou either at the central station or at Guangzhou East Railway Station (Guangzhou Dong), in Tianhe, a 45-minute taxi ride from the city center. All trains between Kowloon and Guangzhou are air-conditioned, but not all between Shenzhen and Guangzhou. Ask for the air-con class when buying a ticket, a small price to pay when temperatures soar in the heat of summer.

By Sea

HONG KONG

If traveling to China from Hong Kong by boat, the choice of destinations includes Guangzhou, Xiamen, Shantou and Shanghai.

There is an overnight steamer between Hong Kong and Guangzhou, which takes 8 hours; there is also a daytime catamaran service, which takes just over 3 hours. Ferry journeys to Shantou take 14 hours; to Xiamen, 20 hours; and to Shanghai, 60 hours. All have restaurants on board.

Hong Kong is linked by hydrofoil with Guangzhou, Huangpu, Guangzhou's commercial port, and the delta cities of Lianhua Shan, Nansha, Shekou, Shunde, Zhongshan and Zhuhai. There are also services between Macau and Shekou. For information on hydrofoil schedules, call 2833 9300 or 2542 3428 in Hong Kong. Most departures are from the Hong Kong-Macau Ferry Terminal at the Shun Tak Center (200 Connaught Road, Hong Kong) and from the China Ferry Terminal, Guangzhou Road, Tsimshatsui.

By day, the most impressive trip is the one between Kowloon and the Bogue port of Nansha, sited at the entrance of the Pearl River, aboard a huge modern catamaran traveling at 35 knots. From the Nansha terminal, a free bus shuttle takes travelers to the White Swan Hotel in Guangzhou. Three high-speed catamaran hydrofoils operate daily (1-hour) between Nansha and Hong Kong: 8.30am, 9.15am, 2pm from Hong Kong, and 11.20am, 4pm and 5pm from Nansha. Tickets can be purchased from the China Ferry Terminal (Tel: 2375 0537) in Hong Kong, the Nansha Terminal (Tel: 498 8312)

or the basement floor of the White Swan Hotel in Guangzhou.

You can also catch a night boat from Hong Kong and Macau to Guangzhou. They run daily except on the last day of each month, leaving either way at dinner time and arriving at sunrise. The departure from Hong Kong sails through the harbor and the view is especially impressive. The *Xinghu*, sailing from Hong Kong, is the most comfortable boat. Departures are from the China Ferry Terminal in Hong Kong and from the Porto Interior in Macau.

There are numerous cruises from Hong Kong along China's coast. They usually stop at Xiamen, Shanghai, Yantai, Nanjing, Qingdao and Dalian.

KOREA

Ferry service is available from Inchon, South Korea, to Weihai, Qingdao and Tianjin. Between Inchon and Weihai takes about 18 hours, departing twice weekly. Between Inchon and Qingdao takes at least a full 24 hours, departing weekly. Between Inchon and Tianjin takes nearly 30 hours, operating every five days. Fares for all services range from US$100 to US$350, depending upon class.

JAPAN

There is a weekly deluxe cruise ship between Shanghai and Japan, alternating every week between Yokohama and Shanghai. There is also a weekly boat between Kobe and Tianjin/Tanggu. Trips take two days, and fares run from US$300 to $1,500 or more.

By Ground

Several of China's international borders are open for crossing. Other parts, like the frontier with Bhutan, are restricted areas. A border crossing with Burma opened in 1996, but the Burmese authorities go out of their way to discourage foreigners from using the crossing.

NEPAL

Crossing via Nepal by bus or taxi has been possible since 1985, with sporadic periods of closed borders. Procure a Chinese visa anywhere else but Nepal, unless part of a tour.

It's possible to travel by road between Kathmandu and Lhasa, but it requires considerable time, not only

for travel, but for bureaucracy, including mandatory tours of Lhasa upon arrival. Independent travelers should note that transport on the Nepal side is good, but scarce on the Tibetan side. Most travelers must plan on a vehicle hire/share to Lhasa.

PAKISTAN

Since 1986, it has been possible to travel the Karakorum Highway between Kashi (Kashgar), in northwest China, and Islamabad. Pakistan requires a visa for most nationalities. Visas are not available at the border for either China or Pakistan.

On both the Pakistani and Chinese side of the border, the roads may be blocked by landslides, and you may have to walk a fair distance, carrying your luggage. Accommodation along the journey is quite modest.

KAZAKHSTAN

There are both a daily bus service and a twice-weekly train service between Urumqi and Almaty, in Kazakhstan.

VIETNAM

In 1995, train service began between Hanoi and Beijing via the Friendship Gate crossing, but it has been plagued by red-tape at the border and has proved to be troublesome, for locals and foreigners alike. From Vietnam to China requires a special visa. One may also cross the border by foot at Hekou (China) and Lao Cai (Vietnam), and at Friendship Gate (Dong Dang, Vietnam/Pingxiang, China).

RUSSIA/MONGOLIA

A journey on the **Trans-Mongolian/Trans-Manchurian railways** between Moscow and Beijing was once one of the world's classic train journeys. Things have changed, and the train now carries a larger number of scoundrels and thieves. Service on the Russian train (both China and Russia run trains on the service) is said to have degraded considerably. Nevertheless, it is an adventure worth considering.

Special Information

Children

The Chinese are fond of children, so traveling with children in China is not difficult. If with toddlers or babies, note that disposable nappies and baby food in jars are not readily available. Children travel at reduced cost on trains and planes. Big hotels offer child-care for a fee.

Disabled

Only in recent years have the needs of disabled people received attention in China. In general, towns, institutions, public transport and sights offer little accessibility for the disabled. Traveling in a group for the disabled certainly reduces these problems considerably. The China National Tourist Offices and CITS have information about whether special trips for the disabled are possible and how they might be organized.

Students

There are no special rules for foreign students in China. International student cards are not recognized in most of China, only the student cards of foreign students studying in China.

Useful Addresses

Public Security Bureau Offices
Beijing: 85 Beichizi Dajie, Tel: 6525 5486, Monday–Friday 8.30am–5pm, Saturday 8.30am–11.30am.
Shanghai: 210 Hankou Lu, Tel: 6321 5380.
Guangzhou: 863 Jiefang Beilu, Tel: 8333 1326.

Visitor Hot Lines:
Shanghai: Tel: 6439 0630
Guangzhou: Tel: 8667 7422
Police: 110
Fire: 119
Local directory assistance: 114
International directory assistance (English): 115

CNTA
China National Tourist Office, London, 4 Glentworth St., London No. 1 UK. Tel: 935 9787, Fax: 487 5842.
Fremdenverkehrsamt der Volksrepublik, China Ilkenhans Strasse 6, D-60433 Frankfurt A.M. Deutschland. Tel: 52 0135, Fax: 52 8490.
Office du Tourisme de China, Paris, 116, Ave des Champs-Elysees, 75008 Paris, France. Tel: 4421 8282, Fax: 4421 8100.
China National Tourist Office, Madrid, Gran Via 88, Grupo 2, Planta 16-8 28013, Madrid, Espana. Tel: 548 0011, Fax: 548 0597.

China National Tourist Office, New York, 350 Fifth Ave, Suite 6413, Empire State Bldg, New York, NY 10118. Tel: 760 9700, Fax: 760 8809.
China National Tourist Office, Los Angeles, 333 West Broadway, Suite 201, Glendale, CA91204 USA. Tel: 545 7505. Fax: 545 7506.
China National Tourist Office, Sydney, Level 19, 44 Market St., Sydney, NSW 2000, Australia. Tel: 299 4057, Fax: 290 1958.
China National Tourist Office, Tokyo, 6F Hachidai Ramamatsu Cho Bldg, 1-27-13 Hamamatsu-cho, Minato-Ku, Tokyo, Japan. Tel: 3433 1461, Fax: 3433 8653.
Office of China International Travel Service, P.O. Box 3281 Tel-Aviv 61030, Israel. Tel: 524 0891, Fax: 522 6281.
China National Tourist Office, Singapore, 1 Shenton Way, #7-05 Robina House, Singapore 068803. Tel: 211 8681, Fax: 221 9267.

Tour Operators

There are countless travel agencies within and outside of China that handle domestic travel arrangements. Prominent among the agencies is **China International Travel Services (CITS)**, formerly and virtually the sole agency handling overseas tourists. It now has branches throughout China, which operate independently. **China Travel Services (CTS)** is a similar organization, originally responsible for domestic tourists and overseas Chinese, but now also catering to foreigners. While the efficiency of both organizations can be brutally lacking in some of their offices, some say CTS is slightly better than CITS.

Agencies may also have business interests extending beyond simply arranging tours and bookings; they may own or partly own hotels. An agency that arranges a tour may do so by contacting agencies in places you will visit, and asking them to deal with local bookings. This means that if you go direct to an agency in the area you are visiting, savings may be possible.

Sometimes, agencies such as CITS may hold tickets for rail journeys, operas, acrobatic performances and concerts even when such tickets are sold out at the stations or venues. Prices will be high, however.

There are also small-scale unlicensed tour operators. Reportedly, some of these use unroadworthy vehicles, take their customers to shops and restaurants that give the guides 'backhanders' (though perhaps this can also happen with licensed operators), and demand mark-ups of 100 percent or more for tickets to tourist sites. Others may be trustworthy, and cheap.

It is also quite possible nowadays – and increasingly common amongst the adventurous – to travel in China without the services of any agency.

Note that within China, agencies – including CITS – have nothing to do with visa extensions or other passport matters. Visit the police for these.

CITS Offices

Beijing, 1 Jian Guo Men Wai Ave, China World Hotel. Tel: 6607 1575, 6608 7124. Open Monday–Saturday 8am–8pm, Sunday 8am–noon.
Chengdu, 65, Sec 2, Remin Rd. S. Tel: 667 9186.
Dalian, 1 Changtong St. Tel: 364 0273.
Guilin, 14 North Ronghu Rd. Tel: 282 2648/283 3905. Open Monday–Sunday 8am–noon, 2.30–5.30pm, 7–9pm; Bing Jiang Nan Rd, Sheraton Hotel. Tel: 282 5588 Ext: 8234. Open Monday–Sunday 8–noon, 1–6pm, 7–10pm.
Guangzhou, No. 1, Shihan Rd. Tel: 8515 2888 Ext. 256. Open Monday–Saturday 8.30am–5pm.
Hangzhou, 1 Shihan Rd. Tel: 515 2888 X 256.
Hong Kong, 6th Fl, Tower 2, South Seas Center 75, Mody Rd, Tsim Sha-Tsui, Kowloon. Tel: 2732 5888, Fax: 2721 7454.
Kunming, 218 Huan Cheng Rd. S. Tel: 313 4019.
Nanjing, 202-1 N Zhong Shan Rd. Tel: 342 1125. Open Monday–Saturday 9am–5pm.
Ningbo, East Seaport Hotel, No. 52 Caihong North Rd. Tel: 737 5751. Open Monday–Saturday 8.30am–5pm.
Suzhou, Nan Lin Hotel. Tel: 529 1642.
Tianjin, 22 You Yi Rd. Tel: 835 5309. Open Monday–Friday 9am–5pm; Saturday 9am–noon.
Wuhan, Rm 303, 1365 Zhongshan Ave, Hankou. Tel: 284 2331. Open Monday–Friday 8.30–11.30am, 2–5pm.
Wuxi, 7 Xing Sheng Rd. Tel: 20 4420. Open Monday–Saturday 9am–5pm.
Xiamen, No. 2 Zhongshan Rd. Tel: 203 1781 or 202 5277. Open Monday–Sunday 8am–5.30pm.

Xi'an, 32 (N) Changan Rd. Tel: 723 1234/526 2066. Open Monday–Sunday 8am–8pm; Sheraton Hotel, 12 Feng Gao Rd. Tel: 426 1888 Ext 1000. Open Monday–Sunday 8am–8pm.

American Express Travel Service Offices

Beijing, L115D West Wing Bldg., China World Trade Center. Beijing 100004. Tel: 6505 2888. Open Monday–Friday 9am–5pm, Saturday 9am–noon.
Guangzhou, 339 Huan Shi Dong Lu, Guangzhou 510060. Tel: 8331 1771. Open Monday–Friday 9–5pm, Saturday 9am–noon.
Shanghai, 206 Retail Plaza, Shanghai Ctr. 1376 Nanjing Rd West, Shanghai 200040. Tel: 6279 8082. Open Monday–Friday 9am–5pm, Saturday 9am–noon.
Xiamen, Rm 27, 2/F Holiday Inn Crowne Plaza Harbour View, 12-8 Zhen Hai Rd. Xiamen 361001. Tel: 212 0268, Fax: 212 0270.

Photography

Taking photographs or videos of military installations is prohibited. As in other countries, some museums, palaces or temples will not allow photographs to be taken, or will charge a fee. Other times, photography is allowed, but without using flash.

Cameras must be declared when arriving in China. No special permit is necessary for video or movie cameras, as long as it is clearly not for professional use.

Practical Tips

Emergencies

Security & Crime

There is still less crime in China than in many other countries, but as vigorous crime crackdowns by the government attest – over 1,000 executions in a two-month period in 1996 – crime is increasingly a problem, particularly in urban areas.

Foreigners are not exempt from be-ing victims of crime. Take the same precautions applicable anywhere, on the street and with valuables in hotels and on public transportation. Pickpockets and bag-slashers can be a problem, especially on crowded trains and buses, and stations. Because of large numbers of migrant workers seeking employment, cities like Guangzhou have higher levels of crime than elsewhere. Nevertheless, in most towns and cities, one needn't worry.

The **Public Security Bureau** (Gongan Ju) is the ever-present police force responsible for *everything* – chasing murderers, quenching dissent, issuing visa extensions. They are usually friendly towards foreigners, even if the rules that they are strictly enforcing seem illogical at times. Also, with serious travel-related disputes – for example, with taxi drivers or hotels – they are usually able to resolve the problem. To stay on their friendly side, don't be caught trying to travel in restricted areas or on an expired visa.

Loss or theft of belongings

If you've lost something, do what one would do anywhere else: Notify the hotel, tour group leader or transportation authorities, and the police, who will usually make a serious effort to recover items. Then, most likely, you might start considering how to replace the lost or stolen items.

Public Security Bureau offices:
Beijing: 85 Beichizi Dajie, Tel: 6525 5486, Monday–Friday 8.30am–5pm, Saturday 8.30am–11.30am.
Shanghai: 210 Hankou Lu, Tel: 6321 5380.
Guangzhou: 863 Jiefang Beilu, Tel: 8333 1326.

Visitor Hot Lines:
Shanghai: Tel: 6439 0630
Guangzhou: Tel: 8667 7422
Police: 110
Fire: 119

Luggage

Forget designer luggage with fine leather trim, useful only for posturing in a hotel lobby. Likewise with shiny aluminum cases which plead to be stolen. Take sturdy, strong luggage. This is especially recommended if traveling independently or away fro the catered tourist venues. Luggage should be lockable, sometimes a requirement for transport.

Medical Services

There is a big difference in China between urban and rural medical services. If traveling in the countryside, there may be no appropriate medical services beyond primary health care, which is a success story in China. Some hospitals in cities have special sections for foreigners and where English is spoken.

Many of the large hotels have their own doctors. Payment must be made on the spot for treatment, medicine and transport.

If planning to visit areas outside of Beijing, Shanghai, Guangzhou and Hong Kong, consider carrying emergency evacuation insurance.

If injured in the deserts of western China, for example, medical and transportation costs could leave you indebted into the next decade.

Two of the largest emergency evacuation companies are SOS Assistance and Asia Emergency Assistance. They have offices in many major cities throughout the world, or contact them in Hong Kong:

International SOS Assistance, 507 Kai Tak Commercial Bldg, 317 Des Voeux Road, Central, Hong Kong. Tel: 2541 6483, Fax: 2544 1677.
Asia Emergency Assistance (AEA), Allied Resources Bldg 9F, 32-38 Ice House St, Central, Hong Kong. Tel: 2810 8898, Fax: 2845 0395. In Beijing: 505 5352.

BEIJING

International Medical Center, Beijing Lufthansa Ctr, 50 Liangmaqiau Lu. Tel: 6465 1561; Fax: 6465 1984. Emergency service 24 hours. Vaccinations and dental services.
Sino-German Polyclinic, Landmark Tower, B-1. Tel: 6501 1983.

SHANGHAI

Shanghai Emergency Center, 68 Haining Lu, Tel: 6324 4010.
Huashan Hospital, 12 Wulumuqi Zhonglu, Tel: 6248 9999.

HONG KONG

Adventist Hospital, No. 40 Stubbs Road, Happy Valley, Tel: 2574 6211.
Central Medical Practice, 1501

Prince's Bldg, Central, Tel: 2521 2567.
Hong Kong Central, 1B Lower Albert Rd, Central, Tel: 2522 3141.

GUANGZHOU

Red Cross Hospital, emergencies: Tel: 8444 6411, in English.
Guangzhou No. 1 People's Hospital, 602 Renmin Bellu, Tel: 8333 3090.
Provincial Hospital No. 1, Foreigners' Dept, 123 Huifu Xilu, Tel: 8777 7812.

Business Hours

Shops are open everyday, including public holidays. Opening hours are usually from 8.30am–9am to 8pm. Government offices and banks are usually open from Monday to Friday, 8.30am to 5.30pm, with a lunch break from noon to 1.30pm. Times are approximate; allow local variations. In western China, for example, offices often open later – they are on Beijing time, but it's before dawn when it's bright daylight in Beijing.

Tipping

Officially, it is still illegal to accept tips in China. Moreover, for a long time, it was considered patronizing. Tourists and visitors in recent years, however, have changed attitudes in areas like Guangzhou and Shanghai. It's also become the custom for travel groups to give a tip to the Chinese travel guides and bus drivers. If you are traveling with a group, ask the guide, who is responsible for the "official" contacts of the group, whether a tip is appropriate and how much.

Tipping is still not common in most restaurants and hotels, although it is accepted in the top-class hotels and restaurants. Note that it is part of the ritual that any gift or tip will, at first, be firmly rejected.

Media

An English-language newspaper, the *China Daily*, is published in China, daily except on Sundays. It is informative and sometimes even a bit bold, depending upon the climate at the moment. Often obtainable from the big hotels for free, it contains the television schedule and a diary of cultural events in Beijing. The sports section is good and informative. Unfortunately,

same-day editions are available only in large cities; elsewhere, it'll be several days late. Overseas editions of the *China Daily* are published in Hong Kong and the United States. Another English-language paper, the *Shanghai Star*, is available in Shanghai.

Most large hotels sell foreign language newspapers and journals, including the *International Herald Tribune*, *The Times*, *Asian Wall Street Journal*, *Time*, *Newsweek*, *Far Eastern Economic Review,* and many more.

The overseas edition of the party newspaper *Renmin Ribao* (*People's Daily*) is usually available in the hotels.

Telephone, Telex & Fax

Telephone: Domestic long-distance calls are cheap, international calls are expensive. Local calls in China, including in the hotels, are usually free of charge. International calls made from hotels typically have high surcharges added to China's ALREADY HIGH IDD rates. Increasingly common in cities are card phones, with cards available in Y20, 50, 100 and 200.

Telex and fax: Most of the big hotels have telex and fax facilities to help business people. Alternatively, central telegraph and post offices offer telex and fax services.

Telegrams: Sending telegrams abroad is relatively expensive. Express telegrams are double the price. There is usually a telegram counter at the hotel; otherwise, go to the central telegraph or post office.

Like many nations expanding their domestic telephone networks, China's telephone numbers can change without too much fanfare. If you hear a funny ringing sound on the line and can't get through, the number may have changed.

Country code for China: 86
Direct-dial international calls: dial 00, then the country code and telephone number.
Home country direct-dial: dial 108, then the country's international area code. For example, to call Britain, dial 108-44, then the domestic area code and number. For the United States and Canada, dial 108-1. (For AT&T, 108-11; MCI, 108-12; Sprint, 108-13.)
Domestic area codes: Add 0 to the codes below if dialing from within China:

Beijing	10
Chengde	314
Chengdu	28
Chongqing	811
Dalian	411
Guangzhou	20
Guilin	773
Hangzhou	571
Hankou	27
Harbin	451
Jilin	432
Kaifeng	378
Kunming	871
Luoyang	379
Nanjing	25
Shanghai	21
Shenyang	24
Suzhou	512
Taiyuan	351
Tianjin	22
Urumqi	991
Wuhan	27
Wuxi	510
Xi'an	29
Xiamen	592
Xinxiang	373
Zhengzhou	371

Getting Around

Orientation

The main means of public transport in the PR of China are the railways, buses and airplanes. In the regions along the big rivers, boats play an important part. All main cities can be reached by plane and train. The road network has been improved in recent years but is still very poor in many areas.

Road names and orientation: Street names are determined by the traditional checkerboard of Chinese urban design. The most important traffic arteries are divided into sectors and laid out in a grid typically based upon the compass points.

Suffixes are added to the primary name to indicate north, south, east or west, and, additionally, to indicate the middle section. The middle section is called *zhong*; *nan* means south; *bei*, north; *dong*, east; and *xi*, west. A main road is *lu*, smaller is *dajie* or *jie*.

On Arrival

You will have to fill in a customs declaration listing all items of value, such as camera, tape recorder, watches and money. Another form asks for details of your health (health declaration). A third requirement is the entry card, on which you fill in details about the length of your stay in China. It will be put with your passport. Keep the customs declaration safe, because you need to hand it in at the end of the trip. The Chinese customs officers may check, when you hand in your customs declaration, whether you are taking out all the items you declared. The loss of the customs declaration can incur a high fine.

There are exchange bureaux at the arrival halls of the airport, railway station and harbour where you can change money. You can also find taxis to your hotel. The Chinese airlines provide buses which will take travellers from the airport, which is often a long way outside the city, to the airline offices in town. The fare is modest.

Be wary of people offering taxis before you reach taxi ranks. Before setting off in a taxi, agree on a price for the journey, or ensure the driver will use the meter.

Domestic Travel

Also see travel descriptions and options in *Getting There*, pages 268–269.

By Air: The following list shows the time needed for flight connections from Beijing to other domestic destinations.

Flight connections from Beijing to	Travel time hrs/min
Chengdu	2.35
Chongqing	2.30
Dalian	1.10
Guangzhou	2.40
Guilin	2.35
Hangzhou	1.50
Harbin	1.40
Hohhot	1.15
Kunming	2.55
Lanzhou	2.10
Nanjing	1.50
Qingdao	1.15
Shanghai	1.50
Taiyuan	1.35
Ürümqi	3.55
Wuhan	1.45
Xi'an	2.00

By Rail: The distance and time needed to travel from Beijing to other domestic destinations are as below:

From Beijing to	Distance km (miles)	Travel time hrs
Chengdu	1,273 (2,048)	34
Chongqing	1,586 (2,552)	40
Datong	249 (400)	8
Dalian	770 (1,239)	19
Guangzhou	1,437 (2,313)	33
Guilin	1,326 (2,134)	31
Hangzhou	1,026 (1,651)	26
Harbin	862 (1,388)	17
Hohhot	423 (680)	14
Kunming	1,975 (3,179)	59
Lanzhou	1,169 (1,882)	33
Luoyang	509 (819)	12
Nanjing	719 (1,157)	15
Qingdao	551 (887)	17
Shanghai	908 (1,462)	17
Suzhou	855 (1,376)	21
Taiyuan	319 (514)	9
Ürümqi	2,345 (3,774)	73
Wuhan	764 (1,229)	16
Wuxi	829 (1,334)	17
Xi'an	724 (1,165)	17

Water Transport

There are regular ferry and boat connections between the large coastal cities in China. The same is true for some of the big rivers, particularly the *Yangzi* and the *Pearl* River (but not the Yellow River). Both the ocean liners and the inland river boats have several classes. You can find out the exact timetable from travel agents or the shipping agencies.

Public Transport

Railways: The Chinese rail network covers 53,400 km (32,467 mi), of which 2,734 miles (4,400 km) are electrified. Average train speed is not very high, mainly due to poor construction. There is no first or second class on Chinese trains, but four categories or classes: *ruanwo* or soft-sleeper; *ruanzuo* or soft-seat; *yingwo* or hard-sleeper, and *yingzuo* or hard-seat. The soft-seat class is usually only available for short journeys. Long distance trains normally only have soft-sleeper or hard-sleeper facilities. The soft-sleeper class has 4-bed compartments with soft beds. It is to be recommended particularly for long journeys. The hard-sleeper class has open, 6-bed compartments. The beds are not really hard, but are not very comfortable either. While you can reserve a place for the first three classes (you always buy a ticket with a place number), this is not essential for the lowest class.

There is always boiled water available on the trains. There are washrooms in the soft-sleeper and hard-sleeper classes. The toilets, regardless of which class, are usually not very hygienic, and it is a good idea to bring your own toilet paper. There are dining cars on long-distance trains which can vary in quality. Trains are usually fully booked and it is advisable to get a ticket well in advance. This is particularly so during the main travel season. There are special ticket counters for foreigners at railway stations. Fares are higher for foreigners than for the Chinese. The price also depends on both the class and the speed of the train; there are slow trains, fast trains, express trains and inter-city trains. Reservations can be made at ticket offices in the town centre or through travel agencies. Be on time, as trains tend to be punctual.

Buses (*gongonqiche*): Overland buses are the most important means of transport in many parts of China, especially where there is as yet no railway line. In most towns and settlements, there are main bus stations for overland buses. They are certainly the cheapest means of transport, but are also correspondingly slow. There are regular breaks during bus journeys; on journeys lasting several days you will usually find simple restaurants and overnight accommodation near the bus stations. Many overland buses have numbered seats and it is advisable to book a ticket and seat well in advance. Modern buses with air conditioning are frequently available in the tourist centres.

Town Transport

The visitor can choose between taxis, buses or bicycles for transport in the cities. In Beijing, Hong Kong and Shanghai there is also the underground. Taxis are certainly the most comfortable form of transport, and can be hired for excursions.

Buses in Chinese towns are always overcrowded. The fare depends on distance, and should be paid to the conductor. Buses are usually easy to use, and timetables or town maps are available everywhere. In some Chinese cities such as Beijing, there are also minibuses for certain routes. They carry a maximum of 16 people. They are a bit more expensive but will stop at any point you want along the route.

You can hire bicycles in many Chinese towns, either at the hotels or at special hiring shops. It is advisable to park the bicycle at guarded parking spaces for a small fee. China too has bicycle thieves and there is a fine for illegal parking.

On Departure

Before leaving by train or plane, you must first hand in your customs declaration, and, on request from the customs official, show the valuables you declared on entry. You could also be asked to produce all the receipts showing what money or travellers cheques you changed.

There is a departure tax.

Where To Stay

Hotels

China's large cities have seen the sprouting of numerous new hotels, most of them at the high end of the market, including many of world-class caliber. Many belong to international hotel chains, or else to international marketing associations, and their management and staff have been trained abroad. Usually the prices of these better hotels are in line with hotel prices in the West.

Tour groups are usually accommodated in good tourist hotels, which are well-appointed. Except in the first-class hotels, take caution with laundry service, particularly with delicate clothes.

Bookings with hotels in the middle and lower price ranges sometimes can be difficult, particularly during the main summer season in May, September and October, when they are hopelessly booked up. Fortunately, if you have confirmed reservations, your room will be waiting, as hotels rarely overbook.

Worth mentioning are a few well-preserved hotels built by the colonial powers in some cities. They include the Peace Hotel (*Heping*) in Shanghai, the People's Hotel (*Renmin Dasha*) in Xi'an and the Friendship Hotel (*Youyibinguan*) in Beijing. Although interiors have been modernized, of course.

Luxury hotels abound in the largest cities. Hong Kong is saturated with them. Rates at all but the cheapest hotels are subject to 10 to 15 percent service surcharge. Rates indicated are for standard rooms.

$$$$$	=	US$200 and up
$$$$	=	US$150–US$200
$$$	=	US$100–US$150
$$	=	US$50–US$100
$	=	below US$50

Beijing

$$$$$

China World Hotel, 1 Jianguomenwai Dajie. Tel: 6505 2266. Top of the line service and accommodations, well located for business. Health club with swimming pool, shopping plaza and business center, plus a variety of Western and Asian restaurants. Part of a huge complex that includes the China World Trade Centre.

Palace Hotel, 8 Jinyu Hutong Wangfujing. Tel: 6512 8899, Fax: 512 9050. 5-star hotel managed by the Peninsula group. Centrally located for shopping and Imperial Palace sights, on a lively downtown alleyway. Restaurants and designer shopping.

$$$$

Kempinski Hotel (Beijing Lufthansa Ctr), 50 Liangmaqiao Lu. Tel: 6465 3388, Fax: 465 3366. Shiny new 5-star hotel with the works. Attached to Youyi Shopping City.

Shangri-La Hotel, 29 Zizhuyuan Rd. Tel: 6841 2211. The Shangri-La offers top-notch accommodation with experienced service staff and friendly surroundings. The hotel is located on the western edge of town, but shuttle buses are available to take guests to the center.

$$$

Hilton Hotel, 1 Dongfong Lu, Dongsanhuanbei Lu. Tel: 6466 2288. New 5-star hotel right off the airport expressway. Posh surroundings, good food.

Hotel New Otani, Changfugong 26 Jianguomenwai Dajie. Tel: 6512 5555, Fax: 513 0810. Japanese joint-venture with swimming pool and health club. Well located for business in the eastern part of the city.

Holiday Inn Crowne Plaza, Beijing 48 Wangfujing Dajie Dengshikou. Tel: 6513 3388. Located on a busy shopping street in central Beijing, close to the Imperial Palace and other sights. Health club and swimming pool.

Hotel Beijing-Toronto, 3 Jianguomenwai Dajie. Tel: 6500 2266. Friendly 4-star lodging in eastern Beijing.

Peace Hotel, 3 Jinyu Hutong Wangfujing. Tel: 6512 8833. Unremarkable rooms, centrally located for shopping and the Imperial Palace. Lively nightlife in the neighborhood.

Guang Dong Regency Hotel, 2 Wangfujing Dajie. Tel: 6513 6666. Comfortable atmosphere and deluxe accommodation in a prime location.

Swissotel Beijing (Hong Kong Macau Centre), Dongsi Shitiao, Lijiao Qiao. Tel: 6501 2288. New luxury highrise hotel northwest of business area.

Traders Hotel (China World Trade Centre), 1 Jianguomenwai Dajie. Tel: 6505 2277. Good solid service, food and accommodation. Well located for business in the east section of the city.

$$

Beijing Bamboo Garden Hotel, 24 Xiaoshiqiao Lane, Jiugulou Dajie. Tel: 6403 2229. Modest and clean rooms that open into a classical-style Chinese garden. The hotel is just one block from the Drum Tower.

Fragrant Hills Hotel, Fragrant Hills Park. Tel: 6259 1166. Sunny modern getaway in the lush hills to the northwest of Beijing, near Summer Palace, but far from the city. Swimming pool, Chinese and Western restaurants.

Jianguo Hotel, 5 Jianguomenwai Dajie. Tel: 6500 2233. A favorite for long-term business travelers to the city. Experienced staff and a comfortable atmosphere. Located in eastern Beijing. Good value.

Holiday Inn Lido Hotel, Jiangtai Lu. Tel: 6437 6688, Fax: 437 6237. A village unto itself catering to short- and long-term guests. Indoor/outdoor swimming, tennis courts, business and shopping facilities. Near the airport.

Novotel 88, Dengshikou Dajie. Tel: 6513 8822. Clean, no frills, centrally located. A real bargain for Beijing.

Qianmen Hotel, Beijing 175, Yongan Lu. Tel: 6301 6688. Standard accommodations in old outer city, near Tiantan. Opera performances nightly.

Xin Qiao Hotel, 2 Dong Jiaomin Xiang, Dongcheng District. Tel: 6513 3366. Elegant old-style hotel located in the former Legation Quarter, close to Tiananmen Square. Peaceful and convenient to transportation.

$

Beijing Friendship Hotel, 3 Baishiqiao Rd. Tel: 6849 8888. An old-style, state-run hotel in the peaceful northwest corner of town. Located near the universities and the Summer Palace.

Ritan Hotel, One Ritan Road, Jianguomenwai. Tel: 6512 5588. Intimate little hotel located inside Ritan Park. Peaceful and reasonably-priced for basic accommodation.

Guangzhou

$$$$

China Hotel, Liuhua Lu, Guangzhou. Tel: 8666 6888; Fax: 8667 7014. Five-star hotel managed by the New World Group of Hong Kong. Restaurants, electronic games arcade and bowling alley. The hotel is across the street from the Canton Trade Fair grounds.

White Swan Hotel, 1 Shamian Nanlu. Tel: 8188 6968; Fax: 8186 1188. One of the finest hotels in China and a member of the Leading Hotels of the World network. The 843-room hotel on Shamian island has stunning views.

$$$

Dongfang Hotel, 120 Liuhua Lu, Guangzhou. Tel: 8666 9900; Fax: 8666 2775. The Dongfang was built in the 1950s by the Soviets and a new wing added in the 1970s. Has managed to retain a lot of charm. Centrally-located and convenient for businessmen, as the China Trade Fair grounds are just opposite. A 5-star hotel.

Garden Hotel, 368 Huangshi Donglu, Guangzhou. Tel: 8333 8989; Fax: 8335 0467. A 5-star hotel located across the street from the largest Friendship Department Store.

Guangdong International Hotel, 336 Huangshi Donglu, Guangzhou. Tel: 8331 1888; Fax: 8331 1666. The newest luxury-class hotel to open in Guangzhou. Has 14 food and beverage outlets and a shopping arcade.

Holiday Inn City Centre Overseas Chinese Village, Huanshi Dong, 28 Guangmin Lu, Guangzhou. Tel: 8776 6999; Fax: 8775 3126. This 430-room hotel, which opened in 1990, is known for its friendly service.

Ramada Pearl Hotel, 9 Mingyue Yilu, Guangzhou. Tel: 8777 2988; Fax: 8776 7481. Part of the Ramada International chain, this 400-room hotel is located in the eastern part of the city.

Forum, 67 Heping Lu, Shenzhen. Tel: 8558 6333; Fax: 8556 1700. Opened in 1990, the Forum is located just west of the railway station. A member of the Inter-Continental hotel and resorts.

Shangri-La, East Side, Railway Station Jianshe Lu, Shenzhen. Tel: 8223 0888; Fax: 8223 9878. Part of the Shangri-La International chain. Luxuriously-appointed 553 rooms with extensive food and beverage outlets.

$$

Equatorial Hotel, 931 Renmin Lu, Guangzhou. Tel: 8667 2888; Fax: 8667 2583. Comprehensive range of food and beverage outlets, business center, health club and discotheque.

Overseas Chinese Hotel, 90 Zhanqian Lu, Guangzhou. Tel: 8666 3488; Fax: 8666 3230. This 400-room hotel has two restaurants, a coffee house and a discotheque.

Century Plaza (Shenzhen), Kinchit Lu, Shenzhen. Tel: 8222 0888; Fax: 8223 4060. Luxury hotel situated in the hub of Shenzhen. Five restaurants, pool, and health and business centers.

Oriental Regent (Shenzhen), Financial Centre Bldg, Shenan Zhonglu, Shenzhen. Tel: 8224 7000; Fax: 8224 7290. Centrally-located, 4-star hotel. Close to nightlife area.

Shenzhen Bay Hotel, Overseas Chinese Town, Shenzhen. Tel: 8660 0111; Fax: 8660 0139. Facing Deep Water Bay and a short walk from attractions like Splendid China, China Folk Culture Village and Windows of the World. This resort-style hotel on the beach offers a full range of recreational facilities.

$

Guangzhou Youth Hostel, 2 Shamian Sijie, Guangzhou. Tel: 8188 4298. Cheap rooms can be found at this hostelry, nicknamed the 'Black Duck', as it faces the luxury White Swan Hotel. A favorite with backpackers.

Victory Hotel, 54 Shamian Sijie, Guangzhou. Tel: 8186 2622; Fax: 8186 2413. Located on the former concession island of Shamian, near the old town. This was one of Guangzhou's top hotels in the 1930s.

Zhongshan Hot Springs Resort, San Xiang, Zhongshan. Tel: 8683 888; Fax: 8683 333. An idyllic retreat from the city. Hotel rooms feature marble baths with hot spring water on tap.

Songtao Hotel, Wan Song Gang, Qixing Crags, Zhaoqing. Tel: 8224 412; Fax: 8224 412. A 3-star hotel situated in the scenic Seven Star Crags area.

Zhuhai Hotel, Jingshan Lu, Zhuhai. Tel: 3833 718; Fax: 8332 339. Luxury hotel with good leisure facilities, including sauna, tennis courts, billiard room, swimming pool, nightclub and mahjong rooms.

Zhuhai Holiday Resort, Shihuashan, Zhuhai. Tel: 8332 038; Fax: 8332 036. Idyllic beachfront 5-star property west of Jiuzhou Harbor. Full range of leisure amenities, including a bowling alley, a roller skating rink, go-cart racing and horse riding.

Shanghai

LUXURY

Garden Hotel, 58 Maoming Nanlu. Tel: 6433 1111, Fax: 6433 8866. A 33-story tower that incorporates the former Cercle Sportif Francais, inject a little of the past into the hotel's modern facilities. Surrounded by a garden, the Garden is popular with Japanese, as it is managed by the Hotel Okura, probably Tokyo's finest hotel.

Hilton International, 250 Hua Shan Rd. Tel: 6248 0000, Fax: 6248 3848. Over 40 stories tall, the Hilton makes an unforgettable first impression with its expansive marble lobby. Popular with both Europeans and Asians. Restaurants include the rooftop Sichuan Court restaurant, with fine views.

Holiday Inn Crowne Plaza, 388 Pan Yu Rd. Tel: 6252 8888, Fax: 6252-8545. Located near the diplomatic neighborhood, the Crowne Plaza follows the elegant design of the chain's top-end hotels everywhere. With full business and recreational facilities, several respected restaurants offer imaginative East-West menus.

JC Mandarin, 1225 Nanjing Xilu. Tel: 6279 1888, Fax: 6279 1822. Conveniently located in the heart of Shanghai's shopping district and on its most commercial avenue, the hotel is within walking distance of the Bund and other sights. Facilities include an indoor pool, gym, and two tennis courts.

Pacific Hotel, 104 Nanjing Lu. Tel: 6327 6226, Fax: 6326 9620. Not one of Shanghai's finer establishments, the hotel is sagging and somewhat Gothic in ambiance. One of Shanghai's older hotels, the granite structure is architecturally interesting: a gold-plated dome with a clock tower crown the roof, and a classically-robust entrance leads into an art-deco lobby.

Peace Hotel, 20 Nanjing Lu. Tel: 6321 1244, Fax: 6329 0300. Located on the Bund and a classic colonial retreat, one of the city's most famous landmarks. When it opened in the 1920s as the Cathay, it was the hotel in China. Somewhat rundown now, but comfortable, the Peace appeals to those who prefer nostalgia to generic creature comforts. Even if not staying here, drop by the bar in the evening to see the Old Jazz Band, a sextet of men in their late 60s.

Portman Shangri-La, Shanghai Center, 1376 Nanjing Xilu. Tel: 6279 8888, Fax: 6279 8999. One of Shanghai's finest hotels, known not only for its central location, but also for its style – Chinese works of art, including statues of horses and camels, adorn the lobby. Chamber music in the lobby each afternoon and evening. The hotel is part of the extensive Shanghai Center, a complex with top restaurants, airline offices, and residential apartments.

Guesthouses

Individual travelers may find accommodation in guesthouses in smaller towns off the beaten tourist track. Guesthouses usually have rooms with two or more beds, and often dormitories are available; there are usually shower and washing facilities, as well. They are recommended as cheap accommodation for backpackers.

Some guesthouses or simple hotels

refuse to take foreign guests, usually because of the rules of Chinese travel agencies or the local police, who often determine where foreigners may stay.

Others

It is practically impossible for foreigners to find accommodation outside of hotels and guesthouses. Private lodgings are unknown because of crowded living conditions. At times, some universities and institutes have guesthouses where foreign visitors can find good, cheap accommodation. Advance booking is not possible.

If going on a long trip or hike in the countryside, especially in Tibet or in areas around the sacred mountains of China, you will come across various types of "long-distance travelers' lodgings". It is advisable to carry a sleeping bag.

Eating Out

What To Eat

For Westerners, the single identifying symbol of Chinese cuisine is the use of chopsticks, which are practical as the food is cut into small pieces. Due to the short supply of fuel over the centuries, it has been necessary to prepare food using a minimum of fuel – small pieces cook quicker.

Only about 10 percent of China's land area is suitable for agriculture. Thus, beef is not a significant source of food; the need to cultivate intensively means grazing is neither possible nor common, except in the extreme north and northwest. Thus, until recently, milk and dairy products were not widely known. In place of animal protein, soybeans have often been a primary source of protein.

Traditionally, food should not only be filling, but it should also have a healing effect. A Chinese meal is based on balance, even the largest and most extravagant banquets.

There are roughly four main styles of Chinese cuisine (this does not take into account the often completely dif-

ferent cooking and eating traditions of the national minorities):

Northern cuisine, with Beijing at its center. The soil around Beijing is fairly poor, thus the food it produces is unvaried. In contrast to the south, where rice is preferred, noodles dishes predominate here. The main vegetable is Chinese cabbage: boiled, steamed, fried, preserved, with a variety of different spices. Special mention should be made of Peking Duck and the Mongolian hotpot, feasts not to be missed if in Beijing. **Haiyang**, in the eastern coastal areas around Shanghai. The predominant food is fish (particularly freshwater) and shellfish. There is a greater choice of vegetables here than in the north. **Cantonese**, the southern cuisine, is the most familiar to Westerners, and the most common in Chinese restaurants around the world. **Sichuan** is famous for its highly-spiced foods, assuring that diners can warm up even in the often humid and cold winters.

The Chinese tend to eat quite early; lunch is often served in Chinese restaurants from 11am. (Hotels and restaurants for foreigners have, of course, adjusted to their preferences.) In the evenings, you won't easily find a meal after 8pm, though this is different in the south, where social life continues until the late evening.

Where To Eat

Chinese meals are best eaten in a group, with diners sharing a variety of dishes; Chinese restaurants are often not suited to individual diners.

The individual traveler is more likely to frequent one of the typical Chinese roadside eateries. Make sure the restaurant is clean and the food has been freshly-prepared and is hot. Bringing one's own chopsticks isn't considered an insult at all. Chinese restaurants are often not heated even during winter (nor are theaters or concert halls), so it is advisable to dress warmly.

Drinking Notes

In most hotel rooms are thermos flasks with hot and cold water, and bags with green or black tea (*hong*, or red). A cup of hot tea, or just "white" tea (hot water), as the Chinese usually drink it, is the most effective way of quenching your thirst. At meal times, Chinese beer, which contain less alcohol than European beer, mineral water or lemonade (often very sweet) are offered in addition to the ubiquitous green tea.

While being in drunk in public is considered unacceptable in China (unlike in Japan, for example), there is a surprisingly large choice of Chinese spirits on offer. The most famous are *maotai jiu*, a 55-percent spirit made of wheat and sorghum that, for centuries, has been produced in Maotai, in Guizhou Province, and *wuliangye jiu*, a spirit made from five different grains. You'll either take to it immediately or not in a lifetime. Chinese wine, both red and white, tend to be very sweet, tasting a bit like sherry. Wine for foreign tastes is also being produced now.

Attractions

Group Travel

The simplest and most comfortable way of travelling to China at a reasonable price is in a group. Participants will have their passage, hotel accommodation and full board, and sightseeing program booked in advance. There are hardly any additional costs apart from drinks and shopping. Sometimes, additional excursions may be on offer once you have arrived, but they are generally not too costly. Some places charge for taking photographs.

The local tour guide is supplied by the Chinese tourist office and is in charge of taking you to the sights.

Specialists will have better knowledge of places of special interest when planning a particular route. Also, the pitfalls of a journey through China have increased rather than diminished in recent years; an experienced tour operator can avoid many difficulties.

Another decisive factor for a successful group trip is the tour guide. While each group with more than ten participants is allocated a permanent Chinese guide in addition to the local guides, their qualifications vary considerably, both in terms of organising the trip and in their knowledge of the country and its sights, and their ability to communicate. The importance of the guide employed by the tour operator shouldn't be underestimated.

A number of tour operaters now offer trips around a theme as well as the traditional routes. A few offer courses in shadow boxing, calligraphy or acupuncture; some even offer language courses.

Individual Travel

There are three ways of travelling in China for the individual traveller. The most comfortable, and of course, most expensive way, is to book a full package tour through an experienced travel agent. Everything is pre-booked, including flights and journeys, accommodation, full board, transfers etc., with the difference that the traveller can choose a route according to their preference. The same is the case for sightseeing: a guide from a China travel agency is available in each town and will help with putting together and arranging a sightseeing program.

The second possibility is booking a mini-package tour. The agent pre-books the flights, accommodation with breakfast, transfers and transport of luggage in China while the traveller is responsible for organising sightseeing. The traveller is met at the airport or railway station of each town and taken to the hotel. Each hotel has a travel agency counter, where you can discuss your plans for sightseeing and have them arranged for a fee.

You can usually have lunch and dinner at your hotel or maybe try a Chinese restaurant while out and about.

The individual tourist may have the most pleasant travel. The most essential bookings have been made (to make them yourself requires a lot of time and strong nerves), and with thorough preparation, you have a good chance of getting to know China beyond the usual tourist routes. You should get a definite booking with an experienced travel agent three months before departure at the latest.

Then, there is also the completely independent travel, without any pre-booking. This form of travelling in China has increased in recent years. The Chinese travel bureaus have partially adapted to it and can help, in the large towns, with buying air and train tickets. You have to arrange your own air and train tickets at each place you visit; unless you speak Chinese, you will probably find it easiest to do this through a travel agency, where it is more likely you will find English-speaking staff. At airports and stations, you will often find that information about destinations is given in Pinyin, or sometimes only in Chinese characters. You shouldn't expect last-minute plans to come through; it can easily happen that you have to wait several days for your railway or air ticket, or abandon your chosen destination and choose a different town for your next visit. You should try and reserve air or rail tickets as soon as you arrive. Tickets cost more for foreigners than for Chinese, and only in rare cases might you succeed (for instance if you have a student card) in getting a ticket at the cost that overseas Chinese pay.

Travel agencies will book hotels for a relatively small fee, though this is typically only the case with hotels in the more expensive range. It is best to approach cheaper hotels or guest houses directly; here, a knowledge of Chinese is an advantage.

Culture

Museums

There are a great variety of museums in China. From the revolution to natural history, everything is captured in exhibitions at various places. Many Chinese museums are not very well administered and not easy for the visitor to appreciate. English labeling is the exception. Recommended below are mainly museums in the field of art and culture. Opening hours are usually between 9am and 5pm.

BEIJING

Museum of Chinese History (Zhongguo Lishi Bowuguan), Tiananmen Square. Tel: 655 8321. On Tiananmen Square. It is one of the most comprehensive and best museums in China covering the entire Chinese history.
Military Museum, Fuxingmenwai Dajie. Tel: 6801 4441.
Museum of the Revolution (Zhongguo Geming Bowuguan), Tiananmen Square. Tel: 655 8321.
Palace Museum in the Imperial Pal-

ace (Gugong Bowuguan). Tel: 6513 2255. The Imperial Palace is one huge museum; occasionally it has special exhibitions.

Lu Xun Museum, Fuchengmennei Dajie. Tel: 6603 7617.

Xu Beihong Memorial Hall, Xinjiekou Beidajie. Tel: 666 1592.

Museum of Chinese Art (Beijing Meishu Zhanlanguan), 1 Wusi Dajie, Chaoyangmennei. Tel: 6401 7076.

The Beijing Agricultural Exhibition Hall (Nongye Zhanlanguan), Sanlitun. Tel: 658 2331.

CHANGSHA

Hunan Provincial Museum. The museum mainly contains objects which were discovered in a Han tomb near Man-wangdui, 3 km (½ mi) east of the museum. They include the perfectly preserved corpse of a 50-year-old woman.

NANJING

Nanjing Museum. 321, Zhongshan Donglu. The most precious exhibit, in addition to pottery, porcelain (including some from the Ming Dynasty), bronzes, tortoise shells and jewellery from various dynasties, is a 2,000-year-old shroud made of 26,000 jade pieces.

SHANGHAI

Shanghai Museum of Art (Yan'an Lu). West of Xizang Lu. It houses one of the best collections of Chinese art history. It has bronzes, pottery, stone figures, weapons as well as an excellent collection of Chinese painting from the Tang dynasty to the end of the Qing dynasty.

ÜRÜMQI

Xinjiang Provincial Museum (Xinjiang Bowuguan). It contains an archaeological exhibition about the Silk Road as well as an exhibition about the minorities in Xinjiang.

WUHAN

Hubei Provincial Museum. It is located on the western shore of Lake Donghu and has finds from a tomb of a prince from the 5th century BC. They include unique bronze chimes with 65 well perserved bronze bells which can still be sounded. Other bronzes and musical instruments were also found in the tomb.

XI'AN

Shaanxi Provincial Museum. The mu-

seum is located in the former Confucian temple found in the south of the town. It has three departments: the history of Xi'an and its surroundings to the end of the Tang Dynasty, Stele forest, and stone sculptures. It also regularly holds special exhibitions.

Museum of the Terracotta Soldiers of the First Qin Emperor. In Lintong county near the tomb of Emperor Qin Shi Huangdi.

Concerts

There are regular concerts of Western classical or traditional Chinese music in various cities. Indigenous or foreign songs and musical performances are often part of the program. Dance performances are also common. In many areas – particularly in those of the national minorities – you can admire performances of local dances and songs on the stage. Ballet is also performed. Young people – though not only them – are very keen on concerts by various pop stars, whether from the PR of China, Hong Kong or even Taiwan. You can find out about time and place of performances in each town from the hotel or through travel agencies.

Operas

There are more than 300 types of opera in China. You can attend performances of traditional opera in virtually every town. The most famous one is the Beijing Opera. The address of the opera and theatre is available from the hotel or from travel agencies. A visit to the Chinese opera is a relaxed affair and occasionally quite noisy. You can leave your evening dress and tie at home; normal day clothes are fine.

BEIJING OPERA

Liyuan Theater, Qianmen Hotel, Yong'an Lu. Daily performances in a large theater.

Gong Wangfu Huayuan. Small theater in the former residence of Prince Gong, just north of Beihai Gongyuan (Park). Performances daily at 7.30pm.

Acrobatics

Acrobatics is popular throughout China. Almost every large town has its own troupe of acrobats. Many of the troupes tour the country. You can get details of time and place of performances locally. In big cities such as

Beijing, Shanghai and Guangzhou, there are permanent performances. In China, acrobatics means a mixture of proper acrobatics, magic and animal acts, and of course clowns. Circus performances are similar.

Festivals

Holidays such as National Day and International Labour Day are fixed on the modern calendar, but most traditional festivals and events are determined by the lunar calendar, which means the date varies a little from year to year.

January / February

The most important festival time is the Lunar New Year, or **Spring Festival**, which falls in late January or early February. Public buildings are festooned with colored lights, people from all over China travel to reunite with families, debts are settled, and there is food consumed – lots of it. On the first days of the lunar year, Chinese visit family and friends. In recent years, a more relaxed atmosphere has brought the revival of old Spring Festival traditions, such as giving *hongbao* – small, red envelopes containing money – to children and young adults. Temple fairs feature martial arts demonstrations, stand-up comic sketches, homemade toys and, of course, food.

Northerners, who have amazing resilience to the bitterly cold winters, partake with gusto in ice-sculpting competitions and winter swimming. The time and duration of the festivals depends on the weather.

Both Beijing and Harbin are noted for their ice-sculpting festivals.

April

On the 12th day of the third lunar month, in the beginning of April, the Chinese honor their deceased ancestors by observing **Qingming**, sometimes referred to as the 'grave-sweeping' day. It is much less impressive nowadays, as people are cremated instead of being buried. Qingming is a time for remembering ancestors, but also for reveling on a warm spring day.

May / June

International Labor Day is a one-day public holiday. Following hot on its heels is **Youth Day**, a commemoration of the May 4th Movement of 1919, reflected by large editorials and government hoopla in the official press. **International Children's Day** is celebrated in earnest on June 1, by letting classes out early and treating children to outings at public parks.

July / August

July 1 is the **Anniversary of the Communist Party**, which was founded in Shanghai in 1921. This means very little to the average citizen but plenty of fun for high-level party members.

The fifth day of the fifth lunar month – usually late July – brings the **Dragon Boat Festival**, marked by dragon boat races in many cities, sometimes involving teams from around the world. It commemorates the memory of Qu Yuan (340–278BC), a poet in the days of the Kingdom of Chu, who, rather than submit to political pressure, drowned himself in the Miluo river, in Hunan. To prevent the fishes from eating his body, the people threw glutinous rice cakes into the river. Nowadays, these *zongzi* are simply eaten to mark the occasion.

August 1 is the **Anniversary of the People's Liberation Army**. Inaugurated in 1927 and formerly marked by enormous parades, it is now noted mainly in the media.

September / October

The **Mid-Autumn Festival** again depends on when the moon reaches its fullest, usually around mid-September. The shops do great business in 'moon cakes' – pastries filled with gooey sesame paste, red-bean and walnut filling. *Tang yuan*, glutinous rice flour balls with sweet fillings in sugar syrup, and *yue bing*, a cake baked specifically for this occasion, are eaten. In the tradition of poets, this is the time to drink a bit of wine and toast the moon.

Late September is normally the time when Chinese communities celebrate the memory of Confucius.

October 1 is the PRC's birthday, **National Day**, celebrated with a two-day public holiday. Government buildings, road intersections and hotels are decked out in lights, and flower arrangements and Sun Yatsen's portrait is displayed in Tiananmen Square. Tens of thousands turn out on the square for picture-taking and general merry-making.

November / December

November and December are quiet months in China, but **Christmas** is gaining momentum as a consumer's celebration. Christian churches hold special services that draw thousands of spectators. In Beijing, for example, it is trendy to exchange greeting cards and presents, while Santa Claus makes the odd shop appearance.

Shopping

What To Buy

Typically "Chinese" goods such as silk, jade and porcelain are still cheaper and of a better quality in Hong Kong than in the People's Republic of China. The choice varies – if you are lucky, the shelves are well stocked and you can find excellent and well-cut silk articles being sold cheaply; if the supply has dried up, you will only find meagre remnants even in Hangzhou, the centre of silk production. You will usually find good quality goods which are produced for export. These are mostly sold in the "Friendship Stores" (*Youyi Shangdian*) and in the hotel shops.

Until recently, it was not usual to bargain and it is still not advisable in the state-owned shops and warehouses. But at the many souvenir stands, it is a good idea to bargain because of the greatly overpriced goods on offer. It is also worth comparing prices in the free markets (if you can read them) and watch how much Chinese customers pay.

When buying antiques, it is essential to check that the official red seal of the shop is on the product. Buying and exporting of antiques is only permitted with this official stamp, otherwise you could meet with great difficulties when leaving the country.

It is worth looking for local products in the smaller towns or in the places where ethnic minorities live. These will be difficult to find anywhere else in China. The most usual articles are craft objects for everyday use or specially worked or embroidered garments.

Import & Export

Antiques that date from before 1795 may not be legally exported. Those that can be taken out of China must carry a small red seal or have one affixed by the Cultural Relics Bureau. All other antiques are the property of the Peoples' Republic of China and, without the seal, will be confiscated without compensation. Beware of fakes; producing new 'antiques' (and the seal) is a thriving industry.

Foreign currency can be imported and exported without restrictions. You may not export more foreign currency than you imported, except with a special permit.

You should not export, nor even buy in the first place, objects made from wild animals, especially from ivory. Most Western countries ban the import of ivory objects, and will confiscate them without compensation.

Shopping Areas

Forget any notions about an austere workers' paradise. Consumerism is the only meaningful 'ism' around China these days.

The number of *dakuan* – the fat cats with portable phones – is increasing. New markets and stores are sprouting up everywhere.

It's advisable to check prices first at state-operated stores, such as the Friendship Store, before buying a similar item in a hotel shop or on the free market. And in the free market, bargain, and be stubborn – but friendly – if interested in an item. Avoid drawn out dickering just for the sport.

Bargaining usually begins with the shopkeeper suggesting a price and the buyer responding with a lower one. In Beijing, the starting price is generally 30 to 50 percent higher than the price shopkeepers will eventually accept. Be persistent, look for missing buttons, stains and other flaws, keep smiling, and walk away if you find the price unacceptable.

Department stores: In every town is a department store selling products for everyday use, from toothpaste to a bicycle. However, the quality of clothing fabric (artificial), the cut and the sizes are usually not up to expectation.

The big department store are state-owned institutions, but many small shops and street stalls – privately owned – have sprung up as well. Here you will often find products from Hong Kong, including higher-quality clothing.

Friendship stores: A visit to the Friendship Store (*Youyi Shangdian*) is an essential part of the program of all tour groups. These stores usually offer a good selection of wares for export: silk fabric, craft articles, electronic devices, clothing and books. Often, there is a whole department offering both traditional and modern medical products and equipment. Individual travelers, too, should take the opportunity to look round these stores from time to time. The Friendship Store in Beijing, for instance, has an excellent food department. A visit to the antiques department in the Friendship Store in Shanghai is also worthwhile.

Some large Friendship Store and warehouses have a delivery section that will send purchases to one's home country. Shops and department stores generally open around 9am and close at 6pm or 7pm.

Markets: Food items such as fruit, vegetables, fish and meat are sold at markets. In the free markets, where prices are more flexible, and sometimes more expensive (off-setting higher quality and availability), there are often additional items, such as wicker baskets, metal and iron bits, and clothes; tailors are sometimes found. In the big towns, numerous street traders offer their wares well into the evening; one can often find jeans or silk blouses from Hong Kong at such places.

Watch how much the Chinese themselves pay. All too often, traders in free markets will happily fleece unwary – foreign – customers.

Beijing

SPECIALTY MARKETS

Silk Alley (Xiushui Shichang) – on Xuishiu Jie and intersecting with Chang'an Lu about 800 m east of the Friendship Store, has been growing in the past few years. As the name implies, vendors flog silk in all shapes and sizes – ties and boxer shorts, dresses and slinky nightgowns – at prices about half of that found in Hong Kong. Just a few blocks away is **Yabaolu Market**, commonly known as the Russian market (open daily 9am–6pm) and on Ritan Lu, opposite Ritan Park. It is a huge clothing market specializing in cotton and wool garments, and also goose-down jackets.

A few blocks straight north of Yabaolu Market is the **Chaowai Flea Market** (open daily 10am–6pm), a favorite shopping ground for resident diplomats and journalists. The front building is filled with antique and classical-style furniture. In the rear building are curios: snuff bottles, ceramics and Mao memorabilia. **Hongqiao Farmers' Market**, on Tiantan Lu (open daily 7am–5.30pm), has the best collection of antique clocks and Mao statues, as well as freshwater pearls.

For traditional Chinese paintings, calligraphy supplies and rare books, poke around at **Liulichang** (open daily 9am–5.30pm), just west of Qianmen district. A bit further afield, but considered to be the most reliable source of antique porcelain in Beijing, is **Jingsong Market** (open daily 9am–6pm) located at East Third Ring Road at the Jingsong east intersection.

Tucked under the southeast corner of the Xizhimen overpass, the **Bird Market** (open daily 7.30am–sunset) is hardly an extension of nature, but it has a wonderful array of feathered creatures. At least as important are the elegant handmade cages, ceramic feeders and other avian paraphernalia sold here.

There are three lively shopping streets in the city center that cater to local customers. **Wangfujing**, **Xidan** and **Dongdan**, which run perpendicular to Chang'an Lu, have mostly inexpensive local goods, with bargains on leather and furs.

At 192 Wangfujing Dajie, check out the **Jianhua Leather Goods Company** (open daily 8am–8.30pm). It has leather jackets for as little as 250 yuan and full-length mink coats running up to 18,000 yuan. Available are suede backpacks, belts and fox pelts.

Further north, along the east side of Wangfujing, is the **Foreign Languages Bookstore**, run by the China News Agency. The first floor has a wide range of books on China. The upper floors have everything from Chinese art and language tapes to computers and a music store.

All three streets are undergoing radical transformation, with more and more boutiques, watch stores and ice-cream shops replacing the old standbys. Xidan and Wangfujing are both undergoing massive rebuilding, which will expand the shopping greatly.

Among the most popular department stores for Chinese products is **Longfu Dasha** (No 95 Longfusi Jie, Chaoyang District; open daily 8.30am–8.30pm). This is the spot to buy China's most famous brands of household products – Flying Pigeon bicycles and Butterfly sewing machines.

ONE-STOP SHOPPING

Capitalism's answer for one-stop shoppers is the glossy, new joint-venture shopping centers that draw China's *nouveau riche*, as well as tourists and mobs of window shoppers. Directly across the street from the Friendship Store is the CIVIC-**Yaohan** (No 22 Jianguomenwai Dajie, open daily 9am–9pm), a Japanese department store full of luxury, trendy imports.

The **Youyi Shopping City** in the Beijing Lufthansa Center (No 52 Liangmaqiao Lu, Chaoyang District; open daily 9am–9pm) carries products with a broader price range. The city's best silk selection – sold by the yard – is offered at reasonable prices.

Stock up on all the beautiful things that China produces – traditional paper cuttings (cheap and easy to pack), jade carvings, kites and chopsticks – at the state-run **Friendship Store** (No 17 Jianguomenwai Dajie; open daily 9am–9pm). The store is also good for getting an estimate of what things outside should cost, and for any last-minute gifts.

Guangzhou

Don't expect the glitz and variety of goods available in Hong Kong. Still, Guangzhou offers interesting shopping and good bargains. Among Chinese cities, Guangzhou is considered to have the widest range of goods, many of which are imported from other parts of the country.

ANTIQUES

The largest private market for antiques is the **Daihe Lu Market**, which sprawls over several lanes. Access the market by the first lane on the right after entering Daihe Lu from Changshou Xilu. There are smaller antique markets nearby; one at the middle lane of the Qingping Market and the other at the Jade Market. Do not buy antiques that the vendor claims are over 100 years old. Even if not trying to rip you off (and most are), a genuine antique that is over a century old cannot be exported if it doesn't carry an official red-wax seal.

Beware of fakes, as new 'antiques' with the official seal is a thriving industry in China. Despite the difficulties, there is still much to buy: *kam muk* (gilded sculptured wood panels), vintage watches, tiny embroidered shoes for Chinese women with bound feet, and beautiful Shiwan porcelain.

If a serious collector, antiques with authentic red-wax seals authorizing export can be bought from government shops. Try the **Guangzhou Antique Shop** (146/162/170 Wende Beilu, Tel: 8333 0175, Fax: 8335 0085) for *kam muk*, calligraphy works, jewelry boxes, paintings, porcelain and silver jewelry.

CLOTHING AND TEXTILES

Guangdong province is a major production center for ready-to-wear clothes and shoes. The biggest variety is to be found at the government-owned **Friendship Stores**. These stores are your best bet for down jackets (one-fifth the price you would pay elsewhere) and cashmere sweaters and scarves. The **Bingfen Fashion Market** on Haizhu Square, the **Gong Lu Fashion Market** on Zhongshan Erlu in Dongshan District, the night market under the Quzhuang Overbridge, and the Xihu Lu night market are also good hunting grounds for apparel.

Of special interest is Guangdong

black-mud silk, which is painstakingly hand-made and dyed as many as 30 times, using the red extract of the gambier root and the iron-rich river mud from the Pearl River. The material stays cool and dry in humid weather. The silk is available from the **Xin Da Xin department store**, at the corner of Beijing Lu and Zhongshan Wulu.

HANDICRAFTS

Paper Cuts: The Renshou Temple in Foshan, previously famous for its paper cuts of scenes from the Cultural Revolution, has remained the major production center for this delicate craft. However, its production nowadays focuses on farm scenes.

Bird cages: The Chinese love songbirds and show them off in splendidly-decorated cages at public parks. Antique cages cost from 100 to 700 yuan; newer ones can be bought at the **Bird Market**, located at the Dongfeng Lu entrance of Liuhua Park.

Seals: You can have your name engraved in Chinese characters on a seal, called a chop in colonial English, at the basement floor of the White Swan Hotel. When selecting your Chinese name, choose auspicious characters and limit yourself to two or three. If you need assistance, the staff at the shop will help you to choose the right combination. The material used can be hard wood, soapstone, crystal or agate. The shop will also sell you the special red ink (*hong yau*) that goes with the seal. Do not buy from side street sellers, as the seals they sell are made of bakelite and colored resin imitations of stone.

JADE AND PEARLS

Jade holds a greater fascination for the Chinese than any other stone. Traditionally, it is worn for good luck, as a protection against sickness and as an amulet for travelers. There are several types of jade: nephrite, tomb jade, jadeite, Imperial jade, and a local variety, *nanyu* jade. Do not buy from open-air private markets, as there are plenty of imitations in the market. Buy from established shops like the **Jade Shop** (12–14 Zhongshan Wulu), **Baoli Yuqi Hang** (220 Zhongshan Silu), **Guangzhou Antique Shop** (696 Wende Lu), and the jewelry shops of the China, Garden and White Swan hotels.

For centuries, pearls have been the

indispensable ornament of the nobility, especially emperors. Most of the pearls on sale in Guangzhou are salt-water southern pearls called *hepu*, cultured in silver-lipped oysters. The largest of these lustrous pearls can have a diameter of 1.2–1.6 cm. Recommended shops are: Guangzhou Gold and Silver Jewelry Center (109 Dade Lu) and Sun Moon Hall (Equatorial Hotel, Renmin Beilu).

MAO MEMORABILIA

In celebration of Mao's 100th birthday in 1993, centennial souvenirs appeared, such as commemorative watches and musical cigarette lighters playing revolutionary ditties. The Daihe Lu antique market has a reasonable variety of Mao artifacts, while the Friendship Stores sell 24K, diamond-studded medals. For badges, the stamp market in People's Park has the best pieces. Prices can be steep.

Language

English is increasingly being used in the People's Republic of China, but on the whole, you will still find it difficult to meet people away from the big hotels and business and tourist centres who speak English, not to mention German or French. It is therefore advisable – especially for individual travellers – to learn some Chinese. Some people joke that, apart from *meiyou* ("it doesn't exist"), the most common words in China are "change money?".

More than a billion people in China, and many other Chinese in Southeast Asia and the United States, speak Chinese. In the People's Republic of China, other languages in addition to Chinese – the language of the Han people, the original Chinese – are spoken in the regions where the national minorities are settled, including Tibetan, Mongolian, Zhuang or Uygur. But everywhere in the People's Republic today, standard Chinese, also called Mandarin, is more or less understood or spoken. Regardless of whether you are in Guangzhou or in Heilongjiang, in Tibet or in Xinjiang, you can get through with standard Chinese.

The Chinese language is divided into several groups of dialect. For instance, a native of Guangzhou or Hong Kong cannot understand someone from Beijing or vice versa, unless both speak standard Chinese. The different dialects have, however, the same grammar and vocabulary; but above all, the writing is the same. The pronunciation may differ, but the written symbols can be understood by all literate Chinese. Thus, a native of Guangzhou and a Beijing citizen can understand each other by simply writing down the symbols.

Since the 1950s, all schools in the People's Republic of China teach standard Chinese or Mandarin – also called Putonghua or common language. It is also used on radio and television. Young Chinese people, particularly, know standard Chinese. Consequently, one can manage throughout the People's Republic – including in Guangzhou – by using standard Chinese. You will immediately notice the difference when you go from Guangzhou to Hong Kong: in Hong Kong, the official language amongst the Chinese is Cantonese.

The transcription of Chinese symbols: Standard Chinese is based on the pronunciation of the northern dialects, particularly the Beijing dialect. There is an officially approved roman writing of standard Chinese, called Hanyu Pinyin (the phonetic transcription of the language of the Han people). Pinyin is used throughout the People's Republic; many public transportation facilities show name places and street names both in symbols and in the romanized transcription.

Most modern dictionaries use the pinyin system. (Taiwan, however, usually uses the older Wade-Giles transliteration system.) This transcription may at first appear confusing if one doesn't see the words as they are pronounced. The city of Qingdao, for example, is pronounced *chingdow*. It would definitely be useful, particularly for individual travellers, to familiarize yourself a little with the pronunciation of pinyin. Even when asking for a place or street

name, you need to know how it is pronounced, otherwise you won't be understood. This guide uses the pinyin system throughout for Chinese names and expressions.

The pronunciation of Chinese: The pronunciation of the consonants is similar to those in English. b, p, d, t, g, k are all voiceless. p, t, k are aspirated, b, d, g are not aspirated. The i after the consonants ch, c, r, sh, s, z, zh is not pronounced, it indicates that the preceding sound is lengthened.

Pinyin/English transcript/Sound
a/a/f**a**r
an /un/r**un**
ang/ung /l**ung**
ao/ou/l**ou**d
b/b/**b**ath
c/ts/ra**ts**
ch/ch/**ch**ange
d/d/**d**ay
e/er/d**ir**t
e (after i,u,y)/a/tram
ei/ay/may
en/en/when
eng/eong/**ng** has a nasal sound
er/or/hon**or**
f/f/**f**ast
g/g/**g**o
h/ch/lo**ch**
i/ee/k**ee**n
j/j/**j**eep
k/k/**c**ake
l/l/**l**ittle
m/m/**m**onth
n/n/**n**ame
o/o/b**o**nd
p/p/tra**pp**ed
q/ch/**ch**eer
r/r/**r**ight
s/s/me**ss**
sh/sh/**sh**ade
t/t/**t**on
u/oo/**sh**oot
u (after j,q,x,y)/as German u+/m**u+d**e
w/w/**w**ater
x/ch/as in Scottish lo**ch**, followed by s
y/y/**y**ogi
z/ds/re**ds**
zh/dj/**j**ungle

It is often said that the Chinese language is monosyllabic. At first sight this may seem the case since, generally, each symbol is one word. However, in modern Chinese, most words are made up of two or three syllable symbols, sometimes more.

Chinese generally lacks syllables,

there are only 420 in Mandarin to represent all symbols in sounds or tones. The tones are used to differentiate – a specifically Chinese practice which often makes it very difficult for foreigners when first learning the Chinese language. Each syllable has a specific sound. These sounds often represent different meanings. For instance, if one pronounces the syllable *mai* with a falling fourth sound (mài) it means to sell; if it is pronounced with a falling-rising third sound, mai, it means to buy. When one reads the symbols carefully this is always clearly shown. To show this again with the simple syllable ma:

> First sound *ma* mother
> second sound *má* hemp
> third sound *ma* horse
> fourth sound *mà* to complain

The Chinese language has four tones and a fifth, 'soundless' sound: The first tone is spoken high pitched and even, the second rising, the third falling and then rising, and the fourth sound falling. The individual tones are marked above the vowel in the syllable in the following way: First tone -, second tone ´, third tone, fourth tone `.

The Chinese sentence structure is simple: subject, predicate, object. The simplest way of forming a question is to add the question particle 'ma' to a sentence in ordinary word sequence. It is usually not possible to note from a Chinese word whether it is a noun, adjective or another form, singular or plural. This depends on the context.

The Chinese language is a language of symbols or pictures. Each symbol represents a one-syllable word. There are in total more than 47,000 symbols, though modern Chinese only use a part of these. For a daily paper, between 3,000 and 4,000 symbols are sufficient. Scholars know between 5,000 and 6,000. Many symbols used to be quite complicated. After 1949, several reforms in the written language were introduced in the People's Republic in order to simplify the written language. Today, the simplified symbols are used throughout the People's Republic, though in Hong Kong and Taiwan, the complex ones are still used.

Many Chinese words are composed of two or more symbols or single-syllable words.

Getting Acquainted

Time Zones

The International Dateline puts Hong Kong resolutely ahead of most of the world. There is no daylight savings so Hong Kong remains GMT +8 all year.

Climate

A historian recently noted that Hong Kong's weather is "trying for half the year". Foreign residents might agree, but few visitors stay long enough for the weather to become oppressive.

In meteorological terms, the climate is tropical (just barely) and monsoonal. Two seasons dominate the year – one consistently hot, wet and humid (the **Southwest Monsoon**, corresponding very roughly to spring/summer), and the other cool and dry (the **Northeast Monsoon**, corresponding to fall/winter). Hong Kong can, however, experience great variations in this general pattern – notably in periods between successive monsoons – and dramatically during **typhoon season**. The word "typhoon" is derived from Cantonese *dai fung* which means "big wind". It is Asia's version of a Western hurricane.

Typhoons

If you are unlucky enough to be here when a full-scale typhoon sweeps in from the South China Sea, you will find out first-hand why it was named *dai fung*, or "big wind", in Cantonese. There is not much you can do except slink back to your hotel and have a typhoon party, which is precisely what many Hong Kong residents do in their homes during these Asian hurricanes.

When a typhoon or **"Severe Tropical Storm"** (which may escalate into a ty-

phoon) comes within a 400-mile radius of Hong Kong, storm signal #1 goes up. The populace is quite blase about a number one signal. A #1 signal can remain aloft for days – sometimes during beautiful pre-storm weather, or be quickly changed to the next important signal #3. Number 3 is the first real alert because it signifies that winds are reaching speeds of 22 to 33 knots with gusts up to 60 knots. At typhoon 8, everything shuts down. Although the MTR may still run, taxis usually charge a premium for driving during the storm.

Never underestimate a typhoon. Too many visitors, mostly from the United States and the Caribbean, probably do because they have seen so many hurricanes. They think typhoons are nothing more than severe rainstorms.

Dry Monsoons

The dry monsoon season begins sometime in September, and brings 3 months of warm (rather than hot) days and usually clear blue skies. Nights are cool, humidity low, and day-to-day temperature changes are slight. The best months to visit are October and November; Hong Kong is predictably chock-a-block with visitors during this period. From December through early January, it is still sunny during the day and cool at night. This period signals a gradual shift to less predictable weather.

Beginning with Chinese New Year – late-January to mid-February – the temperature and clear and dry skies alternate with longer spells of cold wind and dank mist that can run unbroken for weeks. Mountaintops occasionally show night-time frost (the appearance of frost is always a headline story in local tabloids), and beaches at this time of the year are largely deserted.

Hong Kong's rainy season arrives in earnest about the middle of March, when the temperature rises, humidity thickens and trees grow green. Skies can be consistently gray, and heavy afternoon rainstorms become increasingly common. Though quite changeable, this "spring" season generally

stays cool enough to be agreeable with most visitors.

Mid-May to September is high summer, and also the unpredictable typhoon season. Punctuated by cloudbursts, intense tropical sunshine scorches open land and broils even well-tanned skin. Humidity rarely falls below 90 percent, but temperatures rarely top 90–93°F (32–34°C). Airconditioning eases this steamy torpor, so much so that sweaters are sometimes required indoors.

Planning The Trip

What To Wear

Clothing should follow seasons not unlike those in the American Deep South. Dank winter months (January and February) require sweaters, heavy jackets or even a light topcoat. A fickle, cool-to-warm spring (March and April) is best handled with adaptable, all-purpose outfits. High, emphatically tropical summer (May through September) demands the lightest cloths, umbrellas (traditional local models are superb, raincoats a steamy washout) and some sort of protection against fanatic air-conditioning. Much-favoured and dry and temperate fall (October through December) is best suited by middle-weight clothes with a sweater for cool nights during the later months.

Style of dress is happily more a matter of personal taste than public acceptability. The odd habits of visiting "barbarians" long ago ceased to startle residents, and shorts, sandals and haltertops are as popular locally as they are, for most of the year, practical. Obvious opulence, on the other hand, will impress hotel room-clerks – and inspire pajama-clad merchants to new heights in "tourist" pricing. Any semblance of skirt or coat-and-tie mollifies the handful of hotel restaurants requiring "formal dress".

As in most of the world, working businessmen in Hong Kong wear business clothes. Short-sleeved, perm-press "safari-suits" have taken up some of the slack left by the decline of the rumpled linen suit, but otherwise a crisp, cravatted globetrotter look is – sometimes sweatily – de rigueur.

Health

Hong Kong's once well-deserved reputation as a "white man's grave" went out with pirates and the end of the opium trade. Standards of health and medicine today compare fully with the West, and aside from the obvious, travellers need no particular precautions.

Gastric Unrest

In hotels and main-line restaurants (including all those named in these pages), health standards hold up well against any in the world. Order what you like, and worry more about the various glutton's maladies than some indescribable Oriental dysentery.

Off the beaten path, things predictably become more problematic – but rarely exceed even the newest China hand's powers of discretion. Assuming one conquers the obvious oddities (the shirtless chef, the shoeless waiter, the chicken gizzards et al), an obvious question arises: how much local colour is too much? The buzz of a hundred flies is one standard bad sign, as is food served tepid rather than steaming hot. Lack of a refrigerator means nothing in itself, because most Chinese prefer "warm" (freshly killed) meat. A quick glance at the raw ingredients never hurts. As more positive steps, go where the locals seem to go, do as they do by rinsing chopsticks and bowls in hot tea, and drink either more hot tea or anything from a bottle – without ice. Fruit – with the usual tropical caveat about avoiding prepeeled items – is fine for dessert, but the cautious might stick to ice cream.

In the end, though, getting sick results more from bad luck than from anything one does or doesn't do. The hapless – and most travellers to most places seem doomed to this at some point – can minimize debilitation by:

1) Eating nothing solid for 24 hours, then starting slowly on soups and noodles;
2) Drinking copiously (bland liquids only) to stave off dehydration; and
3) Going as easy as it seems reasonable. For persistent diarrhoea or vomiting, obviously seek medical attention.

Drinking Water

The true colonial prefers stronger stuff, the Chinese stick with tea, and many (possibly nostalgic) Western residents insist on boiled or bottled water. Nevertheless, both officially and in fact, straight from the tap is perfectly harmless. It's still not a good idea to ask for a glass of water at a street stall in the New Territories, but several decades have passed since hotel guests had to brush their teeth with gin.

Money Matters

The financial arts are Hong Kong's stock-in-trade. Because it's a strategic centre for international transactions, Hong Kong has banks of every description and there are no local restrictions whatsoever on the import, export, purchase or sale of foreign currency. Anything from credit cards to "black" or "hot" cash can be handled – but there are clearly better and worse ways to go about such money dealings.

Legal Tender

The Hong Kong dollar has a singular distinction: it is the world's last major currency issued not by a government but by local private banks. With unflagging free enterprise, the two leading financial houses here – **The Hongkong and Shanghai Banking Corporation** and **The Standard Chartered** – have recently been joined by the **Bank of China**, China's own state bank, in issuing all the Territory's currency. The notes are emblazoned with grandly styled views of their headquarters, while the likeness of the British Queen and the Coat of Arms have been replaced by the Bauhinia – Hong Kong's flower. The British Queen is confined to coins and one cent notes.

The Hong Kong dollar (HK$) is divided into 100 cents. There are seven standard bills. Each bank uses a different motif, but all share similar denomination colours: $1,000 (gold), $500

(brown), $100 (red), $50 (blue), $20 (orange) and $10 (green). There is also a small and rarely seen one cent (1¢) note that's only slightly larger than a subway ticket. They are blank on one side and make unique souvenirs. Coins include 10¢, 20¢, 50¢, $1, $2 and $5.

Traveller's Cheques

They are sold here by foreign exchange dealers and banks. European or Japanese traveller's cheques are as acceptable as US dollar cheques. Many small merchants here prefer traveller's cheques to credit cards or hard currency, so hold out for more than the going bank rate during any negotiations involving traveller's cheques.

Public Holidays

On public holidays (indicated by asterisk *), banks and offices close. The quiet Chinese New Year, however, usually does not affect tourist-area restaurants and shops.

Undated listings below are normally set at least 6 months in advance; contact the Hong Kong Tourist Association (HKTA) for precise information.

January 1: New Year's Day*
January–February: Chinese New Year*
February–March: Hong Kong Arts Festival; Yuen Siu (Lantern Festival)
March–April: Ching Ming*; Easter (Good Friday, Easter Sunday and Monday)
May: Birthday of Tin Hau; Buddha's Birthday; Tam King's Birthday; Horse Racing Season ends
June: Tuen Ng* (Dragon Boat Festival)
July: Birthday of Lu Pan
August 25: Liberation Day*
September: Mid-Autumn Festival; Horse Racing Season begins
October: Birthday of Confucius; Chung Yueng*
October–November: Asian Arts Festival
December 25: Christmas*
December 26: Boxing Day*

Special Facilities
Children

What about kids who accompany their parents on a trip here? Ocean Park, and its neighbours, Water World and the Middle Kingdom, are natural attractions for kids who are fed up with hotel rooms or shopping in hot humid weather. The Ocean Park, a combination marineland and amusement park, is on quite a large scale while the Water World, though smaller than those giant parks back home, is still spectacular. And, of course, fun.

OTHER ACTIVITIES

There are **Chinese shadow-boxing**, or *tai chi chuan*, demonstrations every morning in the parks (Monday to Saturday 7.30–8.30am) at Chater Gardens and Hong Kong Park, Central, and Victoria Park, Causeway Bay, both in Hong Kong. Also from Monday to Friday 7–8am at Kowloon Park and King George V Park, Kowloon. The Hong Kong Tourist Association sponsors free **kung fu demonstrations**, **puppet shows**, **acrobats**, **jugglers** at Cityplaza on Hong Kong Island and at the Ocean Terminal and New World Centre in Kowloon. Telephone 2801-7177 for the times.

Hong Kong's main zoo is the **Botanical Gardens** in Mid-Levels. There are more than 300 different kinds of birds, many monkeys, a red panda, even a jaguar.

The YMCA on Salisbury Road, Tsimshatsui, Kowloon, has **youth activities** scheduled all year, but especially during the summer. Pop in and see what's going on. You might also want to check the **Girl Guides** (Girl Scouts), the **Brownies** (2332-5523), the **Boy Scouts** (2367-3096) or the **Outward Bound School** (2792-4333) to see what is planned for children.

Practical Tips

Emergencies

Security & Crime

The Hong Kong Police wear light green uniforms in summer, blue ones in winter, and carry handguns. English speaking officers have a small red tab below their serial numbers. In **emergencies** phone 999 and ask for the police, fire department, or ambulance, as required.

Money Thefts: This is a complaint most consulates don't like to hear, but they are usually quite helpful and sympathetic to theft victims. The Hong Kong Police Force is also efficient and helpful. If your hotel is reluctant to assist because of the bad publicity, go to the police directly. Also, the Hong Kong Tourist Association will gladly assist travellers who have been robbed or swindled.

Fraud: To complain about out and out fraud, contact the HKPF "Fraud Squad", Commercial Crimes, tel: 2823-5512. If you find out about a fraudulent sale after you have departed, write to the HKTA or the Consumer Council.

Copyright Infringements: For copyright violations – if you happen to be Messrs. Cartier, Gucci, Lanvin or the like, address your complaints to the Trade Department, 700 Nathan Road, Mongkok, Kowloon, tel: 2737-2333.

Medical Services

CHEMISTS

Don't panic if you suddenly discover that you've run out of your urgently needed prescribed medicine. Hong Kong has modern chemists or dispensaries (as they are called here) and you will not have to make do with ground seahorse or some other traditional remedy. The main pharmacies are Watson, Mannings, Colonial Dispensary and the Victoria Dispensary.

There are also hundreds of Chinese medicine companies which accept prescriptions and usually stock both Western and Asian medicines. These, however, should not be confused with traditional herbalists (with whom they sometimes share premises). Herbalists will happily sell you a dried seahorse, a bit of rhinoceros horn, deer's antler, tiger's penis and a selection of special herbs – all prepared while you wait.

HOSPITALS

In descending order of price, the most notable private hospitals are Matilda (on Mt Kellett Road, The Peak, Hong Kong), Canossa (1 Old Peak Road, above Central District, Hong Kong), The Baptist Hospital (222 Waterloo Road, Kowloon, tel: 2337-4141), and the Adventist. None are cheap, but all are comfortable and offer highest quality specialists and facilities.

CLINICS

For the walking wounded, clinics are a practical and economical alternative, most offering the basic range of specialists in-house. The Hong Kong Adventist Hospital (40 Stubbs Road at Wongneichung Road, above Happy Valley, Hong Kong, tel: 2574-6211) operates an expat-staff out-patient department Sunday through Friday noon, and also has a good dental clinic with 24-hour emergency service. Anderson & Partners, Vio & Partners and Drs Oram & Howard, all have clinics on both sides of the harbour.

PRIVATE PHYSICIANS

Though many people still prefer traditional cures for minor ills, modern Western practices dominate the field. Most doctors took all or part of their training overseas (usually in Britain, North America, Australia or New Zealand), and the medical and dental professions together include several score expatriates. Private physician's fees as well tend to be internationally scaled, particularly room visits by hotel doctors (resident or on-call at most).

ACUPUNCTURISTS

Not every one accepts this traditional type of Chinese medicine so you will have to decide whether the needle treatment is for you. There are many clinics in Hong Kong, but few practitioners speak English or take the time to explain the treatment to a visitor.

Business Hours

Local banking hours are now in the process of gradual extension, but 9am–4.30pm on weekdays, and 9am–noon Saturday (closed Sunday) are normal business hours for foreign exchange services.

Tipping

Though a 10 percent gratuity is added to most hotel and restaurant bills, you are still expected to tip. If the service has been bad, however, collect every penny from the change tray. If the service has been abominable, go up to the restaurant manager and demand that the automatic 10 percent service charge – in your case, non-service charge – be deducted from your bill. Most Chinese restaurants add on a service charge, but some of the smaller, traditional ones do not.

Postal Services

Hong Kong's post offices feature reliable, usually efficient service. Air letters normally take 4 or 5 days to Europe or Australia, 6 to 8 to most destinations in the United States and Canada. Surface packages can vary anywhere from 3 weeks to 3 months.

The most complete and convenient facility is Hong Kong-side's **General Post Office**. Located just off the Star Ferry Concourse, the gleaming white GPO has a full range of package and letter services, including a philatelic window and a ground-floor "General Delivery" counter (Poste Restante, GPO, Hong Kong). Outside working hours (weekdays 8am–6pm, Saturday till 12.30pm, closed Sunday and public holidays), the GPO's stamp machines and letter slots are open round-the-clock.

For large and delicate items, there are reliable commercial packing and shipping firms. For those doing things themselves, the GPO information number (2523-1071) can detail the various regulations on packaging, contents and size.

Telecoms

The international code for Hong Kong is 852.

Local Calls

For directory listing, the English-language phonebooks – three residential (for Hong Kong, Kowloon and the New Territories), a Business Directory, plus the "Yellow Pages" which come in four volumes – are often a better bet than wrangling with the information operators (dial 1081). In a pinch, the Hong Kong Tourist Association's enquiries service, tel: 2801-7177, can handle many local problems. For collect and operator assisted calls (plus direct dialling to China) dial 010; conference or ship to shore, 011; operator-assistance calls to China, 012; and direct dialling enquiries, 013. Cheaper off-peak charges are in effect midnight–7am daily, plus from 1pm Saturday through Sunday.

The emergency number for police/fire/ambulance is 999 – no coin

needed from public phones. For time and temperature dial 18501. An ear-rattling *wai* is the standard Cantonese telephone greeting. Though seemingly rude to most Western ears, the nearest translation is simply "Hello?"

Overseas Calls

International calls can be placed through hotel switchboards (which add a service fee unless they are direct dialled) or directly with **Hong Kong Telecom** at one of its several public offices:

Central District: Exchange Square, Connaught Place (near the Furama Hotel), tel: 2845-1281. Open 24 hours.
Tsimshatsui: Hermes House, 10 Middle Road, tel: 2732-4243. Open 24 hours daily.
Causeway Bay: Lee Gardens Hotel, Hysan Avenue, tel: 2577-0577. Open: Monday to Friday 10am–1pm, 2–6pm, and Saturday 10am–3pm.

Cable & Telex

As with overseas phone calls, these may be placed either through hotels or at any of the Hong Kong Telecom offices listed above.

Tourist Information
Hong Kong Tourist Association (HKTA)

This is a bubbling fount of information – verbally or in the form of numerous brochures advising about everything from eating and shopping to hiking and horse races. Frontline HKTA (Hong Kong Tourist Association) staff seem genuinely interested in helping visitors.

For brochures, maps or basic questions and answers, as well as souvenirs and gifts, the HKTA has walk-in Information & Gift Centres at the airport, at the Kowloon Star Ferry Concourse (8am–6pm weekdays; and 9am–5pm weekends), Jardine House basement (9am–6pm; Saturday till 1pm) on Hong Kong Island. The centre at the airport stays open from 8am–10.30pm daily.

For elusive addresses, lost directions and train or ferry schedules, there is also a telephone enquiries service: 2801-7177 (from 8am–6pm weekdays; 9am–5pm weekends). For serious queries or shopping complaints, the best bet is to contact HKTA Headquarters on the 35th floor of Jardine House.

The HKTA Official Hong Kong Guide (updated monthly) is a good information source. Many hotels also offer this book free with their own name and logo printed on the cover, as does the HKTA.

Overseas, the HKTA maintains offices in Chicago, Frankfurt, London, New York, Osaka, Paris, Rome, Singapore, Sydney, Barcelona, Los Angeles, Toronto, Auckland and Tokyo, and in all Cathay Pacific Airways offices.

Getting Around
Orientation

Getting around Hong Kong is much easier than it seems. Though Cantonese is the language spoken by 98 percent of the population, English is also widely used (if only for English place names which differ from their Cantonese counterparts). It helps, however, to have an address or item written out in Chinese characters by a friend or hotel employee.

Domestic Travel
The Kowloon-Canton Railway

The old Kowloon-Canton Railway is now a modern electrified commuter train. There are 10 stops on this 32-mile (51-km) segment through Kowloon and the New Territories. Single, ordinary, one-way fares for the full run begin at HK$6.50. Don't worry about inadvertently chug-chugging into China. The main railway station is in Hung Hom, Kowloon, and there is a passenger ferry service near that station from the Star Ferry in Central District. Call 2606-9606 for details.

Light Rail Transport

This above ground railway runs between Tuen Muen and Yuen Long in the New Territories.

The Star Ferry

You can always tell the tourists from the residents on Hong Kong's most famous mode of transportation, the

Star Ferry. The tourists are agog at the magnificent site of the world's third busiest harbour – and one of the best natural harbours in the world – as the double-bowed, green and white, two-decker ferries weave their way through the 0.8 nautical mile course between Hong Kong and Tsimshatsui (Kowloon). The residents, on the other hand, are quite content to spend the 7-minute sea voyage with their noses tucked into their own newspapers or racing sheets.

Walla-Wallas

After the MTR closes at 1am and the Star Ferry at 11.30pm, you can still ride across the harbour in a small motorboat called a walla-walla (supposedly named for the hometown – Walla-Walla, Washington, USA – of this craft's original owner). You can also take a taxi or bus through the cross-harbour tunnel, but if you are staying in Tsimshatsui and end up in Central – or vice versa – the direct cross-harbour water route by Star Ferry, MTR or walla-walla is the fastest and cheapest means of transportation. On Hong Kong Island, walla-wallas are located at a pier to the East of the Star Ferry concourse (to the right as you face the harbour, facing City Hall) while in Kowloon, they are located at Kowloon Public Pier (to the left of the Star Ferry as you face the water, opposite the Ocean Terminal).

Local Ferries

There are other ferry services from the Star Ferry, Wanchai and North Point Piers (on Hong Kong) to various destinations in Kowloon, but these are primarily commuter ferries, rarely taken by visitors.

Inter-Island Ferries: There are 236 islands in Hong Kong. A convenient inter-island ferries transportation system is in operation here to service many of them. At the **Outlying Districts Ferry Pier**, Connaught Road, Central, Hong Kong, you'll find double and triple-decker ferries – some with air-conditioning – that regularly travel to the outlying islands. The routes and times are too numerous to mention here, but there is regular service – quite crowded during weekends and holidays – to Lantau, Cheung Chau and Lamma islands (the big three) and many of Hong Kong smaller isles.

The Hong Kong Tourist Association has a complete schedule of all available ferry services and will answer telephone queries at 2801-7177. The **Hong Kong Ferry Company's** enquiry number is 2542-3082.

The **Polly Ferry Company** operates daily services to stops (including Grass Island) along Tolo Harbour and – at weekends and on public holidays – a ferry to Ping Chau. These depart from Ma Liu Shui, near the University KCR station. Call 2771-1630.

Public Transport

Buses

Hong Kong has numerous scheduled buses and bus routes. China Motor Buses are blue while Kowloon Motor Buses are red. With the advent of the cross-harbour tunnel routes, however, they commute on each other's turf.

Minibuses & Maxicabs

Yellow 16-seater vans with a red stripe – called minibuses here – ply all the main routes and make unscheduled stops and charge variable fares. There is a sign in the front indicating their destinations and fare charges. To complicate matters, other yellow 16-seater vans with a green stripe and roof – called maxicabs – run on fixed routes at fixed prices. The maxi-bus terminal in Central is on the eastern side of the Star Ferry carpark.

Trams

On Hong Kong island there are trams running along the north shore from west to east (and vice versa) which pass through the main tourist areas of Central, Wanchai, Causeway Bay and Taikoo Shing Quarry Bay. Sit on the upper deck and watch the real Hong Kong bump and grind by. Looking for an interesting way to entertain? Try a Tram Party. Call 2801-7427 for details.

THE PEAK TRAM

Hong Kong's other "tram" is the century-old Peak Tram, which is not a tram at all but a funicular railway up to The Peak. It is a form of regular local commuter transport and a favourite "tourist attraction". The funicular rises 1,305 ft (397 metres) above sea level in about 10 minutes on a steep journey over 4,500 ft (1,364 metres) of track. It operates from 7am to mid-

night. The Lower Peak Tram Station in Central District is on Garden Road. A free shuttle bus service operates between the Lower Station and the Star Ferry from 9am–7pm daily at 20-minute intervals. There are four intermediate stations before the Upper Peak Tram Station nestled underneath the Peak Tower, a futuristic building on stilts that houses a European restaurant, shops and a supermarket.

Mass Transit Railway (MRT)

The most dramatic change in Hong Kong's public transportation scene is the fully air-conditioned Mass Transit Railway, commonly called the MRT, which in other countries might be called Underground, Tube, Metro or Subway. The system has three lines with around 40 stations, stretching from industrial Kwun Tong (Kowloon) and Tsuen Wan (New Territories) through some of Kowloon's most populated areas, underneath Nathan Road to the Tsimshatsui tourist and entertainment district, and under the harbour to Central, the governmental and financial centre, and along the north shore of Hong Kong Island. (With the MTR, it is easy to reach many of the favourite tourist areas on the island, particularly Wanchai, Causeway Bay and Taikoo Shing.)

Taxis

Have you been introduced to Hong Kong's "national flag" yet? Facetious local wags, tired of fighting for taxis – and being extorted by them during rush hours, holiday periods or late at night – have nicknamed the dirty "vacant" ragflag (supposedly signifying the driver is off duty) as Hong Kong's national standard because of its pesky ubiquitousness.

COMPLAINTS

If you have any trouble with a taxi – say you are victimized, overcharged or you have left your wallet in the back seat – contact the Hong Kong Police special **"taxi hotline"** at 2527-7177. (Don't forget to record the taxi number!)

If a complaint is not resolved, you must be prepared to appear as a witness to the police prosecution. In most cases, the courts will push a tourist's case to the front of its judicial queues to make an example of the offender.

If a constable is nearby, take your complaint directly to him (or threaten to). Such tactics are a marvellous cure for obdurate drivers.

Rickshaws

Hong Kong still has a small number of rickshaws that congregate around Star Ferry concourse on Hong Kong Island. Tourists hire the rickshaws more to pose for pictures than as transportation but the unofficial "official" rate is HK$50–100 for a 5-minute trip around the block. However, because rickshaw-pullers refuse to budge without a round of bartering, the price extracted from visitors is usually more.

Private Transport

Self-drive & Chauffeured Cars: Rental cars, with or without drivers, are also available. **Avis** and **Hertz** are here, along with a couple of dozen local firms. Those under 18 cannot hire any motor vehicles (including cycles and scooters). All visitors with a valid overseas driving licence, however, can drive here for a year. Hotels, through their own transportation services, can usually handle requests for chauffeur-driven cars.

Where To Stay

Whether to stay in Hong Kong or Kowloon is a long-standing debate with die-hard aficionados of both harbour sides. Money is not a factor. The best-heeled (at The Peninsula and the Regent) and shoestring travellers (in the YMCA or Chungking Mansions) are next-door neighbours in Kowloon, though these digs are decidedly, different.

Access to shops and restaurants is also not a consideration. Both sides of the harbour are commercially endowed. The MTR connects various parts of Kowloon and Hong Kong Island in minutes, as does the Star Ferry.

Hotels

Despite certain Hong Kong advantages, most people end up in Kowloon's Tsimshatsui District – probably because it has most of Hong Kong's hotels.

Hong Kong's Central District is considerably more restrained, because it is the business, financial and government centre. Though there is good shopping in Central, it closes at dusk. Hong Kong's Causeway Bay, however, features a wide range of accommodations, late-night shopping and eating. And between Central and Causeway Bay is the "Suzie Wong" bar district of Wanchai, rife with honky-tonk local colour and just down the tram-line from either Central or Causeway Bay.

Hong Kong

$$$$$

Conrad International, Pacific Place, 88 Queensway. Tel: 2521 3838; Fax: 2521 3888. A European-style deluxe boutique hotel. Understated elegance; spacious rooms and good location adjacent to Pacific Place shopping, Admiralty MTR and tramlines.

Grand Hyatt, 1 Harbour Rd, Wanchai. Tel: 2588 1234; Fax: 2802 0677. Probably the most expensive and glitziest hotel in Hong Kong. Luxury on a truly palatial level; overlooking the harbor and only a couple of steps from the HK Convention and Exhibition Centre, the HK Arts Centre.

Island Shangri-La, Pacific Place, Supreme Court Rd, Central. Tel: 2877 3838; Fax: 2521 8742. This gracious oasis lives up to its name. Elegant decor, helpful staff and beautiful, spacious rooms with stunning panoramic views of the harbor or Peak. Great location; adjacent to Hong Kong Park, Pacific Place shopping and Admiralty MTR and tramlines.

Mandarin Oriental, 5 Connaught Rd, Central. Tel: 2522 0111; Fax: 2810 6190. Classy hotel established in 1963 and consistently rated among the world's best. Impeccable service and quality. Full range of facilities including a indoor pool and some of the finest hotel F&B establishments in town. Convenient location.

New World Harbour View, 1 Harbour Rd, Wanchai. Tel: 2802 8888; Fax: 2802 8833. A shade cheaper than the Grand Hyatt but enjoys same prime location overlooking the harbor; with easy access to Kowloon from Wanchai Ferry Pier. Superb recreation facilities.

Ritz-Carlton, 3 Connaught Rd, Central. Tel: 2877 6666; Fax: 2877 6778. Post-modernist exterior gives way to classy traditionalist interior decorated with period art and antiques. Facilities include outdoor pool and good Italian and Japanese restaurants. Convenient location close to Central MTR, Star Ferry, and Admiralty and Central business and commercial districts.

Kowloon Shangri-La, 64 Mody Rd, Tsimshatsui East. Tel: 2721 2111; Fax: 2723 8686. Opulent grandeur and great harbor views. Full range of deluxe facilities including indoor swimming pool and highly rated restaurants. Across from Tsimshatsui East waterfront with easy hoverferry access to Central.

Omni Hong Kong Harbour City, 3 Canton Rd, Tsimshatsui. Tel: 2736 0088; Fax: 2736 0011. Many rooms with magnificent harbor views. Deluxe facilities include an outdoor pool and 5 restaurants. Shopping opportunities are unparalled as it's inside the enormous shopping complex stretching from Ocean Terminal up to the Gateway.

The Peninsula, Salisbury Rd, Tsimshatsui. Tel: 2366 6251; Fax: 2722 4170. Hong Kong's oldest and most prestigious hotel has been a by-word for impeccable service and colonial-style grandeur since it opened in 1928. Extensivle refurbished, with a new 30-storey extension tower. Eight top restaurants and superb location in the heart of Kowloon's shopping, restaurant and entertainment area; close to Tsimshatsui MTR.

The Regent, Salisbury Rd, Tsimshatsui. Tel: 2721 1211; Fax: 2739 4546. Elegant with breathtaking views across Victoria Harbour. Full range of facilities, including a poolside spa, the 1930s-style Club Shanghai nightclub and top-notch Lai Ching Heen and Plume restaurants. Superb location on the waterfront; convenient for Star Ferry and Kowloon's prime commercial and entertainment district.

Sheraton Hong Kong Hotel and Towers, 20 Nathan Rd, Tsimshatsui. Tel: 2369 1111; Fax: 2739 8707. Swish hotel on corner of Nathan and Salisbury roads with full range of deluxe facilities, including an outdoor pool and 5 top-notch restaurants. Good location close to museums, MTR, and Kowloon's prime commercial and entertainment district.

$$$$

Century Hong Kong Hotel, 238 Jaffe Rd, Wanchai. Tel: 2508 8888; Fax: 2598 8866. Modern hotel with good facilities including an outdoor pool, health club and Lao Ching Hing, one of oldest and best Shanghai restaurants in town. Convenient for HK Exhibition and Convention Centre and Wanchai's commercial district.

The Excelsior, 281 Gloucester Rd, Causeway Bay. Tel: 2894 8888; Fax: 2895 6459. Overlooking the colorful Causeway Bay typhoon shelter. Managed by the Mandarin Oriental group, the hotel offers efficient service and a pleasant environment. Close to Causeway Bay's shopping and commercial district and MTR.

Furama Kempinski, 1 Connaught Rd, Central. Tel: 2525 5111; Fax: 2845 9339. Quietly plush business hotel. Good value considering its convenient location to Central MTR, Star Ferry, and Admiralty and the Central district.

Grand Plaza, 2 Kornhill Rd, Quarry Bay. Tel: 2886 0011; Fax: 2886 1738. Modern business hotel with good facilities including golf-putting green, tennis courts, indoor pool and gym. Close to Tai Koo MTR.

Wharney Hotel, 57–73 Lockhart Rd, Wanchai. Tel: 2861 1000; Fax: 2865 6023. Smart modern hotel with good facilities including indoor pool. Located in the heart of Wanchai's commercial and nightlife district, close to HK Convention Centre, MTR and trams.

The Kowloon Hotel, 19–21 Nathan Rd, Tsimshatsui. Tel: 2369 8698; Fax: 2739 9811. Smart, modern business hotel tucked in behind 'The Pen', in the heart of Kowloon's commercial and entertainment district. Close to MTR.

Majestic, 348 Nathan Rd, Yau Ma Tei. Tel: 2781 1333; Fax: 2781 1773. Well-appointed business hotel. Close to Temple Street night market, shops, cinema and Jordan MTR; also well-served by buses.

Nikko, 72 Mody Rd, Tsimshatsui East. Tel: 2739 1111; Fax: 2311 3122. Japanese business hotel with impeccable service and panoramic harbor views. Amenities include an outdoor pool and good Cantonese, French and

Japanese restaurants. Just across from Tsimshatsui East waterfront promenade and convenient for HK Science Museum, Coliseum, Kowloon kcr station and the Cross-Harbour Tunnel.

Omni Marco Polo Harbour City, Canton Rd, Tsimshatsui. Tel: 2736 0888; Fax: 2736 0022. Elegant, Continental style hotel in the middle of enormous Harbour City complex; marginally cheaper than sister-hotel Omni Hong Kong, but lacking views and pool.

Omni Prince Harbour City, Canton Rd, Tsimshatsui. Tel: 2736 1888; Fax: 2736 0066. Similar standard to sister-hotel Omni Marco Polo; with outdoor pool. Very convenient for China Ferry Terminal and Kowloon Park.

Eating Out

What To Eat

No one has ever contradicted the guesstimate that there are more than 5,000 restaurants listed in Hong Kong telephone directories. The exactitude of that figure is debatable, but a hungry fact remains: anywhere you turn, there is a restaurant.

Hong Kong, like Paris, is a place where conversation invariably involves the current merits and demerits of restaurants. New restaurant discovery by an old Hong Kong hand is such important intelligence that the "discoverer" often is rewarded with extra rounds of pink gin. Restaurants in Hong Kong, like those in France, tend to be extensions of one's living room, places where friends and families gather for celebrations and anniversary feasts.

Hong Kong's first eating rule is to be adventurous; get out of your hotel and sample some of the best Chinese, Japanese, Korean, Singaporean, Malayan, Indonesian, Filipino, Thai, Indian and Vietnamese foods in the world. But don't be too surprised if the local Cantonese cuisine (or any other Chinese food served here) looks and tastes different from hometown "Chinese food". It is the real thing here! It is your favourite Chinese restaurant dishes back home that are different.

High Tea

Hong Kong's most well-known place for high tea during the past half century has been the colonnaded lobby of the **Peninsula Hotel**. Anyone who is anyone passes through the Pen's gilded lobby. High tea there is a good place to watch the world go by: "What ho! I say old chappie", and colonial et al. Unfortunately, these days Asian and American tourists seem to outnumber the faithful old Brits at tea time; but it is still the place for this British ritual.

One of the "newer" places for high tea is the lobby of the **Regent**. Opened in late 1980, this hotel is still "new", but while sipping a traditional cuppa in its 40-ft (12-metre) high glass-walled lobby you can marvel at life sailing by in Hong Kong harbour.

Relics & Vestiges

Confucius and the British Empire are paid their respects in institutions such as the **Luk Yu Tea House** located at 26–42 Stanley Street, Central, Hong Kong, tel: 2523-1970, in Chinese, please. Three thousand years of civilization haven't quite ended yet. No fluorescent formica flashes here; blackwood tables, marble-backed benches and brass spittoons do graceful justice to classic Cantonese food and 30-year-old teas. Un-foreign tongues are almost insistently not spoken, and the English menu is pointedly brief. Centrally located, open 7.30am–10pm. Less expensive than it looks.

Things To Do

Your first stop should be at one of the Hong Kong Tourist Association's excellent Information & Gift Centres (Star Ferry Concourse, Kowloon or in the basement of Jardine House, Hong Kong) to collect some of their excellent literature on what-to-do in Hong Kong and how-to-do-it. There are dozens of booklets and pamphlets – everything from the obligatory eating out and shopping to walking tours on the Outlying Islands. The HKTA also runs a variety of tours, including a Housing Tour & Home Visit (see what life in Hong Kong is like outside the tourist and shopping areas), sports (including horse-racing) tours and a New Territories tour. Call 2801-7177. And you can get an early start in planning by visiting one of their overseas offices.

Travel Packages

1) The best trips are usually the simplest, notably **half-day circular tours** of Hong Kong or Kowloon and the New Territories.
2) Particularly with three or four people, the higher priced **limousine tours** are well worth the extra flexibility and speed. Most will happily alter itineraries to suit particular tastes.
3) **Outlying island excursions** are just as easily and comfortably done by ordinary ferry – at as little as one quarter the cost, even including a gourmet-shop picnic lunch.
4) **Tour-group dinners and nightclub shows** are invariably awful, doubly so at Aberdeen's infamous floating restaurants. Save the often considerable sums and have a first-class meal at a real restaurant. But by all means take the pleasant **sunset cruise** which ends up in Aberdeen Harbour. Just refuse to be pressured into dinner on those floating restaurants and return to shore.
5) Avoid Saturdays and Sundays, when time spent sitting in traffic detracts further the time spent at already too-short stopovers.

Culture

Hong Kong does not have a reputation for the arts, performing or otherwise. To tourists, Hong Kong is an interesting venue which can be taken by itself or can serve as a gateway to or exit from China. Its key attractions are shopping and eating. To the business visitor, all the aforementioned is true. Hong Kong is an excellent place to conduct business – the laws, the infrastructure, the geography, and most of all the people, are all present in the right mix. Visitors do not come to Hong Kong for the arts – they do not come to visit museums and see plays or musi-

cals. Yet Hong Kong is by no means a cultural desert. Broadway and West End shows pass through, to say nothing of renown symphony orchestras and opera troupes.

The action takes place at the **Hong Kong Arts Centre**, where, in addition to plays and shows being performed in its theatres, small film festivals are almost a monthly occurrence. Just across the street is the **Hong Kong Academy for Performing Arts** – both buildings are on Harbour Road in Wanchai on Hong Kong Island. Again, it is a superb venue, complete with an outdoor amphitheatre, for all kinds of performances. But more importantly, it is a training ground for budding members, both on stage and behind, of the performing arts. Across the harbour in Kowloon, just adjacent to the Star Ferry, is the **Hong Kong Cultural Centre**. Wing-shaped, it has three first class venues that can stage anything from grand opera to intimate performances. Rarely visited by tourists is the Ko Shan Theatre in Kowloon, an outdoor venue used for pop concerts, operas and variety shows.

There are also local symphonic orchestras, such as the **Hong Kong Philharmonic** and the **Hong Kong Chinese Music Orchestra**, plus several amateur and professional theatres which employ full-time professional musicians and actors. These arts organizations reflect Hong Kong's cosmopolitan and international cultural life.

The **Hong Kong Arts Festival**, in January and February, features an intriguing programme of Western and Eastern art. Renowned orchestras, dance companies, drama groups, opera companies and jazz ensembles are invited to perform here alongside talented local artists. Traditional Chinese herbs blend with Western cultural fare to create a uniquely Hong Kong arts extravaganza.

Another annual arts affair, the **Festival of Asian Arts**, invites artists and performers from various cultural regions in Asia to introduce to Hong Kong audiences their indigenous art forms. During the cultural orgy, Hong Kong is represented by groups that perform traditional Cantonese and Beijing opera, Cantonese drama, multiregional Chinese folk dance and music. Also included are performances by the Hong Kong Philharmonic Orchestra

and the Hong Kong Chinese Music Orchestra. This festival is held during October and November.

Chinese operas, puppet shows, dancing and other "local" cultural fare occur regularly throughout the year, especially during festivals. There are **free weekly Chinese cultural performances** at Cityplaza sponsored by the Hong Kong Tourist Association.

Museums

Museums are rarely considered a tourist attraction in a frantic shopping bazaar like Hong Kong. **The Hong Kong Museum of Art** has a diversified collection, including contemporary and classical paintings, calligraphic scrolls, ceramics, sculpture, lacquerware, jade and cloisonne. Its most distinctive holdings are an extensive collection of oil paintings, drawings, prints, lithographs and engravings of historical Hong Kong. They provide a vivid pictorial record of Sino-British contacts in the 18th and 19th centuries. Contemporary works by Hong Kong artists are also regularly exhibited here.

The Museum of Art is located on Salisbury Road, just next to the Hong Kong Cultural Centre, adjacent to the Star Ferry Concourse in Kowloon. Admission is free. Open: Monday to Saturday (except Thursday) 10am–6pm, Sunday 1–6pm. Admission HK$10 adult, HK$5 student/senior.

The Hong Kong Museum of History has in its permanent collection fine model junks that illustrate the former colony's traditional fishing industry and one of the most comprehensive collections of late 19th- and early 20th-century photographs of Hong Kong that document Fragrant Harbour's historic realities. Also significant is a collection of Hong Kong's coinage and the currencies of nearby Kwangtung Province. With the co-operation of the Hong Kong Archaeological Society, excavated objects, representative of the earliest prehistoric periods, are on display in the museum's archaeological section. Disappearing local arts and crafts, traditional agricultural and fishing implements and rural architectural displays reminiscent of the old New Territories are an important part of the museum's ethnographic collection.

The Museum of History is at 58 Haiphong Road in Kowloon Park.

Open: Monday to Saturday (except Friday) 10am–6pm, Sunday 1–6pm.

The Lei Cheng UK Branch Museum is at the site of a Later Han dynasty (AD 25–220) tomb. In its display halls are funerary wares and models of clay houses typical of that period. This museum-tomb is located at 41 Tonkin Street, Kowloon. Admission is free. Open: Daily (except Thursday) 10am–1pm and 2–6pm, Sunday and public holidays 1–6pm.

The Fung Ping Shang Museum at Hong Kong University is the oldest museum in Hong Kong, founded in 1953. Its excellent bronze collection is divided into three groups: Shang and Chou era (15th–3rd century BC) ritual vessels which testify to the superb achievement of early Chinese metallurgy; decorative mirrors from the Warring States period (480–221 BC) to the T'ang dynasty (AD 618–906); and 966 Nestorian crosses of the Yuan dynasty (AD 1260–1368), the largest collection of its kind in the world. Ceramics including simple pottery of the Third Millenium BC, a number of Ming (AD 1368–1644), and Ch'ing (AD 1644–1900) dynasty paintings and specimens of Buddhist sculptural art from India are also on display.

This museum is located at 94 Bonham Street, Pokfulam, Hong Kong. Open: Daily (except Sunday) 10am–6pm. Free admission.

Museum of Chinese Historical Relics serves as a permanent exhibition site for cultural treasures from China. Twice yearly exhibits. Causeway Centre, 1st floor, 28 Harbour Road, Wanchai, Hong Kong. Open: Monday to Saturday 10am–6pm, Sunday and public holidays 1–6pm.

Hong Kong Space Museum is not really a museum. The Space Theatre, known as a planetarium in other lands, offers between 7 and 10 shows daily, depending on the day. Most shows are in Cantonese, only some in English (call to find out which). However, a simultaneous translation service is available in English, Japanese or Mandarin should you find yourself at a Cantonese show. Arrive 30 minutes ahead to make arrangements. There are also an Exhibition Hall and Hall of Solar

Sciences with excellent exhibitions. Open: Daily (except Tuesday) 2–9.30pm. Call 2734-2722. Open: Weekdays (except Tuesday) 2–8.30pm.

Hong Kong Science Museum, Science Museum Road, Tsimshatsui East, Kowloon. Of the 500 exhibits, more than 60 percent are hands-on which means kids of all ages – including those who paid for an adult ticket to get in – can while away the time watching and experimenting with the mysteries of science. Areas covered include computers, robotics, communications, transportation, electronics and much much more. Open: Tuesday to Friday 1–9pm, Saturday, Sunday and public holidays 10am–9pm. Admission fees.

Hong Kong Railway Museum, Old Taipo Market Railway Station. The station itself dates back to 1913 and is designed in a Chinese style. Historic railway coaches dating from 1911 are lined up. Open: 9am–4pm except Tuesday. Admission free.

Sheung Yiu Folk Museum, Pak Tam Chung Nature Trail, Sai Kung, New Territories. This is another example of Hakka life and lifestyles from days of yore. Be prepared to do a bit of hiking, though. Open: 9am–4pm except Tuesday. Admission free.

Law Uk Folk Museum, 14 Kut Shing Street, Chaiwan, Hong Kong. This is another Hakka home restored to its original state. Open: Daily (except Monday) 10am–1pm, 2–6pm; Sunday and public holidays 1–6pm. Admission free.

Tsui Museum of Art, 10th floor, Rediffusion House, 822 Laichikok Road, Kowloon. A private museum with over 2,000 pieces of Chinese pottery, bronzes, carvings, glassware and furniture. Open: Daily (except Sunday) 10am–4.30pm. Admission HK$20 adult, HK$10 child/student.

There are also two living museums, the **Sung Dynasty Village** (tel: 2741-5111) in Kowloon and the **Middle Kingdom** (tel: 2552-0291) at the Ocean Park, Hong Kong. The former depicts life between 912–1279 and is included on various tours and also sells self-tour visits. The latter, cover-

ing 5,000 years of history, may be visited as part of a trip to the Ocean Park, either on a tour or individually.

Art Galleries
The **Art Gallery of the Chinese University** houses an important collection of paintings and calligraphy by Kwantung artists from the Ming period to modern times. Other impressive displays are a collection of 300 bronze seals of Han and pre-Han provenance, and stone rubbings from monuments of the Han and Sung dynasties. The Art Gallery is located on the campus of the Chinese University in the New Territories. Admission is free. Open: Daily 10am–4.30pm, Sunday and public holidays 12.30–4.30pm.

Pao Sui Loong Galleries of the Hong Kong Arts Centre holds exhibitions from 10am–8pm daily. Admission is free.

Language
General

Hong Kong is officially bilingual (English & Cantonese), which means more on paper than it does on a street corner in North Kowloon. Many residents, of course, can hold their own in one or several of the other Chinese dialects. There is no such thing as spoken "Chinese", only various Chinese dialects. The written language is the same for all areas, which means if two Chinese cannot speak to each other, they can write each other a note, even though each character has a different dialectical pronunciation for the same meaning. For most of the population though, English is at best a few numbers, the ubiquitous "hello", "bye-bye" and a few street and place names.

Taiwan

Getting Acquainted

The Place

Taiwan comprises the main island of Taiwan, the Penghu Archipelago (known in the west as the Pescadores), which is made up of 64 islands, and 21 other islands scattered around the main island. Together, these fill up about 36,000 square kilometers of the Pacific Ocean, with the main island alone occupying 98 percent of that area. Situated just off the southeastern coast of mainland China, Taiwan is bisected by the Tropic of Cancer.

A central mountain range runs parallel to the length of the main island of Taiwan, dividing it into east and west halves. With the Pacific Ocean on the east, which is sculpted by a dramatic coastline, the highland levels off gradually on the western side. The terraced tablelands and alluvial coastal plains, thus formed on the west coast, are home to about 80 percent of Taiwan's 22 million population.

A magnificent 3,952 meters (12,966 ft) in height is Taiwan's highest mountain, Yu Shan.

Time Zones

Taiwan Standard Time is eight hours ahead of Greenwich Mean Time, **GMT +8**. There is no daylight savings time.

Climate

Overlying both tropic and subtropic zones, Taiwan has a tropical climate in the southern and western flatlands, and a subtropical climate in the north and mountainous regions. Its location also subjects it to annual typhoons, which pass through between July and October. Most of these cause little more than strong winds and heavy rains over the island.

Taiwan's climate does not have four distinct seasons, but rather two: a hot season lasting from May till October, and a cold season from December to March. The island remains excessively humid throughout the year and receives abundant rainfall, with the east (uplands) receiving more than the west (lowlands). Except in the northern region, where rainfall is more even, mean annual rainfall in other parts of the island range from 2,500 to 5,000 mm (100 to 200 inches).

Temperature falls with an increase in altitude: snow falls on the summits of the Central Range in the cold season, while lowland Taiwan remains frost-free.

The most pleasant times of the year for travel in Taiwan are March through May and September through November, especially in Taipei.

The People

Etiquette

The Chinese, like the Koreans and Japanese, used to bow and clasp their hands together when being introduced to someone new, but today the Western handshake has displaced the ancient custom. Nevertheless, the Chinese still shy away from boisterous greetings in public, such as hugs, kisses, and resounding slaps on the back. A firm handshake, friendly smile, and slight nod of the head are appropriate gestures of greeting.

In Chinese, a person's family surname precedes both given name and formal title. For example, in the name Li Wu-ping, Li is the surname and Wu-ping is the given name. In the expresson Li jing-li, Li is the surname and *jing-li* (manager) is the title. Most Chinese names consists of three characters – one surname and two given names – but many use only two. The majority of Chinese family names come from the Old Hundred Names (Lao Bai Hsing), first formulated over 3,000 years ago in feudal China. Among the most common are Li, Wang, Chen, Hwang, Chang, Yang, Liang and Sun.

During formal introductions, the Chinese today usually exchange name cards, which has become the tradition throughout Asia. In fact, many people don't even listen to oral introductions, but wait instead to read the person's card. It is a good idea to have some personal name cards printed up before traveling anywhere in the Far East. As the Chinese say, "When entering a new land, follow the local customs".

Some of the most common titles used in Chinese during introductions are:

Hsien-sheng/Mister (as in Li *hsien-sheng*)
Tai-tai/Mrs (Li *tai-tai*)
Hsiao-jye/Miss (Li *hsiao-jye*)
Fu-ren/Madame (Li *fu-ren*)
Lao-ban/Boss (Li *lao-ban*)
Jing-Li/Manager (Li *jing-li*)

The Chinese term *ching-keh* literally means "inviting guests" and refers to the grand Chinese tradition of entertaining friends and associates with lavish generosity, usually at banquets. The Chinese are perplexed when they see Westerners call for their bill at restaurants, then pull out pocket calculators and proceed to figure out precisely how much each person at the table must contribute. The Chinese, on the contrary, almost get into fistfights while arguing for the privilege of paying the bill for the whole table. To the Chinese, inviting guests out for dinner and drinks is a delightful way to repay favors or to cultivate new business relationships, and they do so often. For one thing, this is the type of gift which the giver may always share with the recipients. For another, the very moment you've paid a hefty dinner bill, everyone at the table is immediately obliged to invite you out as their guest sometime in the near future. This way, although the bill is high when it's your turn to *ching-keh*, you only end up paying for one out of 12 banquets. In the final analysis, it all balances out, and everyone takes turns earning the "big face" that comes with being a generous host.

When toasted at dinner parties, it is well-mannered to raise your wine cup with both hands: one holding it and the other touching the base. The host would take his seat opposite (not beside) the guest-of-honor, and it is fitting to have the host's back to the door and the guest-of honor's facing it.

Tea served at the end of a meal is your host's polite insinuation that the party is over and that it is time for you to leave. So don't overstay your welcome even though your host may insist.

What is mere courtesy to the Chinese is often regarded as hypocrisy to Westerners. For example, even though it is late and the host would love to call it a day, he will gently persuade his guest to stay longer. In this case, it is up to the guest to detect from the host's tone what's the best thing to do. But this requires skill and cultural sense. An experienced traveler once ventured, "The rule of thumb is to do the exact opposite that your Chinese friend suggests". Try it if you must, but with discretion.

The Chinese Zodiac

Despite family planning programs, modern birth control, industrialization, the ascendancy of scientific thought, and other pragmatic Western social influences in Taiwan, the Chinese continue to hold great faith in their age-old cosmology. Prior to births, weddings, funerals, major business contracts, grand openings of new buildings, and other important events, most Chinese in Taiwan still consult ancient almanacs, fortune-tellers and geomancers for advice regarding auspicious days.

The Chinese calendar was first devised during the reign of the Yellow Emperor, around 2,700 BC. Thus, the Chinese are currently living in the 48th century, not the 20th, according to this ancient calendar.

In the Chinese lunar calendar, which follows the cycles of the moon rather than the sun, each year is designated by its association with one of the twelve celestial animals, along with one of the Five Cosmic Elements. The animals, in order of sequence, are the Rat, Ox, Tiger, Rabbit, Dragon, Snake, Horse, Ram, Monkey, Chicken, Dog, and Pig. The Five Elements are metal, wood, earth, water, and fire. Since each of the animals is associated in turn with each of the Five Elements, a full cosmic cycle takes 60 years to complete. Then, the sequence repeats itself once again.

Like the Western solar calendar, the Chinese lunar calendar has 12 months, each consisting of 29 or 30 days. To adjust their calendar, the Chinese add an extra month every 30 months. Each month commences with the new moon, and the full moon always falls on the 15th day. Chinese Lunar New Year occurs sometime between January 21 and February 28, and remains the single biggest holiday of the year among Chinese all over the world.

The pervasive influence of the ancient Chinese zodiac and lunar calendar on contemporary Chinese life in Taiwan today is remarkable. Most major Chinese and all local Taiwanese festivals are still determined according to the lunar calendar, which means that every year they fall on a different day on the Western calendar. If you ask a Chinese in Taiwan when his birthday is, he'll ask you whether you mean the Western sun calendar or the Chinese lunar calendar.

The dates for weddings and funerals in Taiwan are always set according to ancient Chinese cosmology. Many Chinese even refuse to travel or embark on new business ventures without considering auspicious dates. Not to do so would invite disaster.

When a modern new skyscraper goes up in Taiwan, the owners routinely consult a Chinese geomancer to determine the optimum position for the main entrance. Called *fengshui* (wind and water), geomancy is the branch of classical cosmology which helps humanity build dwellings in optimum harmony with the elements of the natural environment. Even if the building's owners don't really believe in *fengshui*, they will still follow the geomancer's advice, as they know perfectly well that many prospective buyers and renters will consult their own geomancers about the building prior to moving in.

Even the massive Chiang Kaishek Memorial Hall in downtown Taipei, with its extensive gardens and numerous gates, was laid out according to the laws of Chinese geomancy, in order to provide maximum harmony with the elements and spirits of the cosmos.

The Chinese zodiac is a complex and subtle system, which only fortune-tellers and scholars manage to master completely. But its basic tenets are applied daily in the lives of Chinese people everywhere.

The most popular aspect of the zodiac today is the description of one's basic personality traits according to which animal dominates the year of birth. Professional match-makers still refuse to introduce prospective marriage partners whose signs conflict, and businessmen often attribute unfulfilled contracts, financial failure and other problems to ill cosmology.

Rat: Charming and attractive to the opposite sex. They are hard-working, thrifty and highly resourceful, with remarkable ability to see projects through to the end. Rats hoard their money and are loathe to lend it, but they like to spend lavishly on themselves. Only in love do they grow generous. Though timid and retiring, Rats are easily roused to anger. Frank and honest, Rats also love to gossip.

Ox: Calm and quiet, the Ox inspires confidence and trust in others. Ill-tempered and volatile, the Ox tends to lose control when angry. The Ox is eloquent in speech, alert in mind, and dexterous of hand. The Ox is also stubborn and is not given to passion, which often causes problems with mates. The Ox tends to remain aloof from family.

Tiger: Tigers are courageous and powerful, with strong will-power. They command respect from others and resent authority. Yet they are sensitive and thoughtful, with deep feelings and sympathy for their friends and loved ones. They are said to repel the three evils of thieves, fire and ghosts.

Rabbit: Talented and virtuous, rabbits have conservative tendencies and display good taste. They are both clever and reliable in business, and are usually blessed with good luck. They are tender to those they love, yet often keep a distance from their families. Moody and sometimes arrogant, Rabbits tend to lead tranquil, fortunate lives.

Dragon: Energetic, healthy, and quick to react, Dragons are also stubborn and short-tempered. They are known for honesty and courage, and they inspire trust and confidence in others. Though admired by all, Dragons often worry needlessly about affection. Dragons usually get what they want and are generally the most eccentric people in the zodiac.

Snake: Intense and introverted, Snakes are often distrusted by others and have trouble communicating effectively. They are wise and deep-thinking, but also tend to be vain and selfish. Still, they offer help to those less fortunate than themselves. Money never seems to be a problem for Snakes, nor do they worry about it. They prefer their own judgement to the advice of others. Generally passionate and attractive, Snakes do not make the most faithful marriage partners.

Horse: Optimistic, perceptive and self-confident, Horses are popular with others and rather talkative. Though good-looking and intelligent, they often find themselves at the mercy of the opposite sex. They manage money well and are skillful in their work. Horses love freedom and tend to leave home early.

Ram: Blessed with excellent dispositions, Sheep make fine marriage partners. They are upright, honest and extremely generous, and show great sympathy for those struck by misfortune. They have excellent taste in fashion and are endowed with artistic talents. Gentle, compassionate, and rather shy, Sheep are sometimes puzzled by the vagaries of life.

Monkey: Clever, inventive and original, Monkeys can solve complex problems with ease. However, they are also cunning, inconsistent, and rather mischievous. They love to be the center of attention, but they have little respect for others. They succeed in almost everything they undertake, and are ingenious in handling money. Others respect them for their competence and ability to learn quickly, but their own enthusiasm for projects tends to fizzle out quickly.

Chicken: Outgoing, brave, and highly capable. Chickens embark on many projects, many of which they never complete. They are somewhat eccentric and self-righteous, with strong personal opinions. They tend to be moody, and are highly devoted to their work.

Dog: Dogs are honest, loyal, and

easily trusted by others. They keep secrets very well and have a strong sense of justice. Though they don't possess great wealth, they rarely suffer for lack of funds. They tend to be somewhat cold, sarcastic, and erratic, but they are hard-working and devoted to their friends.

Pig: Honest, polite, and devoted to their tasks, Pigs also place great value on friendship and are loyal. Though quick-tempered, they hate to argue and are affectionate to their mates. They have a tendency towards laziness and love to spend money.

The Government

The Republic of China on Taiwan, as the government officially refers to Taiwan, still marches to the battle cry of Dr. Sun Yatsen, who established a governing system "of the people, by the people and for the people" early in the 20th century.

The government adopted a constitution based on those principles. It incorporates five branches of government called *Yuan* under a president. The executive Yuan resembles the cabinet of Western governments and includes ministries and other offices and departments. Law-making is the function of the Legislative Yuan. The Control Yuan has powers of consent, impeachment, censure and audit. Under the Judicial Yuan are the courts, Council of Grand Justices and other offices that uphold and interpret the law. Finally, the Examination Yuan supervises examinations and personnel.

In addition to the ROC government, the Taiwan Provincial Government and numerous county, city and ethnic minority groups have freely-elected representatives that participate in daily decision-making. The current president of the republic is Lee Teng-hui.

Planning the Trip

What to Wear

During the hot season, appropriate clothing for Taiwan should include light and loose cotton clothing, casual sportswear, and comfortable walking shoes. Men usually need not wear jackets and ties, for even during office hours, most Chinese businessmen prefer to wear leisure suits with open collars to beat the heat. You may want to bring along a lightweight jacket or dress for formal banquets and receptions, but otherwise such clothing is not necessary. If you come for business, it is better to be overdressed, so take your jacket and tie. Most modern offices are air-conditioned.

During the cold season, be sure to bring along some comfortable woolens to help protect you from the bone-chilling, moisture-laden airs of winter in Taiwan. Sweaters, woolen jackets and dresses, warm pants and socks will all come in handy during Taiwan winters, especially in Taipei. People in Taiwan tend to dress a bit more formally on winter evenings than in summer.

During both seasons, it is advisable to bring along some sort of rain-gear. It can burst out in thunderstorms at any moment without forewarning.

Entry Regulations

Visas

Visa-free entry: Citizens of Australia, Austria, Belgium, Canada, France, Germany, Japan, Luxembourg, New Zealand, Netherlands, Portugal, Spain, Sweden, United Kingdom and the United States – with passports valid at least for six month and confirmed onward or return tickets – are allowed visa-free entry to Taiwan at any of its major international ports and harbors, for a period of 14 days. It is **not** possible to extend the validity of such visas.

Visas: Foreigners applying for visitor visas must hold passports or other travel documents which are valid for application, incoming and outgoing travel tickets (or a letter from your travel agent), three photos, and documents stating the purpose of the visit (except for sightseeing or transit) and the completed application form.

Such visitor visas are good for 60 days (unless restricted to two weeks) and may be extended twice for 60 days, for a total of six months' stay. Foreigners entering Taiwan on a visitor visa may not work without official authorization.

Visitors from countries without ROC embassies or consulates may approach the designated ROC representatives in their respective countries for letters of recommendation. These letters of recommendation may then be exchanged for visitor visas at any ROC embassy or consular office en route to Taiwan, or on arrival at Chiang Kaishek International Airport or Kaohsiung International Airport, the only points of entry to Taiwan at which such letters may be exchanged for a visa.

More detailed information regarding ROC visitor visas can be obtained from the **Department of Consular Affairs**, Ministry of Foreign Affairs, 23F, 333 Keelung Road, Sec. 1, Taipei, Taiwan, Tel: (02) 729-7117.

EXTENSIONS

Be sure to apply for extensions at least one or two days before your regular visa expires. To extend a regular tourist visa in Taipei, visit the **Foreign Affairs Department**, National Police Administration, 96 Yenping S. Road, Taipei, tel: (02) 381-8341.

Customs

Inbound Declaration: All inbound passengers must fill a customs declaration form upon arrival in Taiwan.

DUTY-FREE

All personal belongings such as clothing, jewelry, cosmetics, food and similar items may be brought into Taiwan free of duty. Items such as stereo equipments, TV sets and recorders, though also duty-free, must be declared on arrival. Each passenger is also permitted to bring in duty-free one bottle (1 liter) of alcoholic beverage and one carton of tobacco (200 cigarettes, 25 cigars, or 1 pound of pipe tobacco).

GOLD & CURRENCY

On gold in excess of 62.5 grams in weight, duty will be charged.

Although unlimited amounts of foreign currency may be brought into Taiwan, passengers who wish to take excess foreign currency out again must declare the full amount upon arrival. The unused balance may then be declared on the Outbound Passenger Declaration form upon departure from Taiwan.

Otherwise, outbound passengers are limited to taking US$5,000 or the equivalent in other currencies out of Taiwan. No more than NT$40,000 per passenger in local currency may be brought into or out of Taiwan. Visitors who want to bring in more than NT$40,000 in cash must apply for a permit from the Ministry of Finance before entering Taiwan.

PROHIBITED ITEMS

The following items are strictly prohibited from entry into Taiwan:

- counterfeit currency or forging equipment
- gambling apparatus or foreign lottery tickets
- pornographic materials
- publications promoting communism or originating in the few nations or areas still under communist control
- firearms or weapons of any kind and ammunition
- opium, cannabis, cocaine, and other illegal drugs
- toy guns
- all drugs or narcotics of a non-prescription and non-medical nature
- articles which infringe on the patents, trademarks and copyrights of the rightful owners
- animals and pets

OUTBOUND DECLARATION

The outbound passenger declaration form must be completed when carrying any of the following items:

- foreign currency, local currency, gold and silver ornaments in excess of allowed amounts
- any unused foreign currency declared upon arrival
- commercial samples and personal effects such as cameras, calculators, recorders, etc., which you wish to bring back to Taiwan duty-free in

the future
- computer media, diskettes, tapes.

Passengers who have not declared gold, silver and foreign currencies upon arrival and are then discovered to be carrying these items in excess of the legally-designated quantities will have the excess amount confiscated by customs authorities, and may be subject to punishment by law. The designated legal limits are as follows:

- foreign currency – US$5,000 or equivalent, in cash (excluding unused portion of currency declared upon arrival)
- Taiwan currency – NT$40,000 in banknotes and 20 coins (of the types in circulation)
- gold ornaments or coins – 625 grams
- silver ornaments or coins – 625 grams
- articles that may not be taken out of the country include unauthorized reprints or copies of books, records, videotapes, and so on; genuine Chinese antiques, ancient coins and paintings; and items prohibited from entry as firearms, drugs, counterfeit currency, and contraband.

A booklet giving complete customs regulations and hints is available. For further information on Taiwan customs regulations, contact the following government office:
Inspectorate General of Customs, 85 Hsin-Sheng S. Rd, Sec. 1, Taipei. Tel: (02) 741-3181.

Outbound passengers must sometimes open their luggage for security inspection after checking in for flights. This is done at the end of the check-in counters, and if you forget to pay attention to this, your bags may not be loaded onto the aircraft.

AIRPORT TAX

All outbound passengers must pay an exit airport tax of NT$300. You must present the receipt when checking in.

Health

Effective cholera and yellow fever inoculation certificates are required for passengers coming from certain countries or have stayed more than five days in infected areas. Otherwise, health certificates are not normally required. It is very much recommended to have inoculations against Hepatitis A and in some cases, Hepatitis B well in advance if traveling to remote areas.

Currency

Coins come in denominations of NT$1, 5, 10, 50 and 100. Bills come in units of NT$100, 500 and 1,000.

Major foreign currencies can be easily exchanged for the local currency at certain banks, hotels, some shops and all authorized money dealers. In smaller towns or in the countryside, it is nearly impossible to change foreign currency into NT$. If traveling overland, change money before the trip. In smaller towns usually only the **Bank of Taiwan** changes foreign currency; the procedure is complicated, exhausting and time-consuming.

Important: Be sure to obtain receipts of all such transactions: you'll find they save you a lot of hassle with the bank, when you try to reconvert unused New Taiwan dollars on departure. Usually you will get US$ for your surplus NT$. The best for doing this job are the banks at CKS International Airport in Taipei. There is also a bank at Kaohsiung International Airport, but with irregular opening times.

Traveler's checks are also widely accepted at most hotels and other tourist-oriented establishments. This also applies to major credit cards such as American Express, Visa, MasterCard and Diners Club.

Getting There
By Air

Taiwan lies along one of the busiest air routes in Asia, and stopovers there may be included on any round-the-world or regional air tickets at no extra cost. Many international airlines currently provide regular air service to Taiwan. Chinese travel a lot and it is a good idea to make flight reservations as early as possible.

Taipei: A lot of the international air traffic to and from Taiwan goes through the **Chiang Kaishek International Airport** in Taoyuan, about 45 minutes' drive from downtown Taipei. This is one of the safest, most well-designed airports in Asia, fully-

equipped with the latest technology. While you are here, it makes sense to visit the adjoining three-story Chung-Cheng Aviation Museum. More than just a museum exhibiting models of aircraft (about 700), it offers facilities for visitors to test their flying skills or experience the sensation of flying. Also housed within its premises are dioramas and close-circuit TV displays, which trace aviation history from the time of Icarus' flight to modern-day space exploration.

Kaohsiung: In the south of Taiwan is Kaohsiung, with Taiwan's second international airport. Regular air services connect this city to several other Asian destinations.

Special Facilities
Trade Missions

The China External Trade Development Council (CETRA) is designed to assist those who wish to do business with Taiwan, and it displays the full range of products manufactured here. It is an independent, non-profit organization supported by grants from both the government and the local business associations. Its primary purpose is to promote Taiwan's growing trade with other nations. It provides facilities to local and foreign businesses, as well as to visitors with an interest in Taiwan's industries.

CETRA operates an enormous **Display Center and Export Mart** at the Sungshan Airport (domestic), in Taipei, exhibiting the full range of manufactured products available for export from Taiwan. Next to the center is an Export Mart, where Taiwan's major exporters maintain permanent representatives to discuss business and trade with interested foreigners. At the Export Mart, you may also purchase samples of various products at rock-bottom factory prices. The range and quality of the products on display there are impressive: watches and calculators; digital pen/watches and computer games; electronic components and audio-visual equipment; tools and machines; toys and sporting goods; jewelry and handicrafts; and much more. Even if you're not interested in business, it's well worth visiting CETRA's Display Center and Export Mart.

At CETRA's initiative, the **Taipei World Trade Center** (TWTC) was

opened in 1989. The massive TWTC houses four complexes: the Taipei International Convention Center, which can seat 3,300 people and is also equipped with smaller meeting rooms; the Hyatt Regency Hotel, which provide 872 rooms for the luxury and convenience of business people; the exhibition hall, which can accommodate up to 1,313 display booths; and the International Trade Building, which will be able to provide professional assistance to exhibitors, sellers and buyers. The TWTC is the ultimate meeting place with all the modern amenities and essential services.

For information on specific trade shows and dates, contact: CETRA, 5 Hsinyi Rd, Sec. 5, Taipei. Tel: (02) 725-111; fax: (02) 725-1314.

Foreign Representative Offices

American Institute in Taiwan, Taipei 7, Lane 134, Hsinyi Rd, Sec. 3, Taipei. Tel: (02) 709-2000; fax: (02) 702-7675.

American Institute in Taiwan/Kaohsiung, 5F, 2 Chungcheng 3rd Rd, Kaohsiung. Tel: (07) 224-0514; fax: (07) 223-8237.

Anglo-Taiwan Trade Committee, 9F, 199 Jenai Rd, Sec. 2, Taipei. Tel: (02) 322-4242; fax: (02) 394-8673.

Australian Commerce & Industry, Rm 2605, 333 Keelung Rd, Sec. 1, Taipei. Tel: (02) 720-2833; fax: (02) 757-6707.

Australian Trade Delegation, Rm 608, 205 Tunhua N. Rd, Taipei. Tel: (02) 715-5220, fax: (02) 717-3242.

Belgian Trade Association, Rm 901, 131 Minsheng E. Rd, Sec. 3, Taipei. Tel: (02) 715-1215; fax: (02) 712-6258.

Brazil Business Center, Rm 702, 129 Minsheng E. Rd, Sec. 3, Taipei. Tel: (02) 514-9099.

Canadian Trade Office, 13F, 365 Fuhsing N. Rd, Taipei. Tel: (02) 713-7268; fax: (02) 712-7244.

Danish Trade Organization, 4F, 12, Lane 21, Anho Rd, Taipei. Tel: (02) 721-3389, 721-3397; fax: (02) 731-5120.

France Asia Trade Promotion Association, Rm 601, 205 Tunhua N. Rd, Taipei. Tel: (02) 713-8216, 713-3552; fax: (02) 717-1353.

French Institute, Rm 1003, 10F, 205 Tunhua N. Rd Tel: (02) 545-6061; fax: (02) 545-0994.

German Cultural Office, 11F, 24 Hsinhai Rd, Sec. 1, Taipei. Tel: (02) 365-7294; fax: (02) 368-7542.

German Trade Office, 4F, 4 Minsheng E. Rd, Sec. 3, Taipei. Tel: (02) 506-9028; fax: (02) 509-3979.

Indonesian Chamber of Commerce, 3F, 46-1 Chungcheng Rd, Sec. 2, Taipei. Tel: (02) 831-0451; fax: (02) 836-1844.

Institute for Trade & Investment of Ireland, Rm 7B-09, 5 Hsinyi Rd, Sec. 5, Taipei. Tel: (02) 725-1691; fax: (02) 725-1653.

Italian Trade Promotion Office, Rm 2C-14, 5 Hsinyi Rd, Sec 5, Taipei. Tel: (02) 725-1542; fax: (02) 725-1422.

Malaysian Friendship & Trade Center, 8F, 102 Tunhua N. Rd, Taipei. Tel: (02) 713-2626; fax: (02) 718-1877.

Manila Economic & Cultural Office, Rm 803, 47 Chungshan N. Rd, Sec. 3, Taipei. Tel: (02) 585-1125; fax: (02) 594-6080.

Netherlands Trade & Investment Office, Rm B, 5F, 133 Minsheng E. Rd, Sec. 3, Taipei. Tel: (02) 713-5670; fax: (02) 713-0194.

New Zealand Commerce & Industry Office, Rm 812, 333 Keelung Rd, Sec. 1, Taipei. Tel: (02) 757-7060; fax: (02) 757-6972.

Norway Trade Office, 11F, 148 Sungchiang Rd, Taipei. Tel: (02) 543-5484; fax: (02) 561-9044.

Saudi Arabian Trade Office, 65, Lane 2, Yangteh Ave, Sec. 2, Taipei. Tel: (02) 833-2942.

Singapore Trade Office, 9F, 85 Jenai Rd, Sec. 4, Taipei. Tel: (02) 772-1940; fax: (02) 772-1943.

Spanish Chamber of Commerce, 7F-1, 602 Tunhua S. Rd, Taipei. Tel: (02) 325-6234; fax: (02) 754-2572.

Swedish Industries Trade Representative, 96 Chungshan N. Rd, Sec. 2, Taipei. Tel: (02) 562-7601; fax: (02) 531-9504.

Swiss Industries Trade Office, Rm 1614, 333 Keelung Rd, Sec. 1, Taipei. Tel: (02) 720-1001; fax: (02) 757-6984.

Useful Addresses

Tour Operators

Taipei travel agencies operate daily bus-tours for travelers. All buses are air-conditioned, and all tours include bilingual guides. Tickets for these tours may be obtained through any hotel travel desk, or by contacting these agencies directly:

Edison Travel Service, 4F, 190 Sungchiang Rd, Taipei. Tel: (02) 563-5313; fax: (02) 563-4803.

Golden Foundation Tours Corp., 8F, 134 Chunghsiao E. Rd, Sec. 4, Taipei. Tel: (02) 773-3200; fax: (02) 773-4994.

South East Travel Service Co., 60 Chungshan N. Rd, Sec. 2, Taipei. Tel: (02) 567-8111; fax: (02) 564-2256.

Practical Tips

Emergencies

Medical Services

Although medical treatment and dental work cost far less in Taipei than in any Western country or Japan, the quality of medical facilities and services is excellent and up-to-date.

HELP

The following telephone numbers are useful for visitors to Taiwan:

Fire, tel: 119
Police, tel: 110
Traveler info, tel: (02) 717-3737 (from 8am to 8pm)
Foreign Affairs, National Police, tel: (02) 396-9781.
Foreign Affairs, National Police offices:
Taichung, tel: (04) 220-3032.
Kaohsiung, tel: (07) 221-5796.
Tainan, tel: (07) 222-9704.
Keelung, tel: (032) 252-787.

Weights & Measures

In both public markets and small shops throughout Taiwan, vendors still weigh and measure things with traditional Chinese units. If on your own without an interpreter, the following conversion table will help figure out the unit price of items.

Length: The Chinese "foot" is called a *chir*.
1 *chir* = 11.9 inches or 0.99 feet = 0.30 meters
1 *jang* = 10 *chir*

Weight: The Chinese "pound" is called a *catty* or *jin*.
1 *jin* = 1.32 pounds or 0.6 kilograms = 21.2 ounces or 600 grams
The Chinese "ounce" is called a *liang*.
1 *liang* = 1.32 ounces or 37.5 grams
Area: The Chinese measure area in units of *ping* and *jia*
1 *ping* = 36 square feet (6' × 6')
1 *jia* = 2.40 acres

Electricity in Taiwan is 110v (60 cycles).

Business & Banking Hours

Official **government** business hours in Taiwan are 8.30am–12.30pm and 1.30–5.30pm, Monday through Friday, and 8.30am–12.30pm on Saturday, with Sunday closed.

Hours for **banks** are 9am–3.30pm Monday through Friday, and 9am–noon on Saturday, with Sunday closed.

Commercial **business** hours are 9am–5pm Monday through Friday, and 9am–noon on Saturday, with Sunday a day off.

Department **stores** and large shops stay open from 10 or 11am until 9 or 10pm Monday through Saturday, and usually close on Sunday. Many smaller shops and stalls keep longer hours and remain open all week.

Museums are usually closed on Mondays.

Tipping

Generally speaking, heavy tipping is not expected in Taiwan, although token gratuities are always appreciated. Hotels and restaurants automatically add 10 percent service charge to bills, but this money rarely gets distributed among the staff, so a small cash tip of 5 to 10 percent is always welcome in restaurants.

Taiwan taxi drivers do not get upset if you do not tip them, but it is customary to let them "keep the change" in small coins when paying the fare. Taxis still cost far less in Taipei than most places, but the cost of gas and maintenance here is quite high, so drivers appreciate even the smallest tips.

The only places in Taiwan where heavy tips are routinely expected are in wine-houses and dance-halls, where big tipping wins you "big face" and big favors from the ladies.

Media

Despite Taiwan's exotic ambience and traditional culture, it is a modern, highly developed place with complete international services. You need never lose contact with the outside world while traveling in Taiwan, although many visitors prefer to do just that.

Newspapers and Magazines

Two English-language newspapers are published daily in Taiwan: *China Post* (morning) and *China News* (afternoon). In addition to international and regional news culled from major wire services, as well as local features written by their own staff, these newspapers carry financial news, entertainment sections, sports reports and guides to English programs on TV and radio. Most hotel newsstands carry both.

The Government Information Office publishes an illustrated monthly magazine in English, *Free China Review*, which features articles on Chinese culture, travel in Taiwan, and other aspects of life in the Republic of China. Beyond this, the only English periodicals published locally are devoted exclusively to industrial and financial news.

Foreign periodicals available in Taiwan include *Time*, *Newsweek*, *Life*, and several fashion magazines, all of which are sold at English bookstores and hotel newsstands. All foreign publications brought into Taiwan are subject to official government censorship, so don't be surprised if you discover a page or two missing from your magazine.

Radio

There is only one radio station in Taiwan which broadcasts programs entirely in English. International Community Radio Taipei (ICRT) broadcasts popular Western music and other programs in English 24 hours, with international news reports provided on the hour. Phone (02) 861-2280 for details of the broadcasts, on an island-wide frequency of FM 95.3. Chinese radio stations broadcast a wide variety of music, both Western and Chinese.

Television

There are four television stations which broadcast scheduled programs throughout Taiwan, where there is currently an average of one television set per household. These stations are China Television Co. (CTV), Chinese Television System (CTS), Taiwan Television Entreprise (ITV), and People Broadcasting Corporation (PBC). All stations broadcast exclusively in Chinese, but they frequently schedule English-language films and programs from the West. Check the local English-language newspapers for details regarding English-language films and programs on Chinese television.

Postal Services

Taiwan boasts one of the fastest, most efficient postal services in the world. Mail is collected and delivered every day all year, and all incoming mail is sorted and distributed within 48 hours of arrival. Many first-time residents have been astounded on seeing the local postmen trudging through driving rain and howling winds during a major typhoon to deliver a single letter to a remote hillside house. Letters mailed to the United States from Taiwan usually arrive at their destinations within five to seven days of posting. Local mail is delivered within 24 to 48 hours.

Taipei's **Central Post Office** is located at the North Gate intersection, close to the Taipei Railway Station. This is the best place to collect and post mail in Taipei. This office also provides inexpensive cartons and packing services for parcel posting. Post offices in town are open from 8am until 6pm on Monday through Friday, 8am until 1pm on Saturdays. They are closed on Sundays.

Stamps may be purchased at the mail counter of any hotel in Taiwan, and letters may be dropped in any hotel or public mail box, of which there are many in Taiwan. Local mail goes in the green boxes, and international airmail goes into the red boxes. Current rates for letters addressed to destinations in Europe/America are NT$15–17 for letters under 10 grams (plus NT$13–14 for each additional 10 grams), NT$11–12 for postcards, and NT$12–14 for aerograms. Postal rates change from time to time, so be sure to inquire before posting your cards and letters.

Taiwan's decorative and commemorative postage stamps are highly prized in the world of philately. Charming Chinese themes, such as landscape painting, porcelain and calligraphy, are often incorporated into the design of stamps.

Telecoms

Telephone, Fax and Telex
Country Code: 886

Long-distance calls within Taiwan can be made from private or public pay phones by using the following local area codes:

Taipei area, inc. Keelung	02
Kaohsiung	07
Changhua County	04
Chiayi	05
Hsinchu	035
Hualien County	038
Ilan County	039
Miaoli County	037
Nantou County	049
Penghu County	06
Pingtung County	08
Taichung	04
Tainan	06
Taitung County	089
Yunlin County	05

Local city calls may be dialed from any public pay telephone, of which there are many in Taiwan. Local calls cost NT$1 for three minutes, after which the line is automatically cut off. For further conversation, drop in another coin for local calls and dial again. But the best is to use a telephone-card, which will cost you NT$100. Most phones are card phones, and you can phone until the card's cash amount is exhausted.

International calls: On private phones, the overseas operator may be reached by **dialing 100**. Direct-dialing is available from some phones, especially in hotels. International direct dialing rates are calculated every six seconds. Overseas phone calls may also be made at ITA **(International Telecommunications Adminstration)** offices. The main office in Taipei is open 24 hours, seven days a week, and is located at 28 Hangchou S. Rd, Sec. 1, Taipei, tel: (02) 244-3780.

Facsimile: Fax-services are available 24-hours for Taiwan or overseas at the ITA main office. Hotels also provide fax services to guests, often charging an additional fee.

Telegrams: Both international and

domestic telegrams may be sent from the main ITA or branch offices, or from the mail counter of major international tourist hotels. ITA offers both Urgent (12 hours) and Ordinary (24 hours) telegram services.

Visitors who wish to register local cable addresses in Taiwan should do so at ITA's main office.

Telex: Services are available at the main office of ITA, and at major international tourist hotels.

Tourist Offices
Tourist Information

Service and information centers for visitors are located at both the Chiang Kaishek International Airport, in Taoyuan outside of Taipei, and the Kaohsiung International Airport in Kaohsiung. Receptionists at these information counters speak English, and they can help with transportation, accommodations, and other travel requirements.

There are two organizations in Taiwan which oversee and promote the tourism industry. The **Tourism Bureau**, a branch of the Ministry of Communications, is the official government organ responsible for tourism in Taiwan. The **Taiwan Visitors Association** is a private organization that promotes Taiwan tourism abroad and provides travel assistance to visitors in Taiwan. Since neither of these organizations is blessed with a generous budget, the facilities they offer to travelers are limited. Nevertheless, they do their best to assist the inquiring traveler.

At the Sungshan Airport (domestic) in town, you'll find the **Travel Information Service Center.** This facility is designed primarily to provide information on foreign countries to the ever-growing volume of outbound Chinese travelers from Taiwan. However, in addition to audio-visual and printed information on 55 countries, the center also offers a 25-minute audio-visual presentation on the most outstanding tourist attractions in Taiwan. You could also visit the center to familiarize yourself with the culture and conditions of your next Asian destination. The center is open from 8am until 8pm daily, including Sundays and holidays.

Tourist Information Offices

To obtain information regarding tourism in Taiwan, write to the Tourism Bureau's head office in Taipei, or to one of its overseas representatives.

Hong Kong: Rm 904, 9F, Wingshan Tower, 173 Des Voeux Rd, Central, Hong Kong. Tel: (852) 258-10933; fax: (852) 258-10262.

Japan: Tawian Visitors Association, A-9, 5F, Imperial Tower, Imperial Hotel, Uchisaiwai-cho 1-1-1, Chiyoda-ku, Tokyo 100. Tel: (03) 3501-3591/2; fax: (03) 3501-3586.

Korea: Taiwan Visitors Association, Rm 904, 9th Fl., Kyungki Bldg, 115, Samgak-Dong, Chung-Ku, Seoul. Tel: (02) 732-2357/8; fax: (02) 732-2359.

Singapore: Taiwan Visitors Association, 5 Shenton Way, #14-07, UIC Bldg, Singapore 068808.

USA: Tourism Representative, Travel Section, Taipei Economic & Cultural Office,
166 Geary St. (Suite 1605), San Francisco, CA 94108 USA. Tel: (415) 989-8677, 989-8694; fax: (415) 989-7242.
1 World Trade Center (Suite 7953), New York, NY 10048 USA. Tel: (212) 466-0691/0692; fax: (212) 432-6436.
333 North Michigan Ave (Suite 2329), Chicago IL 60601 USA. Tel: (312) 346-1038; fax: (312) 346-1037.

Getting Around
From the Airport

Taipei: The CKS International Airport is about 45 km (28 mi) southwest of Taipei. An airporter bus connects the CKS international Airport with the Taipei Sungshan Airport (domestic), located north from downtown. The journey time is 45 to 60 minutes, the costs per person NT$111. The buses are running frequently every 10 to 20 minutes between 6.20am and 10.30pm. From the Sungshan Airport

bus terminal you are only 10 to 20 minutes (depending on traffic) by cab from most major downtown hotels.

A taxi from the CKS International Airport to downtown Taipei will cost at least NT$1200. For the trip from Taipei to the CKS International Airport the drivers are allowed by law to add a 50% surcharge over the fare shown on the meter.

Kaohsiung: The easiest and best transport is a taxi to the downtown hotels. The airport, located to the south of Kaohsiung, is very close to the city center.

Domestic Travel
By air

Regular scheduled domestic air service in Taiwan is provided by the international flag-carrier China Airlines (CAL), by Far Eastern Air Transport (FAT) and many more domestic airlines. In total, 8 domestic airlines are serving Taiwan and its islands.

Strict security measures are enforced on all domestic flights within Taiwan, and all foreign passengers need to show their passports prior to domestic boarding.

For bookings and other information before arriving in Taiwan, call a travel agent directly. For flight reservations and ticketing in Taiwan, it is the best way to go directly to an airline office; second-best is a travel-agent.

Buses

A special fleet of deluxe express buses serves Taiwan's major towns and cities. Between Taipei and Kaohsiung are frequent scheduled buses. By departure time, almost all buses are fully booked. Come early and wait in a long line for a ticket, or bad news.

The best way to purchase reserved-seat bus tickets in advance is to go directly to the appropriate bus company and buy them one or two days prior to departure. Most hotel travel desks and local travel agencies can make arrangements.

Railway

The Taiwan Railway Administration maintains an extensive railroad network which runs around the island and connects all major cities and towns. Usually the trains are full, and if you do not like to stand the whole trip, a seat reservation is necessary. But without a travel agent, to get one is quite complicated and time-consuming.

The Railway Administration offers three types of services:

Fu Hsing (FH) – air-conditioned, limited express; **Chu Kuang (CK)** – first-class, air-conditioned, express; and **Tsu Chiang (TC)** – electrical multiple units and air-conditioned.

Reservations for first-class express trains in Taiwan must be made at least one, but no more than two, days prior to departure. However, although you may purchase round-trip tickets in advance, reservations for the return trips must be made upon arrival at your destination, also one to two days in advance. Even for local trains, it is highly advisable to purchase tickets at least several hours in advance, and preferably a full day prior to departure. In all cities and towns, advance train tickets may be purchased directly at the main railway station by lining up before the appropriate window. Most hotels and travel agencies will arrange advance train reservations.

Do not expect to see too much on a train ride. Most locals close the windows with the curtain to get some sleep. And they probably will complain heavily if "your" window remains open and sun is shining on "their" head.

Taxis

Sometimes it seems as if there are as many taxis in some towns in Taiwan as people. Stand on the curb and wave your arm in the street: within moments a taxi will glide to a halt by your feet, and the door will automatically swing open as the driver pulls a lever inside.

All taxi fares are calculated according to the meter. Drivers are allowed to charge for waiting time in traffic. If you wish to retain a taxi for a full day, or for a long, round-trip excursion to a specific destination, ask a hotel clerk to negotiate either a set fee for the whole day or discount on the meter fare.

Taiwan taxi meters calculate both time and distance to determine the fare. The meters have three windows. The top left window shows the time taken in minutes and seconds. Top right indicator is the distance in kilometers. The large right window meter shows the fare in NT dollars. From 11pm to 6am, there is an additional 20 percent charge.

Small towns and villages have fixed rates for the use of a taxi within a certain area. It is best to ask locals for the correct rate; even Taiwanese travelers have to do it this way, if they don't want to be overcharged.

Note: Although Taiwan's taxi drivers are almost uniformly friendly and polite, they tend to drive like maniacs. And some are rude also. Many tourists have their wits scared out as their taxi drivers weave carelessly between speeding buses and trucks, narrowly missing pedestrians, run through red lights, careen through swarms of buzzing motorcycles, and screech blindly around corners.

Unfortunately, this sort of driving is the rule rather than the exception in Taiwan. Should you get a particularly reckless driver; tell him to pull over immediately, pay him the fare on the meter (with no tip), and hail another cab. There is never a shortage of cabs in Taipei, day or night, rain or shine.

Very few taxi drivers in Taiwan speak or read English sufficiently well to follow directions given in English. Have your destination written out in Chinese before venturing out by cab. Hotel name cards, local advertisements, even restaurant match-boxes will also suffice to get you around town by taxi.

Car Rentals

It's best to rely on public transportation such as buses, taxis and tour-coaches to get around Taiwanese cities and towns. Trying to drive yourself around the city is a needless risk and could spoil your day. But if you plan an extended tour down-island or along the northern coastline, then renting a car is a fine way to go, for you'll see many more sights and enjoy the freedom to stop whenever and wherever you wish. The North-South Expressway runs like a spinal column down the center of the island from tip to tip, giving access by car to cities and scenic sites along the way. Local roads lead out to the mountains, mineral spas, temples, and other destinations along Taiwan's tourist trail.

Before renting a self-drive car, it is usually the best to ask the hotel for some rental-car company suggestions. You also can phone an Avis, Budget or Hertz reservation center before your trip to Taiwan.

If you like to splurge a bit and see the island in true comfort and convenience, the best way is by air-conditioned (or heated) limousines, driven by chauffeurs who also act as personal guides and interpreters. Any hotel travel desk or local travel agency can arrange a chauffeured limousine. The cost varies accordingly to the type of car.

Motoring Advisories

No matter how well you drive, Taiwan traffic bears the utmost attention. The Chinese have a strong faith in fate, and a big appetite for face. The former factor makes them take incredible chances on the road, while the latter drives them to take up even the slightest challenge from other drivers. The roads themselves are well maintained, however, and give convenient access to all of Taiwan's scenic treasures. With a little bit of luck, you should have no problems on the road if you bear in mind the following points:

• There are millions of motor scooters on the roads, and they constitute the single greatest hazard to automobile drivers. The most spine-chilling sight on the road is a husband and wife on a 90cc motor scooters with five or six infants hanging from the handlebars, gas-tank, fenders and mother's shoulder, speeding through rainy streets among trucks and buses. Steer clear of these.

• Also steer clear of all military vehicles. Military drivers are notorious for their careless driving on public roads. Regardless of the circumstances, military vehicles always have the right of way, and they know it.

• Though roads down south are well marked, the instructions are often in Chinese. So look for route numbers instead of place names, and match them with those on your maps. Route numbers are also inscribed on the stone mileage indicators set along the roadsides.

• Stop and ask directions when in doubt. The further south you drive, the friendlier the people become, and someone is always there to help. Don't attempt to pronounce place names in the countryside, because often people there don't understand Mandarin, at least not when it is spoken by foreigners. Show them the Chinese characters, and their eyes will light up with instant recognition, for these are universal symbols to Chinese the world over.

• Keep your gas-tank at least a third full at all times. In the more remote mountainous and coastal regions, gas stations are few and far between, and often closed at night.

Rapid Transit System

Construction of Taipei's Mass Rapid System began in 1988, when the French contractor started work. First finished was the Mucha–Sungshan Airport Line. It is one of six lines scheduled for Taipei, totaling 88 km (55 mi). The MRT system is scheduled for completion in 1999, but it has encountered many problems. Nevertheless, it is fun to take the Mucha Line and see downtown Taipei from above the traffic. Tickets on the Mucha-Line cost you NT$20 to 35, depending upon distance.

Travel in Taipei

Buses

One of the first things you'll notice in Taipei is the incredible number of public buses on the streets. For budget-minded travelers, buses provide frequent and inexpensive means of transportation to any point within or outside the city limits.

However, unless endowed with an extra measure of Asian patience, it is advisable to avoid the buses during heavy rush hours, which fall between 7.30–9.30am and 5–7pm.

There are two types of city buses: regular and air-conditioned. The regular bus costs about NT$10 per ride and the air-conditioned bus slightly more. Tickets and tokens should be purchased in advance at the little kiosk which you will find at or close to all bus-stops.

City bus service runs continously from about 6am until 11.30pm. To signal the driver to stop at an upcoming station, pull the bell cord. There are so many buses and bus routes within metropolitan Taipei that it is best to ask a hotel clerk or local aquaintance for directions before venturing out. Some bus stops in Taipei have a computer-information machine, indicating in English which buses to take to reach your final destination.

All buses are designated by code numbers, which indicate their routes and final destinations. Once you know the numbers, it is quite easy to get around on buses.

Where to Stay

Hotels

Chinese hotels are renowned for attentive, gracious service rendered with a spirit of pride and genuine desire to please. Visitors are treated as personal guests rather than anonymous patrons, and hospitality is approached more as an art than as an industry. However, Western travelers occasionally encounter frustrations. One reason is the ever-present language barrier: though uniformly trained in English, most Chinese hotel staff understand very little. Yet they'll avoid losing face by pretending to understand, then promptly forget about it. Another reason is cultural: Chinese priorities often differ from a Westerner's, and what seems of vital importance to you, such as punctuality, may seem trivial to the Chinese.

Tourist hotels in Taiwan are ranked in two categories: International Tourist and Regular Tourist. The former offers greater luxury and more varied facilities, while the latter offers lower rates and simpler services.

The hotels in Taipei are extremely expensive. Singles or twins will cost, in international tourist hotels, between NT$4,000–9,000. In Kaohsiung, the cost per room is between NT$2,500–5,000. At other places, expect to pay between NT$1,000–4,000 per night.

Taipei

LUXURY

The Ambassador, 63 Chungshan N. Rd, Sec. 2. Tel: (02) 551-1111; fax: (02) 561-7883. 428 rooms; indoor swimming pool, golfing, banquet and convention facilities, roof-top bar lounge with superb views, convenient access to shops, cocktail lounge.
Asiaworld Plaza Hotel, 100 Tunhwa N.

Rd. Tel: (02) 715-0077; fax: (02) 713-4148. 1057 rooms; huge hotel with 27 bars and restaurants, cinemas, theater restaurant, fitness center, underground parking, convention facilities, department stores, shopping mall with 500 boutiques.
Brother Hotel, 255 Nanking E. Rd, Sec. 3. Tel: (02) 712-3456; fax: (02) 717-3344. 268 rooms; excellent Cantonese dim-sum restaurant, roof-top lounge, well-maintained rooms.
Far Eastern Plaza Hotel Taipei, 201 Tunhua S. Rd, Sec. 2. Tel: (02) 378-8888; fax: (02) 377-7777. 422 rooms; two health clubs and swimming pools, shopping mall with 130 shops adjacent to the hotel
Grand Formosa Regent Taipei, 41 Chungshan N. Rd, Sec. 2. Tel: (02) 523-8000, fax: (02) 523-2828. 552 rooms; 10 different restaurants, health spa and fitness center, roof-top swimming pool.
Hilton International Taipei, 38 Chunghsiao W. Rd, Sec. 1. Tel: (02) 311-5151; fax: (02) 331-9944. 393 rooms; polished, professional service in all departments, award-winning food & beverage facilities; lively disco; sauna, roof garden, jacuzzi pools.
Grand Hyatt Taipei, 2 Sunghsou Road. Tel: (02) 720-1234; fax: (02) 720-111. 872 rooms; next to the convention center, good parking, fitness center with outdoor pool.
Howard Plaza Hotel, 160 Jenai Rd, Sec. 3. Tel: (02) 700-2323; fax: (02) 700-0729. 606 rooms; elegant decor, continental ambience, outdoor swimming pool, health center, sauna, shopping mall.
Lai-Lai Sheraton, 12 Chunghsiao E. Rd, Sec. 1. Tel: (02) 321-5511; fax: (02) 394-4240. 705 rooms; large hotel with many facilities including disco-club, health-club, and several restaurants.
President Hotel, 9 Tenhwei St. Tel: (02) 595-1251; fax: (02) 591-3677. 421 rooms; popular among businessmen; access to nightlife area and highway.
The Ritz Taipei, 155 Minchuan E. Rd. Tel: (02) 597-1234; fax: (02) 596-9222. 200 rooms; small hotel with personalized service, good European food and beverage facilities.
Hotel Royal Taipei, 37-1 Chungshan N. Rd, Sec. 2. Tel: (02) 542-3266; fax: (02) 543-4897. 202 rooms; sauna,

health club, swimming pool, shopping arcade, in the heart of the old business center.

The Sherwood Taipei, 111 Minsheng E. Rd, Sec. 3. Tel: (02) 718-1188; fax: (02) 713-0707. 350 rooms; best hotel in Taiwan, health center with indoor pool and jacuzzi, fitness center and sauna, late check-out until 3pm, four restaurants and a bar, next to the modern business and banking center.

STANDARD

Fortuna Hotel, 122 Chungshan N. Rd, Sec. 2. Tel: (02) 563-1111; fax: (02) 561-9777. 304 rooms.

Fortune Dragon Hotel, 172 Chunghsiao E. Rd, Sec. 4. Tel: (02) 772-2121; fax: (02) 721-0302. 312 rooms.

Gloria, 369 Linshen N. Rd. Tel: (02) 581-8111; fax: (02) 581-5811. 220 rooms.

Golden China Hotel, 306 Sungchiang Rd. Tel: (02) 521-5151; fax: (02) 531-2914. 216 rooms.

The Grand Hotel, 1 Chungshan N. Rd, Sec. 4. Tel: (02) 596-5565; fax: (02) 594-8243. 530 rooms.

Imperial Hotel, 600 Linshen N. Rd. Tel: (02) 596-5111; fax: (02) 592-7506. 327 rooms.

Taipei Miramar, 420 Minchuan E. Rd. Tel: (02) 505-3456; fax: (02) 502-9173. 584 rooms.

Mandarin Hotel, 166 Tunhwa N. Rd. Tel: (02) 581-1201; fax: (02) 712-2122. 351 rooms.

Hotel Rebar Holiday Inn Crown Plaza, 32 Nanking E. Rd, Sec. 5. Tel: (02) 763-5656; fax: (02) 767-9347. 300 rooms.

Riverview, 32 Nanking E. Rd, Sec. 5. Tel: (02) 311-3131; fax: (02) 361-3737. 201 rooms.

Santos Hotel, 439 Chengteh Rd. Tel: (02) 596-3111; fax: (02) 596-3120. 287 rooms.

United Hotel, 200 Kuangfu S. Rd. Tel: (02) 773-1515; fax: (02) 741-2789. 248 rooms.

Kaohsiung

INTERNATIONAL TOURIST

Ambassador Hotel, 202 Minsheng 2nd Rd. Tel: (07) 211-5211; fax: (07) 281-1115, (07) 281-1113. 457 rooms.

Grand Hi-Lai Hotel, 266 Chengkung 1st Rd. Tel: (07) 216-1766; fax: (07) 216-1966. 450 rooms.

Grand Hotel, 2 Yuanshan Rd, Cheng-Ching Lake. Tel: (07) 383-5911; fax: (07) 381-4889. 108 rooms.

Kingdom Hotel, 32 Wufu 2nd Rd. Tel: (07) 551-8211; fax: (07) 521-0403. 312 rooms.

Linden Hotel Kaohsiung, 33 Szuwei 3rd Rd. Tel: (07) 332-2000; fax: (02) 336-1600. 400 rooms.

Major Hotel, 7 Tajen Rd. Tel: (07) 521-2266; fax: (02) 531-2211. 200 rooms.

Summit Hotel, 426 Chiuru 1st Rd. Tel: (07) 384-5526; fax: (07) 384-4739. 210 rooms.

REGULAR TOURIST

Buckingham Hotel, 394 Chihsien 2nd Rd. Tel: (07) 282-2151; fax: (07) 281-4540. 144 rooms.

Duke Hotel, 233 Linsen 1st Rd. Tel: (07) 231-2111; fax: (07) 211-8224. 100 rooms.

Alishan

REGULAR TOURIST

Alishan House, 2 West Alishan, Shanglin Village, Wufeng Hsiang, Chiayi. Tel: (05) 267-9811; fax: (05) 267-9596. 60 rooms.

Hualien

INTERNATIONAL TOURIST

Astar Hotel, 6-1 Meichuan Rd. Tel: (038) 326-111; fax: (038) 324-604. 167 rooms.

Chinatrust Hualien Hotel, 2 Yungsing Rd. Tel: (038) 221-171; fax: (038) 221-185. 237 rooms.

Marshal Hotel, 36 Kungyuan Rd. Tel: (038) 326-123; fax: (038) 326-140. 303 rooms.

Parkview Hotel, 1-1 Lingyuan Rd. Tel: (038) 222-111; fax: (038) 226-999. 360 rooms.

Kenting

INTERNATIONAL TOURIST

Caesar Park Hotel, 6 Kenting Rd, Hengchun Town, Pingtung Hsien. Tel: (08) 886-1888; Fax: (08) 886-1818. 237 rooms.

REGULAR TOURIST

Kenting Hotel, 101 Park Rd, Kenting, Hengchun Town, Pingtung Hsien. Tel: (08) 886-1370; fax: (08) 886-1377. 250 rooms.

Sun Moon Lake

INTERNATIONAL TOURIST

Chinatrust Sun Moon Lake Hotel, 23 Chungcheng Rd, Sun Moon Lake, Nantou. Tel: (049) 855-911; fax: (049) 855 268. 116 rooms.

REGULAR TOURIST

El Dorado Hotel, 5 Mingsheng St, Sun Moon Lake, Nantou. Tel: (049) 85-5855; fax: (049) 85-6656. 54 rooms.

Taichung

INTERNATIONAL TOURIST

Evergreen Laurel Hotel, 6 Taichung Kang Rd, Sec. 2. Tel: (04) 328-9988; fax: (04) 328-8642. 354 rooms.

National Hotel, 257 Taichung Kang Rd, Sec. 1. Tel: (04) 321-3111; fax: (04) 321-3124. 404 rooms.

Park Hotel Taichung, 17 Kungyuan Rd. Tel: (04) 220-5181; fax: (04) 222-5757. 125 rooms.

Plaza International Hotel, 431 Taya Rd. Tel: (04) 295-6789; fax: (04) 293-0099. 305 rooms.

Tainan

INTERNATIONAL TOURIST

Tainan Hotel, 1 Chengkung Rd. Tel: (06) 228-9101; fax: (06) 226-8502. 152 rooms.

BUDGET

Redhill Hotel, 46 Chengkung Rd. Tel: (06) 225-8121; fax: (06) 221-6711. 120 rooms.

Youth Hostels

If you're willing to sleep in dormitories, eat in cafeterias, and travel exclusively by bus, then you can actually tour Taiwan for as little as US$100 per day by utilizing facilities operated by the **China Youth Corps** (CYC). CYC operates a series af Youth Activity Centers and Youth Hostels around the island, and the budget-minded travelers may avail themselves of these facilities. Information and reservations for the hostels and activity centers may be arranged by writing or calling CYC headquarters at 219 Sungkiang Rd, Taipei, tel: (02) 502-5858; fax: (02) 501-1312. For an updated address list, contact the **ROC Tourism Bureau** offices overseas or the **Domestic Tourism Bureau** in Taiwan.

Due to the popularity of these facilities, groups and individuals from overseas who wish to use them should make reservations well in advance. They usually remain fully-booked from July through September, and from January through February. If you have not made prior arrangements, then at least be sure to call ahead to your next intended stop to make sure that hostel accommodations are available.

Rates for room and board vary at different centers, but on the average three meals a day can be had for about NT$250, the price range is between NT$300 to 6,000, with an average of about NT$1,000 to 1,500 per night. Most of these establishments also offer private rooms at higher rates, and some even have spacious bungalows for small groups.

Guest Houses

There are a number of guest houses in the Taipei area which function as small hotels or inns and provide inexpensive accommodations. Weekly and monthly rates may be arranged as well. Ask the **Domestic Tourism Bureau** service centers for addresses and details.

Eating Out

What to Eat

Dining out remains the single greatest pleasure Taiwan holds in store for the traveler. Whether you opt for Chinese or Western cuisine, Japanese sushi or Korean barbecue, the restaurants of Taiwan have something tasty for every palate. The happy marriage of China's highly sophisticated culinary products has given birth to a restaurant industry which never fails to delight even the most experienced epicure. Naturally, when in Taiwan, it's best to do as the Chinese and go for gourmet Chinese cuisine. But if you prefer Western food, the restaurants listed below will serve you a good meal with proper service. Though almost any Chinese eatery in Taiwan serves good food, many of the so-called Western restaurants serve fare that looks and tastes like a careless melange of East and West.

All the restaurants listed are located in Taipei, where travelers generally spend most of their time and do most of their gourmet dining. Once you've mastered dining out in Taipei, you'll be able to make it on your own down-island, where the choice of restaurants and cuisines is less confusing.

When traveling down south, it's generally best to stick with Chinese food, as demand for Western cuisine in the south is not yet sufficiently strong to support genuine gourmet Western restaurants.

Types of Cuisine

Northern Style (Beijing, Mongolia). Recommended dishes: Beijing Duck, Lamb and Leek, Hot and Sour Soup, Celery in Mustard Sauce, Cold Shredded Chicken with Sauce, Sweet and Sour Yellow Fish, Steamed Vegetable Dumplings.

Southern Style (Cantonese). Recommended dishes: Roast Duck, Poached Chicken with Onions and Oil, Greens with Oyster Sauce, Steamed Whole Fish, Assorted *dim-sum*, Roast Pigeon, Cabbage with Cream.

Eastern/Coastal Style (Shanghai). Recommended dishes: West Lake Vinegar Fish, River Eel Sauteed with Leek, Braised Pork Haunch, Sauteed Sweet-Pea Shoots, Drunken Chicken, "Lionhead" meatballs, Braised Beef Loin.

Western/Central Style (Hunan, Szechuan). Recommended dishes: (Szechuan) Steamed Pomfret, Chicken "Duke of Bao", "Grandma's" Beancurd, Fragrant Egg-Sauce, Duck Smoked in Camphor and Tea, Twice-cooked Pork. (Hunan) Frog Legs in Chilli Sauce, Honey Ham, Beggar's Chicken, Minced Pigeon in Bamboo Cup, Steamed Whole Fish.

Taiwanese Food. Recommended dishes: Steamed Crab, Poached Squid, Fresh Poached Shrimp, Shrimp Rolls, Grilled Eel, Sashimi or raw fish, Grilled Clams, Turtle Soup.

Chinese Vegetarian Cuisine. Recommended Dishes: Try the various types of "beef", "pork" and "chicken" made entirely from various forms of soybean curd and/or different types of mushrooms, as well as fresh and crispy vegetables.

Chopsticks

There's nothing more Chinese than chopsticks. The Chinese have been using two sticks to pick up a single grain of rice and one stick to carry two buckets of water ever since time began. Nothing ever appears on the Chinese banquet table that cannot be manipulated single-handedly with a simple pair of chopsticks. Today, as the popularity of Chinese cuisine spreads throughout the world, it is considered *de rigueur* to use chopsticks when eating Chinese food. And in Taiwan you'll find abundant opportunities to practice.

The Chinese only use forks and knives in the kitchen – and when eating Western food. For their own cuisine, they prefer to have everything cut, sliced, diced, or otherwise prepared in the kitchen, so that the food is in bite-sized pieces when served. Those who wield their chopsticks too slowly often miss the choicest morsels whenever a new dish appears on the table.

Chopsticks can also be used to select choice morsels from the best dishes for the guest-of-honor or just for a friend at the table. The polite way to do this is to turn the sticks around so that you use the clean blunt ends to serve food to others.

Last but not least, using the chopsticks makes you a little more Chinese and a little less foreign in Chinese eyes, and this always improves the pleasure of traveling in Taiwan.

But due to hygienical reasons, several restaurants serve now so called set menus with portions of everything on individual plates.

Where to Eat

Restaurants in Taipei

If interested in some typical Chinese food, there are three suggestions for restaurants. The best place to try the perfect Chinese cuisine are the hotel restaurants in Taipei and Kaohsiung. The hotel restaurants are used to serving foreigners, offer nearly-perfect service, and serve probably the best Chinese food available on Taiwan. The Taipei Chinese Food Festival, held in August every year, demonstrates the skills of the hotels master chefs.

Second best suggestion for lunch

and sometimes for dinner is to visit one of the many eateries on the underground floors of the main department stores. Everything is freshly-cooked and the prices are quite low. If you see one eatery with no customers waiting, it is maybe better to go to another, where you have to wait in a line. Several hundred or thousands of Chinese eating at such places can not be wrong.

The third suggestion is to go to an ordinary restaurant. But most taxi drivers will not understand unless you show them the address of the restaurant written in Chinese. Through years of experience they know that Western people like to complain even about an excellent dish, perfectly prepared, because it does not taste the same as at the Chinese restaurant back home. Moreover, Chinese restaurants cater to groups, never individuals. Four people at a table should be the minimum. Do not expect the food to be cheap. Consider also the language barrier – there are so many items on a Chinese menu that most foreigners hesitate to order something "strange", and end up with a dish like rice-and-chicken. That is also one of the reasons why some gourmet Chinese restaurants don't take Western tourists seriously.

Attractions

Tours

The most popular city and island tours offered by travel agencies are briefly introduced below.

Taipei City: This half-day tour covers the National Palace Museum, Martyrs' Shrine, other city sights and offers glimpses of contemporary Chinese urban life along the way. (NT$500).
Taipei by Night: An enduring favorite, this nocturnal tour commences with a traditional Mongolian barbecue dinner, then proceeds to the famous Lungshan Temple and Snake Alley bazaar. (NT$950).
Wulai Aborigine Village: This is a half-

day excursion to the colorful ethnic minority village at Wulai, about an hour's drive out of Taipei. You'll see performances, hike through lush mountain terrain, and enjoy spectacular scenery. (NT$950).
Northern Coast: A half-day tour of Taiwan's scenic northern coastline, this excursion takes you to the port city of Keelung and the fantastic rock formations at Yehliu, then proceeds down the northwest coast back to Taipei. (NT$700).
Taroko Gorge: Taroko Gorge is considered to be one of the wonders of Asia, and it remains the single most popular tourist attraction outside of Taipei. Twelve miles of craggy canyon, enclosed by towering cliffs of marble, which soar up to 3,000 ft high. Taroko Gorge is bisected by the Central Cross-Island Highway, with 38 tunnels cut into solid rock and marble bridges. This tour goes by air to Hualien from Taipei in the morning, then heads up the gorge for a bus tour of breathtaking beauty. Lunch is served in the alpine airs of the Tienhsiang Lodge, then the bus returns to Hualien in time for performances by the Ami tribe, and a tour of Taiwan's biggest marble factory and showroom. The tour returns to Taipei by air around 5pm. (NT$4,000).
Sun Moon Lake: This two-day tour takes you to bucolic Sun Moon Lake, Taiwan's favorite honeymoon resort, located 2,500 ft above sea level in Taiwan's only land-locked county. This year-round resort is famous for its landscape, hiking, temples and pagodas. The tour departs Taipei by air-conditioned bus and arrives in Taichung for lunch. The bus then proceeds to Sun Moon Lake, about an hour's drive from Taichung, passing through green fields of sugar cane, tea, and vegetables, rice paddies, banana and pineapple plantations, and other lush scenery. After checking into a hotel, you'll go for a leisurely two-hour boat cruise on Sun Moon Lake. The second morning is free time. After lunch, the tour will drive back to Taichung and then on to Taipei, arriving back in town by nightfall. (NT$4,500 for double occupancy and NT$5,000 for single occupancy).
Central Cross Island Highway/Sun Moon Lake: The 120-mile-long Central Cross Island Highway, a remarkable feat of engineering by any standards, is known in Taiwan as the Rainbow of

Treasure Island. This three-day tour commences with a morning flight to Hualien from Taipei, followed by a drive through spectacular Taroko Gorge and lunch at the Tienhsiang Lodge. It then proceeds to scenic Lishan for an overnight stay. You'll spend the next morning sightseeing, then depart for Taichung, arriving in time for lunch and some city sightseeing. Next stop is Sun Moon Lake and a second night, touring the lake on the morning of the third day. The tour returns to Taichung by bus after lunch, then onto a train for the return trip to Taipei. (NT$7,500 for double occupancy and NT$9,000 for single occupancy).
Sun Moon Lake/Alishan: This three-day tour features a visit to Alishan, a magnificent resort area of 18 peaks flanking the Central Range in central Taiwan. A 45-mile-long, narrow-gauge railway with diesel trains traverses 80 bridges and passes through 50 tunnels from the town of Chiayi up to Alishan, which at 7,500 ft in altitude is the highest railway station in Asia. From a vantage point atop Chu Shan, you can catch one of the most spellbinding views in all Taiwan: a sea of clouds swirling like water and filling the entire valley between Chu Shan and 3,952-m (12,966 ft) Yu Shan 25 miles away. The latter is the highest peak in northeast Asia and a favorite destination for mountain climbers.

This tour commences with an air-conditioned bus-ride from Taipei to Taichung, then up to Sun Moon Lake for the first night. After a morning tour of the lake, the tour proceeds by bus to Chiayi, where you'll board the mountain railway for the 3-hour ride up to Alishan for the second night. A tour of the mountain the next morning, then a return trip by rail to Chiayi.

From there, you'll board an express bus back to Taipei. (NT$7,500 for double occupancy, NT$9,000 for single occupancy).
Round-the-Island Tour: This four-day tour is an extension of the Central Cross-Island Highway tour, with the addition of a visit to the southern seaport of Kaohsiung, Taiwan's second-largest city. The first day is spent touring Sun Moon Lake. The second day returns to Taichung, then on down to Kaohsiung, including lovely Chengching Lake, then flies to Hualien in the afternoon. After an overnight stay in

Hualien, you'll spend the fourth day driving up Taroko Gorge, then returning to Hualien for Ami performances and a tour of the marble factory. The tour flies back to Taipei around 5pm. (NT$11,000 for double occupancy, NT$13,000 for single occupancy).

Culture

Art Galleries

These galleries exhibit works of art by both established old masters and promising young artists. They display an impressive range of styles, from traditional Chinese landscape painting and calligraphy to contemporary Western abstracts and still-lifs, and the artists employ both Eastern and Western materials and methods. For further information on art and art exhibits in Taipei, contact the **Taipei Art Guild** at 8/F, 218-2, Chunghsiao E. Rd, Sec. 4. Tel: (02) 773-6673.

A spacious **Taipei Fine Arts Museum** has been opened at 1818 Chungshan North Rd, Sec. 3. Tel: (02) 595-7656. This ultra-modern facility frequently sponsors exhibitions of arts and crafts by renowned international and local talents.

Some of the more interesting art galleries an Taipei are listed below:

Apollo Art Gallery, Apollo Bldg, 218-6 Chunghsiao E. Rd, Sec. 4, 2nd Fl. Tel: (02) 781-9332.
Asia Art Center, 117 Chienkuo S. Rd, Sec. 2. Tel: (02) 754-1366.
Cave Gallery, B1, 138 Chunghsiao E. Rd, Sec. 1. Tel: (02) 396-1864.
Crown Center, 50 Lane 120, Tunhwa N. Rd. Tel: (02) 717-1398.
East West Art Gallery, 5/F, Rm 501, 63 Chungking S. Rd, Sec. 1. Tel: (02) 314-8603.
Hsiung Shih Gallery, 5/F, 16, Alley 33, Lane 216, Chunghsiao E. Rd, Sec. 4. Tel: (02) 772-1158.
Kander Arts and Antiquities Gallery, 25-27 Chung S. Rd, Sec. 1. Tel: 314-3210.
Lung-Men Art Gallery, 3/F, 218-1 Chunghsiao E. Rd, Sec. 4, 3rd Fl. Tel: (02) 751-3170.
Ming Sheng Art Gallery, 145B Chungshan N. Rd, Sec. 1. Tel: (02) 581-0858.

Chinese Opera

Taiwan is one of the best places in the world to attend the opera, Chinese style. From the bizarre melodies mouthed by magnificently-costumed performers to the exotic orchestral accompaniment, to the astounding acrobatics and martial arts displays of the performers, a night at a Beijing opera will surely prove entertaining and educational.

There is one place in Taipei where Beijing opera is performed regularly: **National Fu Hsing Dramatic Arts Academy**, 177 Neihu Rd, Sec. 2, Taipei. Tel: (02) 796-2666.

For a taste of Beijing or Taiwan opera, try the television set – live performances are broadcast almost every day. In the back alleys of Taipei and outside the big city, keep your eyes open for the traveling opera companies that set up and perform for several days.

Dance

There is a limited amount of traditional folk dancing in Taiwan, most performed by minority groups. Snippets of ethnic dances can be viewed at the various tourism centers around the island. On the other hand, modern dance has gained popularity in Taiwan in the past decade.

The **Cloud Gate Dance Ensemble**, led by Lin Hwaimin, has spearheaded the movement. It combines both Chinese and Western techniques and ideas, choreographed to the music of contemporary Chinese performers. The group, internationally-acclaimed during tours of the world, holds regular performances in Taipei. Consult your hotel for the schedules of the Cloud Gate ensemble.

Music

Taiwan has produced numerous musicians of world-class standard. Western music is regularly performed at various venues in Taipei by the **Taiwan Provincial Symphony Orchestra** and the **Taipei Municipal Symphony Orchestra**. Consult your hotel or information desk, or such organizations as the National Music Council and the Chinese Classical Music Association for information on scheduled performances. Traditional Chinese music has its roots in both special temple rituals

and folk music. Consider listening to temple music at the elaborate rituals held annually, on September 28, to celebrate the birthday of Confucius.

Handicrafts

If people were classified according to how good they are with their hands, you will definitely find the Taiwanese ranked among the top.

The Taiwanese take great pride in the things they can make with their hands: from lanterns and toys, handbags and baskets, bamboo and rattan crafts, rug and carpets, to knitwear and embroideries.

Their government shoved that pride one rung higher when it erected a four-story, air-conditioned building, housed within it a range of items that have undergone inspection for design and quality, named the building the **Handicraft Exhibition Hall** and opened it officially for public viewing in 1977. Exhibits number more than 1,500 and are from all parts of Taiwan, some produced by cottage industry, and others by regular factories. The Hall, in Tsaotun, is situated on the highway running from Taichung to the Sun Moon Lake and the Hsitou Bamboo Forest. Open daily except Mondays, national and public holidays from 9am to noon and from 2 to 5pm, the hall is well worth the visit.

While in Tsaotun, also call at the **Taiwan Provincial Handicraft Institute**, also operated by the Taiwan Provincial Government. Inside are a factory, kiln and research laboratory.

In Taipei, an excellent selection of local handicrafts are on display for sale at the **Chinese Handicraft Mart**, at #1 Hsu Chou St.. Tel: 321-7233. This is a good place to do souvenir and gift shopping.

Cinemas

It will surprise you that Taiwan residents view more films per year, per capita, than any other people in the world, including Americans. The average citizen of Taiwan sees about three full-length movies per week, and these include both local and foreign films. Taiwan is one of Hollywood's most lucrative markets, and all major Hollywood studios have permanent representatives here.

Most of the foreign films which come to Taiwan are from the United

States, and they are always shown in English, with Chinese subtitles. This means that traveling movie fans need not fear a shortage of Western film entertainment when in Taiwan. On the other hand, since almost all Chinese films are shown with English subtitles, you may also enjoy local gongfu fighting movies, especially if you have never seen one before.

The daily *China Post* and *China News* carry information regarding English films currently playing in Taipei. There are usually three to five performances per day, with the last show beginning around 9pm.

Nightlife

The visitor will find no lack of nightlife in Taipei. The capital city offers sophisticated discotheques, cosy pubs with darts, and a host of piano bars and music lounges for night owls, insomniacs and more...

Food and drink go together in Chinese society. A night on the town usually begins with a meal, not after it. The beer, wine and spirits are ordered along with dinner. And the liquid refreshment rarely stops flowing. "When drinking among intimate friends, even a thousand rounds are not enough", proclaims an ancient Chinese proverb. Again, many of the people of Taiwan take that advice to heart. Inebriation is a form of convivial communication here, an opportunity to drop the formal masks of business and reveal the "inner person".

Since the Chinese are food fanatics who appreciate good cuisine of all kinds, Taipei boasts also a range of Western restaurants, many operated by accomplished European chefs.

MTV and KTV

Besides discos and floor shows, there are other evening diversions. Mushrooming additions to the Taipei night scene are MTV and KTV. Although the name MTV was borrowed from the American cable entertainment show, its similarity ends there. MTV centers offer a wide selection of both Western and Asian movies on laserdisc and videotape. Customers first select a movie and are then assigned to a private room equipped with state-of-the-art monitors abd stereo systems.

KTVs are based on karaoke, long a

favorite form of entertainment in Japan. Now more popular than MTV, KTV venues are elegantly decorated and follow a variety of stylistic themes, from Versailles palaces to high-tech chrome-and-neon space stations. After selecting the appropriate room, customers can order fruit trays, mixed drinks, and snacks while paging through a catalog of traditional, pop, Western and Asian songs. Notepads and pens provided to jot down the desired selections, which are then keyed in via a small terminal in the room. Songs can be selected anytime and are queued in line.

Pubs, bars and wine houses

Taipei abounds with pubs and bars. One of the easiest places to go bar-hopping is the Sugar Daddy Row area around Shuang Cheng Street, near the President Hotel and with lots of establishments within easy walking distance of one another.

One of the quintessential forms of post-dinner activity for groups of Chinese men is the wine house or *jiou-jia*, occasionally referred to by foreigners as "girlie restaurants". Most serve food and expect guests to order several dishes, but the main meal is usually taken elsewhere and guests begin flocking to the wine house about 9pm. The wine house specialties usually include a variety of "potency foods" like Snake Soup, Turtle Stew, Sauteed Eel or Black-fleshed Chicken. All are ballyhooed as aphrodisiacs.

At least four persons should participate in a wine house party and at least one should be a Chinese man who is familiar with the routine. Without enough guests, the party cannot reach that vital stage of excitement which the Chinese call *reh-nau*, literally "hot and noisy". A Chinese-speaking guest helps translate the nuances of the conversation and activity.

A popular method of downing liquor other than toasting is a kind of "rock, paper, scissors" finger game, in which the loser must drain his glass dry. Chinese men engage in this spirited contest in restaurants and pubs throughout Taiwan.

A guest who walks out of such a place sober is considered a cheat or a man with the "capacity of an ocean".

Festivals

General

In addition to ancient festivals such as the Lunar New Year and the Mid-Autumn Moon Festival, and national holidays such as Double-Ten and Dr Sun Yatsen's birthday, there are scores of other local Taiwanese festivals known as *paipai* (pronounced *bye-bye*), which are colorful celebrations held in honor of local city gods and deities. There are over 100 popular city gods in Taiwan, and not only are their birthdays commemorated, each of their "death days" and "deification days" are also occasions for celebration. The sensible government therefore only recognizes the major ones and declares these official public holidays, during which most businesses and public offices are closed.

"Celebration" of *paipai* days begins with the faithful offering the best food and wine to the respective deities, and ends with the devotees themselves gorging the offerings, but not before they are sure that the deities have had their fill. This is usually the time taken for a joss-stick to burn out. Few Taiwanese remain entirely sober on these occasions, and everyone spends a lot of money to *ching-keh*, or "invite friends out". In recent years, the government has tried to dissuade the Taiwanese from indulging in such frequent and extravagant celebrations, branding the custom as wasteful, but the colorful *paipai* tradition is too deeply ingrained in the island's culture to be abandoned. Besides, the relatively well-off people of Taiwan can afford it.

National holidays, which are of more recent origin, follow the solar calendar used in the West, but most festive dates still follow the lunar calendar. Thus, they vary from year to year. Check exact dates at the time of planning for your trip.

January

Foundation Day: On January 1, 1912, Dr Sun Yatsen was inaugurated as the first President of the newly-founded Republic of China. Also on that day, China officially switched from the lunar to the Gregorian calender. This occasion is celebrated annually in Taipei with parades, dragon and lion dances, traditional music, patriotic speeches, and of course, lots of firecrackers.

Lunar New Year: Traditionally called the Spring Festival, the Lunar New Year remains the biggest celebration of the year in Taiwan, as it has for millennia in all Chinese and many Asian communities. The festival is observed in various stages for a full month, from the 16th day of the 12th month, although offices and shops generally close for only a week around the New Year's Day.

Many ancient customs are associated with the Lunar New Year. For example, all outstanding debts must be paid off before New Year's Eve; failure to do so is a grave affront and an omen of bad luck for the coming year. Many wealthy Chinese businessmen in Taiwan keep running accounts in their favorite restaurants and clubs, paying their bills only once a year, just before New Year's Eve. Another custom is exchanging gifts, especially little red envelopes (*hung-bao*) stuffed with "lucky money", the amount depending on the closeness of the relationship between the giver and taker. Everyone dresses up in new clothes at New Year – from hats down to shoes – and this symbolizes renewal and a fresh start in life for the coming year. People visit family and friends and spend a lot of money on entertainment. Indeed, local banks are often plagued with cash shortages at this time of the year. The dominant color is red, which is universally regarded as auspicious among the Chinese; red flowers, red clothing, red streamers, red cakes and candies, and the ubiquitous red envelopes appear everywhere.

At the stroke of midnight on New Year's Eve, the entire island suddenly reverberates to the staccato explosions of millions of firecrackers and skyrockets, as every temple and household in Taiwan lights the fuses which will frighten evil spirits from their thresholds, insuring an auspicious start to the New Year. The Chinese invented gunpowder for this very purpose over 1,000 years ago – long before the West ever knew of it – and the fusillades which mark the Chinese New Year make America's Fourth of July celebrations seem tame by comparison.

The stock phrase to offer all your friends and aquaintances whenever and wherever you encounter them during this period is *kung-hsi-fa-tsai* (pronounced *goong-shee-fah-tsai*), which means "I wish you happiness and prosperity". The witty rhyming retort to this greeting is *hung-bao-na-lai*, or "Hand over a red envelope!"

February

The Lantern Festival: This festival, which falls on the first full moon of the Lunar New Year, marks the end of the Spring Festival. Celebrants appear at night in the streets, parks and temples of Taiwan carrying colorful lanterns with auspicious phrases inscribed on them in elegant calligraphy. This tradition is supposed to insure against evil and illness in the coming year. The festival food associated with this event is a sweet dumpling of glutinous rice-paste stuffed with bean or date paste and called *yuan-hsiao*. Major temples are excellent places to observe the Lantern Festival in full color and pageantry. Prizes are awarded for the most beautiful and original lantern designs.

March

Birthday of Kuanyin, Goddess of Mercy: Kuanyin is one of the most popular Buddhist deities in Taiwan, Korea and Japan. Known for her compassion and love for people, she is one of Taiwan's patron protective deities. Her birthday is celebrated with colorful *paipai* ceremonies in major temples throughout Taiwan.

April

Youth Day: Originally called Revolutionary Martyrs' Day, Youth Day commemorates the deaths of 72 young revolutionaries in China in 1911.

Tomb-Sweeping Day: Traditionally calculated as the 105th day after the Winter Solstice and called the Chingming (Clear and Bright) Festival, Tomb-Sweeping Day in Taiwan is now celebrated annually on April 5, which coincides with the date of President Chiang Kaishek's death, in 1975. Therefore, April 5 is both a traditional Chinese festival and a contemporary national holiday in Taiwan.

During this festival, entire families go out to their ancestral burial grounds to sweep accumulated dirt and debris from the tombs, place fresh flowers around the graves, and perhaps plant some new trees, flowers and bushes in the area.

Buddha's Bathing Festival: This day commemorates the birth of Sakyamuni (the historical Buddha) 2,500 years ago. The festival is marked in temples throughout the island with cleansing-of-Buddha ceremonies, during which all statues of Buddha are ritually washed while monks recite appropriate sutras. Many of the icons are then paraded through the streets to the beat of gongs and drums.

Birthday of Matsu, Goddess of the Sea: One of the biggest *paipai* of the year in Taiwan, this festival is dedicated to Matsu, Goddess of the Sea, patron saint of Taiwan, and guardian deity of the island's fishermen. It is celebrated with great fanfare in over 300 temples where Matsu is enshrined. The biggest festival takes place in central Taiwan, at the Peikang temple near Chiayi. But you can also get an eye and ear full at the famous Lungshan (Dragon Mountain) Temple in downtown Taipei. Sacrificial offerings of roast pig and boiled chickens, billows of smoke from incense and burning paper money, undulating lion and dragon dances, colorful parades, and lavish feasting comprise some of the festivities dedicated to Matsu on her birthday.

May

Dragon Boat Festival: One of China's most ancient festivals, this event commemorates the death of Chu-Yuan, an accomplished poet and upright minister who plunged to his death in a river about 2,500 years ago to protest the corruption and misrule of his king, who had banished him from the court. According to the legend, upon hearing of his tragic death, the local people rowed their boats out on the river and dropped stuffed rice dumplings tightly wrapped in bamboo leaves into the water to supplicate and nourish his spirit, or to distract animals from eating him. These dumplings, called *dzung-dze*, remain this festival's major food item.

The Dragon Boat Festival is celebrated with colorful dragon-boat races, which in recent years have become a major sporting event in Taipei. Teams from all over the island, including several "foreigner teams" from the expatriate community, as well as teams from Singapore, compete for top honors in various divisions. The bows of the boats are carved into elaborate dragon-heads, and the crews row vigorously to the resounding beat of big drums placed at the back of each boat.

June

Birthday of Chenghuang, the City God: This *paipai* festival is celebrated with great pomp and ceremony at Taipei's city-god temple at 61 Tihua St, Sec. 1. The worship of city gods is a practice that has been recorded in China as far back as the early Xia dynasty (2200 BC), and remains one of Taiwan's liveliest celebrations. City gods are said to have the power to protect a city's inhabitants from both natural disasters and enemy intruders, and they also advice the Lord of Heaven and the King of Hell regarding appropriate rewards and punishments for the city's residents after death. No wonder the Chinese pay them such lavish homage!

Among this *paipai's* colorful and highly photogenic festivities are parades with icons of the City God held high upon pedestals, offerings of whole pigs and cows stretched on bamboo racks, processions of celebrants wearing stilts and colorful costumes, lion and dragon dances, lavish feasts, and much more.

July

Chinese Valentine's Day: Chinese Valentine's Day is derived from the legend of the herd boy and the spinning girl. The herd boy (a star formation in the constellation Aquila, west of the Milky Way) and the spinning girl (the star Vega in the constellation Lyra, east of the Milky Way) appear closest together in the sky on this night, and all the magpies on earth are said to ascend to the sky to form a bridge across the Milky Way so that the lovers may cross

over their brief once-a-year tryst. This is a festival for young unmarried girls and for young lovers, who observe the romantic occasion by exchanging gifts, strolling in moonlit parks, and praying in temples for future matrimonial bliss.

August

Ghost Festival: The Chinese believe that on the first day of the 7th lunar month, the gates of hell swing open, permitting the ghosts of deceased relatives to return to their earthly homes for a visit. In order to placate the spirits and discourage their mischief, trays of succulent foods are set out before each home as offering to them, and Buddhist priests are invited to every neighborhood and alley to bless these offerings and supplicate the spirits with prayer. Incense is burned and bundles of paper "clothing" and "money" are set alight for use by the spirits in the other world. These offerings are also meant to prevent the ghosts of criminals and spirits with no living relatives from entering one's home and causing trouble. It is not an auspicious time for marriage or commencing important new ventures. Rites are held daily in all Buddhist temples during the Ghost Festival, which formally ends on the last day of the 7th month, when the spirits return to their underworld abode and the gates slam shut for another year.

September

Confucius' Birthday: This is an official national holiday, celebrated as Teacher's Day, which commemorates the birth of the sage Confucius in 551 BC. Known as China's greatest teacher, Confucius continues to exert profound influence on culture and society in Taiwan. Elaborate traditional ceremonies are held every year on this day, at 6am at Taipei's Confucius Temple, complete with ancient musical instruments, formal court attire, ritual dances, and other Confucian rites as old as the sage himself.

Tickets to attend this ceremony must be arranged in advance through local tourism authorities.

October

Mid-Autumn Moon Festival: The Chinese believe that the harvest moon is the fullest, brightest moon of the year, and they celebrate its annual ap-

pearance by proceeding en masse to parks, hillsides, riverbanks and seashores to gaze at "The Lady in the Moon", nibble on tasty snacks, and drink wine. According to the Chinese legend, Chang-Er, beautiful wife of the Tang emperor Ming-Huang, one day discovered a vial of the Elixir of Immortality specially prepared for her husband and decided to take a sip. But he caught her in the act, and in order to conceal the evidence, she quickly swallowed the entire potion. It took effect instantly and with such intensity that she immediately flew up from earth and landed on the moon. She's been there ever since, and on this night her beauty radiates at her very best.

The festival is celebrated by exchanging gifts of moon cakes, which are large, round pastries stuffed with sweet-bean paste, mashed dates, chopped nuts, minced dried fruits, and other fillings. Exchanging moon cakes also has patriotic overtones, because during the successful overthrow of the Mongol Yuan dynasty by the Chinese Ming, secret plans for the insurrection were concealed in moon cakes and distributed to patriots throughout the empire prior to the uprising.

Double-Ten National Day: "Double-Ten" refers to the 10th day of the 10th month, and commemorates the overthrow of the Manchu Qing dynasty, China's last, by revolutionaries on October 10, 1911. It is by far the most important national holiday of the year in Taiwan, and it is celebrated with massive parades of military hardware and honor guards from all branches of the armed forces, aerial acrobatics by the air force's daring Thunder Tigers, commando-landing demonstrations, patriotic speeches by top government leaders, and displays of folk dancing, sword-fighting, martial arts, and other cultural activites. Most of the action takes place in the huge plaza in front of the Presidential Building, in Taipei.

Hotels and restaurants in Taipei remain packed full throughout the week prior to Double-Ten day, as tens and thousands of overseas Chinese from all over the world pour into town for the festivities. Tourists who visit Taiwan at this time should make early reservations for hotel and airline space.

Restoration Day: This national holiday celebrates the return of Taiwan to Chinese rule after the defeat of Japan in 1945, thereby ending 55 years of Japanese colonial occupation. It is marked with several major athletic events, including regional competition in soccer and basketball for the Presidential Cup awards. Other festivities include lion and dragon dances and bountiful feasting at Taipei's many restaurants and hotels.

Birthday of Chiang Kaishek: This is a national holiday celebrated in Taiwan to commemorate the birth of the late President Chiang Kaishek, in 1887.

November

Birthday of Dr Sun Yatsen: Sun Yatsen, founder and first president of the Republic of China, is regarded as the George Washington of China by Chinese throughout the world, including the Communist mainland. This holiday celebrates his birth in 1866 and is marked with solemn patriotic ceremonies and speeches.

December

Constitution Day: This is an official national holiday which marks the day in 1947 on which the constitution of the Republic of China became effective.

Leisure

Barber Shops & Asian Bath

The Chinese are a sensual people given to creature comforts, and two of the favorite comforts of some Chinese are to relax in the pampered luxury of barber shops and bath houses. In Taiwan, bathing and grooming – like eating and drinking – are regarded as far more than mere neccessities: they are approached as part of the grand art of living.

"Luxurious Tourist Barber Shops" abound throughout Taipei and are easily identified by braces of electrified barber-poles spinning madly by their neon-lit entrances. Stepping inside the automatic doors, you will be greeted by a bevy of young barbermaids clad in long gowns. They will guide you to an empty chair, refresh you with a hot handtowel, offer you hot tea and cigarettes, then proceed to groom you in a style you surely would like to become accustomed.

If you prefer to let your own barber do your hair-cutting and styling, then just go in for a shampoo, manicure and massage. Taipei barbermaids shampoo your hair like nobody else, combining a stimulating scalp massage with the shampoo. While she's blow-drying and combing your hair, you may call for a manicure, pedicure, or whatever other grooming you require. Finally comes the massage – a curiously refreshing finger-pressure massage which covers scalp, neck and spine and sends energy coursing through your nervous system. Those with the time and inclination may then stretch out in reclining position with a towel wrapped over their eyes and indulge in the great Chinese tradition of *hsiou-hsi* ("short rest"). Depending on which services from the girls you require and how long you stay, a visit to a "Luxurious Tourist Barber Shop" in Taipei will run between NT$500 to NT$5,000.

These barber shops cater exclusively to men, but women can get the same stimulating treatment at any Chinese beauty parlor, where shampoos, permanents, hair-styling, manicures and massages are performed in the same luxurious comfort. Almost all international tourist hotels in Taipei have both barber shops and beauty parlors, but these offer contemporary Western-style service and less Chinese flavor. You'll find "Tourist Barber Shops" in all the popular entertainment and shopping districts.

Bath houses and saunas are about as numerous in Taipei as cafes in the West. The Chinese are fanatics about bathing and personal hygiene, and they devote much time to it, often spending hours scrubbing, soaking and relaxing themselves in well-appointed bath houses. Facilities vary from place to place, but generally they include showers, hot and cold pools, whirlpools, saunas, professional massage, snack-bars, lockers and lounging areas. Many a multi-million-dollar deal in Taipei has been concluded in terry-cloth robes or lawyers soothing their weary bones in whirlpool-baths. It's a great way to relax, and it really gets the grit and grime of city air out of your hair and pores.

Remember that in an Asian bath house, you are always expected to thoroughly wash yourself with soap and water before stepping into any of the communal baths or whirlpools. Remember also that modesty is unnecessary, no matter what shape you're in, because the Chinese do not regard nakedness in a bath house as embarassing. Beyond that, simply plunge in and out of the hot and cold pools as the mood strikes you; bake yourself in the sauna; lose yourself in a swirling hot whirlpool; call for a massage and pedicure; relax in the lounge with a cool drink and magazine. A visit to a Taipei bath house will rejuvenate your body and spirit, all for only NT$500–1,500, depending on the services you request.

Almost all bath and saunas in Taipei have separate sections for men and women, and the facilities and services they provide are the same. A number of leading hotels in Taipei have their own sauna and bath facilities.

Language

Chinese is at once the most complex written language and the simplest spoken language in the world. This may sound like a contradiction to Westerners, who are accustomed to alphabetic writing systems based on spoken sounds, but the Chinese system of writing operates wholly independently of the spoken language, and you can learn one without any knowledge of the other.

The Written Language

Chinese writing is based on ideograms, or "idea-pictures", which graphically depict ideas and objects with written characters derived directly from actual diagrams of the subject.

The oldest recorded Chinese characters appeared on oracle bones excavated this century in China and dating from the ancient Shang dynasty (1766–1123 BC). At that time, questions of vital interest to the emperor were inscribed upon the dried shells of giant tortoises, which were then subjected to heat. The heat caused the shells to crack, and diviners then interpreted Heaven's answers to the emperor's questions by "reading" the cracks. The answers were then inscribed on the shells, and they were stored in the imperial archives. Based on the number and complexity of the characters inscribed on these oracle bones, Chinese historians concluded that Chinese written language was first invented during the reign of the Yellow Emperor, around 2700 BC.

The written characters reached their current stage of development about 2,000 years ago during the Han dynasty, and they have changed very little since then, which makes Chinese the oldest ongoing writing system in the world. The importance of China's unique written language cannot be overstated: it held together a vast and complex empire composed of many different ethnic groups, and due to its non-phonetic nature, it formed a written common denominator among China's various and sundry dialects. Once the symbols were learned, they gave the reader access to an enormous wealth of historical and literary writings accumulated in China over five millennia of continuous cultural development. Unlike Egyptian hieroglyphics, for example, which died with the Pharoahs, thereby cutting off subsequent Egyptian generations from their own roots, the Chinese written language evolved continuously from generation to generation, transmitting with it the accumulated treasures of Chinese culture right down to the present era. Small wonder that ancient traditions are so deeply ingrained in the Chinese mind. For example, the simple act of writing one's own surname in Chinese immediately recalls and identifies one with a host of historical and literary heroes, spanning five millennia, who shared the same name.

There are about 50,000 Chinese characters listed in Chinese dictionaries, but the vast majority are either obsolete or used in the highly specialized branches of learning. Three thousand characters are required for basic literacy, such as reading newspapers and business documents, and about 5,000 are required for advanced literary studies. About 2,000 Chinese characters are still used in the written languages of Korea and Japan. Few scholars, however, are capable of using over 6,000 characters without resorting to dictionaries.

The Spoken Language

There are only several hundred vocal sounds in the Chinese spoken language, which means that many written characters must share the same pronunciation. To somewhat clarify matters, the Chinese developed a tonal system which uses four distinctive tones to pronounce each syllable. Even so, many characters share both common syllables and tones, and the only way to be really sure which words are meant when spoken is to consider the entire context of a statement, or demand a written explanation.

Grammatically, spoken Chinese is so simple and direct that it makes other languages seem cumbersome, archaic, and unnecessarily complex by comparison. There are no conjugations, declensions, gender distinctions, tense changes, or other complicated grammatical rules to memorize. The spoken language consists of simple sounds strung together in simple sentence patterns, with the basic "subject/verb/object" construction common to most Western language. Tones, while foreign to Western tongues, come naturally with usage and are not difficult to master. Even within China, the various provinces give different tonal inflections to the various sounds. Proper word-order and correct context are all you need to know about the Chinese grammar.

In Taiwan, the Mandarin dialect (known as *guo-yu*, National Language) has been declared the official lingua franca by the government. Mandarin, which is based upon the pronunciations which prevailed in the old imperial capital of Peking, is by far the most melodious dialect of China.

In addition to Mandarin, there is a local dialect called "Taiwanese" derived from China's Fujian province, ancestral home of the vast majority of Taiwan's Chinese populace. Taiwanese is commonly spoken among locals, especially in the rural regions, and one of Taiwan's major television stations broadcasts programs in that dialect for their benefit. The older generation still speaks some Japanese – a remnant influence of Japan's colonial occupation – and younger people tend to understand at least some basic English. Though English is a required subject for all Chinese students in Taiwan throughout mid-dle and high school, it is spoken fluently by very few.

Getting Acquainted

The Place

Land Divisions: Land is defined from province to the block and street. In the city, land is bound by *si*, city; *ku*, ward; and *dong*, precinct. In rural areas, the land divisions are: *do*, province; *si*, city or large town; *up*, town; *kun*, district; *myon*, township; and *ri*, residential area. Other commonly used Korean words in addresses are *no*, *ro* or *lo* for road or street and *ka* for block.

Time Zones

International time differences are staggered as follows:

Korea	12pm today
Japan	12pm today
Hawaii	5pm yesterday
San Francisco	7pm yesterday
New York	10pm yesterday
London	3am today
Paris	4am today
Bonn	4am today
Bangkok	10am today

For the local time, call 116.

Climate

Korea's location in the mid-latitudes and East Asian Monsoon Belt means four distinct seasons with varying moods. A spring thaw comes in mid-April and lasts little more than two months. Early spring northwesterly gusts bring swirls of golden dust from the Gobi Desert and a light rain. As summer approaches, humid southerlies vie for control and the spring drizzle becomes an occasional downpour by summer (June–October).

July and August are the hottest, most humid months, especially in the inland basin around Taegu; the temperature there climbs into the range between the upper 20°C and lower 30°C (68–86°F). Autumn, by far the most splendid time to be in the country, comes in late October when the air currents shift back to the crisp northerlies. This climatic ideal intensifies by the end of November when the Siberian freeze whips down the peninsula for six months in a cycle of three consecutive cold days followed by four milder days.

The northern inland region of the peninsula has a winter temperature mean of minus 20°C or minus 4°F (Chungkangjin, north Korea, the peninsula's coldest spot, has a temperature mean in January of minus 20.8°C or minus 5.4°F) while the southern provinces, in contrast, winter in less severe temperature (Cheju-do's temperature mean for January is 4°C or 39°F).

The coldest months are January and February when the temperature drops to minus 12° to 1.5°C (10.4° to 34.7°F). The favorable months in Korea are April (10°C or 50°F in Seoul), May (16°C or 60°F), June and September just before and after the summer rains (19°C or 66°F) and in October (12°C or 54°F). You may call 735-0365 in Korea for more detailed information about the weather.

Culture and Customs

National Anthem

Aeguk Ka (Love of Country), the Korean national anthem, was written during the Japanese occupation (composer unknown) and set to music later by Ahn Eak Tai. The national anthem is played throughout the Republic every workday evening over the radio in Korean government offices and in main thoroughfares as the flag is lowered. Proper public protocol – silence and standing at attention – is requested.

The National Flag

The Korean flag, *t'aekuk ki*, was adopted as the national flag in August, 1882, not long after the "Hermit Kingdom" opened its front and back doors to foreign aggressive powers. Appropriately, the flag symbolizes the oriental *yin-yang* (in Korean, *um-yang*) philosophy of the balance and harmony in nature of opposite forces and elements which are in perpetual motion.

The colors of the flag are red, black, and blue against white. The red and blue circle in the center of the flag symbolizes the dualism of the universe. The upper red paisley represents *yang* nature: positive, masculine, active, constructive, light, heat, dignity, etc.; complemented by the lower blue paisley, *um* nature: negative, feminine, passive, destructive, dark, cold, hope, etc. The black trigrams in each corner are also of Chinese origin (from the Tao Te Ch'ing). They basically symbolize the four seasons and cardinal directions. In clockwise starting with the upper left corner, the three solid bars (*K'un*) represent heaven, spring, east and benevolence; the upper right bars (*Kam*): moon, winter, north, and wisdom; lower right bars (*K'on*): earth, summer, west, and righteousness; and lower left bars (*l*): sun, autumn, south, and etiquette.

Civil Defense Alert Drills

Held usually on the 15th of each month the 15-minute civil defense alert drill brings city traffic to a grinding halt. Everyone takes cover in buildings or underground arcades, temporarily abandoning their vehicles.

Korean Names

Korean surnames, most of which are but one syllable, are easy to learn as they are to forget. The problem is that many Koreans share the same romanized surname (although some of the Chinese characters may be written differently). Referring to someone by his surname can only become confusing and futile after meeting many Koreans. To compound the problem, Korean wives retain their maiden names (but they usually will make allowances for foreigners who mistakenly call them by their husband's name). Thus, it is ideal to learn the entire Korean name.

Korean surnames were derived from the Chinese during the early Three Kingdoms period. The most common surnames in order of the most numerous are Kim, Yi (Lee I, Rhee), and Pak (Park), followed by Choi, Chung, and Cho. Throughout the ages, surnames have dictated one's social position, a tradition still honored only in reclusive villages. Whether *yangban* (aristocrat) or *pyongmin* (commoner), however, one's name was recorded in a family tree book, *chokbo*, which traced one's lineage back to the origin of the clan. The *chokbo* is a kind of heirloom still updated and passed on these days.

Given names are usually two syllables and of Chinese origin. Either the first or second character is predetermined and is related to the "theory of the five elements". It is given to all family members of the same generation. The other character is freely selected.

Tojang (House Seals)

Seals, engraved by professional artisans, are as important as personal signatures, especially on legal documents. It, too, was originally a borrowed custom from China, initially a status symbol used by royalty. During the Three Kingdoms period (57 BC–AD 918), a dethroned king had to symbolically transfer power by handing over his imperial seals.

Seals today are more popular than ever as they are used by government offices, companies, and organizations, and for personal flourishes on stationery. The seals are carved of ivory, stone, marble, plastic, wood, smokey topaz, jade, and other materials. The ink is made of sticky scarlet vegetable dye which is permanent.

Planning The Trip

What To Bring

Electricity

The 100 volt current is sufficient and safe for 110 volt electrical devices. It is slowly being converted to 220 volt power.

What To Wear

Influenced by climate and occasion, clothing in Korea follows function rather than style. Business suits are the proper mode, even in the summer, for metropolitan business activities. Otherwise, dress is casual. Mini-skirts and shorts are acceptable, although foreigners are advised to dress more conservatively. An umbrella, sunglasses, and rainy day footwear are practical accessories to pack.

Entry Regulations
Visas & Passports

Visitors to Korea must present a valid passport or travel document, and may stay for 15 days without a visa if they have confirmed out-bound tickets. Most European, and many Asian and South American countries have agreements that permit citizens to stay for longer without a visa. Canadian citizens can stay for 6 months. For more information, consult your local Korean embassy before making travel plans.

Customs

You may bring in 200 cigarettes, 50 cigars, 250 grams of pipe and 100 grams of powdered tobacco, two bottles of liquor and two ounces of perfume. Items for personal use (except certain exclusive goods such as vehicles, guns and musical instruments) may be brought in duty free, but visitors must leave with these items. Literature and items deemed "subversive" or "detrimental to public interest" are prohibited.

Korean antiques dating earlier than 1910 should be checked and appraised by the Arts and Antiques Assessment Office and a permit should be secured. For five or fewer antiques, checking may be done at its Kimp'o Airport office (Tel: 662-0106). A limit of three kilograms of red ginseng with a sales receipt is acceptable.

If you have any other questions regarding customs or immigration, you may call Seoul Immigration Office, Tel: 650-6232, or Kimp'o Customs Office, Tel: 660-5114. There is a 8,000 *won* airport tax.

Health

Except for those whose itineraries include cholera-infected areas, no certificate of vaccination is required.

Currency

Won comes in 1,000, 5,000 and 10,000 denomination notes and 10, 50, 100, and 500 *won* coins. Bank drafts for large amounts (normally drafts of w100,000) are available.

Changing Money

Procuring *won*, Korean currency, outside Korea is virtually impossible. In the country, however, there are foreign exchange counters at the airport, major tourist hotels (which charge a few *won* per exchanged bill or traveler's check), major banks (some with branches in large hotels) and a few major department stores (e.g. Midopa and Lotte) in Seoul. The most viable currencies to carry in Korea are Japanese yen and American dollars. Other foreign currencies are difficult to exchange. Remember to retain all exchange receipts for reconversion on departure. Up to $500 may be reconverted without a receipt.

Credit Cards

American Express, VISA, MasterCard, and Diners Club cards are readily accepted most everywhere.

Banking

Banking hours are 9.30am to 4.30pm Monday through Friday, 9.30am to 1.30pm on Saturdays. You may contact any of the following banks for further information.
Bank of Korea, Tel: 759-4114.
Bank of Seoul, Tel: 771-6000.
Citibank, Tel: 731-1114.
Citizens National Bank, Tel: 771-4000.
Choheung Bank, Tel: 733-2000.
Commercial Bank, Tel: 775-0050.
Export-Import Bank of Korea, Tel: 784-1021.
Hanil Bank, Tel: 771-2000.
Korea Development Bank, Tel: 733-2121.
Korea Exchange Bank, Tel: 729-0114.
Korea First Bank, Tel: 733-0070.
Bank of America, Tel: 729-4500.
Bank of Tokyo, Tel: 752-0111.
Banque Nationale de Paris, Tel: 753-2594.

Chase Manhattan Bank, N.A., Tel: 758-5283.
First National Bank of Chicago, Tel: 316-9700.
Fuji Bank, Tel: 755-1281.
Mitsubishi Bank, Tel: 397-7511.
Sanwa Bank, Tel: 752-7321.
Standard Chartered Bank, Tel: 750 6114.

Public Holidays

January 1, New Year's Day: The first three days of January are recognized by the government as the beginning of a new year according to the lunar calendar. It is celebrated by exchanging greetings, worshipping at family ancestral shrines and eating rice cake soup.
March 1, Samiljol (Independence Day): Observance of the March 1, 1919 independence movement against colonial Japanese rule which features an annual reading of the Korean Proclamation of Independence at Pagoda Park in Seoul.
April 5, Arbor Day: Attention is given to Korea's reforestation program.
Han-sik-il (Cold Food Day) (mid-April): On the 105th day of the lunar calendar, Koreans visit their ancestors' graves with offerings of fruit, rice cakes, meat, wine and other dishes. Traditionally, fires were not lit on this day for reasons long since forgotten.
May 5, Children's Day: This successor to a former "Boy's Day" was proclaimed a national holiday in 1975 to honor Korea's youth and to focus attention on the importance of the family institution in Korea. On this day, children are dolled up, usually in traditional clothes, and taken on holiday excursions to parks and children's centers.
Buddha's Birthday (Mid-May): This "Feast of the Lanterns" day is celebrated on the 8th day of the 4th lunar month in honor of the birth of Buddha. Buddha's Birthday was also designated a national holiday in 1975. It is colorfully commemorated with temple rituals and parades throughout predominantly Buddhist Korea.
June 6, Memorial Day: On this solemn holiday, the nation remembers and honors war heroes. Memorial services are conducted throughout the nation, but perhaps the biggest tribute is paid at the National Cemetery in Seoul.
July 17, Constitution Day: A legal national holiday to commemorate the proclamation of the Constitution of the Republic of Korea on July 17, 1948. Patriotic gatherings are held in town squares and other such public places throughout the country.
August 15, Liberation Day: A national holiday commemorating Japanese acceptance of Allied surrender terms in 1945 and thereby releasing Korea from some 36 years of Japanese colonial domination. This day also marks the formal proclamation of the Republic of Korea in 1948. This is a day of speeches, parades and other such activities by Korean patriots.
Ch'usok (September or October): Ch'usok – which occurs on the 15th day of the 8th lunar month – is the Korean counterpart to America's Thanksgiving. On this day, people visit family tombs and make food offerings to their ancestors. Traditional Korean costumes color every street in a festive and classical way.
October 3, National Foundation Day: Also called Tan'gun Day, this national holiday recalls the day in mythical times when Tan'gun, the legendary son of a bear-woman, was born and became Korea's first human king. Tan'gun's reign is said to have begun in 2333 BC, continuing till 1122 BC.
December 25, Christmas Day: Because of a large Christian community, Christmas is observed as a national holiday in Korea in about the same way as it is observed in most Occidental countries.

Getting There

By Air

Kimp'o International Airport, 24 km (15 miles) west of Seoul, receives more than 500 flights weekly from most world destinations. It is served from the United States by Korean Air (Korea's national flag carrier), Japan Airlines, United Airlines, and Northwest Airlines among others. Carriers routed through Seoul include Cathay Pacific, China Airlines, Malaysian Airline System and Singapore Airlines.

Seoul can often be added as a stopover on north-east Asia air tickets at no extra cost. It is less than 13 hours from the US West Coast, 2.5 hours from Tokyo, 3.5 hours from Hong Kong, and 1.5 hours from Beijing.

You can call Kimp'o Airport Information, (02) 660-2200, or any of the airlines in Seoul below:

Air Canada, Tel: (02) 779-5654.
Air France, Tel: (02) 773-3151.
Air India, Tel: (02) 778-0064.
Air New Zealand, Tel: (02) 779-1671.
Alitalia Airlines, Tel: (02) 779-1676.
All Nippon Airways, Tel: (02) 752-5500.
Asiana Airlines, Tel: (02) 774-4000.
British Airways, Tel: (02) 774-5511.
Cathay Pacific, Tel: (02) 773-0321.
China Airlines, Tel: (02) 755-1523.
Continental, Tel: (02) 773-0100.
Delta Airlines, Tel: (02) 754-1921.
Garuda Indonesia, Tel: (02) 773-2092.
Japan Airlines, Tel: (02) 757-1711.
Japan Air System, Tel: (02) 752-9090.
KLM Royal Dutch Airlines, Tel: (02) 755-7040.
Korean Air, Tel: (02) 756-2000.
Lufthansa German Airlines, Tel: (02) 538-8141.
Malaysia Airlines, Tel: (02) 777-7761.
Northwest Airlines, Tel: (02) 734-7800.
Philippine Airlines, Tel: (02) 774-3581.
Qantas Airways, Tel: (02) 777-6871.
Singapore Airlines, Tel: (02) 755-1226.
Swissair, Tel: (02) 757-8901.
Thai Airways International, Tel: (02) 754-9960.
United Airlines, Tel: (02) 757-1691.
Vietnam Airlines, Tel: (02) 775-7666.

By Sea

The overnight *Pukwan* and *Kampu* ferries linking Pusan to Shimonoseki, Japan, depart from both ports at 6pm every day and arrive at 8.30am. First and second class "western style" berths are available on this 952-passenger ferry. The adaptable traveller, however, may want to try the economy Japanese-style "suite" – a communal cabin with a mat-padded floor (blankets and straw pillows are provided). Tickets range from US$65 to US$110 with discounts for round trip passengers, and students and children under 12. For more information contact: the Osaka office (06) 345-2245, Shimonoseki (0832) 24-3000, Seoul (02) 738-0055, Pusan (051) 464-2700.

The *Kukjae Ferry* connects Kobe and Osaka and Pusan. Contact Osaka (06) 266-1111, Pusan (051) 463-7000 or Seoul (02) 754-7786. Also, the *Fukuoka International Ferry* goes from Okinawa to Fukuoka to Yosu. Contact Fukuoka (092) 272-5151, Seoul (02) 776-4927 or Yosu (0662) 629-689.

A speedier way to cross the water

from Japan is by jetfoil linking Nagasaki and Cheju-do.

If approaching Korea from China, you can take the Weidong Ferry from Qingdao and Weihai in Shandong Province, to Inchon, the port west of Seoul. It leaves Weihai on Wednesday and Friday and returns Tuesday and Thursday. The Qingdao-Inchon ferry leaves every Saturday and returns Monday. For tickets call Seoul (02) 711-8230.

Practical Tips

Emergencies
Loss of Belongings
To recover lost possession, including those left in taxis, contact the nearest police box or ask the hotel front desk clerk to help you do so. Call the Seoul police Lost and Found Center at 298-1282.

Medical Services
Many kinds of medicines and health care goods – from bottled sweetened vitamin tonics to contraceptives – are available at local pharmacies. Many drugs are imported. Except for the sales of narcotics and barbiturates, there is little government control over these business, and drugs are sometimes diluted or mixed, repackaged, and then sold. Placebos are not unheard of. Hospital pharmacies are more reliable drug outlets.

If immunizations are needed, they are administered at the International Clinic at Severance Hospital which uses disposable needles for preventive measures, and at the Seoul Quarantine Office to the right of the USO compound in Kalwol-dong, Yongsan-gu.

Dentists and optometrists are generally reliable and their work is reasonably priced.

Major hotels have house doctors. For medical attention in hospitals, below are some of their phone numbers.
Cheil Hospital, Tel: 274-1231.
Ewha Women's University Hospital, Tel: 760-5114.
Hanyang Hospital, Tel: 290-8114.

Korea University Hospital, Tel: 920-5114/6114.
Kyunghee University Hospital, Tel: 958-8114.
National Medical Center, Tel: 265-9131.
Seoul Adventist Hospital, Tel: 244-0191.
Seoul Red Cross Hospital, Tel: 737-4581.
Seoul National University Hospital, Tel: 760-2114.
Severance Hospital (International Clinic), Tel: 361-5114.
Chungang Hospital (International Clinic), Tel: 224-3114.

OTHER EMERGENCY NUMBERS
Police: 112
Fire: 119
Ambulance: 119

Business Hours
Banks: Weekdays: 9.30am–4.30pm; Saturdays: 9.30am–1.30pm; Sunday & Public Holidays: Closed.
Embassies: Weekdays: 9am–5pm Saturdays, Sundays & Public Holidays: Closed.
Department Stores: Weekdays & Saturdays: 10.30am–8pm; Sundays & Public Holidays: *10.30am–8pm.
Private Companies: Weekdays: **9am–6pm; Saturdays: **9am–1pm; Sundays & Public Holidays: Closed.
Government Offices: Weekdays: 9am–6pm; Saturdays: 9am–1pm; Sundays & Public Holidays: Closed.
Post Offices: Weekdays: 9am–6pm; Saturdays: 9am–1pm; Sundays & Public Holidays: Closed.

* Closed once a week on a weekday.
** Private Companies tend to start earlier and close later.

Tipping
This western custom is expected only in businesses which cater primarily to westerners. A 10–15 percent service charge is automatically added to major hotel room and restaurant tabs (read the bill to make sure before tipping). Airport baggage porters are tipped generously at the exit door according to a set standard. Taxi drivers do not expect a tip unless they perform extra service. And unless requested for, they may not return the change if it is

small. Bellhops usually receive around w150 tip per bag.

Media
Newspapers & Magazines
There are 10 national dailies, five economic dailies and three sports dailies, plus two English newspapers. The two English-language papers, *The Korea Herald* (Tel: 756-7711) and *The Korea Times* (Tel: 732-4161), use international wire services and are available at news-stands and bookstores except during the New Year holidays (January 1st to the 3rd), and on special national holidays. The Pacific edition of *Stars and Stripes*, a US military newspaper, is sold at US military installations and areas nearby, and to subscribers in Seoul. *The Asian Wall Street Journal* and *The Far Eastern Economic Review* are also circulated locally.

Weeklies, semi-weeklies, bi-weeklies, monthlies and bi-monthlies flood the bookstores. The popular English language periodicals are the Korea Economic weekly and the monthly Korea Economic Report. *Time* and *Newsweek* are prominently displayed in bookstores. (Other foreign publications are available at diplomatic mission libraries.) Among the distinguished local periodicals with a readership of over 30,000 are *Wolgan Chosun*, and *Shin Dong-a*. For advice on cultural material call the Royal Asiatic Society at 763-9483.

Radio & Television
In the winter of 1980, Korean radio broadcasting was consolidated into three broadcasting stations: Korean Broadcasting Systems (KBS), a government-owned station; Munhwa Broadcasting Company, owned by a semi-government foundation; and the Christian Broadcasting System, which was established by religious sponsors in 1945. US Armed Forces Korea Network (AFKN) offers English programs with news every hour on the hour, 24 hours a day, to its military community.

Television broadcasting in Korea began in 1956 with a privately-owned, commercial station which burned down three years later. On December 31, 1961, the government established its own network, the Korea Broadcasting Service (KBS-TV). Presently, there are three major Korean networks: KBS-TV,

KBS2-TV and MBC-TV (Munhwa Broadcasting Company). A fourth network, AFKN-TV (American Forces Korean Network), caters essentially to the US military community and to others peripherally. Broadcasting hours vary from station to station (shorter on weekdays, longer on weekends). Daily program schedules are listed in the English-language papers.

If you have any queries as to the media, you may call the Seoul Foreign Correspondents Club at 734-3275.

Postal Services

The first modern post office was opened in 1884 in Seoul on An'guk Street to the right of the Chogyesa Buddhist temple. It was burned during a political riot soon after opening, but was reconstructed into a Communications Memorial Center in 1969. On display are old telegram sheets designed in 1904, a map showing the layout of telephone subscribers in Inch'on in 1900, official seals, records, documents and other relics. In addition, a collection of stamps – dating from the first issues – is also displayed. All these stamps, from the T'aekuk-design stamp in 1884 to the 1978 dedication of the Sejong Cultural Center, present the commemoration of some key historical events in the country. Commemorative stamps are sold here, as well as at regular post offices and in up'yo (stamp) shops around town. The memorial is open business hours weekdays and until noon on Saturday.

The contemporary central post office, however, is located on Chungmu Street across from the Chinese Embassy, a block east of Shinsegye Department Store. The Kwanghwamun post office branch is located near the corner of T'aep'yong-no and Chong-no. General post office hours are 9am to 6pm Monday to Saturday.

Aerograms cost w500 and postcards w370. A 10-gram airmail letter to Europe, North America and Middle East is w440, and to Hong Kong or Japan, w370. Letters to the US and Europe take 5–7 days. You may make further enquiries at the Central Post Office (Tel: 752-0007), Kwanghwa-mun Post Office (Tel: 732-0007) or International Post Office (Tel: 777-0020).

Telecoms

Local Calls: Public pay phones take four w10 coins per intra-city call. The call automatically disconnects after three minutes. Inter-city and overseas calls cannot be placed from these phones.

Domestic Long-distance Calls: To place a direct dial inter-city call, use the following prefixes before the desired phone number:

Anyang	0343
Ch'olwon	0353
Ch'ongju	0441
Ch'unch'on	0361
Cheju City	064
Chonju	0652
Inch'on	032
Iri	0653
Kanghwa-Si	0349
Kangnung	0391
Kumi	0546
Kuri	0346
Kwangju	062
Kyongju	0561
Masan	0551
Mokp'o	0631
P'ohang	0562
Pusan	051
Seoul	02
Sogwip'o	0642
Songnam	0342
Suwon	0331
Taegu	053
Taejon	042
Uijongbu	0351
Ulsan	0522

Overseas Calls: Overseas calls can be dialed direct from major hotels by dialing the international access code (001) plus a country code and the number. To call from private lines, you must dial the operator and calls are placed immediately. To book a call dial 0077 and if you have further enquiries on international calls, you may dial 0074 for International Call Information. General information is given at 114.

Telegrams

Telegrams can be written and sent at any telephone office. They may also be sent by phone: dial 115 for domestic telegrams and 0075 for international. Charges for domestic telegrams are w500 for the first 20 syllables and w80 for each extra 5 syllables. If sent in English, telegrams cost w80 a word. For express service the rate is doubled. International rates per word are: North America: w240, Europe: w450, Japan, Taiwan: w240, Hong Kong: w270 and the Philippines: w310.

Tourist Information

A wide range of tour information and related services are readily available at the Tourist Information Center (TIC) of the Korean National Tourism Corporation (CPO Box 903, Seoul. Tel: 02-729-9600). It is equipped with an information desk, reservation and ticketing desk, tourism exhibition hall, book and souvenir shop and a small theater. It is open daily from 9am to 6pm.

There are also information counters at Kimp'o, Kimhae, and Cheju International Airports. They provide you with city maps, brochures and useful information on tours, shopping, dining and accommodations.

Seoul: Kim'po Airport Information Counter, Tel: (02) 665-0088.

Pusan: Kimhae Airport Information Counter , Tel: (051) 98-1100.

Cheju: Cheju Airport Information Counter, Tel: (064) 42-0032.

Other information centers in Seoul are: (prefix 02)

Head Office: Tourist Information Center (TIC), Tel: 729-9600.

City Hall, Tel: 735-8688.

Kimp'o Airport, Tel: 665-0088.

Seoul Railway Station, Tel: 392-7811.

Seoul Express Bus Terminal, Tel: 537-9198.

Chongno Center, Tel: 272-0348.

Myongdong Center, Tel: 757-0088.

Itaewon Center, Tel: 794-2490.

Alternatively, you can enquire at the **Korea Tourist Association,** Tel: (02) 556-2356.

Useful Telephone Numbers

The telephone numbers of some noted organizations are:

American Chamber of Commerce, Tel: 752-3061.

Japanese Chamber of Commerce, Tel: 755-6672.

Korea Red Cross, Tel: 755-9301.

Korea Trade Promotion Corporation, Tel: 551-4181.

Korean UNESCO, Tel: 568-5115.

Lions International, Tel: 734-5111.

Seoul JAYCEES, Tel: 244-6015.
Seoul Rotary Club, Tel: 266-1860.
YMCA, Tel: 730-9391.
YWCA, Tel: 779-7561.

Getting Around

From The Airport

The airport bus has three lines which run every 10 minutes. Follow the signs at the airport to the stop in front of the terminal. No. 600 runs through downtown to the Walker Hill Hotel, No. 600-1 runs through downtown to Tongdaemun, and No. 601 runs south of the river to the Olympic Sports Complex. Tickets cost w800 and the trip can take between 45 and 90 minutes depending on the time of day.

The two Korean carriers run limousine bus services from the airport: Korean Air has four routes and charges w4,000; Asiana has one route and charges w3,000. For route information check with the ticket desks. You can call the Korean Air desk at 660-7940.

City bus #41 runs every five minutes from the airport to Midop'a Department Store in downtown Seoul. It cost w350 and the pick-up point is at the bus terminal, located next to the airport parking lot. However, for the traveler with a lot of baggage, the city bus is not recommended.

Korean Air also runs several limousine buses.

Domestic Travel

By Air

Two airlines, Korean Air and Asiana Airlines conduct all domestic air travel within Korea. Daily flights from Seoul to Cheju-do (65 minutes), Pusan (60 minutes), and Kwangju (50 minutes) are available on both domestic carriers. Flights from Seoul to Taegu (40 minutes), Yosu (60 minutes), Sokch'o (40 minutes), Chinju (60 minutes), and Ulsan (50 minutes), are available only on Korean Air. Tickets are available at major hotels and tourist and travel

agencies. Security at the airport is tight; passengers and baggage are checked and umbrellas, cameras, knives, and certain other articles are withheld during the flight. Tourist passports are necessary.

By Sea

Numerous ferries and fishing boats make regular connections between the coasts and the outlying islands. The schedules change frequently and boats will cancel trips at any time if the weather gets bad. Travel arrangements should be made with travel agents and time should be allowed for last minute changes if you travel during the monsoon season.

Several routes on the south coast in the Hallyo Waterway may be traveled either by ferry or by hydrofoil. Although the hydrofoil is faster, it is small and cramped. If time allows, the ferry is by far the more pleasant mode of transportation and it allows the passengers to take in some scenery. There's not much of a view from the hydrofoil and those prone to seasickness should definitely avoid it. You may call any of the following ferry terminals for further details.

Pusan, Tel: (051) 466-0518 international, (051) 469-0116 domestic.
Cheju, Tel: (064) 57-0117.
Kunsan, Tel: (0654) 42-0115.
Inch'on, Tel: (032) 884-4247.
Masan, Tel: (0551) 45-0116.
Mokp'o, Tel: (0631) 43-0116.
P'ohang, Tel: (0562) 44-3118.
Yosu, Tel: (0662) 63-0116.

By Rail

The introduction of the locomotive to Korea was not without political motives. Several foreign powers, including Russia, Japan, France, and the United States, bid hard for the contract, which was eventually awarded to an American, James R. Morse. Soon after initiating construction, Morse, beset with financial difficulties, was forced to pass the project to the Japanese. The Korean government directed Japan to complete the line in the standard gauge system Morse used rather than import arrow gauge rails in from Japan. The first railroad, which linked Seoul to Inch'on, was opened in September 1899. Other major lines were laid by the Japanese, including lines originating in Mokp'o, Masan, and

Pusan to Seoul and to Sinuiju in North Korea, which linked with the Trans-Siberian Railway. At one time, a serious traveler could travel by train from Pusan to Paris. The railroad suffered considerable damage during various wars, but since 1953 the railway system in South Korea has been steadily modernized over the years to accommodate tourists comfortably.

Today four kinds of service are available in Korea's efficient and fast intercity train system: the *Bidulgi*, the slow train which stops at each station; the *Saemaul*, fast, comfortable and air-conditioned and which usually has a dining car; and the *Tongil* and the *Mugunhwa*, also comfortable, fast and air-conditioned and which may also have a dining car and sleeper facilities. For information, call:

Seoul	(02) 392-7811/5051
Pusan	(051) 463-7551
Taejon	(042) 26-7788
Taegu	(053) 955-7789
Kyongju	(0561) 43-8053

By Road

Inter-city Buses: Eight expressways cut across the farmlands and mountains of Korea: the Kyungjin (Seoul-Inch'on); Yongdong (Yongin-Kangnung); Tonghae (Kangnung-P'ohang); Kuma (Taegu-Masan); Kyongbu (Seoul-Pusan); Namhae (Masan-Kwangju); Honam (Kwangju-Taejon); and the '88 Olympic (Taegu-Kwangju) Expressways.

There are four kinds of inter-city buses: the *Udeung kosok*, which is the most comfortable and includes a public phone; the *Kosok* express bus, the *Chikhaeng* (first class local and direct route) and the *Wanhaeng* (round about with frequent stops). Because of the high rate of occupancy, it is advisable to buy bus tickets in advance for a reserved seat. Listed below are eight main bus stations in Seoul and their more popular destinations (check Seoul map for locations):

Kangnam Bus Terminal: Located across the Han River in Banpo-dong; provides the only express bus service to cities out of Seoul. Tel: 591-3402, 535-4151.
Tongbu Bus Terminal: In Majang-dong; several meters away from city bus #41 stop; service to Ch'unch'on, Sorak, Sokch'o, Yangyang, Yongmun-sa, Kangnung, Yoju, Chungju, Kwangju, Wonju, and Andong. Tel: 279-4160.

Nambu Bus Terminal: In south Yongsan along the main road; service to Kanghwa-do, Kosam, Taech'on Beach, Puyo, Kongju, Chonju, Songni-san, Ch'ongju, Taejon. Tel: 521-8550.

Sinchon Bus Terminal: Service to Kanghwa-do: 6am–8pm; trip takes 1 hour 15 minutes. Tel: 324-0611.

Dong Sooul Bus Terminal: Located beside Kangbyon Subway station on the Han River; services to east and south of Seoul. Tel: 458-4851.

Sangbong Bus Terminal: Located in Sangbong-dong and covers northern region, including Uijongbu and Tongduchon. Tel: 435-2122.

Seoul Sobu Bus Terminal: In Pulang-dong (northern Sodaemun-gu); service to Haengju-sansong, Uijongbu. Tel: 356-3517.

Public Transport

The majority of people living in Seoul depend on public transportation. Previous government statistics show that 70 percent of the traffic was handled by 8,725 city buses; 11 percent by subway; and 7 percent by 64,475 taxis. Now "radio call" taxis and privately chauffeured cars are common.

Three transportation alternatives to and from downtown Seoul are: the airport bus mentioned above (w800), regular city buses (w350), and taxis.

City Buses

During less hectic commuting hours, getting around on the local city bus can be interesting, quick and cheap. The driver usually turns up his radio so all may listen to the local baseball game, a melodrama, or to the latest rock'n roll or classical hits. Confucian ethics generally prevail on board the bus: students offer their seats to mothers toting babies and to grandfolks, and out of mutual consideration, those seated relieve those standing of their schoolbooks and shopping bags. Smoking is prohibited.

Buses run frequently from 5am to around 11.45pm daily. Tokens available at most stops cost w320. Fares paid in cash cost an extra 30 won payable upon entrance.

In addition to the regular city buses, there are express buses, which follow similar routes but with fewer stops and for a somewhat higher fare (w700). These are designed for commuter use and generally make few stops downtown.

A word of caution: beware of pickpockets on the bus and at crowded bus stops.

Destinations are written on the side of the bus in han'gul and on street signs at the bus stops. Route maps for the entire system are virtually non-existent and change so frequently that it is impossible to keep track. The routes are mapped out on a panel inside the bus, but destinations are again written only in han'gul. The best way to get around the matter is to take the subway, and with directions from a hotel concierge or a business partner, it is possible to brave the crowds. Two rules of thumb: when the bus comes, run to where it stops and leap on; at the other end, get to the exit before the bus stops and jump off just as fast.

Taxis

Taxis are lined in front of the customs exit door ready to whisk passengers off to any destination.

By far the most expedient public transport, taxis are everywhere – weaving in and out of city traffic and darting along rural roads. Fare for regular cabs begins at w1,000 for the first 2 kilometers (1.24 miles) and w100 for each additional 279 meters. The meter also runs on time when movement is slower than 15 kilometers per hour and w100 is charged for every 67 seconds in addition to the basic fare. The special black taxis are more expensive: w3,000 for the first two kilometers and w200 for each additional 400 meters. You may call for these taxi services in Seoul at (02) 414-0150/2. Another higher class of taxi in Korea is "Hotel Taxi" which is found near major hotels. Call (02) 333-1238 for this service.

Cabs may be hailed to curbside and shared with other passengers bound in the same direction. Each passenger pays only for the distance he travels (two or more traveling as one party pay as one passenger). This taxi-sharing system is called hapsong.

After midnight, passengers are expected to pay a 20 percent surcharge on taxi fares. The driver should have a chart available listing officially calculated surcharge totals. Long-distance rides can be bargained for. Few drivers understand English, so try to have your destination written in han'gul before entering the cab.

US military ID holders may also use Army-Air Force Exchange taxis, which charge slightly higher rates in dollars.

Kiamaster pick-up trucks transport bulky baggage and packages at metered and negotiated rates.

Subway

The subway costing w350 anywhere in the city is also heavily used and it is the most convenient form of public transportation for visitors. Korea's subway system opened in August 1974, covers 131.6 km with four lines and hooks up with the Korean National Railroad. From Seoul Railway Station, it goes to six major destinations: Chongnyang-ni Train Station and Songbuk district to the north, and, to Inch'on (39 km west), Suwon (41.5 km south), Chamsil and Kuro. Trains run from 5am to midnight at three minute intervals during rush hours, and six minute intervals at other times. Smoking is prohibited in the cars. Following are points of interest within walking distance of each subway stop within the city walls:

City Hall (T'aepyong-no): City Hall, Toksu Place, British Embassy, major hotels, banks, department stores, Seoul Tourist Information Center.

Chonggak (Chong-no): Posin-gak (city bell tower), bookstores (with foreign language sections), Korean National Tourism Corporation, Ch'ogye-sa (Buddhist Temple), Communications Memorial Center, Seoul Immigration Office, Kyongbok Palace, National Museum, Folk Museum, Embassies of USA, Japan, and Canada, Sejong Cultural Center, Yi Sun-sin statue at Kwanghwa-mun Intersection.

Chong-no 3-ka: Pagoda Park and shopping arcade, Chongmyo (Royal Confucian Shrine), Insa-dong (Mary's Alley antique shops, art galleries, etc).

Chong-no 5-ka: East Gate marketplace, herb shops.

Tongdae-mun: Tongdae-mun (East Gate), Seoul Baseball Stadium.

Private Transport

Car Rentals

Foreigners are advised to avoid driving in Korea. The accident rate is one of the highest in the world and, in a legal dispute, foreigners tend to come off worse unless accompanied or supported by a local.

However, for the brave there are car rental firms. They will need to see your passport to prove you are over 21 and an international drivng license to show you have over one year's driving experience.

The cost of hiring a car ranges from w35,500 a day for a small Tico to around 200,000 a day for a Grandeur 3.5. Rental firms include: VIP (a joint venture with Avis) at Seoul tel: (02) 839-0015, Kumho, a joint venture with Hertz at (02) 798-1515 and Daehan at (02) 585-0801. For other companies available in Seoul and other provinces, call the Korea Car Rental Union at (02) 533-2503.

Where To Stay

Hotels

For all the comforts, conveniences, and privacy of home, nothing beats western-style hotels which range in standard and price.

Seoul (Prefix 02)

SUPER DELUXE

Hilton International, 395 Namdaemunno 5-ga, Chung-ku, Tel: 753-7788, Fax: 754-2510.

Grand Hyatt, 747-7 Hannam-dong, Yongsan-ku, Tel: 797-1234, Fax: 798-6953.

Inter-Continental, 159-8 Samsung-dong, Kangnam-ku, Tel: 555-5656, Fax: 559-7990.

Lotte, 1 Sogong-dong, Chung-ku, Tel: 771-1000, Fax: 752-3758.

Lotte World, 40-1 Chamsil-dong, Songp'a-ku, Tel: 419-7000, Fax: 417-3655.

Plaza, 23 Taep'yongro 2-ga, Chung-ku, Tel: 771-2200, Fax: 756-3610.

Ritz Carlton, 602 Yeoksam-dong, Kangnam-ku, Tel: 3451-8000, Fax: 556-8855.

Seoul Renaissance, 676 Yeoksam-dong, Kangnam-ku, Tel: 555-0501, Fax: 553-8118.

Sheraton Walker Hill, Kwangjang-dong, Songdong-ku, Tel: 453-0121, Fax: 452-6867.

Shilla, 202 Changch'ung-dong 2-ga, Chung-ku, Tel: 233-3131, Fax: 233-5073.

Swiss Grand, 201-1 Hongeun-dong, Seodaemun-ku, Tel: 356-5656, Fax: 356-7799.

Westin Chosun, 87-1 Sogong-dong, Chung-ku, Tel: 771-0500, Fax: 752-1443.

DELUXE

Capital, 22-76 Itaewon-dong, Yongsan-ku, Tel: 792-1122, Fax: 796-0918.

Garden, 169-1 Tohwa-dong, Map'o-ku, Tel: 717-9441, Fax: 715-9411.

King Sejong, 61-3 Chungmuro 2-ga, Chung-ku, Tel: 753-6000, Fax: 776-4009.

Koreana, 61-1 Taepyongro 1-ga, Chung-ku, Tel: 730-9911, Fax: 734-0665.

Nam Seoul, 615-21 Yeoksam-dong, Kangnam-ku, Tel: 552-7111, Fax: 556-8855.

New World, 112-5 Samsong-dong, Kangnam-ku, Tel: 557-0111, Fax: 557-0141.

Novotel, 603 Yeoksam-dong, Kangnam-ku, Tel: 567-1101, Fax: 564-4573.

Palace, 63-1 Banp'o-dong, Soch'o-ku, Tel: 532-5000, Fax: 532-0399.

President, 188-3 Uljiro1-ga , Chung-ku, Tel: 753-3131, Fax: 752-7417.

Ramada Olympia, 108-2 P'yongch'ang-dong, Chongro-ku, Tel: 396-6600, Fax: 396-6633.

Riverside, 6-1 Chamwon-dong, Soch'o-ku, Tel: 543-1001, Fax: 543-5310.

Riviera, 53-7 Ch'ongdam-dong, Kangnam-ku, Tel: 541-3111, Fax: 546-6111.

Royal, 6 Myong-dong 1-ga, Chung-ku, Tel: 756-1112, Fax: 756-1119.

Sofitel Ambassador, 186-54 Changch'ung-dong 2-ga , Chung-ku, Tel: 275-1101, Fax: 272-0773.

Tower, 5-5 San Changch'ung-dong 2-ga, Chung-ku, Tel: 236-2121, Fax: 235-0276.

FIRST CLASS

Crown, 34-69 Itaewon-dong, Yongsan-ku, Tel: 797-4111, Fax: 796-1010.

Hamilton, 119-25 Itaewon-dong, Yongsan-ku, Tel: 794-0171, Fax: 796-7884.

Mammoth, 620-69 Chonnung-dong, Tongdaemun-ku, Tel: 962-5611, Fax: 960-3335.

Manhattan, 13-3 Yoido-dong, Yongdungpo-ku, Tel: 780-8001, Fax: 784-2332.

New Kukje, 29-2 Taep'yongro 1-ga, Chung-ku, Tel: 732-0161, Fax: 732-1774.

New Seoul, 29-1 Taep'yongro 1-ga, Chung-ku, Tel: 735-9071, Fax: 735-6212.

New Star, 24 Sokchun dong, Songp'a ku, Tel: 420-0100, Fax: 412-1932.

Pacific, 31-1 Namsan-dong 2-ga, Chung-ku, Tel: 777-7811, Fax: 755-5582.

Seokyo, 354-5 Seokyo-dong, Mapo-ku, Tel: 333-7771, Fax: 333-3388.

Pusan (Prefix 051)

SUPER DELUXE

Hyatt Regency Pusan, 1405-16 Chung-dong, Haeundae-ku, Tel: 743-1234, Fax: 743-1250.

Paradise Beach, 1408-5 Chung-dong, Haeundae-ku, Tel: 742-2121, Fax: 742-2100.

Westin Chosun Beach, 737 Ui-dong, Haeundae-ku, Tel: 742-7411, Fax: 742-1313.

DELUXE

Commodore, 743-80 Yongju-dong, Chung-ku, Tel: 466-9101, Fax: 462-9101.

Sorabol, 37-1 Taech'ong-dong 1-ga, Chung-ku, Tel: 463-3511, Fax: 463-3510.

FIRST CLASS

Arirang, 1204-1 Choryang-dong, Tong-ku, Tel: 463-5001, Fax: 463-2800.

Empire, 398-14 Deochon 3-dong, Puk-ku, Tel: 337-8811, Fax: 337-8820.

Grand, 1413-6 Onch'on 3-dong, Tongnae-ku, Tel: 506-0093, Fax: 505-4283.

Kukje, 830-62 Pomil 2-dong, Tong-ku, Tel: 642-1330, Fax: 642-6595.

Mirabo, 1124-25 Yonsan-dong, Tongnae-ku, Tel: 866-7400, Fax: 866-8770.

Tongnae, 212 Onch'on-dong, Tongnae-ku, Tel: 555-1121, Fax: 555-6717.

Inchon (Prefix 032)

DELUXE

Songdo Beach, 812 Tongch'un-dong, Nam-ku, Tel: 865-1311, Fax: 865-1325.

FIRST CLASS

New Star, 29 Shinheung-dong 3-ga, Chung-ku, Tel: 883-9841, Fax: 882-8307.
Olympos, 3-2 Hang-dong 1-ga, Chung-ku, Tel: 762-5181, Fax: 763-5281.

SECOND CLASS

Bosung, 141-8 Juan-dong, Nam-ku, Tel: 433-2221, Fax: 433-2228.

THIRD CLASS

Paegun, 182-200 Shipchong-dong, Buk-ku, Tel: 529-4411, Fax: 529-4419.
Soobong, 618-2 Tohwa-dong, Nam-ku, Tel: 868-6611, Fax: 868-4333.

Chejo-Do (Prefix 064)

SUPER DELUXE

Cheju Grand, 263-15 Yon-dong, Cheju city, Tel: 47-5000, Fax: 42-3150.
Hyatt Regency, 3039-1 Saekdal-dong, Sogwip'o, Tel: 33-1234, Fax: 32-2039.
Shilla, 3039-3 Saekdal-dong, Sogwip'o, Tel: 38-4466, Fax: 38-3982.

DELUXE

Cheju KAL, 1691-9 2-do1-dong Cheju city, Tel: 53-6151, Fax: 52-4187.
Cheju Nam Seoul, 291-30 Yon-dong, Cheju city, Tel: 42-4111, Fax: 46-4111.
Lagonda, 159-1 Yongkam1-dong, Cheju city, Tel: 58-2500, Fax: 55-0027.
Oriental, 1197 3-do 2-dong, Cheju city, Tel: 52-8222, Fax: 52-9777.
Prince, 731-3 Sohong-dong, Sogwip'o, Tel: 32-9911, Fax: 32-9900.
Sogwipo KAL, 486-3 T'opyong-dong, Sogwip'o, Tel: 32-9851, Fax: 32-3190.

Inns

Yogwan: Korean guests might request *pori ch'a* (barley tea), *yo* and *ibul* (mattress and blanket, respectively), *pyogae* (pillow), *ondol* (heated floor), and inexpensive home-cooked Korean meals. Some inns prepare a communal hot bath. Prices range from w17,000 to w40,000.

Yoinsuk: The *yoinsuk*, another type of Korean inn, offers lodging in a private compound and isn't as consistently clean, convenient, nor as appealing as the *yogwan*. But the room rates are usually lower and accommodation is native all the way.

Boarding House (*Hasuk Chip*). The *hasuk chip* (boarding house) has its place among students, working bachelors, and itinerants. Rooms are rented by the month, usually to long-term residents. Rent includes very simple home-cooked meals.

Rented Rooms (*Setbang*). For the working foreigner, the *setbang* – a rented room in a local home – is yet another option. Except for the fact that he happens to share the same roof with others, the tenant is generally on his own.

Youth Hostels

A chain of youth hostels has been established in many of the provinces, and such facilities are open to international members. Membership is open at any of their branches. Some of the hostels, such as the Seoul Bando Youth Hostel and the Puyo Youth Hostel, are a combination hostel-hotel, with communal rooms as well as plush, private rooms and suites. Below is a list of youth hostels in Korea.

Eating Out

What To Eat

Barbecue Meat Restaurant (*Pul Koki Jip*). Beef (*so-koki*) and pork (*toechi-koki*) and short rib (*kal bi*) are marinated in soy sauce, sesame oil, garlic, green onions, and toasted sesame seeds, then char-broiled.

Raw Fish Restaurant (*Saengson Hoe Jip*). Fresh raw fish is served sliced with a soy sauce (*kan-chang*) or red pepper sauce (*cho-chang*). Other kinds of fish dishes such as *maeun t'ang* (hot pepper soup of fish, soybean curd, egg, and vegetables) are served.

Ginseng Chicken Dish Restaurant (*Samgyae T'ang Jip*). Chicken stuffed with rice, white ginseng, and dried oriental dates are steamed and served hot. Deep-fried chicken and other chicken dishes are also served.

Dumplings Restaurant (*Mandoo Jip*). Meat, vegetables, and sometimes soybean curd are stuffed into a dumpling

and steamed, fried or boiled in a broth. Chinese-style cookie pastries baked in the restaurant fill the display window.

Noodles Restaurant (*Poonsik Jip*). Noodle dishes are the specialty but so are easily prepared rice dishes. Some of the popular dishes are *Momil kooksoo* – buckwheat noodles served with a sweet radish sauce; *Naeng-myon* – cold potato flour or buckwheat flour noodles topped with sliced meat, vegetables, a boiled egg, and a pepper relish sauce and ice; *K'ong kooksoo* – wheat noodles in fresh soymilk; *Odaeng kooksoo* – wheat noodles topped with oriental fishcake in a broth; *Ramyon* – instant noodles in instant broth; *Udong* – long, wide wheat noodles with onions, fried soybean curd, red pepper powder, and egg; *Pipim-pap* – rice topped with parboiled fern bracken, bluebell root, soy-sprouts, spinach, and a sunny-side-up egg, accompanied with a bowl of broth; and *Chap Chae* – rice vermicelli stir-fried with vegetables and meat slices.

Steamed Rice Restaurant (*Paekpan Jip*). A bowl of rice is served with a variety of *kimch'i, namul* (parboiled vegetables), fish, and soup (usually made of soybean paste) – the basic Korean meal. Other simple dishes, such as *naengmyon* and *pipim-pap* are often on the menu. In the evening, the *paekpan jip* switches into a *makkolli jip* (see *Nightlife* section).

Dog Meat Soup (*Posin T'ang Jip*). *Posin-hada* means to build up one's strength. Thus, to the people, dog meat soup, *Posin t'ang*, is considered to be a delicacy. Other popular Korean dishes include: *Sinsullo* – chopped vegetables, meat, quail egg, fish balls, and gingko nuts in a brazier; *Sollong t'ang* – rice in a beef and bone stew; and *Pindaettok* – the Korean bean flour and egg pancake filled with different combinations of vegetables and meat.

Chinese Shantung restaurants are as popular as Korean restaurants. They are designated by a red or green door plaque draped with a red strip of cloth. Homemade wheat noodles with various sauces make for a slurpy meal. *Tchajangmyon* is a popular order consisting of pork, seafood, and vegetable tidbits stir-fried in a sweet-sour black bean sauce, and topped with a boiled egg.

Japanese restaurants complete with *sushi* (laver-covered rice rolls), _sashimi_ (raw fish), and _tempura_ (deep-fried batter-covered fish and vegetables) bars are scattered all over Seoul, and are even more common in the southern part of Pusan.

Drinking Notes

Water: Potable water is available in hotels. In establishments for locals, _bori ch'a_ (roasted barley boiled in water), distinguished by its light brown color, is served instead. Another popular water substitute is _sungnyung_, tea boiled from browned rice gathered from the bottom of a rice pot. It is also quite safe to drink water which spring from certain mountain sites at temples in the countryside. Unboiled tap water is never advised for drinking. Bottled water can be purchased for use in private residences from Diamond Water. The company will deliver the water, which costs w600 per 1.8 liters, to your doorstep on a regular basis (Tel: 335-5171).

Tearooms (_Tabang_): _Tabang_ (or _tasil_) is one of the most common signs in any Korean town. Koreans go to the _tabang_ for everything but tea (in fact, the tea is free) or coffee. It is where businessmen strike deals, where students practice English with "native speakers", where friends gather to gossip, joke, and listen to music, and where lovers tryst. It is also where the honk, grind and smoke of the city is rivaled – but nobody complains. A cup of thin coffee is but a token to hours of socializing. The _tabang_ has become a vital institution in contemporary Korean culture; a meeting hall outside the home and office for young and old, male and female. And with ten million souls in the capital alone, there is always room for one more tearoom to open above, below, or next to all the others. Unlike teahouses or coffeeshops elsewhere, the Korean _tabang_ provides a personal delivery service: a girl dressed in a uniform will deliver a hot cup of coffee in a scarf-wrapped thermos bottle to customers who call in orders and clearly indicate their whereabouts.

Attractions

Things To Do

Businessmen visiting Korea, like readers of economic journals around the world, know that Koreans are reputed to be among the most diligent workers on earth, logging endless hours to keep production at a peak, and to ensure the perpetual prosperity of the country's export-oriented economy.

Foreign residents too, both old-time and new, generally concur with this characterization, but also know that the "Land of the Morning Calm" harbors some of the world's most hearty and enthusiastic drinkers, who are often loath to abandon their watering holes before dawn.

These two stereotypes do seem to complement each other, since a people who work hard might naturally be expected to play hard as well, but there is yet a third side to the modern-day Korean – a passive but pleasing contrast to the other two, which is somewhat less well known to the outside world.

During the Yi Dynasty, a proper Confucian gentleman might have found calm and contentment in an after-dinner ritual with his pipe, filling its small brass bowl with Korean tobacco, and drawing slowly through the long bamboo stem to cool the soothing smoke. His descendants today can seek diversion in a variety of establishments offering all manner of indulgences and female companionship. These range from beer halls where the waitress might share a drink and squeeze one's hand, to secret salons where the whiskey flows freely and the customer's every wish is his hostess-cum-partner's command.

Somewhere between those ancient and modern extremes on the spectrum of hedonistic delights, there lie a number of common pleasures available, in startlingly similar forms, to contemporary Koreans ranging from day laborers to tycoons.

When a Korean has been working or playing (or both) with perhaps more zeal than wisdom, he is likely to seek refuge and relief through one of the few such simple pleasures which remain amid the excesses and inconstancies of urban industrialization. Depending on his whim, he might well choose a bathhouse or a barber shop, both of which abound in every urban setting, as well as in most sizable rural communities.

Barber & Massage

A haircut is so much more than cutting hair in a Korean barber shop (_ibalso_). One can easily spend an hour, and perhaps two, in laid-back languor as a crew of young ladies and gentlemen attend to nails, whiskers, face, ears, muscles, aches and – not to be forgotten – hair.

The actual clipping is mere prologue, a ritual of 10 minutes or so more aptly termed a "trim", lest the customer be tempted to wait too long before his next visit. A manicure is usually begun just about the time one's stockinged feet get comfortably settled on a cushion placed over the sink, and it inevitably lasts much longer than the haircut.

The sequence is not strictly prescribed, but those interested in a shave generally get one quite soon after the haircut. Young ladies traditionally perform this service, which is not always limited to the conventional heavier growths of whiskers; upper cheeks, noses, foreheads and even selected parts of the ear are all fair game for a well-trained and unrestrained Korean razor maid.

The next step is often a face massage (_massaji_ in Korean, after the Japanese rendering of the English). This can, with luck, encompass the scalp as well, along with those chronically understimulated muscles and vessels around the base of the skull. Between soothing applications of a hot towel, the young lady in charge might apply a plastic-like facial pack, peeled off later like congealed glue, or perhaps just a simple layer of cold cream. In either case, as the face is absorbing allied benefits, the lady will produce an ear spoon, preferably made of bamboo, and carefully begin to excavate hidden reserves of wax – unless the client recalls the old doctor's dictum that only one's elbows are to enter one's ears. When the delicate digging is done, each ear is given an unnerving twirl with a tool resembling a doll house duster – a tickling sensation comparable to hearing kittens' claws on a blackboard.

By this point, someone has no doubt already begun a body massage (anma in Korean, from two Chinese characters roughly meaning "press" and "rub"). This can coincide with other services, and can involve a number of people who come, go, and reappear, according to the needs of other customers. It is not uncommon to have three or four girls and fellows at work in a single curtained cubicle, each kneading a separate extremity. One of them is usually a young man equally well versed in Oriental finger pressure therapy and the orthopedic limitations of the human anatomy – although he occasionally loses his feel for the fine line between stimulation and pain.

Even as a joint effort, a body massage can last half an hour or longer. Ordinarily, it concludes with an extraordinary ritual. First one's wrists, then palms, and then fingers are firmly massaged. Next the young lady gives each finger a sharp, snapping tug, perhaps to realign the knuckles. Finally, she interlocks her fingers with the client's, bends his hand backward, and, while gently running her thumbnails across the taut palm, blows on it ever so softly, telegraphing tingling signals up well past the elbow.

After all this, it's time for a nap, presuming the customer has time. (If he doesn't, he should have postponed his visit until another day.) A towel placed over his eyes softens any harsh visual stimuli, and he is left to dreams and fantasies.

Later on, someone eventually has to mention the code word "shampoo", and the customer knows his respite is nearly over. Not only is the barber chair about to be raised abruptly to the upright position, but that foot-supporting cushion will also be removed from the sink. Within seconds, said groggy gent is roused from his delightful daydreams – not just sitting up, but bent over a basin, head soaked and soapy.

The end comes quickly. A brief towel fluffing is followed by the barber's final touch – the "turai" (dry) with a comb and hand-held blower – as the client receives a ritual offering: a cigarette and a shot of sweet yogurt drink. Then it's time to button up, straighten up, settle the tab (US$5 to $10) and bid a fond, but hardly final, farewell to tonsorial therapy.

Bathhouse (Mogyokt'ang)

Just as a visit to the barber shop involves more than a simple haircut, so a call at the bathhouse offers much more than a mere turn in the tub. For the seeker of a slightly more active treatment for weary bones, the bathhouse (mogyokt'ang) presents a moderate alternative to the passive pleasures of the barber's chair.

At the baths, one is free to set one's own schedule, regimen, timing and style. That last choice offers perhaps the widest variety of options, and the images conjured up by the behavior of an ordinary bathhouse's clientele might run the gamut – from scolded puppies to walruses in rut.

There is quite a range of bathhouse types as well, but all offer the same basic accoutrements, focusing on the same essential enjoyment of a steamy, soothing soak. As visitors to Japan may already know, the proper form is to bathe before entering the communal tub, and in Korea too, soap and dirt should be kept out of the bathwater.

One begins by soaping up, shampooing and rinsing down, either by dipping a basin at the edge of the main tub, or under a shower, if there is one. Next should come a leisurely soak in the central tub, where muscles can relax and pores dilate. Then, back on the curb-like lip ringing the tub, it's time to commence some serious scrubbing, again using a basin.

Westerners seem to cling to the illogical conviction that towels should be kept dry, although they only perform their rightful function by getting wet. In the mogyokt'ang, a handtowel is just the right size, doubling both as an ample washcloth and as a fig leaf substitute – for modesty's sake – as one moves around. Small red washcloths are available, too – very abrasive, but very popular for doing away with dead and dying skin and stubborn city grit. And for the patron who doesn't savor the strain of a vigorous scrub, attendants are usually on hand to rub, rub, rub with cloths until the customer's skin approaches the hue of that raspy red fabric.

A scrubbing session is by far the most apropos opportunity for a shave. Steam, suds and sweat combine to create the fleeting impression that there is no blade in the razor – an innocent illusion swiftly given the lie if one later slaps on a little aftershave.

All that accounts for the literal "mogyok" (bathing) in mogyokt'ang, but one is no more restricted to a mere bath in a bathhouse than to only a haircut in a barber shop. Time and the facilities at hand are the only limits, and none but the improvident take towel in hand with less than an hour or two to kill.

Nearly every ordinary bathhouse (taejungt'ang, or "masses' bath") offers, in addition to the central tub and showers, an extra-hot tub, a cold tank and, in many cases, a sauna dock as well. These present many alternatives to the basic cycle of bathe, soak, bathe.

The properly heated hot tank greets the bather with a sharp tingling sensation that is easily mistaken for pain, but which gradually mellows into simply stimulating heat. (If the tank is overheated, on the other hand, it turns out to be real pain.) The sauna is often so hot that it hurts to inhale quickly, and persons with abnormal blood pressure or heat sensitivity are advised to exercise appropriate caution.

Alternate visits to the sauna and hot tub, interspersed with breathtaking plunges into the cold tank, can give the pores a healthy workout. A few such rounds, however, can leave one a bit light-headed, not a little enervated, and frankly ready for a short nap. A well-planned bathhouse will have a mezzanine, where those with the time can stretch out and doze off.

The last step in the bathing area is usually a final rinse under the shower – hot or cold, or both. But that is hardly the end. There is more to enjoy out in the dressing room. After all that time in the baths, most patrons seem to feel it a bit abrupt simply to dress and leave. Smokers smoke; thinkers sit and think; trimmers trim (a nail clipper is usually available); and browsers read ads on the walls for products such as soap, ginseng nectar, and "Happiness" – a mysterious compound touted as an aid to a happy married life. Some people, of course, simply dry themselves at considerable leisure, perhaps in front of a fan, but better yet, while grabbing one last cat-nap. (That soggy handtowel, once wrung out, turns out to be quite up to the task.)

Gentlemen can get the same finishing touch they would in a barber shop, while on the ladies' side, bathers can relax one last time under a hair dryer. Eventually though, everyone has to leave. Korean bathhouses, incidentally, close around 8pm, hours earlier than the counterpart *ofuro* in Japan, but they open earlier as well, about 5 or 6am.

Culture

Korea's cultural history is vividly displayed in numerous museums (municipal and national) and cultural centers. Drama theaters and libraries present more contemporary perspectives. Listed below are the larger public and private museums and cultural centers. For a more definitive list, refer to the cultural map in the Korean Art feature section.

Museums

National Museum and National Folklore Museum. Located on the grounds of Kyongbok Palace, the National Museum houses excavated and national treasures. The National Folklore Museum just west of the National Museum renders articles and settings of traditional treasures: Palsang-jon (the five-story pagoda at Popju-sa), Hwaomsa and Kumsan-sa.

National Museum of Contemporary Art. A permanent collection of Korean modern art and special shows during the year are held in this museum at Seoul Grand Park.

Onyang Folk Museum. The largest and finest collection of Korean folk art is exhibited in Onyang, a pleasant country town southwest of Seoul. It is especially rich in crafts, but is limited in folk painting.

Puyo and Kongju National Museums. Museum collections include archaeological finds made in the vicinities of these two ancient Paekche (18 BC–AD 660) capitals. At the Kongju National Museum, treasures on display are from King Muryong's tomb, excavated in 1971. The tomb itself is a few miles away and is open to the public.

Kwangju National Museum. This two-storey museum in Chollapuk-do was recently built specially to house Yuan Dynasty bounty salvaged from a sunken 600-year-old Chinese ship discovered in west coast waters in 1976. Cholla-do treasures are displayed on the second floor.

Kyongju National Museum. Opened in 1975 on the site of an ancient Silla building, the Kyongju National Museum is located on the outskirts of Kyongju town. Silla dynasty articles, including the famous Emille Bell, the largest Buddhist temple bell in Korea (cast in AD 771), are on display. There is also a folk museum in the center of the town.

Ancient Tombs (*Tumuli*) Park, Kyongju. This cluster of 21 tombs built before the unification of Silla lies on the eastern fringe of the city. Excavation from 1973 to 1975 led to the discovery of King Mich'u's tomb (reign: AD 262–285) and the tomb with the mysterious "Flying Horse" painted on a saddle. Some of the original relics and some replicas (many originals are in the National Museum) are exhibited.

The Korean Folk Village. In Suwon, a complete traditional Korean village has been recreated for visitors to wander through and observe the folk customs and lifestyle. Food and drink are prepared and sold at profitable prices.

Emileh Museum. The world's largest collection of Korean folk painting is newly housed in Songni-san, near Popju Temple. The Emileh Museum is privately owned by Zo Zayong, author of several art and cultural books about Korea.

Sejong University Museum. Located in eastern Seoul near Children's Park, this museum is one of six folk museums in Korea. Over 3,000 articles, especially of traditional dress, ornaments, furniture, and art paintings are on display.

Concerts

Open Music Hall. Periodic Korean and western concerts are given here on the western slopes of Namsan near the Central National Library.

Sejong Cultural Center. Opened in 1978 near Kwanghwamun, the Sejong Cultural Center (81-3, Sejongno, chongno-gu. Tel: 02-399-1514), holds foreign and Korean classical and contemporary concerts and dramatic plays.

Theaters

Drama Center. The Drama Center (Tel: 02-778-0261) is off Namsan Street, at 8-19, Yejang-dong, Chung-gu. Everything from P'ansori to Shakespeare is performed. Check the newspapers for current performances.

Korea House. Situated on the slopes of Namsan off Toegyero. Korea House stages free folk dance performances at 3pm on Saturday and Sunday. Art displays decorate the rooms and Korea-related books are sold in their bookshop. A Korean restaurant overlooks an oriental garden. Tel: 266-9101.

National Classical Music Institute. Just past Tower Hotel on the slopes of Namsan is the school where many of the nation's finest classical musicians of different genres, including Royal Court musicians, practice and teach their art. Performances are given in the concert hall. Check the entertainment section of newspapers for engagements. Tel: 02-274-1151.

Space Center. Housed in an architectural artpiece near the Secret Garden of Ch'angdok Palace (219, Wonsodong, Chongno-gu), the Space Center (Tel: 02-763-0771) stages a variety of shows from classical *kayakum* (Korean zither) solos to Dixieland jazz to drama. The Center also publishes a cultural magazine called *Space*.

Other Modern Drama Theaters in Seoul:

Madang Cecil Theater, 3-7, Chong-dong, Chung-gu. Tel: (02) 737-8836.

Elcanto Art Theater, 50, Myong-dong 1-ga, Chung-gu. Tel: (02) 776-8035.

Mun Ye Theater, 130-47, Tongsung-dong, Chongno-gu. Tel: (02) 744-0686.

National Theater, San 14-67, Changch'ung-dong 2-ga, Chung-gu. Tel: (02) 274-1151.

Silhum Theater, 609-1, Shinsa-dong, Kangnam-ku. Tel: (02) 515-7661.

Libraries

Royal Asiatic Society (RAS). The RAS is the Korean chapter of an international British association. Its office is in the Christian Center Building (136-46 Yunjidong, Chongno-gu. Tel: 763-9483) near Chongno 5-ka. There you'll find most books written locally in English about Korea and a complete collection of their magazine, *Transactions*, which contains Korea-related articles that have been written by lecturing members since 1900. Visitors are welcome to sign up for tours conducted by the RAS and by an affiliate, the Korea Art Club.

Korean Research Center. The Korean Research Center is located in Socho-dong (Tel: 535-3130). The Center publishes cultural research articles in Korea with some translations in English but also provides a quiet library of old and recent Korea-related books written by foreign explorers, diplomats, and expatriates. Some current periodicals written in other languages are available. The Center is open weekdays from 9am to 5pm.

United States Information Service (USIS). USIS (Tel: 397-4114) offers a library for public viewing and study. Passport identification is needed. Art gallery hours are 8.30am to 5pm weekdays and library hours are 9.30am to 6pm weekdays.

UNESCO Library. Back issues of the *Korea Journal* and *The Courier*, as well as Korean cultural magazines are available, the latter in English, French, and Spanish. The Library is also stocked with other reference publications.

Ewha, Sogang, Yonsei, and other universities also invite foreigners to use their library.

Nightlife

There are at least five kinds of *sul jip* (liquor house).

Pubs

The common bar or pub is usually a small, simple cafe which serves liquor and beer. *Anju* (hors d'oevres) are served at an additional cost in most places. The cheapest liquor is *soju* (sweet potato wine).

Beer Halls

Beer (*maekchu*) comes either bottled (*pyong*) or as a draft (*saeng*). *Anju* are pricey but are nevertheless customarily ordered.

Cabarets

Often located in narrow alleyways in Mugyo-dong and Myong-dong in Seoul, cabarets are easy to notice because of the loud band music, neon signs and/or bow-tied doormen attempting to lure in passers-by. Dance hostesses inside do their part and expect a tip for their

efforts. Highballs and beer are served. Patronize these *jip* with caution or with a good Korean friend. Closing time is midnight. Salons are exclusive cabarets in a tidier setting (which customers pay for).

Gambling

Blackjack, anyone? Gambling is limited to Cheju-do plus one venue per province. There are **casinos** in five hotels where one can gamble at roulette, poker, bacarat, craps, dice, *tai-sai* and other games of chance. Casinos' business hours differ from hotel to hotel. Gaming parlors are located at the following places:

Sheraton Walker Hill Hotel (Seoul), San-21, Kwangjang-dong, Singdong-gu. Tel: (02) 453-0121/31.

Olympos Hotel (Inch'on), 3-2, Hang-dong 1-ga, Chung-gu. Tel: (032) 762-5181.

Paradise Beach Hotel (Pusan), 1408-5, Chung-dong, Haeundae-gu. Tel: (051) 742-2121.

Songnisan Hotel (Ch'ungch'ongpuk-do), 198, Sanae-ri, Naesonghi-myon, Poun-gun. Tel: (0433) 42-5281.

Cheju KAL Hotel (Cheju-do), 1691-9, 2-do, 1-dong, Cheju. Tel: (064) 53-6151.

Hyatt Regency Cheju, 3039-1 Saektal-dong, Sogwip'o. Tel: (064) 33-1234.

Shopping

What To Buy

Korea's unique arts and crafts and the towns which traditionally produce the best of particular products are:

Bamboo craft: Tamyang
Brassware: Ansong, Taegu
Hemp cloth: Hansan, Andong
Lacquerware: Wonju
Oriental paper: Chonju
Pottery: Ich'on
Porcelain: Ansong

Ruchecraft: Kanghwa City
Silk: Ch'unch'on, Kanghwa City

Seoul Shopping

Popular merchandise and where to shop for them in Seoul include:

Antiques: Ahyon-dong, Insa-dong, Chungang Sijang (Central market), It'aewon
Brassware: It'aewon
Boutique goods: Myong-dong, Idae-ap
Calligraphy paint brushes – Insa-dong, Kyonji-dong
Korean costumes: Tongdae-mun Sijang, and most other marketplaces
Korean cushions and blankets: Insa-dong, marketplaces
Korean herbal medicine: Chong-no 5-ka, Chong-no 6-ka
Name seals (custom-made name seals in stylistic characters carved of hard wood, stone): along the busy streets
Oriental paper: Insa-dong, Kyonji-dong
Silk Brocade: Tongdae-mun Sijang (2nd floor), Chong-no 2-ka, Myong-dong (K'o Silk Shop)
Custom-tailored men's suits: hotels, Myong-dong
Sweatsuits and athletic shoes and gear: It'aewon, Namdae-mun Sijang (across the Tokyu Hotel)
Topaz, "smokey topaz", amethyst, jade: underground arcades

UNDERGROUND ARCADES

Specialty shops can be found in underground shopping malls. Don't let the price tags intimidate you from bargaining. The larger more centrally located arcades are: Namdaemun Arcade, Myong-dong Arcade, Sogong Arcade, Hangram Arcade, Ulchi-ro Arcade, Lotte Center 1st Avenue Arcade, Arcade Bando-Chosun.

MARKETPLACES

Seoul marketplaces run on for blocks. Anyone who has anything to sell is out there – from the button merchant to the antique dealer to the rice cake *ajumoni*, including *chige* (A-frame) bicycle and Kiamaster delivery men and haggling shoppers. The distinguishing feature of Korean markets, however, is that shops with the same goods tend to group together, and even set up the shops the same way. Merchants say they are not hurt by competition caused by the close proximity; instead, the area becomes known for specializing in, say, second-hand books, sinks or antiques.

BOOKSTORES

Reading material in English or European languages are difficult to locate in Seoul but there are several places where titles can be regularly found. The major hotels have bookstores which carry periodicals although they are usually late in coming and are extremely expensive. For the latest issues (also at high prices), the most reliable bookstore is in the basement of the Kyobo Building which is near the American Embassy on Taepyong-ro 2-ga.

Used books and magazines can be found in Myong-dong just across from the Chinese Embassy. There are several small shops here overflowing with books and old magazines which are sold for much less than their original cost. You can also trade in your own used paperbacks or bargain for lower prices, particularly if you purchase several books at a time.

On the outskirts of It'aewon, about halfway toward the third tunnel through Namsan, there is another foreign bookstore which both buys and sells. The titles here are limited, however, especially adventure stories and war novels. The owner also drives a rather hard bargain.

Language

Survival Korean

Korean *han'gul* is romanized in two ways: by the Ministry of Education system and by the McCune-Reischauer system, an internationally recognized romanization scheme. Both romanizations are used in literature, maps, and signs, which can confuse those unacquainted with the language. Thus, learning the Korean alphabet, which is simple, would prove most beneficial, especially for the lone traveler.

Provided below are commonly used questions and statements romanized according to the McCune-Reischauer system. No matter what village, town or city in Korea you visit, you should be able to survive with the following common questions and statements. At least this simple lesson will lead you to a taxi, bus or train station, and then to food, shelter and a hot bath.

Numeral System

The following is a list of basic numbers and their Korean pronunciation:

1/*Il*
2/*Ee*
3/*Sam*
4/*Sa*
5/*O*
6/*Yuk*
7/*Ch'il*
8/*P'al*
9/*Ku*
10/*Ship*
11/*Ship-il*
20/*Ee-ship*
30/*Sam-ship*
40/*Sa-ship*
50/*O-ship*
60/*Yuk-ship*
70/*Ch'il-ship*
80/*P'al-ship*
90/*Ku-ship*
100/*Paek*
200/*Ee-paek*
300/*Sam-paek*
567/*O-paek yuk-ship ch'il*
1,000/*Ch'on*
2,000/*Ee-ch'on*
4,075/*Sa-ch'on ch'il-ship o*
10,000/*Man*
13,900/*Man Sam-ch'on ku-baek*

Useful Phrases

the airport/*konghang*
the subway/*cho-hach'ol*
the taxi/*taeksi*
Seoul train station/*Seoul yok*
express bus terminal/*Kosok t'ominal*
the ticket office/*p'yo p'a-nun kos-i*
entrance/*ipku*
exit/*ch'ulku*
the public bathhouse or private bathroom/*mogyokt'ang*
the restroom/*hwajang-sil*
the restaurant/*sik-tang, umsik-chom*
the tea or coffee house/*tabang*
the bank/*unbaeng*
the hotel/*hotel*
a good Korean inn/*cho-un yogwan*
the post office/*uch'e-guk*
the post box/*kyongch'al-so*
the embassy/*daesa-kwan*
the International.../*Kukche-Chonsin*-Telecommunication Office/ *chonhwakuk*

Useful Questions & Sentences

How many kilometers is it from here?/ *Yogi-so myot kilo im-nikka?*
How long does it take to go there?/ *Olmana kollimnikka?*
It takes 30 minutes/1 hour./*Samship-pun/han si-gan kollimnida.*
Please call a taxi for me./*Taeksi jom pullo ju-seyo.*
Just a moment, please./*Cham-kkan man kitari-seyo.*
Please go straight./*Ttok paro ka-seyo.*
Please stop here./*Sewo ju-seyo.*
What is this place called?/*Yogi-nun odi imnikka?*
Hello (to get the attention of a waiter, sales clerk, etc.)/*Yobo-seyo.*
I will have coffee (or) please give me some coffee./*K'op'i-rul chu-seyo.*
May I have more beer?/*Maekchu to ju-seyo.*
May I have the bill?/*Kaesanso-rul chu-seyo.*
Do you have amethyst? (see index-glossary for other items)/ *Chasujong iss-umnikka?*
Please show me another one./*Tarun kos-ul poyo ju-seyo.*
How much does it cost; what is the price?/*Olma imnikka?*
Can you give me a discount?/ *Tisukauntu rul hal-su iss-umnikka?*
It's too expensive./*Nomu pissamnida.*
Thank you./*Kamsa-hamnida.*
I will buy this./*Ee Kos-ul sa kess-umnida.*
Good-bye (said to somebody not departing)./*Annyong-hi ke-seyo.*
Good-bye (said to somebody who is also departing)./*Annyong-hi ka-seyo.*
Can you speak English?/*Yong-o halsu-issum-nikka?*
Do you understand me?/*Ee hae ha-seyo?*
Please bring me some.../*...chom katta ju-seyo.*
...beer/*maekchu...*
...cold drinking water/*naeng su...*
...hot water (for bathing)/*ttugo-un mul...*
...barley tea/*pori ch'a...*
...Korean food/*Han chong sik...*
Good morning/Good afternoon/Good evening./*Annyong ha-simnikka.*
Excuse me./*Sille-hamnida.*
I am sorry./*Mian-hamnida.*
You are welcome./*Ch'onman-eyo.*
Yes/*Ne.*
No/*Anio.*

Japan

Getting Acquainted

The Place

Japan is made up of four main islands, Honshu, Hokkaido, Kyoshu and Shikoku, and several thousand smaller ones that stretch nearly 3,000 km (1,900 miles) in the temperate and sub-tropical zones, between 20° and 45° latitude. The total land area is 377,435 sq. km (145,728 sq. miles), 85 percent of which is mountainous. The country is divided into four different climatic and cultural zones by mountain ranges: the Japan Sea and Pacific Ocean on the northeast half, and the Japan Sea and Inland Sea on the southwest half. The famed Mount Fuji, seen on clear days from many places in and around Tokyo, is the country's highest mountain at 3,776 meters (2.3 miles). The population of Japan is about 125 million.

Climate

"Japan has four seasons" is a phrase you will hear often, though it is still not clear why the Japanese feel that it is a feature unique to their country. The climate in Tokyo can be a bit of everything, and in recent years, the manifestation of the "four seasons" has not been all that clear, but generally in spring most of Japan is pleasant until May. In June begins the rainy season which should last about a month, but often longer. The summers are hot and sticky through to September. The typhoons usually come through in August and September. Fall begins in late September and lasts through mid-November and is cool and pleasant. The winter lasts from mid-November to the end of February or beginning of March.

The People

Population density: 326 persons per square kilometer
Life expectancy at birth: 76 male; 82 female

Life expectancy has been steadily rising for the last three decades, and the "greying" of Japan is becoming a major social concern. In 1985, only 10.3 percent of the population was 65 or older; in the year 2000 it is expected to reach 16.2 percent.

Retirement age for salaried employees, stable at 55 during most of the post-war era, is now gradually being raised to 60 by many major companies. Private and national pension plans are provided, covering 99 percent of the country's working population.

Government

Form: Parliamentary Democracy
Head of State: Emperor Akihito (born December 23, 1933, took office January 7, 1989)

While it is generally felt that the emperor's actual power is less than that of, say, the queen of England, his social, cultural and political influence is much stronger than intended by the allied powers who, during the occupation of Japan following World War II, "guided" the drafting of Japan's present constitution.

Although Article 1 of that document states the the "Emperor shall be the symbol of the State," and that he derives his position from the will of the people, the exact powers of the emperor are not specifically defined.
Prime Minister: (President of majority party in Lower House, currently – and since 1955 except 1993–1996 – the LDP)

Education

Japan's public education system is tax-funded (although many private schools exists). Compulsory for all children are 6 years junior high school (enrolment 100 percent); high school (3 years) is elective (enrolment over 00 percent nationwide, nearly 100 percent in urban areas); higher education at college/university (4 years) or trade schools is also elective (over 30 percent of all high school graduates go on to higher educational studies).

The school year begins in April; vacations include about 40 days in summer and around 10 days each for spring and New Years.

The three-year high school program is compressed to two in many of the best high schools to allow students to prepare for college entrance exams.

There are about 95 national, 34 public and 31 private 4-year universities/colleges in Japan. The quasi-national radio/TV network NHK runs the University of the Air that combines radio and TV and correspondence.
Literacy: 99 percent
Juku: These "after-school schools" are estimated to number about 200,000, earn ¥500 billion annually, and attract as many as 1.5 million elementary and 2 million high school students. In the main, they focus on preparing students for entrance exams.

Customs and Culture

At work and in most formal situations, the Japanese may seem a very reticent and reserved people, lacking in spontaneity or personality. There are books and theories explaining this behavior, but it only provides one side of the picture. Japanese (especially men) can become extremely raucous when drinking, and often let out their real opinions and feelings after a few drinks.

On the crowded trains you will find yourself being pushed and bumped around. You do not need to be polite here; just push along with everyone else. It is often said that "the Japanese are only polite with their shoes off," which means that they are polite and courteous with people they know well and would be indoors with (where shoes are almost always removed).

The Japanese distinguish between inside and outside the home. Inside the entrance to all homes (and some restaurants) is an area for removing shoes. You then step up into the living area, wearing slippers or in your stockinged feet. (Slippers are never worn on *tatami* mats, however.) Taking shoes off keeps the house clean, besides being more relaxing, and it also increases the amount of usable space, since you can sit on the floor without worrying about getting dirty. The toilet, however, is one area of the house that is considered "dirty," so separate slippers are provided there.

The custom of bowing has, in many cases, become somewhat a conditioned reflex. Foreigners, in general, are not expected to bow, and this is especially evident if a Japanese person first reaches out to shake hands.

As to punctuality and keeping appointments, the Japanese have a reputation for not being very punctual. At several of the famous "meeting places" you can observe people waiting, often for an hour or more, for someone. After several apologies and explanations, everything is usually forgotten and forgiven.

The way the Japanese usually speak and express themselves gives a very good picture of their culture. Direct statements of fact are most often avoided as this implies that the speaker has a superior knowledge, and this is considered impolite. Therefore, much "beating around the bush" is done which often leads to misunderstandings and seems like a waste of time to foreigners, but this must be taken into consideration when dealing with the Japanese.

When eating with Japanese, if you don't know what to do, just watch what the people around you are doing and do as they do. Below are a few helpful tips:

- Do not rest your chopsticks vertically in your rice, as this is associated with death.
- Do not pass food from chopstick to chopstick, as this is only done with the cremated bones of the dead at funeral services.
- When drinking beer or sake, one person will pour for the other, who will hold up his glass while it is being filled. Each person takes turns at pouring until enough is drunk and people will often begin to pour their own.

In any case, whatever happens, foreigners are usually forgiven for any breach of etiquette, so there's no need to spend time worrying about what is right and wrong. Japanese behavior in general is situational, and the Japanese themselves often do not know the right thing to do in any given situation. "It all depends on the situation," remarks the smart alec, but it's often fun for everyone involved when one of "us" makes a slip. Sometimes it actually does help to break the ice and put everyone in a more relaxed mood.

Planning The Trip

Getting There

The most practical way of entering Japan is by air and through one of its several international airports. **New Tokyo International Airport (Narita Airport)**, 60 km (37 mi) from Tokyo city center, is the busiest and one of the two main gateways to Japan. Flights on China Airlines are served by **Haneda Airport**, Tokyo's domestic airport located between Tokyo and Yokohama. Osaka's 24-hour, offshore **Kansai International Airport**, the other main gateway, serves routes plying the Americas, Europe and Asia. **Nagoya Airport** connects flights to and from various points in the Pacific and the Americas. Three airports on Kyushu – **Fukuoka**, **Kumamoto** and **Kagoshima** – serve those from cities in Europe, Korea and mainland Asia. Three major domestic airlines maintain air routes throughout Japan: Japan Air Lines (JAL), All Nippon Airways (ANA) and Japan Air Systems (JAS).

There is an airport tax for all passengers departing on international flights.

Entry Regulations
Visas and passports

A proper visa is necessary for foreigners living in Japan and engaged in business or study. Passengers with con-

firmed departure reservations can obtain a stopover pass for up to 72 hours.

Visitors from the following countries are not required to obtain a visa prior to arrival in Japan, provided they do not intend to stay for more than 90 days nor receive remuneration in Japan: Argentina, Bahamas, Bangladesh, Barbados, Belgium, Canada, Chile, Colombia, Costa Rica, Cyprus, Denmark, Dominican Republic, El Salvador, Finland, Greece, Guatemala, Holland, Honduras, Iceland, Israel, Italy, Lesotho, Luxembourg, Malaysia, Malta, Mauritius, Norway, Pakistan, Peru, Portugal, San Marino, Singapore, Spain, Surinam, Sweden, Tunisia, Turkey, Uruguay, USA.

Visitors from the following countries may reside in Japan for up to 6 months providing they are not earning an income: Austria, Germany, Ireland, Liechtenstein, Mexico, Switzerland and the United Kingdom.

Extension of Stay

Foreigners wishing to extend their stay in Japan must report, in person, to the Immigration Bureau within two weeks before their visa expiration. Present your passport, a statement with the reasons why you want an extension of stay, and documents certifying the reasons. The fee is ¥4,000.

Foreigners living in Japan must obtain a re-entry permit from the Immigration Bureau if they leave Japan and plan to return. Present, in person, your passport and certificate of alien registration (held by foreign residents in Japan) along with the appropriate re-entry form to the Immigration Office. The fee for a single re-entry is ¥3,000 and for a multiple re-entry ¥6,000.

Those wishing to transfer visas to new passports must report to the Immigration Bureau in Tokyo. Present both old and new passports and certificate of alien registration.

Immigration Information. Tel: (03) 3213-8523 or 3213-8527. Open Monday–Friday 9.30am–noon, 1–4pm. Answers to questions regarding immigration rules, regulations and restrictions. Languages: English, Chinese, Korean, Spanish, Portuguese, and Thai.
Tokyo Regional Immigration Bureau, 1st Otemachi Common Government Office 2nd Floor, 1-3-1 Otemachi, Chiyoda-ku, Tokyo. Tel: (03) 3213-

8523–8527. Open 9am–noon, 1–4pm. Closed on Saturday and Sunday.
Shibuya Immigration Office, 1-3-5 Jinnan, Shibuya-ku (just beyond "In the Room" dept. Store). Tel: (03) 5458-0370 or (03) 3286-5241. Open Monday–Friday 9am–noon, 1–5pm.
Hakozaki Immigration Branch Office, Tokyo City Air Terminal, 42-1 Nihombashihakozaki, Chuo-ku. Tel: (03) 3664-3046. Open 9am–noon, 1–5pm. Closed on Saturday and Sunday.
Yokohama Regional Immigration Bureau. Tel: (045) 681-6801.
Osaka Immigration Information, Tel: (06) 774-3409. Visa/Immigration Information in Osaka. Language: English, Chinese, Portuguese, Spanish. Open Monday–Friday 9.30am–12 noon, 1pm–4.30pm.
Automated Immigration Information, Tel: (03) 3213-8141. Usage: with a touch-tone phone, enter 1 for Japanese, 2 for English. Dial the code number for the information you want (about 800 available). The code list is available at immigration/ward offices.

Alien Registration

Foreigners planning to stay in Japan for more than three months are required to register at the ward office in their residing area. The application must be made in person within 90 days. The applicant must have his/her passport containing the proper visa and two photographs (3 cm x 4 cm).

If the alien registration card is lost or defaced, report to the ward office within 14 days. Take your passport and two new photographs and you will be issued a new one.

For visitors under 16 years of age, applications may be made by a parent or legal guardian by producing the applicant's passport. No photograph is necessary.

Ward office hours are from 8.45am–5pm. Monday through Friday, and 8.45am–12.30pm on Saturdays.
Tokyo Metropolitan Government, Tokyo Daisan Chosha, 3-5-1 Marunouchi, Chiyoda-ku, Tokyo, tel: (03) 3211-4433. English service is available on Monday and Thursday from 1–4pm.

Information regarding alien status and visas presented above is general and subject to change. For further information contact your appropriate embassy, consulate or the Japan Immigration Bureau.

Customs

Japan strictly bans the import and use of narcotic drugs, firearms and ammunition. If caught in possession of any of these, the offender will not face the death penalty, but can expect no leniency. Many a foreigner is still sitting in a Japanese prison, long forgotten by everyone but himself. Pornographic magazines and videos showing any pubic hair are technically forbidden in Japan.

This issue of films and magazines displaying pubic hair is a curious one. Photographs in *Playboy* magazine, for example, are literally sanded to obliterate pubic hair, but maybe only every other photo. Yet at convenience stores like 7-Eleven, teenage boys can buy magazines with very, very explicit photographs or *manga* illustrations. Likewise, films sometimes will have fuzzy flesh-colored spots or electronic mosaics floating over offending parts. Other films are shown untouched.

You can bring in any currency, personal ornaments and other valuables into Japan, but there is an official limit of ¥5 million that can be taken out.

You are also allowed to bring with you into Japan, free of tax, three 760 ml (25 fl oz) bottles of spirits, 400 cigarettes and 100 cigars or a total of 500 g of tobacco, and 2 fl oz (50 g) of perfume.

Health

In general, levels of hygiene are very high, and it is very unlikely that you will become ill as a result of eating or drinking something. The tap water, though heavily chlorinated, is potable. Most food is of a high standard. However, because the Japanese place so much emphasis on presentation and how food looks, there is wide use of chemical fertilizers in Japan, and therefore it is not recommended to eat the peels of fruits and some vegetables.

Toilets: Apart from major hotels and some train stations, most toilets in Japan are of the Asian squatting type, which takes some getting used to, but are supposed to be the most hygienic (no part of your body actually touches them) and physiologically best. In Tokyo and other major cities, they are slowly being replaced with Western-style toilets in many establishments.

By law, every coffee shop and restaurant etc. must have its own toilet, or access to one in the same building.

Electricity

The power supply is 100 volts AC. Eastern cities in Japan, including Tokyo, run on 50 cycles, while those in the west such as Kyoto, Osaka and Nagoya, use 60 cycles. Hotels have adaptors for shavers and hair dryers.

Currency

The unit of currency is the yen (indicated as ¥), and the coins are ¥1, ¥5, ¥10, ¥50, ¥100 and ¥500. Bills are ¥1,000, ¥5,000 and ¥10,000. Foreign currencies are accepted at a very limited number of hotels, restaurants and souvenir shops. You can buy yen at foreign exchange banks and other authorized money changers on presentation of your passport. At the international airport at Narita, the bank is open 24 hours.

Traveler's checks are useful only at banks and major hotels. Elsewhere, they are virtually worthless. Many banks in Japan will issue international traveler's checks.

Major credit cards, such as American Express, Diner's Club, MasterCard and Visa, are accepted at establishments in and around Tokyo and Osaka/Kyoto, and there is no surcharge for their use. Unfortunately, acceptance is sporadic. It is often quite difficult for a merchant to get approval for a purchase with a foreign-issued credit card. If they refuse your card, don't get testy. Carry lots of cash instead, just in case.

Banks

Despite the wide use of computers and on-line systems, Japanese banks are often slow and inefficient in many fields. Especially when transferring money in or out of the country, you can expect the process to take a long time and to be costly. Also, small neighborhood branches are often not able to process any international transactions. In order to send money out of the country, or cash foreign checks, you will find it much easier to go to a major branch, where someone will be able to speak English and usually understand what you want to do. The bank charges for remitting money out of the country are expensive.

Banks are open Monday to Friday between 9am and 3pm for normal banking. Cash dispensers are open from 9am to 6pm on weekdays, and 9am to 2pm on Saturdays. Most cash dispensers, however, cannot be used for cash advances on credit cards *not* issued by a Japanese bank. Even if there is a logo for Visa or MasterCard, almost always it is for a Japanese bank-issued card only.

Public Holidays

January 1 – Ganjitsu (New Year's Day)
January 15 – Seijin no Hi (Coming-of-Age Day)
February 11 – Kenkoku Kinen no Hi (National Foundation Day)
March 21 – Shumbun no Hi (Vernal Equinox Day)
April 29 – Midori no Hi (Greenery Day)
May 3 – Kempo Kinembi (Constitution Memorial Day)
May 4 – Kokumin no Kyujitsu (National Holiday)
May 5 – Kodomo no Hi (Children's Day)
September 15 – Keiro no Hi (Respect-for-the-Aged Day)
September 23 – Shubun no Hi (Autumnal Equinox Day)
October 10 – Taiiku no Hi (Sports Day)
November 3 – Bunka no Hi (Culture Day)
November 23 – Kinro Kansha no Hi (Labor Thanksgiving Day)
December 23 – Tenno Tanjobi (Emperor's Birthday)

If a holiday falls upon Sunday, the following Monday will be a 'substitute holiday'.

Special Facilities
Disabled

In general, Japan is not user-friendly for the disabled. Doors, elevators, toilets and just about everything else have not been designed for wheelchairs, nor are there any regulations regarding access for the disabled. It is a struggle for the disabled to get around Japan, but it can be done.

Forget about using a wheelchair in train or subway stations, much less trains, during rush hour, 7–9am and 5–7pm. The crowds are just too thick, and too rude.

To arrange assistance – in advance – at **Tokyo Station**, call the JR English InfoLine at (03) 3423-0111. They will make arrangements at Tokyo Station for you.

It is possible to reserve a special seat for wheelchairs on the *shinkansen*, or bullet train. Reservations can be made from one month to two days before departure. You must also reserve ahead to use the elevators for the shinkansen platforms.

In many stations, staff will help with escalators and elevators, although a wait of half an hour to an hour may be involved.

Useful Addresses
Tourist Offices

Tourists may write or contact any of the following offices of the Japan National Travel Organization for assistance:

JNTO OVERSEAS OFFICES

Australia: Level 33, The Chifley Tower, 2 Chifley Square, Sydney, NSW 2000. Tel: (02) 232-4522, fax: (02) 232-1494.
Brazil: Av. Paulista, 509-S/405, 01311-000 Sao Paulo, S.P. Tel: (011) 289-2931, fax: (011) 288-5738.
Canada: 165 University Ave, Toronto, Ont. M5H 3B8. Tel: (416) 366-7140, fax: (416) 366-4530, e-mail: jnto@inforamp.net
France: 4-8, rue Sainte-Anne, 75001 Paris. Tel: (01) 42-96-20-29, fax: (01) 40-20-92-79.
Germany: Kaiserstrasse 11, 60311 Frankfurt /M. Tel: (069) 20353, fax: (069) 284281, e-mail: info@jntofra.rhein-main.com
Hong Kong: Suite 3704-05, 37/F, Dorset House, Taikoo place, Quarry Bay. Tel: 2968-5688, fax: 2968-1722.
Korea: 10th fl., Press Center Bldg, 25 Taepyongno1-ga, Chung-gu, Seoul. Tel: (02) 732-7525, fax: (02) 732-7527.
Switzerland: 13 rue de Berne, 1201 Geneva. Tel: (022) 731-81-40, fax: (022) 738-13-14.
Thailand: 3/61, 13th fl., Wall Street Tower Bldg, Suriwong Road, Bangkok 10500. Tel: (02) 233-5108, fax: (02) 236-8356.
United Kingdom: Heathcoat House, 20 Savile Row, London W1X 1AE. Tel: (0171) 734-9638, fax: (0171) 734-4290, e-mail: jntolon@dircon.co.uk
United States

New York: One Rockefeller Plaza, Suite 1250, New York, NY 10111. Tel: (212) 757-5640, fax: (212) 307-6754, e-mail: jntonyc@interport.net.
Chicago: 401 North Michigan Ave., Suite 770, Chicago, IL 60611. Tel: (312) 222-0874, fax: (312) 222-0876, e-mail: jntochi@aol.com
San Francisco: 360 Post St, Suite 601, San Francisco,CA 94108. Tel: (415) 989-7140, fax: (415) 398-5461, e-mail: sfjnto@aol.com
Los Angeles: 624 South Grand Ave, Suite 1611, Los Angeles, CA 90017. Tel: (213) 623-1952, fax: (213) 623-6301, e-mail: hideki.tomioka@sit.com

DOMESTIC OFFICES OF JNTO

Head office: 10-1, Yurakucho 2-chome, Chiyoda-ku, Tokyo 100. If you have message or questions, please send e-mail to JNTO. Mail to: jnto@jnto.go.jp. It may take some time until you get the answer from JNTO.

Tourist Information Centers (TICs):
Tokyo TIC, Kotani Bldg, 6-6 Yurakucho 1-chome, Chiyoda-ku, Tokyo 100. Tel: (03) 3502-1461. Open from 9am to 5pm on weekdays, 9am to 12 noon Saturday, closed Sundays and national holidays.
Narita TIC, Airport Terminal Bldg, Narita, Chiba Pref. 282. tel: (0475) 32-8711.
Kyoto Office (TICs): 1st fl., Kyoto Tower Bldg, Higashi-Shiokojicho, Shimogyo-ku, Kyoto 600. Tel: (075) 371-5649. Open from 9am to 5pm weekdays, 9am to 12 noon Saturday, closed on Sunday and holidays.

Japan Travel-Phone is a nationwide toll-free service offering travel-related information and language assistance. It is operated by JNTO.

If within Tokyo or Kyoto, call the respective TIC offices. You will be connected to an English-speaking travel officer. Service is available daily between 9am and 5pm. All numbers are toll-free.
Eastern Japan: (0088) 22-2800 or (0120) 222-800.
Western Japan: (0088) 22-4800 or (0120) 444-800.

Practical Tips

Emergencies
Security and Crime
About 13 million crimes are reported a year, about one-eighth the number reported in the United States in the same year. Murders and violent assaults each average about 1.5 per 100,000 population. Although the crime rate has risen by 20 percent in Japan over the past decade, its growth is far lower, and the arrest/conviction rate remarkably higher, than in other industrialized nations.

Emergency Numbers
Police (crime and accidents): 110
Fire and ambulance: 119
Police, info in English: (03) 3501-0110

Japan Hotline, information and help about everything, in English, 10am–4pm weekdays, tel: (03) 3586-0110.
For **hospital information**, call (03) 5285-8181 in Tokyo (English, Chinese, Korean, Thai and Spanish spoken).

Loss of Belongings
Fortunately, the Japanese are quite honest about turning in found items. If you've lost a wallet packed with cash or a camera, or simply an overnight bag with dirty socks, chances are you will recover it.
JR trains: Items left on trains will usually be kept for a couple of days at the nearest station. After that, they are taken to one of the major stations to be stored for five more days. Inquiries can be made in Japanese to lost-and-found centers at Tokyo Station (03) 3231-1880, or Ueno Station (03) 3841-8069. In English, inquiries can be made with the JR East Infoline (03) 3423-0111 from 10am to 6pm weekdays.
Subways: Things left on Tokyo's Eidan trains are stored for three or four days at the station nearest to where the item was found, then taken to a lost-and-found center. In Japanese, call

the center at (03) 3834-5577, 9.30am–7pm weekdays, 9.30am–4pm Saturday. On the Toei trains, or on Tokyo city-operated buses inquire about lost property at terminals the same day, or call the lost-and-found center, in Japanese, at (03) 3815-7229, from 9am–6pm weekdays.
Taxis: All taxi companies in Tokyo report unclaimed items to a single center, the Tokyo Taxi Kindaika Center. Call (03) 3648-0300, in Japanese.
Police: At last resort, contact the police. The Tokyo Metropolitan Police Department maintains an immense – a *very* immense – lost-and-found center in Iidabashi, with everything from forgotten umbrellas (zillions of them) to bags full of cash. Call (03) 3814-4151, 8.30am–5.15pm weekdays. English sometimes, Japanese mostly.

Medical Services
Try to remember that you are in Japan, and must be prepared to adapt to the Japanese system. Although some doctors may speak English, the receptionist and nursing staff will not, so it is advisable to bring along a Japanese friend or someone else who can speak both languages. Most hospitals and clinics do not have appointment systems, so you have to be prepared to wait your turn, however frustrating that may be. Here is a list of hospitals and clinics in Tokyo where you would have no problem in being understood or treated. They all have different hours and systems.

HOSPITALS IN TOKYO
International Catholic Hospital (Seibo Byoin), 2-5-1 Nakaochiai, Shinjuku-ku. Tel: (03) 3951-1111. Open Monday–Saturday 8–11am. Closed Sunday and 3rd Saturday.
Red Cross Medical Center (Nisseki), 4-1-22 Hiroo, Shibuya-ku. Tel: (03) 3400-1311. Open Monday–Friday 8.30–11am; Saturday 8.30–10.30am. Closed Sunday.
St Luke's International Hospital (Seiroka Byoin), 10-1 Akashicho, Chuo-ku. Tel: (03) 3541-5151. Open Monday–Saturday 8.30–11am. Closed Sunday.
International Clinic, 1-5-9 Azabudai, Minato-ku. Tel: (03) 3582-2646. Open Monday–Friday 9am–noon, 2.30–5pm; Saturday 9am–noon. Closed Sunday.
Toho Fujin Women's Clinic, 5-3-10

Kiba, Koto-ku. Tel: (03) 3630-0303. Open Monday–Saturday 1–5pm. Closed Sunday.

Left Luggage
If possible, carry as little luggage as possible when traveling in Japan. Trains and stations, especially, are not designed for travelers with more than a small overnight bag. If you think you can make all your Tokyo train and subway connections while hauling several large bags, forget it. The train/subway map looks neat and tidy. But station connections are serious hikes with no carts or porters available, and lots of steep stairs. Hotels, of course, will usually store luggage for guests heading off on adventures.

International Airports. For security reasons, bombs in particular, the international airports have no coin lockers. There are checkrooms, however, at Narita airport:
ABC Skypartners: between the South Wing and the Central Building. ¥400 or ¥800/day per bag, with no time limit for storage. 7am–10pm.
GPA (Green Port Agency): South Wing, 1F and 4F. ¥400/day per bag, 30 day limit. 7am–10pm.
Train and subway stations. Most train and subway stations have coin lockers of varying sizes for ¥200 to ¥500 per day, depending on station and size of the locker. Time limit is 3 days. After that, contents are removed.

Checkrooms for large bags are located at several main JR stations. Luggage can be stored for up to two weeks, ¥400/day per bag for the first five days, ¥800/day per bag for each additional day.
Tokyo Station, outside Yaesu south exit, 8.30am–6pm.
Ueno Station, in front of central exit, 8am–8pm.
Shin Osaka Station, outside the central exit, 5am–10pm.
Kyoto Station, Karasuma central exit and Hachijo central exit, 8am–8pm.

Business Hours
Officially, business is done on a 9am to 5pm basis, but this is in theory only. The Japanese will often do overtime till 8 or 9pm. In general, **government** offices are open from 8.30 or 9am to 4 or 5pm Monday to Friday, and from

9am to noon on the 1st and 3rd Saturday of the month. **Main post offices** are open 9am to 7pm Monday to Friday, 9am to 5pm on Saturday, and 9am to noon on Sunday and holidays. **Branch post offices** are open 9am to 5pm Monday to Friday. **Department stores** are open daily from 10am to 7.30 or 8pm, except that they tend to close the store only twice or three times a month, which varies with each store. **Restaurants** are open for lunch from 11.30am to 2pm and for dinner from 5 to 9 or 10pm. **Major companies and offices** are open from 9am to 5pm Monday to Friday. Some are also open on Saturday mornings. **Most shops** open between 9 and 11am and close between 6 and 8pm.

Tipping

No tipping remains the rule in Japan, except for unusual or exceptional services. Porters at large stations and airports charge around ¥300 per piece.

Telecoms

To use the public telephones, which are colored either green, red, pink, or yellow, just insert a ¥10 coin and dial the number desired. ¥10 for three minutes. Yellow and green phones accept ¥100 coins, which make them more convenient for long-distance calls, but no change is returned for unused portions thereof.

Most common are the green phones, all taking prepaid telephone cards, and some taking only prepaid cards, no coins. Telephone cards can be obtained at any Nippon Telegraph and Telephone (NTT) office, KDD office, other stores, or through special vending machines near phones.

International calls can be made only from specially-marked – in English and Japanese – green telephones. Increasingly, dark gray card phones are appearing in hotels and at airports. They have computer connections, both analog and digital.

Japan's country code: 81
Domestic area codes start with zero:
Fukuoka: 092
Hiroshima: 082
Kagoshima: 099
Kyoto: 075
Nagasaki: 0958

Nagoya: 052
Naha: 098
Narita: 0476
Osaka: 06
Sapporo: 011
Sendai: 022
Tokyo: 03
Yokohama: 045

KDD Information, international telephone information, in English: 0057 (toll free).
NTT Information, domestic telephone directory information, in English. 9am–5pm weekdays.
Tokyo, tel: (03) 5295-1010.
Narita, tel: (0476) 28-1010.
Yokohama, tel: (045) 322-1010.
Hiroshima, tel: (082) 262–1010
English telephone directory from **NTT**. Tel: (03) 5256-3141, fax: (03) 5256-3148.
City Source, free English telephone directory from NTT. Tel: (03) 5256-3141, fax: (03) 5256-3148.
Osaka, tel: (06) 571-7866, fax: (06) 571-4185.
Japan Hotline (NTT/KDD), broad-based, hard-to-find phone numbers. Tel: (03) 3586-0110. Monday–Friday, 10am–4pm.

International

While there are several international carriers, person-to-person, collect and credit card calls can be made only through KDD: 0051

Toll-Free Numbers

Domestic telephone numbers that begin with "0120" or "0088" are toll-free, or "free-dial", calls

Telegrams

Domestic: 115
Overseas: (03) 3344-5151
Central Post Office
Domestic: (03) 3284-9539 (Japanese)
International: (03) 3284-9540 (Japanese)
For telegram inquiries, call: Tokyo, (03) 3346-2521; Yokohama, (045) 671-4347.

Getting Around

On Arrival

From Narita Airport

A taxi to downtown Tokyo from Narita costs between ¥20,000 and ¥30,000, depending on destination and traffic. Most people prefer either the bus or train, a tenth of the price of a taxi. Either way, it's 2–3 hours by road.

Bus: A regular limousine bus service runs between Narita and TCAT (Tokyo City Air Terminal) in downtown Tokyo, to Tokyo and Shinjuku Stations, and to most major hotels in Tokyo. Tickets (just under ¥3,000) are bought at the airport after clearing immigration and customs. There are several routes depending on destination. Buses are boarded outside the terminal at the curb, and will accept any amount of luggage at no extra charge. The buses leave every 20 minutes or so, taking two to three hours to arrive. There are also buses to Yokohama and Haneda, the domestic airport.

Trains: There are two train alternatives into Tokyo: the Keisei Skyliner and the JR Narita Express. Both are twice as fast as by taxi or bus, but not as convenient.

In terms of connections, the Narita Express is more convenient, stopping at JR Stations in Chiba, Tokyo (Station), Shinjuku, Ikebukuro, Yokohama and Ofuna. The Skyliner stops just at Ueno Station and nearby Nippori. Both take about the same time to reach Tokyo, an hour, and both have no restrictions on luggage. (Be warned, however, that carrying luggage through train and subway stations in Japan, especially in Tokyo, is a feat of considerable effort with long hikes and Fuji-like climbs. If carrying more than one piece of luggage, and if not taking the limousine bus directly to a hotel, consider a baggage delivery service.)

The Narita Express costs about ¥3,000 for regular class, and tickets must be bought in advance. The Skyliner costs ¥1,740 and tickets can be bought in advance or at the Ueno Keisei Station for the next train.

The Skyliner is far more comfortable than the Narita Express (unless traveling in first class, which is a delight). Narita Express's regular seats are small with almost no leg room: usually you sit facing another seat, knee to knee, in groups of four. When traveling with families, the Japanese prefer this style. But for the arriving traveler trying to shake jet lag, or exhausted from last-minute sightseeing before leaving Japan, this arrangement leaves a lot to be desired, especially for the price and especially when the train is overcrowded. (JR permits standing passengers when trains are full, making them even fuller.)

The Keisei Skyliner, on the other hand, is never overbooked or crowded, and the seats are quite comfortable with lots of leg room. Considering the difference in price, the Skyliner is far and away the better deal, both in price and in comfort. If one isn't carrying a lot of luggage, a connection can be made at Ueno Station to JR trains or the subway.

Note: If making a domestic airline connection, take the taxi, bus or train into Tokyo and make the connection at Haneda Airport. No domestic flights are made out of Narita. The limousine bus will take you directly from Narita to Haneda, as will a very expensive taxi.

Baggage delivery: Most residents of Japan take advantage of Japan's fast and reliable delivery network. After clearing immigration and customs, take your luggage to the ABC counter in the main terminal (there are several). Often a line indicates the counter. For about ¥1,500 per bag, ABC will deliver the bag by the following day wherever you are. If carrying more than a couple of bags, consider this alternative.

From Kansai Int'l Airport

The new Kansai International Airport (KIX) has replaced Osaka Airport (Itami) as the international air terminus for the Kansai region. However, some domestic flights still fly from Itami. The second largest and the first 24-hour-operation airport in Japan, Kansai International Airport, opened on September 4, 1994. It is located southeast Osaka Bay, 5 km off the coast and about 60 km from JR Shin-Osaka Station for shinkansen train connections.

KIX, constructed on an artificial island in Osaka Bay, and one of the world's most expensive – ¥2,600 departure tax – is architecturally impressive and extremely functional. All international and domestic connections at KIX are made at the same terminal in a matter of minutes. (Note: Make sure to confirm that domestic flight connections are from KIX and not Itami-Osaka Airport.) Despite being on an island, getting to and from KIX is relatively easy: two railways, two expressways, some 10 limousine bus lines, and four high-speed ferries connect the island to every point in the Kansai.

For your travel information, the **Kansai Tourist Information Center** is located in the arrival lobby (1st Fl.) and is open daily from 9am to 9pm. For handling currency exchange, there are 10 banks at the airport, with one or more open from 6am to 11pm. Your Japan Rail Pass can be exchanged either at the JR West Information Center in the International Arrivals Lobby (1st Fl, open daily, 8am to 9pm), at the TiS-Travel Service Center (open daily, 10am to 6pm), or at the green-colored Midori-no-madoguchi Reservations Ticket Office (open daily, 5.30am to midnight) of JR Kansai Airport Station.

TO/FROM OSAKA

Train: JR (Japan Railway) Haruka Express, reserved seating, runs between KIX and Osaka's Tennoji Station (29 min), and Shin Osaka Station (45 min), where you catch the shinkansen, or bullet train. The JR Kuko-Kaisoku connects KIX with Osaka's Tennoji Station (45 min) and Namba Station's Osaka City Air Terminal (O-CAT), which offers express baggage check-in (60 min).

For JR train information tel: (0724) 56-6242.

Nankai Railroad also connects KIX with Osaka's Namba Station. Three trains make the run. For Nankai train information tel: (0724) 56-6203.

Bus: There are a number of deluxe buses between KIX and various Osaka hotels and rail stations. These take about an hour, on a good day, and are a bit cheaper than the train. For bus information call Keihan Bus Co. tel: (07240) 55-2500.

Ferry: Two high-speed ferries connect KIX with Osaka's Tenpozan port (40 min). For ferry information tel: (06) 575-1321.

TO/FROM KYOTO

Train: JR Haruka Express, reserved seats, connects Kyoto Station with KIX (75 min). For JR train information tel: (075) 351-4004.

Bus: A Keihan bus leaves from Uji, south of Kyoto, for KIX and takes about 2 hours. For bus Keihan bus information call tel: (0724) 55-2500.

TO/FROM KOBE

Bus: You can connect by bus from KIX to Kobe's Sannomiya Station (90 min). For bus information call Keihan Bus Co. Tel: (0724) 55-2500.

Ferry: The Kobe Jet Shuttle is the best and fastest way to get to or from Kobe. The Jet Shuttle runs between KIX and the Kobe City Air Terminal (K-CAT) on Port Island (30 min), where free bus service is provided to Kobe's Sannomiya Station. For Jet Shuttle information tel: (078) 306-2411.

TO/FROM SOUTHERN ISLANDS

Ferries: Two high-speed ferries connect KIX with Awaji and Shikoku Islands: To Tsuna and Sumoto on Awaji Island (40 min), for information tel: (0799) 24-3333. To Tokushima on Shikoku Island (82 min), for information tel: (06) 575-2101.

TO/FROM NARA

Bus: A bus runs from KIX to Nara JR Station (95 min). For bus information call Keihan Bus Co. tel: 0724-55-2500.

Public Transport
Rail

JR Train Information, in English, information only, no reservations, 10am–6pm weekdays, tel: (03) 3423-0111.

Japan has one of the most efficient and extensive rail networks in the world. Rail service is provided by **Japan Railways (JR)** and several regional private lines. The trains on important routes run every few minutes. Trains – such as JR's **shinkansen**, sometimes called the bullet train, which travels at speeds of up to 170 mph (275 kph) – offer alternatives to air and long-distance bus travel. Between Tokyo and Kyoto, travel times are the same for both air and shinkansen. The train, however, is from city center to city center; air, from airport to airport.

The **subway** systems in Japan are clean, safe, and convenient. It is faster than congested road transportation. However, Japanese trains are notorious for being crowded, especially during morning and evening rush hours. Trains and subways are sometimes packed to more than three times their specified capacity, though it actually feels like a lot more.

All subway stations post a timetable. Regular service is Monday through Saturday. The Sunday and holiday schedule has slightly fewer runs. Trains run until around after midnight, so be sure to check the time of the last train. All subway and train stations have a route map with fares for each stop near the ticket machines. However, it is not always in English. Your present location is indicated with a red mark. The fares are regulated on a station-to-station basis, so if you cannot determine the fare required, just purchase the cheapest ticket available. You can pay the difference, if needed, upon arrival at your destination. The ticket machine will dispense the ticket and give the correct change. A child's ticket is half fare.

Most ticket machines accept coins only, although some will take ¥1,000 notes or prepaid cards. There is usually a machine that gives change or sells prepaid cards nearby.

Transportation cost savings can be made by buying a *teiki* (train pass), valid for one, three or six months. Major subway and train stations issue passes. Another way to save on train fares is to buy a *kaisuken*, a series of 11 tickets between two destinations for the price of 10. Lastly, one-day tickets good on either subway lines or JR trains are available.

Station arrivals are announced in Japanese inside the trains but are often difficult to understand. There is usually a map of the stops on the line and connecting lines above the train doors. The names of the stations are most often written in both Japanese and English.

Timetables and subway maps in Japanese can be obtained at most stations. Subway maps in English are available in various English-language publications and at some major train and subway stations.

Taxis

Taxis are the most convenient way of getting around, but unfortunately, also the most expensive. The basic fare in Tokyo is ¥650 for the flag drop. A short trip can easily run ¥3,000 to ¥5,000. Once again, no tipping is expected or required. Taxis are readily available on almost every street corner, and can certainly be found at every major hotel and railway station. There is a red light on in the front window if the taxi is free and available.

Don't touch the door when getting in or out of a taxi. The doors on taxis are opened and closed by the driver, who has a lever in the front, so when you've hailed a taxi and it stops, just wait for the door to open, and after arriving at your destination and paying, again the door will open by itself. You can get out and just walk away without trying to close the door.

Most taxi drivers do not speak any language other than Japanese, so it can be helpful to have your destination written in Japanese.

Private Transport

You will need an international driving license or a Japanese one. However, be warned that driving in Japan can be a headache and tedious. The major cities seem to be in a perpetual stage of renovation; there is always construction work going on somewhere, and road divisions are often not easy to see. The streets are narrow, crowded and often confusing. Most street signs are in Japanese.

Remember that in Japan, driving is on the left-hand side of the road. Renting a car will cost from about ¥6,000 for 6 hours, or from ¥10,000 for 24 hours.

You can obtain the *Driver's Map of Japan* issued by the JAF Publishing Co. 9-3, Shiba Sakaecho, Minato-ku, Tokyo. Tel. (03) 3433-8731.

Where To Stay

Hotels

There are hotels everywhere, but unfortunately few of them are up to international standards. Those that are reflect it in their price. However, convenience is a very dear commodity here, so often you are paying for the location more than the service or luxury. Below is a brief listing of major hotels in alphabetical order. Please note that the rankings are according to prices of single or twin rooms. In most hotels and all *ryokan,* you are provided with a *yukata* robe, toothbrush, razor, shower cap, etc.

Many hotels offer only twin beds, which are the most popular arrangement in Japan. Smoking rooms may have a thick stench of stale smoke.

Finally, hotel rooms are quite compact. Even a ¥20,000 room in a deluxe hotel can be snug. So-called business hotels, generally found in the moderate and budget categories (and a few in the expensive category), have rooms that are not just snug, but cramped. Expect submarine-style spaciousness.

Western-style hotels offer rooms whose rates may vary from ¥8,000 to ¥30,000. There are hotels which also provide Japanese-style guest rooms and landscaped gardens. Others have restaurants serving Continental food as well as local *sukiyaki, sushi, tempura.*

Ryokan (Japanese-style inns) exude an atmosphere of traditional Japanese living. They charge an average of ¥9,000 per person, depending on the type of bath facilities offered.

There are about 80,000 ryokan in Japan, of which 2,000 are members of the Japan Ryokan Association (JRA), who ensure that a high standard of service is maintained. Guests sleep in rooms covered with *tatami* (straw) mats, on *futon.* The baths are communal, though there are usually separate baths for men and women. Morning and evening meals are served in the guest's room.

Minshuku are bed-and-breakfast lodgings without the frills (toiletries and *yukata* gowns etc). Rates are from ¥5,000 up. The Japan National Tourist Organization (JNTO) lists some 230 minshuku for overseas visitors.

Japan Minshuku Center Booking office, B1, Tokyu Kotsu Kaikan Bldg, 2-10-1, Yurakucho, Tokyo. Tel: (03) 3216-6556 (English spoken). 10am–6pm, Monday–Saturday, closed Sunday & national holidays. Average fee: ¥6,000–¥13,000 per person with 2 meals. Guarantee ¥1,000 (per person per night). Commission ¥500 (per MInshuku). Reservation by phone is basically not accepted. Reservation for high tourist season (July–August, April 29–May 5, December 25–January 4, weekends) can only be accepted for more than 2 persons per room. Rooms are mostly Japanese-style.

Tokyo

EXPENSIVE

Akasaka Prince Hotel, 1-2 Kioicho, Chiyoda-ku. Tel: (03) 3234-1111. One of the Prince chain. Very modern and efficient, and great views from every room.
Akasaka Tokyu Hotel, 2-14-3 Nagatacho, Chiyoda-ku. Tel: (03) 3580-2311. One of the most conveniently located hotels in Akasaka; it is just minutes away from all the action.
ANA Hotel Tokyo, 1-12-33 Akasaka, Minato-ku. Tel: (03) 3505-1111. An exquisite hotel in the heart of Ark Hills, a popular office and shopping complex. Down the hill from Roppongi. Convenient for business and fun.
Capitol Tokyu Hotel, 2-10-3 Nagatacho, Chiyoda-ku. Tel: (03) 3581-4511. Formerly the Tokyo Hilton. A very comfortable and relaxing setting, blending Japanese and Western design. Excellent restaurants and pool (summer only).
Century Hyatt Tokyo, 2-7-2 Nishi Shinjuku, Shinjuku-ku. Tel: (03) 3349-0111. One of the buildings amidst all the skyscrapers of Shinjuku. Japanese-style Hyatt service and accommodation. Health facilities and disco.
Crowne Plaza Metropolitan, 1-6-1 Nishi-Ikebukuro, Toshima-ku. Tel: (03) 3980-1111. Three minutes from Ikebukuro Station's west exit, Ikebukuro's finest hotel.

Hotel Okura, 2-10-4 Toranomon, Minato-ku. Tel: (03) 3582-0111. Officially rated the 2nd-best hotel in the world. Health facilities, excellent restaurants and executive salon.
Hotel New Otani, 4-1 Kioicho, Chiyoda-ku. Tel: (03) 3265-1111. The largest hotel in Asia. Health facilities, a 400-year-old Japanese garden, and very good location.
Imperial Hotel, 1-1-1 Uchisaiwaicho, Chiyoda-ku. Tel: (03) 3504-1111. First built in 1890, with a new tower completed in 1983. Pool, shopping arcade, several excellent restaurants. Convenient to government offices and Ginza.
Keio Plaza Hotel, 2-2-1 Nishi Shinjuku, Shinjuku-ku. Tel: (03) 3344-0111. A 45-story skyscraper on the west side of Shinjuku. Near the Tokyo Metropolitan Government Office towers. Health facilities and executive salon.
Miyako Hotel, 1-1-50 Shiroganedai, Minato-ku. Tel: (03) 3447-3111. Affiliated with the famous Miyako Hotel in Kyoto. Health facilities and quiet, though not too convenient.
New Takanawa Prince Hotel, 3-13-1 Takanawa, Minato-ku. Tel: (03) 3442-1111. Addition to the Takanawa Prince. All of the rooms have private balconies. Pool (summer only).
Roppongi Prince Hotel, 3-2-7 Roppongi, Minato-ku. Tel: (03) 3587-1111. A few minutes from Roppongi Station. Outdoor heated pool.
Palace Hotel, 1-1-1 Marunouchi, Chiyoda-ku. Tel: (03) 3211-5211. Old but quiet and peaceful surroundings overlooking the Imperial Palace moats and gardens.
Royal Park Hotel, 2-1-1 Nihombashi, Kakigaracho, Chuo-ku. Tel: (03) 3667-1111. Next door to the Tokyo City Air Terminal. Indoor swimming pool, fitness club, Japanese garden and executive floors. Convenient to many different locations.
Takanawa Prince Hotel, 3-13-1 Takanawa, Minato-ku. Tel: (03) 3447-1111. Convenient to Shinagawa and the southwest part of Tokyo. Traditional Japanese garden. Pool (summer only).
Tokyo Hilton International, 6-6-2 Nishi Shinjuku, Shinjuku-ku. Tel: (03) 3344-5111. Completed in 1984 and follows in the tradition of the former Hilton. Health facilities and executive salon.
Tokyo Prince Hotel, 3-3-1 Shibakoen, Minato-ku. Tel: (03) 3432-1111. Another of the Prince chain. Located next

to Zojo-ji temple. Pleasant outdoor garden restaurant, which is very popular in summer. Pool (summer only).

MODERATE

Asakusa View Hotel, 3-17-1 Nishiasakusa, Taito-ku. Tel: (03) 3842-2111. Good location for sightseeing and shopping in downtown Asakusa. There is always something happening.
Diamond Hotel, 25 Ichibancho, Chiyoda-ku. Tel: (03) 3263-2211. Just a few minutes from Hanzomon Station. Nice quiet area.
Fairmont Hotel, 2-1-17 Kudan Minami, Chiyoda-ku. Tel: (03) 3262-1151. Old British style. About six minutes from Kudanshita Station, right in front of the Imperial Palace moat.
Ginza Dai-Ichi Hotel, 8-13-1 Ginza, Chuo-ku. Tel: (03) 3542-5311. Conveniently located, less than five minutes from Shimbashi Station.
Ginza Nikko Hotel, 8-4-21 Ginza, Chuo-ku. Tel: (03) 3571-4911. About four minutes from Shimbashi Station.
Ginza Tokyu Hotel, 5-15-9 Ginza, Chuo-ku. Tel: (03) 3541-2411. Reasonably priced hotel located close to the Kabuki-za Theater in Ginza.
Haneda Tokyu Hotel, 2-8-6 Haneda Kuko, Ota-ku. Tel: (03) 3747-0311. Right next to Haneda Airport. Shuttle service between hotel and airport.
Hillport Hotel, 23-19 Sakuragaoka-cho, Shibuya-ku. Tel: (03) 3462-5171. A three-minute walk from Shibuya Station. Excellent access to restaurants, department stores and theaters.
Hilltop Hotel, 1-1 Surugadai, Kanda, Chiyoda-ku. Tel: (03) 3293-2311. Five minutes from Ochanomizu Station. An and very pleasant hotel. This is an old favorite of writers and artists. Excellent food and service.
Hotel Atamiso, 4-14-3 Ginza, Chuo-ku. Tel: (03) 3541-3621. Convenient to the Kabuki-za (*Kabuki* Theater) and to all Ginza shopping. Two minutes from Higashi Ginza on the Hibiya line. Formerly a *ryokan*, it opened as a Western-style hotel in 1984.
Hotel Grand Palace, 1-1-1 Iidabashi, Chiyoda-ku. Tel: (03) 3264-1111. Downtown location. Ten minutes by car to Tokyo Station and TCAT.
Hotel Ibis, 7-14-4 Roppongi, Minato-ku. Tel: (03) 3403-4411. Trendy decor with 200 rooms located where a lot of the action can be found.
Hotel New Kanda, 2-10 Kanda, Awaji-

cho, Chiyoda-ku. Tel: (03) 3258-3911. Quiet and yet only a 5-minute walk to noisy Akihabara electronic quarter.

Hotel Park Side, 2-11-18 Ueno, Taito-ku. Tel: (03) 3836-5711. Overlooking Ueno Park. Very delightful atmosphere. Easy access to public transport.

Mitsui Urban Hotel, 8-6-15 Ginza, Chuo-ku. Tel: (03) 3572-4131. Great location.

President Hotel, 2-2-3 Minami Aoyama, Minato-ku. Tel: (03) 3497-0111. Located near the Crown Prince's residence and the Roppongi and Aoyama areas.

Shiba Park Hotel, 1-5-10 Shibakoen, Minato-ku. Tel: (03) 3433-4141. Quiet and cozy, away from all the noise.

Shibuya Tokyu Inn, 1-24-10 Shibuya, Shibuya-ku. Tel: (03) 3498-0109. Good location.

Shimbashi Dai-Ichi Hotel, 1-2-6 Shimbashi, Minato-ku. Tel: (03) 3501-4411. Very central location. Convenient for business, shopping and sightseeing.

Shinagawa Prince Hotel, 4-10-30 Takanawa, Minato-ku. Tel: (03) 3440-1111. Year-round sports facilities.

Shinjuku Prince Hotel, 1-30-1 Kabuki-cho, Shinjuku-ku. Tel: (03) 3205-1111. Right in the heart of exciting Shinjuku.

Sunshine City Prince Hotel, 3-1-5 Higashi-Ikebukuro, Toshima-ku. Tel: (03) 3988-1111. A modern hotel located in the Sunshine City complex.

Washington Hotel, 3-2-9 Nishi Shinjuku, Shinjuku-ku. Tel: (03) 3343-3111. Very modern, very reasonable and very convenient, though the rooms are rather small.

Yaesu Fujiya Hotel, 2-9-1 Yaesu, Chuo-ku. Tel: (03) 3273-2111. One minute from Tokyo Station.

BUDGET

Taisho Central Hotel, 1-27-7 Takadanobaba, Shinjuku-ku. Tel: (03) 3232-0101. Just one minute from Takadanobaba Station on the JR Yamanote Line.

Dai-Ichi Inn Ikebukuro, 1-42-8 Higashi Ikebukuro, Toshima-ku. Tel: (03) 3986-1221. Good for shopping, business.

Hotel Sunroute Ikebukuro, 1-39-4 Higashi-Ikebukuro, Toshima-ku. Tel: (03) 3980-1911. Convenient location. Minutes away from Ikebukuro Station on the JR Yamanote Line.

Ryogoku River Hotel, 2-13-8 Ryogoku, Sumida-ku. Tel: (03) 3634-1711. One-minute from Ryogoku Station. Good for *sumo* watching if a tournament is on.

Tourist Hotel, 3-18-11 Higashi Ueno, Taito-ku. Tel: (03) 3831-0237. Minutes away from Ueno Station.

Attractions

The following lists museums, galleries and theaters in Tokyo.

Museums and Art Galleries

In Japan, there are more than 1,400 museums and art galleries and their numbers are increasing year by year.

Listed are art galleries, folk history museums, treasure houses and folk art museums. Major science museums and those of a unique nature are also included.

These institutions are arranged geographically from north to south and are classified roughly by district and city according to their location.

SAPPORO (HOKKAIDO)

Historical Museum of Hokkaido, 53-2 Konopporo, Atsubetsucho, Atsubetsu-ku, Sapporo 061-004. Tel: (011) 898-0456. 40 minutes by bus from Sapporo Station, 5 minutes by bus from Shinrinkoen Station or 10 minutes by taxi from Shin-Sapporo Station. Palaeontological and biological specimens, archeological remains, implements and utensils used by the Ainu and immigrants, progress of colonization and industries of Hokkaido. Open 9.30am–4.30pm, closed Mondays and national holidays.

The Natural History Museum of Agriculture, Hokkaido University, 8-chome, Nishi, Kita-Sanjo, Chuo-ku, Sapporo 060 (in the botanical garden). Tel: (011) 251-8010. 10-minutes walk from Sapporo Station. Specimens of fauna and flora peculiar to Hokkaido, implements and utensils of the old Ainus and Gilyaks are on display. Open 29 April –3 November 9am–4pm, closed Mondays and 4 November–28 April.

NORTHEASTERN HONSHU

Munakata Shiko Memorial Museum of Art, 2-1-2, Matsubara, Aomori, Aomori Pref. 030. Tel: (0177) 77-4567. 15 minutes by bus from Aomori Station. Prints and paintings by Munakata Shiko (1903–75), Aomori's best-known artist. Open April–September 9.30am–4.30pm; October–March 9.30am–4pm, closed Mondays, holidays and end of every month.

Chusonji Treasury, Chusonji, Hiraizumicho, Nishiiwaigun, Iwate Pref. 029-41. Tel: (0191) 46-2211. 5 minutes by bus from Hiraizumi Station to Chusonji bus stop, then a 20-minute walk. A fine collection of the art of the late Heian period, some 800 years ago. The collection includes Buddhist images, paintings and other cultural and historical relics of that period. Open April–October 8am–5pm; November–March 8.30am–4.30pm.

Homma Museum of Art, 7-7, Onaricho, Sakata, Yamagata Pref. 998. Tel: (0234) 24-4311. 5-minute walk from Sakata Station. Japanese paintings, calligraphy, prints, swords and various articles associated with the local culture and the folk arts. Many were the property of the Homma family, wealthy merchants in Sakata. Open April–October 9am–5pm; November–March 9am–4.30pm, closed Mondays of December–March.

Chido Museum, 10-18, Kachu-Shinmachi, Tsuruoka, Yamagata Pref. 997. Tel: (0235) 22-1199. 10 minutes by bus from Tsuruoka Station. Art objects, archaeological relics and folk items related to the rural customs of the area, and some of the possessions of the Sakai family, a feudal lord of the region. They are housed in a group of buildings among which are the former police station, government office and an old farm house. Open 9am–5pm, closed 28 December–1 January.

Sendai City Museum, Sannomaruato, Kawauchi, Sendai, Miyagi Pref. 980. Tel: (022) 225-2557. 10 minutes by bus from Sendai Station. *Samurai* armors, swords, old costumes and other art objects, many of which were possessed by the Date family, the well-known feudal lord of Sendai. Also on display are Japanese paintings, ukiyo-e, and pottery. Open 9am–4.45pm, closed Mondays and the day following national holidays.

Kurita Museum, 1542, Komabacho, Ashikaga, Tochigi Pref. 329-42. Tel: (0284) 91-1026. 10-minute walk from Tomita Station. A large collection of Imari and Nabeshima porcelains. There is a branch of this museum in Tokyo. (See Tokyo section.) Open 9.30am–5pm

Mashiko Reference Collection Museum, 3388, Mashiko, Mashiko-machi, Haga-gun, Tochigi Pref. 321-42. Tel: (0285) 72-5300. One hour by bus from Utsunomiya Station. Works of late Shoji Hamada and his collection. (Eastern and Western ceramics, fabrics, furniture, paintings etc.) Open 9.30am–4.30pm, closed Mondays, 28 December–4 January and all February.

TOKYO

Bridgestone Museum of Art, 1-10-1, Kyobashi, Chou-ku, Tokyo 104. Tel: (03) 3563-0241. 5-minute walk from Tokyo Station (Yaesuguchi side). Western paintings, prints, sculpture, pottery and metal items, and paintings by contemporary Japanese artists. Open 10am–5.30pm, closed Mondays.

Communications Museum, 2-3-1, Otemachi, Chiyoda-ku, Tokyo 100. Tel: (03) 3244-6821. 1-minute walk from Otemachi subway station. A large collection of postage stamps and various data on communications. Open 9am–4.30pm; Fridays 9am–6.30pm, closed Mondays.

Furniture Museum, JIC Building, 3-10, Harumi, Chuo-ku, Tokyo 104. Tel: (03) 3533-0098. 15 minutes by bus from Ginza. Old Japanese furniture. Open 10am–4.30pm, closed Wednesdays.

The Gotoh Museum, 3-9-25, Kaminoge, Setagaya-ku, Tokyo 158. Tel: (03) 3703-0661. 4-minute walk from Kaminoge Station on the Tokyu Oimachi Line. Fine arts and crafts of ancient Japan, China and other Oriental nations. Open 9.30am–4.30pm, closed Mondays and the day following a national holiday.

Hatakeyama Collection, 2-20-12, Shiroganedai, Minato-ku, Tokyo 108. Tel: (03) 3447-5787. 6-minute walk from Takanawadai subway station. Fine arts and crafts of ancient Japan, Korea and China. Many objects are relating to the tea ceremony. A tea ceremony room on the upper floor. Open April–September 10am–5pm; October–March 10am–4.30pm, closed Mondays.

Idemitsu Museum of Arts, 9th floor of Kokusai Building, 3-1-1, Marunouchi, Chiyoda-ku, Tokyo 100. Tel: (03) 3213-9402. 3-minute walk from Yurakucho Station. Zenga by Zen priest Sengai, Japanese ceramics, crafts & paintings, hand-painted Ukiyo-e and Chinese ceramics, crafts & bronzes. Open 10am–5pm, closed Mondays.

The Japan Folk Crafts Museum, 4-3-33, Komaba, Meguro-ku, Tokyo 153. Tel: (03) 3467-4527. 5-minute walk from Komaba-Todaimae Station on the Keio-Inokashira Line. Folk art of various parts of Japan and Korea, and other countries of the world, mostly assembled by Yanagi Soetsu. Open 10am–5pm, closed Mondays.

Japanese Sword Museum, 4-25-10, Yoyogi, Shibuya-ku, Tokyo 151. Tel: (03) 3379-1386. 10-minute walk from Sangubashi Station on the Odakyu Line. Works of noted swordsmiths, both ancient and modern. Open 9am–4pm, closed Mondays.

Kite Museum, 5th floor of Taimeiken Building, 1-12-10, Nihombashi, Chuo-ku, Tokyo 103. Tel: (03) 3271-2465. 2-minute walk from Nihombashi subway station. Kites collected from throughout Japan and other countries. Open 11am–5pm, closed Sundays and national holidays.

Museum of Maritime Science, 3-1, Higashi-Yashio, Shinagawa-ku, Tokyo 135 (in the reclaimed land area). Tel: (03) 3528-1111. 20 minutes by bus from Shinagawa Station. Various nautical exhibits housed in a ferro-concrete replica of a 60,000-ton liner in the seaside park. Open 10am–5pm daily.

Matsuoka Museum of Art, 8th floor of Matsuoka Tamuracho Building, 5-22-10, Shimbashi, Minato-ku, Tokyo 105. Tel: (03) 3437-2787. 3-minute walk from Onarimon subway station. Oriental ceramics and Japanese paintings, and Egyptian, Greek, Roman and Indian sculptures. Open 10am–5pm, closed Mondays.

Meiji Jingu Treasure Museum, 1-1, Kamizonocho, Yoyogi, Shibuya-ku, Tokyo 151. Tel: (03) 3379-5511. 13-minute walk from JR Yoyogi Station or 5 minutes walk from Sangubashi Station on the Odakyu Line. Objects used by the Emperor Meiji (1852–1912). Open March–October 9am–4.30pm; November–February 9am–4pm, closed 3rd Friday.

Meiji Memorial Picture Gallery, Meiji Jingu Gaien, Meiji-jingu Gaien, 9, Kasumigaoka, Shinjuku-ku, Tokyo 160. Tel: (03) 3401-5179. 3-minute walk from Shinanomachi Station. Pictures showing the main events in the reign of the Emperor Meiji. Open 9am–4.30pm daily.

National Museum of Modern Art, Tokyo, 3, Kitanomaru-koen, Chiyoda-ku, Tokyo 102 (in Kitanomaru Park). Tel: (03) 3214-2561. 5-minute walk from Takebashi subway station. Japanese paintings, sculptures, prints, and calligraphy. Open 10am–5pm, closed Mondays.

Crafts Gallery, National Museum of Modern Art, Tokyo, 1, Kitanomaru-koen, Chiyoda-ku, Tokyo 102 (in Kitanomaru Park). Tel: (03) 3211-7781. 7-minute walk from Takebashi subway station. Contemporary Japanese handicrafts. Open 10am–5pm, closed Mondays.

National Science Museum, 7-20, Ueno-koen, Taito-ku, Tokyo 110 (in Ueno Park). Tel: (03) 3822-0111. 5-minute walk from Ueno Station. Exhibits in the field of natural history and physical sciences and technology. Open 9am–4.30pm, closed Mondays.

National Museum of Western Art, 7-7, Ueno-koen, Taito-ku, Tokyo 110 (in Ueno Park). Tel: (03) 3828-5131. 3-minute walk from Ueno Station. Works of famous Western painters and sculptors, mostly French artists from the 19th century to the recent past. Open 9.30am–5pm, closed Mondays.

Nezu Institute of Fine Arts, 6-5-1, Minami-Aoyama, Minato-ku, Tokyo 107. Tel: (03) 3400-2536. 10-minute walk from Omotesando subway station. Japanese paintings, calligraphy, sculpture, ceramics, lacquer and Chinese bronzes, Korean ceramics; a Japanese garden in which there are several tea houses. Open 9.30am–4.30pm, closed Mondays.

NHK Broadcast Museum, 2-1-1, Atago, Minato-ku, Tokyo 105. Tel: (03) 5400-6900. 6-minute walk from Kamiyacho subway station. Materials showing the history of the development of radio and TV broadcasting in Japan. Open 9.30am–4.30pm, closed Mondays.

Sumo Museum, 1-3-28, Yokoami, Sumida-ku, Tokyo 130. Tel: (03) 3622-0366. 1-minute walk from Ryogoku Station. Records and documents concerning the history of sumo (Japanese wrestling) since the 18th century. Open 9.30am–4.30pm, closed Saturdays, Sundays and national holidays.

Ukiyo-e, Ota Memorial Museum of Art, 1-10-10, Jingumae, Shibuya-ku, Tokyo 150. Tel: (03) 3403-0880. 3-minute walk from Meiji-Jingumae subway station and Harajuku Station. A large collection of ukiyo-e woodblock prints collected by Mr. Seizo Ota. Open 10.30am–5.30pm, closed Mondays and 25th–end of each month.

The Okura Shukokan, 2-10-3, Toranomon, Minato-ku, Tokyo 105. Tel: (03) 3583-0781. 8-minute walk from Kamiyacho subway station or 10 minutes walk from Toranomon subway station. Fine arts and crafts of ancient Japan and other Asian countries. Adjacent to Okura Hotel. Open 10am–4pm, closed Mondays.

Paper Museum, 1-1-8, Horifune, Kita-ku, Tokyo 114. Tel: (03) 3911-3545. 1-minute walk from JR Oji Station. Various kinds of Japanese paper. Products and utensils for the making of handmade paper. Open 9.30am–4.30pm, closed Mondays and national holidays.

Pentax Gallery, Kasumicho Corporation, 3-21-20, Nishi-Azabu, Minato-ku, Tokyo 106. Tel: (03) 3401-2186. 8-minute walk from Roppongi subway station. Cameras. Open 10am–5pm, closed Sundays and national holidays.

Hiraki Ukiyo-e Museum, 6th floor, Yokohama Sogo Department Store, 2-18-1, Takashima, Nishi-ku, Yokohama, Kanagawa Pref. 220. Tel: (045) 465-2233. Adjacent to Yokohama Station. Hikaki collection of ukiyo-e prints. Open 10am–7pm, closed Tuesdays.

Science Museum, 2-1, Kitanomaru-koen, Chiyoda-ku, Tokyo 102 (in Kitanomaru Park). Tel: (03) 3212-8471. 5-minute walk from Takebashi subway station. Machinery of the latest type. Open 9.30am–4.50pm.

Suntory Museum of Art, 11th floor of Suntory Building, 1-2-3, Moto-Akasaka, Minato-ku, Tokyo 107. Tel: (03) 3470-1073. 3-minute walk from Akasakamitsuke subway station. Japanese lacquer, ceramics, glass, costumes, masks and other fine arts. A tea ceremony room is in the museum. Open 10am–5pm; Fridays 10am–7pm, closed Mondays.

Tobacco and Salt Museum, 1-16-8, Jinnan, Shibuya-ku, Tokyo 150. Tel: (03) 3476-2041. 8-minute walk from

Shibuya Station or 10 minutes walk from Harajuku Station. Items and documents relating to smoking and salt. Special exhibits: – "Ukiyo-e prints depicting smoking custom" and others – on the 4th floor. Open 10am–6pm, closed Mondays, 1st Tuesday of June and 29 December–3 Janurary.

Tokyo Central Museum, 5th floor of Ginza Boeki Building, 2-7-18, Ginza, Chuo-ku, Tokyo 104. Tel: (03) 3564-4600. 3-minute walk from Ginza subway station. Contemporary paintings, sculptures, prints, calligraphy and handicrafts. Open 10am–6pm, closed Mondays.

Hara Museum of Contemporary Art, 4-7-25, Kita-Shinagawa, Shinagawa-ku, Tokyo 140. Tel: (03) 3445-0651. 15-minute walk from Shinagawa Station. Collection of paintings and sculptures, after 1950 up to now, by leading artists of America, Europe and Japan. Open 11am–5pm; Wednesdays 11am–8pm, closed Mondays.

Tokyo Metropolitan Art Museum, 8-36, Ueno-koen, Taito-ku, Tokyo 110 (in Ueno Park). Tel: (03) 3823-6921. 7-minute walk from Ueno Station. Works of contemporary Japanese artists. Open 9am–5pm, closed 3rd Monday. (Gallery for Museum is closed on every Monday.)

Tokyo National Museum, 13-9, Ueno-koen, Taito-ku, Tokyo 110 (in Ueno Park). Tel: (03) 3822-1111. 10-minute walk from Ueno Station. The largest museum in Japan. Fine arts and archaeology of Japan including many that are designated as National Treasures or Important Cultural Properties. Also collections of Chinese, Korean and Indian art and archaeology. Open 9am–4.30pm, closed Mondays.

Transportation Museum, 1-25, Kanda Sudacho, Chiyoda-ku, Tokyo 101. Tel: (03) 3251-8481. 4-minute walk from Awajicho subway station or 5 minutes walk from Akihabara Station. Various items showing the progress of railways and other means of transportation in Japan. Open 9.30am–5pm, closed Mondays. (Open daily in August, 26 March–6 April.)

Tsubouchi Memorial Theater Museum, Waseda University, Waseda University, 1-6-1, Nishi-Waseda, Shinjuku-ku, Tokyo 169. Tel: (03) 3203-4141, ext. 5214. 6-minute walk from Waseda subway station. Items and documents connected with the

Oriental and Occidental theaters. Open 9am–5pm, Sundays 10am–5pm, closed national holidays.

Yamatane Museum of Art, 8th and 9th floors of Yamatane Building, 7-12, Nihombashi-Kabutocho, Chou-ku, Tokyo 103. Tel: (03) 3669-7643. 1-minute walk from Kayabacho subway station. Japanese paintings of the Meiji period to the present. Tea ceremony rooms adjoin the museum. Open 10am–5pm, closed Mondays.

VICINITY OF TOKYO

Japan Open-air Folkhouse Museum, 7-1-1, Masugata, Tama-ku, Kawasaki, Kanagawa Pref. 214. Tel: (044) 922-2181. 15-minute walk from Muko-gaoka-yuen Station on the Odakyu Line. Outdoor museum featuring old and rare Japanese farmhouses. Open 9.30am–4pm, closed Mondays.

Toshiba Science Institute, 1, Komukai-Toshibacho, Saiwai-ku, Kawasaki, Kanagawa Pref. 210. Tel: (044) 511-2300. 10 minutes by bus from Kawasaki Station to Komukai-koban bus stop and then 3-minute walk to the institute. The newest technologies, concepts and visitor-operated displays on electricity along with electronic products. Open 9am–5pm, closed Saturdays, Sundays and holidays.

Silk Museum, 2nd floor of Silk Center Building, 1, Yamashitacho, Naka-ku, Yokohama, Kanagawa Pref. 231. Tel: (045) 641-0841. 10-minute walk from Kannai Station or 15 minutes walk from Sakuragicho Station. Silk goods of various kinds and educational materials relating to silk. Open 9am–4.30pm, closed Mondays. (When Monday falls on a holiday, it is closed on Tuesday.)

Kanagawa Prefectural Kanazawa-Bunko Museum, 142, Kanazawacho, Kanazawa-ku, Yokohama, Kanagawa Pref. 236. Tel: (045) 701-9069. 10-minute walk from Kanazawa-Bunko Station on the Keihin-Kyuko Line. Sculpture, paintings, calligraphy, historical documents and a large library of the Chinese and Japanese classics. This Kanazawa Bunko was founded about 1260 by the Hojo family. Open 9am–4.30pm, closed Mondays, last two days of every 2 months and the day following national holidays.

Kamakura Museum, 2-1-1, Yukino-shita, Kamakura, Kanagawa Pref. 248 (in the precincts of the Tsurugaoka

Hachiman-gu). Tel: (0467) 22-0753. 15-minute walk from Kamakura Station. Paintings, sculpture and other art objects of the 12th–16th centuries. Open 9am–4pm, closed Mondays.

Museum of Modern Art, Kanagawa, Annex; 2-1-53, Yukinoshita, Kamakura, Kanagawa Pref. 248 (in the precincts of the Tsurugaoka Hachiman-gu). Tel: (0467) 22-5000, 7718. 10-minute walk from Kamakura Station. Japanese and foreign art: paintings, sculpture, prints, from the 19th century to the present. Open 10am–5pm, closed Mondays and the day following national holidays.

KYOTO

Chishaku-in Temple Storehouse, Higashiyama-Shichijo, Higashiyama-ku, Kyoto 605 (in the grounds of the Chishaku-in Temple). Tel: (075) 541-5361. Near Higashiyama-Shichijo bus stop. Japanese paintings on walls and screens of the Momoyama period (1573–1615). The Japanese garden is one of the best gardens in Kyoto. Open 9am–4pm.

Costume Museum, 5th floor of Izutsu Building, Shin-Hanayacho-Horikawa-kado, Shimogyo-ku, Kyoto 600. Tel: (075) 361-8388. 10-minute walk from Kyoto Station (near NishiHongan-ji). Japanese costumes, from ancient to modern times, displayed on life-sized dolls. Open 9am–5pm, closed Sundays and national holidays.

Domoto Art Museum, 26, Kamiyanagicho, Hirano, Kita-ku, Kyoto 603. Tel: (075) 463-1348. Near Ritsumeikan Daigaku-mae bus stop. Japanese paintings, prints, ceramics by the famous artist, Domoto Insho (1891–1975). Open 9.30am–5pm, closed Mondays.

Taiga, Ike Art Museum, 57, Matsuomangokucho, Nishikyo-ku, Kyoto 615. Tel: (075) 381-2832. In front of Kokedera bus stop operated by the Kyoto Bus. *Sumi-e* (black and white paintings) and calligraphy by Ike Taiga (1723–1776). Open 10am–5pm, closed Wednesdays.

Kawai Kanjiro's House, Kaneicho, Gojozaka, Higashiyama-ku, Kyoto 605. Tel: (075) 561-3585. 2-minute walk from Umamachi bus stop. Works of the famous potter, Kawai Kanjiro (1890–1966), the folkcraft objects used in his traditionally-styled Japanese house. His workroom and 2 kilns

are preserved. Open 10am–5pm, closed Mondays, 24 December–7 January and 10–20 August.

Koryuji Reihoden Treasury, 36, Uzumasa Hachigaokacho, Ukyo-ku, Kyoto 616 (in the grounds of the Koryuji Temple). Tel: (075) 861-1461. Near Uzumasa Station on the Keifuku Linc. Japanese sculpture, calligraphy, documents, and costumes, owned by the temple. The wooden image of Miroku Bosatsu is especially famous nationwide. Open March–November 9am–5pm; December–February 9am–4.30pm.

Kyoto Municipal Museum of Art, 124, Enshojicho, Okazaki, Sakyo-ku, Kyoto 606 (in Okazaki Park). Tel: (075) 771-4107. In front of Kyoto Kaikan Bijutsukan-mae bus stop. Works of modern Japanese artists. Japanese paintings of the Kyoto School are predominant. Open 9am–5pm, closed Mondays. (Open when Monday falls on a holiday.)

Kyoto Yuzen Dyeing Hall, 6, Mamedacho, Nishikyogoku, Ukyo-ku, Kyoto 615. Tel: (075) 311-0025. 5-minute walk from Nishikyogoku Station on the Hankyu Line. Demonstration of the process of Yuzen dyeing and display and sale of Yuzen products. Open 9am–5pm, closed Mondays.

Kyoto National Museum, 527, Chayamachi, Higashiyama-ku, Kyoto 605 (near the Sanjusangendo Hall). Tel: (075) 541-1151. 13 minutes by bus from Kyoto Station. Fine arts and archaeology of Japan, mainly from the Museum Collection. Many of exhibits include the art treasures principally from the shrines and temples in and around Kyoto. Open 9am–4.30pm, closed Mondays.

National Museum of Modern Art, Kyoto, Enshojicho, Okazaki, Sako-ku, Kyoto 606 (in Okazaki Park). Tel: (075) 761-4111. In front of Kyoto Kaikan Bijutsukan-mae bus stop. Contemporary arts of Japan and other countries. Open 9.30am–5pm, closed Mondays.

The Raku Museum, Aburanokoji, Nakadachiuri Agaru, Kamigyo-ku, Kyoto 602. Tel: (075) 414-0304. 5-minute walk from Horikawa Nakadachiuri bus stop. Open 10am–4.30pm, closed Mondays.

Sen'oku Hakkokan (Sumitomo Collection), 24, Shimo-Miyanomaecho, Shishigadani, Sakyo-ku, Kyoto 606. Tel: (075) 771-6411. Near Higashi

Tennocho bus stop. Open March–June and September–November 10am–4pm, closed Mondays and national holidays. (Open when Monday falls on a holiday.)

Toji Treasure House, 1, Kujocho, Minami-ku, Kyoto 601 (in the grounds of the Toji Temple). Tel: (075) 691-3325. 15-minute walk from the southwest exit of Kyoto Station (Hachijo-guchi exit). Buddhist statues, paintings, sutras and other objects owned by the temple. Open 9am–4.30pm.

OSAKA AND VICINITY

Fujita Museum of Art, 10-32, Amijimacho, Miyakojima-ku, Osaka 534. Tel: (06) 351-0582. 7-minute walk from Katamachi Station. Japanese and Chinese fine arts and crafts. Many objects are related to the tea ceremony. Open mid-March–mid-June and mid-September–early December 10am–4pm, closed Mondays.

Open Air Museum of Old Japanese Farm Houses, 1-2, Hattori-Ryokuchi, Toyonaka, Osaka Pref. 560. Tel: (06) 862-3137. 13-minute walk from Ryokuchi-koen Station on the Kita-Osaka Kyuko Line. Old Japanese farmhouses are reassembled and put on display in a village setting. Open April–October 9.30am–5pm, November–March 9.30am–4pm, closed Mondays.

Mint Museum, 1-1-7, Temma, Kita-ku, Osaka 530 (in the grounds of the Osaka Mint Bureau). Tel: (06) 351-8509. 15-minute walk from Minami-Morimachi subway station. Japanese coins from the feudal days to the present times. Open 9am–4pm, closed Saturdays, Sundays and national holidays.

National Museum of Art, Osaka, 10-4, Senri-Banpaku-Koen, Suita, Osaka Pref. 565 (in Expo Park). Tel: (06) 876-2481. Get off at JR Ibaraki Station, Hankyu Railways Ibarakishi Station, then take the bus to Nihon Teien-mae bus stop and then a 10-minute walk. Contemporary paintings and other works of art relating to the interchange of fine arts between the East and the West. Open 10am–5pm, closed Wednesdays. (Open when Wednesday falls on a holiday, but closed on the following day.)

National Museum of Ethnology, 10-1, Senri-Banpaku-Koen, Suita, Osaka Pref. 565 (in Expo Park). Tel: (06) 876-2151. 15-minute walk from Nihon

Teien-mae bus stop. Display of artifacts from Japan and other countries and booths for individual viewing of films relating to the exhibits. Open 10am–5pm, closed Wednesdays.

Osaka Japan Folk Crafts Museum, 10-5, Senri-Banpaku-Koen, Suita, Osaka Pref 565 (in Expo Park). Tel: (06) 877-1971. 10-minute walk from Nihon Teien-mae bus stop. Japanese folk craft objects which have been chosen with great care. Open 9.30am–5pm (last admittance at 4pm), closed Wednesdays. (Open when Wednesday falls on a holiday, but closed on the following day.)

Osaka City Museum, 1-1, Osakajo, Chou-ku, Osaka 540 (in the grounds of the Osaka Castle). Tel: (06) 941-7177. 15-minute walk from Morinomiya Station. Materials and records connected with the history, economy, and culture of Osaka. Open 9.15am–4.45pm, closed every 2nd and 4th Monday of the month. (Open when the 4th Monday falls on a holiday, but closed on the following day.)

Osaka Municipal Museum of Art, 1-82, Chausuyamacho, Tennoji-ku, Osaka 543 (in Tennoji Park). Tel: (06) 771-4874. 8-minute walk from Tennoji Station (Subway or JR). Japanese, Chinese, and Korean art objects, both ancient and modern. Open 9.30am–5pm, closed Mondays.

Osaka Museum of Natural History, 1-23, Nagai-koen, Higashi-Sumiyoshi-ku, Osaka 546 (in Nagai Park). Tel: (06) 697-6221. 10-minute walk from Nagai subway station. Material for study of natural science. Open 9.30am–4.30pm, closed Mondays.

Modern Transportation Museum, 3-11-10, Namiyoke, Minato-ku, Osaka 552. Tel: (06) 581-5771. Near JR Bentencho Station. Various items relating to air, land, and sea transportation and more specifically the modernizing of the Japanese National Railways. Open 9.30am–5pm, closed Mondays. (Open daily during spring holiday season and summer holiday season.)

KOBE AND VICINITY

Hakutsuru Art Museum, 6-1-1, Sumiyoshi-Yamate, Higashi-Nada-ku, Kobe 658. Tel: (078) 851-6001. 15-minute walk from Mikage Station on the Hankyu Line. Chinese bronzes, ceramics, lacquer ware, and ancient

Japanese art objects. Open mid-March–end May and mid-September–end November 10am–4.30pm, closed Mondays and the day following national holidays.

Hyogo-ken Togei-kan, 5th floor of Zentan Kaikan Building, 4-5-1, Shimo-Yamatedori, Chou-ku, Kobe 650. Tel: (078) 321-0709. 3 minute walk from JR Motomachi Station. A large collection of Japanese ceramics. Among the pieces, Tamba ware are predominant. Open 10am–5pm, closed Mondays.

Hyogo Prefectural Museum of Modern Art, Kobe, 3-8-30, Harada-dori, Nada-ku, Kobe 657. Tel: (078) 801-1591. 5-minute walk from Hankyu Ojikoen Station on the Hankyu Kobe Line. Contemporary arts of Japan and other countries. Open 10am–5pm, closed Mondays.

Kobe City Museum, 24 Kyomachi, Chou-ku, Kobe 650. Tel: (078) 391-0035. 10-minute walk from JR Sannomiya Station. A newly-opened museum of archaeology and history of Kobe. It also houses a fine collection of Japanese paintings and art objects of the 16th to 17th centuries produced under the influence of Portugal and Spain (Namban Art), Kohmoh Art (the 17th to 19th centuries, influenced by Holland) and old maps. Open 10am–5pm, closed Mondays and the day following national holidays.

Tekisui Art Museum, 13-3, Yama-Ashiyacho, Ashiya, Hyogo Pref. 659. Tel: (0797) 22-2228. 8-minute walk from Ashiyagawa Station on the Hankyu Line. Japanese art objects, collection of toys and games, Kyoto wares. Open 10am–5pm, closed Mondays, mid-July–mid-September and mid-December–mid-January.

Ceramic Art and Crafts

Japan is a country of earthenware, a ceramic-loving nation and a storehouse of ceramic art and crafts. The origin of Japanese ceramic art is generally regarded to date back to the beginning of the 13th century, when Chinese ceramics were introduced.

The development of the art was stimulated in the 16th century because of the popularity of the tea ceremony, and new kilns were opened in various parts of the country. The one in Arita, constructed in 1598 by a Korean potter who came from Korea that year, deserves special mention.

During the years of the Edo Period (1603–1867), many daimyo (feudal lords) encouraged the efforts of their potters and ordered them to make certain ceramic articles of exquisite shapes and designs.

Afterwards, because of the Meiji Restoration, some potters who were engaged in their work under the patronage of the daimyo, had to stop their work. On the other hand, there had been very many potters, protected by tradesmen, who kept firing their kilns and continued to create Japanese ceramic works of art.

The characteristics of Japanese ceramics are: (1) their expression is gentle and suave; (2) they are noted for their irregularity and freedom, simplicity and homeliness; and (3) they are free from artificiality and monotony. The decorations on Japanese wares are quiet and not piquant. Gentleness of expression, which is the chief feature of Japanese ceramics, has been influenced by Japanese taste, fostered by the unique climatic conditions and geographical features of the country.

There are a large number of kilns in Japan, each with a long history.

Tea Ceremony (in English)

Imperial Hotel (Toko-an), 1-1-1 Uchisaiwai-cho, Chiyoda-ku, Tokyo. (4F the Main Wing). Tel: (03) 3504-1111. Near Hibiya Station on Hibiya, Chiyoda, or Toei Mita Line. Open 10am–4pm. Closed on Sunday and holidays. Fee, 20-min. participation periods. Advanced reservation is required.

Hotel Okura (Chosho-an), 2-10-4 Toranomon, Minato-ku, Tokyo. (7F of the Main Bldg.). Tel: (03) 3582-0111. Near Toranomon Station on Ginza Line or Kamiyacho Station on Hibiya Line. Open daily 11am–5pm. Fee, 20–30-min. participation periods. Advanced reservation is required.

Hotel New Otani, 4-1 Kioi-cho, Chiyoda-ku, Tokyo. (7F of Tower Bldg.). Tel: (03) 3265-1111, ext. 2443. Near Akasaka-mitsuke Station on Ginza or Marunouchi Line. Open Thursday, Friday and Saturday 11am–noon, 1–4pm. Fee, 15–20-min. participation periods. No reservation is needed if guests total less than 5 or 6.

Chado Kaikan, 3-39-17 Takadanobaba, Shinjuku-ku, Tokyo. Tel: (03) 3361-2446. 15-minute walk from Takadanobaba Station or take a bus for Otakibashi-Shako to Takadanobaba 4-chome stop. Open Monday–Thursday 10.30am–2.30pm. Closed on holidays. Fee, 1-hour participation periods. Advanced reservation is required. **Kenkyusha Nihongo Center**, 1-2 Kagurazaka, Shinjuku-ku, Tokyo. Tel: (03) 5261-8940. 5-min. walk from the west exit of Iidabashi Station on JR Sobu Line, or the B-3 exit of Iidabashi Station on Yurakucho or Tozai Line. Open Monday 6–8pm; Friday 2–4pm or 6–8pm. Fee, 2-hour participation periods. Advanced reservation is required. **Happoen** (Muan), 1-1-6 Shiroganedai, Minato-ku, Tokyo. Tel: (03) 3443-3111. 15-min. walk from Meguro Station on JR Yamanote Line. Open daily, when tour groups participate in the tea ceremony 10am–6pm. Only up to 1 or 2 persons can join the tea ceremony with them. Tea is served to the guests seated on chairs and not on tatami. Fee, 30-min. participation periods. Private tea ceremony is available (¥20,000 + ¥800 X the number of persons).

Imperial Palace Visits

Any visit to the Imperial residence is an honor and a privilege. Only the grounds of Tokyo's Imperial Palace are opened to the public on January 2 and December 23, Emperor Akihito's birthday, a national holiday (Tenno Tanjobi). The Imperial Palace and villas in Kyoto are open by appointment only, through the Imperial Household Agency.

To see the **Kyoto Imperial Palace**, **Shugakuin Imperial Villa**, or **Katsura Imperial Villa**, apply for permission at the Imperial Household Agency office on the Palace grounds in Kyoto. Admission to the Palace and villas is free. For palace tours, you must apply – with passport – 30 minutes before tour times: 10am and 2pm weekdays and Saturday morning. (The palace is closed on Sundays and national holidays.) While the palace is open on Saturday mornings, the agency office is closed, so you need to apply on weekdays. Only overseas visitors can apply and visit on the same day. Japanese must apply months in advance or wait for the week in April and October when the palace is open to the general public – a good time to avoid visiting. Palace tours begin at Seisho gate in the middle of the western wall and take about an hour; most, but not all, are

conducted in English, but an English-language pamphlet is provided. You must also apply to the same office for visits to either of the imperial villas; this can normally be done a few days before your intended visit. Some restrictions do apply on children, so check with the Imperial Household Agency office before your visit. Your hotel can be helpful in pre-planning any visit. It might seem like a lot of work, but then, how many imperial residences have you ever visited?

Imperial Household Agency, Kyoto Palace – Kyoto Gosho, 3 Kyoto Gyoen, Kamigyo-Ku, Kyoto 602. Tel: (075) 211-1215. Office hours are 9am to 4.30pm weekdays only.

Festivals

General

Festivals, or matsuri seem to be happening at any given time somewhere in Tokyo, and indeed have been an important part of Japanese life for hundreds of years. Many of the festivals have their roots in the long history of Japan's agricultural society. In today's ever modernizing Japan, they are one of the few occasions when the Japanese can dress up and live a nostalgic past. Below is a short list of the main national holidays and the most important festivals. For information on upcoming events going on during any particular week or month, please consult TIC or any of the tourist publications.

January

The first **sumo** tournament of the year, **Hatsubasho**, is held for fifteen days at the **Kokugikan** in mid January.

February

On the 3rd is **Setsubun**, the traditional bean throwing ceremony that is meant to purify the home of evil. Roasted beans are scattered from the inside of

the house to the outside while people shout, *"Oni wa soto"* (Devils, go out!), and from the outside of the home to the inside while *"Fuku wa uchi"* (good luck, come in) is shouted. The same ceremony is also held at temples and shrines.

March

On the 3rd of the month is **Hina Matsuri** (Girl's Day), a festival for little girls. Small *Hina* dolls, representing imperial court figures, are displayed at home and in several public places.

April

From early to mid April is **Ohanami** (Cherry Blossom viewing), one of the important spring rites. People love to turn out and picnic, drink *sake* and sing songs under the pink blossoms.

On the 8th is **Hana Matsuri** (Birthday of Buddha), when commemorative services are held at various temples such as **Gokokuji Temple, Sensoji Temple, Zojoji Temple and Hommonji Temple**.

May

In mid May, the **Natsubasho** (summer *sumo* tournament) is held for fifteen days at the **Kokugikan**.

On the 3rd Sat. and Sun. the **Sanja Matsuri** is held. This is one of the big *Edo* festivals honoring the three fishermen who found the image of *Kannon* in the river. The **Asakusa Shrine** is a great place to go at this time to see the dancing, music and many portable shrines.

June

On the second Sunday is **Torigoe Jinja Taisai**, a night time festival, when the biggest and heaviest portable shrine in Tokyo is carried through the streets by lantern light. It all happens at the **Torigoe Shrine**.

From the 10th to the 16th is **Sanno Sai**, another big *Edo* festival featuring a *gyoretsu* (people parading in traditional costumes) on Saturday at the **Hie Shrine**.

July

From the 6th to the 8th is the **Asagao Ichi** (Morning Glory Fair), when over one hundred merchants set up stalls selling the morning flower at **Iriya Kishibojin**.

On the 7th is the **Tanabata Matsuri**,

a festival celebrating the only day of the year when, according to the legend, the Weaver Princess (Vega) and her lover the Cowherder (Altair) can cross the Milky Way to meet. People write their wishes on pieces of colored paper, hang them on bamboo branches, and then float them down a river the next day.

On the 9th and 10th is the *Hozuki Ichi* (Ground Cherry Fair) at **Sensoji Temple** from early morning to midnight. A visit to this temple on the 10th is meant to be equal to 46,000 visits at other times.

On the last Saturday of July, the *Sumidagawa Hanabi Taikai* (Sumida River Fireworks) is held. This is the biggest fireworks display in Tokyo, and the best places to watch the display is between the **Kototoi** and **Shirahige bridges**, or at the **Komagata Bridge**.

August
Between the 13th and the 16th is the *Obon* festival, when people return to their hometowns to clean up the graves and offer prayers to the souls of departed ancestors. The traditional *Bon Odori* folk dances are held all over around this time.

October
From mid to late October is Chrysanthemum viewing time. There are flower displays dotted around the cities.

November
The 15th is *Shichi-Go-San* (Three-Five-Seven), a ceremony for 5-year-old boys and 3- and 7-year-old girls. The children usually dress up in *kimono* and are taken to visit a shrine.

December
The 14th is *Gishi Sai*, a memorial service for the famous *47 Ronin* who, on this day in 1702, avenged the death of their master and later committed ritual suicide. They are buried at the **Sengakuji Temple** where the service is held.

On the 31st at the stroke of midnight, every temple bell throughout the country begins to toll. The bells toll 108 times representing the 108 evil human passions. This is called *Joya no Kane*, and the general public is allowed to strike the bells at various temples.

Shopping

Shopping Areas

Japan is a very expensive place to shop, but there are still bargains to be had if you look them up. The quality of Japanese products is well known, and there are some items which can only be bought in Japan. Certain areas promote only certain kinds of merchandise, which means that some domestic travel is involved for the serious shopper.

Following is a guide to the main shopping attractions in the cities and other areas throughout Japan.

In and Around Tokyo
Akihabara: The electronic jungle of the world featuring hundreds of discount stores.

Aoyama: High-class fashion boutiques.

Asakusa: Traditional Japanese toys, souvenirs, workmen's clothes, etc.

Ginza: The most expensive shopping center. Several major department stores are located here, such as **Hankyu**, **Matsuya**, **Matsuzakaya**, **Mitsukoshi**, **Printemps**, **Seibu** and **Wako**, and exclusive boutiques. Also some traditional Japanese goods stores.

Harajuku: Another fashion area, though mostly geared to the young, which makes shopping relatively cheap. Several antique shops, and **Kiddyland** for the kids.

Hibiya: Mostly antique shops, jewelry shops, and art galleries.

Kanda and **Jimbocho:** Many second-hand bookstores.

Nihombashi: A good place to pick up traditional craft work. Two of Japan's oldest department stores, **Mitsukoshi** and **Takashi-maya** are located here.

Roppongi: Several antique shops in the area, the **Axis** design building which features interior design as its main theme, and Seibu's **Wave** building which specializes in audio-visual equipment.

Shibuya: A good place to start with, Shibuya has a little bit of everything. **Tokyu Hands** is a must to visit; probably the most complete do-it-yourself department store in the world. Also here are the **Seibu**, **Tokyu** and **Marui** departments stores, the **Parco** "fashion buildings" besides the hundreds of small boutiques geared to young shoppers.

Shinjuku: Several big camera and electronic discount stores such as **Yodobashi** and **Sakuraya**. Also, **Isetan** and **Marui** department stores.

Ueno: **Ameyoko** is good for cheap food, cosmetics, clothing and toys. One of the few open markets in Tokyo. The shops in the back streets sell traditional Japanese goods.

ANTIQUES
In most of the shops listed here, the staff speak English and are helpful. Watch out for badly restored pieces that have been given a quick coat of glossy lacquer and sold like new at steep prices.

Antique Gallery Kikori, Hanae Mori Building, B1, 3-6-1 Kita Aoyama, Minato-ku. Tel: (03) 3407-9363. Small but interesting selection of *tansu* and other items.

Antique Gallery Meguro, Stork Building, 2nd Fl, 2-24-18 Kamiosaki, Shinagawa-ku. Tel: (03) 3493-1971. Antique market of sorts covering 740 sq. meters (885 sq. yards) that houses several small antique shops.

Edo Antiques, 2-21-12 Akasaka, Minato-ku. Tel: (03) 3584-5280. Large selection of *tansu* and *hibachi*.

Hasabe-ya Antiques, 1-5-24 Azabu Juban, Minato-ku, tel: (03) 3401-9998

Harumi Antiques, 9-6-14 Akasaka, Minato-ku. Tel: (03) 3403-1043. Mostly *tansu* that have been restored, but some unrestored pieces can be purchased.

Japan Old Folkcraft and Antique Center (Tokyo Komingu Kotto-kan), 3-9-5 Minami Ikebukuro, Toshima-ku. Tel: (03) 3980-8228. 35 dealers covering 600 sq. meters (718 sq. yards) and displaying various antique items.

Oriental Bazaar, 5-9-13 Jingæmae,

Shibuya-ku. Tel: (03) 3400-3933. Apart from antiques, it is also a nice place to browse and pick up traditional Japanese toys, paper (*washi*), *kimono*, etc.

CERAMICS

Besides workshops, department stores are the best places for Japanese ceramics offered at reasonable prices. On back streets, small shops also sell ceramics but prices are higher.

Iseryu Shoten, 3-8-2 Ningyocho, Nihombashi, Chuo-ku, tel: (03) 3661-4820. Closed Sundays and holidays.

Saga Toen, 2-13-13 Nishi Azabu, Minato-ku, tel: (03) 3400-3682.

Tachikichi & Co. Ltd, 6-13 Ginza, Chuo-ku, tel: (03) 3571-2924.

DEPARTMENT STORES

Daimaru, 1-9-1 Marunouchi, Chiyoda-ku, tel: (03) 3212-8011. Closed Thursdays.

Isetan, 3-14-1 Shinjuku, Shinjuku-ku, tel: (03) 3352-1111. Closed Wednesdays.

Marui, 3-30-16 Shinjuku, Shinjuku-ku, tel: (03) 3354-0101. 10.30am–7.30pm. Closed 2nd or 3rd Wednesday.

Matsuya, 1-4-1 Hanakawado, Taito-ku, tel: (03) 3842-1111. Closed Thursdays.

Matsuzakaya, 3-29-5 Ueno, Taito-ku, tel: (03) 3832-1111.

Mitsukoshi, 1-7-4 Muromachi, Nihombashi, Chuo-ku, tel: (03) 3241-3311. Closed Mondays.

Printemps, 3-2-1 Ginza, Chuo-ku, tel: (03) 3567-0077. 10am–7pm. Closed Wednesdays.

Seibu (Main Store), 1-28-1 Minami Ikebukuro, Toshima-ku, tel: (03) 3981-0111. Closed Thursdays.

Sogo, 1-11-1 Yurakucho, Chiyoda-ku, tel: (03) 3284-6711. Closed Tuesdays.

Takashimaya, 2-4-1 Nihombashi, Chuo-ku, tel: (03) 3211-4111. Closed Wednesdays.

Tokyu, 2-24-1 Dogenzaka, Shibuya-ku, tel: (03) 3477-3111. Closed Thursdays.

JAPANESE PAPER (*WASHI*)

Haibara, 2-7-6 Nihombashi, Chuo-ku, tel: (03) 3272-3801. Closed Sundays and holidays.

Isetatsu, 2-18-9 Yanaka, Taito-ku, tel: (03) 3823-1453.

Kurodaya, 1-2-11 Asakusa, Taito-ku,

tel: (03) 3845-3830. Closed Mondays.

Kyækyodo, 5-7-4 Ginza, Chuo-ku, tel: (03) 3571-4429.

Ozu Shoten, 2-6-3 Nihombashi Honcho, Chuo-ku, tel: (03) 3663-8788. Closed on Sundays

Washikobo, 1-8-10 Nishi Azabu, Minato-ku, tel: (03) 3405-1841. Closed Sundays and public holidays.

KIMONOS (ANTIQUE)

These shops specialize in antique *kimono*, *obi*, traditional blue and white textiles, *furoshiki*, *hanten*, etc. Prices from ¥1,000 up.

Flea markets (see list under *Flea Markets*) also sell them, and you can usually pick up very beautiful old *kimono* and *obi* in good condition.

Ayahata, 2-21-2 Akasaka, Minato-ku, tel: (03) 3582-9969. Closed Sundays and public holidays.

Hayashi Kimono, International Arcade, 1-7 Uchisaiwaicho, Chiyoda-ku, tel: (03) 3581-9826.

Ikeda, 5-22-11 Shiroganedai, Minato-ku, tel: (03) 3445-1269. Closed Sundays.

Konjaku Nishimura, Hanae Mori Building, B1, 3-6-1 Kita Aoyama, Minato-ku, tel: (03) 3498-1759. Closed Thursdays.

LACQUERWARE (*SHIKKI*)

Bushi, Axis Building, B1 5-17-1 Roppongi, Minato-ku, tel: (03) 3587-0317. Closed Mondays.

Heiando, 3-10-11 Nihombashi, Chuo-ku, tel: (03) 3272-2871. Closed Sundays and public holidays.

Inachu Japan, 1-5-2 Akasaka, Minato-ku, tel: (03) 3582-4451.

Kuroeya, Kuroeya Kokubu Building, 2nd Floor, 1-2-6 Nihombashi, Chuo-ku, tel: (03) 3271-3356. Closed Saturdays, Sundays and public holidays.

MUSICAL INSTRUMENTS

Bachi Ei Gakkiten (*Shamisen*), 2-10-11 Ningyocho, Nihombashi, Chuo-ku, tel: (03) 3666-7263. Closed Sundays and holidays.

Kikuya Shamisen Ten (*Shamisen*), 3-45-11 Yushima, Bunkyo-ku, tel: (03) 3831-4733. Closed Sundays and holidays.

Tsurukawa Gakki Honten (*Koto*), 1-12-11 Kyobashi, Chuo-ku, tel: (03) 3561-1872. Closed Sundays and holidays.

Ishida Biwa Ten (*Biwa*), 3-8-4 Toranomon, Minato-ku, tel: (03) 3431-6548.

Closed Sundays and holidays.

Chikuyusha (*Shakuhachi*), 3 San-eicho, Shinjuku-ku, tel: (03) 3351-1270. Closed Sundays and public holidays.

Miyamoto Unosuke Shoten (drums), 6-1-15 Asakusa, Taito-ku, tel: (03) 3874-4131. Closed Sundays and public holidays.

PAPER LANTERNS

Hanato, 2-25-6 Asakusa, Taito-ku, tel: (03) 3841-6411. 10am–9pm. Closed 2nd and 4th Tuesdays.

Kashiwaya, 2-3-13 Shintomi, Chuo-ku, tel: (03) 3551-1362. Closed Sundays.

UMBRELLAS (*KASA*)

Hasegawa Hakimonoten, 2-4-4 Ueno, Taito-ku, tel: (03) 3831-3933. Closed Sundays.

Iidaya, 1-31-1 Asakusa, Taito-ku, tel: (03) 3841-3644.

WOODBLOCK PRINT (*UKIYOE*)

Asakusa Okuramae Shobo, 3-10-12 Kuramae, Taito-ku, tel: (03) 3866-5894. Closed on Sundays, but will stay open for appointments. Specialist on books and prints on *Edo* and *sumo*.

Hara Shobo, 2-3 Jimbocho, Kanda, Chiyoda-ku, tel: (03) 3261-7444. All types of prints old and new, from the highest quality to a "bargain drawer." English is spoken here.

Matsushita Associates, Inc., 6-3-12 Minami Aoyama, Shibuya-ku, tel: (03) 3407-4966. Closed Sundays and public holidays.

Oya Shobo, 1-1 Kanda, Jimbocho, Chiyoda-ku, tel: (03) 3291-0062. Closed Sundays.

Sakai Kokodo Gallery, 1-2-14 Yurakucho, Chiyoda-ku, tel: (03) 3591-4678.

BOOKSTORES

There are bookstores all over Tokyo, and it is quite acceptable to browse through the books and magazines in the shop without having to buy them, so don't feel guilty. In spite of the large number of bookstores, there are relatively few that specialize in English books. Below is a list of the major stores that stock foreign books and books on Japan. They are usually helpful when phoning about information on books in stock. Besides these places, you can also get foreign newspapers and magazines in most hotels.

Aoyama Book Center. Tel: (03) 3479-0479. Open daily 10–5.30am; Sunday and holidays 10am–10pm. 1 minute from Roppongi Station (Hibiya Line).

Kinokuniya, 3-17-7 Shinjuku, Shinjuku-ku. Tel: (03) 3354-0131. Open 10am–7pm. Closed 3rd Wednesday of each month. Foreign books on the 6th floor.

Libro (Ikebukuro Branch), 1-28-1 Minami Ikebukuro, Toshima-ku (Seibu Dept. SMA BIF, B2F). Tel: (03) 5992-8800. Open daily 10am–8pm, except Tuesday.

Maruzen, 2-3-10 Nihombashi, Chuo-ku. Tel: (03) 3272-7211. Open 10am–6pm. Closed Sunday. Foreign books on the 3rd floor.

Jena (pronounced "yena"), 5-6-1 Ginza, Chuo-ku. Tel: (03) 3571-2980. Weekdays 10.30am–7.50pm; Sunday 12.30–6.45pm. Closed holidays. Foreign books on the 3rd floor.

Sanseido, 1-1 Kanda Jimbocho, Chiyoda-ku. Tel: (03) 3233-3312. Open 10am–7.30pm. Closed Tuesday. Foreign books on 5th floor.

Kitazawa Shoten, 2-5-3 Kanda Jimbocho, Chiyoda-ku. Tel: (03) 3263-0011. Open 10am–6pm. Closed Sunday. Second-hand books on the 2nd floor, and English and American literature on the 1st floor.

Biblos, F1 Bldg, 4th Floor, 1-26-5 Takadanobaba, Shinjuku-ku. Tel: (03) 3200-4531. Open daily 10.30am–7.30pm; Sunday and holidays 11am–6.30pm. Closed 3rd Sunday of each month.

National Book Store, National Azabu Supermarket 2nd Floor, 4-5-2 Minami Azabu, Minato-ku. Tel: (03) 3442-3181. Open daily 9.30am–6.30pm.

Sports and Leisure

Sumo Tournaments

Six tournaments annually, each lasting for 15 days, are held in January, May and September in Tokyo, in March in Osaka, in July in Nagoya, and in November in Fukuoka. During the tourna-

ment, matches are televised daily from 4–6pm. Matches by junior wrestlers begin at about 10am; by senior wrestlers at 3pm on the first and the last days, and at 3.30pm on other days.

TOKYO

January, May and September: Kokugikan Sumo Hall, 1-3-28 Yokoami, Sumida-ku, Tokyo. Tel: (03) 3623-5111. Near JR Ryogoku Station.

OSAKA

March: Osaka Furitsu Taiikukaikan (Osaka Prefectural Gymnasium), 3-4-36 Namba Naka, Naniwa-ku, Osaka. Tel: (06) 631-0121. Near Namba subway station.

NAGOYA

July: Aichi Ken Taiikukan (Aichi Prefectural Gymnasium), 1-1 Ninomaru, Naka-ku, Nagoya. Tel: (052) 971-2516. 15 minute by car from Nagoya Station. Tickets are sold from 9am. Competition starts from 9.20am.

FUKUOKA

November: Fukuoka Kokusai Center Sogo Hall, 2-2 Chikuko-Honcho, Hakata-ku, Fukuoka. Tel: (092) 272-1111.

Admission for Tokyo: Chair Seat A ¥7,500; Chair Seat B ¥5,500; Chair Seat C ¥3,000; Unreserved Seat Y1,500.

Tickets for the Tokyo tournaments are sold at the office of the Nihon Sumo Kyokai at Kokugikan Sumo Hall in Ryogoku as well as at ticketing bureaus in downtown Tokyo. *Very difficult to obtain tickets.*

Language

Although more and more foreigners are making the effort to learn Japanese, and learn it to a high degree of fluency, few Japanese expect foreigners to be able to speak their language.

Unfortunately, this lack of confidence in the ability of others to speak their language is not matched by a high level of proficiency in foreign languages on the part of the Japanese themselves. The number who can communicate effectively in any foreign language is very small, in spite of the fact that the majority of them have studied English for at least six years.

However, it is rare for the foreign visitor to Japan to be in a situation where absolutely nobody can be found to help out. Indeed, some Japanese will go to extraordinary lengths to help the bewildered tourist, using a curious blend of smiles, gestures and Japanese together with the odd recognizable word of English as a fairly effective means of communication. Simply looking helpless will often be enough to attract assistance.

The visitor will have few language problems within the confines of airports and the major Western-style hotels, but outside these the going can get tough for those who are unescorted. Quite apart from being unable to communicate verbally, the hapless visitor will also have the disconcerting experience of being almost totally illiterate.

The written language is made up of three different sets of characters: two simple homegrown syllabaries, *hiragana* and *katakana,* consisting of forty-six characters each; and the much more formidable Chinese ideograms, *kanji.* Knowledge of just under two thousand of these is necessary to read a daily newspaper. While the expenditure of the enormous effort required to memorize this number of kanji (it takes the Japanese most of their school career to do so) is clearly unjustifiable for those with only a passing interest in the language, a few hours spent learning the two syllabaries (on the plane trip to Japan, for example) would not be time completely wasted for those who can afford it. Hiragana can be useful for identifying which station your train has stopped at; the platforms are plastered with hiragana versions of the station name so that children who have not yet learned kanji can see where they are. Station names are usually (but not always) posted in Roman script as well, but not always as obviously. Katakana is useful in that it is used to transliterate foreign words. Western-style restaurants often simply list the foreign names for the dishes on their menus in katakana. Listed in the table below are the two syllabaries.

Pronunciation: With its small number of simple and unvarying vowel sounds, the pronunciation of Japanese should be easy for those who speak Western languages, which are rich in vowel sounds. The consonants should also present few problems (with the possible exception of l/r, ts and f – the only way to learn these is to have someone demonstrate them for you), and Japanese has nothing like the dreaded tonal system of Chinese to frustrate the student.

Vowels have but one sound, much like Spanish. Don't be sloppy with their pronunciations.

a – between fat and the u in but
e – like the e in egg
i – like the i in ink *
o – like the o in orange
u – like the u in butcher *

* When they occur in the middle of words, i and u are often almost silent. For example, *Takeshita* is really pronounced *Takesh'ta* while *sukiyaki* sounds more like *s'kiyaki*.

In spite of the seemingly simple pronunciation of Japanese, a lot of foreigners manage to mangle the language into a form which is almost impossible for the native speaker to understand. It is mainly intonation that is responsible for this. It would be fallacious to claim that the Japanese language has no rise and fall in pitch – just listen to a group of schoolgirls conversing on the train to confirm this – but it is certainly "flatter" in character than Western languages.

It is important to avoid stressing syllables within words; whereas an English speaker would naturally stress either the second or third syllable of *Hiroshima,* for example, in Japanese the four syllables should be stressed equally. Another problem lies in long (actually double) vowel sounds. These are often indicated by a line above the vowel, or simply by a double vowel, e.g. *Iidabashi.* To pronounce these long vowels properly, it is simply necessary to give the vowel sound double length. However, many publications, including this book and most English newspapers in Japan, ignore these long double vowels.

Greetings

Good morning/*Ohayo gozaimasu*
Hello (afternoon)/*Konnichiwa*
Good evening/*Kombanwa*
Good night/*Oyasumi nasai*
Goodbye/*Sayonara (Shitsure shimasu* for formal occasions)
How do you do?/*Hajime mashite!*
How are you?/*Ogenki desuka?*
It's good to see you again./*Shibaraku desu* (informally,*domo* is enough.)
My name is.../*...to moshimasu*
I'm American/*Amerika-jin desu*
I'm British/*Igirisu-jin desu*
I'm Australian/*Osturaraia-jin desu*
I'm Canadian/*Kanada-jin desu*

Asking for Directions

Excuse me, where is the **toilet**?
*Sumimasen. **Toire** wa doko desu ka?*
Excuse me, is there a **post office** near here?
*Sumimasen. Kono chikaku ni, **yubin-kyoku** wa arimasu-ka?*

Out Shopping

This one/*Kore*
That one (near the other person)/*Sore*
That one (near neither of you)/*Are*
Do you have...?/*...(wa) arimasu-ka?*
Could you show me that one please?
Sore o misete kudasai.
How much is it?/*Ikura desu-ka?*
Don't you have anything cheaper?
Mo sukoshi yasui no arimasen-ka?
Can I try it on?
Shichaku shite mo ii desu-ka?
Do you accept (credit) cards?
(Kurjitto) kado tsukaemasu-ka?
I'll take this./*Kore o kudasai.*
Three of these, please.
Kore o mittsu kudasai.

Boarding the Train

Ticket (office)/*Kippu (uriba)*
A single ticket to Sendai, please.
Sendai made, katamichi ichi-mae kudasai.
Two returns to Nikko, please.
Nikko made, ofuku ni-mae kudasai.
Reserved seat/*Shitei seki*
Unreserved seat/*Jiyuseki*
First class car/*Guriin* (Green) *sha*
Which platform does the train for Nagoya leave from?
Nagoya yuki wa namban sen desuka?
Thank you (very much)/*(Domo) arigato gozaimasu* (informally, *domo* is enough)
Don't mention it./*Doitashimashite*

Thanks for the meal.
Gochisosama deshita.
Here you are./*Dozo*
After you./*Dozo*
Sure, go ahead./*Dozo* (in answer to "May I...?")

Days/Time

(Un) Sunday/*Nichi-yobi (ni)*
(Next) Monday/*(Raishu no) Getsu-yobi*
(Last) Tuesday/*(Senshu no) Ka-yobi*
(Every) Wednesday/*(Maishu) Sui-yobi*
(This) Thursday/*(Konshu no) Moku-yobi*
Friday/*Kin-yobi*
Saturday/*Do-yobi*
Yesterday/*Kino*
Today/*Kyo*
This morning/*Kesa*
This evening/*Konya*
Tomorrow/*Ashita*
What time is it?/*Nan-ji desu ka?*

Numbers

Counting is very complicated in Japanese! Counting up to ten on their fingers, the Japanese will go: *ichi, ni, san, shi (yon), go, roku, shichi* (or *nana), hachi, ku* (or *kyu), ju.* If they are counting bottles, they will go: *ip-pon, ni-hon, sam-bon, yon-hon,go-hon, rop-pon, nana-hon, hap-pon, kyu-hon, jup-pon.* Depending on what is being counted, the suffix will change. You will be fairly safe with numbers that don't need suffixes:

One/*Hitotsu*
Two/*Futatsu*
Three/*Mittsu*
Four/*Yottsu*
Five/*Itsutsu*
Six/*Muttsu*
Seven/*Nanatsu*
Eight/*Yattsu*
Nine/*Kokonotsu*
Ten/*To*

If you want five of something, simply point at it and say, *Itsutsu kudasai.*

Photography by
Adams, B.J. 85
Alfter, Emil 232, 233, 251
Apa 313, 110/111, 277L
Central News Agency, Inc. 150
China Steel Corporation 188L
Chung, Nedra 208
Chyou Su-liang ("Smiley") 187
Colosio 59
Corrance, Douglas 291
Davis, Greg 202, 215, 217, 220, 224/225, 238
Debnicki, Kryzstus 50
Deep-Rooted Tree Publishing House 236
Dobson, Richard 135
Evrard, Alain 34, 99L, 100, 103L/R, 121, 128/129, 131, 139, 159, 196/197, 211, 235, 237, 254, 292
Gorazd, Vilhar 278, 285, 290R, 300, 305, 308
Gottschalk, Manfred 124, 138
Heaton, D.J. 181, 231R, 298, 326
Hessel, Peter 51L, 52, 53, 82, 86
Höfer, Hans 62, 63
Hollingsworth, Jack 24/25, 26
Hong Kong Museum of Art Collection (Auguste Borget) 96/97, 122
Jezierski, Ingo 2
Jopp, Carol 322
Karnow, Catherine 39, 290L, 307R
Kim, Chu-ho 209
Kowall, Earl 98, 106L/R, 107, 130, 136
Kucera, Ron 310L/R
Kugler, Jean 118, 123, 293, 299, 301L, 303, 324, 327, 336
Kwang Hwa Mass Communications 151, 230
Laude, Olivier 10/11, 40
Lawson, Lyle 205, 206, 227R, 234, 243, 246/247, 256, 334
Lee, Nam Soo 253
Leo Haks Collection 105
Liau, Chung Ren 44R, 92, 126, 127L/R
Lim, Sukje 244, 245
Lucero, Pat 79, 80, 81, 83, 84, 87
Lueras, Leonard 12/13, 14/15, 198/199, 204, 207R, 213, 218, 219, 221, 222, 223, 228, 240, 241, 242, 248, 249, 250, 252, 255, 258/259, 260, 261
Martorano, Tony 104
McGregor, Keith 18/19, 88/89, 90/91, 112, 120
McLeod, Robert 304, 307, 312, 315
Morgenstern, Manfred 30, 31, 32, 33, 42, 43, 45, 54, 58, 64, 66L, 67, 70/71, 72, 73, 75L/R
Museum of Yamato Bunkakan, Nara, Japan, courtesy of A. Yoshida 212

Nakayama, Ben 320
National Museum of Korea & the Center for Korean Studies, University of Hawaii 214
National Palace Collection 20
National Palace Museum 154/155
Nichols, R.C.A. 115
Nichols, Robin 229
Oey, Eric M. 156
Pansegrau, Erhard 44L, 49, 51R, 66R, 69, 70/71
Photobank 23, 35, 36, 37, 38, 46, 55, 65, 74, 76/77, 78, 226, 273
Purcell, Carol 302
Reichelt, G.P. 108, 125, 134
Rivas-Micoud, Miguel 277R, 297
Rocovits, Dan 144/145, 152, 153, 157, 163, 175
Rutherford, Scott 1, 16/17, 262/263, 264/265, 274, 275, 276, 279, 280, 281, 282, 283, 284, 294/295, 296, 321, 323, 325, 328, 305, 308, 335, 337, 338
Salmoiraghi, Frank 167, 173, 174, 177, 178, 180, 185
Samuel Moffett Collection 207L
Seiden, Allan 162, 190
Seitelman, Mi 231L
Shimbun, Mainichi 272
Sibley, Norman 257
Straiton, Ken 332, 333
Tainan Hostorical Museum 1498
Thailer, Mark 158R
Tokyo National Museum 268/269, 270L/R, 271, 286L/R, 287, 289
Tovy, Adina 109, 117
Van Riel, Paul 171
Wah 148, 203
Wandel, Elke 41, 61
Wassman, Bill 101, 102, 114R, 116, 119, 133, 137, 140, 142/143, 160, 161, 165, 168/169, 170, 172, 176, 179, 182, 183, 186, 188R, 189, 191, 192, 193, 194, 195
Webb, Michael 56/57, 316, 318
Weber-Lui, Kosima 48, 6
Wheeler, Nik 309, 311
Zanghi, Joseph 141, 288, 301

Maps Berndtson & Berndtson

Visual Consultant V. Barl

I n d e x

Taiwan

I n d e x

KOREA

Japan

A
B
C
D
E
F
G
I
J
a
b
c
d
e
f
g
h
j
k
l

The Insight Approach

The book you are holding is part of the world's largest range of guidebooks. Its purpose is to help you have the most valuable travel experience possible, and we try to achieve this by providing not only information about countries, regions and cities but also genuine insight into their history, culture, institutions and people.

Since the first Insight Guide – to Bali – was published in 1970, the series has been dedicated to the proposition that, with insight into a country's people and culture, visitors can both enhance their own experience and be accepted more easily by their hosts. Now, in a world where ethnic hostilities and nationalist conflicts are all too common, such attempts to increase understanding between peoples are more important than ever.

Insight Guides:
Essentials for understanding

Because a nation's past holds the key to its present, each Insight Guide kicks off with lively history chapters. These are followed by magazine-style essays on culture and daily life. This essential background information gives readers the necessary context for using the main Places section, with its comprehensive run-down on things worth seeing and doing. Finally, a listings section contains all the information you'll need on travel, hotels, restaurants and opening times.

As far as possible, we rely on local writers and specialists to ensure that the information is authoritative. The pictures, for which Insight Guides have become so celebrated, are just as important. Our photojournalistic approach aims not only to illustrate a destination but also to communicate visually and directly to readers life as it is lived by the locals.

Compact Guides
The "great little guides"

As invaluable as such background information is, it isn't always fun to carry an Insight Guide through a crowded souk or up a church tower. Could we, readers asked, distil the key reference material into a slim volume for on-the-spot use?

Our response was to design Compact Guides as an entirely new series, with original text carefully cross-referenced to detailed maps and more than 200 photographs. In essence, they're miniature encyclopedias, concise and comprehensive, displaying reliable and up-to-date information in an accessible way.

Pocket Guides:
A local host in book form

However wide-ranging the information in a book, human beings still value the personal touch. Our editors are often asked the same questions. Where do *you* go to eat? What do *you* think is the best beach? What would you recommend if I have only three days? We invited our local correspondents to act as "substitute hosts" by revealing their preferred walks and trips, listing the restaurants they go to and structuring a visit into a series of timed itineraries.

The result is our Pocket Guides, complete with full-size fold-out maps. These 100-plus titles help readers plan a trip precisely, particularly if their time is short.

Exploring with Insight:
A valuable travel experience

In conjunction with co-publishers all over the world, we print in up to 10 languages, from German to Chinese, from Danish to Russian. But our aim remains simple: to enhance your travel experience by combining our expertise in guidebook publishing with the on-the-spot knowledge of our correspondents.